CLYMER™

MERCRUISER

STERN DRIVE SHOP MANUAL

1986-1994 Alpha One, Bravo One, Bravo Two & Bravo Three

The World's Finest Publisher of Mechanical How-To Manuals

INTERTEC PUBLISHING

P.O. Box 12901, Overland Park, Kansas 66282-2901

Copyright ©1995 Intertec Publishing Corporation

FIRST EDITION
First Printing July, 1988

SECOND EDITION
Revised to include 1989 models
First Printing May, 1989
Second Printing April, 1990
Third Printing January, 1991

THIRD EDITION
Updated by Mark Jacobs to include 1990 models
First Printing February, 1992
Second Printing January, 1993

FOURTH EDITION
Updated by Mark Jacobs to include 1991-1992 models
First Printing December, 1993
Second Printing December, 1994
Third Printing June, 1995

FIFTH EDITION
Updated by Mark Jacobs to include 1993-1994 models
First Printing October, 1995

Printed in U.S.A.

ISBN: 0-89287-655-7

Library of Congress: 95-75411

Tools shown in Chapter Two courtesy of Thorsen Tool, Dallas, Texas. Test equipment shown in Chapter Two courtesy of Dixson, Inc., Grand Junction, Colorado.

Technical illustrations courtesy of Mercury Marine with additional illustrations by Mitzi McCarthy and Steve Amos.

With thanks to Valley Marine, Burbank, California.

COVER: Photographed by Mark Clifford, Mark Clifford Photography, Los Angeles, California. Boat courtesy of Galaxie Boat Center in Canyon Country, Canyon Country, California.

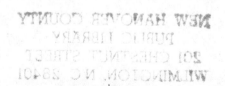

INTERTEC BOOKS
President and CEO Raymond E. Maloney
General Manager Randy Stephens

The following books and guides are published by Intertec Publishing.

CLYMER™ SHOP MANUALS
Boat Motors and Drives
Motorcycles and ATVs
Snowmobiles
Personal Watercraft

ABOS®/INTERTEC BLUE BOOKS® AND TRADE-IN GUIDES
Recreational Vehicles
Outdoor Power Equipment
Agricultural Tractors
Lawn and Garden Tractors
Motorcycles and ATVs
Snowmobiles and Personal Watercraft
Boats and Motors

AIRCRAFT BLUEBOOK-PRICE DIGEST®
Airplanes
Helicopters

AC-U-KWIK® DIRECTORIES
The Corporate Pilot's Airport/FBO Directory
International Manager's Edition
Jet Book

I&T SHOP SERVICE™ MANUALS
Tractors

INTERTEC SERVICE MANUALS
Snowmobiles
Outdoor Power Equipment
Personal Watercraft
Gasoline and Diesel Engines
Recreational Vehicles
Boat Motors and Drives
Motorcycles
Lawn and Garden Tractors

Contents

Quick Reference Data

TUNE-UP SPECIFICATIONS

Model	Spark plugs Type	Gap (in.)	Breaker points Dwell (degrees)	Gap (in.)
120, 2.5L	AC-MR43T	0.035	28-34	0.022
140, 3.0L (with Delco distributor)	AC-MR43T	0.035	28-34	0.022
3.0L (with Prestolite distributor)	AC-MR43T	0.035	39-45	0.016
3.0L, 3.0LX (with DDIS ignition)	AC-MR42LTS	0.035	Note 1	Note 1
3.0L, 3.0LX (with EST ignition)	AC-MR43T	0.035	Note 2	Note 2
165, 170, 180, 190, 3.7L, 3.7LX	AC-R42CTS	0.035	28-34	0.022
175, 185, 205, 4.3L, 4.3LX	AC-MR43T	0.035	Note 3	Note 3
200, 230, 5.0L, 5.0LX	AC-MR43T	0.035	Note 3	Note 3
260, 5.7L, 350 Magnum	AC-MR43T	0.035	Note 3	Note 3
7.4L, 454 Magnum, 502 Magnum	AC-MR43T	0.035	Note 3	Note 3

Model	Initial timing (degrees BTDC)	Maximum Advance (degrees BTDC)	Idle rpm (in gear)	Full throttle range (rpm)
120, 2.5L	8	37 @ 2,000 rpm	650-700	4,200-4,600
140, 3.0L (with Delco distributor)	6	35 @ 2,000 rpm	650-700	4,200-4,600
3.0L (with Prestolite distributor)	8	26 @ 2,000 rpm	650-700	4,200-4,400
3.0L (with DDIS ignition)	8	28 @ 4,600 rpm	650-700	4,400-4,800
3.0L, 3.0LX (with EST ignition)	1	23 @ 4,800 rpm	650-700	4,400-4,800
3.0LX (with DDIS ignition)	8	28 @ 4,200 rpm	650-700	4,400-4,800
165, 170, 3.7L	4	33 @ 2,000 rpm	650-700	4,200-4,600
180, 190, 3.7LX	4	33 @ 2,000 rpm	650-700	4,400-4,800
175, 185, 205, 4.3L, 4.3LX	8	22 @ 2,500 rpm	650-700	4,400-4,800
200, 5.0L, 230, 5.0LX, 260, 5.7L	8	Note 4	650-700	4,200-4,600
350 Magnum	8	32 @ 3,800 rpm	650-700	4,400-4,800
7.4L	8	32 @ 3,700 rpm	650-700	4,200-4,600
454 Magnum	8	32 @ 3,700 rpm	650-700	Note 5
502 Magnum	8	28 @ 5,000 rpm	650-700	4,600-5,000

Model	Firing order	Oil pressure @ 2,000 rpm (psi)	Fuel pressure (psi)	Compression pressure (psi)
All 4-cylinder	1-3-4-2	30-60	5-6.5	140
165, 170, 3.7L, 180, 190, 3.7LX	1-3-4-2	15 minimum	3-6	150
175, 185, 205, 4.3L, 4.3LX	1-6-5-4-3-2	30-55	3-7	180
200, 5.0L	1-8-4-3-6-5-7-2	30-55	5.5-7	150
230, 5.0LX	1-8-4-3-6-5-7-2	30-55	5.5-7	155
260, 5.7L, 350 Magnum	1-8-4-3-6-5-7-2	30-55	5.5-7	150
7.4L	1-8-4-3-6-5-7-2	35-70	5.5-7	150
454 Magnum, 502 Magnum	1-8-4-3-6-5-7-2	30-70	3-7	150

1. Digital, distributorless ignition system (DDIS).
2. Electronic spark timing (EST) ignition system.
3. Thunderbolt IV breakerless ignition system.
4. Ignition amplifier module identification mark V8-24—32° BTDC @ 3,700 rpm; V8-24S—32° BTDC @ 4,600 rpm; V8-22—30° BTDC @ 3,400 rpm; V8-22A—30° BTDC @ 4,400 rpm.
5. 1986 and 1987 models—4,200-4,600 rpm; 1988-on models—4,600-5,000 rpm.

APPROXIMATE ENGINE OIL CAPACITIES

Model	Capacity (with filter)[1]
Inline 4-cylinder	
120, 2.5L, 140, 3.0L, 3.0LX	4.0 qt.
165, 170, 3.7L	5.5 qt.
180, 190, 3.7LX	6.5 qt.
V6	
175, 185, 205, 4.3L, 4.3LX	4.5 qt.
V8	
200, 5.0L	5.0 qt.
230, 5.0LX, 260, 5.7L, 350 Magnum	5.5 qt.
7.4L, 454 Magnum	7.0 qt.
502 Magnum	8.0 qt.
502 Magnum (Mark V)[2]	7.0 qt.

1. All capacities in this table are approximate. To ensure correct oil level and prevent overfilling the engine, always use the dipstick as recommended in the text.
2. Mark V engines can be identified by the fuel pump mounted on the belt-driven seawater pump.

MERCRUISER MODELS

Model/hp	Displacement	Drive unit	Gear ratio	Full throttle engine operating range
1986				
120	2.5L (153 cid)	Alpha One	1.98:1	4,200-4,600 rpm
140	3.0L (181 cid)	Alpha One	1.98:1	4,200-4,600 rpm
170	3.7L (224 cid)	Alpha One	1.84:1	4,200-4,600 rpm
185	4.3L (262 cid)	Alpha One	1.84:1	4,400-4,800 rpm
190	3.7L (224 cid)	Alpha One	1.84:1	4,400-4,800 rpm
200	5.0L (3.5 cid)	Alpha One	1.65:1	4,200-4,600 rpm
205	4.3L (262 cid)	Alpha One	1.84:1	4,400-4,800 rpm
230	5.0L (305 cid)	Alpha One	1.50:1	4,200-4,600 rpm
260	5.7L (350 cid)	Alpha One	1.50:1	4,200-4,600 rpm
350 Magnum	5.7L (350 cid)	Alpha One	1.50:1	4,200-4,600 rpm
454 Magnum	7.4L (454 cid)	Alpha One	1.32:1	4,200-4,600 rpm
1987				
2.5L/120	2.5L (153 cid)	Alpha One	1.98:1	4,200-4,600 rpm
3.0L/130	3.0L (181 cid)	Alpha One	1.98:1	4,200-4,600 rpm
165	3.7L (224 cid)	Alpha One	1.84:1	4,400-4,800 rpm
175	4.3L (262 cid)	Alpha One	1.84:1	4,400-4,800 rpm
180	3.7L (224 cid)	Alpha One	1.84:1	4,400-4,800 rpm
200	5.0L (305 cid)	Alpha One	1.65:1	4,200-4,600 rpm
205	4.3L (262 cid)	Alpha One	1.84:1	4,400-4,800 rpm
230	5.0L (305 cid)	Alpha One	1.50:1	4,200-4,600 rpm
260	5.7L (350 cid)	Alpha One	1.50:1	4,200-4,600 rpm
350 Magnum	5.7L (350 cid)	Alpha One	1.50:1	4,200-4,600 rpm
454 Magnum	7.4L (454 cid)	Alpha One	1.32:1	4,200-4,600 rpm

(continued)

MERCRUISER MODELS (continued)

Model/hp	Displacement	Drive unit	Gear ratio	Full throttle engine operating range
1988-1989				
2.5L/120	2.5L (153 cid)	Alpha One	1.98:1	4,200-4,600 rpm
3.0L/130	3.0L (181 cid)	Alpha One	1.98:1	4,200-4,600 rpm
3.7L/165	3.7L (224 cid)	Alpha One	1.84:1	4,400-4,800 rpm
4.3L/175	4.3L (262 cid)	Alpha One	1.84:1	4,400-4,800 rpm
3.7LX/180	3.7L (224 cid)	Alpha One	1.84:1	4,400-4,800 rpm
5.0L/200	5.0L (305 cid)	Alpha One	1.65:1	4,200-4,600 rpm
4.3LX/205	4.3L (262 cid)	Alpha One	1.84:1	4,400-4,800 rpm
5.0LX/230	5.0L (305 cid)	Alpha One	1.50:1	4,200-4,600 rpm
5.7L/260	5.7L (350 cid)	Alpha One	1.50:1	4,200-4,600 rpm
350 Magnum/270	5.7L (350 cid)	Alpha One	1.50:1	4,200-4,600 rpm
7.4L/330	7.4L (454 cid)	Bravo One	1.50:1	4,200-4,600 rpm
454 Magnum/365	7.4L (454 cid)	Alpha One	1.32:1	4,600-5,000 rpm
454 Magnum/365	7.4L (454 cid)	Bravo One	1.50:1	4,600-5,000 rpm
1990[1]				
3.0L/115	3.0L (181 cid)	Alpha One	1.98:1	4,200-4,600 rpm
3.0LX/135	3.0L (181 cid)	Alpha One	1.98:1	4,400-4,800 rpm
4.3L/155	4.3L (262 cid)	Alpha One	1.84:1	4,400-4,800 rpm
4.3LX/175	4.3L (262 cid)	Alpha One	1.84:1	4,400-4,800 rpm
5.0L/180	5.0L (305 cid)	Alpha One	1.65:1	4,200-4,600 rpm
5.0LX/205	5.0L (305 cid)	Alpha One	1.50:1	4,200-4,600 rpm
5.7L/230	5.7L (350 cid)	Alpha One	1.50:1	4,200-4,600 rpm
350 Magnum/240	5.7L (350 cid)	Alpha One	1.50:1	4,200-4,600 rpm
7.4L/300	7.4L (454 cid)	Bravo One	1.50:1	4,200-4,600 rpm
454 Magnum/360	7.4L (454 cid)	Bravo One	1.50:1	4,600-5,000 rpm
502 Magnum/410	8.2L (502 cid)	Bravo One	1.36:1	4,400-4,800 rpm
1991[1]				
3.0L/115	3.0L (181 cid)	Alpha One	1.98:1	4,200-4,600 rpm
3.0LX/135	3.0L (181 cid)	Alpha One	1.98:1	4,400-4,800 rpm
4.3L/155	4.3L (262 cid)	Alpha One	1.84:1	4,400-4,800 rpm
4.3LX/175	4.3L (262 cid)	Alpha One	1.84:1	4,400-4,800 rpm
5.0L/180	5.0L (305 cid)	Alpha One	1.65:1	4,200-4,600 rpm
5.0LX/205	5.0L (305 cid)	Alpha One	1.50:1	4,200-4,600 rpm
5.7L/230	5.7L (350 cid)	Alpha One	1.50:1	4,200-4,600 rpm
5.7L/240	5.7L (350 cid)	Bravo Two	2:1	4,200-4,600 rpm
350 Magnum/240	5.7L (350 cid)	Alpha One	1.50:1	4,200-4,600 rpm
7.4L/300	7.4L (454 cid)	Bravo One	1.5:1	4,200-4,600 rpm
7.4L/300	7.4L (454 cid)	Bravo Two	2:1	4,200-4,600 rpm
454 Magnum/350	7.4L (454 cid)	Bravo One	1.5:1	4,600-5,000 rpm
502 Magnum/390	8.2L (502 cid)	Bravo One	1.36:1	4,600-5,000 rpm
1992[1]				
3.0L/115	3.0L (181 cid)	Alpha One	1.98:1	4,200-4,600 rpm
3.0LX/135	3.0L (181 cid)	Alpha One	1.98:1	4,400-4,800 rpm
4.3L/155	4.3L (262 cid)	Alpha One	1.84:1	4,400-4,800 rpm
4.3LX/175	4.3L (262 cid)	Alpha One	1.84:1	4,400-4,800 rpm
5.0L/180	5.0L (305 cid)	Alpha One	1.65:1	4,200-4,600 rpm

(continued)

MERCRUISER MODELS (continued)

Model/hp	Displacement	Drive unit	Gear ratio	Full throttle engine operating range
1992[1] (continued)				
5.0LX/205	5.0L (305 cid)	Alpha One	1.50:1	4,200-4,600 rpm
5.7L/230	5.7L (350 cid)	Alpha One	1.50:1	4,200-4,600 rpm
5.7L/250	5.7L (350 cid)	Bravo Two	2.2:1	4,400-4,800 rpm
350 Magnum/250	5.7L (350 cid)	Alpha One	1.50:1	4,400-4,800 rpm
7.4L/300	7.4L (454 cid)	Bravo One	1.5:1	4,400-4,800 rpm
7.4L/300	7.4L (454 cid)	Bravo Two	2:1	4,200-4,600 rpm
454 Magnum/350	7.4L (454 cid)	Bravo One	1.5:1	4,600-5,000 rpm
502 Magnum/390	8.2L (502 cid)	Bravo One	1.36:1[2]	4,600-5,000 rpm
1993				
3.0L/115	3.0L (181 cid)	Alpha One	1.98:1	4,200-4,600 rpm
3.0LX/135	3.0L (181 cid)	Alpha One	1.98:1	4,400-4,800 rpm
4.3L/160	4.3L (262 cid)	Alpha One	1.84:1	4,400-4,800 rpm
4.3LX/180	4.3L (262 cid)	Alpha One	1.84:1	4,400-4,800 rpm
5.0L/190	5.0L (305 cid)	Alpha One	1.65:1	4,200-4,600 rpm
5.0LX/205	5.0L (305 cid)	Alpha One	1.50:1	4,200-4,600 rpm
5.7L/235	5.7L (350 cid)	Alpha One	1.50:1	4,200-4,600 rpm
5.7L/250	5.7L (350 cid)	Bravo Two	2.2:1	4,400-4,800 rpm
350 Magnum/250	5.7L (350 cid)	Alpha One	1.5:1	4,400-4,800 rpm
7.4L/300	7.4L (454 cid)	Bravo One	1.5:1	4,200-4,600 rpm
7.4L/300	7.4L (454 cid)	Bravo Two	2.0:1	4,200-4,600 rpm
7.4L/300	7.4L (454 cid)	Bravo Three	2.0:1	4,200-4,600 rpm
454 Magnum/350	7.4L (454 cid)	Bravo One	1.5:1	4,600-5,000 rpm
502 Magnum/390	8.2L (502 cid)	Bravo One	1.36:1[2]	4,600-5,000 rpm
1994				
3.0L/115	3.0L (181 cid)	Alpha One	1.98:1	4,200-4,600 rpm
3.0LX/135	3.0L (181 cid)	Alpha One	1.98:1	4,200-4,600 rpm
4.3L/160	4.3L (262 cid)	Alpha One	1.84:1	4,400-4,800 rpm
4.3LX/180	4.3L (262 cid)	Alpha One	1.84:1	4,400-4,800 rpm
5.0L/190	5.0L (305 cid)	Alpha One	1.65:1	4,200-4,600 rpm
5.0LX/205	5.0L (305 cid)	Alpha One	1.50:1	4,200-4,600 rpm
5.7L/235	5.7L (350 cid)	Alpha One	1.50:1	4,200-4,600 rpm
5.7L/250	5.7L (350 cid)	Bravo Two	2.2:1	4,400-4,800 rpm
5.7L/250	5.7L (350 cid)	Bravo Three	2.0:1	4,400-4,800 rpm
350 Magnum/250	5.7L (350 cid)	Alpha One	1.5:1	4,400-4,800 rpm
7.4L/300	7.4L (454 cid)	Bravo One	1.5:1	4,200-4,600 rpm
7.4L/300	7.4L (454 cid)	Bravo Two	2.0:1	4,200-4,600 rpm
7.4L/300	7.4L (454 cid)	Bravo Three	2.0:1	4,200-4,600 rpm
454 Magnum/350	7.4L (454 cid)	Bravo One	1.5:1	4,600-5,000 rpm

1. Horsepower rated at the propeller shaft.
2. Also available in 1.5:1 gear ratio.

RECOMMENDED LUBRICANTS, SEALANTS AND ADHESIVES

Lubricants	Part No.
Quicksilver 4-cycle Marine Engine Motor Oil	92-13831A12
Quicksilver Premium Blend Gear Lube	92-755812A4
Quicksilver High Performance Gear Lubricant	92-816026A4*
Quicksilver Special Lubricant 101	92-13872A1
Quicksilver 2-4-C Multi-Lube	92-90018A12
Quicksilver Anti-Corrosion Grease	92-78376-12

Sealants	Part No.
Quicksilver Perfect Seal	92-34227-1
Quicksilver RTV Sealant	92-91600-1
Quicksilver Liquid Neoprene	92-25711-1
Quicksilver Insulating Compound	92-25711

Adhesives	Part No.
3M Brand Adhesive	92-25234
Quicksilver Bellows Adhesive	92-86166
Locquic Primer "T"	92-59327-1
Loctite No. 35	92-59328-1
Loctite Type "A" (271)	92-32609

Miscellaneous	Part No.
Quicksilver Corrosion Guard	92-78379
Quicksilver Marine Fuel System Treatment and Stabilizer	92-78383A12
Quicksilver Power Tune	92-15104-12
Quicksilver Storage Seal	92-86145-12
Quicksilver Light Gray Primer	92-78374-12
Quicksilver Phantom Black Spray Paint	92-78373-12
Quicksilver Spray Paint Leveler	92-75996-12

* The manufacturer recommends using only high performance gear lubricant (part No. 92-816026A4) in gearcase on 502 Magnum models.

Introduction

This Clymer shop manual covers the service and repair of all MerCruiser Alpha One (1986-1990), Alpha One Generation II (1991-on), Bravo One, Bravo Two and Bravo Three stern drive units used for pleasure boating from 1986-1994. Step-by-step instructions and hundreds of illustrations guide you through jobs ranging from simple maintenance to complete overhaul.

This manual can be used by anyone from a first time amateur to a professional mechanic. Easy to read type, detailed drawings and clear photographs give you all the information you need to do the work right.

Having a well-maintained engine and stern drive will increase your enjoyment of your boat as well as assure your safety offshore. Keep this manual handy and use it often. It can save you hundreds of dollars in maintenance and repair bills and make yours a reliable, top-performing boat.

Chapter One

General Information

This detailed, comprehensive manual contains complete information on maintenance, tune-up, repair and overhaul. Hundreds of photos and drawings guide you through every step-by-step procedure.

Troubleshooting, tune-up, maintenance and repair are not difficult if you know what tools and equipment to use and what to do. Anyone not afraid to get their hands dirty, of average intelligence and with some mechanical ability, can perform most of the procedures in this book. See Chapter Two for more information on tools and techniques.

A shop manual is a reference. You want to be able to find information fast. Clymer books are designed with you in mind. All chapters are thumb tabbed and important items are indexed at the end of the book. All procedures, tables, photos, etc., in this manual assume that the reader may be working on the machine or using this manual for the first time.

Keep this book handy in your tool box. It will help you to better understand how your machine runs, lower repair and maintenance costs and generally increase your enjoyment of your marine equipment.

MANUAL ORGANIZATION

This chapter provides general information useful to marine owners and mechanics.

Chapter Two discusses the tools and techniques for preventive maintenance, troubleshooting and repair.

Chapter Three describes typical equipment problems and provides logical troubleshooting procedures.

Following chapters describe specific systems, providing disassembly, repair, assembly and adjustment procedures in simple step-by-step form. Specifications concerning a specific system are included at the end of the appropriate chapter.

NOTES, CAUTIONS AND WARNINGS

The terms NOTE, CAUTION and WARNING have specific meanings in this manual. A NOTE provides additional information to make a step or procedure easier or clearer. Disregarding a NOTE could cause inconvenience, but would not cause damage or personal injury.

A CAUTION emphasizes areas where equipment damage could result. Disregarding a CAUTION could cause permanent mechanical damage; however, personal injury is unlikely.

A WARNING emphasizes areas where personal injury or even death could result from negligence. Mechanical damage may also occur. WARNINGS *are to be taken seriously*. In some cases, serious injury or death has resulted from disregarding similar warnings.

TORQUE SPECIFICATIONS

Torque specifications throughout this manual are given in foot-pounds (ft.-lb.) and either Newton meters (N.m) or meter-kilograms (mkg). Newton meters are being adopted in place of meter-kilograms in accordance with the International Modernized Metric System. Existing torque wrenches calibrated in meter-kilograms can be used by performing a simple conversion: move the decimal point one place to the right. For example, 4.7 mkg = 47 N.m. This conversion is accurate enough for mechanics' use even though the exact mathematical conversion is 3.5 mkg = 34.3 N.m.

ENGINE OPERATION

All marine engines, whether 2- or 4-stroke, gasoline or diesel, operate on the Otto cycle of intake, compression, power and exhaust phases.

4-stroke Cycle

A 4-stroke engine requires two crankshaft revolutions (4 strokes of the piston) to complete the Otto cycle. **Figure 1** shows gasoline 4-stroke engine operation. **Figure 2** shows diesel 4-stroke engine operation.

2-stroke Cycle

A 2-stroke engine requires only 1 crankshaft revolution (2 strokes of the piston) to complete the Otto cycle. **Figure 3** shows gasoline 2-stroke engine operation. Although diesel 2-strokes exist, they are not commonly used in light marine applications.

FASTENERS

The material and design of the various fasteners used on marine equipment are not arrived at by chance or accident. Fastener design determines the type of tool required to work with the fastener. Fastener material is carefully selected to decrease the possibility of physical failure or corrosion. See *Galvanic Corrosion* in this chapter for more information on marine materials.

Threads

Nuts, bolts and screws are manufactured in a wide range of thread patterns. To join a nut and bolt, the diameter of the bolt and the diameter of the hole in the nut must be the same. It is just as important that the threads on both be properly matched.

The best way to determine if the threads on two fasteners are matched is to turn the nut on the bolt (or the bolt into the threaded hole in a piece of equipment) with fingers only. Be sure both pieces are clean. If much force is required, check the thread condition on each fastener. If the thread condition is good but the fasteners jam, the threads are not compatible.

Four important specifications describe every thread:
   a. Diameter.
   b. Threads per inch.
   c. Thread pattern.
   d. Thread direction.

Figure 4 shows the first two specifications. Thread pattern is more subtle. Italian and British

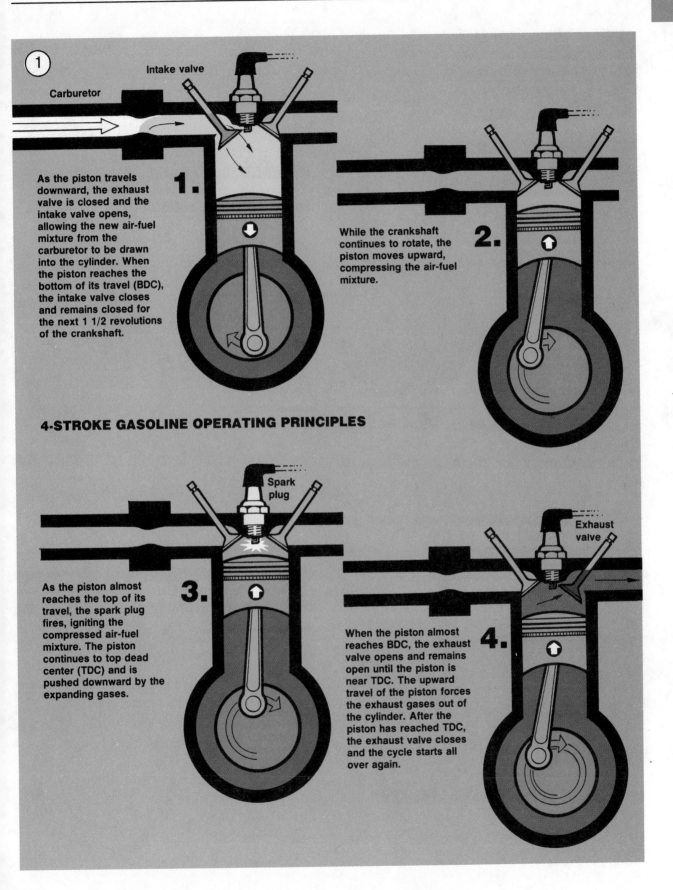

① **Carburetor** | **Intake valve**

1. As the piston travels downward, the exhaust valve is closed and the intake valve opens, allowing the new air-fuel mixture from the carburetor to be drawn into the cylinder. When the piston reaches the bottom of its travel (BDC), the intake valve closes and remains closed for the next 1 1/2 revolutions of the crankshaft.

2. While the crankshaft continues to rotate, the piston moves upward, compressing the air-fuel mixture.

4-STROKE GASOLINE OPERATING PRINCIPLES

Spark plug

3. As the piston almost reaches the top of its travel, the spark plug fires, igniting the compressed air-fuel mixture. The piston continues to top dead center (TDC) and is pushed downward by the expanding gases.

Exhaust valve

4. When the piston almost reaches BDC, the exhaust valve opens and remains open until the piston is near TDC. The upward travel of the piston forces the exhaust gases out of the cylinder. After the piston has reached TDC, the exhaust valve closes and the cycle starts all over again.

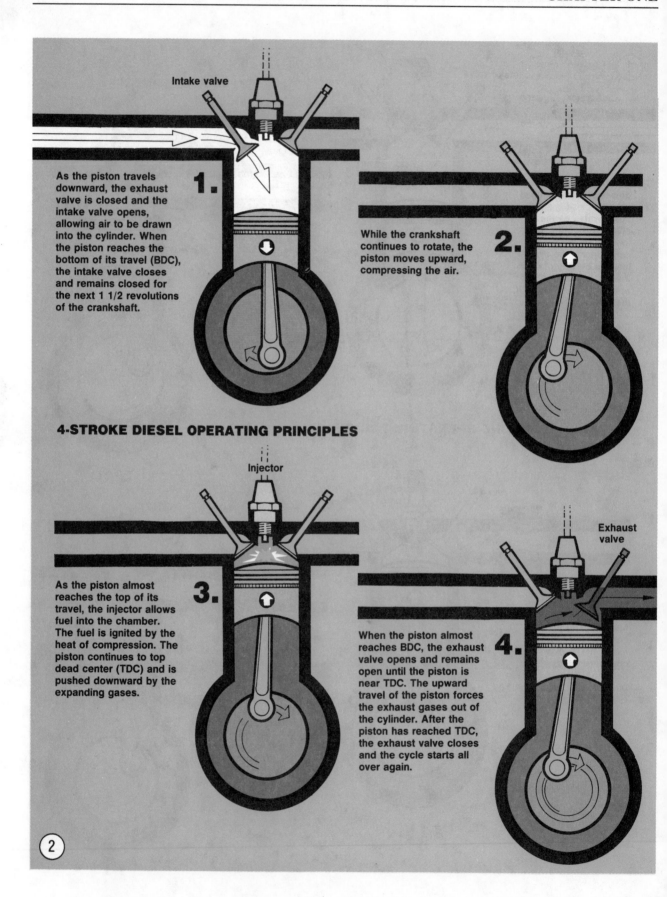

Intake valve

As the piston travels downward, the exhaust valve is closed and the intake valve opens, allowing air to be drawn into the cylinder. When the piston reaches the bottom of its travel (BDC), the intake valve closes and remains closed for the next 1 1/2 revolutions of the crankshaft.

1.

While the crankshaft continues to rotate, the piston moves upward, compressing the air.

2.

4-STROKE DIESEL OPERATING PRINCIPLES

Injector

As the piston almost reaches the top of its travel, the injector allows fuel into the chamber. The fuel is ignited by the heat of compression. The piston continues to top dead center (TDC) and is pushed downward by the expanding gases.

3.

Exhaust valve

When the piston almost reaches BDC, the exhaust valve opens and remains open until the piston is near TDC. The upward travel of the piston forces the exhaust gases out of the cylinder. After the piston has reached TDC, the exhaust valve closes and the cycle starts all over again.

4.

②

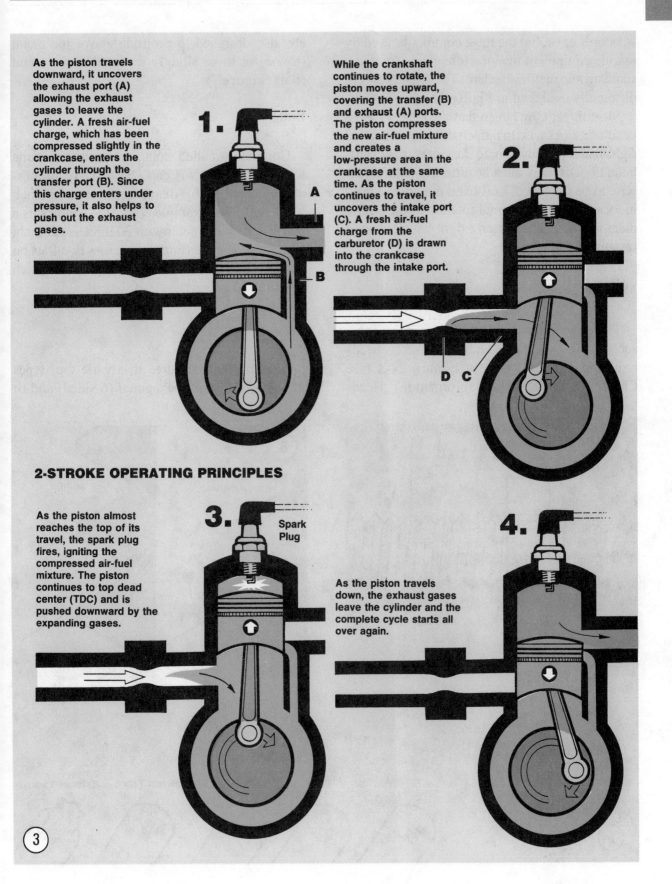

As the piston travels downward, it uncovers the exhaust port (A) allowing the exhaust gases to leave the cylinder. A fresh air-fuel charge, which has been compressed slightly in the crankcase, enters the cylinder through the transfer port (B). Since this charge enters under pressure, it also helps to push out the exhaust gases.

1.

A

B

While the crankshaft continues to rotate, the piston moves upward, covering the transfer (B) and exhaust (A) ports. The piston compresses the new air-fuel mixture and creates a low-pressure area in the crankcase at the same time. As the piston continues to travel, it uncovers the intake port (C). A fresh air-fuel charge from the carburetor (D) is drawn into the crankcase through the intake port.

2.

D C

2-STROKE OPERATING PRINCIPLES

As the piston almost reaches the top of its travel, the spark plug fires, igniting the compressed air-fuel mixture. The piston continues to top dead center (TDC) and is pushed downward by the expanding gases.

3. Spark Plug

As the piston travels down, the exhaust gases leave the cylinder and the complete cycle starts all over again.

4.

③

standards exist, but the most commonly used by marine equipment manufacturers are American standard and metric standard. The threads are cut differently as shown in **Figure 5**.

Most threads are cut so that the fastener must be turned clockwise to tighten it. These are called right-hand threads. Some fasteners have left-hand threads; they must be turned counterclockwise to be tightened. Left-hand threads are used in locations where normal rotation of the equipment would tend to loosen a right-hand threaded fastener.

Machine Screws

There are many different types of machine screws. **Figure 6** shows a number of screw heads requiring different types of turning tools (see Chapter Two for detailed information). Heads

are also designed to protrude above the metal (round) or to be slightly recessed in the metal (flat) (**Figure 7**).

Bolts

Commonly called bolts, the technical name for these fasteners is cap screw. They are normally described by diameter, threads per inch and length. For example, 1/4-20 × 1 indicates a bolt 1/4 in. in diameter with 20 threads per inch, 1 in. long. The measurement across two flats on the head of the bolt indicates the proper wrench size to be used.

Nuts

Nuts are manufactured in a variety of types and sizes. Most are hexagonal (6-sided) and fit

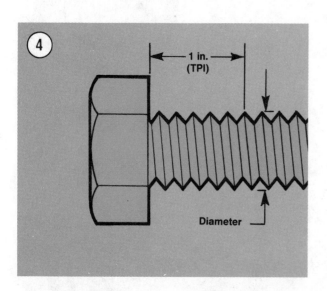

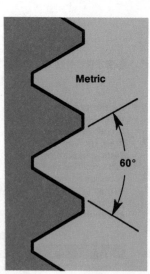

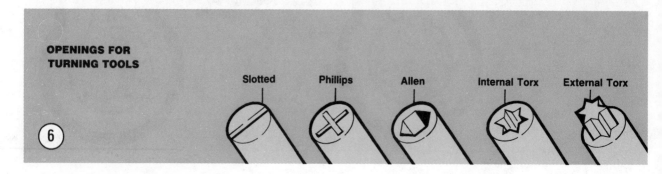

on bolts, screws and studs with the same diameter and threads per inch.

Figure 8 shows several types of nuts. The common nut is usually used with a lockwasher. Self-locking nuts have a nylon insert that prevents the nut from loosening; no lockwasher is required. Wing nuts are designed for fast removal by hand. Wing nuts are used for convenience in non-critical locations.

To indicate the size of a nut, manufacturers specify the diameter of the opening and the threads per inch. This is similar to bolt specification, but without the length dimension. The measurement across two flats on the nut indicates the proper wrench size to be used.

Washers

There are two basic types of washers: flat washers and lockwashers. Flat washers are simple discs with a hole to fit a screw or bolt. Lockwashers are designed to prevent a fastener from working loose due to vibration, expansion and contraction. **Figure 9** shows several types of lockwashers. Note that flat washers are often used between a lockwasher and a fastener to provide a smooth bearing surface. This allows the fastener to be turned easily with a tool.

Cotter Pins

Cotter pins (**Figure 10**) are used to secure special kinds of fasteners. The threaded stud

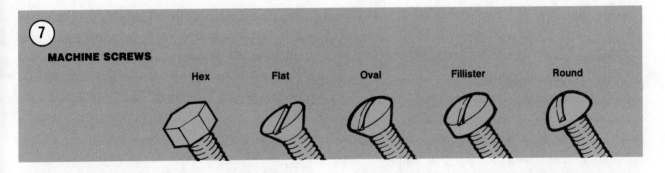

(7) MACHINE SCREWS

Hex   Flat   Oval   Fillister   Round

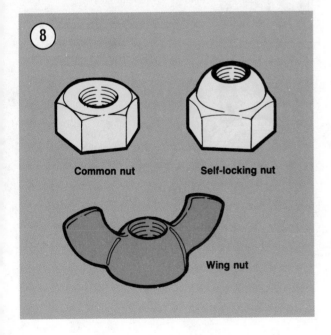

(8)

Common nut   Self-locking nut

Wing nut

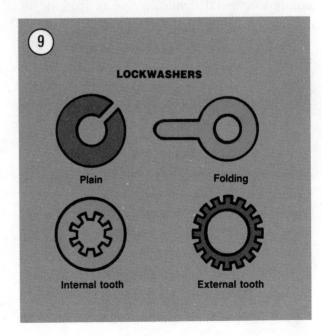

(9)

LOCKWASHERS

Plain   Folding

Internal tooth   External tooth

must have a hole in it; the nut or nut lock piece has projections that the cotter pin fits between. This type of nut is called a "Castellated nut." Cotter pins should not be reused after removal.

Snap Rings

Snap rings can be of an internal or external design. They are used to retain items on shafts (external type) or within tubes (internal type). Snap rings can be reused if they are not distorted during removal. In some applications, snap rings of varying thickness can be selected to control the end play of parts assemblies.

LUBRICANTS

Periodic lubrication ensures long service life for any type of equipment. It is especially important to marine equipment because it is exposed to salt or brackish water and other harsh environments. The *type* of lubricant used is just as important as the lubrication service itself; although, in an emergency, the wrong type of lubricant is better than none at all. The following paragraphs describe the types of lubricants most often used on marine equipment. Be sure to follow the equipment manufacturer's recommendations for lubricant types.

Generally, all liquid lubricants are called "oil." They may be mineral-based (including petroleum bases), natural-based (vegetable and animal bases), synthetic-based or emulsions (mixtures). "Grease" is an oil which is thickened with a metallic "soap." The resulting material is then usually enhanced with anticorrosion, antioxidant and extreme pressure (EP) additives. Grease is often classified by the type of thickener added; lithium and calcium soap are commonly used.

4-stroke Engine Oil

Oil for 4-stroke engines is graded by the American Petroleum Institute (API) and the So-

ciety of Automotive Engineers (SAE) in several categories. Oil containers display these ratings on the top or label (**Figure 11**).

API oil grade is indicated by letters, oils for gasoline engines are identified by an "S" and oils for diesel engines are identified by a "C." Most modern gasoline engines require SF or SG graded oil. Automotive and marine diesel engines use CC or CD graded oil.

Viscosity is an indication of the oil's thickness, or resistance to flow. The SAE uses numbers to indicate viscosity; thin oils have low numbers and thick oils have high numbers. A "W" after the number indicates that the viscosity testing was done at low temperature to simulate cold weather operation. Engine oils fall into the 5W-20W and 20-50 range.

Multi-grade oils (for example, 10W-40) are less viscous (thinner) at low temperatures and more viscous (thicker) at high temperatures. This allows the oil to perform efficiently across a wide range of engine operating temperatures.

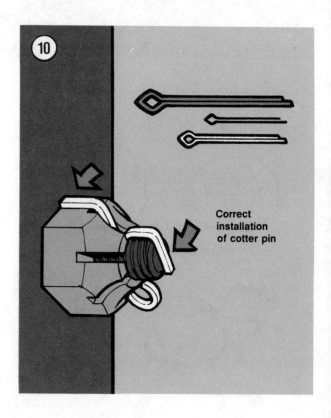

Correct installation of cotter pin

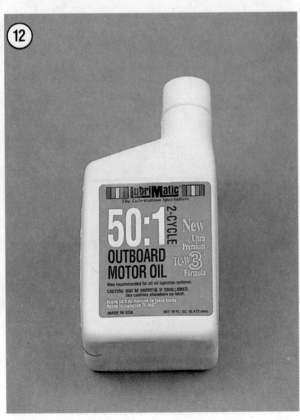

2-stroke Engine Oil

Lubrication for a 2-stroke engine is provided by oil mixed with the incoming fuel-air mixture. Some of the oil mist settles out in the crankcase, lubricating the crankshaft and lower end of the connecting rods. The rest of the oil enters the combustion chamber to lubricate the piston, rings and cylinder wall. This oil is then burned along with the fuel-air mixture during the combustion process.

Engine oil must have several special qualities to work well in a 2-stroke engine. It must mix easily and stay in suspension in gasoline. When burned, it can't leave behind excessive deposits. It must also be able to withstand the high temperatures associated with 2-stroke engines.

The National Marine Manufacturer's Association (NMMA) has set standards for oil used in 2-stroke, water-cooled engines. This is the NMMA TC-W (two-cycle, water-cooled) grade (**Figure 12**). The oil's performance in the following areas is evaluated:

   a. Lubrication (prevention of wear and scuffing).
   b. Spark plug fouling.
   c. Preignition.
   d. Piston ring sticking.
   e. Piston varnish.
   f. General engine condition (including deposits).
   g. Exhaust port blockage.
   h. Rust prevention.
   i. Mixing ability with gasoline.

In addition to oil grade, manufacturers specify the ratio of gasoline to oil required during break-in and normal engine operation.

Gear Oil

Gear lubricants are assigned SAE viscosity numbers under the same system as 4-stroke engine oil. Gear lubricant falls into the SAE 72-250 range (**Figure 13**). Some gear lubricants are multi-grade; for example, SAE 85W-90.

Three types of marine gear lubricant are generally available: SAE 90 hypoid gear lubricant is designed for older manual-shift units; Type C gear lubricant contains additives designed for electric shift mechanisms; High viscosity gear lubricant is a heavier oil designed to withstand the shock loading of high-performance engines or units subjected to severe duty use. Always use a gear lubricant of the type specified by the unit's manufacturer.

Grease

Greases are graded by the National Lubricating Grease Institute (NLGI). Greases are graded by number according to the consistency of the grease; these ratings range from No. 000 to No. 6, with No. 6 being the most solid. A typical multipurpose grease is NLGI No. 2 (**Figure 14**). For specific applications, equipment manufacturers may require grease with an additive such as molybdenum disulfide (MOS^2).

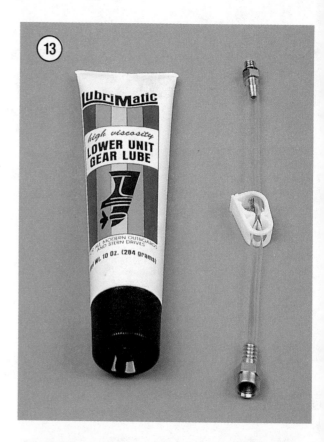

GASKET SEALANT

Gasket sealant is used instead of pre-formed gaskets on some applications, or as a gasket dressing on others. Two types of gasket sealant are commonly used: room temperature vulcanizing (RTV) and anaerobic. Because these two materials have different sealing properties, they cannot be used interchangeably.

RTV Sealant

This is a silicone gel supplied in tubes (**Figure 15**). Moisture in the air causes RTV to cure. Always place the cap on the tube as soon as possible when using RTV. RTV has a shelf life of one year and will not cure properly when the shelf life has expired. Check the expiration date

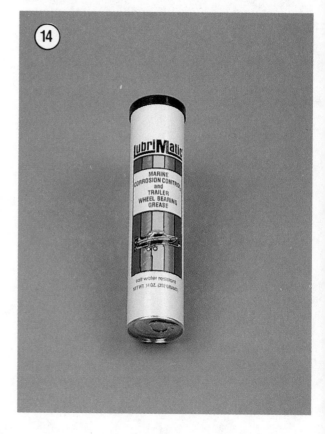

on RTV tubes before using and keep partially used tubes tightly sealed. RTV sealant can generally fill gaps up to 1/4 in. (6.3 mm) and works well on slightly flexible surfaces.

Applying RTV Sealant

Clean all gasket residue from mating surfaces. Surfaces should be clean and free of oil and dirt. Remove all RTV gasket material from blind attaching holes because it can create a "hydraulic" effect and affect bolt torque.

Apply RTV sealant in a continuous bead 2-3 mm (0.08-0.12 in.) thick. Circle all mounting holes unless otherwise specified. Torque mating parts within 10 minutes after application.

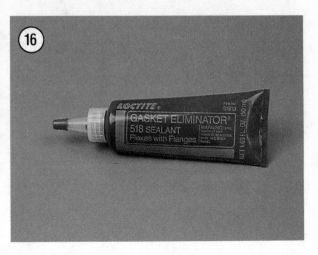

Anaerobic Sealant

This is a gel supplied in tubes (**Figure 16**). It cures only in the absence of air, as when squeezed tightly between two machined mating surfaces. For this reason, it will not spoil if the cap is left off the tube. It should not be used if one mating surface is flexible. Anaerobic sealant is able to fill gaps up to 0.030 in. (0.8 mm) and generally works best on rigid, machined flanges or surfaces.

Applying Anaerobic Sealant

Clean all gasket residue from mating surfaces. Surfaces must be clean and free of oil and dirt. Remove all gasket material from blind attaching holes, as it can cause a "hydraulic" effect and affect bolt torque.

Apply anaerobic sealant in a 1 mm or less (0.04 in.) bead to one sealing surface. Circle all mounting holes. Torque mating parts within 15 minutes after application.

GALVANIC CORROSION

A chemical reaction occurs whenever two different types of metal are joined by an electrical conductor and immersed in an electrolyte. Electrons transfer from one metal to the other through the electrolyte and return through the conductor.

The hardware on a boat is made of many different types of metal. The boat hull acts as a conductor between the metals. Even if the hull is wooden or fiberglass, the slightest film of water (electrolyte) within the hull provides conductivity. This combination creates a good environment for electron flow (**Figure 17**). Unfortunately, this electron flow results in galvanic corrosion of the metal involved, causing one of the metals to be corroded or eaten away by the process. The amount of electron flow (and, therefore, the amount of corrosion) depends on several factors:

    a. The types of metal involved.

    b. The efficiency of the conductor.

    c. The strength of the electrolyte.

Metals

The chemical composition of the metals used in marine equipment has a significant effect on the amount and speed of galvanic corrosion. Certain metals are more resistant to corrosion than others. These electrically negative metals are commonly called "noble;" they act as the cathode in any reaction. Metals that are more subject to corrosion are electrically positive; they act as the anode in a reaction. The more noble metals include titanium, 18-8 stainless steel and nickel. Less noble metals include zinc, aluminum and magnesium. Galvanic corrosion becomes more severe as the difference in electrical potential between the two metals increases.

In some cases, galvanic corrosion can occur within a single piece of metal. Common brass is a mixture of zinc and copper, and, when immersed in an electrolyte, the zinc portion of the mixture will corrode away as reaction occurs between the zinc and the copper particles.

Conductors

The hull of the boat often acts as the conductor between different types of metal. Marine equipment, such as an outboard motor or stern drive unit, can also act as the conductor. Large masses of metal, firmly connected together, are more efficient conductors than water. Rubber mountings and vinyl-based paint can act as insulators between pieces of metal.

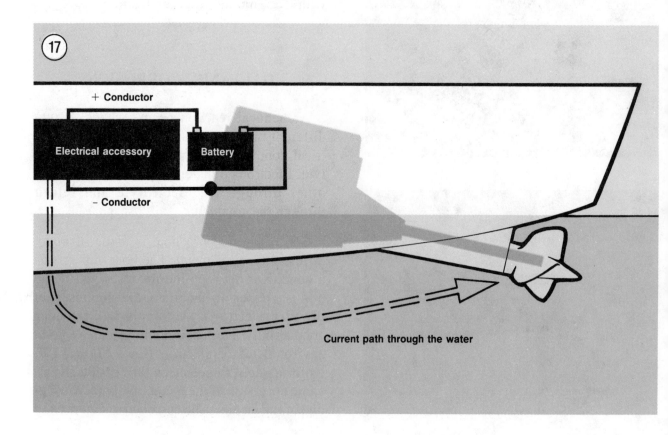

(17)

+ Conductor

Electrical accessory   Battery

- Conductor

Current path through the water

Electrolyte

The water in which a boat operates acts as the electrolyte for the galvanic corrosion process. The better a conductor the electrolyte is, the more severe and rapid the corrosion.

Cold, clean freshwater is the poorest electrolyte. As water temperature increases, its conductivity increases. Pollutants will increase conductivity; brackish or saltwater is also an efficient electrolyte. This is one of the reasons that most manufacturers recommend a freshwater flush for marine equipment after operation in saltwater, polluted or brackish water.

PROTECTION FROM GALVANIC CORROSION

Because of the environment in which marine equipment must operate, it is practically impossible to totally prevent galvanic corrosion. There are several ways by which the process can be slowed. After taking these precautions, the next step is to "fool" the process into occurring only where *you* want it to occur. This is the role of sacrificial anodes and impressed current systems.

Slowing Corrosion

Some simple precautions can help reduce the amount of corrosion taking place outside the hull. These are *not* a substitute for the corrosion protection methods discussed under *Sacrificial Anodes* and *Impressed Current Systems* in this chapter, but they can help these protection methods do their job.

Use fasteners of a metal more noble than the part they are fastening. If corrosion occurs, the larger equipment will suffer but the fastener will be protected. Because fasteners are usually very small in comparison to the equipment being fastened, the equipment can survive the loss of material. If the fastener were to corrode instead of the equipment, major problems could arise.

Keep all painted surfaces in good condition. If paint is scraped off and bare metal exposed, corrosion will rapidly increase. Use a vinyl- or plastic-based paint, which acts as an electrical insulator.

Be careful when using metal-based antifouling paints. These should not be applied to metal parts of the boat, outboard motor or stern drive unit or they will actually react with the equipment, causing corrosion between the equipment and the layer of paint. Organic-based paints are available for use on metal surfaces.

Where a corrosion protection device is used, remember that it must be immersed in the electrolyte along with the rest of the boat to have any effect. If you raise the power unit out of the water when the boat is docked, any anodes on the power unit will be removed from the corrosion cycle and will not protect the rest of the equipment that is still immersed. Also, such corrosion protection devices must not be painted because this would insulate them from the corrosion process.

Any change in the boat's equipment, such as the installation of a new stainless steel propeller, will change the electrical potential and could cause increased corrosion. Keep in mind that when you add new equipment or change materials, you should review your corrosion protection system to be sure it is up to the job.

Sacrificial Anodes

Anodes are usually made of zinc, a far from noble metal. Sacrificial anodes are specially designed to do nothing but corrode. Properly fastening such pieces to the boat will cause them to act as the anode in *any* galvanic reaction that occurs; any other metal present will act as the cathode and will not be damaged.

Anodes must be used properly to be effective. Simply fastening pieces of zinc to your boat in random locations won't do the job.

You must determine how much anode surface area is required to adequately protect the equipment's surface area. A good starting point is provided by Military Specification MIL-A-818001, which states that one square inch of new anode will protect either:

a. 800 square inches of freshly painted steel.
b. 250 square inches of bare steel or bare aluminum alloy.
c. 100 square inches of copper or copper alloy.

This rule is for a boat at rest. When underway, more anode area is required to protect the same equipment surface area.

The anode must be fastened so that it has good electrical contact with the metal to be protected. If possible, the anode can be attached directly to the other metal. If that is not possible, the entire network of metal parts in the boat should be electrically bonded together so that all pieces are protected.

Good quality anodes have inserts of some other metal around the fastener holes. Otherwise, the anode could erode away around the fastener. The anode can then become loose or even fall off, removing all protection.

Another Military Specification (MIL-A-18001) defines the type of alloy preferred that will corrode at a uniform rate without forming a crust that could reduce its efficiency after a time.

Impressed Current Systems

An impressed current system can be installed on any boat that has a battery. The system consists of an anode, a control box and a sensor. The anode in this system is coated with a very noble metal, such as platinum, so that it is almost corrosion-free and will last indefinitely. The sensor, under the boat's waterline, monitors the potential for corrosion. When it senses that corrosion could be occurring, it transmits this information to the control box.

The control box connects the boat's battery to the anode. When the sensor signals the need, the control box applies positive battery voltage to the anode. Current from the battery flows from the anode to all other metal parts of the boat, no matter how noble or non-noble these parts may be. This battery current takes the place of any galvanic current flow.

Only a very small amount of battery current is needed to counteract galvanic corrosion. Manufacturers estimate that it would take two or three months of constant use to drain a typical marine battery, assuming the battery is never recharged.

An impressed current system is more expensive to install than simple anodes but, considering its low maintenance requirements and the excellent protection it provides, the long-term cost may actually be lower.

PROPELLERS

The propeller is the final link between the boat's drive system and the water. A perfectly

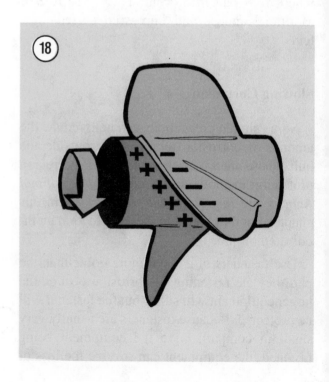

maintained engine and hull are useless if the propeller is the wrong type or has been allowed to deteriorate. Although propeller selection for a specific situation is beyond the scope of this book, the following information on propeller construction and design will allow you to discuss the subject intelligently with your marine dealer.

How a Propeller Works

As the curved blades of a propeller rotate through the water, a high-pressure area is created on one side of the blade and a low-pressure area exists on the other side of the blade (**Figure 18**). The propeller moves toward the low-pressure area, carrying the boat with it.

Propeller Parts

Although a propeller may be a one-piece unit, it is made up of several different parts (**Figure 19**). Variations in the design of these parts make different propellers suitable for different jobs.

The blade tip is the point on the blade farthest from the center of the propeller hub. The blade tip separates the leading edge from the trailing edge.

The leading edge is the edge of the blade nearest to the boat. During normal rotation, this is the area of the blade that first cuts through the water.

The trailing edge is the edge of the blade farthest from the boat.

The blade face is the surface of the blade that faces away from the boat. During normal rotation, high pressure exists on this side of the blade.

The blade back is the surface of the blade that faces toward the boat. During normal rotation, low pressure exists on this side of the blade.

The cup is a small curve or lip on the trailing edge of the blade.

The hub is the central portion of the propeller. It connects the blades to the propeller shaft (part of the boat's drive system). On some drive systems, engine exhaust is routed through the hub; in this case, the hub is made up of an outer and an inner portion, connected by ribs.

The diffuser ring is used on through-hub exhaust models to prevent exhaust gases from entering the blade area.

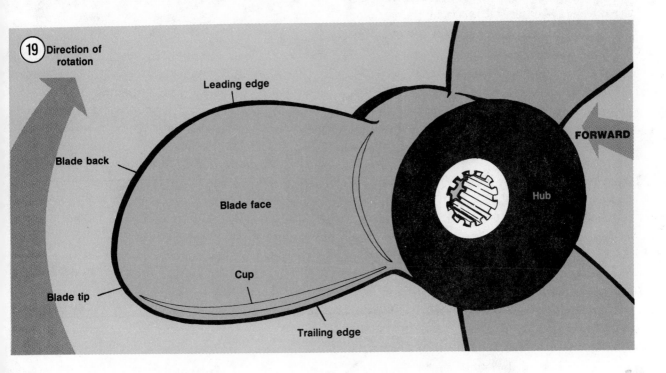

19 Direction of rotation

Leading edge

FORWARD

Blade back

Blade face

Hub

Cup

Blade tip

Trailing edge

Propeller Design

Changes in length, angle, thickness and material of propeller parts make different propellers suitable for different situations.

Diameter

Propeller diameter is the distance from the center of the hub to the blade tip, multiplied by

2. That is, it is the diameter of the circle formed by the blade tips during propeller rotation (**Figure 20**).

Pitch and rake

Propeller pitch and rake describe the placement of the blade in relation to the hub (**Figure 21**).

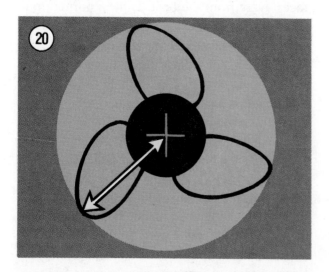

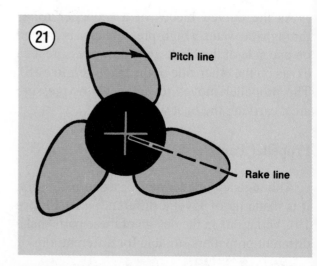

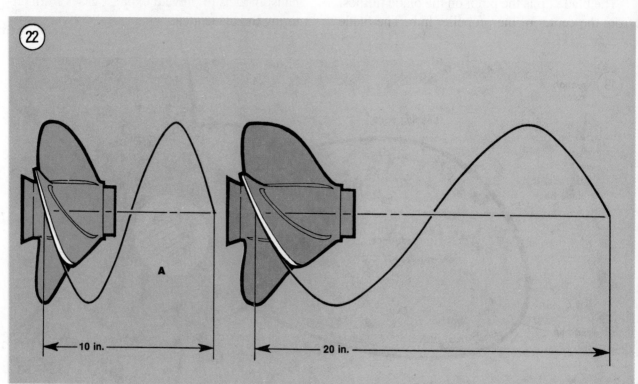

Pitch is expressed by the theoretical distance that the propeller would travel in one revolution. In A, **Figure 22**, the propeller would travel 10 inches in one revolution. In B, **Figure 22**, the propeller would travel 20 inches in one revolution. This distance is only theoretical; during actual operation, the propeller achieves about 80% of its rated travel.

Propeller blades can be constructed with constant pitch (**Figure 23**) or progressive pitch (**Fig-ure 24**). Progressive pitch starts low at the leading edge and increases toward to trailing edge. The propeller pitch specification is the average of the pitch across the entire blade.

Blade rake is specified in degrees and is measured along a line from the center of the hub to the blade tip. A blade that is perpendicular to the hub (A, **Figure 25**) has 0° of rake. A blade that is angled from perpendicular (B, **Figure 25**) has a rake expressed by its difference from perpen-

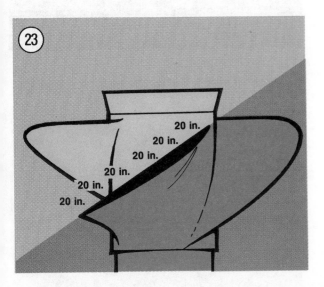

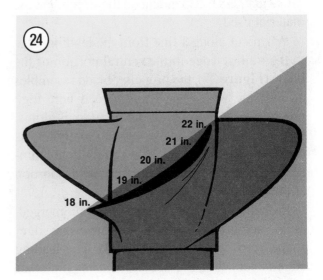

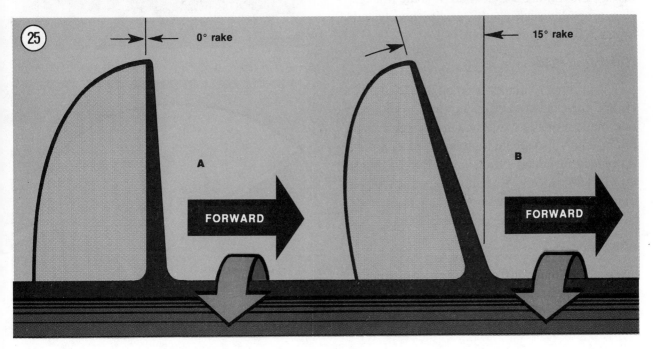

dicular. Most propellers have rakes ranging from 0-20°.

Blade thickness

Blade thickness is not uniform at all points along the blade. For efficiency, blades should be as thin as possible at all points while retaining enough strength to move the boat. Blades tend to be thicker where they meet the hub and thinner at the blade tip (**Figure 26**). This is to support the heavier loads at the hub section of the blade. This thickness is dependent on the strength of the material used.

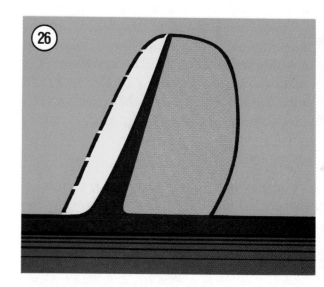

When cut along a line from the leading edge to the trailing edge in the central portion of the blade (**Figure 27**), the propeller blade resembles an airplane wing. The blade face, where high pressure exists during normal rotation, is almost flat. The blade back, where low pressure exists during normal rotation, is curved, with the thinnest portions at the edges and the thickest portion at the center.

Propellers that run only partially submerged, as in racing applications, may have a wedge-shaped cross-section (**Figure 28**). The leading edge is very thin; the blade thickness increases toward the trailing edge, where it is the thickest. If a propeller such as this is run totally submerged, it is very inefficient.

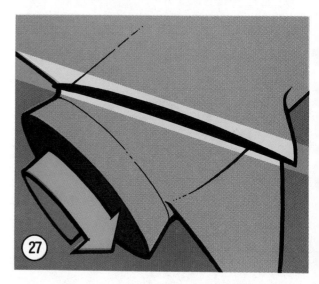

Number of blades

The number of blades used on a propeller is a compromise between efficiency and vibration. A one-blade propeller would be the most efficient, but it would also create high levels of vibration. As blades are added, efficiency decreases, but so do vibration levels. Most propellers have three blades, representing the most practical trade-off between efficiency and vibration.

Material

Propeller materials are chosen for strength, corrosion resistance and economy. Stainless steel, aluminum and bronze are the most commonly used materials. Bronze is quite strong but

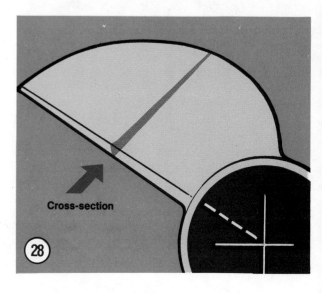

Cross-section

rather expensive. Stainless steel is more common than bronze because of its combination of strength and lower cost. Aluminum alloys are the least expensive but usually lack the strength of steel. Plastic propellers may be used in some low horsepower applications.

Direction of rotation

Propellers are made for both right-hand and left-hand rotation although right-hand is the most commonly used. When seen from behind the boat in forward motion, a right-hand propeller turns clockwise and a left-hand propeller turns counterclockwise. Off the boat, you can tell the difference by observing the angle of the blades (**Figure 29**). A right-hand propeller's blades slant from the upper left to the lower right; a left-hand propeller's blades are the opposite.

Cavitation and Ventilation

Cavitation and ventilation are *not* interchangeable terms; they refer to two distinct problems encountered during propeller operation.

To understand cavitation, you must first understand the relationship between pressure and the boiling point of water. At sea level, water will boil at 212° F. As pressure increases, such as within an engine's closed cooling system, the boiling point of water increases—it will boil at some temperature higher than 212° F. The opposite is also true. As pressure decreases, water will boil at a temperature lower than 212° F. If pressure drops low enough, water will boil at typical ambient temperatures of 50-60° F.

We have said that, during normal propeller operation, low-pressure exists on the blade back. Normally, the pressure does not drop low enough for boiling to occur. However, poor blade design

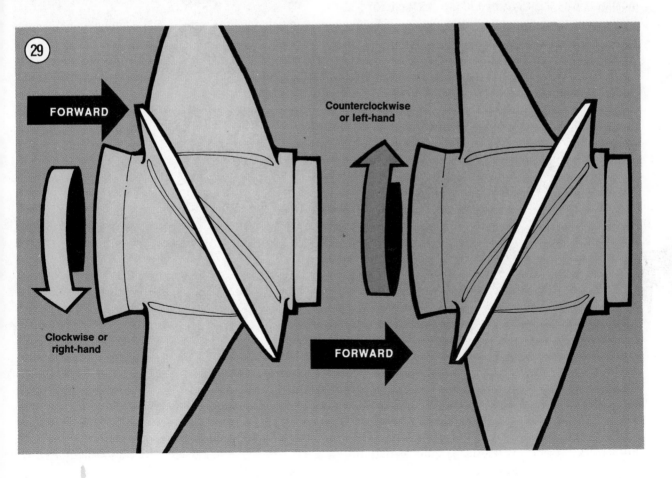

FORWARD

Counterclockwise or left-hand

Clockwise or right-hand

FORWARD

or selection, or blade damage can cause an unusual pressure drop on a small area of the blade (**Figure 30**). Boiling can occur in this small area. As the water boils, air bubbles form. As the boiling water passes to a higher pressure area of the blade, the boiling stops and the bubbles collapse. The collapsing bubbles release enough energy to erode the surface of the blade.

This entire process of pressure drop, boiling and bubble collapse is called "cavitation." The damage caused by the collapsing bubbles is called a "cavitation burn." It is important to remember that cavitation is caused by a decrease in pressure, *not* an increase in temperature.

Ventilation is not as complex a process as cavitation. Ventilation refers to air entering the blade area, either from above the surface of the water or from a through-hub exhaust system. As the blades meet the air, the propeller momentarily over-revs, losing most of its thrust. An added complication is that as the propeller over-revs, pressure on the blade back decreases and massive cavitation can occur.

Most pieces of marine equipment have a plate above the propeller area designed to keep surface air from entering the blade area (**Figure 31**). This plate is correctly called an "antiventilation plate," although you will often *see* it called an "anticavitation plate." Through hub exhaust systems also have specially designed hubs to keep exhaust gases from entering the blade area.

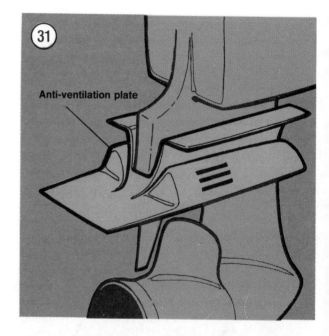

Anti-ventilation plate

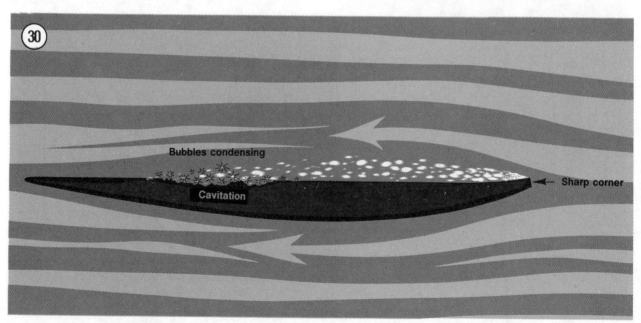

Bubbles condensing

Cavitation

Sharp corner

Chapter Two

Tools and Techniques

This chapter describes the common tools required for marine equipment repairs and troubleshooting. Techniques that will make your work easier and more effective are also described. Some of the procedures in this book require special skills or expertise; in some cases, you are better off entrusting the job to a dealer or qualified specialist.

SAFETY FIRST

Professional mechanics can work for years and never suffer a serious injury. If you follow a few rules of common sense and safety, you too can enjoy many safe hours servicing your marine equipment. If you ignore these rules, you can hurt yourself or damage the equipment.

1. Never use gasoline as a cleaning solvent.
2. Never smoke or use a torch near flammable liquids, such as cleaning solvent. If you are working in your home garage, remember that your home gas appliances have pilot lights.
3. Never smoke or use a torch in an area where batteries are being charged. Highly explosive hydrogen gas is formed during the charging process.

4. Use the proper size wrenches to avoid damage to fasteners and injury to yourself.
5. When loosening a tight or stuck fastener, think of what would happen if the wrench should slip. Protect yourself accordingly.
6. Keep your work area clean, uncluttered and well lighted.
7. Wear safety goggles during all operations involving drilling, grinding or the use of a cold chisel.
8. Never use worn tools.
9. Keep a Coast Guard approved fire extinguisher handy. Be sure it is rated for gasoline (Class B) and electrical (Class C) fires.

BASIC HAND TOOLS

A number of tools are required to maintain marine equipment. You may already have some of these tools for home or car repairs. There are also tools made especially for marine equipment repairs; these you will have to purchase. In any case, a wide variety of quality tools will make repairs easier and more effective.

Keep your tools clean and in a tool box. Keep them organized with the sockets and related drives together, the open end and box wrenches together, etc. After using a tool, wipe off dirt and grease with a clean cloth and place the tool in its correct place.

The following tools are required to perform virtually any repair job. Each tool is described and the recommended size given for starting a tool collection. Additional tools and some duplications may be added as you become more familiar with the equipment. You may need all standard U.S. size tools, all metric size tools or a mixture of both.

Screwdrivers

The screwdriver is a very basic tool, but if used improperly, it will do more damage than good. The slot on a screw has a definite dimension and shape. A screwdriver must be selected to conform with that shape. Use a small screwdriver for small screws and a large one for large screws or the screw head will be damaged.

Two types of screwdriver are commonly required: a common (flat-blade) screwdriver (**Figure 1**) and Phillips screwdrivers (**Figure 2**).

Screwdrivers are available in sets, which often include an assortment of common and Phillips blades. If you buy them individually, buy at least the following:

a. Common screwdriver—5/16 × 6 in. blade.
b. Common screwdriver—3/8 × 12 in. blade
c. Phillips screwdriver—size 2 tip, 6 in. blade.

Use screwdrivers only for driving screws. Never use a screwdriver for prying or chiseling. Do not try to remove a Phillips or Allen head screw with a common screwdriver; you can damage the head so that the proper tool will be unable to remove it.

Keep screwdrivers in the proper condition and they will last longer and perform better. Always keep the tip of a common screwdriver in good condition. **Figure 3** shows how to grind the tip to the proper shape if it becomes damaged. Note the parallel sides of the tip.

Pliers

Pliers come in a wide range of types and sizes. Pliers are useful for cutting, bending and crimping. They should never be used to cut hardened objects or to turn bolts or nuts. **Figure 4** shows several types of pliers.

Each type of pliers has a specialized function. General purpose pliers are used mainly for holding things and for bending. Locking pliers are used as pliers or to hold objects very tightly, like a vise. Needlenose pliers are used to hold or bend small objects. Adjustable or slip-joint pliers can

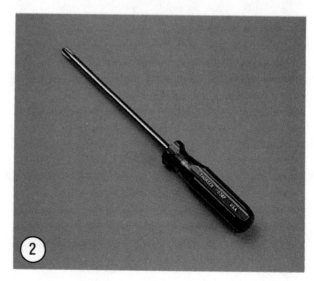

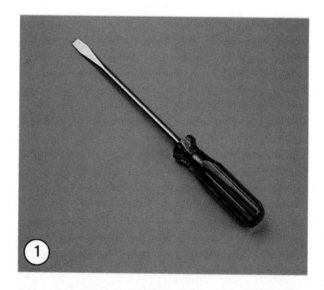

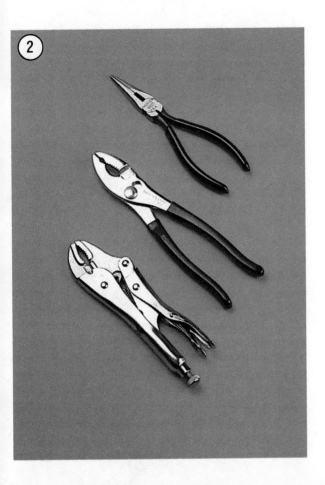

be adjusted to hold various sizes of objects; the jaws remain parallel to grip around objects such as pipe or tubing. There are many more types of pliers. The ones described here are the most commonly used.

Box and Open-end Wrenches

Box and open-end wrenches are available in sets or separately in a variety of sizes. See **Figure 5** and **Figure 6**. The number stamped near the end refers to the distance between two parallel flats on the hex head bolt or nut.

Box wrenches are usually superior to open-end wrenches. An open-end wrench grips the nut on only two flats. Unless it fits well, it may slip and round off the points on the nut. The box wrench grips all 6 flats. Both 6-point and 12-point openings on box wrenches are available. The 6-point gives superior holding power; the 12-point allows a shorter swing.

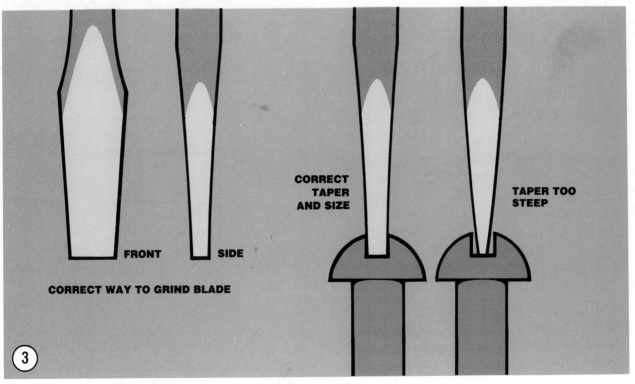

FRONT   SIDE

CORRECT WAY TO GRIND BLADE

CORRECT TAPER AND SIZE   **TAPER TOO STEEP**

Combination wrenches, which are open on one side and boxed on the other, are also available. Both ends are the same size.

Adjustable Wrenches

An adjustable wrench can be adjusted to fit nearly any nut or bolt head. See **Figure 7**. However, it can loosen and slip, causing damage to the nut and maybe to your knuckles. Use an adjustable wrench only when other wrenches are not available.

Adjustable wrenches come in sizes ranging from 4-18 in. overall. A 6 or 8 in. wrench is recommended as an all-purpose wrench.

Socket Wrenches

This type is undoubtedly the fastest, safest and most convenient to use. See **Figure 8**. Sockets, which attach to a suitable handle, are available with 6-point or 12-point openings and use 1/4, 3/8 and 3/4 inch drives. The drive size indicates

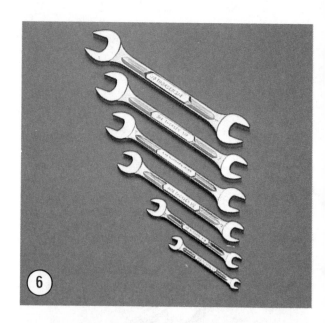

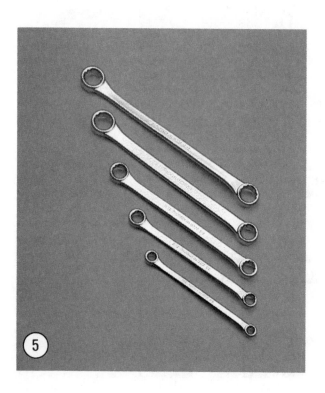

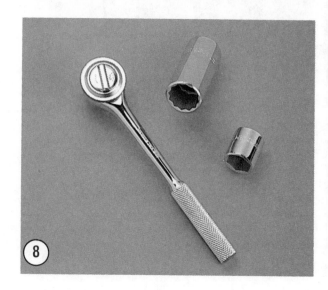

the size of the square hole that mates with the ratchet or flex handle.

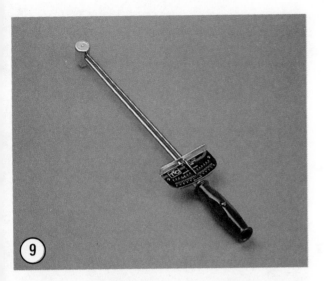

Torque Wrench

A torque wrench (**Figure 9**) is used with a socket to measure how tight a nut or bolt is installed. They come in a wide price range and with either 3/8 or 1/2 in. square drive. The drive size indicates the size of the square drive that mates with the socket. Purchase one that measures up to 150 ft.-lb. (203 N•m).

Impact Driver

This tool (**Figure 10**) makes removal of tight fasteners easy and eliminates damage to bolts and screw slots. Impact drivers and interchangeable bits are available at most large hardware and auto parts stores.

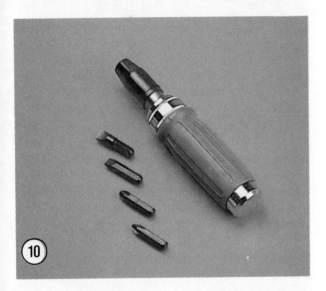

Circlip Pliers

Circlip pliers (sometimes referred to as snapring pliers) are necessary to remove circlips. See **Figure 11**. Circlip pliers usually come with several different size tips; many designs can be switched from internal type to external type.

Hammers

The correct hammer is necessary for repairs. Use only a hammer with a face (or head) of rubber or plastic or the soft-faced type that is filled with buckshot (**Figure 12**). These are sometimes necessary in engine tear-downs. *Never* use a metal-faced hammer as severe damage will result in most cases. You can always produce the same amount of force with a soft-faced hammer.

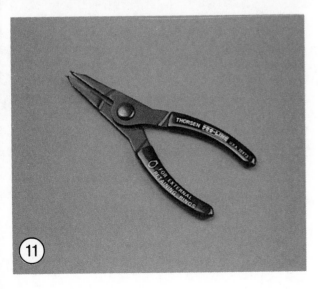

Feeler Gauge

This tool has either flat or wire measuring gauges (**Figure 13**). Wire gauges are used to measure spark plug gap; flat gauges are used for all other measurements. A non-magnetic (brass) gauge may be specified when working around magnetized parts.

Other Special Tools

Some procedures require special tools; these are identified in the appropriate chapter. Unless otherwise specified, the part number used in this book to identify a special tool is the marine equipment manufacturer's part number.

Special tools can usually be purchased through your marine equipment dealer. Some can be made locally by a machinist, often at a much lower price. You may find certain special tools at tool rental dealers. Don't use makeshift tools if you can't locate the correct special tool; you will probably cause more damage than good.

TEST EQUIPMENT

Multimeter

This instrument (**Figure 14**) is invaluable for electrical system troubleshooting and service. It combines a voltmeter, an ohmmeter and an ammeter into one unit, so it is often called a VOM.

Two types of multimeter are available, analog and digital. Analog meters have a moving needle with marked bands indicating the volt, ohm and amperage scales. The digital meter (DVOM) is ideally suited for troubleshooting because it is easy to read, more accurate than analog, contains internal overload protection, is auto-ranging (analog meters must be recalibrated each time the scale is changed) and has automatic polarity compensation.

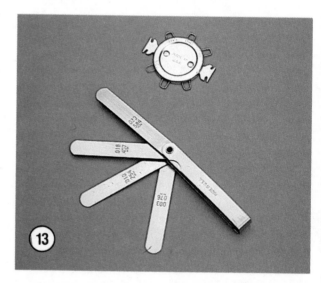

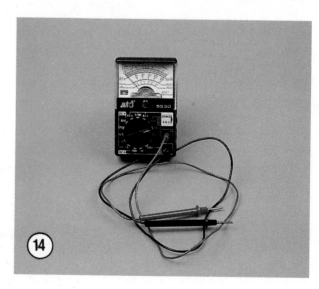

Strobe Timing Light

This instrument is necessary for dynamic tuning (setting ignition timing while the engine is running). By flashing a light at the precise instant the spark plug fires, the position of the timing mark can be seen. The flashing light makes a moving mark appear to stand still opposite a stationary mark.

Suitable lights range from inexpensive neon bulb types to powerful xenon strobe lights. See **Figure 15**. A light with an inductive pickup is best because it eliminates any possible damage to ignition wiring.

Tachometer/Dwell Meter

A portable tachometer is necessary for tuning. See **Figure 16**. Ignition timing and carburetor adjustments must be performed at the specified idle speed. The best instrument for this purpose is one with a low range of 0-1000 or 0-2000 rpm and a high range of 0-6000 rpm. Extended range (0-6000 or 0-8000 rpm) instruments lack accuracy at lower speeds. The instrument should be capable of detecting changes of 25 rpm on the low range.

A dwell meter is often combined with a tachometer. Dwell meters are used with breaker point ignition systems to measure the amount of time the points remain closed during engine operation.

Compression Gauge

This tool (**Figure 17**) measures the amount of pressure present in the engine's combustion chamber during the compression stroke. This indicates general engine condition. Compression readings can be interpreted along with vacuum gauge readings to pinpoint specific engine mechanical problems.

The easiest type to use has screw-in adapters that fit into the spark plug holes. Press-in rubber-tipped types are also available.

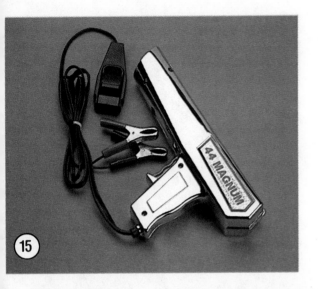

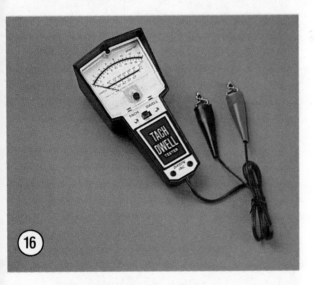

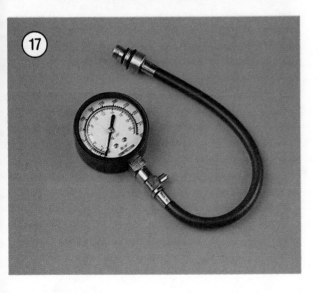

Vacuum Gauge

The vacuum gauge (**Figure 18**) measures the intake manifold vacuum created by the engine's intake stroke. Manifold and valve problems (on 4-stroke engines) can be identified by interpreting the readings. When combined with compression gauge readings, other engine problems can be diagnosed.

Some vacuum gauges can also be used as fuel pressure gauges to trace fuel system problems.

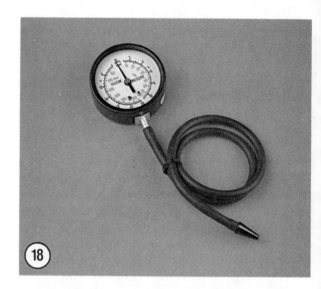

Hydrometer

Battery electrolyte specific gravity is measured with a hydrometer (**Figure 19**). The specific gravity of the electrolyte indicates the battery's state of charge. The best type has automatic temperature compensation; otherwise, you must calculate the compensation yourself.

Precision Measuring Tools

Various tools are needed to make precision measurements. A dial indicator (**Figure 20**), for example, is used to determine run-out of rotating parts and end play of parts assemblies. A dial indicator can also be used to precisely measure piston position in relation to top dead center; some engines require this measurement for ignition timing adjustment.

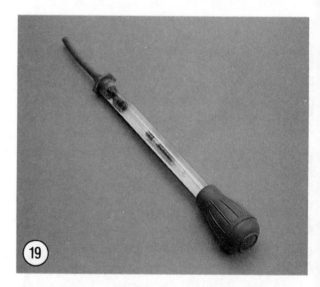

Vernier calipers (**Figure 21**) and micrometers (**Figure 22**) are other precision measuring tools used to determine the size of parts (such as piston diameter).

Precision measuring equipment must be stored, handled and used carefully or it will not remain accurate.

SERVICE HINTS

Most of the service procedures covered in this manual are straightforward and can be performed by anyone reasonably handy with tools.

It is suggested, however, that you consider your own skills and toolbox carefully before attempting any operation involving major disassembly of the engine or gearcase.

Some operations, for example, require the use of a press. It would be wiser to have these performed by a shop equipped for such work, rather than trying to do the job yourself with makeshift equipment. Other procedures require precise measurements. Unless you have the skills and equipment required, it would be better to have a qualified repair shop make the measurements for you.

Preparation for Disassembly

Repairs go much faster and easier if the equipment is clean before you begin work. There are special cleaners, such as Gunk or Bel-Ray Degreaser, for washing the engine and related parts. Just spray or brush on the cleaning solution, let it stand, then rinse away with a garden hose. Clean all oily or greasy parts with cleaning solvent as you remove them.

> *WARNING*
> *Never use gasoline as a cleaning agent. It presents an extreme fire hazard. Be sure to work in a well-ventilated area when using cleaning solvent. Keep a Coast Guard approved fire extinguisher, rated for gasoline fires, handy in any case.*

Much of the labor charged for repairs made by dealers is for the removal and disassembly of other parts to reach the defective unit. It is frequently possible to perform the preliminary operations yourself and then take the defective unit in to the dealer for repair.

If you decide to tackle the job yourself, read the entire section in this manual that pertains to it, making sure you have identified the proper one. Study the illustrations and text until you have a good idea of what is involved in completing the job satisfactorily. If special tools or replacement parts are required, make arrangements to get them before you start. It is frustrating and time-consuming to get partly into a job and then be unable to complete it.

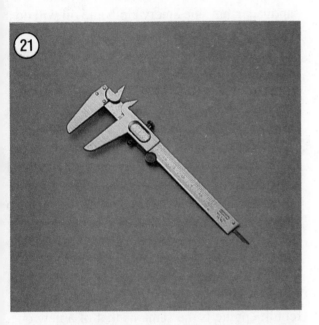

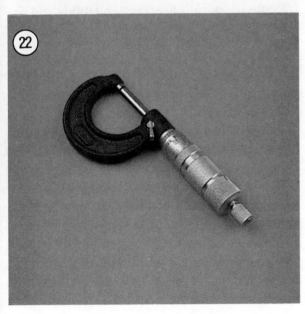

Disassembly Precautions

During disassembly of parts, keep a few general precautions in mind. Force is rarely needed to get things apart. If parts are a tight fit, such as a bearing in a case, there is usually a tool designed to separate them. Never use a screwdriver to pry apart parts with machined surfaces (such as cylinder heads and crankcases). You will mar the surfaces and end up with leaks.

Make diagrams (or take an instant picture) wherever similar-appearing parts are found. For example, head and crankcase bolts are often not the same length. You may think you can remember where everything came from, but mistakes are costly. There is also the possibility you may be sidetracked and not return to work for days or even weeks. In the interval, carefully laid out parts may have been disturbed.

Cover all openings after removing parts to keep small parts, dirt or other contamination from entering.

Tag all similar internal parts for location and direction. All internal components should be reinstalled in the same location and direction from which removed. Record the number and thickness of any shims as they are removed. Small parts, such as bolts, can be identified by placing them in plastic sandwich bags. Seal and label them with masking tape.

Wiring should be tagged with masking tape and marked as each wire is removed. Again, do not rely on memory alone.

Protect finished surfaces from physical damage or corrosion. Keep gasoline off painted surfaces.

Assembly Precautions

No parts, except those assembled with a press fit, require unusual force during assembly. If a part is hard to remove or install, find out why before proceeding.

When assembling two parts, start all fasteners, then tighten evenly in an alternating or crossing pattern if no specific tightening sequence is given.

When assembling parts, be sure all shims and washers are installed exactly as they came out.

Whenever a rotating part butts against a stationary part, look for a shim or washer. Use new gaskets if there is any doubt about the condition of the old ones. Unless otherwise specified, a thin coat of oil on gaskets may help them seal effectively.

Heavy grease can be used to hold small parts in place if they tend to fall out during assembly. However, keep grease and oil away from electrical components.

High spots may be sanded off a piston with sandpaper, but fine emery cloth and oil will do a much more professional job.

Carbon can be removed from the cylinder head, the piston crown and the exhaust port with a dull screwdriver. *Do not* scratch either surface. Wipe off the surface with a clean cloth when finished.

The carburetor is best cleaned by disassembling it and soaking the parts in a commercial carburetor cleaner. Never soak gaskets and rubber parts in these cleaners. Never use wire to clean out jets and air passages; they are easily damaged. Use compressed air to blow out the carburetor *after* the float has been removed.

Take your time and do the job right. Do not forget that the break-in procedure on a newly rebuilt engine is the same as that of a new one. Use the break-in oil recommendations and follow other instructions given in your owner's manual.

SPECIAL TIPS

Because of the extreme demands placed on marine equipment, several points should be kept in mind when performing service and repair. The following items are general suggestions that may improve the overall life of the machine and help avoid costly failures.

1. Unless otherwise specified, use a locking compound, such as Loctite Threadlocker, on all bolts and nuts, even if they are secured with lockwashers. Be sure to use the specified grade

of thread locking compound. A screw or bolt lost from an engine cover or bearing retainer could easily cause serious and expensive damage before its loss is noticed.

When applying thread locking compound, use a small amount. If too much is used, it can work its way down the threads and stick parts together that were not meant to be stuck together.

Keep a tube of thread locking compound in your tool box; when used properly, it is cheap insurance.

2. Use a hammer-driven impact tool to remove and install screws and bolts. These tools help prevent the rounding off of bolt heads and screw slots and ensure a tight installation.

3. When straightening the fold-over type lockwasher, use a wide-blade chisel, such as an old and dull wood chisel. Such a tool provides a better purchase on the folded tab, making straightening easier.

4. When installing the fold-over type lockwasher, always use a new washer if possible. If a new washer is not available, always fold over a part of the washer that has not been previously folded. Reusing the same fold may cause the washer to break, resulting in the loss of its locking ability and a loose piece of metal adrift in the engine.

When folding the washer, start the fold with a screwdriver and finish it with a pair of pliers. If a punch is used to make the fold, the fold may be too sharp, thereby increasing the chances of the washer breaking under stress.

These washers are relatively inexpensive and it is suggested that you keep several of each size in your tool box for repairs.

5. When replacing missing or broken fasteners (bolts, nuts and screws), always use authorized replacement parts. They are specially hardened for each application. The wrong 50-cent bolt could easily cause serious and expensive damage.

6. When installing gaskets, always use authorized replacement gaskets *without* sealer, unless designated. Many gaskets are designed to swell when they come in contact with oil. Gasket sealer will prevent the gaskets from swelling as intended and can result in oil leaks. Authorized replacement gaskets are cut from material of the precise thickness needed. Installation of a too thick or too thin gasket in a critical area could cause equipment damage.

MECHANIC'S TECHNIQUES

Removing Frozen Fasteners

When a fastener rusts and cannot be removed, several methods may be used to loosen it. First, apply penetrating oil, such as Liquid Wrench or WD-40 (available at any hardware or auto supply store). Apply it liberally and allow it penetrate for 10-15 minutes. Tap the fastener several times with a small hammer; do not hit it hard enough to cause damage. Reapply the penetrating oil if necessary.

For frozen screws, apply penetrating oil as described, then insert a screwdriver in the slot and tap the top of the screwdriver with a hammer. This loosens the rust so the screw can be removed in the normal way. If the screw head is too chewed up to use a screwdriver, grip the head with locking pliers and twist the screw out.

Avoid applying heat unless specifically instructed because it may melt, warp or remove the temper from parts.

Remedying Stripped Threads

Occasionally, threads are stripped through carelessness or impact damage. Often the threads can be cleaned up by running a tap (for internal threads on nuts) or die (for external threads on bolts) through threads. See **Figure 23**.

Removing Broken Screws or Bolts

When the head breaks off a screw or bolt, several methods are available for removing the remaining portion.

If a large portion of the remainder projects out, try gripping it with vise-grip pliers. If the projecting portion is too small, file it to fit a wrench or cut a slot in it to fit a screwdriver. See **Figure 24**.

If the head breaks off flush, use a screw extractor. To do this, centerpunch the remaining portion of the screw or bolt. Drill a small hole in the screw and tap the extractor into the hole. Back the screw out with a wrench on the extractor. See **Figure 25**.

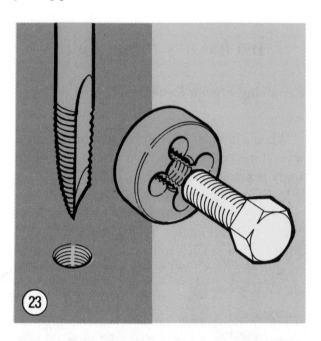

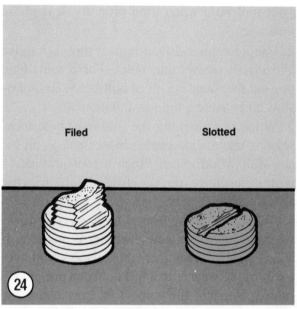

Filed   Slotted

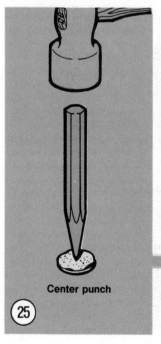

Center punch

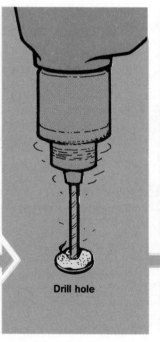

Drill hole

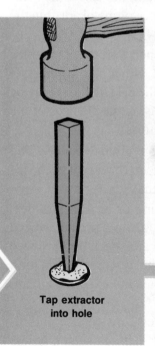

Tap extractor into hole

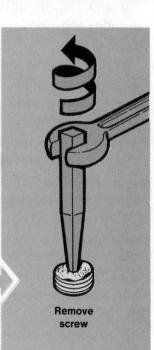

Remove screw

Chapter Three

Troubleshooting

Every internal combustion engine requires an uninterrupted supply of fuel and air, proper ignition and adequate compression. If any of these is lacking, the engine will not run.

Troubleshooting is a relatively simple matter when it is done logically. The first step in any troubleshooting procedure is to define the symptoms as fully as possible and then localize the problem. Subsequent steps involve testing and analyzing those areas which could cause the symptoms. A haphazard approach may eventually solve the problem, but it can be very costly in terms of wasted time and unnecessary parts replacement.

There are two axioms to remember about troubleshooting:

1. The source of the problem is seldom where you think it is.

2. When all else fails, go back to basics—simple solutions often solve complex-appearing problems.

Never assume anything. Don't overlook the obvious. If the engine suddenly quits when running or refuses to start, check the easiest and most accessible spots first. Make sure there is fuel in the tank, and that the spark plugs and all wiring harnesses are properly connected. Something as simple as a loose terminal connection on the ignition coil can allow the primary wire to come off while boating, especially if the vessel has been subjected to turbulent waters. It is costly and embarrassing to call for help in such a case.

You should be familiar enough with the engine compartment to know which wires go where. If a quick visual check of the obvious does not turn up the cause of the problem, look a little further. Learning to recognize and describe symptoms accurately will make repairs easier for you or a technician at the shop. Saying that "it won't run" isn't the same as saying "it quit at high speed and wouldn't restart."

Gather as many symptoms together as possible to aid in diagnosis. Note whether the engine lost power gradually or all at once, what color smoke (if any) came from the exhaust and so on. Remember, the more complicated engine systems become, the easier it is to troubleshoot them because symptoms point to specific problems.

After the symptoms are defined, test and analyze those areas which could cause the problem(s). You don't need fancy or complicated test equipment to determine if repairs can be performed at home.

The electrical system is the weakest link in the chain. More problems result from electrical malfunctions than from any other source. Keep this in mind before you blame the fuel system and start making unnecessary carburetor adjustments. A few simple checks can keep a small problem from turning into a large one. They can also save a large repair bill and time lost while the boat sits in a shop's service department.

On the other hand, be realistic and don't attempt repairs beyond your abilities or with makeshift tools. Stripping the threads on a carburetor fuel inlet while trying to change the fuel filter will cost you several hundred dollars for a new carburetor. Marine service departments also tend to charge heavily for putting together a disassembled engine or other component that may have been abused. Some won't even take on such a job. Use common sense and don't get in over your head or attempt a job without the proper tools.

Proper lubrication, maintenance and periodic tune-ups as described in Chapter Four will reduce the necessity for troubleshooting. Even with the best of care, however, every marine engine is prone to problems which will eventually need troubleshooting.

If replacement components are to be installed, do *not* use automotive parts. While marine components such as carburetors, starters, alternators, etc. may appear to be the same as automotive components, they are not. Marine components have been designed to withstand the unique requirements of marine service, as well as to provide a measure of safety that is not required of automotive service. For example, a marine starter is flashproofed to prevent possible igni-

tion of fuel vapors in the bilge. The use of an automotive starter as a replacement can result in an explosion or fire and possible serious injury or loss of boat and life.

This chapter contains brief descriptions of each major operating system and troubleshooting procedures to be used. The troubleshooting procedures analyze common symptoms and provide logical methods of isolation. These are not the only methods. There may be several approaches to a problem, but all methods used must have one thing in common to be successful—a logical, systematic approach.

Troubleshooting diagrams for individual systems are provided within the chapter. Master troubleshooting charts (**Table 1** and **Table 2**) and model coverage (**Table 3**) are provided at the end of the chapter.

STARTING SYSTEM

The starting system consists of the battery, starter motor, starter solenoid, assist solenoid, ignition switch, shift control (if so equipped) and the necessary connecting wiring and fuses. See **Figure 1**, typical. MerCruiser engines may use a Delco-Remy or Prestolite marine starter motor.

Starting system problems are relatively easy to find. In most cases, the trouble is a loose or dirty connection.

Delco-Remy Starting System Operation

When the ignition switch is turned to START with the shift control in NEUTRAL, the slave solenoid closes and battery current is transmitted to the starter solenoid, which mechanically engages the starter with the engine flywheel. Once the engine has started and the ignition switch is released, the slave solenoid is de-energized. Without current to hold the solenoid in position, the starter motor overrunning clutch disengages the starter pinion from the flywheel.

Prestolite Starting System Operation

When the ignition switch is turned to START with the shift control in NEUTRAL, the slave solenoid closes and battery current is transmitted to the starter motor. A spiral-cut sleeve attached to the armature forces the starter pinion gear to engage with the engine flywheel. A calibrated spring keeps the drive engaged until the crankshaft speed reaches a level high enough to keep the engine running under its own power. At that point, the spring allows the pinion to reverse on its splines and disengage the drive from the flywheel.

On-boat Testing

Two of these procedures require a fully charged 12-volt battery, to be used as a booster, and a pair of jumper cables. Use the jumper cables as outlined in *Jump Starting,* Chapter Eleven, following all of the precautions noted. Disconnect the wiring harness and leads at the rear of the alternator before connecting a booster battery for these tests. This will protect the alternator diodes from possible damage.

Slow cranking starter

1. Connect the 12-volt booster battery to the engine's battery with jumper cables. Listen to the starter cranking speed as the engine is cranked. If the cranking speed sounds normal, check the battery for loose or corroded connections or a low charge. Clean and tighten the connections as required. Recharge the battery if necessary.

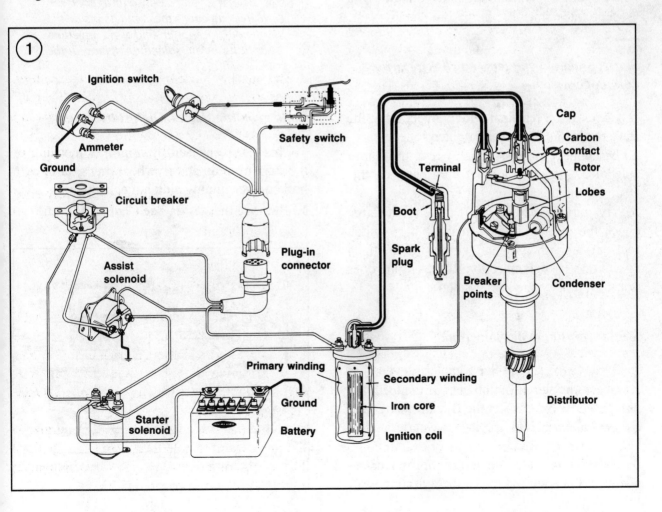

2. If cranking speed does not sound normal, clean and tighten all starter solenoid connections and the battery ground on the engine.

3. Repeat Step 1. If the cranking speed is still too slow, replace the starter.

Starter solenoid clicks, starter does not crank

1. Clean and tighten all starter and solenoid connections. Make sure the terminal eyelets are securely fastened to the wire strands and are not corroded.

2. Remove the battery terminal clamps. Clean the clamps and battery posts. Reinstall the clamps and tighten securely.

3. If the starter still does not crank, connect the 12-volt booster battery to the engine's battery with the jumper cables. If the starter still does not crank, replace it.

Starter solenoid chatters (no click), starter does not crank

1. Check the S terminal wire connection at the starter solenoid. Clean and tighten if necessary.

2. Disconnect the S terminal wire at the starter solenoid. Connect a jumper wire between this terminal and the positive battery post.

3. Try starting the engine. If the engine starts, check the ignition switch, neutral start switch (cut-out) and the system wiring for an open circuit or a loose connection. If the engine does not start, replace the starter solenoid.

Starter spins but does not crank

1. Remove the starter. See Chapter Eleven.

2. Check the starter pinion gear. If the teeth are chipped or worn, inspect the flywheel ring gear for the same problem. Replace the starter and/or ring gear as required.

3. If the pinion gear is in good condition, disassemble the starter and check the armature shaft

for corrosion. See *Brush Replacement,* Chapter Eleven for disassembly procedure. If no corrosion is found, the starter drive mechanism is slipping. Replace the starter with a new or rebuilt marine unit.

Starter will not disengage when ignition switch is released

This problem is usually caused by a sticking solenoid, but the pinion may jam on the flywheel ring gear on an engine with many hours of operation.

> *NOTE*
> *A low battery or loose or corroded battery connections can also cause the starter to remain engaged with the flywheel ring gear. Low voltage at the starter can cause the contacts inside the solenoid to chatter and weld together, resulting in the solenoid sticking in the ON position.*

Loud grinding noises when starter runs

This can be caused by improper meshing of the starter pinion and flywheel ring gear or by a broken overrunning clutch mechanism.

1. Remove the starter. See Chapter Eleven.

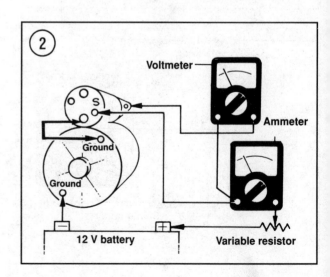

2. Check the starter pinion gear. If the teeth are chipped or worn, inspect the flywheel ring gear for the same problem. Replace the starter and/or ring gear as required.

3. If the pinion gear is in good condition, disassemble the starter and check the overrunning clutch mechanism (Delco-Remy) or Bendix drive (Prestolite). See *Brush Replacement*, Chapter Eleven for disassembly procedure.

Starter Resistance Test

The following test will determine the amount of voltage reaching the starter motor during cranking and will indicate if excessive resistance is present in the circuit.

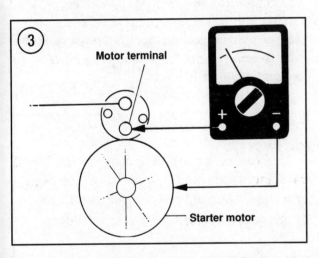

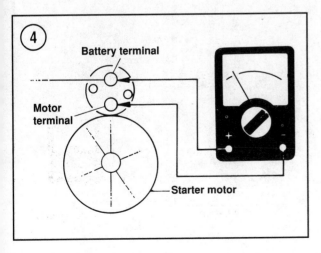

Delco-Remy starter

Refer to **Figure 2** for this procedure.

1. Check the battery and cable condition. Clean the terminals, replace suspect cables or recharge the battery as required.

2. Start the engine and warm to normal operating temperature.

3. Shut the engine off. Disconnect the distributor primary lead at the coil negative terminal to prevent the engine from starting.

4. Connect the positive lead of a voltmeter to the bottom terminal on the solenoid, then ground the negative lead to the starter frame. See **Figure 3**.

> *CAUTION*
> *Do not crank the engine for more than 10 seconds in Step 5. Wait for at least 2 minutes before recranking the engine or it may overheat and damage the starter motor.*

5. Crank the engine for a few seconds while noting the voltmeter reading. If it reads less than 9 volts, connect the voltmeter as shown in **Figure 4**.

6. While cranking the engine, switch the voltmeter from its high to low scale, take the reading, then switch the meter back to its high scale and stop cranking the engine. If the voltmeter reading is more than 1/10 volt, replace the solenoid.

7. If the voltmeter reads less than 1/10 volt in Step 6, check the current draw of the solenoid windings:

   a. Remove the solenoid terminal screw (**Figure 2**) and bend the field leads enough so they will not touch the terminal. Ground the solenoid M terminal to the starter motor frame with a jumper wire.

   b. Connect a battery, a carbon pile and an ammeter with a 0-100 amp scale in series with the solenoid S terminal as shown in **Figure 2**. Ground the starter frame to the negative battery terminal.

   c. Connect the voltmeter between the solenoid frame and S terminal.

d. Adjust the carbon pile slowly until the voltmeter shows 10 volts, then note the ammeter scale. The current draw of both windings in parallel should be 47-55 amps at 10 volts (room temperature).

e. Remove the jumper wire installed between the M terminal and starter frame. Readjust the carbon pile until the voltmeter shows 10 volts, then note the ammeter scale. The current draw of the hold-in winding should be 14.5-16.5 amps at 10 volts (room temperature).

f. If the solenoid windings do not perform as specified, replace the solenoid.

CHARGING SYSTEM

The charging system consists of the alternator, voltage regulator, battery, ignition switch, starter and/or assist solenoid, instrument panel ammeter or voltmeter, the necessary connecting wiring and fuses.

A drive belt driven by the engine crankshaft pulley turns the alternator, which produces electrical energy to charge the battery. As engine speed varies, the voltage output of the alternator varies. The regulator maintains the voltage to the electrical system within safe limits. The ammeter or voltmeter on the instrument panel signals when charging is not taking place.

All models (except 224 cid models) use a Motorola or a Mando (Korean) alternator with a transistorized voltage regulator attached to the rear of the alternator housing. The output rating is stamped on the alternator frame. **Figure 5** shows the Motorola and Mando charging circuit. All 224 cid models use the direct drive alternator charging system described in this chapter.

Complete troubleshooting of the charging system requires test equipment and skills which the average home mechanic does not possess. However, there are basic tests which can be done to pinpoint most problems.

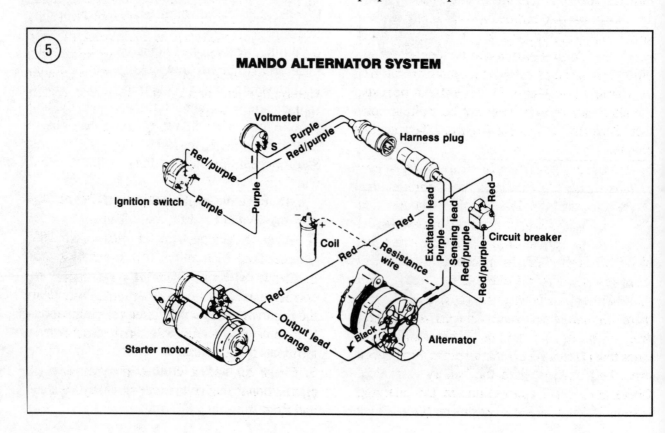

⑤ MANDO ALTERNATOR SYSTEM

Charging system troubles are generally caused by a defective alternator, voltage regulator, battery or a blown fuse. They may also be caused by something as simple as incorrect drive belt tension.

The following are symptoms of problems you may encounter.

1. *Battery dies frequently, even though the ammeter or voltmeter indicates no discharge*—This can be caused by a drive belt that is slightly loose. Grasp the alternator pulley with both hands and try to turn it. If the pulley can be turned without moving the belt, the drive belt is too loose. As a rule, keep the belt tight enough so that it can be deflected only about 1/2 in. under moderate thumb pressure applied between the pulleys. The battery may also be at fault; test the battery condition as described in Chapter Eleven.

2. *Ammeter/voltmeter needle does not move or charging system warning lamp does not light when ignition switch is turned ON*—This may indicate a defective ignition switch, battery, voltage regulator or ammeter/voltmeter/warning lamp. Try to start the engine. If it doesn't start, check the ignition switch and battery. If the engine starts, remove and test the ammeter/voltmeter/warning lamp bulb. If the problem persists, the alternator brushes may not be making contact. Perform the *System Circuitry Test* in this chapter.

3. *Ammeter needle fluctuates between "Charge" and "Discharge" or warning lamp flashes on and off*—This usually indicates that the charging system is working intermittently. Check drive belt tension first, then check all electrical connections in the charging circuit. As a last resort, check the alternator.

4. *Ammeter needle stays on "Discharge," voltmeter indicates less than 12 volts or warning lamp comes on and stays on*—This usually indicates that no charging is taking place. First check drive belt tension, then the battery condition. Check all wiring connections in the charging system. If this does not locate the problem, check

the alternator and voltage regulator as described in this chapter.

5. *Battery requires frequent addition of water or lamp require frequent replacement*—The alternator is probably overcharging the battery. The voltage regulator is most likely at fault.

6. *Excessive noise from the alternator*—Check for loose mounting brackets and bolts. The problem may also be worn bearings or (in some cases) lack of lubrication. If an alternator whines, a shorted diode may be the problem.

MOTOROLA CHARGING SYSTEM TROUBLESHOOTING

A transistorized regulator is attached to the rear of the alternator. The transistorized regulator contains excitation and sensing circuits. The excitation circuit connected to the ignition switch sends a small amount of current to the alternator rotor field winding, initiating output during starting. As a result, the Motorola alternator builds voltage more quickly than other units which rely on residual magnetism to build up voltage during initial startup. The sensing circuit allows the regulator to sense resistance inside the alternator (internally) and outside the alternator (externally).

System Circuitry Test

This test checks the output, excitation and sensing circuits.

1. Check the alternator drive belt tension. See Chapter Ten.
2. Check the battery terminals and cables for corrosion and/or loose connections. Disconnect the negative battery cable, then the positive battery cable. Clean the cable clamps and battery terminals if necessary.
3. Check all wiring connections between the alternator and engine to make sure they are clean and tight.

4. Connect the positive voltmeter lead to the alternator output terminal. Connect the negative voltmeter lead to the alternator ground terminal. See **Figure 6**.

5. Move the engine wire harness back and forth while observing the voltmeter scale. The meter should indicate a steady battery voltage reading (approximately 12 volts). If the reading varies or if no reading is obtained, check for poor connections or damaged wiring. Correct as necessary.

6. Connect the positive voltmeter lead the alternator regulator terminal. Connect the negative voltmeter lead to the alternator ground terminal. See Test No. 1, **Figure 7**.

7. Turn the ignition switch ON. The voltmeter should read 1.5-2.5 volts. If voltmeter reading is not within specifications, remove the alternator and have it bench tested by a dealer or qualified specialist.

8. If no reading is obtained, unplug the white or purple lead at the regulator. Connect the positive voltmeter lead to the disconnected wire. Connect the negative voltmeter lead to a good ground. See Test No. 2, **Figure 7**.

9. If the voltmeter reads battery voltage (approximately 12 volts) in Step 8, replace the voltage regulator. If there is still no voltage reading, check the excitation circuit for poor connections or damaged wiring. Correct as necessary.

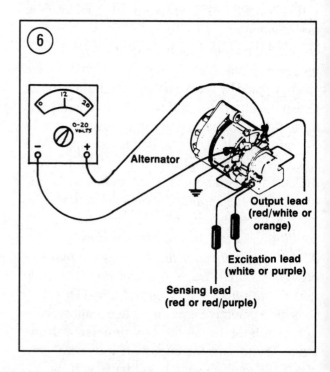

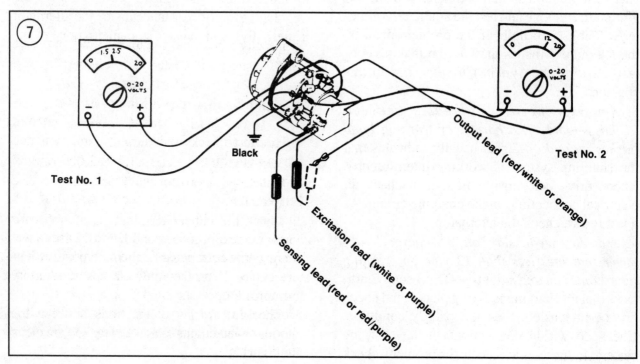

10. Unplug the red or red/purple voltage regulator lead. Connect a voltmeter between the regulator lead and the alternator ground terminal. See **Figure 8**.

11. If the voltmeter does not indicate battery voltage (approximately 12 volts) in Step 10, check the red or red/purple wire for poor connections or damaged wiring. Correct as necessary.

Current Output Test

Refer to **Figure 9** for this procedure.

1. Disconnect the negative battery cable.

2. Disconnect the red/white or orange lead at the alternator output terminal. Connect the positive lead of a 0-50 amp DC ammeter to the output terminal and the negative lead to the disconnected wire.

3. Reconnect the negative battery cable.

4. Disable the ignition system to prevent the engine from starting.

5. Turn all accessories on and crank the engine for 15-20 seconds to remove any surface charge from the battery.

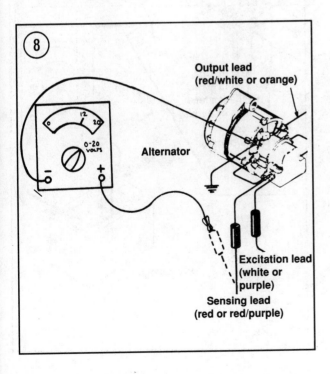

(8)

Output lead
(red/white or orange)

Alternator

0-20 VOLTS

Excitation lead
(white or purple)

Sensing lead
(red or red/purple)

6. Turn all accessories off and reconnect the coil lead to the distributor cap.

7. Connect the tachometer to the engine according to manufacturer's instructions. Connect a carbon pile across the battery.

8. Start the engine and run at 1,500-2,000 rpm. Adjust the carbon pile to obtain maximum alternator output. The ammeter should read a minimum of 30 amps.

9. If a lower output reading (or none) is obtained, shut the engine off. Connect a jumper lead between the alternator output and regulator terminals. Repeat Steps 4-8.

    a. If the ammeter reading is now within specifications, remove the alternator and have the diode trio replaced by a dealer or qualified electrical shop.

    b. If the low reading remains, perform the *Voltage Regulator Test* in this chapter.

Voltage Regulator Test

Refer to **Figure 10** for this procedure.

1. Connect the positive voltmeter lead to the positive battery terminal. Connect the negative voltmeter lead to the negative battery terminal.

2. Connect a tachometer to the engine according to manufacturer's instructions.

3. Start the engine and run at fast idle (1,000-1,500 rpm) until it reaches normal operating temperature.

4. Bring engine speed to 1,500-2,000 rpm and note the voltmeter reading. If the voltage regulator is working correctly, the reading should be between 13.9-14.7 volts.

5. If the reading is above 14.7 volts, check for a poor connection or damaged wiring. Correct as necessary. If connections and wiring are good, perform Step 7 and Step 8 of *System Circuitry Test* in this chapter. If the sensing circuitry is good, replace the voltage regulator as described in this chapter.

6. If the reading is less than 13.9 volts, stop the engine. Remove the 4 regulator attaching screws and pull the regulator far enough from the alternator end frame to connect a jumper lead between the field and regulator terminals. See **Figure 11**.

7. Start the engine, watch the voltmeter and gradually increase engine speed to 1,500 rpm. Do not let voltage exceed 16 volts.

8. If the voltmeter reads 14.5 volts or more in Step 7, replace the voltage regulator as described in this chapter. If the voltmeter reading is less than 14.5 volts, remove the alternator and have it bench tested by a dealer or qualified electrical shop.

MANDO CHARGING SYSTEM TROUBLESHOOTING

The Mando alternator contains excitation and sensing circuits similar to those used with the Motorola alternator.

System Circuitry Test

This test check the output, excitation and sensing circuits.

1. Check the alternator drive belt tension. See Chapter Ten.

2. Check the battery terminals and cables for corrosion and/or loose connections. Disconnect the negative battery cable, then the positive battery cable. Clean the cable clamps and battery terminals if necessary.

3. Check all wiring connections between the alternator and engine to make sure they are clean and tight.

4. Connect the positive voltmeter lead to the alternator output terminal. Connect the negative

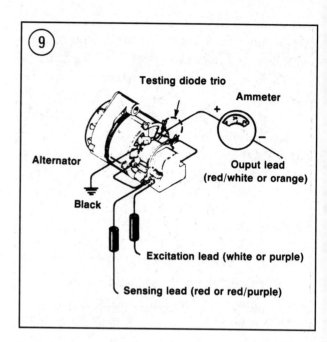

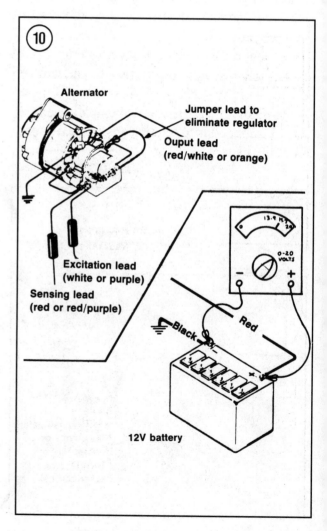

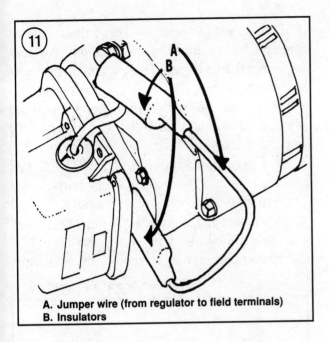

A. Jumper wire (from regulator to field terminals)
B. Insulators

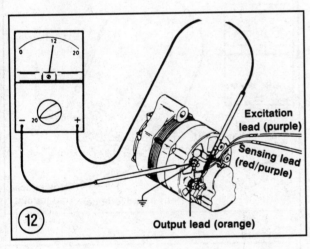

Excitation lead (purple)

Sensing lead (red/purple)

Output lead (orange)

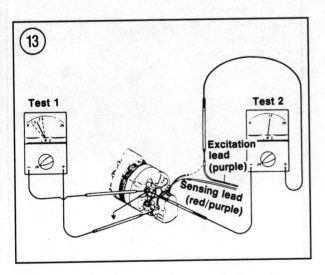

Test 1

Test 2

Excitation lead (purple)

Sensing lead (red/purple)

voltmeter lead to the alternator ground terminal. See **Figure 12**.

5. Move the engine wire harness back and forth while observing the voltmeter scale. The meter should indicate a steady battery voltage reading (approximately 12 volts). If the reading varies or if no reading is obtained, check for poor connections or damaged wiring. Correct as necessary.

6. Connect the positive voltmeter lead to the alternator regulator terminal. Connect the negative voltmeter lead to the alternator ground terminal. See Test No. 1, **Figure 13**.

7. Turn the ignition switch on. The voltmeter should read 1.3-2.5 volts. If voltmeter reading is not within specifications, remove the alternator and have it bench tested by a dealer or qualified specialist.

8. If no reading is obtained, unplug the purple excitation lead and connect it to the positive voltmeter lead. Connect the negative voltmeter lead to a good ground. See Test No. 2, **Figure 13**.

9. If the voltmeter reads battery voltage (approximately 12 volts) in Step 8, replace the voltage regulator. If there is still no voltage reading, check the excitation circuit for poor connections or damaged wiring. Correct as necessary.

10. Unplug the red/purple voltage sensing lead and connect it to the positive voltmeter lead. See **Figure 14**.

11. If the voltmeter does not indicate battery voltage (approximately 12 volts) in Step 10, check the red/purple sensing lead for poor connections or damaged wiring and correct as required.

Current Output Test

The procedures and specifications are the same as given under *Motorola Charging System Current Output Test* in this chapter. Refer to **Figure 15** for test connections.

Voltage Regulator Test

The procedures and specifications are the same as given under *Motorola Charging System Voltage Regulator Test* in this chapter. Refer to **Figure 16** for test connections.

CLYMER QUICK TIP

The charging system seems to be working properly, but 1 or 2 cells of your unsealed battery require water quite frequently. A visual inspection of the battery and charging system turns up nothing and you suspect an overcharge condition.

Remove the battery from the engine compartment and check the case carefully for a crack before having the alternator tested. When only 1 or 2 cells are thirsty, the chances are good that the battery has been damaged from moving around in the battery case or from a battery hold-down that was tightened excessively.

DIRECT DRIVE ALTERNATOR CHARGING SYSTEM

A direct drive alternator charging system is used on MerCruiser 1986 170 and 190 models and 1987-on 165, 180, 3.7L and 3.7LX models. This system is nearly maintenance-free, since it has no brushes, pulleys, belts or bearings. The stator windings (**Figure 17**) are installed on a laminated core attached to the engine front cover. Permanent magnets affixed to the alternator rotor rotate around the stationary stator windings to produce alternating current. A remote diode rectifier changes the alternating current to direct current.

A water-cooled voltage regulator is used with this system.

Constant High Output Test

1. Disconnect the negative battery cable.
2. Connect a tachometer to the engine according to its manufacturer's instructions.

3. Disconnect the orange wire at the regulator and connect an ammeter between the wire and its terminal. See **Figure 18**. Reconnect the negative battery cable.
4. Disconnect one of the yellow/red wires at the regulator and tape it out of the way where it will not contact any metal.
5. Start the engine and run at 1,000 rpm. The ammeter should show no current output If it does, there is a stator short to ground.
6. Reconnect the yellow/red wire. Disconnect the other yellow/red wire and repeat Step 4. If there is no current output, replace the regulator.

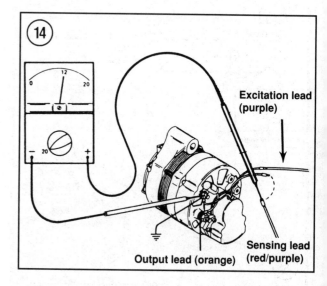

(14)

Excitation lead (purple)

Output lead (orange)   Sensing lead (red/purple)

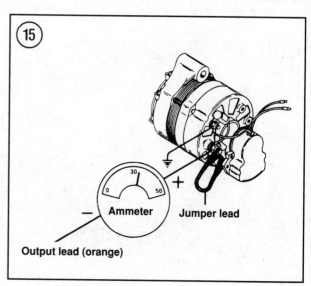

(15)

— Ammeter   Jumper lead

Output lead (orange)

No Output Test

1. Disconnect both yellow/red leads and the orange lead at the regulator. See **Figure 19**. Check resistance between the regulator case and the yellow/red wire studs with an ohmmeter. Replace the regulator if a reading near zero is obtained.

2. Disconnect both yellow/red leads and connect an ohmmeter between the two leads (**Figure**

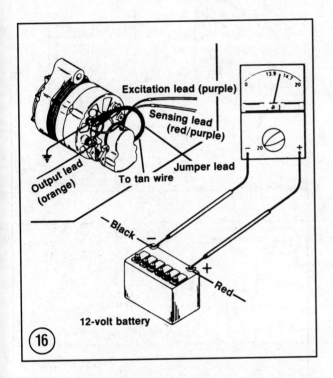

Excitation lead (purple)

Sensing lead (red/purple)

Output lead (orange)

To tan wire

Jumper lead

Black −

Red +

12-volt battery

16

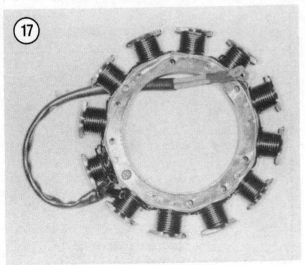

17

20). Replace the stator if the resistance exceeds 1 ohm.

3. Reconnect all regulator leads and disconnect the red/purple sensing lead (**Figure 19**). Connect an ammeter between the red/purple lead and regulator terminal. Start the engine and run at 1,000 rpm. If any charging current is indicated, replace the regulator.

4. If there is no output in Step 3, reconnect the red/purple lead. Connect the ammeter as shown in **Figure 18**. Connect one yellow/red terminal to ground with a jumper lead (**Figure 21**). Run the engine at 1,000 rpm and note the ammeter reading. Ground the other yellow/red terminal and note the reading. If the output is less than 10 amps at either terminal stud, replace the regulator.

RECTIFIER TEST

A Magneto Analyzer (part No. C-91-31800) is recommended for this test. If not available, the test can be performed with either an ohmmeter or a self-powered test lamp.

1. Calibrate the magneto analyzer by setting the selector switch to the No. 3 position and connecting the small red/black test leads together. Turn the adjustment knob to align the needle with the "set" position on the scale. After the meter is calibrated, disconnect the red/black leads.

> *NOTE*
> *If an ohmmeter is used in Steps 2-7, it should show continuity in only one direction when testing positive or negative diodes. A self-powered test lamp will light in one direction and not in the other if the diodes are good.*

2. Connect the small red tester lead to either alternator terminal on the rectifier. Connect the small black tester lead to the positive rectifier terminal. See **Figure 22**. The meter needle should move to the right of scale No. 3.

3

3. Reverse position of the tester leads on the rectifier terminals. The meter needle should move to the left of scale No. 3.

4. Repeat Step 2 and Step 3 with the other rectifier alternator terminal. If the meter needle does not react as specified, one or more of the positive diodes is defective.

5. Connect the small red tester lead to either alternator terminal on the rectifier. Connect the small black tester lead to the rectifier ground bolt. See **Figure 22**. The meter needle should move to the left of scale No. 3.

6. Reverse position of tester leads on the rectifier terminals. The meter needle should move to the right of scale No. 3.

7. Repeat Step 5 and Step 6 with the other rectifier alternator terminal. If the meter needle does not react as specified, one or more of the negative diodes is bad.

IGNITION SYSTEM

All MerCruiser engines except the 3.0L and 3.0LX are equipped with either a mechanical contact breaker-point ignition or a Thunderbolt (breakerless) ignition system. On 3.0L and 3.0LX models, either a digital distributorless ignition system (DDIS) or an electronic spark timing (EST) ignition system is used. Most problems involving failure to start, poor performance or rough running stem from trouble in the ignition system. Many novice troubleshooters assume that these symptoms point to the fuel system instead of the ignition system (remember our axioms?).

Note the following performance symptoms:

a. Engine misses.

b. Stumbles on acceleration (misfiring).

c. Loss of power at high speed (misfiring).

d. Hard starting (if at all).

e. Rough idle.

These symptoms may be caused by one or more of the following:

a. Spark plug(s).

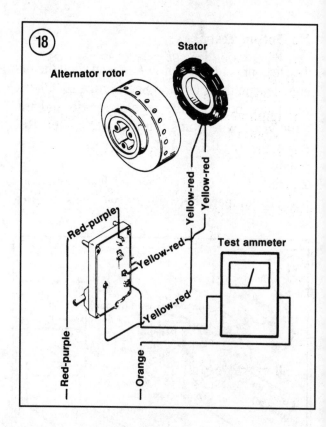

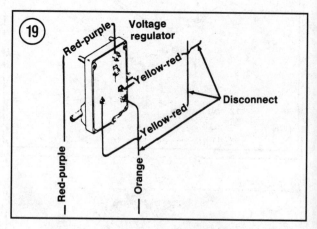

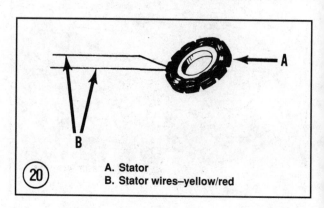

A. Stator
B. Stator wires—yellow/red

b. Secondary wire(s).

c. Distributor cap and rotor.

d. Ignition coil.

e. Ignition amplifier (Thunderbolt ignition).

f. Ignition sensor (Thunderbolt ignition).

g. Motion sensor (DDIS ignition).

h. Ignition module (EST ignition).

i. Pickup coil (EST ignition).

Most of the symptoms can also be caused by a carburetor that is worn or improperly adjusted, or a fuel pump that is about to fail. But considering the law of averages, the odds are far better that the source of the problem will be found in the ignition rather than the fuel system.

Ignition system troubles may be roughly divided between those affecting only one cylinder and those affecting all cylinders. If the problem affects only one cylinder, it can only be in the distributor (or coil pack on DDIS ignition) associated with that particularly cylinder. If the problem affect all cylinders (weak or no spark), then the trouble is most likely located in the ignition coil, rotor, distributor or motion sensor or associated wiring.

Some tests of the ignition system require running the engine with a spark plug or ignition coil wire disconnected. The safest way to do this is to disconnect the wire with the engine stopped, then hold its end next to a metal surface with insulated pliers as shown in **Figure 23**, typical.

WARNING
Never disconnect a spark plug or ignition coil wire when the engine is run-

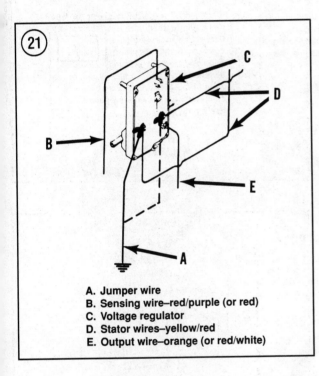

A. Jumper wire
B. Sensing wire—red/purple (or red)
C. Voltage regulator
D. Stator wires—yellow/red
E. Output wire—orange (or red/white)

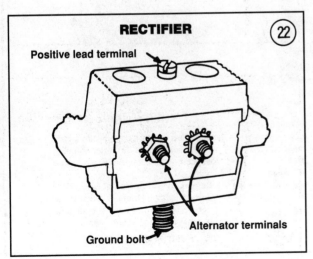

RECTIFIER

Positive lead terminal

Alternator terminals

Ground bolt

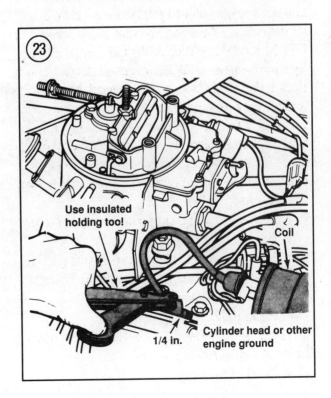

Use insulated holding too!

Coil

1/4 in.

Cylinder head or other engine ground

(24)

SPARK PLUG CONDITION

NORMAL

- Identified by light tan or gray deposits on the firing tip.
- Can be cleaned.

GAP BRIDGED

- Identified by deposit buildup closing gap between electrodes.
- Caused by oil or carbon fouling. If deposits are not excessive, the plug can be cleaned.

OIL FOULED

- Identified by wet black deposits on the insulator shell bore and electrodes.
- Caused by excessive oil entering combustion chamber thorough worn rings and pistons, excessive clearance between valve guides and stems, or worn or loose bearings. Can be cleaned. If engine is not repaired, use a hotter plug.

CARBON FOULED

- Identified by black, dry, fluffy carbon deposits on insulator tips, exposed shell surfaces and electrodes.
- Caused by too cold a plug, weak ignition, dirty air cleaner, too rich a fuel mixture, or excessive idling. Can be cleaned.

LEAD FOULED

- Identified by dark gray, black, yellow, or tan deposits or a fused glazed coating on the insulator tip.
- Caused by highly leaded gasoline. Can be cleaned.

WORN

- Identified by severely eroded or worn electrodes.
- Caused by normal wear. Should be replaced.

FUSED SPOT DEPOSIT

- Identified by melted or spotty deposits resembling bubbles or blisters.
- Caused by sudden acceleration. Can be cleaned.

OVERHEATING

- Identified by a white or light gray insulator with small black or gray brown spots and with bluish-burnt appearance of electrodes.
- Caused by engine overheating, wrong type of fuel, loose spark plugs, too hot a plug, or incorrect ignition timing. Replace the plug.

PREIGNITION

- Identified by melted electrodes and possibly blistered insulator. Metallic deposits on insulator indicate engine damage.
- Caused by wrong type of fuel, incorrect ignition timing or advance, too hot a plug, burned valves, or engine overheating. Replace the plug.

ning. *The high voltage in the ignition system could cause serious injury or even death.*

Spark plug condition is an important indicator of engine performance. Spark plugs in a properly operating engine will have slightly pitted electrodes and a light tan insulator tip. **Figure 24** shows a normal plug and a number of others which indicate trouble in their respective cylinders.

> *WARNING*
> *Be certain the engine compartment is well ventilated and that no gasoline vapors are present during ignition system troubleshooting.*

The troubleshooting procedures outlined in **Figure 25** will help isolate ignition malfunctions in breaker-point systems quickly. These procedures assume the battery and starting system are in acceptable condition and able to crank the engine at its normal speed.

3

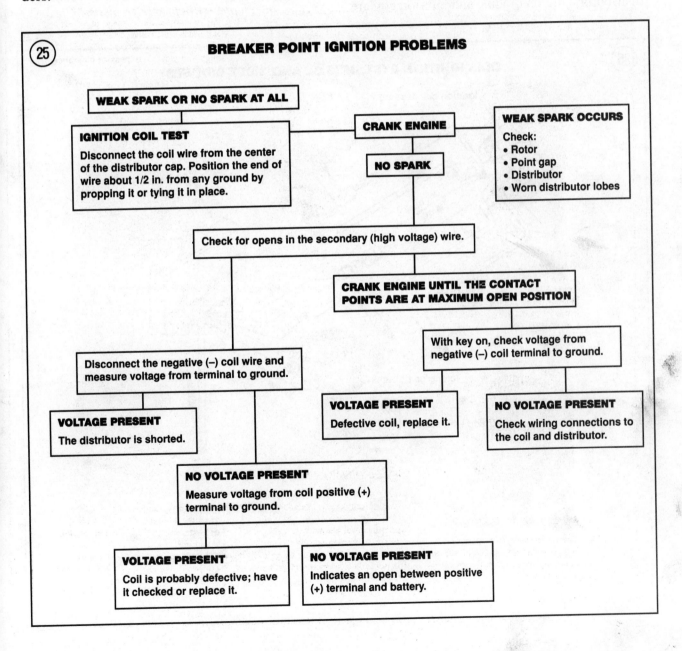

(25) BREAKER POINT IGNITION PROBLEMS

WEAK SPARK OR NO SPARK AT ALL

IGNITION COIL TEST
Disconnect the coil wire from the center of the distributor cap. Position the end of wire about 1/2 in. from any ground by propping it or tying it in place.

CRANK ENGINE

NO SPARK

WEAK SPARK OCCURS
Check:
• Rotor
• Point gap
• Distributor
• Worn distributor lobes

Check for opens in the secondary (high voltage) wire.

CRANK ENGINE UNTIL THE CONTACT POINTS ARE AT MAXIMUM OPEN POSITION

With key on, check voltage from negative (–) coil terminal to ground.

Disconnect the negative (–) coil wire and measure voltage from terminal to ground.

VOLTAGE PRESENT
Defective coil, replace it.

NO VOLTAGE PRESENT
Check wiring connections to the coil and distributor.

VOLTAGE PRESENT
The distributor is shorted.

NO VOLTAGE PRESENT
Measure voltage from coil positive (+) terminal to ground.

VOLTAGE PRESENT
Coil is probably defective; have it checked or replace it.

NO VOLTAGE PRESENT
Indicates an open between positive (+) terminal and battery.

Thunderbolt Ignition System Troubleshooting

WARNING
Be certain the engine compartment is well ventilated and that no gasoline vapors are present during ignition system troubleshooting.

Use the following test procedures to isolate a malfunction in the Thunderbolt ignition system.
1. Make sure all terminal connections at the distributor, ignition module and ignition coil are clean and tight. Make sure the battery is in acceptable condition and fully charged. Make sure the distributor clamp screw is securely tightened.
2. Disconnect the ignition coil wire from the distributor cap. Position the end of the wire approximately 1/2 in. from a good engine ground (**Figure 23**). Crank the engine and check for spark.

NOTE
Prior to performing Step 3 on Alpha One models, disconnect the white/green shift interrupter switch wire from its bullet

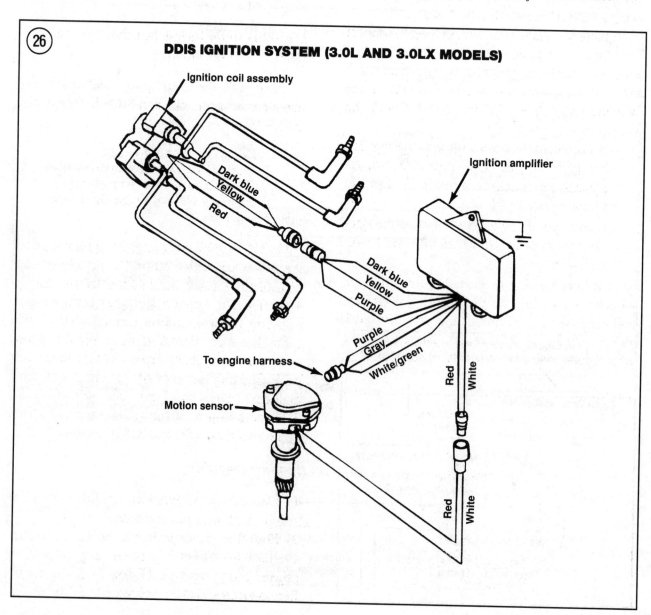

(26) **DDIS IGNITION SYSTEM (3.0L AND 3.0LX MODELS)**

Ignition coil assembly

Dark blue
Yellow
Red

Ignition amplifier

Dark blue
Yellow
Purple

Purple
Gray
White/green

To engine harness

Red
White

Motion sensor

Red
White

connector at the distributor. Also remove the gray tachometer wire from the ignition coil negative (–) terminal.

3. If no spark is noted in Step 2, place the ignition switch in the ON position (engine not running). Connect a voltmeter between a good engine ground and the positive (+) terminal on the ignition coil and note the voltage.

4. If no voltage is noted in Step 3, check the engine wiring harness, instrument panel wiring harness, battery cables and ignition switch for open or shorted circuits. Repair or replace the wiring harness or switch as necessary.

5. If battery voltage is present in Step 3, connect the voltmeter between ground and the white/red wire terminal at the distributor (ignition switch ON). If no voltage is noted, disconnect the white/red wire from the distributor. Check the voltage at the white/red wire.

   a. If no voltage is noted, replace the ignition amplifier. If battery voltage is noted, replace the ignition sensor inside the distributor. See Chapter Eleven.

   b. If battery voltage is noted, replace the ignition sensor inside the distributor. See Chapter Eleven.

6. If battery voltage is present at the white/red wire terminal (Step 5), disconnect the ignition coil wire from the distributor and provide a spark gap as shown in **Figure 23**. Disconnect the white/green wire from the distributor. Place the

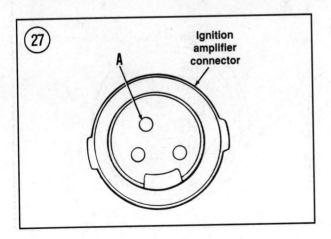

ignition switch in the ON position, then strike the white/green wire against a good engine ground.

   a. If a normal spark is noted at the coil wire, replace the ignition sensor (Chapter Eleven).

   b. If no spark is noted at the coil wire, replace the ignition coil and repeat Step 5. If normal spark is now noted, the original ignition coil is defective. If no spark is noted after replacing the ignition coil, the ignition amplifier is defective. Reinstall the original coil and replace the ignition amplifier. See Chapter Eleven.

Digital Distributorless Ignition System (DDIS) Troubleshooting

Make sure the spark plugs and spark plug wires are in acceptable condition before testing the DDIS system.

> *WARNING*
> *Be certain the engine compartment is well ventilated and that no gasoline vapors are present during ignition system troubleshooting.*

On DDIS ignition, a motion sensor replaces the conventional distributor. The sensor provides crankshaft position information to the ignition amplifier. The ignition amplifier controls ignition coil output, ignition timing advance and contains a speed limiter to prevent engine speed from exceeding 5,000 rpm. The ignition coil pack assembly consists of 2 coils; 1 coil fires cylinders 1 and 4 and 1 coil fires cylinders 2 and 3. Refer to **Figure 26** for a diagram of the DDIS system used on 3.0L and 3.0LX models.

Ignition amplifier

1. Disconnect the ignition amplifier from the coil pack at the 3-pin connector.

2. Place the ignition switch in the RUN position. Connect a voltmeter between a good engine ground and terminal A, **Figure 27** of the amplifier connector. Battery voltage should be noted.

3. Disconnect the engine wiring harness from the ignition amplifier at the 3-pin connector.

4. Connect the voltmeter between engine ground and terminal A, **Figure 28** of the engine harness connector. With the ignition switch in the RUN position, battery voltage should be noted.

5. If the voltage measured in Step 2 and Step 4 varies more than 1/2 volt, the ignition amplifier is defective and must be replaced. See Chapter Eleven.

Ignition coil pack

NOTE
Resistance specifications for the ignition coil assembly are based on measurements taken at room temperature (68°F). Actual resistance values will vary according to ambient temperature and temperature of the component tested.

1. Place the ignition switch in the OFF position.

2. Disconnect the ignition coil from the ignition amplifier at the 3-pin connector.

3. Check coil primary winding resistance by connecting the ohmmeter between terminals A and B, **Figure 29**, then between terminals A and C, **Figure 29**. Coil primary resistance should be 1.9-2.5 ohms.

4. To check coil secondary winding resistance, disconnect the spark plug wires from the coil.

5. Connect the ohmmeter between the No. 1 and No. 4 high tension towers, then between the No. 2 and No. 3 high tension towers.

6. Coil secondary resistance should be 11,300-15,500 ohms.

7. Replace the ignition coil pack assembly if primary or secondary resistance is not as specified.

8. Connect the ohmmeter between each primary terminal (**Figure 29**) and engine ground. Next, connect the ohmmeter between each high tension tower (**Figure 30**) and engine ground. If continuity is noted between any connection and ground, the coil is shorted and must be replaced.

Motion sensor

NOTE
Resistance specifications for the motion sensor are based on measurements taken at 68°F (room temperature). Actual resistance values will vary according to ambient temperature and temperature of the component tested.

1. Make sure the ignition switch is in the OFF position.

2. Disconnect the motion sensor from the ignition amplifier at the 2-pin connector.

3. Connect an ohmmeter between the motion sensor terminals in the 2-pin connector and note the resistance.

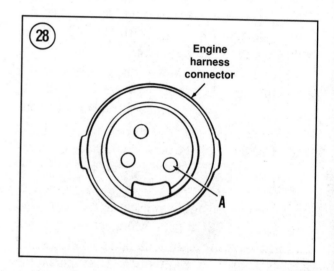

(28) Engine harness connector

A

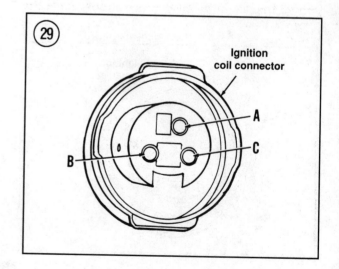

(29) Ignition coil connector

A

C

B

4. Motion sensor resistance should be 140-180 ohms. If not, replace the motion sensor assembly. See Chapter Eleven.

Shift interrupter switch

1. Disconnect the engine harness from the ignition amplifier at the 3-pin connector. Connect an ohmmeter between engine ground and terminal A, **Figure 31** of the engine harness connector. No continuity should be noted. If continuity is

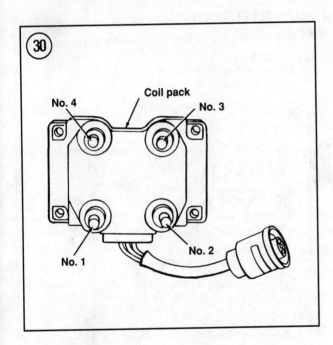

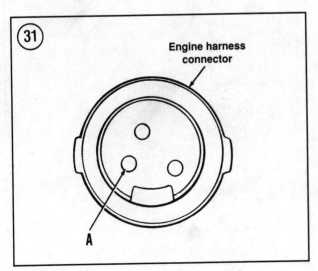

present, either the shift interrupter switch is defective, or the switch circuit is shorted to ground. Repair the circuit or replace the switch as necessary.

> *NOTE*
> *The shift interrupter switch is normally open. When shifting from forward or reverse gear into neutral, the switch will close momentarily.*

Electronic Spark Timing (EST) Troubleshooting

> *WARNING*
> *Be certain the engine compartment is well ventilated and that no gasoline vapors are present during ignition system troubleshooting.*

EST ignition is used on late 1991-on 3.0L and 3.0LX models. EST ignition is a breakerless, electronic ignition system consisting of a distributor, pickup coil, electronic ignition module, ignition coil, battery, ignition switch and related circuitry. A centrifugal spark advance mechanism is not used; spark advance and dwell are controlled electronically by the ignition module. The ignition module and pickup coil are contained inside the distributor. **Figure 32** shows an exploded view of the distributor components.

> *NOTE*
> *The electronic timing advance must be disabled before initial timing can be checked or adjusted. See Chapter Four.*

Prior to testing the ignition system, be sure the spark plugs and spark plug wires are in acceptable condition. Check the distributor cap and rotor for corrosion, cracks, carbon tracks or excessive wear. Replace the distributor cap and rotor as necessary. Inspect the pickup coil and ignition module connections for corrosion or loose connections.

The ignition module can only be tested with a module tester such as Kent-Moore Module

Tester part No. J24642, or equivalent. However, a defective ignition module will cause the ignition system to display one of two failures, no spark or no ignition timing advance. If either of these failures are noted, and all other ignition components test good, replace the ignition module as described in Chapter Eleven. Kent-Moore tools are available from: Kent-Moore Tool & Equipment Division, 29784 Little Mack, Roseville, Michigan 48066. The pickup coil and

ignition coil can be tested using a conventional ohmmeter.

Pickup coil test

NOTE
Resistance specifications for the pickup coil are based on measurements taken at 68°F (room temperature). Actual resistance values will vary according to am-

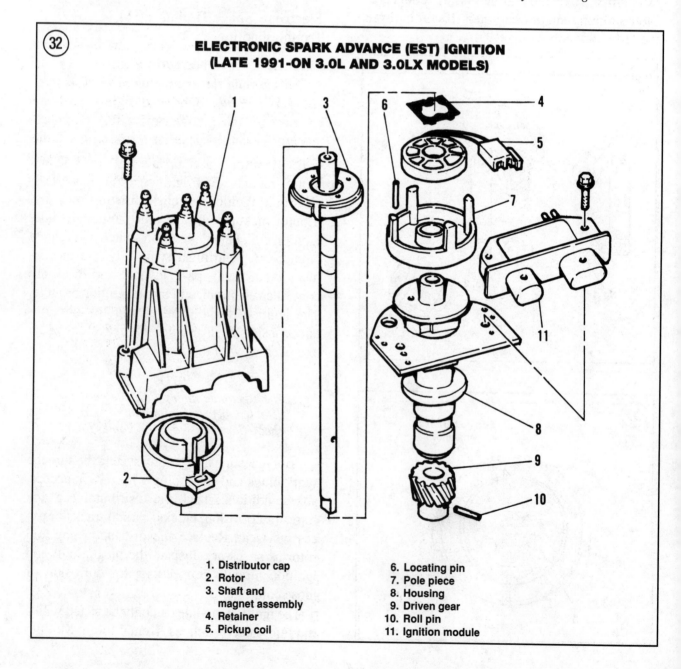

32

**ELECTRONIC SPARK ADVANCE (EST) IGNITION
(LATE 1991-ON 3.0L AND 3.0LX MODELS)**

1. Distributor cap
2. Rotor
3. Shaft and
   magnet assembly
4. Retainer
5. Pickup coil

6. Locating pin
7. Pole piece
8. Housing
9. Driven gear
10. Roll pin
11. Ignition module

bient temperature and temperature of the component tested.

Check the pickup coil for open or shorted windings using an ohmmeter as follows:

1. Make sure the ignition switch is in the OFF position. Disconnect the negative battery cable from the battery.

2. Remove the distributor cap, allowing the spark plug wires to remain attached. Remove the rotor.

3. Disconnect the pickup coil connector from the ignition module. See **Figure 33**.

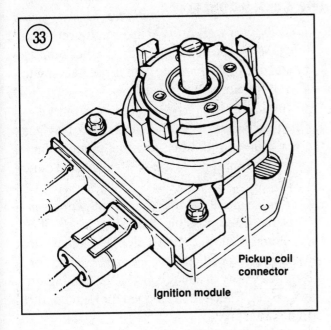

Pickup coil connector

Ignition module

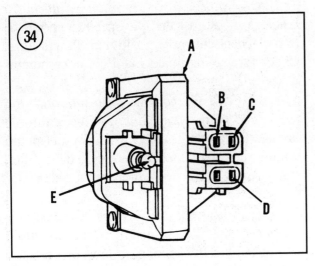

4. Calibrate the ohmmeter on the R × 1000 scale. Connect the ohmmeter leads between the distributor housing and either terminal of the pickup coil connector. Note the ohmmeter reading.

5. Repeat Step 4 at the remaining pickup coil terminal.

6. The ohmmeter should indicate infinity (no continuity) at both connections. If any continuity is present between either pickup coil terminal and the distributor housing, the coil is shorted and must be replaced.

7. Calibrate the ohmmeter on the R × 1000 scale. Connect the ohmmeter leads between the two terminals in the pickup coil connector.

8. Pickup coil resistance should be a constant 500-1,500 ohms. Bend and lightly pull the pickup coil wires while noting the ohmmeter reading to locate intermittent open circuits. If the resistance is not a constant 500-1,500 ohms, replace the pickup coil as described in Chapter Eleven.

Ignition coil test

> *NOTE*
> *Resistance specifications for the ignition coil are based on measurements taken at 68°F (room temperature). Actual resistance values will vary according to ambient temperature and temperature of the component tested.*

Check the ignition coil for open or shorted windings using an ohmmeter as follows:

1. Make sure the ignition switch is in the OFF position. Disconnect the negative cable from the battery.

2. Disconnect the coil high tension lead and both primary connectors from the coil.

3. Calibrate the ohmmeter on the R × 100 scale. Connect the ohmmeter leads between the 12-volt input terminal (B, **Figure 34**) and the coil frame (A, **Figure 34**). No continuity should be noted. If continuity is present, the coil is shorted and must be replaced.

4. Calibrate the ohmmeter on the R × 1 scale. Connect the ohmmeter between the 12-volt input terminal (B, **Figure 34**) and terminal (D, **Figure 34**). Resistance should be approximately 0.4 ohms. If not, replace the coil.

5. Next, connect the ohmmeter leads between the 12-volt input terminal (B, **Figure 34**) and the tachometer terminal (C, **Figure 34**). Resistance should be approximately 0.4 ohm. If not, replace the coil.

6. Calibrate the ohmmeter on the R × 1000 scale. Connect the ohmmeter between the 12-volt input terminal (B, **Figure 34**) and the high tension terminal (E, **Figure 34**). Resistance should be 7,800-8,800 ohms. If not, replace the coil.

CLYMER QUICK TIP

If the engine runs roughly after you or someone else has worked on it, check the spark plug wire routing. The wire may have been connected to the plugs correctly, but improperly routed, resulting in a condition known as cross-fire or induction leakage.

Cross-fire is caused by induced magnetism whenever ignition cables are positioned closely together and in parallel for a distance. It is most likely to occur between consecutive firing cylinders when the cylinders are located side-by-side in the engine block.

FUEL SYSTEM

Fuel system problems should be isolated to the fuel pump, fuel line, fuel filter or carburetor. The following procedures assume that the ignition system is working properly and is correctly adjusted.

1. *Engine will not start*—Make sure there is gas in the tank and that it is being delivered to the carburetor. Remove the flame arrestor, look into the carburetor throat and operate the throttle linkage several times. There should be a stream of fuel from the accelerator pump discharge tube each time the linkage is moved (**Figure 35**). If not, check the fuel pump pressure as described in Chapter Nine. Also check the float condition and adjustment. If the engine will not start, check the automatic choke parts for sticking or damage. If necessary, rebuild or replace the carburetor as described in Chapter Nine.

2. *Engine runs at fast idle*—Check the choke setting, idle speed and mixture adjustments.

3. *Rough idle or engine miss with frequent stalling*—Check choke linkage for proper adjustment. Check throttle stop screw adjustment. Check for sticking throttle plates. Set idle speed to specifications. Check float adjustment.

4. *Engine "diesels" (continues to run) when ignition is switched off*—Check ignition timing and idle speed (probably too fast). Check linkage to make sure the fast idle cam is not hanging up. Check for engine overheating.

5. *Stumbling when accelerating from idle*—Check accelerator pump action (Step 1). Check for a clogged fuel filter, low fuel pump volume, plugged bowl vents or a power valve that is stuck closed.

6. *Engine misses at high speed or lacks power*—This indicates possible fuel starvation. Check accelerator pump action (Step 1). Check float setting and needle valve action. Check for a plugged pump discharge nozzle or leaking nozzle gasket. Check for a clogged fuel filter or dirty flame arrestor.

7. *Engine stalls on deceleration or during a quick stop*—Adjust the idle speed to specifications. Check throttle positioner functioning. Check for leaking intake manifold or carburetor gasket(s).

8. *Engine will not reach wide-open throttle, top speed and power are reduced*—Check throttle linkage for binding. Check for low fuel pump volume, incorrect float drop, a clogged fuel filter, stuck power valve or an inoperative secondary system.

9. *Engine surges at cruising speed*—Check for a plugged fuel filter. Adjust float level and drop. Check for low fuel pump volume or pressure.

Check fuel for contamination. Check for blocked air bleeds or leaking plugs/lead seals.

10. *Black exhaust smoke*—Check for an excessively rich mixture. Check idle speed adjustment and choke setting. Check for excessive fuel pump pressure, leaky float or worn needle valve.

11. *Excessive fuel consumption*—Check for an excessively rich mixture or misblended gasohol. Check choke operation. Check idle speed and mixture adjustments. Check for excessive fuel pump pressure, leaky float or worn needle valve.

CLYMER QUICK TIP
Contrary to what manufacturers would have you believe, the composition material used in floats does gradually absorb fuel over a period of time. Such fuel absorption increases the weight of the float and prevents it from operating properly when set to correct specifications.

To check a composition float for fuel absorption, remove it from the carburetor, hold it between a thumb and finger and gently press a fingernail into the surface. If moisture appears where your fingernail pressed, the float has started to absorb fuel.

Since floats are quite expensive, the best way to determine if fuel absorption has affected float performance is to weigh it with an inexpensive float scale available in most auto supply stores. The scale comes with weight specifications for all new floats and can immediately pinpoint a fuel system problem that's often overlooked.

CLYMER QUICK TIP
Your fuel economy has dropped off considerably and you can smell gasoline fumes. You suspect a leak in the fuel system, but a quick check turns up no signs of the tell-tale stains such a leak

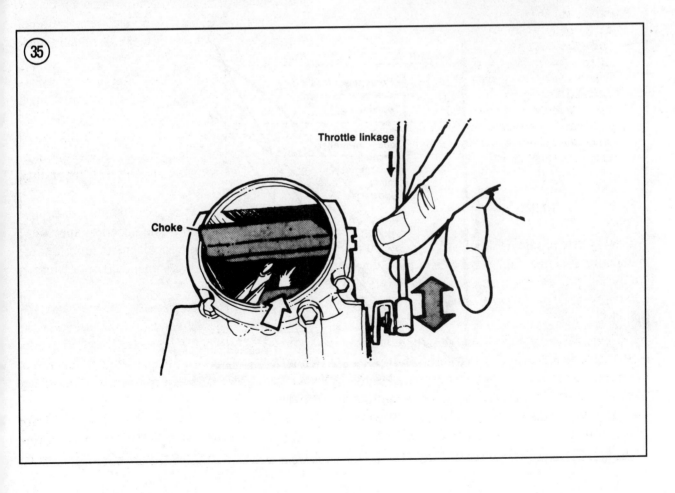

35

Throttle linkage

Choke

would leave on the carburetor or intake manifold. It's not an uncommon problem with Rochester Quadrajet carburetors.

The Quadrajet contains 2 brass plugs in the secondary fuel well which tend to leak over a period of time. The solution requires carburetor removal and disassembly to reach the plugs. After scraping the area around each plug clean, seal it with epoxy. Let the epoxy cure for 24-48 hours before reassembling the carburetor.

ENGINE PERFORMANCE

Elevation and weather have definite effects on the wide-open throttle power of any internal combustion engine. As elevation increases, the air gets thinner and the engine air-fuel mixture becomes richer. Installation of a lower pitch propeller will regain some of the lost performance, but the basic problem remains; The diameter of the propeller is too large for the reduced power available. Your MerCruiser dealer can calculate how much diameter must be removed from a lower pitch propeller to provide good performance at high elevations. You may find it helpful to make a gear ratio change to provide more reduction.

Heat and humidity affect the density of the air in a similar manner. This is particularly noticeable when your engine is propped out on a cool,

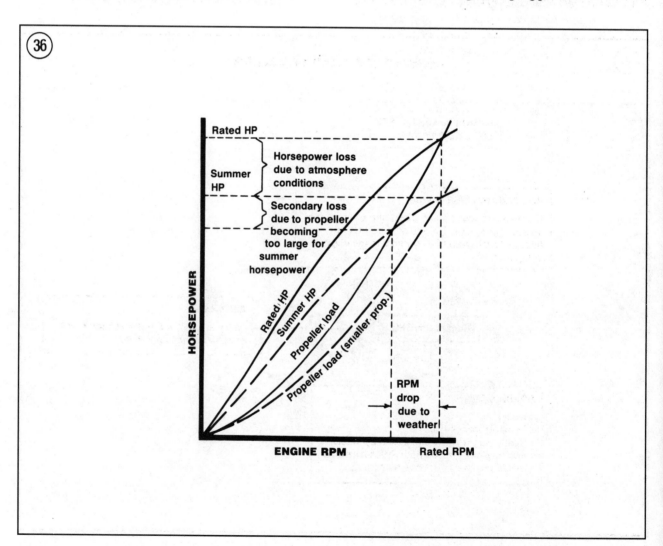

dry spring day or seems to lose its pep during hot, humid August days. You may lose up to 14 percent of the available horsepower, resulting in a 2-3 mph reduction in speed and an inability to get the boat on plane. **Figure 36** shows the relationship between horsepower and weather conditions.

A number of factors can make the engine difficult or impossible to start or cause rough running, poor performance and so on. The majority of novice troubleshooters immediately suspect the carburetor as the cause of the problem. In most cases, however, the problem lies in the ignition system.

The troubleshooting procedures outlined in **Figures 37-40** and **Table 1** will help you solve most engine performance problems in a systematic manner.

ENGINE OVERHEATING

There are numerous causes of engine overheating, some of which are often overlooked during troubleshooting.

a. A loose alternator belt—this prevents the engine circulating water pump from operating at the proper speed.

b. Excessively advanced or retarded ignition timing.

c. A plugged or restricted water passage in the stern drive due to operation while the drive unit was submerged in sand or silt.

3

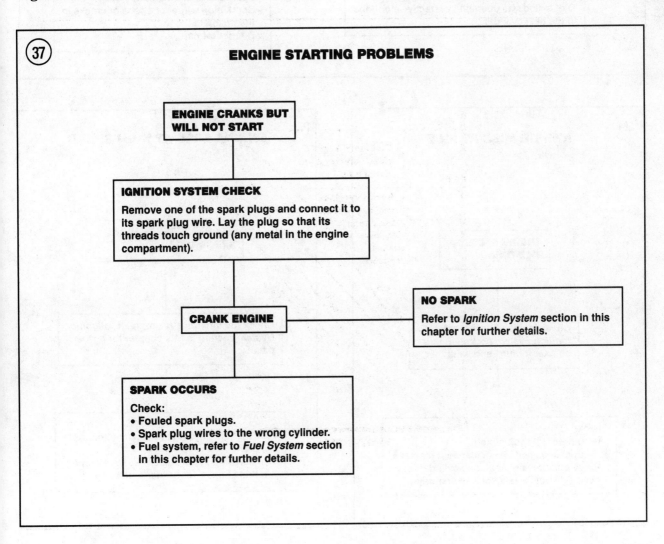

(37) ENGINE STARTING PROBLEMS

ENGINE CRANKS BUT WILL NOT START

IGNITION SYSTEM CHECK

Remove one of the spark plugs and connect it to its spark plug wire. Lay the plug so that its threads touch ground (any metal in the engine compartment).

CRANK ENGINE

NO SPARK

Refer to *Ignition System* section in this chapter for further details.

SPARK OCCURS

Check:
• Fouled spark plugs.
• Spark plug wires to the wrong cylinder.
• Fuel system, refer to *Fuel System* section in this chapter for further details.

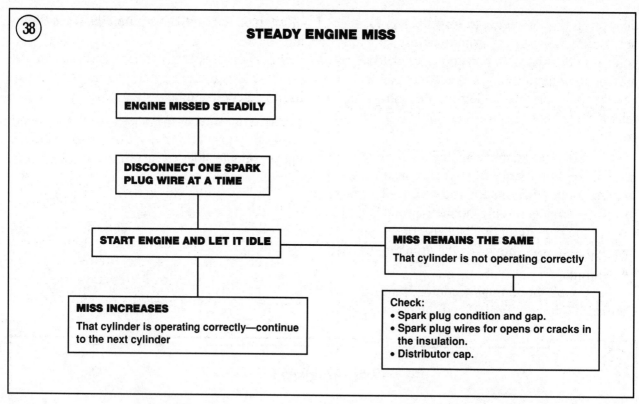

(38) **STEADY ENGINE MISS**

ENGINE MISSED STEADILY

DISCONNECT ONE SPARK PLUG WIRE AT A TIME

START ENGINE AND LET IT IDLE

MISS REMAINS THE SAME

That cylinder is not operating correctly

MISS INCREASES

That cylinder is operating correctly—continue to the next cylinder

Check:
• Spark plug condition and gap.
• Spark plug wires for opens or cracks in the insulation.
• Distributor cap.

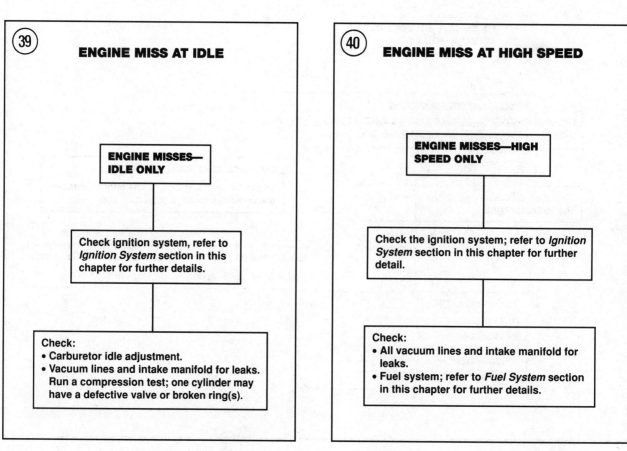

(39) **ENGINE MISS AT IDLE**

ENGINE MISSES— IDLE ONLY

Check ignition system, refer to *Ignition System* section in this chapter for further details.

Check:
• Carburetor idle adjustment.
• Vacuum lines and intake manifold for leaks. Run a compression test; one cylinder may have a defective valve or broken ring(s).

(40) **ENGINE MISS AT HIGH SPEED**

ENGINE MISSES—HIGH SPEED ONLY

Check the ignition system; refer to *Ignition System* section in this chapter for further detail.

Check:
• All vacuum lines and intake manifold for leaks.
• Fuel system; refer to *Fuel System* section in this chapter for further details.

d. Water supply hoses that are defective inside—this is most often the result of delamination, in which the hose disintegrates from inside.

e. A plugged or restricted inlet screen on the stern drive lower unit.

f. A worn or damaged engine circulating or stern drive water pump.

g. Leakage of air or exhaust into the suction side of the stern drive water pump.

h. Too much oil in the crankcase—excessive oil will cause overheating at wide-open throttle.

i. A defective thermostat—see Chapter Ten.

ENGINE OIL PRESSURE INDICATOR

Proper oil pressure is vital to the engine. If oil pressure is insufficient, the engine can destroy itself in a comparatively short time.

The oil pressure warning circuit monitors oil pressure constantly. If pressure drops below a predetermined level, the warning light comes on.

Obviously, it is vital that the warning circuit be in working order to signal low oil pressure. Each time you turn on the ignition, but before starting the engine, the warning light should come on. If it doesn't, the trouble is in the warning circuit, not the oil pressure system. See **Figure 41** to troubleshoot the warning circuit.

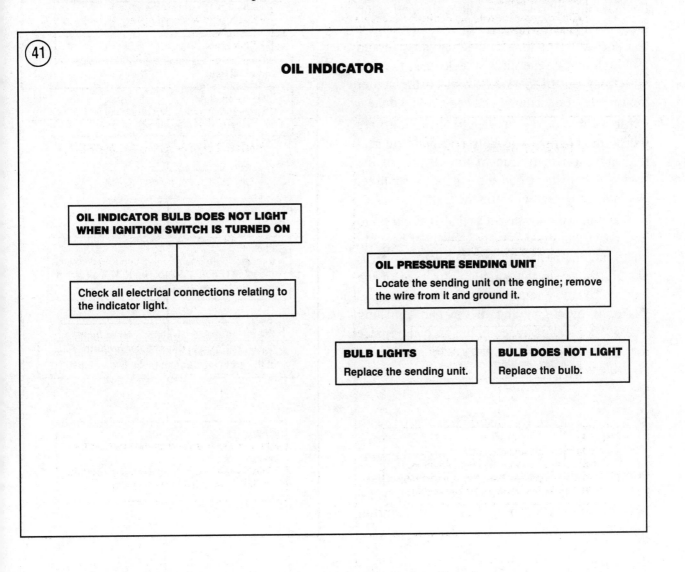

41

OIL INDICATOR

OIL INDICATOR BULB DOES NOT LIGHT WHEN IGNITION SWITCH IS TURNED ON

Check all electrical connections relating to the indicator light.

OIL PRESSURE SENDING UNIT
Locate the sending unit on the engine; remove the wire from it and ground it.

BULB LIGHTS
Replace the sending unit.

BULB DOES NOT LIGHT
Replace the bulb.

Once the engine is running, the warning light should remain off. If the warning light comes on or acts erratically while the engine is running, there is trouble with the engine oil pressure system. *Stop the engine immediately.* Refer to **Figure 42** for possible causes of the problem.

ENGINE OIL LEAKS

Like automotive engines, MerCruiser marine engines are subject to oil leaks. Boat installation, however, may make it difficult to determine exactly where the leak is. Many owners of new boats discover oil in the bilge. Generally, this oil leaks into the sealed flywheel housing through the rear main oil seal if the boat is shipped at too high an angle. It is not a serious problem and is self-correcting, as long as the boat is not stored at a high angle. The oil that leaks past the seal will spray out of the water vent on the starter motor side of the engine and can be wiped up.

More common oil leaks are found as hours are put on the engine. A leaking rear main oil seal will allow oil to run down the outside of the flywheel housing when the engine is running. Replacing the seal will stop the leak.

A leaking oil pan gasket will also allow oil to drip down the outside of the flywheel housing when the engine is running. The leaking oil is usually found on the starter motor side of the engine. The most common cause of a leaking pan gasket is overtightening of the pan attaching screws. If a leak is traced to the oil pan, replace the gasket and check the pan gasket surface for possible warpage.

ENGINE NOISES

Often the first evidence of an internal engine problem is a strange noise. That knocking, clicking or tapping sound which you never heard before may be warning you of impending trouble.

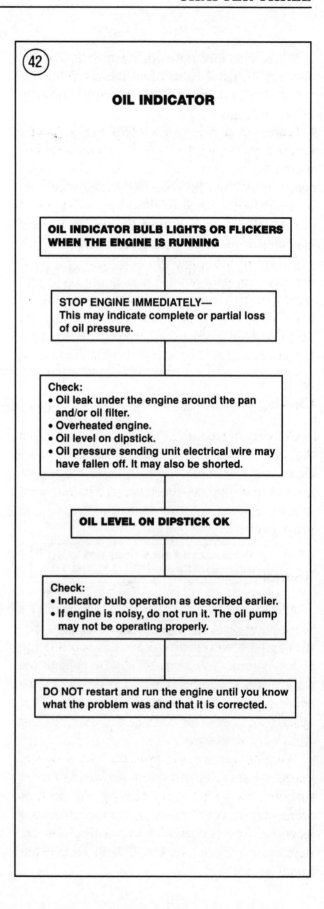

(42)

OIL INDICATOR

OIL INDICATOR BULB LIGHTS OR FLICKERS WHEN THE ENGINE IS RUNNING

STOP ENGINE IMMEDIATELY—
This may indicate complete or partial loss of oil pressure.

Check:
• Oil leak under the engine around the pan and/or oil filter.
• Overheated engine.
• Oil level on dipstick.
• Oil pressure sending unit electrical wire may have fallen off. It may also be shorted.

OIL LEVEL ON DIPSTICK OK

Check:
• Indicator bulb operation as described earlier.
• If engine is noisy, do not run it. The oil pump may not be operating properly.

DO NOT restart and run the engine until you know what the problem was and that it is corrected.

While engine noises can indicate problems, they are difficult to interpret correctly; inexperienced mechanics can be seriously misled by them.

Professional mechanics often use a special stethoscope (which looks like a doctor's stethoscope) for isolating engine noises. You can do nearly as well with a "sounding stick" which can be an ordinary piece of doweling, a length of broom handle or a section of small hose. By placing one end in contact with the area to which you want to listen and the other end near your ear, you can hear sounds emanating from that area. The first time you do this, you may be horrified at the strange sounds coming from even a normal engine. If you can, have an experienced friend or mechanic help you sort out the noises.

Clicking or Tapping Noises

Clicking or tapping noises usually come from the valve train and indicate excessive valve clearance. A sticking valve may also sound like a valve with excessive clearance. In addition, excessive wear in valve train components can cause similar engine noises.

Knocking Noises

A heavy, dull knocking is usually caused by a worn main bearing. The noise is loudest when the engine is working hard, such as accelerating at low speed. You may be able to isolate the trouble to a single bearing by disconnecting the spark plugs one at a time. When you reach the spark plug nearest the bearing, the knock will be reduced or disappear.

Worn connecting rod bearings may also produced a knock, but the sound is usually more metallic. As with a main bearing, the noise is worse during acceleration. It may increase just as you go from acceleration to coasting. Disconnecting the spark plugs will help isolate this knock as well.

A double knock or clicking usually indicates a worn piston pin. Disconnecting spark plugs will isolate this to a particular piston; however, the noise will *increase* when you reach the affected piston.

A loose flywheel and excessive crankshaft end play also produces knocking noises. While similar to main bearing noises, they are usually intermittent, not constant, and they do not change when spark plugs are disconnected. When caused by a loose flywheel or coupling, the noise is generally heard at idle or during rapid deceleration. It is a good idea to recheck flywheel/coupler nut torque whenever the engine is removed from the boat.

Some mechanics confuse piston pin noise with piston slap (excessive piston clearance). The double knock will distinguish piston pin noise. Piston slap will always be louder when the engine is cold.

ENGINE TROUBLESHOOTING

These procedures assume the starter cranks the engine over normally. If not, refer to the *Starter* section of this chapter.

Engine Won't Start

This can be caused by the ignition or fuel system. Refer to *Ignition System* section of this chapter and perform a spark intensity test. If sparks occur, the problem is more likely in the fuel system. If they do not occur, check the ignition system.

Engine Misses Steadily

Remove one spark plug wire at a time and ground the wire. If engine miss increases, that cylinder is working properly. Reconnect the wire and check another. When a wire is disconnected and engine miss remains the same, that cylinder is not firing. Perform a spark intensity test as described in this chapter. If no spark occurs for the suspected cylinder, check the distributor cap, wire and spark plug. See Chapter Four. If a spark occurs properly, check cylinder compression and intake manifold vacuum (Chapter Four).

Engine Misses Erratically at All Speeds

Intermittent problems can be difficult to locate. This could be in the ignition system, exhaust system or fuel system. Start with the secondary ignition wiring and follow the troubleshooting procedures for each system to isolate the cause.

Engine Misses at Idle Only

The problem could be in the ignition system or carburetor idle adjustment. Adjust the idle mixture and inspect the idle circuit for restrictions.

Engine Misses at High Speed Only

Check the accelerator pump operation and fuel pump delivery. Look for a restricted fuel line. Check the spark plugs and wires.

Low Performance at All Speeds, Poor Acceleration

Usually an ignition or fuel system problem. May also be an intake manifold or carburetor vacuum leak.

> *CLYMER QUICK TIP*
> *To check for a leaking V6 or V8 intake manifold gasket, use a garden hose to run water along the mating surface on each side with the engine idling. The V-design of the engine will allow enough water to accumulate to temporarily seal any leak. If the engine idle suddenly smooths out, the gasket is leaking.*

Although oil or carburetor cleaner is often used to troubleshoot this problem, water is preferred, as it is both cleaner and safer. Water does not leave the messy residue of oil and is not dangerous like carburetor cleaner.

Tighten the bolts on a leaking intake manifold first to see if this eliminates the problem. However, tightening the manifold on engines which use a metal valley cover with laminated gasket sections will not work. The laminated gasket material is causing the leak and the entire valley cover will have to be replaced.

Excessive Fuel Consumption

Check for a plugged or restricted air cleaner filter element. Misblended gasohol will also cause the problem, although there will be performance problems at the same time.

Engine Overheats

Usually caused by a cooling system problem, although late ignition or valve timing can be responsible. Check the coolant level in the cooling system. Check the condition of the drive belt. Check the cooling system hoses for leaks and loose connections.

Engine Stalls As It Warms Up

The choke valve may be stuck closed, the engine idle speed may be set too low, or the vacuum choke break may be defective.

Engine Stalls After Idling or Slow-speed Cruising

This can be caused by a defective fuel pump, overheated engine, incorrect float level or idle adjustment, or a defective PCV valve.

Engine Stalls After High-speed Cruising

Vapor lock within the fuel lines caused by an overheated engine and/or hot weather is the usual cause of this trouble. Inspect and service the cooling system (Chapter Ten). If the problem persists, change to a different fuel or shield the fuel line from engine heat.

Engine Backfires

There are several possible reasons for this problem; incorrect ignition timing, overheating, excessive carbon, spark plugs with an incorrect heat range, hot or sticking valves and/or a cracked distributor cap.

Smoky Exhaust

Blue smoke indicates excessive oil consumption, usually caused by worn piston rings. Black smoke indicates an excessively rich fuel mixture.

Excessive Oil Consumption

This can be caused by external leaks through broken seals or gaskets, or by burning oil in the combustion chambers. Check the oil pan and the front/rear of the engine for signs of oil leakage. If the oil is not leaking externally, valve stem clearances may be excessive, valve seals may be defective, piston rings may be worn, or cylinder walls may be scored.

COOLING SYSTEM

The temperature gauge usually signals cooling system problems before there is any damage. As long as you stop the engine at the first indication of trouble, serious damage is unlikely.

With standard cooling systems in which seawater is drawn into the engine, circulated and then expelled, cooling system problems are generally mechanical—a faulty pump, defective thermostat, loose or broken drive belt or passages plugged with contamination or foreign material.

Closed cooling systems are more complex in that they use a heat exchanger which transfers heat from the engine coolant to seawater without the two coming in contact. The "closed" portion of the cooling system is pressurized (like an automotive cooling system) and uses a 50/50 mixture of ethylene glycol antifreeze and pure soft water. This system should be checked periodically to make sure it can withstand 15 psi.

Heat exchangers used in closed cooling systems collect salt, lime and other contaminants in their passages, leading to a gradual decrease in cooling efficiency. For this reason, they should be removed every 2 years and the seawater passages cleaned with a wire brush and compressed air.

STERN DRIVE UNIT

In normal straight-ahead operation, a stern drive makes very little noise. Changing direction to port or starboard will increase the noise level from the universal joints, but it should not be objectionable.

If U-joint noise is suspected, attach a flush-test device (Chapter Four) and run the engine at idle. Have an assistant turn the stern drive first to port and then to starboard while you listen for noise at the gimbal housing. Any unusual noise during this test indicates either U-joint wear or a defective gimbal bearing.

Propeller damage may occur without being obvious. If the propeller has hit many underwater objects, it may slip on its hub.

If water leaks into the boat, inspect the gimbal housing seal, U-joint bellows or shift cable bellows.

A shift handle that is difficult to move may be caused by a problem in the stern drive, transom shift cable, shift box or remote control cable. To isolate the trouble, disconnect the remote control

3

cable at the transom plate. If shifting is still difficult, the shift cable or control box is at fault. If shifting is normal, the problem is in the stern drive. Have an assistant turn the propeller by hand while you move the shift cable back and forth between the stern drive and transom plate. If the cable does not move freely, replace it.

Tilt/trim system problems may be mechanical, electrical or hydraulic. Any of these can prevent the stern drive from moving to a full up or full down position. First check to make sure that the stern drive is in forward gear. If it is in reverse, the shift interlock switch will prevent the power trim system from operating.

Mechanical problems result from frozen U-joints, lack of proper lubrication or non-use over a lengthy period. Electrical problems involve the pump motor wiring circuit. Hydraulic problems are most often caused by low or contaminated hydraulic fluid.

Table 1 ENGINE TROUBLESHOOTING

Trouble	Probable cause	Correction
Starter will not start engine	Discharged battery	Charge or replace battery
	Corroded battery terminals	Clean terminals
	Loose connection in starting circuit	Clean and tighten all connections
	Defective starting switch	Replace switch
	Starting motor brushes dirty	Clean or replace brushes
	Jammed Bendix gear	Loosen starter motor to free gear
	Faulty starter motor	Replace motor
Starter turns but does not crank engine	Partially discharged battery	Charge or replace battery
	Defective wiring or wiring capacity too low	Locate and replace defective wiring
	Broken Bendix drive	Remove starter motor and repair drive
Engine will not start	Empty fuel tank	Fill tank with proper fuel
	Flooded engine	Remove spark plugs and crank engine several times; replace spark plugs
	Water in fuel system	Clean fuel tank, lines and carburetor; refill with proper fuel
	Inoperative or sticking choke valve	Check choke, linkage and carburetor; check choke rod/cable for proper operation
	Improperly adjusted carburetor	Adjust carburetor
	Clogged fuel lines or defective fuel pump	Disconnect fuel line at carburetor. If fuel does not flow freely when engine is cranked, clean fuel line and sediment bowl (if so equipped). If fuel still does not flow freely after cleaning, repair or replace fuel pump
Engine will not start	Air leak around intake manifold	Check for leak by squirting oil around intake connections; if leak is found, tighten manifold and replace gaskets if necessary.

(continued)

Table 1 ENGINE TROUBLESHOOTING (continued)

Trouble	Probable cause	Correction
Engine will not start (continued)	Loose spark plugs	Check all plugs for proper seating, gasket and tightness; replace all damaged plugs and gaskets
	Loosely seating valves	Check for broken or weak valve springs, warped stems, carbon and gum deposits and insufficient tappet clearance
	Damaged cylinder head gasket	Check for leaks around gasket when engine is cranked; if a leak is found, replace gasket
	Worn or broken piston rings	Replace worn or broken rings; check cylinders for out-of-round and taper
Engine will not start (Ignition system)	Ignition switch OFF or defective	Turn on switch or replace defective compoment
	Fouled or broken spark plugs	Remove plugs and check for cracked porcelain, dirty points or improper gap
	Improperly set, worn or pitted distributor points; defective ignition coil	Remove center wire from distributor cap and hold within 3/8 in. of engine block. Crank engine. A clean, sharp spark should jump between wire and block when points open. Clean and adjust points. If spark is weak or yellow after point adjustment, replace condenser. If spark is still weak or not present, replace ignition coil.
	Wet, cracked or broken distributor cap	Dry inside surfaces of cap with clean cloth. Inspect for cracks or other defects; replace if necesary.
	Engine timing off	Set engine timing
Hard starting when cold	Choke out of adjustment	Check choke adjustment
	Stale or sour fuel	Drain fuel tank and refill with fresh fuel
	Defective fuel pump	Replace fuel pump
	Malfunction in ignition system	Check ignition system
	Improper engine timing	Check and adjust timing
Hard starting when hot	Choke out of adjustment	Check choke adjustment
	Incorrect spark plugs	Replace with plugs of the proper heat range
	Defective coil and/or condenser	Test and replace if necessary
	Water in fuel	Drain and clean fuel tank, lines and carburetor; refill with proper fuel
Excessive coolant temperatures	No water circulation	Check for clogged water lines and restricted inlets/outlets. Check for broken or stuck thermostat. Look for worn or damaged water pump or water pump drive.
	Defective thermostat	Replae thermostat
No oil pressure	Defective gauge	Replace gauge
	No oil in engine	Refill with proper grade oil
	Dirt in pressure relief valve	Clean oil pump valve
	Defective oil pump, oil line leak or broken oil pump drive	Check oil pump and oil pump drive for worn or broken parts; tighten all oil line connections
Low oil pressure	Oil leak in pressure line	Inspect all oil lines; tighten all connections
	Weak or broken pressure relief valve spring	Replace relief valve spring
	Worn oil pump	Replace oil pump
	Worn or loose bearings	Replace bearings

(continued)

3

Table 1 ENGINE TROUBLESHOOTING (continued)

Trouble	Probable cause	Correction
Oil pressure too high	Engine oil viscosity too thick	Drain crankcase and replace with oil of proper viscosity
	Pressure relief valve stuck	Clean or replace valve
	Dirt or obstructions in lines	Drain and clean oil system; check for bent or flattened oil lines and replace where necessary
RPM loss	Damaged propeller	Repair or replace propeller
	Misalignment	Realign engine to stern drive
	Dirty boat bottom	Clean boat bottom
Vibration	Msifiring or preignition	See "Preignition" portion of this table
	Loose mount or mounting bolts	Tighten
	Loose crankshaft balancer or flywheel	Tighten bolts
	Loose alternator	Tighten bolts
	Propeller shaft bent or out-of-line	Repair or replace
	Propeller bent or pitch out-of-true	Repair or replace
Preignition	Defective spark plugs	Check all spark plugs for broken porcelain, burned electrodes or incorrect gap; replace all defective plugs or clean and reset gap
	Improper timing	Set timing
	Engine carbon	Remove cylinder head and clean out carbon
	Engine overheating	See "Excessive coolant temperature" portion of this table
Backfiring	Insufficient fuel reaching engine due to dirty lines, strainer or blocked fuel tank vent; water in fuel	See "Engine will not start" portion of this table
	Improper distributor adjustment	See "Engine will not start" portion of this table
Sludge in oil	Infrequent oil changes	Drain and refill with proper weight oil
	Water in oil	Drain and refill; if trouble persists, check for cracked block, cracked head or defective head gasket
	Dirty oil filter	Replace oil filter

Table 2 STERN DRIVE TROUBLESHOOTING

Trouble	Probable cause	Correction
Gear housing noise	Contaminated lubricant	Disassemble, clean, inspect and reassemble; fill with clean lubricant
	Incorrectly installed propeller	Remove propeller and reinstall correctly
	Damaged propeller	Replace propeller
	Incorrect gear alignment/shimming	Check and correct alignment shimming as required
	Worn, loose or damaged parts	Disassemble unit and replace parts as required

(continued)

3

Table 2 STERN DRIVE TROUBLESHOOTING (continued)

Trouble	Probable cause	Correction
Drive shaft housing noise	Low lubricant level	Add lubricant
	Worn/dirty U-joint bearings	Clean/repair as required
	Worn/dirty gimbal or transmission output bearing	Clean/repair as required
	Contaminated lubricant	Disassemble, clean, inspect and reassemble; fill with clean lubricant
	Transom too thin	Shim transom plates
	Incorrect gear alignment/shimming	Check and correct alignment/shimming as required
	Worn, loose or damaged parts	Disassemble unit and replace parts as required
	Engine misaligned	Align with proper tools
	Worn engine coupler	Replace coupler
MerCruiser Alpha 1 or Bravo 1 will not slide into bell housing	Misaligned U-joint and engine coupling shaft splines	Rotate propeller counterclockwise to align splines
	Shift shaft coupler in bell housing not aligned	Align coupler in forward gear position
	Misaligned engine	Align with proper tools
	Misaligned gimbal housing bearing	Align with engine alignment shaft
	Damaged shaft or coupling splines	Replace shaft or coupling
Hard steering (power steering)	Loose drive belt	Adjust belt tension
	Fluid level low	Fill reservoir to proper level
	Leaking hoses or air in system	Locate and correct
	Defective pump	Replace pump
	Restricted hoses	Locate and correct
	Defective cylinder	Replace cylinder
	Control valve	Adjust as required
	Loose mounting bracket adjusting screw	Tighten screw and locknut
Hard steering (Ride-Guide)	Damaged cable	Replace cable
	Incorrect cable length	Install proper length cable
	Corroded cable	Lubricate or replace as required
	Linkage nuts too tight	Retorque nuts
	Insufficient rack or rotary head lubrication	Disassemble and lubricate rack

Table 3 MERCRUISER MODELS

Model/hp	Displacement	Drive unit	Gear ratio	Full throttle engine operating range
		1986		
120	2.5L (153 cid)	Alpha One	1.98:1	4,200-4,600 rpm
140	3.0L (181 cid)	Alpha One	1.98:1	4,200-4,600 rpm
170	3.7L (224 cid)	Alpha One	1.84:1	4,200-4,600 rpm
185	4.3L (262 cid)	Alpha One	1.84:1	4,400-4,800 rpm
190	3.7L (224 cid)	Alpha One	1.84:1	4,400-4,800 rpm
200	5.0L (3.5 cid)	Alpha One	1.65:1	4,200-4,600 rpm
205	4.3L (262 cid)	Alpha One	1.84:1	4,400-4,800 rpm
	(continued)			

Table 3 MERCRUISER MODELS (continued)

Model/hp	Displacement	Drive unit	Gear ratio	Full throttle engine operating range
1986 (continued)				
230	5.0L (305 cid)	Alpha One	1.50:1	4,200-4,600 rpm
260	5.7L (350 cid)	Alpha One	1.50:1	4,200-4,600 rpm
350 Magnum	5.7L (350 cid)	Alpha One	1.50:1	4,200-4,600 rpm
454 Magnum	7.4L (454 cid)	Alpha One	1.32:1	4,200-4,600 rpm
1987				
2.5L/120	2.5L (153 cid)	Alpha One	1.98:1	4,200-4,600 rpm
3.0L/130	3.0L (181 cid)	Alpha One	1.98:1	4,200-4,600 rpm
165	3.7L (224 cid)	Alpha One	1.84:1	4,400-4,800 rpm
175	4.3L (262 cid)	Alpha One	1.84:1	4,400-4,800 rpm
180	3.7L (224 cid)	Alpha One	1.84:1	4,400-4,800 rpm
200	5.0L (305 cid)	Alpha One	1.65:1	4,200-4,600 rpm
205	4.3L (262 cid)	Alpha One	1.84:1	4,400-4,800 rpm
230	5.0L (305 cid)	Alpha One	1.50:1	4,200-4,600 rpm
260	5.7L (350 cid)	Alpha One	1.50:1	4,200-4,600 rpm
350 Magnum	5.7L (350 cid)	Alpha One	1.50:1	4,200-4,600 rpm
454 Magnum	7.4L (454 cid)	Alpha One	1,32:1	4,200-4,600 rpm
1988-1989				
2.5L/120	2.5L (153 cid)	Alpha One	1.98:1	4,200-4,600 rpm
3.0L/130	3.0L (181 cid)	Alpha One	1.98:1	4,200-4,600 rpm
3.7L/165	3.7L (224 cid)	Alpha One	1.84:1	4,400-4,800 rpm
4.3L/175	4.3L (262 cid)	Alpha One	1.84:1	4,400-4,800 rpm
3.7LX/180	3.7L (224 cid)	Alpha One	1.84:1	4,400-4,800 rpm
5.0L/200	5.0L (305 cid)	Alpha One	1.65:1	4,200-4,600 rpm
4.3LX/205	4.3L (262 cid)	Alpha One	1.84:1	4,400-4,800 rpm
5.0LX/230	5.0L (305 cid)	Alpha One	1.50:1	4,200-4,600 rpm
5.7L/260	5.7L (350 cid)	Alpha One	1.50:1	4,200-4,600 rpm
350 Magnum/270	5.7L (350 cid)	Alpha One	1.50:1	4,200-4,600 rpm
7.4L/330	7.4L (454 cid)	Bravo One	1.50:1	4,200-4,600 rpm
454 Magnum/365	7.4L (454 cid)	Alpha One	1.32:1	4,600-5,000 rpm
454 Magnum/365	7.4L (454 cid)	Bravo One	1.50:1	4,600-5,000 rpm
1990[1]				
3.0L/115	3.0L (181 cid)	Alpha One	1.98:1	4,200-4,600 rpm
3.0LX/135	3.0L (181 cid)	Alpha One	1.98:1	4,400-4,800 rpm
4.3L/155	4.3L (262 cid)	Alpha One	1.84:1	4,400-4,800 rpm
4.3LX/175	4.3L (262 cid)	Alpha One	1.84:1	4,400-4,800 rpm
5.0L/180	5.0L (305 cid)	Alpha One	1.65:1	4,200-4,600 rpm
5.0LX/205	5.0L (305 cid)	Alpha One	1.50:1	4,200-4,600 rpm
5.7L/230	5.7L (350 cid)	Alpha One	1.50:1	4,200-4,600 rpm
350 Magnum/240	5.7L (350 cid)	Alpha One	1.50:1	4,200-4,600 rpm
7.4L/300	7.4L (454 cid)	Bravo One	1.50:1	4,200-4,600 rpm
454 Magnum/360	7.4L (454 cid)	Bravo One	1.50:1	4,600-5,000 rpm
502 Magnum/410	8.2L (502 cid)	Bravo One	1.36:1	4,400-4,800 rpm
(continued)				

Table 3 MERCRUISER MODELS (continued)

Model/hp	Displacement	Drive unit	Gear ratio	Full throttle engine operating range
1991[1]				
3.0L/115	3.0L (181 cid)	Alpha One	1.98:1	4,200-4,600 rpm
3.0LX/135	3.0L (181 cid)	Alpha One	1.98:1	4,400-4,800 rpm
4.3L/155	4.3L (262 cid)	Alpha One	1.84:1	4,400-4,800 rpm
4.3LX/175	4.3L (262 cid)	Alpha One	1.84:1	4,400-4,800 rpm
5.0L/180	5.0L (305 cid)	Alpha One	1.65:1	4,200-4,600 rpm
5.0LX/205	5.0L (305 cid)	Alpha One	1.50:1	4,200-4,600 rpm
5.7L/230	5.7L (350 cid)	Alpha One	1.50:1	4,200-4,600 rpm
5.7L/240	5.7L (350 cid)	Bravo Two	2:1	4,200-4,600 rpm
350 Magnum/240	5.7L (350 cid)	Alpha One	1.50:1	4,200-4,600 rpm
7.4L/300	7.4L (454 cid)	Bravo One	1.5:1	4,200-4,600 rpm
7.4L/300	7.4L (454 cid)	Bravo Two	2:1	4,200-4,600 rpm
454 Magnum/350	7.4L (454 cid)	Bravo One	1.5:1	4,600-5,000 rpm
502 Magnum/390	8.2L (502 cid)	Bravo One	1.36:1	4,600-5,000 rpm
1992[1]				
3.0L/115	3.0L (181 cid)	Alpha One	1.98:1	4,200-4,600 rpm
3.0LX/135	3.0L (181 cid)	Alpha One	1.98:1	4,400-4,800 rpm
4.3L/155	4.3L (262 cid)	Alpha One	1.84:1	4,400-4,800 rpm
4.3LX/175	4.3L (262 cid)	Alpha One	1.84:1	4,400-4,800 rpm
5.0L/180	5.0L (305 cid)	Alpha One	1.65:1	4,200-4,600 rpm
5.0LX/205	5.0L (305 cid)	Alpha One	1.50:1	4,200-4,600 rpm
5.7L/230	5.7L (350 cid)	Alpha One	1.50:1	4,200-4,600 rpm
5.7L/250	5.7L (350 cid)	Bravo Two	2.2:1	4,400-4,800 rpm
350 Magnum/250	5.7L (350 cid)	Alpha One	1.50:1	4,400-4,800 rpm
7.4L/300	7.4L (454 cid)	Bravo One	1.5:1	4,400-4,800 rpm
7.4L/300	7.4L (454 cid)	Bravo Two	2:1	4,200-4,600 rpm
454 Magnum/350	7.4L (454 cid)	Bravo One	1.5:1	4,600-5,000 rpm
502 Magnum/390	8.2L (502 cid)	Bravo One	1.36:1[2]	4,600-5,000 rpm
1993				
3.0L/115	3.0L (181 cid)	Alpha One	1.98:1	4,200-4,600 rpm
3.0LX/135	3.0L (181 cid)	Alpha One	1.98:1	4,400-4,800 rpm
4.3L/160	4.3L (262 cid)	Alpha One	1.84:1	4,400-4,800 rpm
4.3LX/180	4.3L (262 cid)	Alpha One	1.84:1	4,400-4,800 rpm
5.0L/190	5.0L (305 cid)	Alpha One	1.65:1	4,200-4,600 rpm
5.0LX/205	5.0L (305 cid)	Alpha One	1.50:1	4,200-4,600 rpm
5.7L/235	5.7L (350 cid)	Alpha One	1.50:1	4,200-4,600 rpm
5.7L/250	5.7L (350 cid)	Bravo Two	2.2:1	4,400-4,800 rpm
350 Magnum/250	5.7L (350 cid)	Alpha One	1.5:1	4,400-4,800 rpm
7.4L/300	7.4L (454 cid)	Bravo One	1.5:1	4,200-4,600 rpm
7.4L/300	7.4L (454 cid)	Bravo Two	2.0:1	4,200-4,600 rpm
7.4L/300	7.4L (454 cid)	Bravo Three	2.0:1	4,200-4,600 rpm
454 Magnum/350	7.4L (454 cid)	Bravo One	1.5:1	4,600-5,000 rpm
502 Magnum/390	8.2L (502 cid)	Bravo One	1.36:1[2]	4,600-5,000 rpm

(continued)

3

Table 3 MERCRUISER MODELS (continued)

Model/hp	Displacement	Drive unit	Gear ratio	Full throttle engine operating range
		1994		
3.0L/115	3.0L (181 cid)	Alpha One	1.98:1	4,200-4,600 rpm
3.0LX/135	3.0L (181 cid)	Alpha One	1.98:1	4,200-4,600 rpm
4.3L/160	4.3L (262 cid)	Alpha One	1.84:1	4,400-4,800 rpm
4.3LX/180	4.3L (262 cid)	Alpha One	1.84:1	4,400-4,800 rpm
5.0L/190	5.0L (305 cid)	Alpha One	1.65:1	4,200-4,600 rpm
5.0LX/205	5.0L (305 cid)	Alpha One	1.50:1	4,200-4,600 rpm
5.7L/235	5.7L (350 cid)	Alpha One	1.50:1	4,200-4,600 rpm
5.7L/250	5.7L (350 cid)	Bravo Two	2.2:1	4,400-4,800 rpm
5.7L/250	5.7L (350 cid)	Bravo Three	2.0:1	4,400-4,800 rpm
350 Magnum/250	5.7L (350 cid)	Alpha One	1.5:1	4,400-4,800 rpm
7.4L/300	7.4L (454 cid)	Bravo One	1.5:1	4,200-4,600 rpm
7.4L/300	7.4L (454 cid)	Bravo Two	2.0:1	4,200-4,600 rpm
7.4L/300	7.4L (454 cid)	Bravo Three	2.0:1	4,200-4,600 rpm
454 Magnum/350	7.4L (454 cid)	Bravo One	1.5:1	4,600-5,000 rpm

1. Horsepower rated at the propeller shaft.
2. Also available in 1.5:1 gear ratio.

Chapter Four

Lubrication, Maintenance
And Tune-up

All gasoline engines used with MerCruiser drives are based on automotive engines. The average pleasure boat engine, however, is subjected to operating conditions which are far more severe than those encountered by the average automobile engine. This is particularly true if the engine uses raw water cooling and is used in salt or polluted water. Regular preventive maintenance and proper lubrication will pay dividends in longer engine and stern drive life, as well as safer boat operation.

This chapter provides the basis for such a program. The lubrication and maintenance intervals provided in **Table 1** are those recommended by Mercury Marine for normal operation. When the boat is used for continuous heavy-duty, high speed operation or under other severe operating conditions, maintenance and lubrication should be performed more frequently. If the boat is not used regularly, moisture and dirt will collect in and on the engine and stern drive. This eventually leads to rust, corrosion and other damage.

Active use of the boat will help prevent such deterioration.

It is also a good idea to keep the engine and accessory units clean and free of dirt, grime and grease buildup. Such a buildup will eventually reduce the engine's capacity for cooling by preventing heat from radiating from the metal. Keeping the engine clean will ensure that it can perform at its top efficiency and has the added benefit of allowing you to locate leaks almost immediately, as they will be far more apparent on a clean engine than on one that has been allowed to accumulate a coating or buildup of contamination.

Tables 1-6 are at the end of the chapter.

PREOPERATIONAL CHECKS

Before starting the engine for the first time each day, perform the following checks:

1. Remove the engine compartment cover or hatch and check for the presence of raw gasoline fumes. If the boat is equipped with a bilge blower, turn it on for a few minutes. If strong fumes can be smelled, determine their source and correct the problem before proceeding.

WARNING
Always have a Coast Guard-approved fire extinguisher close at hand when working around the engine.

2. Check the engine oil level with the dipstick as described in this chapter. Add oil if the level is low.

3. Check the electrolyte level in each battery cell as described in this chapter. Add distilled water if necessary.

4. Check the power steering pump fluid level, if so equipped.

5. Check the condition of all drive belts. If a belt is in doubtful condition, replace it. Spare belts are difficult to obtain offshore.

6. Check all water hoses for leaks, loose connections and general condition. Repair or replace as required.

7. Check the oil level in the stern drive unit as described in this chapter. Add lubricant if necessary.

8. Check the fluid level in the trim/tilt reservoir, if so equipped. Add fluid if required.

9. Check the bilge for excessive water; if present, drain or pump dry.

10. Check the propeller for nicks, dents, missing metal, etc. Repair or replace the propeller if damaged.

11. Turn on the fuel tank valve(s).

12. Connect the battery cables to the battery (if disconnected).

13. Reinstall the engine compartment cover or hatch.

STARTING CHECKLIST

After performing the preoperational checks, observe the following starting checklist:

1. If equipped with a bilge blower, operate it for at least 5 minutes before starting the engine.

2. Make sure the stern drive unit is fully down and in operating position.

3. If the engine is cold, prime it by operating the throttle one or two times.

4. Make sure the gearshift lever is in NEUTRAL.

WARNING
Always have a fully charged fire extinguisher at hand before attempting to start the engine.

5. Start the engine and let it run at idle speed for a few minutes.

CAUTION
Prolonged operation of the engine with the gearshift lever in NEUTRAL can cause damage to gears in the stern drive unit due to improper circulation of the lubricant.

6. Note the gauges and warning lights to make sure that the engine is not overheating, that proper oil pressure is present and that the battery is not discharging. If any of these conditions occur, shut the engine down at once. Determine the cause and correct the problem before proceeding.

POST-OPERATIONAL CHECKS

Perform the following maintenance after each use.

1. If the boat was used in salt or polluted water, flush the cooling system with freshwater as described in this chapter. This will minimize corrosion and buildup of deposits in the cooling system.

2. Disconnect the battery cables from the battery, negative cable first. You may want to re-

move the battery from the boat to prevent its theft.

3. Shut off the fuel tank valve(s).

4. Top off the fuel tank(s), if possible. This will minimize the possibility of moisture condensation in the tank(s).

5. If water is present in the bilge, either drain or pump dry.

6. Wash the interior and exterior surfaces of the boat with freshwater.

COOLING SYSTEM FLUSHING

Flushing procedures differ depending upon the location of the water pump. Regardless of pump location, cooling water must *always* circulate through the stern drive whenever the engine is running to prevent damage to the pump impeller. On models equipped with a closed cooling system and a seawater pump in addition to the seawater pump in the drive unit, *both* pumps must be supplied with cooling water.

> *WARNING*
> *When the cooling system is flushed, make sure that there is sufficient space to the side and behind the propeller and that no one is standing in the vicinity. If possible, remove the propeller to prevent the possibility of serious personal injury.*

Standard Cooling System

A flush-test device must be used with this procedure to provide cooling water. **Figure 1** shows a typical unit in use.

1. Attach the flush-test device directly over the intake holes in the gear housing. Connect a hose between the device and the water tap.

> *CAUTION*
> *Do not use full water tap pressure in Step 2.*

2. Partially open the water tap to allow a low-pressure flow of water into the device.

> *CAUTION*
> *Do not run the engine above idle speed while flushing the system in Step 3.*

3. Place the gearshift lever in NEUTRAL. Start the engine and run at normal idle until the engine reaches normal operating temperature, as shown on the temperature gauge.

4. Watch the water being flushed from the cooling system. When the flow is clear, shut the engine off.

5. Shut the water tap off. Disconnect and remove the flush-test device from the gear housing.

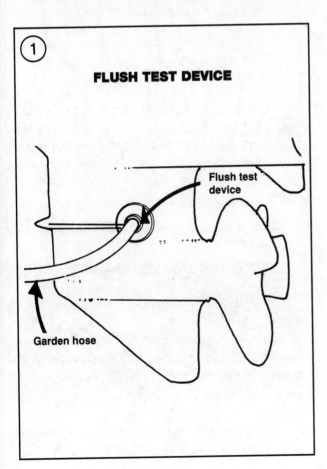

FLUSH TEST DEVICE

Flush test device

Garden hose

Closed Cooling System

If the engine is to be flushed with the boat still in the water, a seawater petcock must be installed between the water pickup and pump inlet.

1. If the boat is to remain in the water for this procedure, close the seawater petcock.

2. Loosen the water intake hose clamp and remove the hose from the water pump inlet. **Figure 2** shows a typical location.

3. Connect a length of garden hose between the water pump inlet and a water tap.

> *CAUTION*
> *Do not use full water tap pressure in Step 4.*

4. Partially open the water tap to allow a low-pressure flow of water into the pump inlet.

> *CAUTION*
> *Make sure that water is being discharged from the exhaust outlets in Step 5. If not, shut the engine off immediately and check the flushing hose connections.*

5. Place the remote control handle in NEUTRAL. Start the engine and run at idle until the engine reaches normal operating temperature, as shown by the temperature gauge.

6. Watch the water being flushed from the cooling system. When the flow is clear, shut the engine off.

7. Shut the water tap off and remove the garden hose from the water pump inlet and water tap. Reconnect the water intake hose to the pump inlet and tighten the clamp securely.

8. Open the seawater petcock.

ENGINE MAINTENANCE AND LUBRICATION

The maintenance tasks discussed in this section should be performed at the intervals indicated in **Table 1**. These intervals are only guidelines, however. Consider the frequency and extent of boat use when establishing the actual intervals. You should perform the tasks more frequently if the boat is used under severe service conditions.

Engine Oil Level Check

All engines will consume a certain amount of oil as a lubricating and cooling agent. The rate of consumption is highest during a new engine's break-in period, but should stabilize after approximately 100 hours of operation. It is not

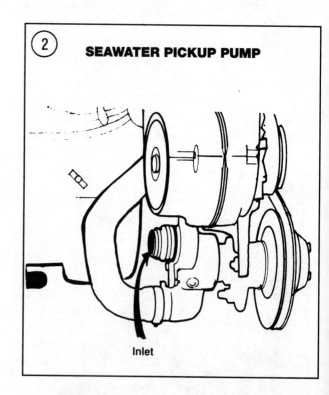

② **SEAWATER PICKUP PUMP**

Inlet

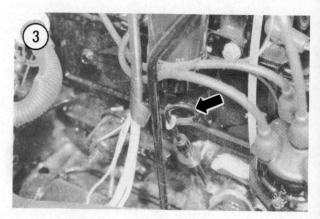

③

unusual for a 4-cylinder engine to consume up to a quart of oil in 5-10 hours of wide-open throttle operation.

For this reason, you should check the oil level at least every week. If the boat is used more frequently, check the level each time the engine is shut down, allowing approximately 5 minutes for the oil in the upper end to drain back into the crankcase oil pan.

1. With the boat at rest in the water and the engine off, pull out the dipstick. See **Figure 3** (inline) or **Figure 4** (V6 and V8) for typical locations. Wipe it with a clean rag or paper towel, reinsert it and pull it out again. Note the oil level on the dipstick.

NOTE
Some dipsticks have ADD and FULL lines. Others read ADD 1 QT. and OP-ERATING RANGE. In either case, keep the oil level between the two lines.

2. Top up to the FULL or OPERATING RANGE mark on the dipstick if necessary, using Quicksilver 4-cycle Marine Engine Oil. If this is not available, any good quality automotive oil carrying an API designation of SG may be used. See **Table 2** for the proper single viscosity oil to be used (Mercury Marine does not recommend the use of multi-viscosity oil). Remove the oil filler cap and add oil through the hole in the valve cover. See **Figure 5** (inline) or **Figure 6** (V6 and V8), typical.

Engine Oil and Filter Change

The engine oil and filter should be changed at the end of the 20 hour break-in period, then as specified in **Table 2** according to oil viscosity. At a minimum, the oil and filter should be changed at least once per season. Mercury Marine recommends the use of its Quicksilver 4-cycle SAE 40 motor oil. If this is not available, any good quality automotive oil carrying an API designation of SF or SG may be used. See **Table 2** for the proper single viscosity oil (Mercury Marine does not recommend the use of multi-viscosity oil) according to the lowest ambient temperature expected during the period the boat will be used.

Most installations do not leave enough space to permit the use of the oil pan drain plug. For this reason, an oil drain suction pump (part No. C-91-34429 or equivalent) is the most common device used to drain the crankcase oil. The pump has a long, flexible hose which is inserted into the oil dipstick tube and fed into the crankcase. Several makes of pumps are available from marine supply dealers. Some are hand-operated, some are motorized and others are designed to be operated with an electric drill (**Figure 7**).

The used oil should be discharged into a sealable container and properly disposed of. There are several ways to discard the old oil safely. Many auto supply stores sell an oil disposal kit which contains a quantity of sawdust-like material designed to absorb the oil. After pouring the oil into the bag containing this material, the bag is sealed and the entire box disposed of.

Plastic bleach and milk containers are also excellent for oil disposal. The oil can then be taken to a service station for recycling.

> *NOTE*
> *Check local regulations before disposing of oil. Never dump used oil overboard or on the ground.*

Oil filters are the disposable spin-on type. An inexpensive oil filter wrench can be obtained from any auto parts or marine supply store. This wrench is handy in removing oil filters, but should *not* be used to install the new filter. A firm fit is all that is required; overtightening the filter can damage it and/or cause an oil leak.

Some 1987 and later models are equipped with a remote oil filter assembly mounted at the top rear of the upper drive (**Figure 8**). This assembly is available as a kit (part No. 92043A5) for installation on 200, 230 and 260 models with PlusPower (TM) exhaust elbows. See your MerCruiser dealer for availability and installation.

> *CAUTION*
> *Mercury Marine specifically states that automotive oil filters containing a filter within a filter and offering "double filtration" should not be used on any MerCruiser installation.*

The installed angle of the engine affects oil level in the crankcase. To assure that the oil is drained and replaced properly, perform the following procedure with the boat at rest in the water.

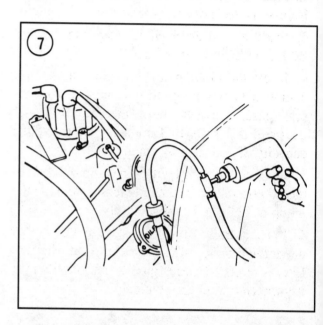

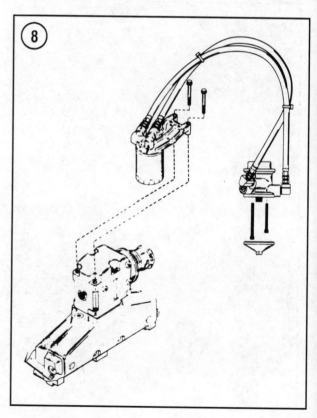

1. Start the engine and warm to normal operating temperature under load, then shut it off.

2. Remove the dipstick, wipe it clean with a lint-free cloth or paper towel and place it to one side out of the way. See **Figure 3** (inline) or **Figure 4** (V6 and V8), typical.

3. Insert the oil drain pump hose into the dipstick tube as far as it will go.

4. Insert the other pump hose into a sealable container large enough to hold the oil from the crankcase. Most engine crankcases hold 4-7 quarts of oil. Refer to **Table 3** to determine the capacity of your engine crankcase.

5. Operate the pump until it has removed all of the oil possible from the crankcase. Remove the pump hose from the dipstick tube.

6. Place a drain pan or other suitable container under the filter to catch any oil spillage when the filter is removed. See **Figure 9** (remote filter) or **Figure 10** (all others), typical.

7. Unscrew the filter counterclockwise. Use the filter wrench if the filter is too tight or too hot to remove by hand.

8. Wipe the gasket surface on the engine block clean with a paper towel.

9. Coat the neoprene gasket on the new filter with a thin coat of clean engine oil.

10. Screw the new filter onto the engine *by hand* until the gasket just touches the engine block. At this point, there will be a very slight resistance when turning the filter.

11. Tighten the filter another 1/2-3/4 turn *by hand*. If the filter wrench is used, the filter will probably be overtightened. This can damage the filter or cause an oil leak.

12. Remove the oil filler cap from the valve cover. See **Figure 5** (inline) or **Figure 6** (V6 and V8), typical.

13. Reinstall the dipstick in the dipstick tube.

14. Refer to **Table 3** to determine the crankcase capacity of your engine. Pour the specified

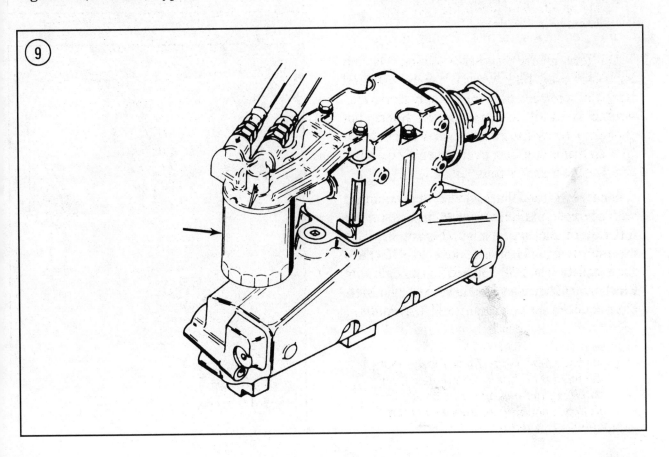

amount of oil into the valve cover opening and install the oil filler cap. Wipe up any spills on the valve cover with a clean cloth as they occur.

NOTE
Check the area under and around the oil filter for leaks while the engine is running in Step 15.

15. Start the engine and let it idle for 5 minutes, then shut the engine off.

16. Wait approximately 5 minutes, then remove the dipstick. Wipe the dipstick clean with a lint-free cloth or paper towel and reinsert it in the dipstick tube. Remove the dipstick a second time and check the oil level. Add oil, if necessary, to bring the level up to the FULL or OPERATING RANGE mark, but do not *overfill*.

Power Steering Service

If equipped with power steering, check the fluid level in the pump reservoir after the first 20 hours of operation, then at 50 hour intervals or at least once a year. Top up if necessary with Quicksilver Power Trim and Steering Fluid or DEXRON II automatic transmission fluid.

Fuel System Service

This service is particularly important, especially if the boat is equipped with fiberglass fuel tanks. Some types of fiberglass tanks contain a residue of particles which will prematurely clog the filter. Others contain a wax used in their manufacture which dissolves in gasoline. This wax is trapped by the filter but since it cannot be seen, the filter appears to be clean. The resulting lean-out condition can only be cured by installing a new filter.

All fuel lines should be checked for deterioration or loose connections at the intervals specified in **Table 1** and replaced or tightened as required.

Remove and clean the fuel filter sediment bowl (if used) whenever moisture or contamination can be seen. The sediment bowl is located on the fuel pump (**Figure 11**).

Replace canister-type filters (**Figure 12**) and carburetor fuel inlet filters (**Figure 13**) at least once a year; more often if operating conditions are severe.

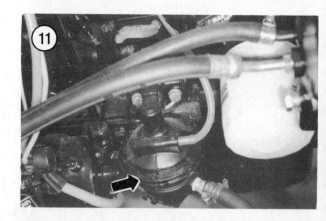

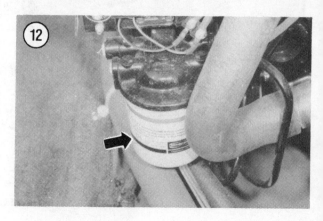

4

NOTE

In areas where only poor quality fuel is available or where moisture tends to condense in fuel tanks, it is advisable to install an inline fuel filter to remove moisture and other contaminants. These are sold as accessory items by marine supply dealers.

Fuel Pump Sediment Bowl Filter Replacement

Refer to **Figure 14** for this procedure.

1. Loosen the sediment bowl yoke screw. Swing the yoke over the bowl. Remove the bowl and filter spring.
2. Remove and discard the filter and bowl gasket.
3. Wash the bowl thoroughly in clean solvent and blow dry with compressed air.
4. Installation is the reverse of removal. Tighten the yoke screw securely. Start the engine and check for leaks.

Canister-type Filter Replacement

This type of fuel filter looks like an oil filter (**Figure 12**) and is replaced using a procedure similar to that for oil filter replacement. Unscrew the filter canister from the filter adapter (using a filter wrench, if necessary) and discard. Wipe the neoprene gasket on the new filter with a thin film of clean engine oil and screw the filter onto the adapter until it is snug—do not overtighten. Start the engine and check for leaks.

Carburetor Fuel Inlet Filter Replacement

Refer to **Figure 15** for this procedure.

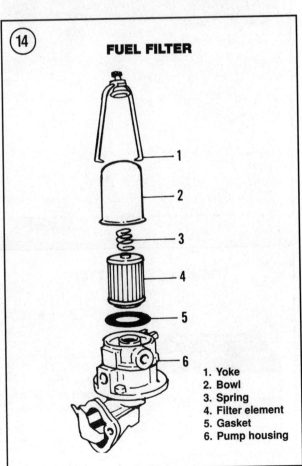

FUEL FILTER

1. Yoke
2. Bowl
3. Spring
4. Filter element
5. Gasket
6. Pump housing

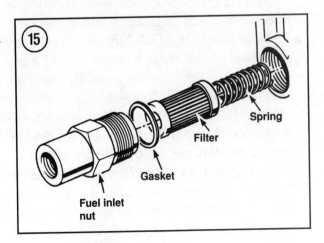

Spring
Filter
Gasket
Fuel inlet nut

1. Remove the flame arrestor or cover (**Figure 16**, typical) if necessary to provide adequate working clearance.

2. Place one wrench on the carburetor inlet nut. Place a second wrench on the fuel line connector nut. Hold the fuel inlet nut from moving and loosen the connector nut.

3. Disconnect the fuel line from the inlet nut fitting. Remove the inlet nut from the carburetor.

4. Remove the filter element and spring from the carburetor fuel inlet.

5. Remove and discard the inlet nut gasket.

6. Installation is the reverse of removal. Make sure the end of the filter with the hole faces the inlet nut. Use a new gasket. Tighten the inlet nut and connector nut snugly.

7. Install the flame arrestor, if removed. Start the engine and check for leaks.

Fuel Quality

Gasoline blended with alcohol and sold for marine use is widely available, although this fact may not be advertised and it is not legally required to be labeled as such in many states. Using such fuel is not recommended unless you can determine the nature of the blend. A mixture of 10 percent ethanol alcohol and 90% unleaded gasoline is called gasohol.

Fuel with an alcohol content tends to slowly absorb moisture from the air. When the moisture content of the fuel reaches approximately one half of one percent, it combines with the alcohol and separates from the fuel. This separation does not normally occur when gasohol is used in an automobile, as the tank is generally emptied within a few days after filling it.

The problem does occur in marine use, however, because boats often remain idle for days or even weeks between start-ups. This length of time permits separation to take place. The water-alcohol mixture settles at the bottom of the tank where the fuel pickup carries it into the fuel line. Since the engine will not run on this mixture, it

is necessary to drain the fuel tank, flush out the fuel system with clean gasoline and then remove and clean the spark plugs before the engine can be started. If it is necessary to operate an engine on gasohol, do not store such fuel in the tank(s) for more than a few days, especially in climates with high humidity.

Some methods of blending alcohol with gasoline now make use of cosolvents as suspension agents to prevent the water-alcohol from separating from the gasoline. Regardless of the method used, however, alcohol mixed with gasoline in any manner can cause numerous and

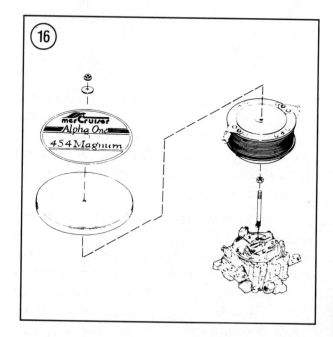

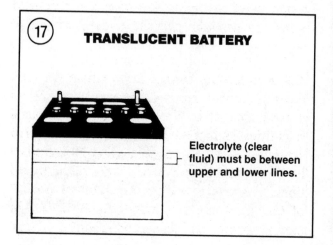

TRANSLUCENT BATTERY

Electrolyte (clear fluid) must be between upper and lower lines.

serious problems with a marine engine and fuel system. Among them are performance problems (such as vapor lock, hard starting or a low-speed stall), fuel tank corrosion and deterioration of fuel lines and other nonmetallic fuel system components (O-ring seals, inlet needle tips, accelerator pump cups and gaskets).

The following is an accepted and widely used field procedure for detecting alcohol in gasoline. Use any small transparent bottle or tube that can be capped and provided with graduations or a mark at approximately 1/3 full. A pencil mark on a piece of adhesive tape is sufficient.

1. Fill the container with water to the 1/3 full mark.

2. Add gasoline until the container is almost full. Leave a small air space at the top.

3. Shake the container vigorously, then allow it to set for 3-5 minutes. If the volume of water appears to have increased, alcohol is present. If the dividing line between the water and gasoline becomes cloudy, reference the center of the cloudy band.

The detection procedure is performed with water as a reacting agent. However, if cosolvents have been used as suspension agents in alcohol blending, the test will not show the presence of alcohol unless ethylene glycol (automotive antifreeze) is used instead of water as a reacting agent. It is suggested that a gasoline sample be tested twice using the detection kit: first with water and then with ethylene glycol (automotive antifreeze).

The procedure cannot differentiate between types of alcohol (ethanol, methanol, etc.) nor is it considered to be absolutely accurate from a scientific standpoint, but it is accurate enough to determine whether or not there is sufficient alcohol in the fuel to cause the user to take precautions. Maintaining a close watch on the quality of fuel used can save hundreds of dollars in marine engine and fuel system repairs.

Flame Arrestor

The flame arrestor (**Figure 16**, typical) serves as an air filter and as a safety precaution against engine backfiring that might cause a dangerous explosion in the engine compartment. Remove and service the flame arrestor every 100 hours of operation or once per season. Wash in solvent and air dry thoroughly. Make sure the air inlet screen is not deformed and reinstall the flame arrestor.

Battery

Remove the battery vent caps and check battery electrolyte level. On translucent batteries, it should be between the marks on the battery case (**Figure 17**). On black batteries, it should be about 3/16 in. above the plates or even with the bottom of the filler wells. See **Figure 18**. Test the battery condition with a hydrometer (**Figure 19**). See Chapter Eleven.

STERN DRIVE LUBRICATION (ALPHA ONE [EXCEPT GENERATION II])

The lubrication tasks described in this section should be performed at the intervals indicated in **Table 1**. These intervals are only guidelines, however. Consider the frequency and extent of boat use when setting actual intervals and perform the tasks more frequently if the boat is used under severe service conditions.

Stern drive capacities are listed in **Table 4**; recommended lubricants are provided in **Table 5**. Lubricate all Alpha One stern drives with Quicksilver Premium Blend Gear Lube. Use of regular automotive grease or other substitute lubricant will result in premature failure.

An oil reservoir kit is available as an accessory. This allows you to check the oil level in the drive unit from inside the boat when it is in the water.

Dispose of old lubricant properly. Disposal methods discussed under *Engine Oil and Filter Change* in this chapter are applicable.

Fluid Check (Without Reservoir Kit)

> *WARNING*
> *Since the lubricant expands when hot, its level should be checked when the unit is cool. The expanded lubricant may spray out if the oil vent plug is removed when the unit is hot and can cause serious burns.*

1. With the drive unit in a vertical position (anti-ventilation plate level), unscrew and remove the oil vent plug from the port side of the drive shaft housing (**Figure 20**).

2. Carefully check the oil level. It should be even with the bottom edge of the vent hole. If oil level is correct, check the condition of the sealing washer on the plug. Reinstall vent plug with a

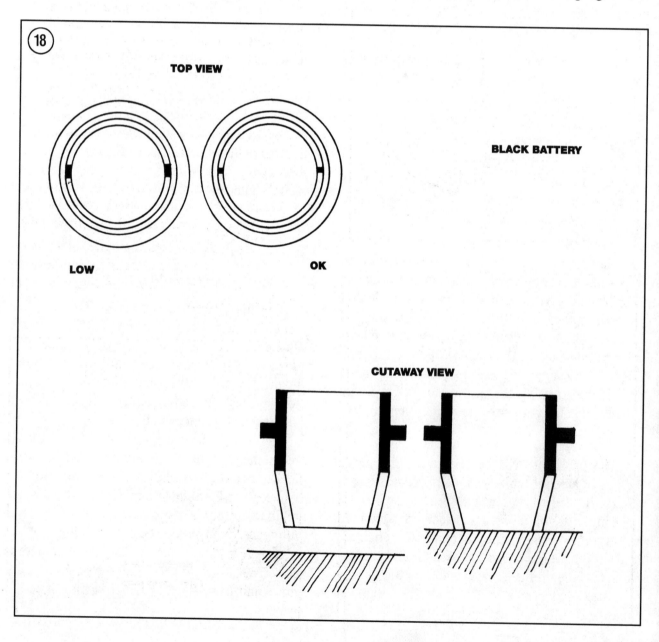

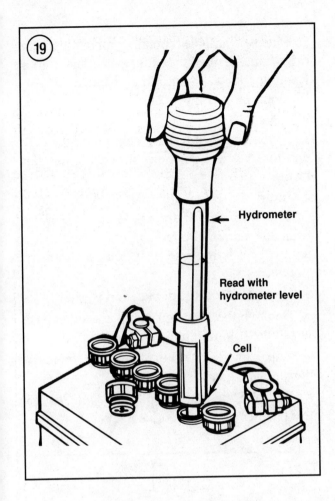

Hydrometer

Read with
hydrometer level

Cell

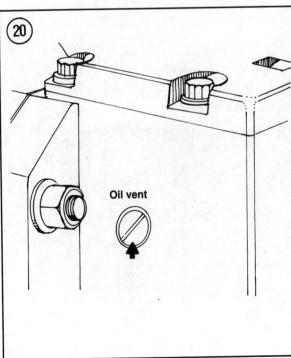

Oil vent

new washer, if the old one is damaged or deteriorated.

3. If oil level is not correct:

  a. Temporarily reinstall the vent plug to create an air lock inside the unit.

> *CAUTION*
> *The lubricant in the stern drive should be periodically checked for water contamination. To check for water, trim the drive unit to the fully OUT position. Remove the fill/drain plug and take a small sample of the lubricant. If the lubricant is milky brown or if water is evident, a leak is present that must be repaired before the unit is returned to service. On 1987 and later models, a magnetic fill/drain plug is used. Check the magnetic tip of the plug for metallic particles which could indicate internal problems. Thoroughly clean the tip before reinstalling the plug.*

  b. Remove the oil fill/drain plug (**Figure 21**) and insert lubricant pump (part No. 91-26150) or equivalent in the fill/drain hole.

  c. Remove the oil vent plug and inject lubricant from the pump through the oil fill/drain hole until it spurts from the vent hole in an air-free stream.

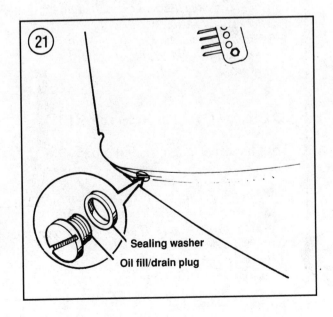

Sealing washer
Oil fill/drain plug

CAUTION
The unit should not require more than 2 ounces of lubricant. If it does, an oil leak is probable and the unit should not be used until it is checked for leakage and any problem corrected.

d. Reinstall the oil vent plug and washer.
e. Remove the lubricant pump and quickly reinstall the fill/drain plug and washer.
f. Wipe any excess lubricant from the drive housing and gearcase.
g. Repeat Step 1 and Step 2 to recheck lubricant level.

Fluid Check (With Reservoir Kit)

WARNING
If the lubricant in the reservoir is milky brown or if water is mixed with it, the drive unit has an internal leak which must be corrected before it is returned to service.

Check the lubricant level in the reservoir (A, **Figure 22**). If the fluid level is below the FULL mark on the reservoir, remove the cover (B, **Figure 22**) and add sufficient lubricant to bring the level to the mark. Reinstall cover tightly.

CAUTION
The unit should not require more than 2 ounces of lubricant. If it does, an oil leak is probable and the unit should not be used until it is checked for leakage and any problem corrected.

Fluid Change (Without Reservoir Kit)

1. Trim the drive unit to its full out position.

CAUTION
When the oil fill/drain plug is removed in Step 2, let a small quantity of fluid drain on your fingers. If the lubricant is milky brown or if water is mixed with it, the drive unit has an internal leak which must be corrected before it is returned to service.

2. Place a suitable container underneath the drive unit so that the fluid can drain into it. Remove the oil vent plug (**Figure 20**) and fill/drain plug (**Figure 21**). Allow the lubricant to drain *completely*.

3. When lubricant has drained, return the drive unit to a vertical position (antiventilation plate level).

4. Insert lubricant pump (part No. 91-26150) or equivalent in the fill/drain hole. Inject lubricant from the pump through the oil fill/drain hole until it spurts from the vent hole in an air-free stream.

5. Reinstall the oil vent plug and washer.

6. Remove the lubricant pump and quickly reinstall the fill/drain plug and washer.

7. Wipe any excess lubricant from the drive housing and gearcase.

8. Repeat Step 1 and Step 2 of *Fluid Check* in this chapter to check lubricant level.

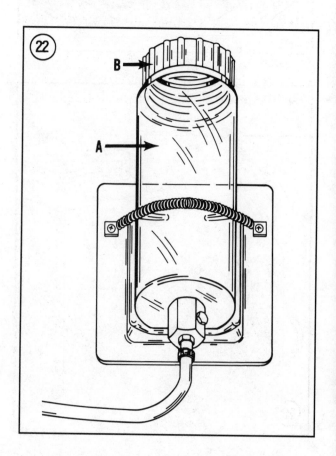

Fluid Change (With Reservoir Kit)

1. Trim the drive unit to its full out position.

> *WARNING*
> *When the oil fill/drain plug is removed in Step 2, let a small quantity of fluid drain on your fingers. If the lubricant is milky brown or if water is mixed with it, the drive unit has an internal leak which must be corrected before it is returned to service.*

2. Place a suitable container underneath the drive unit so that the fluid can drain into it. Remove the oil fill/drain plug (**Figure 21**). Allow the lubricant to drain *completely*.

3. Remove the reservoir from its bracket (**Figure 22**). Remove the cover and drain the lubricant into a suitable container.

4. Unscrew and remove the adapter and hose from the drive shaft housing oil vent hole. See **Figure 23**.

5. When lubricant has drained, return the drive unit to a vertical position (anti-ventilation plate level).

6. Insert lubricant pump (part No. 91-26150) or equivalent in the fill/drain hole. Inject lubricant from the pump through the oil fill/drain hole

until it spurts from the vent hole in an air-free stream.

7. Temporarily plug the oil vent hole to create an air-lock in the drive unit.

8. Remove the lubricant pump and quickly reinstall the fill/drain plug and washer.

9. Wipe any excess lubricant from the drive housing and gearcase.

10. Reinstall the adapter and hose to the drive shaft housing oil vent hole. Tighten adapter securely.

11. Reinstall oil reservoir to its bracket. Fill reservoir to its FULL mark and reinstall the cover tightly.

12. Loosen the adapter fitting at the drive shaft housing vent hole. Let lubricant flow until there are no air bubbles in the stream, then retighten the fitting securely. Repeat Step 9.

13. Recheck fluid level in oil reservoir and top up, if required. Do *not* fill the reservoir above the FULL mark.

STERN DRIVE LUBRICATION (ALPHA ONE GENERATION II, BRAVO ONE, BRAVO TWO AND BRAVO THREE)

The lubrication tasks described in this section should be performed at the intervals indicated in **Table 1**. These intervals are only guidelines, however. Consider the frequency and extent of boat use when setting actual intervals and perform the tasks more frequently if the boat is used under severe service conditions.

Stern drive capacities are listed in **Table 4** and the recommended lubricants are provided in **Table 5**. Lubricate Alpha One (Generation II), Bravo One, Bravo Two and Bravo Three stern drives (except 502 Magnum models) with Quicksilver Premium Blend Gear Lube. Quicksilver High-Performance Gear Lube *must* be used in the Bravo One drive unit used on 502 Magnum models. The manufacturer recommends using High-Performance Gear Lube in

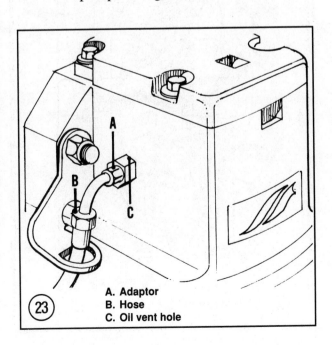

A. Adaptor
B. Hose
C. Oil vent hole

(23)

Alpha One Generation II and Alpha One SS models; however, it is not mandatory. Do not mix Quicksilver Premium Blend and High-Performance lubricants. The use of regular automotive gear lube or other substitute lubricants will result in premature drive unit failure.

The lube oil monitor (**Figure 24**) is standard on 1989-on Bravo One, all Bravo Two and Bravo Three and 1994 Alpha One models. The lube oil monitor is optional on Alpha One models prior to 1994. The lube oil monitor allows the drive unit oil level to be checked and added to from inside the boat. The reservoir is equipped with a lubricant level warning sensor that activates the audio warning system should the drive unit oil

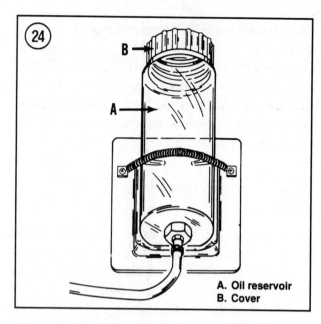

A. Oil reservoir
B. Cover

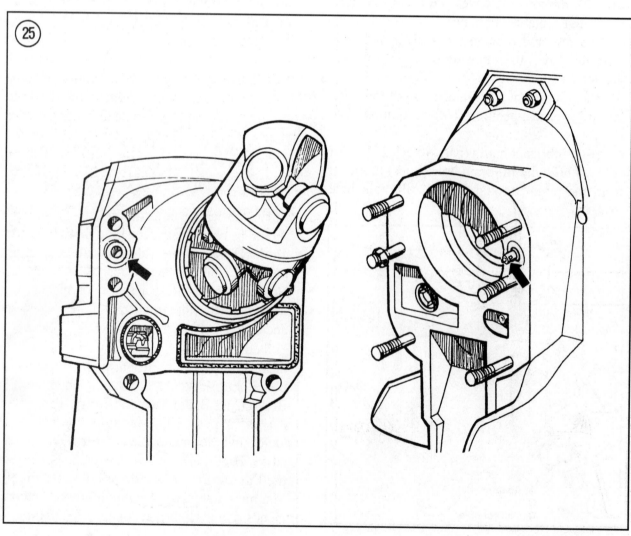

level become low. Unlike the external reservoir connection used on early Alpha One models (**Figure 23**), the connection is internal on Bravo One, Bravo Two, Bravo Three and Alpha One Generation II models. A check valve connector permits easy removal and installation of the drive unit. See **Figure 25**.

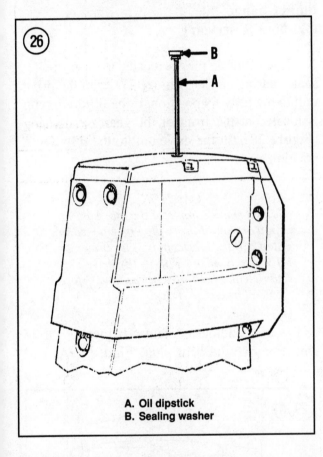

A. Oil dipstick
B. Sealing washer

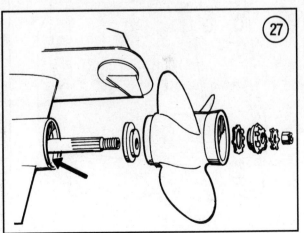

Fluid Check
(Without Reservoir)

1. Bring the stern drive to a vertical position (antiventilation plate level).

2. Unscrew and remove the oil level dipstick on the top of the upper gear housing (**Figure 26**). If the oil level is at the line on the dipstick, reinstall the dipstick with the sealing washer. Tighten the dipstick securely. If the oil level is low, continue at Step 3.

NOTE
On late Bravo One models, the drive unit fill/drain plug is located in the propeller shaft bearing carrier. On models so equipped, the propeller and forward thrust hub must be removed to access the fill/drain plug. See Chapter Fourteen for propeller removal/installation procedure.

3. On late Bravo One models, remove the propeller and thrust hub, then remove the fill/drain plug located in the propeller shaft bearing carrier (**Figure 27**). On all other models, remove the fill/drain plug from the gear housing (**Figure 28**). Insert lubricant pump (part No. 91-26150, or equivalent) into the fill/drain plug hole.

4. Remove the vent plug (**Figure 29**A), then inject the lubricant from the pump into the

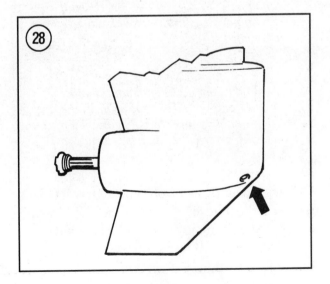

fill/drain plug hole until the lubricant is even with the bottom of the fill/drain plug hole. Note that the vent plug is on the port side on Alpha One models.

CAUTION
If more than 2 ounces of lubricant is required to fill the drive unit, a leak is probable. Repair the leakage before returning the unit to service.

5. Reinstall the oil vent plug and washer. Tighten the plug to 17 in.-lb. (2 N•m).
6. Remove the lubricant pump and quickly reinstall the fill/drain plug and washer. Tighten the plug to 17 in.-lb. (2 N•m).
7. Wipe any excess lubricant from the drive unit.
8. Repeat Step 1 and Step 2 to recheck the lubricant level.
9. After operating the unit, recheck the lubricant level (Step 1 and Step 2).

Fluid Check
(With Reservoir)

CAUTION
On models equipped with an oil reservoir, do not remove the dipstick, or check the drive unit oil level using the dipstick. If the dipstick is removed on models equipped with a reservoir, an overfull condition will result which can damage drive unit oil seals.

CAUTION
If the lubricant in the reservoir is milky brown or if water is mixed with it, the drive unit has an internal leak which must be corrected before it is returned to service.

Check the lubricant level in the reservoir (**Figure 24**). If the fluid level is below the FULL mark on the reservoir, remove the cover and add sufficient lubricant to bring the level to the mark. Reinstall cover tightly.

CAUTION
The unit should not require more than 2 ounces of lubricant. If it does, an oil leak is probable and the unit should not be used until it is checked for leakage and any problem corrected.

Fluid Change
(Without Reservoir)

1. If the fill/drain plug is located in the propeller shaft bearing carrier (**Figure 27**), trim the drive unit to the fully IN position. If the fill/drain plug is located at the front of the gearcase housing (**Figure 28**), tilt the drive unit to the fully OUT position.

CAUTION
Take a small sample of the lubricant as soon as the fill/drain plug is removed in Step 2. If the lubricant is milky brown or if water is mixed with it, the drive unit has a leak which must be repaired before it is returned to service.

2. Place a suitable container below the drive unit. Remove the vent plug (**Figure 29**A) and

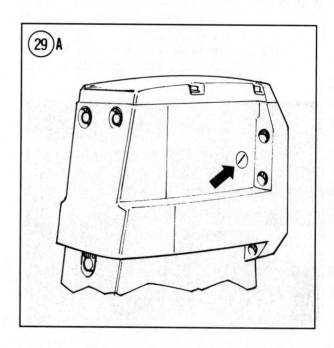

fill/drain plug (**Figure 27** or **Figure 28**). Allow the gear housing to drain completely.

3. After the lubricant is completely drained, return the drive unit to the vertical position (if tilted OUT).

4. Insert lubricant pump (part No. 91-26150, or equivalent) into the fill/drain plug hole until an air-free stream flows from the vent plug hole.

5. Reinstall the vent plug and seal washer. Tighten the plug to 17 in.-lb. (2 N·m).

6. Remove the lubricant pump and quickly reinstall the fill/drain plug and seal washer. Tighten the plug to 17 in.-lb. (2 N·m).

7. Wipe any excess lubricant from the drive unit.

8. Check the fluid level by repeating Step 1 and Step 2 under *Fluid Check* in this chapter. After operating the unit, recheck the fluid level and add lubricant as necessary.

Fluid Change (With Reservoir)

1. If the fill/drain plug is located in the propeller shaft bearing carrier (**Figure 27**), trim the drive unit to the fully IN position. If the fill/drain plug is located at the front of the gearcase housing (**Figure 28**), tilt the drive unit to the fully OUT position.

CAUTION
Take a small sample of the lubricant as soon as the fill/drain plug is removed in

Step 2. If the lubricant is milky brown or if water is mixed with it, the drive unit has a leak which must be repaired before it is returned to service.

2. Place a suitable container under the drive unit. Remove the vent plug (**Figure 29**A) and the fill/drain plug (**Figure 27** or **Figure 28**) and allow the gear housing to drain completely.

3. After all lubricant is completely drained, return the drive unit to the fully IN position (if tilted OUT).

4. Remove the reservoir from its bracket (**Figure 24**). Remove the cover and drain the lubricant into a suitable container.

5. Insert the lubricant pump (part No. 91-26150, or equivalent) into the fill/drain hole. Inject lubricant from the pump through the oil fill/drain hole until it spurts from the vent hole in an air-free stream.

6. Reinstall the oil vent plug and washer. Tighten the plug to 17 in.-lb. (2 N·m).

7. Remove the lubricant pump and quickly reinstall the fill/drain plug and washer. Tighten the plug to 17 in.-lb. (2 N·m).

8. Wipe any excess lubricant from the drive housing and gearcase.

9. Reinstall the oil reservoir to its bracket. Fill the reservoir to its FULL mark and reinstall the cover tightly.

FUEL PUMP HOUSING (MARK V ENGINES)

On Mark V engines (1991-on 7.4L and 1992-on 454 and 502 Magnum), the fuel pump is driven by the belt-driven seawater pump. The lubricant level in the fuel pump housing should be checked periodically and filled if necessary.

1. Check the lubricant level by removing the upper fill plug (**Figure 29**B) on the fuel pump housing.

2. The lubricant should be even with the plug hole.

3. If necessary, add Quicksilver High-Performance Gear Lube (part No. 92-816026A4) into the fill plug hole until the lubricant is even with the plug hole.

4. Reinstall the plug and tighten securely.

GENERAL LUBRICATION POINTS

The following lubrication fittings should be serviced at 100 hour intervals or at least once a season.

Shift Cable

1. Lubricate the shift cable pivot points marked "A" in **Figure 30** with SAE 20 or SAE 30 motor oil.

2. Lubricate the shift cable pivot points marked "B" in **Figure 30** with Quicksilver 2-4-C Multi-Lube.

Propeller Shaft

The Quicksilver lubricants specified in this procedure are listed in their order of effectiveness.

1. Remove the propeller and lubricate the prop shaft (**Figure 31**) with Special Lubricant 101, 2-4-C Multi-Lube or Perfect Seal.

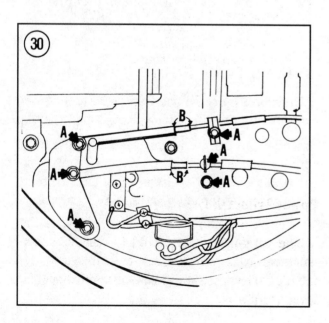

2. Reinstall propeller on prop shaft and tighten the self-locking nut to 55 ft.-lb. (75 N•m).

Steering System

Refer to **Figure 32** (power steering) or **Figure 33** (non-power steering) for this procedure.

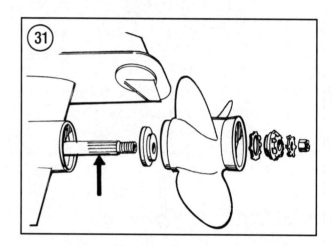

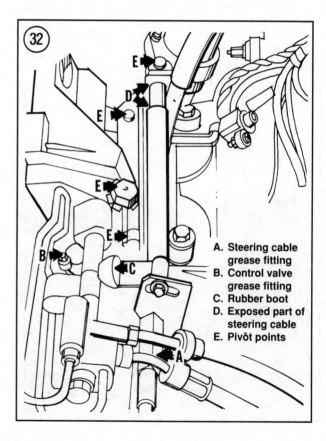

A. Steering cable grease fitting
B. Control valve grease fitting
C. Rubber boot
D. Exposed part of steering cable
E. Pivôt points

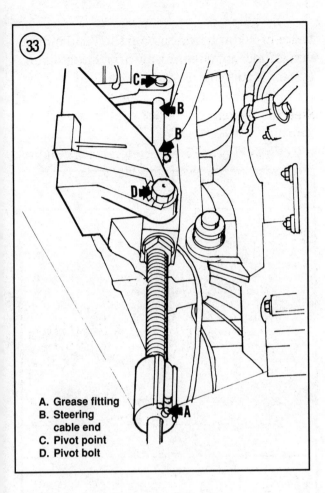

A. Grease fitting
B. Steering cable end
C. Pivot point
D. Pivot bolt

1. Fully retract the transom end of the steering cable into its housing. Lubricate the steering cable grease fitting with Quicksilver 2-4-C Multi-Lube.

2. Fully extend the transom end of the steering cable and lubricate the exposed part of the cable with Quicksilver Special Lubricant 101.

3. Lubricate all steering system pivot points (including tie bar pivot points on dual installations) with SAE 20 or SAE 30 motor oil.

4. For power steering:

   a. Lubricate the control valve grease fitting with Quicksilver 2-4-C Multi-Lube until lubricant can be seen around the rubber boot.

   b. Check the power steering unit and all linkages for loose, missing or damaged components. If any require replacement, see your MerCruiser dealer as soon as possible to have the deficiency corrected.

Transom Gimbal Housing, Swivel Shaft, Swivel Pin, Hinge Pins and Gimbal Bearing

NOTE
*The grease fitting shown in **Figure 34** has been removed on late Alpha and Bravo models equipped with self-lubricating swivel pin bushings.*

Refer to **Figure 34** and **Figure 35** and lubricate all fittings with Quicksilver 2-4-C Multi-Lube.

Power Trim/Tilt Lubrication

The trim/tilt unit reservoir, hydraulic pump and motor are a combined self-contained unit. At the start of each season, check the reservoir fluid level as follows.

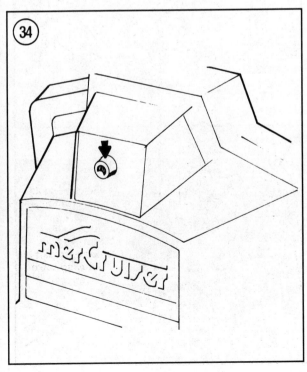

Prestolite Pump

1. Place the drive unit in its full in/down position.

2. Remove the fill screw from the pump housing (**Figure 36**).

3. If the lubricant level is not up to the bottom of the fill screw hole threads, top up with SAE 10W-30 or SAE 10W-40 motor oil.

4. Operate the drive unit through its range 6-10 times to purge any air from the system. Return the drive unit to its full in/down position and recheck the fluid level. If it is still not correct, repeat the procedure.

5. When fluid level is correct, install and tighten the fill screw securely. Make sure the vent screw at the bottom of the pump is backed out 2 full turns.

Oildyne/Eaton Pump (Old Style)

> *CAUTION*
> *The fill/vent screw (**Figure 37**) provides a vent for the pump reservoir. The screw must be backed off 1 full turn after bottoming or pump damage or failure can occur.*

1. Place the drive unit in the fully in/down position.

2. Remove the fill/vent screw from the pump housing (**Figure 37**). Wipe the screw with a lint-free cloth and reinsert but do not thread into place.

3. Wait a few seconds, then remove the screw from the housing and check the fluid level on the dipstick.

4. If the fluid level is not between the ADD and FULL marks on the dipstick, add sufficient Quicksilver Power Trim and Steering Fluid or Dexron II automatic transmission fluid to bring the fluid level to the correct position on the dipstick. *Do not* overfill the reservoir.

5. Reinstall the fill/vent screw. Thread the screw into the pump body until fully bottomed, then

back off 1 full turn. Raise and lower the drive unit 2 times to purge any air from the hydraulic system. Return the drive unit to its fully in/down position, then recheck the fluid level on the dipstick. Add fluid if necessary, then repeat this step.

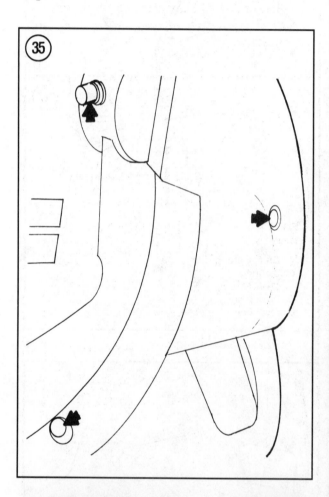

Oildyne/Singer Pump (New Style)

> *CAUTION*
> *The vent screw (A, **Figure 38**) on models so equipped, must be backed off 2 full turns after bottoming out to properly vent the pump reservoir. The fill cap (B, **Figure 38**) provides the vent on pump assemblies not equipped with a vent screw.*

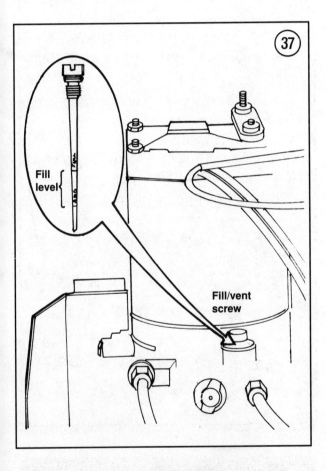

Fill level

Fill/vent screw

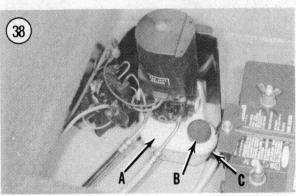

A   B   C

1. Place the drive unit in its fully down/in position.

2. Check the fluid level in the translucent plastic reservoir (C, **Figure 38**). If it is not within the embossed lines on the reservoir, remove the oil fill cap (B, **Figure 38**) and top up as required with Quicksilver Power Trim and Steering Fluid or Dexron II automatic transmission fluid to bring the fluid level to the correct position on the reservoir.

3. Operate the drive unit through its range 2 times to purge any air from the system. Return the drive unit to its fully in/down position and recheck the fluid level in the reservoir. If it is still not correct, repeat the procedure.

4. When fluid level is correct, install and tighten the oil fill cap.

ENGINE TUNE-UP

A smooth running, dependable marine engine is more than a convenience. At sea, it can mean your life. To keep your engine running right, you must follow a regular program of preventive maintenance.

Part of any preventive maintenance program is a thorough engine tune-up. A tune-up is a series of accurate adjustments necessary to restore maximum power and performance. In addition, some ignition parts which deteriorate with use must be replaced.

Engine tune-ups are generally recommended at 50-hour intervals. If the engine is used infrequently, a tune-up should be performed at least once a season. Tune-up specifications are provided in **Table 6** at the end of the chapter. Late-model engines may have a decal containing the engine serial number and tune-up specifications (**Figure 39**). If so equipped, follow the specifications given on the decal (even if they differ from those provided in **Table 6**).

A tune-up consists of the following:

a. Compression check

b. Ignition system work

c. Carburetor inspection and adjustment

Careful and accurate adjustment is crucial to a successful engine tune-up. Each procedure in this section must be performed exactly as described and in the order presented.

> *WARNING*
> *Marine components are more expensive than comparable automotive parts (contact breaker points, distributors, carburetors, etc.), but they are designed to operate in a different environment. Automotive parts should **not** be substituted for safety reasons, as well as long component life. Major reasons for this are found in Section 183.410 (a) of the Coast Guard Electrical and Fuel Systems Standards.*

Compression Check

Check the compression of each cylinder before attempting a tune-up. A compression test measures the compression pressure that builds up in each cylinder. Its results can be used to assess general cylinder and valve condition. In addition, it can warn of developing problems inside the engine. If more than a 20-lb. difference exists between the highest and lowest reading cylinders, the engine cannot be tuned to develop its maximum power.

1. If the boat is not in the water, install a flush-test device to provide water before operating the engine.

2. Warm the engine to normal operating temperature, then shut it off.

3. Remove the flame arrestor (**Figure 40**, typical) and make sure that the choke and throttle valves are completely open.

> *NOTE*
> *During compression testing, the ignition system must be disabled to prevent sparking and possible ignition system damage while cranking the engine.*

4. Disable the ignition system by performing the following:

    a. 3.0L and 3.0LX with DDIS ignition—Disconnect the motion sensor from the ignition amplifier module at the 2-pin connector.

    b. 3.0 and 3.0LX with EST ignition—Disconnect the upper 2-pin connector (purple and gray wires) from the ignition coil.

    c. All others—Disconnect the ignition coil high tension lead at the distributor cap tower. Ground the lead to a good engine ground.

5. Remove the spark plugs as described in this chapter.

6. Connect a remote start switch to the starter solenoid or assist solenoid according to manufacturer's instructions. Leave the ignition switch in the OFF position.

NOTE
The No. 1 cylinder is the front cylinder on all inline engines. It is the front cylinder on the port side of V6 and V8 engines.

7. Connect a compression tester to the No. 1 cylinder according to manufacturer's instructions (**Figure 41**).

8. Crank the engine at least 5 turns with the remote start switch or until there is no further increase in compression shown on the tester gauge.

9. Remove the compression tester and record the reading. Relieve the tester pressure valve.

10. Repeat Steps 7-9 for each remaining cylinder.

When interpreting the results, actual readings are not as important as the difference between readings. Any variation of less than 20% is acceptable. Greater differences indicate that engine repair is required because of worn or broken rings, leaky or sticking valves or a combination of all.

If the compression test indicates a problem (excessive variation in readings), isolate the cause with a wet compression test. This is performed in the same way as the dry test, except that about 1 tablespoon of heavy engine oil (at least SAE 30) is poured down the spark plug hole before performing Steps 7-9. If the wet compression readings are much greater than the dry compression readings, the trouble is probably caused by worn or broken rings. If there is little difference between the wet and dry readings, the problem is probably due to leaky or sticking valves. If 2 adjacent cylinders read low on both tests, the head gasket may be leaking between the cylinders.

Use a vacuum gauge and compare the vacuum gauge and compression tester readings to isolate the problem more closely. **Figure 42** provides interpretation of vacuum gauge readings.

Ignition System

Four different ignition systems are used on engines covered in this manual.

   a. Breaker-point ignition system.

   b. Thunderbolt IV breakerless ignition system.

   c. Digital distributorless ignition (DDIS) system.

   d. Electronic spark timing (EST) ignition system.

The breaker point ignition system may be equipped with a Delco-Remy or Mallory distributor. **Figure 43** (breaker points), **Figure 44** (Thunderbolt IV) and **Figure 45** (DDIS) show the major ignition components and wiring of the ignition system. **Figure 46** shows the distributor, ignition coil and related wiring used on EST ignition systems.

Total ignition service is presented for all mechanical breaker point systems. Service to Thunderbolt IV, EST and DDIS ignition systems is limited to replacement of spark plugs, inspection and repair of wiring and checking/adjusting ignition timing.

Spark plug removal

CAUTION
Whenever the spark plugs are removed, dirt from around them can fall into the spark plug holes. This can cause expensive engine damage.

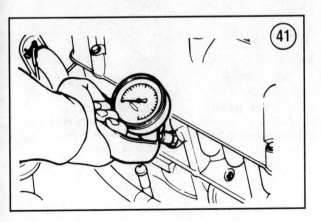

(42)

1. NORMAL READING
Reads 15 in. at idle.

2. LATE IGNITION TIMING
About 2 in. too low at idle

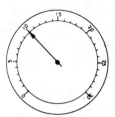

3. LATE VALVE TIMING
About 4 to 8 inches low at idle.

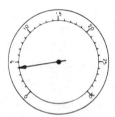

4. INTAKE LEAK
Low steady reading.

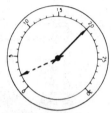

5. NORMAL READING
Drops to 2, then rises to 25 when accelerator is rapidly depessed and released.

6. WORN RINGS, DILUTED OIL
Drops to 0, then rises to 18 when acceleration is rapidly depressed and released.

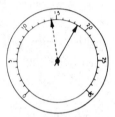

7. STICKING VALVE(S)
Normally steady. Intermittently flicks downward about 4 in.

8. LEAKY VALVE
Regular drop about 2 inches.

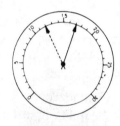

9. BURNED OR WARPED VALVE
Regular, evenly spaced down-scale flick about 4 in.

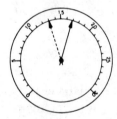

10. WORN VALVE GUIDES
Oscillates about 4 in.

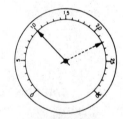

11. WEAK VALVE SPRINGS
Violent oscillation (about 10 in.) as rpm increases. Often steady at idle.

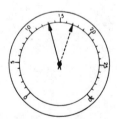

12. IMPROPER IDLE MIXTURE
Floats slowly between 13-17 in.

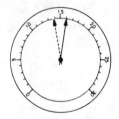

13. SMALL SPARK GAP or DEFECTIVE POINTS
Slight float between 14-16 in.

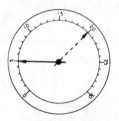

14. HEAD GASKET LEAK
Gauge floats between 5-19 in.

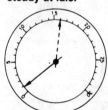

15. RESTRICTED EXHAUST SYSTEM
Normal when first started. Drops to 0 as rpm increases. May eventually rise to about 16.

4

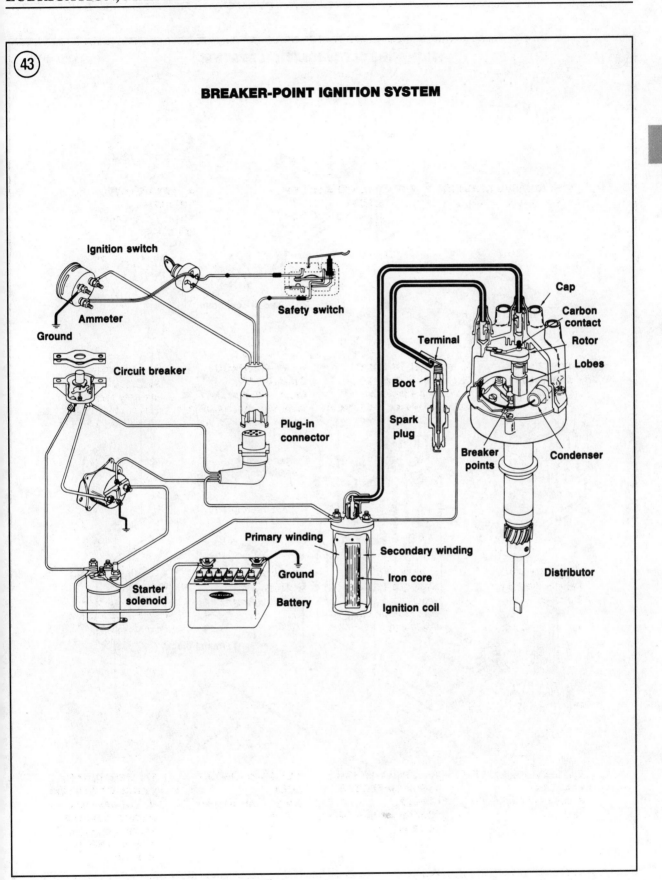

43

BREAKER-POINT IGNITION SYSTEM

Ignition switch

Ammeter

Ground

Circuit breaker

Plug-in connector

Safety switch

Terminal

Boot

Spark plug

Breaker points

Cap

Carbon contact

Rotor

Lobes

Condenser

Starter solenoid

Primary winding

Ground

Battery

Secondary winding

Iron core

Ignition coil

Distributor

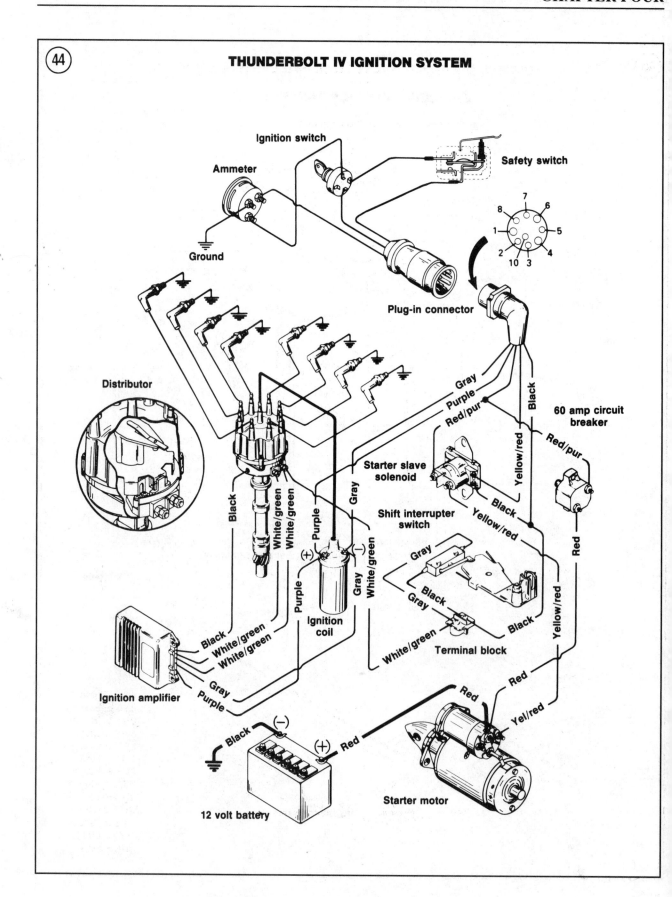

44 THUNDERBOLT IV IGNITION SYSTEM

4

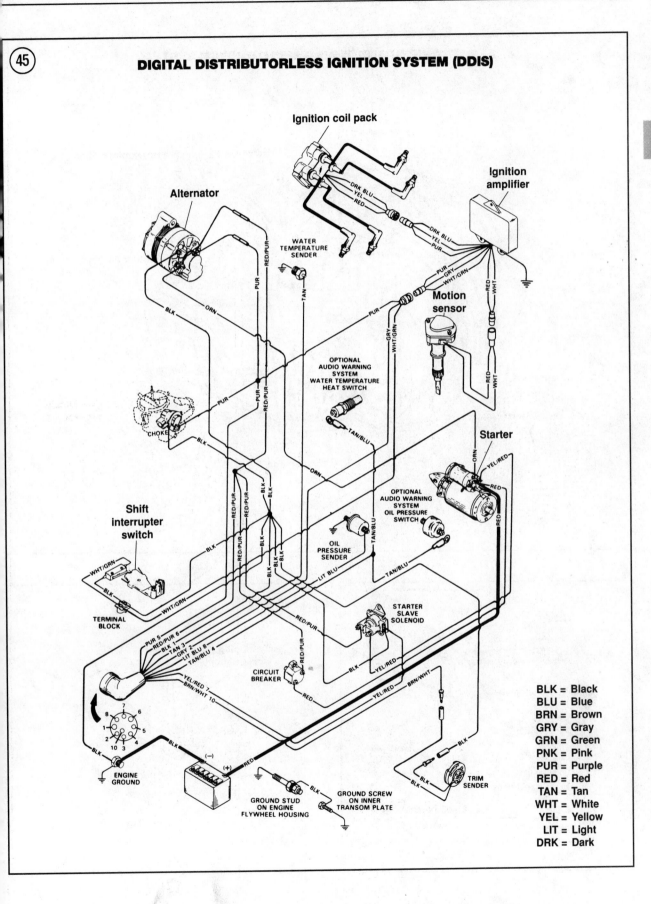

45 DIGITAL DISTRIBUTORLESS IGNITION SYSTEM (DDIS)

BLK = Black
BLU = Blue
BRN = Brown
GRY = Gray
GRN = Green
PNK = Pink
PUR = Purple
RED = Red
TAN = Tan
WHT = White
YEL = Yellow
LIT = Light
DRK = Dark

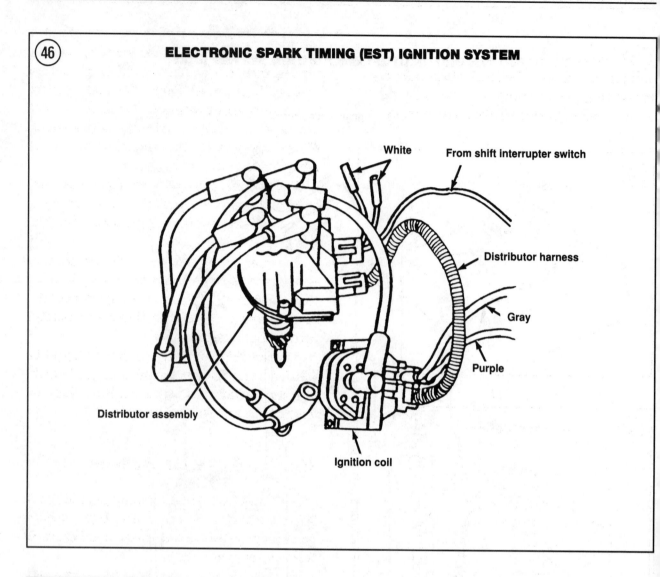

(46) ELECTRONIC SPARK TIMING (EST) IGNITION SYSTEM

White

From shift interrupter switch

Distributor harness

Gray

Purple

Distributor assembly

Ignition coil

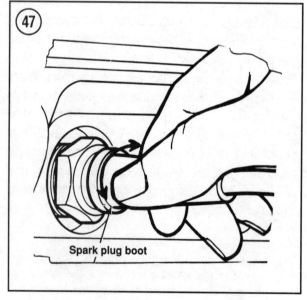

(47)

Spark plug boot

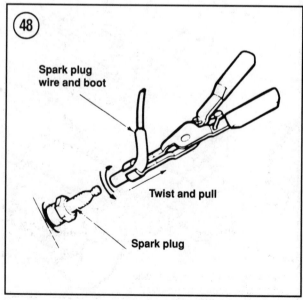

(48)

Spark plug wire and boot

Twist and pull

Spark plug

1. Blow out any foreign matter that may have accumulated around the spark plugs with compressed air. Use a compressor if you have one or a can of inert gas available at photo stores.

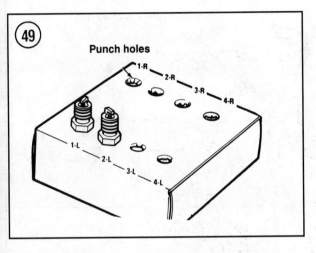

Punch holes

1-R
2-R
3-R
4-R
1-L
2-L
3-L
4-L

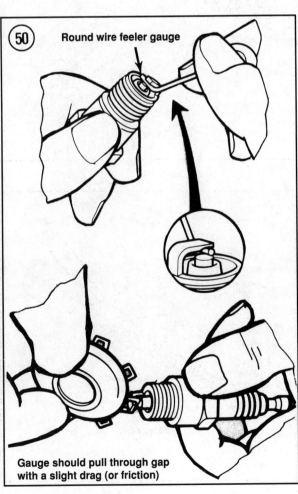

Round wire feeler gauge

Gauge should pull through gap
with a slight drag (or friction)

2. Disconnect the spark plug wires by twisting the wire boot back and forth on the plug insulator while pulling upward (**Figure 47**). Pulling on the wire instead of the boot may break it. In some cases, you may find spark plug wire removal pliers (**Figure 48**) useful, especially when working around a warm or hot engine.

3. Remove the plugs with an appropriate size spark plug socket. Keep the plugs in order so you know which cylinder each came from. See **Figure 49**.

4. Examine each spark plug and compare its appearance with the illustrations in Chapter Three. Electrode appearance is a good indicator of performance in each cylinder and permits early recognition of trouble.

5. Discard the plugs. Although they could be cleaned, regapped and reused if in good condition, they seldom last very long. New plugs are inexpensive and far more reliable.

Spark plug gapping and installation

New plugs should be carefully gapped to ensure a reliable, consistent spark. Use a special spark plug tool with a wire gauge. See **Figure 50** for two common types.

1. Remove the plugs from their boxes. Tapered plugs do not use gaskets. Some plug brands may have small end pieces that must be screwed on before the plugs can be used.

2. Determine the correct gap setting from **Table 6**. Insert the appropriate size wire gauge between the electrodes. If the gap is correct, there will be a slight drag as the wire is pulled through. If there is no drag or if the wire will not pull through, bend the side electrode with the gapping tool (**Figure 51**) to change the gap, then remeasure with the wire gauge.

CAUTION
Never try to close the electrode gap by tapping the spark plug on a solid surface. This can damage the plug inter-

*nally. Always use the gapping/adjusting
tool to open or close the gap.*

3. Apply a drop of engine oil to the threads of
each spark plug. Screw each plug in by hand until
it seats. Very little effort is required. If force is
necessary, the plug is cross-threaded. Unscrew it
and try again.

4. Tighten the spark plugs. If you have a torque
wrench, tighten to 15-20 ft.-lb. (20-30 N•m). If
not, tighten the plugs with your fingers, then
tighten an additional 1/16 turn (tapered seat
plug) or 1/4 turn (gasket-type plug) with the plug
wrench.

5. Reinstall the wires to their correct cylinder
location.

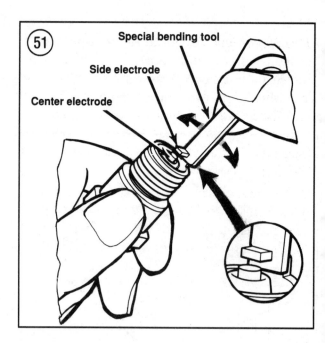

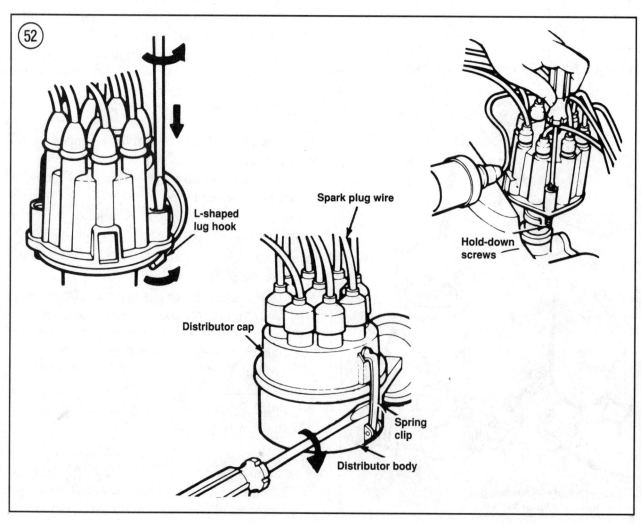

Distributor cap, wires and rotor

1. Wipe all ignition wires with a cloth slightly moistened in kerosene. Carefully bend each wire and inspect the insulation, cable nipple and spark plug boot for abrasions, cracks or deterioration. Clean any corroded terminals. Replace wires as required.

2. Unsnap, unscrew or turn the distributor cap attachment devices as required and remove the cap. See **Figure 52**. Pull cap straight up and off the distributor to prevent rotor blade damage.

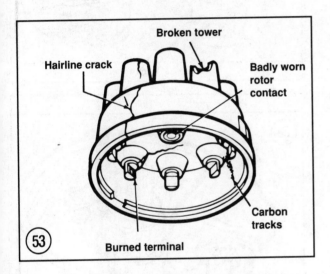

Broken tower
Hairline crack
Badly worn rotor contact
Carbon tracks
Burned terminal

53

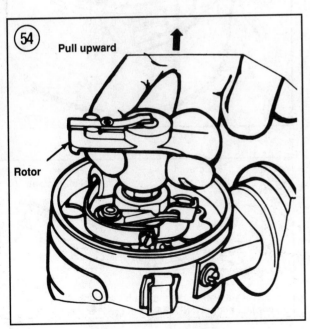

54
Pull upward
Rotor

3. Check the carbon button and electrodes inside the distributor cap for dirt, corrosion or arcing. See **Figure 53**. Check the cap for cracks and make sure the vent screen is clean and fits correctly. Replace the cap and rotor as a set if necessary.

4. Lift the rotor straight up and off the distributor shaft (**Figure 54**). Wipe the rotor with a clean, damp cloth. Check for burns, arcing, cracks and other defects. Replace the rotor and cap as a set if necessary.

5. To reinstall, align the tang inside the rotor with the slot in the distributor shaft. Press rotor onto shaft until it is fully seated.

6. Grasp the rotor, twist it clockwise and then release it. The rotor should return quickly to its original position when released. If not, the distributor advance mechanism requires service. This should be done by a dealer.

7. Install the distributor cap. Snap the clips in place, turn the cap latches or tighten the screws as required. See **Figure 52**.

Contact breaker point replacement

The expendable ignition parts (breaker points and condenser) should be replaced during a tune-up. Copy the distributor number and use it to obtain the correct replacement parts. Set breaker point dwell angle to specifications (**Table 6**), then check ignition timing.

> *CAUTION*
> *Breaker point sets used in marine distributors have corrosion-resistant springs. Do not use automotive breaker points as a replacement. Use only NMMA marine-approved parts.*

1. Remove the distributor cap and rotor as described in this chapter.

2. Loosen the primary terminal nut and disconnect the primary lead. See **Figure 55**, typical.

3. Unscrew the retaining screw(s) from the condenser and breaker assembly. Note the location

of the ground wire so it may be reinstalled in the same place, then remove the condenser and breaker point assembly from the distributor. See **Figure 56**, typical.

NOTE
*On distributors using a felt lubricating cam wick (**Figure 57**), install a new wick and proceed with Step 5.*

4. Wipe the cam and breaker plate clean. See **Figure 58**. Lightly coat the cam with special distributor grease. Never use oil or common grease; they will break down under the high temperature and frictional load and are likely to find their way onto the contact points.

5. Install the new contact breaker assembly and condenser in the distributor, but do not tighten the locking screw. Make sure the ground wire,

condenser lead and primary lead are installed exactly as they were before. Double check the connections and screw to ensure that they are tight.

6. With the points closed, make certain the contact surfaces are properly aligned with each other (**Figure 59**). Make adjustments as required,

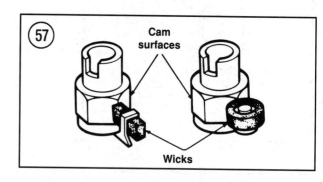

Cam surfaces

Wicks

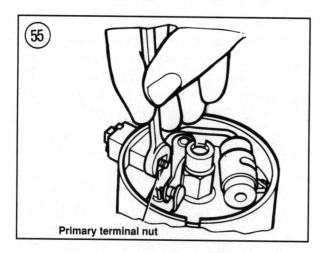

Primary terminal nut

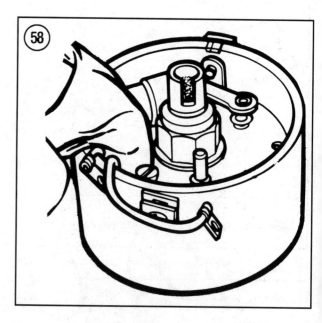

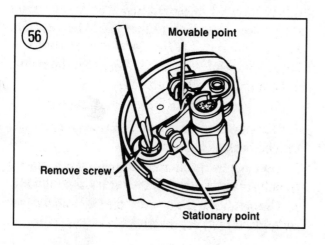

Movable point

Remove screw

Stationary point

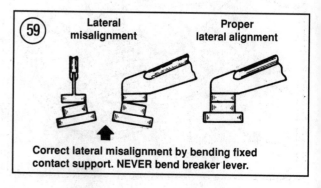

Lateral misalignment

Proper lateral alignment

Correct lateral misalignment by bending fixed contact support. NEVER bend breaker lever.

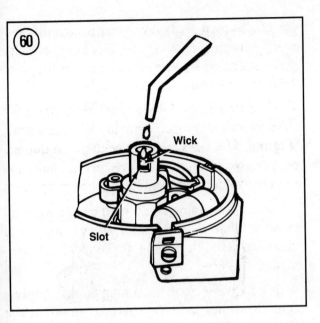

Wick

Slot

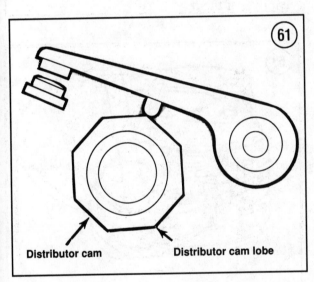

Distributor cam　　　Distributor cam lobe

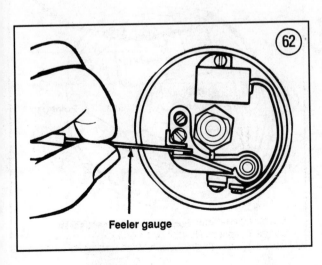

Feeler gauge

bending the stationary arm of the point set only. If reusing old points, they should not be re-aligned.

7. Check inside of the distributor shaft. If a felt wick is installed, lubricate with 1-2 drops of SAE 30 engine oil (**Figure 60**).

8. Adjust breaker point gap as described in this chapter.

Breaker Point Gap Adjustment

There are two ways to adjust the breaker point gap.

　　a. Feeler gauge

　　b. Dwell meter

The dwell meter method is the most accurate.

To set the gap with a feeler gauge:

1. Disconnect the ignition coil high tension (thick) lead and ground it to the engine block.

2. Connect a remote starter button to the starter solenoid or assist solenoid according to its manufacturer's instructions and crank the engine over until the breaker point rubbing block rests precisely on a distributor cam lobe, as shown in **Figure 61**. At this position, the points are open to their fullest.

3. Insert a flat feeler gauge between the open points (**Figure 62**) and compare the gap to specifications (**Table 6**). Gap adjustment is made either with an adjusting screw or with a screwdriver inserted in the slotted hole in the point set/breaker plate. See **Figure 63**. When a slight drag is felt on the gauge blade, tighten the locking screw. Recheck gap to make sure the points did not move during tightening.

To adjust point gap with a dwell meter:

1. Remove the distributor cap and rotor as described in this chapter.

2. Connect a dwell meter and remote starter switch according to manufacturer's instructions.

3. Crank the engine with the remote starter switch and read the dwell angle on the meter.

4. Adjust the dwell by varying the breaker point gap. Decrease the gap to increase dwell; increase the gap to decrease dwell.

5. Tighten the breaker point locking screw.

6. Repeat Step 3 to recheck the dwell.

7. Install the distributor rotor and cap as described in this chapter.

Ignition Timing

The manufacturer does not recommend using a timing light equipped with an adjustable spark advance dial. This type of timing light has a control dial that can be used to indicate the amount of timing advance an ignition system is providing. The manufacturer has determined that adjustable timing lights have the potential for considerable inaccuracy in the amount of timing advance indicated. Under-advanced or over-advanced ignition timing can result in loss of power and/or major engine damage, especially on models equipped with electronic ignition. If this type of timing light must be used, its accuracy must be checked frequently to prevent maladjusted ignition timing.

CAUTION
Never operate the engine without water circulating through the gear housing to the engine. If the engine is run in a dry condition, it will damage the water pump and may result in engine damage.

Some form of cooling water is required whenever the engine is running. The use of a test tank is recommended, however, the timing procedure may be performed with the boat in the water, or with a flushing device connected to the gear housing.

All models except 3.0L and 3.0LX equipped with EST ignition

NOTE
The No. 1 cylinder is the front cylinder on all inline engines. It is the front cyl-
inder on the port side of GM V6 and V8 engines.

1. Connect a suitable timing light to the No. 1 spark plug lead according to its manufacturer's instructions.

2. Connect a shop tachometer to the engine according to its manufacturer's instructions. Do not rely on the boat tachometer.

3. Locate the timing marks on the engine timing cover or block and crankshaft pulley or harmonic balancer. See **Figure 64** for typical arrangements.

4. If necessary, clean the timing marks. Apply a coat of white paint or chalk to improve the visibility of the marks.

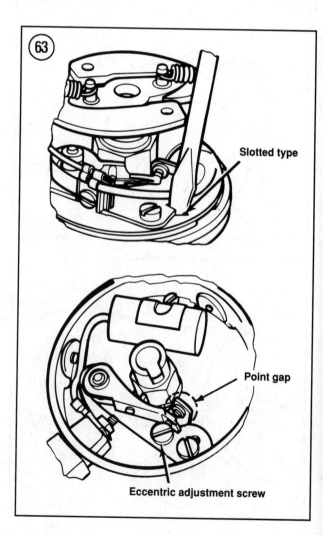

Slotted type

Point gap

Eccentric adjustment screw

5. Start the engine and allow to warm to normal operating temperature. Be sure that sufficient cooling water is flowing through the gear housing to the engine.

6. With the engine running at slow idle, point the timing light at the timing marks. Refer to **Table 6** for timing specifications. If the engine timing is correct, the correct moving mark will appear to stand still opposite the stationary mark.

7. If the timing marks are not properly aligned, loosen the hold-down clamp bolt at the base of the distributor just enough to allow the distributor body to be turned by hand. On some engines, it may be more convenient to use an automotive distributor wrench to loosen and tighten the hold-down clamp bolt. See **Figure 65**, typical.

NOTE
On models equipped with digital distributorless ignition system (DDIS), a crankshaft motion sensor assembly is installed where the distributor would be located. To adjust initial timing on models so equipped, first make sure the engine is running at 900 rpm or below. Then loosen the bolt securing the hold-down clamp and rotate the sensor housing as necessary to align the timing marks.

8. Slowly rotate the distributor body clockwise or counterclockwise as required until the timing marks come into alignment. See **Figure 66**.

9. Tighten the hold-down bolt (**Figure 65**) without moving the distributor. Recheck the timing after tightening the bolt. Repeat Steps 6-8 if further adjustment is necessary.

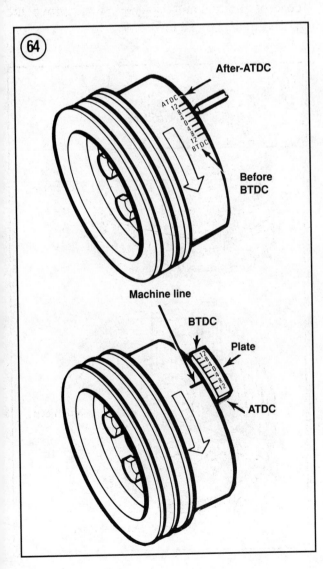

After-ATDC

ATDC
12
8
4
0
4
8
12
BTDC

Before BTDC

Machine line

BTDC

Plate

ATDC

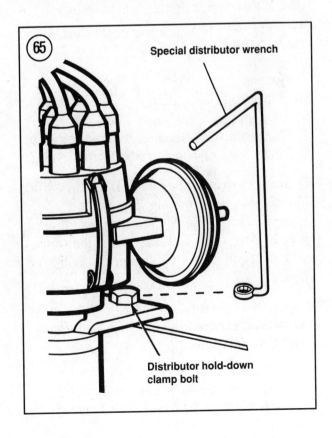

Special distributor wrench

Distributor hold-down clamp bolt

10. After adjusting initial timing, check the operation of the spark advance system. With the engine operating at slow idle, note the position of the timing marks using the timing light.

> *NOTE*
> *If timing advance does not perform as described in Step 11 and Step 12, the centrifugal advance (breaker-point ignition) or the ignition amplifier (breakerless ignition) is not operating properly.*

11. Gradually increase the engine speed to approximately 1,800 rpm while observing the timing marks. The timing should advance steadily as engine speed increases.

12. Decrease the engine speed to slow idle whole observing the timing marks. The timing should return to the initial setting as engine speed nears idle speed.

3.0L and 3.0LX models equipped with EST ignition

> *NOTE*
> *The No. 1 cylinder is the front cylinder on all inline engines.*

1. Connect a suitable timing light to the No. 1 spark plug lead according to its manufacturer's instructions.

2. Connect a shop tachometer to the engine according to its manufacturer's instructions. Do not rely on the boat tachometer.

3. Locate the timing marks on the engine timing cover and crankshaft pulley. If necessary, clean the timing marks and apply white paint or chalk to increase the visibility of the marks.

4. Start the engine and allow to warm to normal operating temperature. Make sure sufficient cooling water is flowing through the gear housing to the engine.

> *NOTE*
> *The timing advance system must be disabled (Step 5) to check or adjust initial timing. The jumper lead used in Step 5*

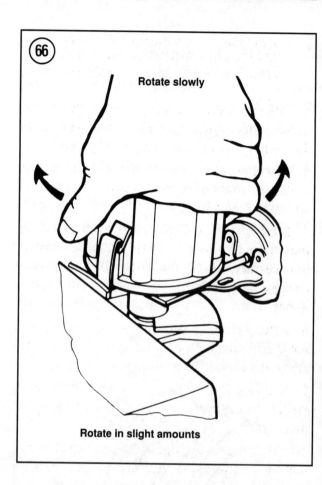

Rotate slowly

Rotate in slight amounts

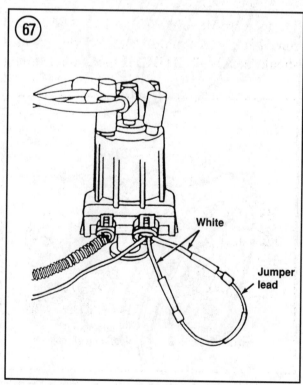

White

Jumper lead

should be fabricated using a short length of 16 gauge wire and 2 male bullet terminals attached to the ends of the wire.

5. With the engine running at idle speed, connect a jumper lead across the 2 white wires at the distributor 3-pin connector. See **Figure 67**.

6. Disconnect the wires at the shift interrupter switch. Connect the wires together to bypass the interrupter switch.

7. Point the timing light at the timing marks. The initial timing should be 1° BTDC. If adjustment is necessary, loosen the distributor hold-down clamp bolt (**Figure 65**) and rotate the distributor as necessary.

8. After the timing is properly adjusted, tighten the distributor hold-down clamp bolt, then recheck the timing. Repeat Step 7 if necessary.

9. Reconnect the wires to the shift interrupter switch and remove the jumper lead from the distributor.

10. With the timing light still connected, verify that the timing advanced to 10-14° BTDC after the jumper lead (**Figure 67**) was removed.

11. Increase the engine speed to 2,400-2,800 rpm and check timing. Total timing advance should be 25-29° BTDC. If the correct timing

advance is not noted, the ignition module is defective and must be replaced.

Carburetor

Refer to specifications in **Table 6** for the proper idle speed for your engine. Do not remove the flame arrestor for this procedure.

1. Connect a tachometer according to its manufacturer's instructions.

2. Locate the idle mixture screw(s) on your carburetor. This is usually a spring-loaded screw near the carburetor base. See **Figure 68**, typical.

3. Locate the idle speed screw on the carburetor throttle linkage. See **Figure 68**, typical.

4. Start the engine and run at fast idle (1,500 rpm) until normal operating temperature is reached.

5. Once the engine is warmed up, bring it back to a normal idle. Shift into FORWARD gear (idle position).

6. Disconnect the throttle cable brass barrel from the anchor stud. Do not lose the anchor stud spacer.

7. Note the idle speed on the tachometer. If necessary, adjust the idle stop screw to bring the idle speed back within specifications (**Table 6**).

8. Adjust the idle mixture screw clockwise until engine speed begins to drop (lean mixture). If the carburetor has 2 mixture screws, repeat the adjustment with the second screw.

9. Adjust the idle mixture screw counterclockwise until engine speed begins to drop (rich mixture). If the carburetor has 2 mixture screws, repeat the adjustment with the second screw.

10. Turn each screw (one at a time) to the midpoint between Step 8 and Step 9 until maximum engine smoothness and rpm is obtained.

11. Readjust idle speed to bring it back within specifications, if necessary.

12. Shut the engine off and remove the tachometer. Reconnect the throttle cable and make sure that the throttle valves are fully open with the remote control in its full forward position.

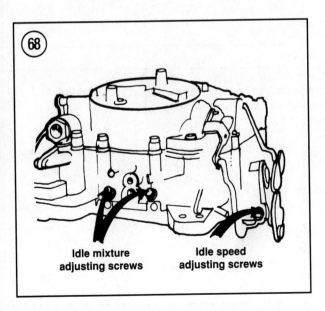

(68)

Idle mixture adjusting screws   **Idle speed adjusting screws**

Table 1 MERCRUISER MAINTENANCE SCHEDULE

	ENGINE
Weekly	Check battery
	Check engine oil level
	Check power steering fluid level
	Check power trim pump fluid level
	Check transom assembly and drive unit for corrosion or impact damage
After first 20 hours of operation	Check battery
	Check cooling system condition
	Check and adjust drive belt tension
	Inspect all electrical connections
	Clean flame arrestor
	Replace inline, carburetor and/or fuel pump filter element
	Check fuel lines and connections
	Change engine oil and filter
Every 50 hours of operation or 60 days	Check battery
	Check and adjust drive belt tension
	Check fuel lines and connections
	Check for loose, missing or damaged components
	Check power steering fluid level
Every 100 hours of operation or 120 days	Inspect breaker points[1]
	Check cooling system condition
	Clean crankcase vent system
	Clean flame arrestor
	Change engine oil and filter
	Clean vent-type oil filler cap
	Check and lubricate throttle and shift linkage points
	Check hose condition
	Check continuity circuit (if so equipped)
	Check engine alignment
Once each year	Perform 100 hours check
	Check alternator rear screen[2]
	Lubricate distributor cam[2]
	Check electrical connections
	Replace fuel filter
	Check for loose, missing or damaged components
	Inspect spark plug condition
	Clean and paint exterior surfaces
	STERN DRIVE
Weekly	Check stern drive lubricant level
	Check condition of trim tab, anodic bolt heads and other sacrificial anodes
	Check gear housing water pickups for debris or growth
After first 20 hours of operation	Check engine and drive alignment
	Check bellows and clamps[2]
	Check engine mount, drive, steering cable and trim cylinder fasteners for tightness
	Lubricate gimbal bearing[2]
	Lubricate hinge pins[3]
	Lubricate power steering control valve
	Lubricate upper and lower swivel pins[2]
	Check level of all fluids
	Lubricate steering cable and lever[3]
	Lubricate U-joint coupling splines
	Check propeller condition and lubricate prop shaft splines

(continued)

Table 1 MERCRUISER MAINTENANCE SCHEDULE (continued)

STERN DRIVE (continued)	
Every 50 hours of operation or 60 days	Lubricate hinge pins[3] Check propeller condition and lubricate prop shaft splines Check level of all fluids Lubricate steering cable[3] Lubricate steering linkage[2] Lubricate exposed portion of steering cable Lubricate power steering control valve
Every 100 hours of operation or 120 days	Lubricate transom gimbal bearing assembly swivel shaft and bearing Lubricate U-joint shaft splines and cross bearings Check trim cylinder fasteners for tightness Lubricate upper and lower swivel pins[2] Lubricate propeller shaft splines[2][4]
Once each year	Perform 100 hours checks Check propeller for damage Replace Alpha One water pump impeller Remove, disassemble and clean Bravo One seawater pump Spray exterior surfaces with rust preventative Test output of MerCathode II system (if so equipped) Inspect and lubricate steering head and remote control Inspect and lubricate shift cable Inspect steering system for loose, damaged or missing components

1. Does not apply to Thunderbolt IV, EST or DDIS ignition.
2. Perform more frequently if operated in salt water.
3. Every 30 days in salt water; every 60 days in fresh water.
4. Lubricate during each installation. Make certain that nut is secure.

Table 2 ENGINE OIL VISCOSITY

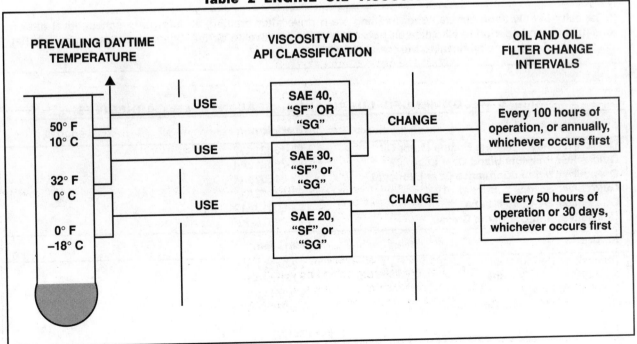

Table 3 APPROXIMATE ENGINE OIL CAPACITIES

Model	Capacity (with filter)[1]
Inline 4-cylinder	
120, 2.5L, 140, 3.0L, 3.0LX	4.0 qt.
165, 170, 3.7L	5.5 qt.
180, 190, 3.7LX	6.5 qt.
V6	
175, 185, 205, 4.3L, 4.3LX	4.5 qt.
V8	
200, 5.0L	5.0 qt.
230, 5.0LX, 260, 5.7L, 350 Magnum	5.5 qt.
7.4L, 454 Magnum	7.0 qt.
502 Magnum	8.0 qt.
502 Magnum (Mark V)[2]	7.0 qt.

1. All capacities in this table are approximate. To ensure correct oil level and prevent overfilling the engine, always use the dipstick as recommended in the text.
2. Mark V engines can be identified by the fuel pump mounted on the belt-driven seawater pump.

Table 4 APPROXIMATE STERN DRIVE CAPACITIES

Model	Capacity*
Alpha One	32 oz. (0.98 liters)
Alpha One (with lube oil monitor)	54 oz. (1.6 liters)
Bravo One	64 oz. (1.95 liters)
Bravo One (with lube oil monitor)	86 oz. (2.54 liters)
Bravo Two	80 oz. (2.4 liters)
Bravo Two (with lube oil monitor)	102 oz. (3.0 liters)
Bravo Three (with lube oil monitor)	3 qt. (2.9 liters)

* Capacity is only approximate. When refilling stern drive after draining all lubricant, recheck level after a one-minute run-in period to eliminate air pockets which may develop during filling. If necessary, top up after rechecking to bring the lubricant to the correct level.

Table 5 RECOMMENDED LUBRICANTS, SEALANTS AND ADHESIVES

Lubricants	Part No.
Quicksilver 4-cycle Marine Engine Motor Oil	92-13831A12
Quicksilver Premium Blend Gear Lube	92-755812A4
Quicksilver High Performance Gear Lubricant	92-816026A4*
Quicksilver Special Lubricant 101	92-13872A1
Quicksilver 2-4-C Multi-Lube	92-90018A12
Quicksilver Anti-Corrosion Grease	92-78376-12
Sealants	**Part No.**
Quicksilver Perfect Seal	92-34227-1
Quicksilver RTV Sealant	92-91600-1
Quicksilver Liquid Neoprene	92-25711-1
Quicksilver Insulating Compound	92-25711

(continued)

Table 5 RECOMMENDED LUBRICANTS, SEALANTS AND ADHESIVES (continued)

Adhesives	Part No.
3M Brand Adhesive	92-25234
Quicksilver Bellows Adhesive	92-86166
Locquic Primer "T"	92-59327-1
Loctite No. 35	92-59328-1
Loctite Type "A" (271)	92-32609

Miscellaneous	Part No.
Quicksilver Corrosion Guard	92-78379
Quicksilver Marine Fuel System Treatment and Stabilizer	92-78383A12
Quicksilver Power Tune	92-15104-12
Quicksilver Storage Seal	92-86145-12
Quicksilver Light Gray Primer	92-78374-12
Quicksilver Phantom Black Spray Paint	92-78373-12
Quicksilver Spray Paint Leveler	92-75996-12

* The manufacturer recommends using only high performance gear lubricant (part No. 92-816026A4) in gearcase on 502 Magnum models.

Table 6 TUNE-UP SPECIFICATIONS

Model	Spark plugs		Breaker points	
	Type	Gap (in.)	Dwell (degrees)	Gap (in.)
120, 2.5L	AC-MR43T	0.035	28-34	0.022
140, 3.0L (with Delco distributor)	AC-MR43T	0.035	28-34	0.022
3.0L (with Prestolite distributor)	AC-MR43T	0.035	39-45	0.016
3.0L, 3.0LX (with DDIS ignition)	AC-MR42LTS	0.035	Note 1	Note 1
3.0L, 3.0LX (with EST ignition)	AC-MR43T	0.035	Note 2	Note 2
165, 170, 180, 190, 3.7L, 3.7LX	AC-R42CTS	0.035	28-34	0.022
175, 185, 205, 4.3L, 4.3LX	AC-MR43T	0.035	Note 3	Note 3
200, 230, 5.0L, 5.0LX	AC-MR43T	0.035	Note 3	Note 3
260, 5.7L, 350 Magnum	AC-MR43T	0.035	Note 3	Note 3
7.4L, 454 Magnum, 502 Magnum	AC-MR43T	0.035	Note 3	Note 3

Model	Initial timing (degrees BTDC)	Maximum advance (degrees BTDC)	Idle rpm (in gear)	Full throttle range (rpm)
120, 2.5L	8	37 @ 2,000 rpm	650-700	4,200-4,600
140, 3.0L (with Delco distributor)	6	35 @ 2,000 rpm	650-700	4,200-4,600
3.0L (with Prestolite distributor)	8	26 @ 4,000 rpm	650-700	4,200-4,400
3.0L (with DDIS ignition)	8	28 @ 4,600 rpm	650-700	4,400-4,800
3.0L, 3.0LX (with EST ignition)	1	23 @ 4,800 rpm	650-700	4,400-4,800
3.0LX (with DDIS ignition)	8	28 @ 4,200 rpm	650-700	4,400-4,800
165, 170, 3.7L	4	33 @ 2,000 rpm	650-700	4,200-4,600
180, 190, 3.7LX	4	33 @ 2,000 rpm	650-700	4,400-4,800
175, 185, 205, 4.3L, 4.3LX	8	22 @ 2,500 rpm	650-700	4,400-4,800
200, 5.0L, 230, 5.0LX, 260, 5.7L	8	Note 4	650-700	4,200-4,600
350 Magnum	8	32 @ 3,800 rpm	650-700	4,400-4,800
7.4L	8	32 @ 3,700 rpm	650-700	4,200-4,600
454 Magnum	8	32 @ 3,700 rpm	650-700	Note 5
502 Magnum	8	28 @ 5,000 rpm	650-700	4,600-5,000

(continued)

Table 6 TUNE-UP SPECIFICATIONS (continued)

Model	Firing order	Oil pressure @ 2,000 rpm (psi)	Fuel pressure (psi)	Compression pressure (psi)
All 4-cylinder	1-3-4-2	30-60	5-6.5	140
165, 170, 3.7L, 180, 190, 3.7LX	1-3-4-2	30-60	3-6	150
175, 185, 205, 4.3L, 4.3LX	1-6-5-4-3-2	30-55	3-7	180
200, 5.0L	1-8-4-3-6-5-7-2	30-55	5.5-7	150
230, 5.0LX	1-8-4-3-6-5-7-2	30-55	5.5-7	155
260, 5.7L, 350 Magnum	1-8-4-3-6-5-7-2	30-55	5.5-7	150
7.4L	1-8-4-3-6-5-7-2	35-70	5.5-7	150
454 Magnum, 502 Magnum	1-8-4-3-6-5-7-2	30-70	3-7	150

1. Digital, distributorless ignition system (DDIS).
2. Electronic spark timing (EST) ignition system.
3. Thunderbolt IV breakerless ignition system.
4. Ignition amplifier module identification mark V8-24—32° BTDC @ 3,700 rpm; V8-24S—32° BTDC @ 4,600 rpm; V8-22—30° BTDC @ 3,400 rpm; V8-22A—30° BTDC @ 4,400 rpm.
5. 1986 and 1987 models—4,200-4,600 rpm; 1988-on models—4,600-5,000 rpm.

Chapter Five

Lay-up, Cooling System Service and Fitting Out

LAY-UP

Boats that are to be stored for more than 4 or 5 weeks should be carefully prepared. This is necessary to prevent damage to the engine and the stern drive unit from freezing, corrosion or fuel system contamination. Preparation for lay-up should begin, if possible, while the boat is still in the water.

If the boat has been removed from the water, a supply of cooling water must be made available to the engine. This can be accomplished in one of two ways. The stern drive unit can be submerged in a test tank, or a garden hose may be attached to the cooling system using a flush/test device available from your MerCruiser dealer. See Chapter Four. If a flush/test device is used, you should remove the propeller to prevent any possible interference and always start the water flow before starting the engine.

The suggestions for lay-up preparation which follow are based on recommendations made by Mercury Marine. See Chapter Four for lubricants recommended by Mercury Marine.

In-the-water Preparation

1. If the boat is not in the water, attach a flushing/test device to the stern drive. See *Cooling System Flushing*, Chapter Four.
2. Make sure the fuel contains Quicksilver Marine Fuel Treatment and Stabilizer. Refer to the container for the recommended amount to add according to the size of your tank and the amount of fuel inside. This additive prevents gum and varnish from forming in the fuel system.
3. Start the engine and run under load (boat in water) or at idle (boat out of water and a flushing adapter used) until it reaches normal operating temperature, then shut the engine off.
4. Drain the engine oil and install a new oil filter (**Figure 1**, typical). See Chapter Four.
5. Refill the crankcase with the proper amount of fresh SG engine oil. Add one pint of Quicksilver Engine Oil Supplement to the crankcase. See Chapter Four.
6. Make sure the stern drive is in its full-down position. Restart the engine and run at fast idle (1,000-1,500 rpm) for several minutes to circu-

late the fresh oil throughout the engine. Check for leaks around the new filter and oil pan while the engine is running.

7. Shut the engine off and wait approximately 5 minutes, then check the oil level on the dipstick (**Figure 2**, typical location). See Chapter Four. Add oil, if necessary, to bring the level up to the FULL mark on the dipstick.

8. Remove the flame arrestor cover, if so equipped, and flame arrestor (**Figure 3**) from the carburetor air horn and restart the engine. Increase engine speed to a fast idle (1,000-1,500 rpm) and slowly pour a can of Quicksilver Storage Seal into the carburetor intake to fog the internal surfaces of the induction system. When the can of Storage Seal has approximately 2 ounces remaining in it, decrease engine speed to a normal idle and kill the engine by quickly pouring the remaining Storage Seal into the carburetor. If the engine does not stall at this point, shut the ignition off immediately.

> *NOTE*
> *If Quicksilver Storage Seal is not available, pour about one cup of SAE 20 SG engine oil into the carburetor. Kill the engine by quickly pouring in 2 oz. of SAE 20 SG engine oil.*

9. Clean the flame arrestor with solvent, blow dry with compressed air, if available, and reinstall on the carburetor.

10. Install a new fuel filter canister on all engines so equipped. See **Figure 4**, typical. If equipped with a sediment bowl fuel filter (**Figure 5**, typical), remove and clean the bowl, then install a new filter before reinstalling it to the fuel pump.

11. Install a new filter in the carburetor fuel inlet nut, if so equipped. See **Figure 6**, typical.

> *WARNING*
> *Be sure to have a Coast Guard-approved fire extinguisher at hand before performing Step 12.*

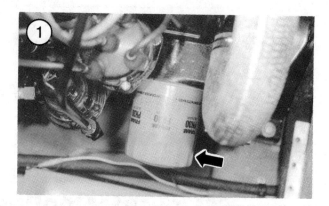

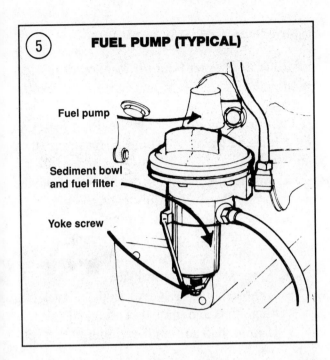

FUEL PUMP (TYPICAL) ⑤

Fuel pump

Sediment bowl
and fuel filter

Yoke screw

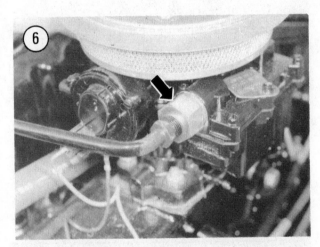

⑥

⑦

12. Close the fuel shut-off valve, if so equipped, and completely drain the fuel tank of all gasoline.

WARNING
Since gasoline is an extreme fire hazard, always store it in a sealed metal container away from heat, sparks and flame.

13. Remove the boat from the water, keeping the bow higher than the stern if possible to assist in draining the exhaust system.

5

Out-of-water Preparation

1. Adjust trailer or cradle so that the engine is in a level position. Lower the stern drive unit to its full-down position.

2. Loosen drive belt tension and inspect condition of all belts; replace as required. Tighten accessory unit adjusting bolts without placing tension on drive belts.

3. Drain the cooling system as described in this chapter.

4. Check all hoses for signs of deterioration, cracks or other defects. Replace hoses as required.

5. Remove the spark plugs and pour 1 oz. of Quicksilver Storage Seal or SAE 20 SF or SG engine oil into each cylinder.

6. Disable the ignition system by performing the following:

    a. 3.0L and 3.0LX with DDIS ignition—Disconnect the motion sensor from the ignition amplifier module at the 2-pin connector.

    b. 3.0L and 3.0LX with EST ignition—Disconnect the 2-pin connector (purple and gray wires) from the ignition coil.

    c. All others—Disconnect the ignition coil high tension lead at the distributor cap tower (**Figure 7**). Ground the lead to a good engine ground.

7. Crank the engine with the starter for 15-20 seconds to coat the cylinder walls with oil.

8. Wipe up any excess oil from the plug holes. Wipe a thin film of SAE 20 engine oil on the

spark plug threads. Reinstall the spark plugs and reconnect the ignition wires or coil lead.

9. Remove the valve cover(s) and check for signs of condensation in the rocker arm area. Carefully wipe away any oil/water mixture found. Coat valve mechanism and inside of rocker arm cover(s) generously with Storage Seal or SAE 20 engine oil. Reinstall the valve cover(s) using new gasket(s).

10. Refill the closed cooling system, if so equipped, as described in this chapter.

11. Cover the flame arrestor and carburetor with a plastic bag and tape tightly in place. This prevents moisture from entering the carburetor and intake manifold.

12. Remove the battery from the boat. Tape vent holes closed and clean battery case with baking soda solution to remove any traces of corrosion and acid, then rinse with cold water. Check electrolyte level in each cell and top up with distilled water as required. Cover terminals with distilled water as required. Cover terminals with a light coat of petroleum jelly. Store the battery in a cool, dry place.

NOTE
Remove the battery from storage every 30-45 days. Check electrolyte level and slow-charge for 5-6 hours at 6 amperes.

13. Tape the exhaust outlets closed to prevent moisture from entering the exhaust manifolds and valve chambers.

14. Cover through-hull fuel tank ventilators with tape to help keep moisture out of the fuel tanks.

15. Clean the engine exterior thoroughly and retouch any blemishes with engine touch-up paint. Apply a film of Quicksilver Corrosion Guard on exterior surfaces or wipe down with a rag coated with Storage seal or SAE 20 engine oil to leave a light coating on exterior surfaces.

Stern Drive Unit

Refer to Chapter Four for location of lubrication points listed below and type of lubricant to be used.

1. Insert a length of wire in the drive shaft and gear housing water drain holes to make sure they are open.

2. Lubricate the following components with the appropriate Quicksilver lubricant.
   a. Steering cable grease fitting.
   b. Extended portion of steering cable.
   c. Steering system pivot points.
   d. Power steering control valve.
   e. Gimbal housing swivel shaft, swivel pin, hinge pins and gimbal bearing.
   f. U-joint shaft and engine coupling shaft splines.
   g. U-joint bearings.

3. Remove the propeller. Lubricate the propeller shaft and reinstall the propeller.

4. Check the condition of the bellows and clamps. Replace bellows or tighten clamps as required.

5. On Alpha One drives, check water pump impeller; replace if worn, hardened or set.

CAUTION
Do not paint sacrificial zinc rings, plugs or bars, if present. These must be left

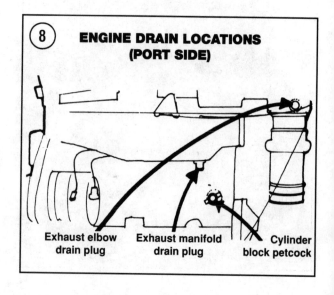

(8) **ENGINE DRAIN LOCATIONS (PORT SIDE)**

Exhaust elbow drain plug   Exhaust manifold drain plug   Cylinder block petcock

unpainted in order to prevent damage from galvanic corrosion.

6. Remove all marine growths and deposits from the stern drive unit. Clean and repaint metal surfaces that have become exposed with touch-up paint.

7. Wipe or spray exterior surfaces of stern drive with Quicksilver Corrosion Guard.

8. Store stern drive in its normal full-down position. If the unit is stored in a tilted-up position, the universal joint bellows may develop a "set" that will lead to premature bellows failure once the stern drive is returned to service.

COOLING SYSTEM DRAINING

The engine cooling system must be properly drained for storage during the winter months in areas where temperatures fall below 32° F (0° C). If it is not, the engine block may be cracked by expansion of frozen water.

Inline engines tend to crack horizontally just below the core plugs or along the upper edge below the cylinder head. A V-block will usually

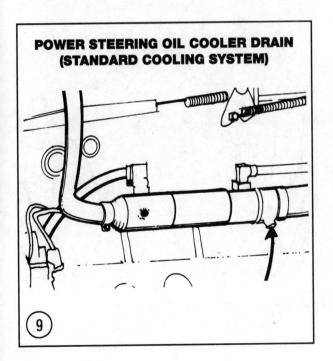

POWER STEERING OIL COOLER DRAIN (STANDARD COOLING SYSTEM)

⑨

crack near the hydraulic lifters or in the valley of the block below the intake manifold.

The following procedures are designed to help you prevent unnecessary engine damage during winter storage.

To assure that the cooling system is completely drained, adjust the trailer or cradle so that the forward end of inline engines is higher than the aft end. With V6 and V8 engines, adjust the trailer or cradle so that the engine is level—the bow of the boat will be higher than the stern.

Standard Cooling System (Inline Engines)

1. Place suitable containers under the exhaust manifold and engine block drain points, if space permits. This will prevent water from draining into the bilge.

2. Cover any exposed components such as the alternator or starter motor with plastic to protect them from water during this procedure.

3. Open the drain valve on the port side of the engine block and remove the exhaust manifold drain plug. Remove the exhaust elbow drain plug, if so equipped. See **Figure 8** for typical locations.

4. If equipped with an elbow riser, remove the drain plug from the front of the riser.

5. If equipped with power steering, remove the drain plug from the lower-aft end of the power steering cooler unit. See **Figure 9**, typical.

6. Remove the lower end of all cooling system hoses from the engine, circulating pump and exhaust manifold. Lower the hoses and allow them to completely drain. Then, reconnect the hoses and clamp securely.

7. Allow cooling system to drain *completely*, then coat drain plug threads with Quicksilver Perfect Seal and reinstall. Close engine block drain valve.

Closed Cooling System
(Inline Engines)

The freshwater section of a closed cooling system need not be drained during winter months, provided it is kept filled with a 50/50 solution of pure soft water and ethylene glycol antifreeze. However, the seawater section *must* be drained *completely.*

Seawater section (except MerCruiser 4-cylinder engine)

1. Place containers under drain points, if space permits. This will prevent water from draining into the bilge.
2. Remove the exhaust manifold drain plug. Remove the exhaust elbow drain plug, if so equipped.
3. If equipped with an exhaust elbow riser, remove the drain plug from the riser.
4. If equipped with power steering, remove the drain plug from the bottom of the power steering cooler. See **Figure 10**, typical.
5. Refer to **Figure 11** and disconnect the seawater inlet hose (A), remove the drain plug from the aft end of the heat exchanger (B) and remove the zinc anode (C), if so equipped.
6. Examine the zinc anode (if so equipped) for erosion. If it is less than 25 percent eroded, coat the anode threads with Quicksilver Perfect Seal and reinstall. If more than 25 percent of the anode is gone, install a new one.
7. Allow the seawater section to drain *completely,* then reinstall the drain plug threads with Quicksilver Perfect Seal and reinstall. Reconnect the seawater inlet hose to the heat exchanger (A, **Figure 11**).

Seawater section (MerCruiser 4-cylinder engine)

Refer to **Figure 12** (typical) for this procedure.

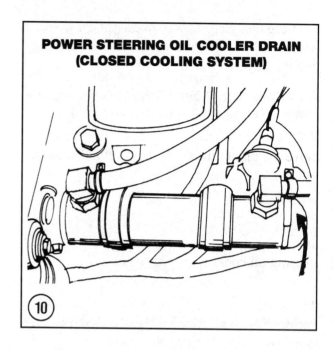

POWER STEERING OIL COOLER DRAIN (CLOSED COOLING SYSTEM)

10

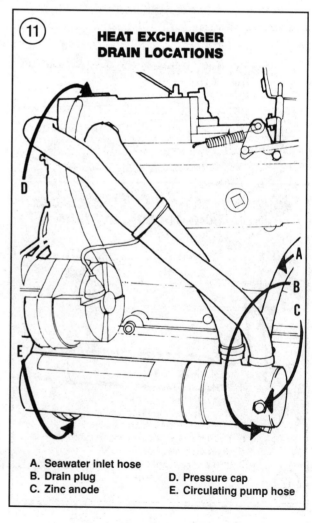

11

HEAT EXCHANGER DRAIN LOCATIONS

A. Seawater inlet hose
B. Drain plug
C. Zinc anode
D. Pressure cap
E. Circulating pump hose

1. Place containers under drain points, if space permits. This will prevent water from draining into the bilge.

2. Remove the exhaust elbow drain plug and heat exchanger seawater drain plug.

3. If equipped with an exhaust elbow riser, remove the drain plug from the front of the riser.

4. Disconnect the seawater inlet hose at the water-cooled voltage regulator.

5. If equipped with power steering, remove the drain plug from the lower-aft end of the power steering oil cooler. See **Figure 10**.

6. Allow seawater section to drain *completely*, then coat drain plug threads with Quicksilver Perfect Seal and reinstall. Reconnect seawater inlet hose to the voltage regulator.

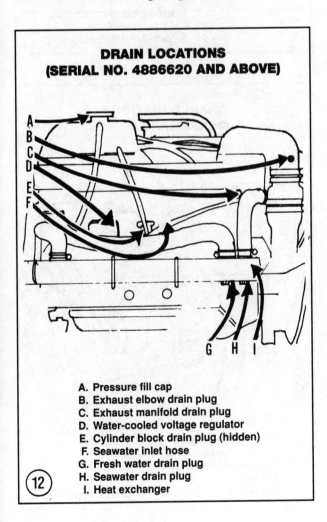

DRAIN LOCATIONS (SERIAL NO. 4886620 AND ABOVE)

A. Pressure fill cap
B. Exhaust elbow drain plug
C. Exhaust manifold drain plug
D. Water-cooled voltage regulator
E. Cylinder block drain plug (hidden)
F. Seawater inlet hose
G. Fresh water drain plug
H. Seawater drain plug
I. Heat exchanger

(12)

Freshwater section
(except MerCruiser 4-cylinder engine)

1. Place containers under drain points, if space permits. This will prevent coolant from draining into the bilge.

2. Remove the pressure fill cap from the reservoir. See D, **Figure 11**.

3. Open the engine block drain valve on the port side of the block. See **Figure 8** for typical location.

4. Disconnect the circulating pump-to-heat exchanger hose (E, **Figure 11**) from the front of the heat exchanger. Lower the hose to let the coolant drain.

5. Remove the coolant recovery hose, if so equipped, from the mounting bracket. Drain the coolant.

6. Allow the freshwater section to drain *completely*, then close the engine block drain valve. Reconnect the circulating pump hose to the heat exchanger.

Freshwater section
(MerCruiser 4-cylinder engine)

Refer to **Figure 12**, typical for this procedure.

1. Place containers under drain points, if space permits. This will prevent coolant from draining into the bilge.

2. Remove the pressure fill cap from the reservoir.

3. Remove the heat exchanger, exhaust manifold and engine block drain plugs.

4. Remove the circulating pump drain plug at the bottom of the front cover. See **Figure 13**.

5. Remove the coolant recovery reservoir, if so equipped, from the mounting bracket. Drain the coolant.

6. Allow the freshwater section to drain *completely*, then coat the drain plug threads with Quicksilver Perfect Seal and reinstall.

5

Standard Cooling System
(V6 and V8 Engines)

1. Place containers under the drain points, if space permits. This will prevent water from draining into the boat bilge.

2A. *Models prior to 1990*—Remove the exhaust manifold and elbow drain plugs from both sides of the engine. Open the cylinder block drain valve on each side of the engine. See **Figure 14** and **Figure 15**. Allow all water to drain. If necessary, insert a wire into the drain holes or petcocks to ensure that foreign material is not obstructing the drain.

> *NOTE*
> *On 1990-on V6 and V8 models (built after October 1, 1989), the exhaust manifold drain holes and petcocks have been eliminated. In addition, the cylinder block drain petcocks have been eliminated and drain plugs installed in their place. To drain the exhaust manifolds, the coolant hose must be removed from the manifold elbow as described in the following procedure.*

2B. *1990-on*—Loosen the clamp and remove the coolant hose from the exhaust manifold el-

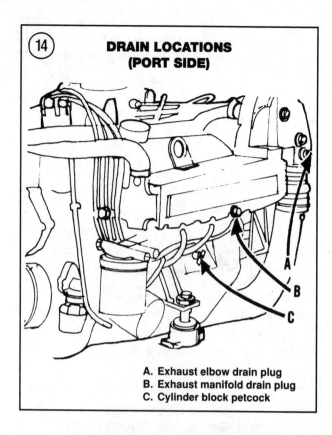

14 **DRAIN LOCATIONS (PORT SIDE)**

A. Exhaust elbow drain plug
B. Exhaust manifold drain plug
C. Cylinder block petcock

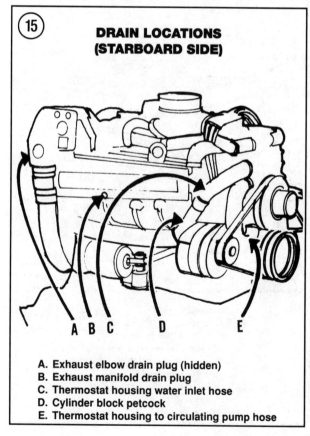

15 **DRAIN LOCATIONS (STARBOARD SIDE)**

A. Exhaust elbow drain plug (hidden)
B. Exhaust manifold drain plug
C. Thermostat housing water inlet hose
D. Cylinder block petcock
E. Thermostat housing to circulating pump hose

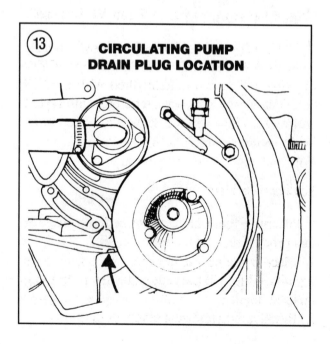

13 **CIRCULATING PUMP DRAIN PLUG LOCATION**

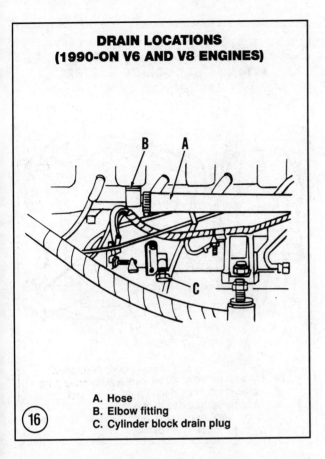

**DRAIN LOCATIONS
(1990-ON V6 AND V8 ENGINES)**

A. Hose
B. Elbow fitting
C. Cylinder block drain plug

(16)

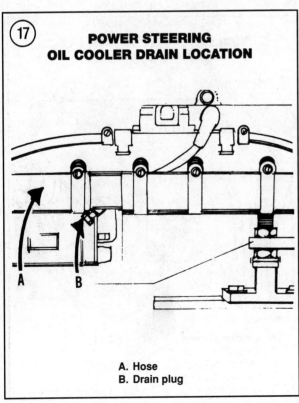

(17)

**POWER STEERING
OIL COOLER DRAIN LOCATION**

A. Hose
B. Drain plug

bow fitting on each side of the engine. See **Figure 16**. Remove the cylinder block drain plugs from each side of the engine. Allow all water to drain. If necessary, insert a wire into each drain hole to ensure that foreign material is not obstructing the drain.

3. If equipped with exhaust elbow risers under the exhaust elbows, remove the drain plug from each riser.

NOTE
*If the power steering oil cooler has no drain plug, remove hose A in **Figure 17**.*

4A. *Power steering*—Remove the drain plug from the lower-aft end of the power steering oil cooler. See B, **Figure 17**.

4B. *Non-power steering*—Disconnect the water inlet hose at the thermostat housing. Lower the hose to let the water drain from the lowest point.

5. Disconnect the circulating pump hose at the pump and lower the hose to drain the water.

6. Allow the cooling system to drain *completely,* then coat the drain plug threads with Quicksilver Perfect Seal and reinstall.

7. Close the engine block drain valves and reconnect the hoses.

Closed Cooling System (V6 and V8 Engines)

The freshwater section of a closed cooling system need not be drained during winter months, provided it is kept filled with a 50/50 solution of pure soft water and ethylene glycol antifreeze. However, the seawater section *must* be drained *completely.*

Seawater section

Refer to **Figure 18** and **Figure 19**, typical for this procedure.

1. Place containers under drain points, if space permits. This will prevent water from draining into the bilge.

2. Remove both exhaust elbow drain plugs.

5

3. If equipped with water distribution blocks under the exhaust elbows, remove the drain plug from each block. See **Figure 20**.

4. If equipped with exhaust elbow rises, remove the drain plug at the front of each riser.

5. Remove the heat exchanger drain plug.

6. If equipped with power steering, remove the drain plug from the bottom of the power steering oil cooler, if so equipped. See **Figure 17**.

7. Disconnect the inlet and outlet hoses from the aft end of the seawater pump. See **Figure 21**, typical. Be sure to reconnect the hoses to their proper fitting.

8. Disconnect the coil secondary (thick) lead from the center distributor tower and ground it to the engine block.

9. Crank the engine over to purge any water remaining in the seawater pickup pump.

10. Allow the seawater section to drain *completely*, then coat the drain plug threads with Quicksilver Perfect Seal and reinstall the plugs.

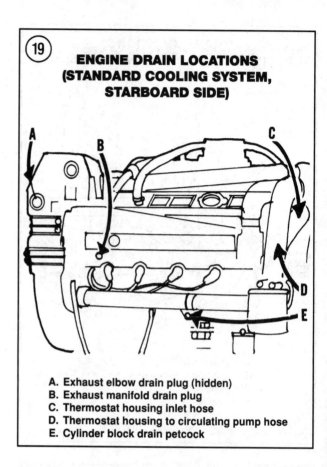

(19)

ENGINE DRAIN LOCATIONS (STANDARD COOLING SYSTEM, STARBOARD SIDE)

A. Exhaust elbow drain plug (hidden)
B. Exhaust manifold drain plug
C. Thermostat housing inlet hose
D. Thermostat housing to circulating pump hose
E. Cylinder block drain petcock

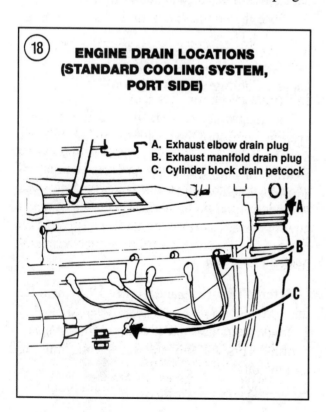

(18)

ENGINE DRAIN LOCATIONS (STANDARD COOLING SYSTEM, PORT SIDE)

A. Exhaust elbow drain plug
B. Exhaust manifold drain plug
C. Cylinder block drain petcock

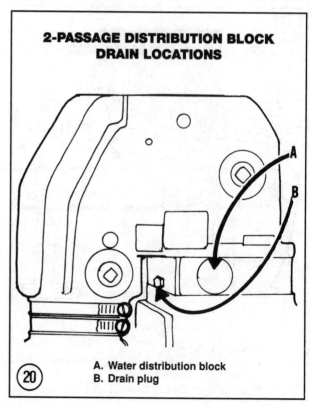

2-PASSAGE DISTRIBUTION BLOCK DRAIN LOCATIONS

A. Water distribution block
B. Drain plug

(20)

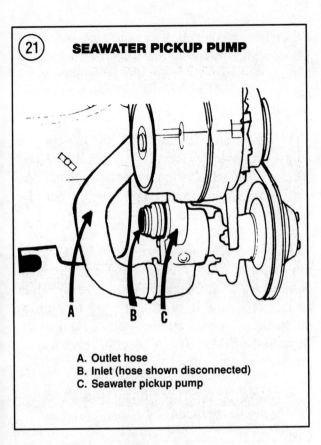

SEAWATER PICKUP PUMP

A. Outlet hose
B. Inlet (hose shown disconnected)
C. Seawater pickup pump

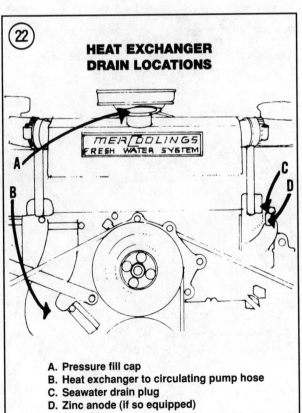

HEAT EXCHANGER DRAIN LOCATIONS

MER*COOLINGS FRESH WATER SYSTEM

A. Pressure fill cap
B. Heat exchanger to circulating pump hose
C. Seawater drain plug
D. Zinc anode (if so equipped)

11. Close the engine block drain valves, reconnect all hoses and reinstall the coil secondary (thick) lead.

Freshwater section

1. Place containers under drain points, if space permits. This will prevent coolant from draining into the bilge.
2. Remove the pressure fill cap from the heat exchanger reservoir. See **Figure 22**.
3. Remove the exhaust manifold drain plugs and open the drain valve on both sides of the block.
4. Disconnect the circulating pump hose at the pump and drain the water in it.
5. Remove the coolant recovery hose, if so equipped, from the mounting bracket. Drain the coolant from the reservoir.
6. Allow the freshwater section to drain *completely,* then coat drain plug threads with Quicksilver Perfect Seal and reinstall the plugs.
7. Close the engine block drain valves. Reconnect the circulating pump hose.

COOLING SYSTEM REFILLING

In Preparation For Storage

Under normal circumstances, the freshwater section of a closed cooling system would not be drained until just before the boat is to be returned to service from winter storage. The following procedures pertain to standard cooling systems and are designed to provide additional protection against freeze damage during winter temperatures.

CAUTION
Do not run the engine after performing the storage service procedure that follows. Before returning the boat to service, drain the coolant as described in this chapter and tighten all fasteners and clamps to specifications.

Inline engines

1. Remove the water distribution block cover. See **Figure 23**, typical.
2. Remove the thermostat and gasket. Discard the gasket.
3. Disconnect the hose at the manifold front end cap. See **Figure 24**, typical.
4. Pour a 50/50 solution of pure soft water and ethylene glycol antifreeze into the water distribution block until the cylinder head, block and manifold are full.
5. Reinstall the thermostat with a new gasket. Tighten the water distribution block cover securely and install the hose to the manifold front end cap.

V6 and V8 engines

1. Loosen the hose clamps at the manifold front end caps. See A, **Figure 25**, typical. Remove hoses from end caps.
2. Remove the thermostat housing cover. See B, **Figure 25**, typical.
3. Remove the thermostat and gasket. Discard the gasket.
4. Pour a 50/50 solution of pure soft water and ethylene glycol antifreeze into the thermostat housing until it is full.
5. Pour the coolant solution into the opening in each manifold end cap until the level reaches the top of the cap.
6. Install the thermostat with a new gasket. Tighten the thermostat housing cover screws snugly (B, **Figure 25**).
7. Connect the hoses to the manifold front end caps and snug down the clamps. See A, **Figure 25**, typical.

Returning the Engine to Service

Most ethylene glycol antifreeze solutions used in closed cooling systems tend to become corrosive after approximately 3 years of use or if a blown head gasket allows exhaust gases to enter the cooling system. While such corrosive tendencies will not cause significant damage to the engine, they do produce loose particles that can plug the coolant side of the heat exchanger.

The increased usage of aluminum components in engines, water pumps, manifolds and recovery tanks has led to the development of an antifreeze formulation recommended for use with aluminum engines.

This new type antifreeze formula should be used with all MerCruiser marine engine closed cooling systems. Check the antifreeze container and make sure it meets one of the major automakers' specifications, such as Ford specification ESE-M97B44-A or GM specification 1825M.

1. Remove the pressure fill cap from the reservoir or heat exchanger.

2. Fill the freshwater section with a 50/50 mixture of pure soft water and ethylene glycol antifreeze until the fluid level is approximately one inch below the top of the filler neck.

CAUTION
Water must flow through the seawater pump in Step 3 or possible damage to the pump and engine may occur.

3. If the boat is not in the water, connect a flushing device and adjust water flow. Start the engine and run at about 1,000 rpm, adding coolant to the heat exchanger as necessary to maintain the coolant level at approximately 1 in. below the top of the filler neck. When the engine reaches normal operating temperature and coolant level remain constant, reinstall the pressure fill cap.

4. If equipped with a coolant recovery system, remove the reservoir cap and fill with coolant to the FULL mark on the reservoir.

5. Check for leaks while the engine is running and note the position of the engine temperature gauge—it should be normal.

WARNING
Do not remove the pressure fill cap when the engine is warm or hot. You may be seriously scalded or burned by coolant escaping under pressure.

6. Shut the engine off and allow it to cool for 30 minutes. Turn the pressure fill cap to the first

detent and allow any pressure to escape, then remove the cap.

7. Recheck the coolant level in the reservoir or heat exchanger and all coolant as required to bring it to a midpoint between the ADD and FULL marks when the engine is at normal operating temperature.

COOLING SYSTEM CONVERSION

Standard cooling system can be converted to a closed cooling system on some models. **Figure 26** shows the components of the front-mounted closed cooling kit (part No. 18390A2) available from Mercruiser dealers for the 7.4L and 454 Magnum Bravo One models.

FITTING OUT

Preparing the boat for use after storage is relatively easy if the engine and stern drive unit were properly prepared before storage. The following suggestions for fitting out are based on recommendations made by Mercury Marine.

1. Clean the engine and stern drive unit with a solvent such as kerosene to remove any accumulated dirt and preservative oil. Retouch any paint blemishes.

NOTE
*If the boat is to be left in the water for an extended period of time, it may be advisable to cover the underwater surfaces (including the stern drive unit) with an antifouling paint. Do **not** use a paint containing copper or mercury, as these elements may increase galvanic corrosion.*

2. Remove any protective covers installed on the flame arrestor, carburetor, exhaust outlets or fuel tank ventilators.

3. Drain antifreeze from standard cooling systems, if installed.

4. Make sure all drain valves and plugs are tightly closed and that all cooling system hoses are securely clamped in place.

5. Inspect all hoses for cracks, weak walls and leaks. Replace any that appear questionable.

6. Check all through-hull fittings for leaks and proper valve operation.

7. Remove, clean and reinstall the flame arrestor.

8. Check the fuel system. Refill the tanks if they were drained. Turn the fuel shut-off valve(s) ON and check all fuel lines for leaks.

9. Check battery electrolyte level and fill if necessary. Make certain battery has a full charge; recharge if necessary. Clean the battery terminals and install the battery, making certain the cables are connected with proper polarity. Cover battery terminals with a light coat of petroleum jelly.

10. Drain preservative oil from stern drive unit. Refill with oil of the proper viscosity and grade. See Chapter Four.

11. Check the crankcase oil level. Add oil, if necessary. If oil was not changed at time of lay-up or if engine has been in storage for an

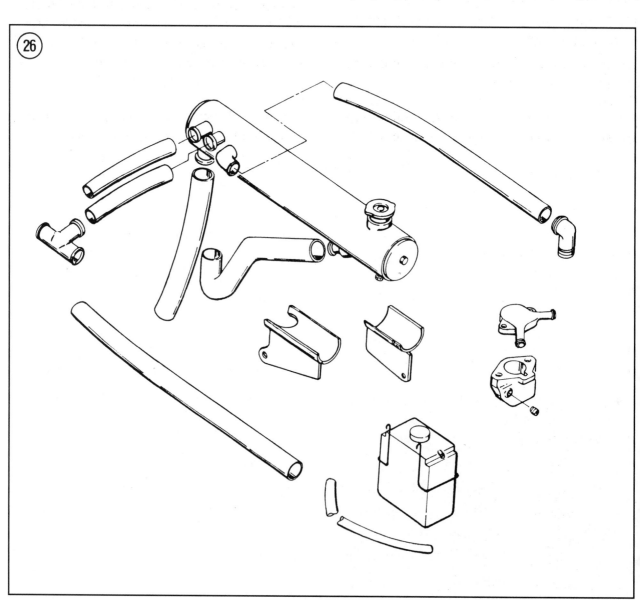

(26)

extended period of time, change the oil and oil filter.

12. Check the power steering and power trim hydraulic pump oil levels, if so equipped, and top up as required.

13. Check and adjust drive belt tension. See Chapter Ten.

14. Make a thorough check of the boat, engine and stern drive for loose or missing fasteners. Pay particular attention to the stern drive transom connection. Tighten, replace or take such other corrective actions as may be necessary.

15. Examine sacrificial zinc elements and replace if more than 25% eroded.

16. Remove the distributor cap and examine the distributor contact breaker points, if so equipped. Replace point set if any wear is evident. If old points are to be reused, clean thoroughly with alcohol or acetone to remove any traces of oil.

Clean the inside of the distributor cap with a soft cloth and then reinstall.

WARNING
If your boat is not equipped with a bilge blower, make sure the engine cover or hatch is open and properly supported before performing Step 17. This will prevent the buildup of any fumes that might result in an explosion if there is a fuel leak.

17. Provide a source of water for engine cooling. Make certain a Coast Guard-approved fire extinguisher is handy, then start the engine. While the engine is warming up, watch the instrument panel gauges to make certain that all systems are operating as they should. You should also check for any signs of fuel, oil or water leaks.

18. Proceed with engine tune-up. See Chapter Four for instructions and specifications.

5

Chapter Six

Gm Inline Engines

This chapter covers the GM 2.5L and 3.0L 4-cylinder inline engines used with MerCruiser 120, 2.5L, 140, 3.0L and 3.0LX models.

The cylinders are numbered from front to rear: 1-2-3-4. The firing order is 1-3-4-2.

Rocker arms are retained on individual threaded shoulder studs. A ball-pivot valve train is used, with camshaft motion transferred through hydraulic lifters to the rocker arms by pushrods.

The gear-driven camshaft is located above the crankshaft in the engine block and supported by 4 bearings. The oil pump mounted at the bottom front of the engine block on the starboard side is driven by the distributor shaft. The distributor is driven by a gear on the camshaft.

The crankshaft is supported by 5 main bearings, with the rear bearing providing the crankshaft thrust surfaces. Crankshaft rotation is counterclockwise when seen from the drive unit end of the engine.

The cylinder block is cast iron with full length water jackets around each cylinder.

Engine specifications (**Table 1**) and tightening torques (**Table 2** and **Table 3**) are at the end of the chapter.

ENGINE SERIAL NUMBER AND CODE

The engine serial number and model designation is stamped on a plate mounted on the right-hand rear side of the engine block above the starter motor (**Figure 1**) or located on a decal on the engine. If the plate or decal is missing, you can determine the model by checking the last 2 letters of the engine code stamped on the front of the cylinder block. This code number is found on all factory engines and all replacement partial assemblies.

The number is found on the starboard side near the distributor (**Figure 2**). This information indicates if there ar unique parts or if internal changes have been made during the model year. It is important when ordering replacement parts for the engine.

SPECIAL TOOLS

Where special tools are required or recommended for engine overhaul, the tool numbers are provided. Mercury Marine tool part numbers have a "C" prefix. GM tool part numbers have a "J" prefix. While GM tools can sometimes be rented from rental dealers, they can be purchased from Kent-Moore Tool & Equipment Division, 29784 Little Mack, Roseville, MI 48006.

GASKET SEALANT

Gasket sealant is used instead of preformed gaskets between some mating surfaces on the

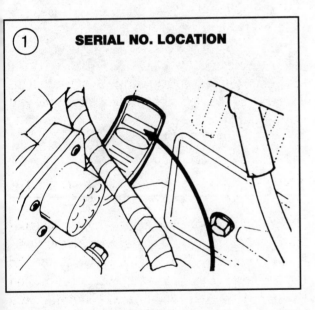

① SERIAL NO. LOCATION

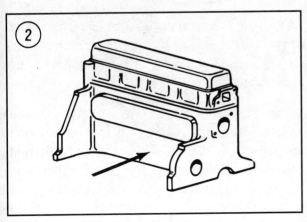

②

engines covered in this chapter. Two types of gasket sealant are available: room temperature vulcanizing (RTV) and anaerobic. Since these 2 materials have different sealing properties, they cannot be used interchangeably.

Room Temperature Vulcanizing (RTV) Sealant

This is a silicone gel supplied in tubes and available from your MerCruiser dealer. Moisture in the air causes RTV to cure. Always place the cap on the tube as soon as possible when using RTV. RTV has a shelf life of approximately one year and will not cure properly when the shelf life has expired. Check the expiration date on RTV tubes before using and keep partially used tubes tightly sealed.

Applying RTV Sealant

Clean all gasket residue from mating surfaces. They should be clean and free of oil and dirt. Remove all RTV gasket material from blind attaching holes, as it can cause a hydraulic lock and affect bolt torque.

Unless otherwise specified, apply RTV sealant in a continuous bead 3-5 mm (1/8-3/16 in.) thick. Apply the sealant on the inner side of all mounting bolts. Torque mating parts within 10-15 minutes after application or the sealant will have started to cure. If this happens, the old sealant must be removed and new sealant applied.

Anaerobic Sealant

This is also a gel supplied in tubes. It cures only in the absence of air, as when squeezed tightly between 2 machined mating surfaces. For this reason, it will not spoil if the cap is left off the tube. It should not be used if one mating surface is flexible.

6

Applying Anaerobic Sealant

Clean all gasket residue from mating surfaces. They should be clean and free of oil and dirt. Remove all gasket material from blind attaching holes, as it can cause a hydraulic lock and affect bolt torque.

Unless otherwise specified, apply anaerobic sealant in a 1 mm (0.04 in.) or less continuous bead to one sealing surface. Apply the sealant on the inner side of all mounting holes. Torque mating parts within 15 minutes after application or the sealant will have started to cure.

REPLACEMENT PARTS

Various changes are made to automotive engine blocks used for marine applications. Numerous part changes are required due to operation in fresh and saltwater. For example, the cylinder head gasket must be corrosion resistant. Marine engines use head gaskets of copper or stainless steel instead of the standard steel used in automotive applications. Brass expansion or core plugs must be used instead of the steel plugs found in automotive blocks.

Since marine engines are run at or near maximum rpm most of the time, the use of special valve lifters, springs, pistons, bearings, camshafts and other heavy-duty moving components is necessary for maximum life and performance.

For these reasons, automotive-type parts should not be substituted for marine components. In addition, Mercury Marine recommends that only Quicksilver parts be used. Parts offered by other manufacturers may look alike, but may not be manufactured to Mercury's specifications. Any damage resulting from the use of other than Quicksilver parts is not covered by the Mercury Marine warranty.

ENGINE REMOVAL

Some service procedures can be performed with the engine in the boat; others require removal. The boat design and service procedure to be performed determines whether the engine must be removed.

Although some installations may use a drive shaft extension, the stern drive unit *must* be removed from the boat for engine removal on all models.

WARNING
The engine is heavy, awkward to handle and has sharp edges. It may shift or drop

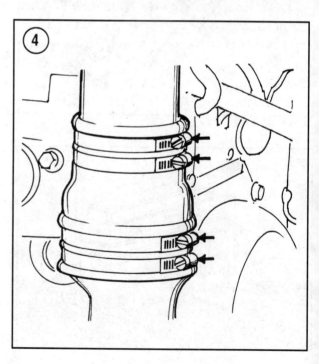

suddenly during removal. To prevent serious injury, always observe the following precautions.
1. Never place any part of your body where a moving or falling engine may trap, cut or crush you.
2. If you must push the engine during removal, use a board or similar tool to keep your hands out of danger.
3. Be sure the hoist is designed to lift engines and has enough load capacity for your engine.
4. Be sure the hoist is securely attached to safe lifting points on the engine.
5. The engine should not be difficult to lift with a proper hoist. If it is, stop lifting, lower the engine back onto its mounts and make sure the engine has been completely separated from the vessel.

Without Drive Shaft Extension

1. Remove the stern drive unit. See Chapter Twelve.
2. Remove the engine hood cover and all panels that interfere with engine removal. Place the cover and panels to one side out of the way.
3. Disconnect the negative battery cable, then the positive battery cable. As a precaution, remove the battery from the boat.
4. Unplug the instrument harness connector from the engine harness receptacle.
5. Disconnect the fuel inlet line from the tank to the fuel filter pump. Cap the line and plug the

pump fitting to prevent leakage and the entry of contamination.
6. Disconnect the throttle cable from the carburetor. See A, **Figure 3**, typical. If necessary, remove the cable from the anchor plate (B, **Figure 3**).
7. Locate the trim sender wires at the engine harness bracket terminal block. Disconnect the trim sender wires from the terminal block.
8. Disconnect the power trim pump wires (red and black) from the engine, if so equipped.
9. Disconnect the shift cutout switch wires from the shift plate terminal block (located on exhaust manifold), if so equipped.
10. Disconnect the water inlet hose.
11. Unclamp and disconnect the exhaust elbow bellows (**Figure 4**).
12. Disconnect both shift cables from the shift plate on the exhaust manifold or valve cover. See **Figure 5**, typical.
13. Disconnect any ground leads or accessories connected to the engine. If equipped with power steering, use a flare nut wrench to loosen and disconnect both power steering hydraulic lines from the control valve. Cap the lines and plug the control valve fittings to prevent leakage and the entry of contamination. Secure the lines at a point higher than the engine power steering pump during the remainder of this procedure to prevent damage or the loss of fluid.
14. Attach a suitable hoist to the engine lifting brackets. The hoist must have a minimum lift capacity of 1,500 lb. Raise the hoist enough to remove all slack.

NOTE
At this point, there should be no hoses, wires or linkage connecting the engine to the boat or stern drive unit. Recheck this to make sure nothing will hamper engine removal.

15. Unbolt the rear (**Figure 6**) and front (**Figure 7**) engine mounts from the boat. Do not loosen or move the mounts at the engine attaching points or a complete realignment will be required when the engine is reinstalled.

6

16. Remove the engine from the boat with the hoist.

With Drive Shaft Extension

1. Remove the engine hood cover and all panels that interfere with engine removal. Place the cover and panels to one side out of the way.

2. Disconnect the negative battery cable, then the positive battery cable. As a precaution, remove the battery from the boat.

3. Unplug the instrument harness connector from the engine harness receptacle.

4. Disconnect the fuel inlet line from the tank to the fuel pump at the pump. Cap the line and plug the pump fitting to prevent leakage and the entry of contamination.

5. Disconnect the throttle cable from the carburetor. See A, **Figure 3** (typical). If necessary, remove the cable from the anchor plate. See B, **Figure 3** (typical).

6. Locate the trim sender brown and white wires at the engine harness plug bracket terminal block. Disconnect the trim sender wires from the terminal block and remove the hoses from the clamps holding the power steering hoses, if so equipped.

7. Disconnect the black and white/green shift cut-out switch wires from the engine harness.

8. Disconnect the water inlet hose from the thermostat housing.

9. Unclamp and disconnect the exhaust pipe from the exhaust hose.

10. Remove the top shield, then the bottom shield. See **Figure 8**.

11. Unbolt and disconnect the drive shaft from the output flange. See **Figure 9**.

12. Disconnect both shift cables from the shift plate. See **Figure 5** (typical).

13. Disconnect any ground leads or accessories connected to the engine. If equipped with power steering, use a flare nut wrench to loosen and disconnect both power steering hydraulic lines from the control valve on the transom plate. Cap

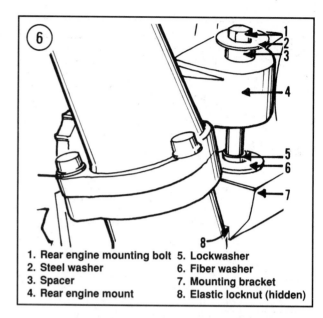

1. Rear engine mounting bolt
2. Steel washer
3. Spacer
4. Rear engine mount
5. Lockwasher
6. Fiber washer
7. Mounting bracket
8. Elastic locknut (hidden)

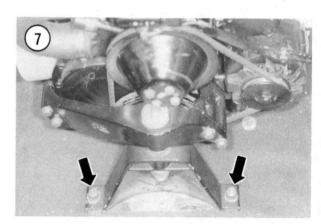

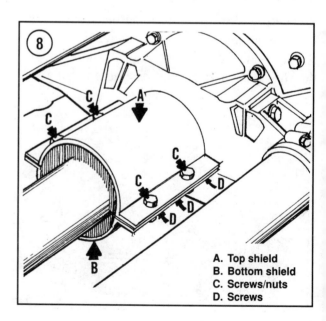

A. Top shield
B. Bottom shield
C. Screws/nuts
D. Screws

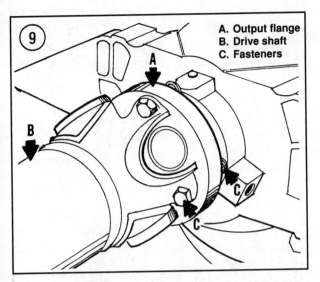

A. Output flange
B. Drive shaft
C. Fasteners

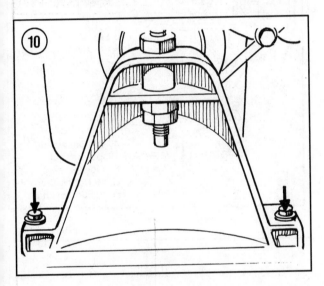

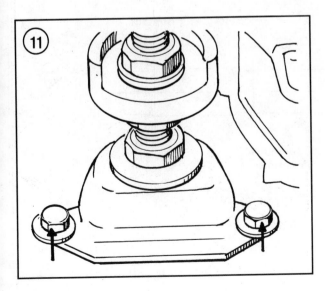

the lines and plug the control valve fittings to prevent leakage and the entry of contamination. Secure the lines at a point higher than the engine power steering pump during the remainder of this procedure to prevent damage or the loss of fluid.

14. Attach a suitable hoist to the engine lifting brackets. The hoist must have a minimum lift capacity of 1,500 lb. Raise the hoist enough to remove all slack.

NOTE
At this point, there should be no hoses, wires or linkage connecting the engine to the boat or stern drive unit. Recheck this to make sure nothing will hamper engine removal.

15. Unbolt the rear (**Figure 10**) and front (**Figure 11**) engine mounts from the boat. Do not loosen or move the mounts at the engine attaching points or a complete realignment will be required when the engine is reinstalled.

16. Remove the engine from the boat with the hoist.

ENGINE INSTALLATION

Without Drive Shaft Extension

Engine installation is the reverse of removal, plus the following:

1. Wipe the engine coupling splines with Quicksilver Engine Coupler Spline Grease.

2. Fit a large fiber washer on top of each transom plate engine support, then install a double wound lockwasher inside each fiber washer. See **Figure 12**.

3. Install hose clamps on the rubber exhaust elbow bellows and lower the engine over the transom plate mounting brackets. Let rear engine mounts rest on the transom plate engine supports but do not remove the hoist tension.

CAUTION
Elastic stop nuts should never be used more than twice. It is a good idea to replace such nuts with new ones each time they are removed. Never use worn-out stop nuts or non-locking nuts.

4. Install one steel washer and spacer on each rear mount bolt. Install bolts downward through the engine mounts, washers and brackets. See **Figure 6**. Thread a new elastic stop nut on each bolt and tighten to 35-40 ft.-lb. (47-54 N•m).

5. Install front engine mount fasteners and tighten securely.

6. Use guide bolts to align the engine to the bell housing. It may be necessary to rotate the crankshaft slightly to align the engine coupling splines with the drive shaft. You may also rotate the drive shaft by placing the outdrive in forward gear and rotating the propeller.

CAUTION
If the alignment tool specified in Step 7 is not available, take the boat to a Mer-Cruiser dealer for proper alignment. Drive shaft/coupling spline misalignment can cause serious damage.

7. Using alignment tool part No. 91-805475A1 (Alpha One Generation II) or part No. 91-57797A3 (all others), check engine alignment as follows:

NOTE
A new alignment tool (part No. 91-805475A1) is necessary to align the engine on Alpha One Generation II

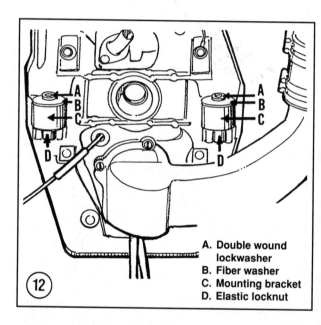

A. Double wound lockwasher
B. Fiber washer
C. Mounting bracket
D. Elastic locknut

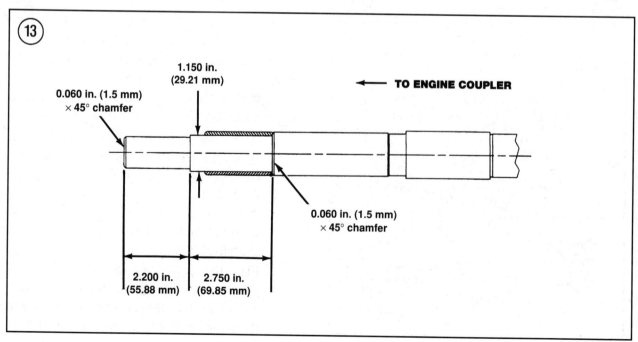

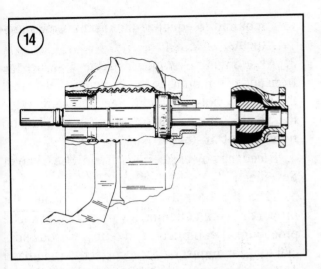

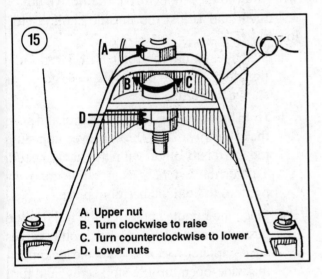

A. Upper nut
B. Turn clockwise to raise
C. Turn counterclockwise to lower
D. Lower nuts

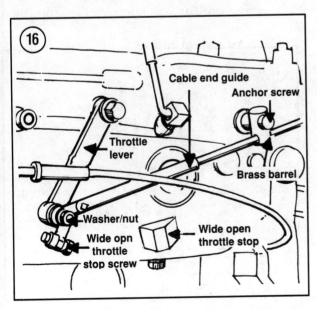

Cable end guide

Anchor screw

Throttle lever

Brass barrel

Washer/nut

Wide opn throttle stop screw

Wide open throttle stop

models. However, if the new alignment tool is not available, alignment tool (part No. 91-57797A3) can be modified to the dimensions shown in Figure 13 and used on Alpha One Generation II engines. The new tool (part No. 91-805475A1) or the modified tool (part No. 91-57797A3) can be used to align the engine on ALL current models and older models that used alignment tool (part No. 91-57797A3).

6

a. Coat the solid end of the tool with Quick-silver 2-4-C Multi-Lube and insert it from outside the boat through the U-joint bellows into the gimbal bearing (**Figure 14**).

b. Index the bearing and drive shaft with the engine coupling splines. If indexing is difficult, raise or lower the engine with the hoist as required to permit indexing with no resistance.

c. Loosen the locknut on both front engine mounts (**Figure 15**) and thread the adjusting nut up or down as required to properly position the front of the engine to maintain the desired alignment. Make sure that each side of the engine is raised or lowered the same amount to prevent cocking the front of the engine.

d. Tighten the locknuts securely, then recheck alignment by repeating sub-step a.

8. Attach and adjust the throttle cable as follows:

a. With the remote control in NEUTRAL (idle position), fasten the cable end guide as shown in **Figure 16**.

b. Hold the throttle cable brass barrel and push the cable toward the throttle lever, adjusting the barrel to align with the anchor stud or threaded manifold hole. Tighten the fasteners securely, but do not overtighten, to hold the barrel in place.

c. Place the remote control in the full throttle position and make sure the throttle valves are completely open. Loosen the locknut on the wide-open throttle stop screw and turn screw until it just contacts the stop, then turn it in another 1/4 turn. Tighten the locknut securely.

d. Place the remote control back in NEU-TRAL (idle position) and make sure the idle stop screw rests against the stop. If it does not, repeat this procedure.

9. If equipped with power steering, tighten the large power steering fitting to 20-25 ft.-lb. (27-34 N•m). Tighten the small fitting to 96-108 in.-lb. (11-12 N•m). Bleed the power steering system. See Chapter Seventeen.

10. Fill the engine with an oil recommended in Chapter Four.

11. Fill the cooling system, if equipped with a closed system. See Chapter Five.

12. Adjust the drive belts. See Chapter Ten.

13. Adjust the timing as required. See Chapter Four.

With Drive Shaft Extension

Engine installation is the reverse of removal, plus the following:

1. After connecting the drive shaft to the output flange, tighten fasteners to 50 ft.-lb. (68 N•m). Relieve the hoist tension and slide the engine fore or aft as necessary to provide a 1/4 in. clearance between the flange shoulder and extension shaft housing bearing. See **Figure 17**.

2. To obtain correct engine/drive shaft lateral alignment:

   a. Measure the distance between the center of the bearing support attaching bolts on the inner transom plate and shaft extension housing grease fitting. See A, **Figure 18**. If the distances are not equal, slide the aft end of the engine in the direction required to equalize the distance measurements.

   b. Measure the distance between the center of the bearing support bolts and the rear engine mount adjusting bolt. See B, **Figure 18**. If the distances are not equal, slide the front end of the engine in the direction

required to equalize the distance measurements.

3. After engine alignment is correct, secure the front and rear mounts to the stringers, then install the top and bottom shield. See **Figure 8**. Wipe the shield screws with Loctite Type 242 and tighten to 30 ft.-lb. (41 N•m).

4. Bleed the power steering system. See Chapter Seventeen.

5. Take the boat to a MerCruiser dealer for proper drive unit alignment with the engine. The procedure is complicated, requires various special tools and must be done correctly or damage will result to the engine/drive shaft/drive unit.

6. Attach and adjust the throttle cable as follows:

   a. With the remote control in NEUTRAL (idle position), fasten the cable end guide as shown in **Figure 16**.

   b. Hold the throttle cable brass barrel and push the cable toward the throttle lever, adjusting the barrel to align with the anchor stud. Tighten the fasteners securely (do not overtighten) to hold the barrel in place.

   c. Place the remote control in the full throttle position and make sure the throttle valves are completely open. Loosen the locknut on the wide-open throttle stop screw and turn screw until it just contacts the stop, then

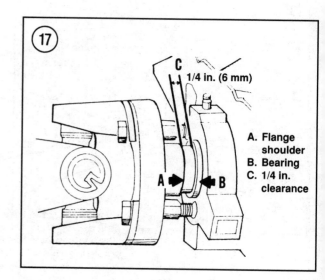

A. Flange shoulder
B. Bearing
C. 1/4 in. clearance

1/4 in. (6 mm)

turn it in another 1/4 turn. Tighten the locknut securely.

d. Place the remote control back in neutral (idle position) and make sure the idle stop screw rests against the stop. If it does not, repeat this procedure.

7. If equipped with power steering, tighten the large power steering fitting to 20-25 ft.-lb. (27-34 N·m). Tighten small fitting to 96-108 in.-lb. (11-12 N·m). Bleed the power steering system. See Chapter Seventeen.

8. Fill the engine with an oil recommended in Chapter Four.

9. Fill the cooling system, if equipped with a closed system. See Chapter Five.

10. Adjust the drive belts. See Chapter Ten.

11. Adjust the timing as required. See Chapter Four.

DISASSEMBLY CHECKLISTS

To use the checklists, remove and inspect each part in the order mentioned. To reassemble, go through the checklists backwards, installing the parts in order. Each major part is covered in its own section in this chapter, unless otherwise noted.

Decarbonizing or Valve Service

1. Remove the valve cover.
2. Remove the intake and exhaust manifolds.
3. Remove the rocker arms.
4. Remove the cylinder head.
5. Remove and inspect the valves. Inspect the valve guides and seats, repairing or replacing as required.
6. Assemble by reversing Steps 1-5.

Valve and Ring Service

1. Perform Steps 1-5 of *Decarbonizing or Valve Service*.
2. Remove the oil pan and oil pump.
3. Remove the piston with connecting rods.
4. Remove the piston rings. It is not necessary to separate the pistons from the connecting rods

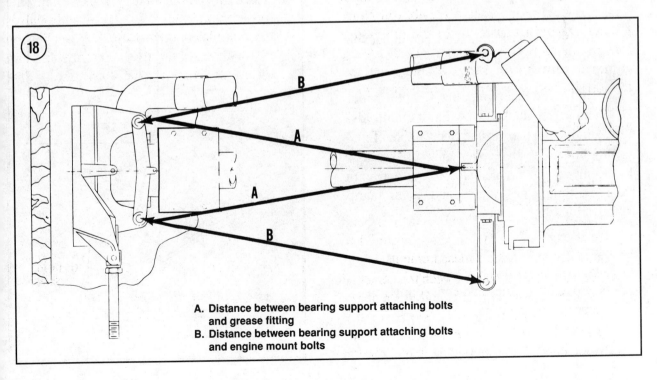

(18)

A. Distance between bearing support attaching bolts and grease fitting
B. Distance between bearing support attaching bolts and engine mount bolts

6

unless a piston, connecting rod or piston pin needs repair or replacement.

5. Assemble by reversing Steps 1-4.

General Overhaul

1. Remove the engine from the boat.
2. Remove the flywheel.
3. Remove the mount brackets and oil pressure sending unit from the engine.
4. If available, mount the engine on an engine stand. These can be rented from equipment rental dealers. The stand is not absolutely necessary, but it will make the job much easier.
5. Remove the following accessories or components from the engine, if present.

    a. Alternator and mounting bracket

    b. Power steering pump and mounting bracket

    c. Spark plug wires and distributor cap

    d. Carburetor and fuel lines

    e. Oil dipstick and tube

    f. Seawater pump, if so equipped

6. Check the engine for signs of coolant or oil leaks.
7. Clean the outside of the engine.
8. Remove the distributor. See Chapter Eleven.
9. Remove all hoses and tubes connected to the engine.
10. Remove the fuel pump. See Chapter Nine.
11. Remove the intake and exhaust manifolds.
12. Remove the thermostat. See Chapter Ten.
13. Remove the valve cover and rocker arms.
14. Remove the crankshaft pulley, harmonic balancer, timing case cover and water pump. Remove the timing gears.
15. Remove the camshaft.
16. Remove the cylinder head.
17. Remove the oil pan and oil pump.
18. Remove the pistons and connecting rods.
19. Remove the crankshaft.
20. Inspect the cylinder block.
21. Assemble by reversing Steps 1-19.

VALVE COVER

Removal/Installation

1. Disconnect the crankcase ventilation hose at the valve cover.
2. Disconnect the spark plug cables at the plugs and remove the plug cable retainers from their brackets on the cover.
3. Remove any other accessory unit that might interfere with valve cover removal.
4. Remove the cover attaching fasteners and load spreaders, if used.
5. Rap the valve cover with a soft-faced mallet to break the gasket seal. Remove the valve cover. Discard the gasket, if used.

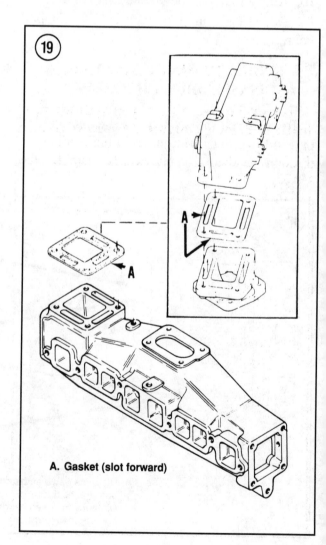

A. Gasket (slot forward)

6. Clean any gasket residue from the cylinder head and valve cover with degreaser and a putty knife.

7. Coat one side of a new gasket with an oil-resistant sealer. Install the gasket sealer-side down in the valve cover. Gasket tabs must engage cover notches.

8. Position the valve cover on the cylinder head.

9. Install the attaching fasteners (with load spreaders, if used) and tighten to specifications (**Table 2**).

10. Install the spark plug cable retainers on the valve cover brackets. Connect the wires to the appropriate spark plugs. See Chapter Four.

11. Install the crankcase ventilation hose in the valve cover.

INTAKE/EXHAUST MANIFOLDS

The intake and exhaust manifolds are combined in one unit. **Figure 19** shows a typical

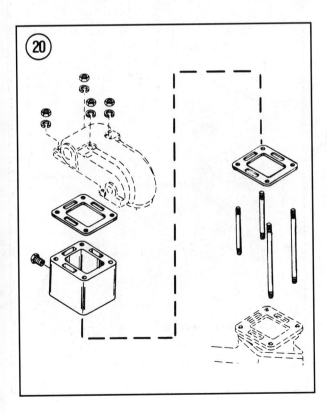

manifold assembly. **Figure 20** shows the accessory high riser kit components.

All 1989 models with thru transom exhaust are equipped with mufflers as standard equipment to reduce exhaust noise. The mufflers are installed between the exhaust elbows and transom and are easily disassembled for replacement or cleaning of the internal element.

Removal/Installation

Refer to **Figure 19** and **Figure 20** (typical), as required for this procedure.

1. Disconnect the negative battery cable.

2. Open the cylinder block water drain and allow all water to drain. Drain the exhaust manifold and elbow.

3. Disconnect the throttle cable from the carburetor. See A, **Figure 3**, typical. If necessary, remove the cable from the anchor plate. See B, **Figure 3**, typical.

4. Disconnect and remove the fuel line between the carburetor and fuel pump.

5. Disconnect both shift cables from the shift plate on the exhaust manifold. See **Figure 5**, typical.

6. Disconnect the water inlet hose.

7. Unclamp and disconnect the exhaust elbow bellows (**Figure 4**).

8. Disconnect the crankcase ventilation line from the valve cover.

9. Remove the slave solenoid and wiring harness clamps from the manifold.

10. Disconnect the shift cutout switch wires from the shift plate terminal block (located on exhaust manifold), if so equipped.

11. Disconnect the electric choke lead and any other electric wires that will interfere with manifold removal.

12. Loosen and remove the manifold assembly fasteners. Pry the manifold loose and remove it from the cylinder head. Remove and discard the manifold gasket.

13. Remove the exhaust elbow and adapter.

14. If equipped with a high riser which requires disassembly, refer to **Figure 20**.

15. Clean all gasket residue from the cylinder head and manifold assembly with degreaser and a putty knife.

16. If the manifold is being replaced, transfer the carburetor and all other components to the new manifold.

17. Install a new gasket on the cylinder head. Position the manifold on the cylinder head studs. Make sure gasket is properly aligned and install the manifold against the cylinder head.

18. Install the manifold attaching fasteners. Tighten the manifold fasteners to specifications (**Table 2**) working from the center to the ends.

19. If equipped with a high riser which was removed, refer to **Figure 20** and reinstall, using new gaskets coated with Quicksilver Perfect Seal on both sides.

20. Reverse Steps 1-11 to complete installation. Use new gaskets and position as shown in **Figure 19**. Coat all electrical connections with Quicksilver Neoprene Dip.

Inspection

1. Check the manifold assembly for cracks or distortion. Replace if distorted or if cracks are found.

2. Check the mating surfaces for nicks or burrs. Small burrs may be removed with an oilstone.

3. Place a straightedge across the manifold flange/mating surfaces. If there is any gap between the straightedge and surface, measure it with a flat feeler gauge. Measure each manifold from end to end and from corner to corner. If the mating surface is not flat within 0.006 in. (0.15 mm) per foot of manifold length, replace the manifold.

4. Inspect the engine exhaust ports for rust or corrosion. Replace manifold if excessive rust or corrosion are found.

5. Check water passage in exhaust elbow for clogging.

6. Remove pipe plugs in manifold and exhaust elbow, if so equipped. Check for sand, silt or other foreign matter.

ROCKER ARM ASSEMBLIES

Removal/Installation

Each rocker arm moves on its own pivot ball. The rocker arm and pivot ball are retained by a nut.

It is not necessary to remove the rocker arm for pushrod replacement; simply loosen the nut and move the arm away from the pushrod. To remove the entire assembly, refer to **Figure 21** (typical), and proceed as follows.

1. Remove the valve cover as described in this chapter.

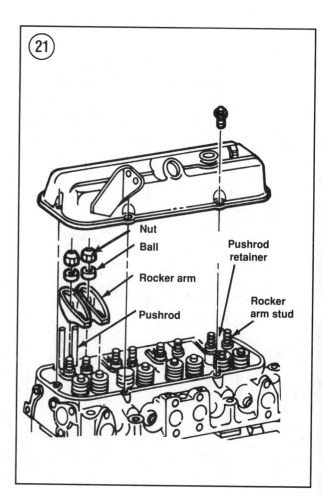

Nut
Ball
Rocker arm
Pushrod
Pushrod retainer
Rocker arm stud

2. Remove each rocker arm nut, ball, rocker arm and pushrod.

3. Place each rocker arm and pushrod assembly in a separate container or use a rack to keep them separated for reinstallation in the same position from which they were removed.

4. Lubricate the rocker arms and balls with engine oil.

5. Install the pushrods, making sure that each fits into its lifter socket.

6. Install the rocker arms, balls and nuts. If new rocker arms or balls are being installed, coat contact surfaces with engine oil or Molykote.

7. Adjust the valve clearance as described in this chapter.

8. Install the rocker arm cover as described in this chapter.

Inspection

1. Clean all parts with solvent and use compressed air to blow out the oil passages in the pushrods.

2. Check each rocker arm, ball, nut and pushrod for scuffing, pitting or excessive wear, replace as required. If one component is worn, replace all components servicing that valve.

3. Check pushrods for straightness by rolling them across a flat, even surface such as a pane of glass. Replace any pushrods that do not roll smoothly.

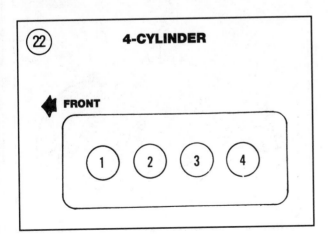

4. If a pushrod is worn from lack of lubrication, replace the corresponding lifter and rocker arm as well.

Valve Clearance Adjustment

Valve adjustment is required only when the cylinder head valve train has been disassembled. Adjust the valves with the lifter on the base circle of the camshaft lobe.

1. Rotate the crankshaft until the pulley notch aligns with the zero mark on the timing tab. This positions the No. 1 cylinder at TDC. This position can be verified by placing a finger on the No. 1 cylinder rocker arms as the pulley notch nears the zero mark. If the valves are moving, the engine is in the No. 4 firing position; rotate the crankshaft pulley one full turn to reach the No. 1 firing position.

NOTE
The intake valves are those closer to the intake ports. The exhaust valves are closer to the exhaust ports.

2. With the engine in the No. 1 firing position, refer to **Figure 22** and adjust the following valves:

    a. Intake: 1, 2 and 4

    b. Exhaust: 1 and 3

3. To adjust each valve, back off the adjusting nut until lash is felt at the pushrod, then turn the nut to remove all lash. When lash has been removed, the pushrod will not rotate. Turn the nut in another one turn to center the lifter plunger. See **Figure 23**.

4. Rotate the crankshaft one full turn to realign the pulley notch and the timing tab zero mark in the No. 4 firing position. Refer to **Figure 22** and adjust the following valves:

    a. Intake: 3

    b. Exhaust: 2 and 4

5. Install the valve cover as described in this chapter.

CRANKSHAFT PULLEY AND TORSIONAL DAMPER

Pulley Removal/Installation (2.5L)

1. Remove the alternator drive belt. See Chapter Ten.

2. Remove the pulley attaching bolts. Remove the pulley from the hub.

3. Install puller part No. J-6978-E or equivalent to the pulley hub with pulley attaching bolts and remove the hub. See **Figure 24**.

4. Lubricate the timing gear cover seal lip with clean engine oil.

5. Position the hub on the end of the crankshaft. Then, carefully drive the hub onto the crankshaft using a soft-face mallet. Continue striking the hub until it is fully seated.

6. Reinstall and adjust alternator drive belt.

See Chapter Ten.

Torsional Damper Removal/Installation (3.0L)

If engine is being serviced in the boat, attach a suitable hoist to support the front of the engine and remove the front mount bracket.

1. Remove the alternator drive belt. See Chapter Ten.

2. Remove the torsional damper retaining bolt, if so equipped.

3. Install puller part No. J-6978-E or equivalent to the damper with the pulley attaching bolts and remove the torsional damper from the crankshaft. See **Figure 25**, typical.

4. Lubricate the front cover seal lip and the contact areas on the torsional damper and crankshaft with clean engine oil.

5. Install tool part No. J-22197 to damper (**Figure 26**), place damper and tool against crankshaft and drive damper onto the crankshaft until fully seated. Remove the tool.

6. Reinstall and adjust alternator drive belt (Chapter Ten). If front mounting bracket was removed, reinstall and remove the hoist.

TIMING GEAR COVER AND SEAL

Cover Removal/Installation

1. Remove the engine from the boat as described in this chapter.

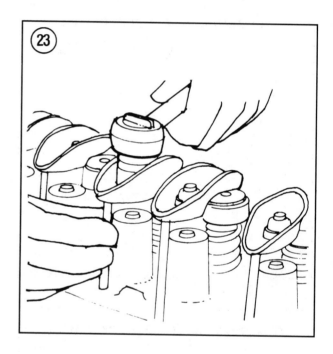

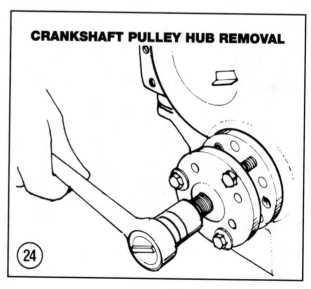

CRANKSHAFT PULLEY HUB REMOVAL

2. Remove the crankshaft pulley (2.5L) or torsional damper (3.0L) as described in this chapter.

3. Remove the oil pan as described in this chapter.

4. Unbolt and remove the front cover from the engine block. Remove and discard the gasket.

5. Installation is the reverse of removal. Use a new front cover gasket coated on both sides with Quicksilver Perfect Seal. Insert alignment tool part No. J-23042 through the timing gear cover seal and position the timing gear cover on the engine block. Work carefully to prevent damage to the oil seal or movement of the gasket.

Seal Replacement

The seal can be replaced without removing the front cover. If the cover has been removed and seal replacement is necessary, support the cover on a clean workbench and perform Steps 2-4.

1. Remove the crankshaft pulley (2.5L) or torsional damper (3.0L) as described in this chapter.

2. Pry the old seal from the cover with a large screwdriver. Work carefully to prevent damage to the cover seal surface.

3. Clean the seal recess in the cover with solvent and blow dry with compressed air.

4. Position a new seal in the cover recess with its open end facing the inside of the cover. Drive seal into place with installer part No. J-23042. See **Figure 27**.

5. Reinstall the crankshaft pulley (2.5L) or torsional damper (3.0L) as described in this chapter.

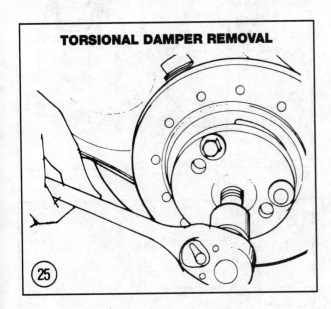

TORSIONAL DAMPER REMOVAL

㉕

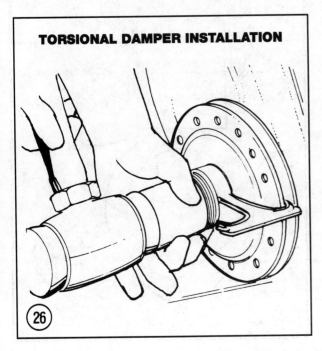

TORSIONAL DAMPER INSTALLATION

㉖

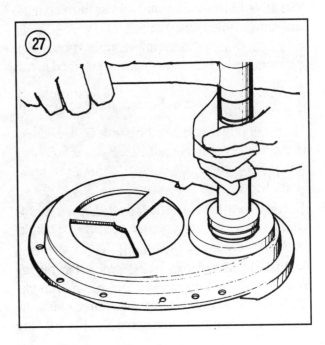

㉗

CAMSHAFT

Lobe Lift Measurement

Camshaft lobe lift can be measured with the camshaft in the block and the cylinder head in place.

1. Remove the valve cover as described in this chapter.

2. Remove the rocker arm assemblies as described in this chapter.

3. Remove the spark plugs. See Chapter Four.

4. Install a dial indicator on the end of a pushrod. A piece of rubber tubing will hold the dial indicator plunger in place on the center of the pushrod. See **Figure 28**, typical.

5. Rotate the crankshaft in the normal direction of rotation until the valve lifter seats on the heel or base of the cam lobe (**Figure 29**). This positions the pushrod at its lowest point.

6. Set the dial indicator at zero, then slowly rotate the crankshaft until the pushrod reaches its maximum travel. Note the indicator reading and compare to specifications (**Table 1**).

7. Repeat Steps 4-6 for each pushrod. If all lobes are within specifications in Step 6, reinstall the rocker arm assemblies and adjust the valves as described in this chapter.

8. If one or more lobes are worn beyond specification, replace the camshaft as described in this chapter.

9. Remove the dial indicator and reverse Steps 1-3.

Removal/Installation

1. Remove the valve cover as described in this chapter.

2. Crank the engine over until the No. 1 piston is at the top of its compression stroke. The timing mark on the pulley/damper will align with the TDC mark on the timing gear cover and the distributor rotor will point to the No. 1 spark plug

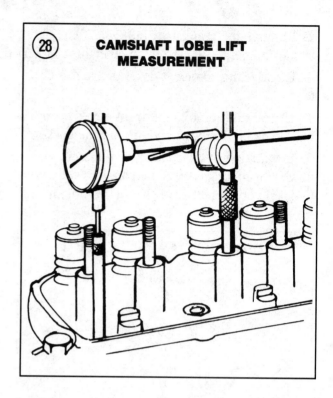

(28) **CAMSHAFT LOBE LIFT MEASUREMENT**

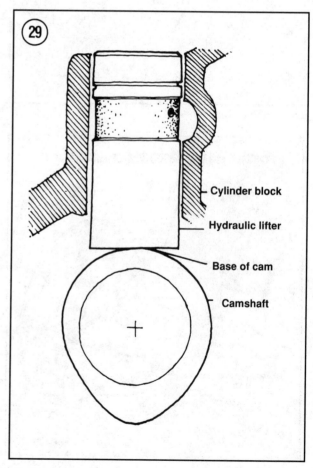

(29)

Cylinder block

Hydraulic lifter

Base of cam

Camshaft

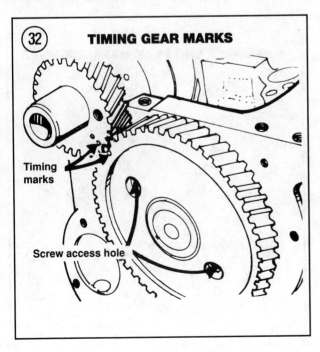

TIMING GEAR MARKS

Timing marks

Screw access hole

terminal in the distributor cap. Remove the distributor (Chapter Eleven).

3. Remove the timing gear cover as described in this chapter.

4. Remove the fuel pump. See Chapter Nine

5. Loosen the rocker arm adjusting nuts, swivel the arms off the pushrods and remove the pushrods. Identify each pushrod for reinstallation in its original location.

6. Remove the valve lifter covers (**Figure 30**) and discard the gaskets.

7. Remove the valve lifters with a pencil-type magnet. Place them in a rack in order of removal for reinstallation in their original locations. **Figure 31** shows lifter location, with one lifter removed.

8. Rotate the camshaft to align the timing gear marks (**Figure 32**).

9. Working through the screw access holes in the camshaft gear (**Figure 32**), remove the 2 camshaft thrust plate screws.

> *CAUTION*
> *Do not cock the camshaft during removal. This can damage the camshaft or its bearing thrust surfaces.*

10. Carefully withdraw the camshaft from the front of the engine with a rotating motion to avoid damage to the bearings.

11. Installation is the reverse of removal. Coat the camshaft lobes with GM EOS lubricant (or equivalent). Lubricate the cam journals with heavy engine oil before reinstalling in the block. Check gear runout and backlash as described in this chapter.

Inspection

1. Check the journals and lobes for signs of wear or scoring. Lobe pitting in the toe area is not sufficient reason for replacement unless the lobe lift loss exceeds specifications.

NOTE
If you do not have precision measuring equipment, have Step 2 done by a machine shop.

2. Measure the camshaft journal diameters with a micrometer (**Figure 33**) and compare to specifications (**Table 1**). Replace the camshaft if one or more journals do not meet specifications.

3. Suspend the camshaft between V-blocks and check for warpage with a dial indicator. See **Figure 34**. Replace if the runout is greater than 0.0015 in.

4. Check the distributor drive gear for excessive wear or damage.

5. Check camshaft gear and thrust plate for wear or damage. Insert a flat feeler gauge between the thrust plate and camshaft to measure end play. See **Figure 35**. If end play exceeds specifications (**Table 1**), remove the camshaft gear as described in this chapter and replace the thrust plate.

Camshaft/Crankshaft Gear Runout and Backlash

1. Install a dial indicator as shown in **Figure 36**. Rotate camshaft 360° to check runout. If camshaft gear runout exceeds 0.004 in., replace the gear.

3. Install dial indicator as shown in **Figure 37** to check gear teeth backlash. If backlash is not between 0.004-0.006 in., replace both gears.

Bearing Replacement

Camshaft bearings can be replaced without complete engine disassembly. Replace bearings in complete sets. Camshaft bearing and installer tool part No. J-6098 is required for bearing replacement.

1. Remove the camshaft as described in this chapter.

2. Remove the crankshaft as described in this chapter. Leave pistons in cylinder bores.

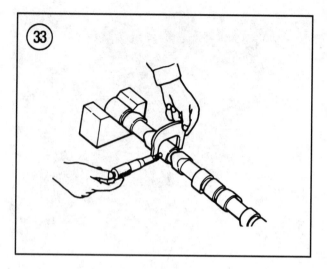

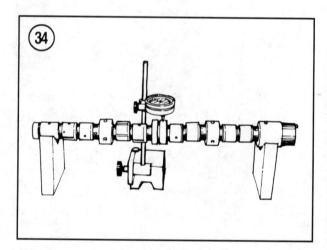

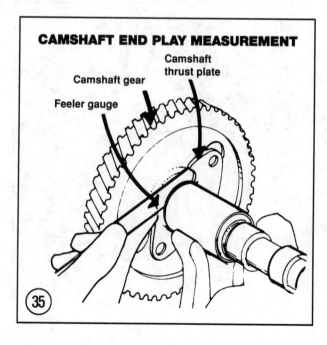

CAMSHAFT END PLAY MEASUREMENT

Camshaft gear

Camshaft thrust plate

Feeler gauge

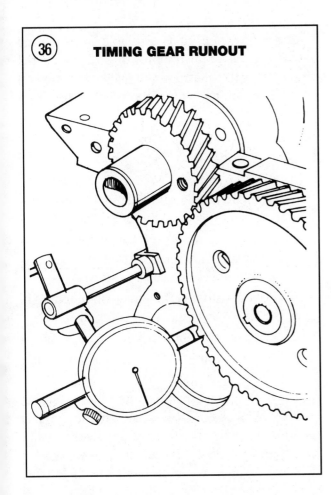

36 **TIMING GEAR RUNOUT**

3. Drive the camshaft welch plug from the rear of the cylinder block.

4. Secure the connecting rods to the side of the engine to keep them out of the way while replacing the cam bearings.

5. Install the nut and thrust washer to tool part No. J-6098. Index the tool pilot in the front cam bearing. Install the puller screw through the pilot.

6. Install tool part No. J-6098 with its shoulder facing the front intermediate bearing and the threads engaging the bearing.

7. Hold the puller screw with one wrench. Turn the nut with a second wrench until the bearing has been pulled from its bore. See **Figure 38**.

8. When bearing has been removed from bore, remove tool and bearing from puller screw.

9. Repeat Steps 5-8 to remove the center bearing.

10. Remove the tool and index it to the rear bearing to remove the rear intermediate bearing from the block.

11. Remove the front and rear bearings by driving them toward the center of the block.

6

CAUTION
Improper alignment of the rear bearing during Step 12 will restrict oil pressure reaching the valve train.

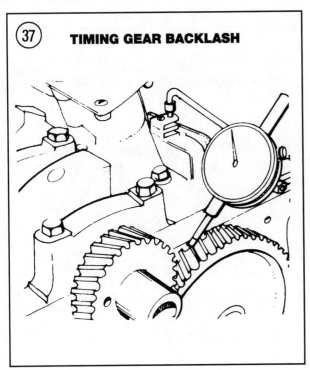

37 **TIMING GEAR BACKLASH**

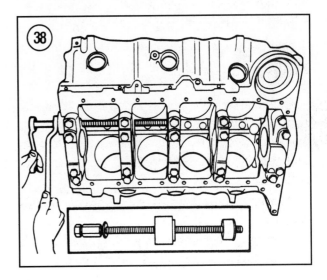

38

12. Installation is the reverse of removal. Use the same tool to pull the new bearings into their bores. Bearing oil holes must align with those in the block. Since the oil hole is on the top of the bearings (and cannot be seen during installation), align bearing oil hole with hole in bore and mark opposite side of bearing and block at bore to assist in positioning the oil during installation.

> *CAUTION*
> *On early models, be sure front camshaft bearing does not block timing gear oil nozzle. Bearing should be recessed approximately 1/8 in. from front face of cylinder block. Later models do not use a timing gear oil nozzle and a plug is used to seal the nozzle hole.*

13. Wipe a new camshaft welch plug with Quicksilver Perfect Seal and install it flush to 1/32 in. deep to maintain a level surface on the rear of the block.

Timing Gear Replacement

If inspection indicates that the camshaft, gear or thrust plate should be replaced, press the gear from the camshaft with an appropriate size support sleeve. Position the thrust plate so that it will not be damaged by the Woodruff key in the shaft when it separates from the gear. If the gear is to be reused, support its hub before applying pressure or it will be ruined. Install the camshaft gear by pressing it onto the shaft, then check end play as described in Step 5, under *Inspection* in this chapter.

OIL PAN

Ease of oil pan removal will depend on the installation within a given boat. In some cases, the oil pan can be removed without removing the engine. In others, engine removal will be required to provide sufficient working space and clearance for oil pan removal.

A modification kit is available from marine dealers to assist in draining the oil when the engine is in the boat. This kit can be installed on any engine oil pan when the engine is removed for service.

Oil Leaks

Constant oil leakage around the oil pan can be caused by one of several factors:

a. Excessive torquing of the oil pan screws (squeezing the 2-piece gasket out and causing the rubber end seals to split)

b. Gaskets with insufficient crush (contact) in certain areas to make a good seal

c. Defective or improperly installed seals.

d. Mis-machining of the crankshaft and/or block

On installations manufactured after October 1985, GM used RTV sealant on the oil pan gaskets and end seals. This was replaced in January 1986 by a new 2-piece "high swell" gasket which expanded when exposed to oil. In May 1986, a one-piece soft silicone rubber gasket (part No. 27-14901A1) superseded all previous gaskets (**Figure 39**). The soft rubber fills in small

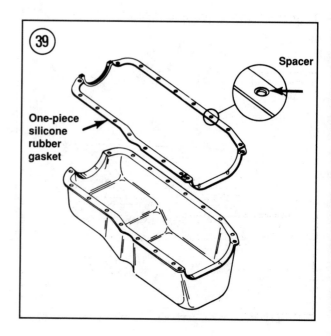

One-piece silicone rubber gasket

Spacer

gaps that might otherwise leak; metal spacers around each of the screws prevent damage from excessive torque. The oil pan on 1987 and later models was changed to provide more gasket crush in the rear main bearing area. The one-piece silicone rubber gasket should be used as a replacement whenever the oil pan is removed from earlier models.

If oil leakage continues to be a problem after installation of a one-piece silicone rubber gasket, remove the engine from the boat. Remove the oil pan and measure at the following areas:

a. Crankshaft diameter at the seal area (it should be 2.43-2.432 in.)

b. Inside diameter of the seal shoulder (it should be 2.775-2.778 in.)

If the measurements are not within the specifications provided, the crankshaft and/or block were incorrectly machined. See your MerCruiser dealer.

Removal

Refer to **Figure 39** (1-piece gasket) or **Figure 40** (2-piece gasket) as appropriate for this procedure.

1. Remove the engine as described in this chapter.

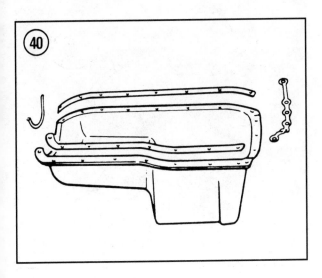

2. Place a suitable container under the oil pan drain plug. Remove the plug and let the crankcase drain. Reinstall the drain plug.

3. If mounted in an engine stand, rotate the engine 180° to place the oil pan in an upright position.

4. Remove the starter motor. See Chapter Eleven.

5. Remove the oil pan attaching screws. Remove the oil pan.

6. Remove and discard the 2-piece pan gasket and the front/rear seals (1985) or the 1-piece silicone rubber gasket (1986-on).

Inspection and Cleaning

1. Clean any gasket residue from the oil pan rail on the engine block, rear main bearing cap, front cover and the oil pan sealing flange with degreaser and a putty knife.

2. Clean the pan thoroughly in solvent and check for dents or warped gasket surfaces. Straighten or replace the pan as required.

Installation

Refer to **Figure 39** for this procedure.

1. Install a new 1-piece gasket on the pan flanges. Insert a screw on each side and at each end of the pan to position the gasket.

2. Carefully position the oil pan in place, make sure the gasket is not misaligned and tighten the screws inserted in Step 3 finger-tight.

3. Install the remaining screws and tighten all to specifications (**Table 2**). Work from the center outward in each direction.

4. Reinstall the starter motor. See Chapter Eleven.

5. Install the engine in the boat as described in this chapter and fill the crankcase with an oil recommended in Chapter Four.

OIL PUMP

Removal/Installation

1. Remove the oil pan as described in this chapter.

> *NOTE*
> *The oil pump pickup tube and screen are a press fit in the pump housing and should not be removed unless replacement is required.*

2. Loosen the pickup tube bracket bolt (A, **Figure 41**). Remove the bracket attaching nut (B, **Figure 41**).

3. Remove the oil pump attaching bolts (**Figure 42**). Remove the oil pump, gasket and pickup tube/screen as an assembly.

4. To install, align the pump gear shaft slot with the distributor shaft drive tang.

5. Install pump to block. Tighten pump attaching bolts and bracket fasteners to specifications (**Table 2**).

6. Reinstall the oil pan as described in this chapter.

Disassembly/Assembly

Refer to **Figure 43** for this procedure.

1. Remove the cover screws, cover and gasket. Discard the gasket.

2. Mark the gear teeth to ensure reassembly with identical gear indexing and then remove the idler and drive gear with shaft from the body.

3. Remove the pressure regulator valve pin, regulator, spring and valve.

4. Remove the pickup tube/screen assembly *only* if it needs replacement. Secure the pump body in a soft-jawed vise and separate the tube from the cover.

> *CAUTION*
> *Do not twist, shear or collapse the tube when installing it in Step 5.*

5. If the pickup tube/screen assembly was removed, install a new one. Secure the pump body in a soft-jawed vise. Apply sealer to the new tube and gently tap in place with a soft-faced mallet. See **Figure 44**.

6. Lubricate all parts thoroughly with clean engine oil before reassembly.

7. Assembly is the reverse of disassembly. Index the gear marks, install a new cover gasket and rotate the pump drive shaft by hand to check for smooth operation. Tighten cover bolts to specifications (**Table 2**).

Inspection

> *NOTE*
> *The pump assembly and gears are serviced as an assembly. If one or the other*

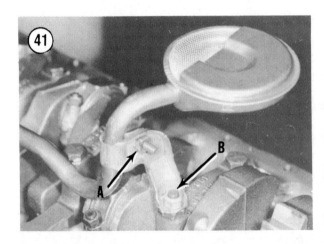

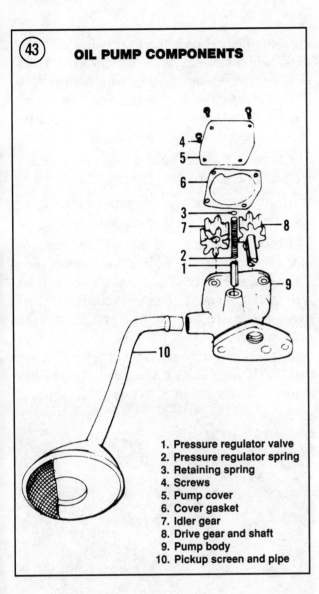

(43) **OIL PUMP COMPONENTS**

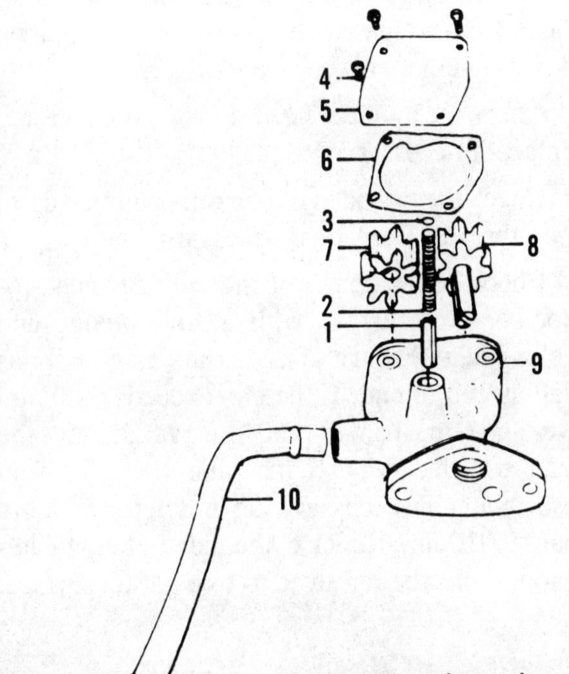

1. Pressure regulator valve
2. Pressure regulator spring
3. Retaining spring
4. Screws
5. Pump cover
6. Cover gasket
7. Idler gear
8. Drive gear and shaft
9. Pump body
10. Pickup screen and pipe

(44)

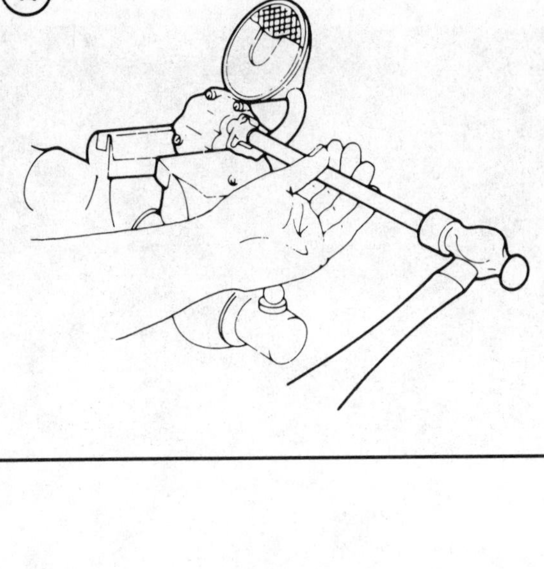

is worn or damaged, replace the entire pump. No wear specifications are provided by the manufacturer.

1. Clean all parts thoroughly in solvent. Brush the inside of the body and the pressure regulator chamber to remove all dirt and metal particles. Dry with compressed air, if available.
2. Check the pump body and cover for cracks or excessive wear.
3. Check the pump gears for damage or excessive wear.
4. Check the drive gear shaft-to-body fit for excessive looseness.
5. Check the inside of the pump cover for wear that could allow oil to leak around the ends of the gears.
6. Check the pressure regulator valve for a proper fit.

CYLINDER HEAD

Removal

Perform Steps 1-8 if engine is in boat. If engine has been removed from the boat, begin with Step 9.

1. Open the engine block drain valves and drain all water from the block.
2. Remove the manifold assembly as described in this chapter.
3. Disconnect the fuel line support clamps. Remove the fuel line.
4. Disconnect the cooling hoses at the water distribution housing (**Figure 45**).
5. Disconnect the temperature sending lead and remove the water distribution housing.
6. Disconnect and remove the ignition coil (except DDIS ignition). See **Figure 46**, typical.
7. Remove the circuit breaker bracket and engine lifting eye.
8. Disconnect all spark plug cables. Remove the spark plugs. See Chapter Four.
9. Remove the valve cover as described in this chapter.

10. Loosen the rocker arms and rotate them to one side. Remove the pushrods and identify each for reinstallation in its original position.

11. Loosen the cylinder head bolts, working from the center of the head to the end in each direction.

12. Remove the head bolts. Rap the end of the head with a soft-faced hammer to break the gasket seal. Remove the head from the engine.

CAUTION
Place the head on its side to prevent damage to the spark plugs or head gasket surface.

13. Remove and discard the head gasket. Clean all gasket residue from the head and block mating surfaces.

Decarbonizing

1. Without removing the valves, remove all deposits from the combustion chambers, intake ports and exhaust ports. Use a fine wire brush dipped in solvent or make a scraper from hardwood. Be careful not to scratch or gouge the combustion chambers.

2. After all carbon is removed from the combustion chambers and ports, clean the entire head in solvent.

3. Clean away all carbon on the piston tops. Do not remove the carbon ridge at the top of the cylinder bore.

4. Remove the valves as described in this chapter.

5. Clean the pushrod guides, valve guide bores and all bolt holes. Use a cleaning solvent to remove dirt and grease.

6. Clean the valves with a fine wire brush or buffing wheel.

Inspection

1. Check the cylinder head for signs of oil or water leaks before cleaning.

2. Clean the cylinder head thoroughly in solvent. While cleaning, look for cracks or other visible signs of damage. Look for corrosion or foreign material in the oil and water passages. Clean the passages with a stiff spiral brush, then blow them out with compressed air.

3. Check the cylinder head studs for damage and replace if necessary.

4. Check the threaded rocker arm studs for damaged threads. Replace if necessary.

5. Check for warpage of the cylinder head-to-block gasket surface with a straightedge and feeler gauge (**Figure 47**). Measure diagonally, as well as end to end. If the gap exceeds 0.003 in. over any 6 in. span, or 0.007 in. overall, have the head resurfaced by a machine shop. If head resurfacing is necessary, do not remove more than 0.010 in. Replace the head if a greater amount must be removed to true gasket surface.

Installation

1. Make sure the cylinder head and block gasket surfaces and bolt holes are clean. Dirt in the block bolt holes or on the head bolt threads will affect bolt torque.

2. Recheck all visible oil and water passages for cleanliness.

3. Fit a new head gasket over the cylinder dowels on the block.

4. Carefully lower the head onto the cylinder block, engaging the dowel pins.

5. Wipe all head bolt threads with Quicksilver Perfect Seal or equivalent. Install and tighten the head bolts finger-tight.

6. Tighten the head bolts 1/2 turn at a time following the sequence shown in **Figure 48** until the specified torque is reached. See **Table 2**.

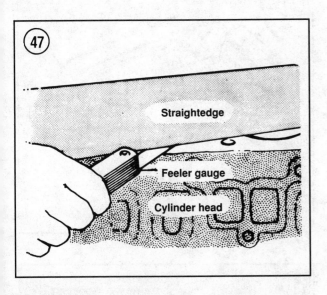

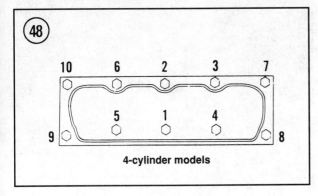

4-cylinder models

CAUTION
Retorque the head bolts during the 20-hour checkup. This will prevent possible poor engine performance, a blown head gasket, burned valves and other engine problems from developing.

7. If engine is in the boat, reverse Steps 1-10 of *Removal* in this chapter to complete installation. If engine is out of the boat, reverse Step 9 and Step 10 of *Removal* in this chapter. Adjust the valves as described in this chapter. Check and adjust ignition timing as required. See Chapter Four.

6

VALVES AND VALVE SEATS

Servicing the valves, guides and valve seats must be done by a dealer or machine shop, since they require special knowledge and expensive machine tools. Others, while possible for the home mechanic, are difficult or time-consuming. A general practice among those who do their own service is to remove the cylinder head, perform all disassembly except valve removal and take the head to a dealer or machine shop for inspection and service. Since the cost is low relative to the required effort and equipment, this is usually the best approach, even for experienced mechanics. The following procedures are given to acquaint the home mechanic with what the dealer or machine shop will do.

Valve Removal

Refer to **Figure 49** for this procedure.

1. Remove the cylinder head as described in this chapter.

2. Remove the rocker arm assemblies as described in this chapter.

3. Compress the valve spring with a compressor like the one shown in **Figure 50**. Remove the valve keys or cap locks and release the spring tension.

4. Remove the valve spring cap, shield, spring and damper assembly.

5. Remove and discard the valve stem seal. See **Figure 51**. Remove the shim and spacer, if used.

> *CAUTION*
> *Remove any burrs from the valve stem lock grooves before removing the valves or the valve guides will be damaged.*

6. Remove the valve and repeat Steps 3-5 on each remaining valve.

7. Arrange the parts in order so they can be returned to their original positions when reassembled.

Inspection

1. Clean the valves with a fine wire brush or buffing wheel. Discard any cracked, warped or burned valves.

2. Measure valve stems at the top, center and bottom for wear. A machine shop can do this when the valves are ground. Also measure the length of each valve and the diameter of each valve head.

> *NOTE*
> *Check the thickness of the valve edge or margin after the valves have been ground. See **Figure 52**. Any valve with a margin of less than 1/32 in. should be discarded.*

3. Remove all carbon and varnish from the valve guides with a stiff spiral wire brush.

> *NOTE*
> *The next step assumes that all valve stems have been measured and are within specifications. Replace valves with worn stems before performing this step.*

4. Insert each valve into the guide from which it was removed. Holding the valve just slightly off its seat, rock it back and forth in a direction parallel with the rocker arms. This is the direc-

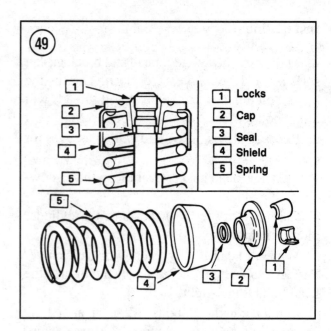

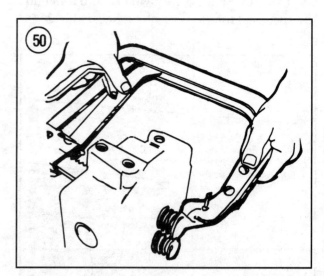

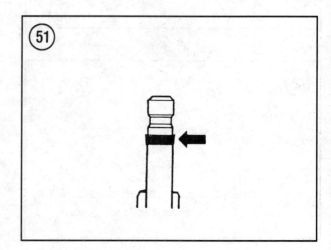

tion in which the greatest wear normally occurs. If the valve stem rocks more than slightly, the valve guide is probably worn.

5. If there is any doubt about valve guide condition after performing Step 4, have the valve guide measured with a valve stem clearance checking tool. Compare the results with specifications in **Table 1**. Worn guides must be reamed for the next oversize valve stem.

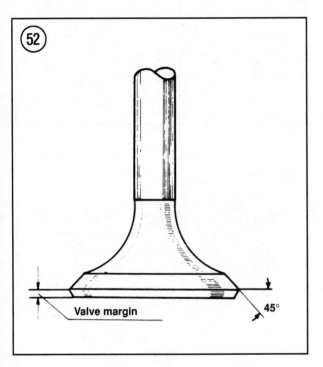

Valve margin   45°

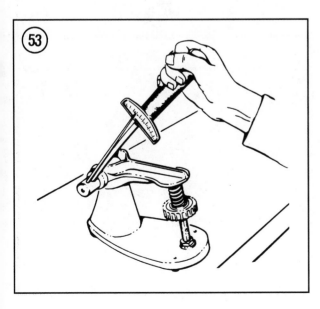

6. Test the valve springs under load on a spring tester (**Figure 53**). Replace any springs that test more than 10 lb. (45 N) out of specification (**Table 1**).

7. Inspect the valve seat inserts. If worn or burned, they must be reconditioned. This is a job for a dealer or machine shop, although the procedure is described in this chapter.

8. Check each spring on a flat surface with a steel square. See **Figure 54**. Slowly revolve the spring 360° and note the space between the top of the coil and the square. If it exceeds 5/16 in. (7.9 mm) at any point, replace the spring.

9. Check each valve lifter to make sure it fits freely in the block and that the end that contacts the camshaft lobe is smooth and not worn excessively.

6

Valve Guide Reaming

Worn valve guides must be reamed to accept a valve with an oversize stem. These are available in 3 sizes for both intake and exhaust valves. Reaming must be done by hand (**Figure 55**) and is a job best left to an experienced machine shop.

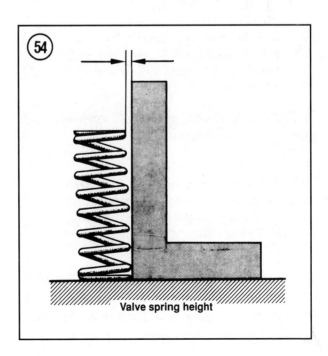

Valve spring height

The valve seat must be refaced after the guide has been reamed.

Valve Seat Reconditioning

1. Cut the valve seats to the specified angle (**Table 1**) with a dressing stone. See **Figure 56**. Remove only enough metal to obtain a good finish.

2. Use tapered stones to obtain the specified seat width when necessary.

3. Coat the corresponding valve face with Prussian blue dye.

4. Insert the valve into the valve guide.

5. Apply light pressure to the valve and rotate it approximately 1/4 turn.

6. Lift the valve out. If it seats properly, the dye will transfer evenly to the valve face.

7. If the dye transfers to the top of the valve face, lower the seat. If it transfers to the bottom of the valve face, raise the seat.

Valve Installation

NOTE
Install all parts in the same positions from which they were removed.

1. Coat the valves with engine oil and install them in the cylinder head.

2. Install new oil seals on each valve. Seal should be flat and not twisted in the valve stem groove.

3. Drop the valve spring shim/spacer around the valve guide boss. Install the valve spring over the valve, then install the spring retainer.

4. Compress the springs and install the locks. Make sure both locks seat properly in the upper groove of the valve stem.

5. Measure the installed spring height between the top of the valve seat and the underside of the spring retainer, as shown in **Figure 57**. If height is greater than specifications, install an extra

spring seat shim about 1/16 in. thick and remeasure the height.

VALVE LIFTERS

Removal/Installation

1. Remove the rocker arm assemblies, pushrods and lifter covers as described in this chapter.

2. Remove the valve lifters. This can be done without special tools, although tool part No. J-3049 will make the job easier and faster.

3. Installation is the reverse of removal.

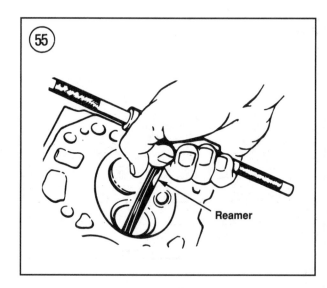

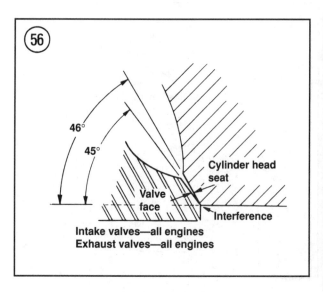

Inspection

Keep the lifters in proper sequence for installation in their original position in the cylinder block. Clean lifters in solvent and wipe dry with a clean, lint-free cloth. Inspect and test the lifters separately to prevent intermixing of their internal parts. If any part requires replacement, replace the entire lifter.

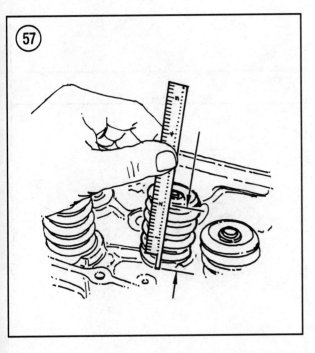

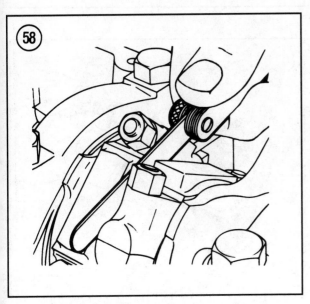

Inspect all parts. If any lifter shows signs of pitting, scoring, galling, non-rotation or excessive wear, discard it. Check the lifter plunger. It should drop to the bottom of the body by its own weight when dry and assembled.

PISTON/CONNECTING ROD ASSEMBLY

Piston/Connecting Rod Removal

1. Remove the engine as described in this chapter.
2. Place a suitable container under the oil pan and remove the drain plug. Let the crankcase oil drain, then reinstall the drain plug.
3. Remove the manifold assembly as described in this chapter.
4. Remove the cylinder head as described in this chapter.
5. Remove the oil pan and oil pump as described in this chapter.
6. Rotate the crankshaft until one piston is at bottom dead center. Pack the cylinder bore with clean shop rags. Remove the carbon ridge at the top of the cylinder bores with a ridge reamer. These can be rented for use. Vacuum out the shavings, then remove the shop rags.
7. Rotate the crankshaft until the connecting rod is centered in the bore. Measure the clearance between the connecting rod and the crankshaft journal flange with a flat feeler gauge (**Figure 58**). If the clearance exceeds specifications (**Table 1**), replace the connecting rod during reassembly.

NOTE
*Mark the cylinder number on the top of each piston with quick-drying paint. Check the cylinder numbers or identification marks on the connecting rod and cap. If they are not visible, make your own (**Figure 59**).*

6

8. Remove the nuts holding the connecting rod cap. Lift off the cap, together with the lower bearing insert.

> *NOTE*
> *If the connecting rod caps are difficult to remove, tap the studs with a wooden hammer handle.*

9. Use the wooden hammer handle to push the piston and connecting rod from the bore.

10. Remove the piston rings with a ring remover (**Figure 60**).

11. Repeat Steps 6-10 for all remaining piston/connecting rods.

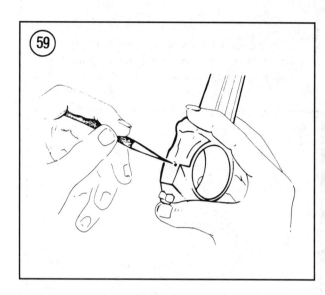

Piston Pin Removal/Installation

The piston pins are press-fitted to the connecting rods and hand-fitted to the pistons. Removal requires the use of a press and support stand. This is a job for a dealer or machine shop equipped to fit the pistons to the pins, ream the pin bushings to the correct diameter and install the pistons and pins on the connecting rods.

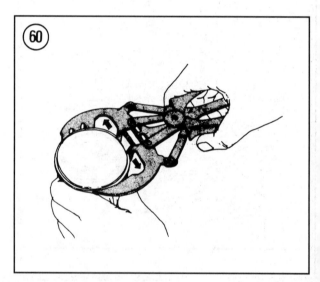

Piston Clearance Check

Unless you have precision measuring equipment and know how to use it properly, have this procedure done by a machine shop.

1. Measure the piston diameter with a micrometer (**Figure 61**) just below the rings at a right angle to the piston pin bore.

2. Measure the cylinder bore diameter with a bore gauge (**Figure 62**). **Figure 63** shows the points of normal cylinder wear. If dimension A exceeds dimension B by more than 0.003 in., the cylinder must be rebored and a new piston/ring assembly installed.

3. Subtract the piston diameter from the largest cylinder bore reading. If it exceeds the specifications in **Table 1**, the cylinder must be rebored and an oversized piston installed.

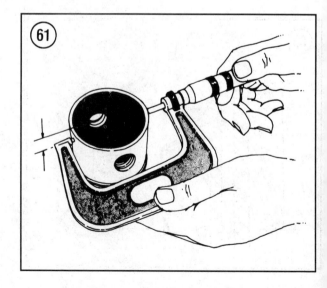

NOTE
Obtain the new piston and measure it to determine the correct cylinder bore oversize dimension.

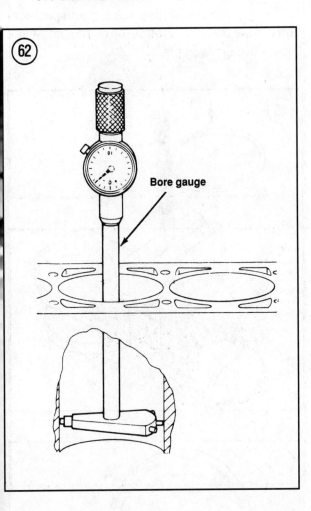

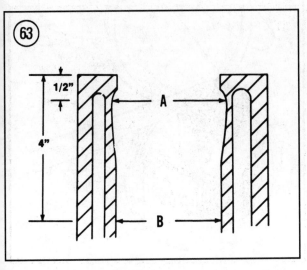

Piston Ring Fit/Installation

1. Check the ring gap of each piston ring. To do this, position the ring at the bottom of the ring travel area and square it by tapping gently with an inverted piston. See **Figure 64**.

NOTE
If the cylinders have not been rebored, check the gap at the bottom of the ring travel, where the cylinder is least worn.

2. Measure the ring gap with a feeler gauge as shown in **Figure 65**. Compare with specifications in **Table 1**. If the measurement is not within specification, the rings must be replaced as a set. Check gap of new rings as well. If the gap is too small, file the ends of the ring to correct it (**Figure 66**).

3. Check the side clearance of the rings as shown in **Figure 67**. Place the feeler gauge alongside the ring all the way into the groove. If the measurement is not within specifications (**Table 1**), either the rings or the ring grooves are worn. Inspect and replace as required.

4. Using a ring expander tool (**Figure 68**), carefully install the oil control ring, then the com-

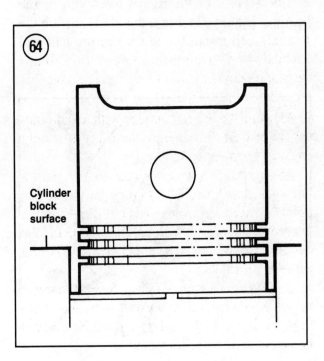

pression rings. Oil rings consist of 3 segments. The wavy segment goes between the flat segments to act as a spacer. See **Figure 69**. Upper and lower flat segments are interchangeable. The second compression ring is tapered. The top of each compression ring is marked and must face upward.

5. Position the ring gaps as shown in **Figure 70**.

Connecting Rod Inspection

Have the connecting rods checked for straightness by a dealer or machine shop. When installing new connecting rods, have them checked for misalignment before installing the piston and piston pin. Connecting rods can spring out of alignment during shipping or handling.

Connecting Rod Bearing Clearance Measurement

1. Place the connecting rods and upper bearing halves on the proper connecting rod journals.

2. Cut a piece of Plastigage the width of the bearing (**Figure 71**). Place the Plastigage on the journal, then install the lower bearing half end cap.

NOTE
Do not place Plastigage over the journal oil hole.

3. Tighten the connecting rod cap to specification (**Table 2**). Do not rotate the crankshaft while the Plastigage is in place.

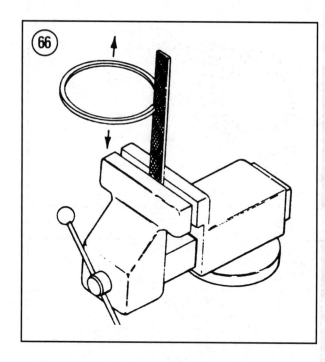

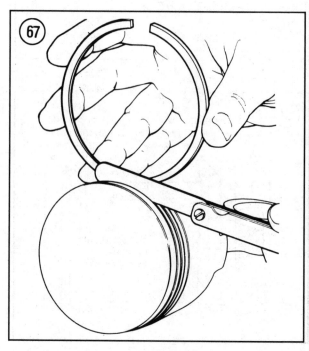

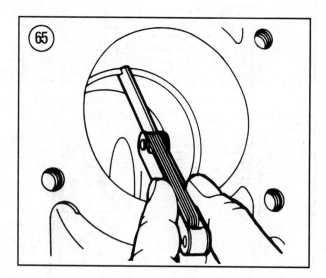

4. Remove the connecting rod caps. Bearing clearance is determined by comparing the width of the flattened Plastigage to the markings on the

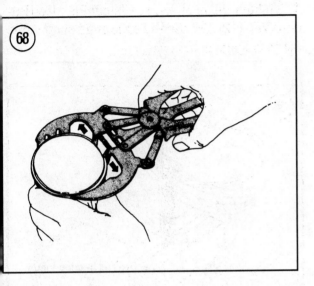

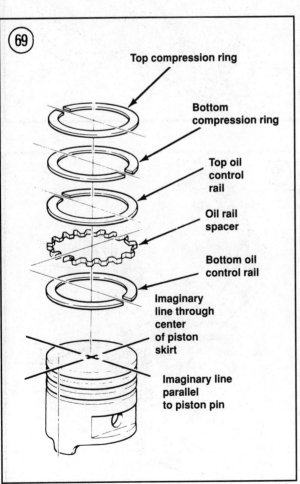

Top compression ring

Bottom compression ring

Top oil control rail

Oil rail spacer

Bottom oil control rail

Imaginary line through center of piston skirt

Imaginary line parallel to piston pin

envelope (**Figure 72**). If the clearance is excessive, the crankshaft must be reground and undersize bearings installed.

Piston/Connecting Rod Installation

1. Make sure the pistons are correctly installed on the connecting rods, if they were separated. The small rod bearing tang should be on the same side as the arrow or notch in the piston head. See **Figure 73**, typical.

2. Make sure the ring gaps are positioned as shown in **Figure 70**.

3. Slip short pieces of hose over the connecting rod studs to prevent them from nicking the

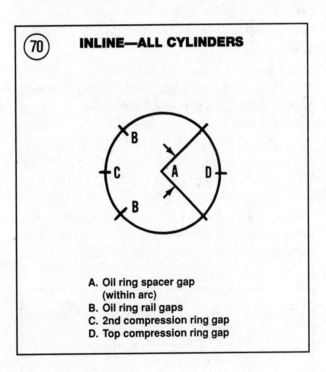

INLINE—ALL CYLINDERS

A. Oil ring spacer gap (within arc)
B. Oil ring rail gaps
C. 2nd compression ring gap
D. Top compression ring gap

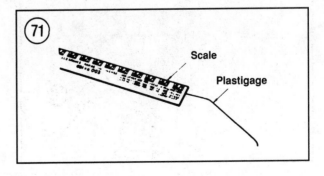

Scale

Plastigage

6

crankshaft. Tape will work if you do not have the right diameter hose, but it is more difficult to remove.

4. Immerse the entire piston in clean engine oil. Coat the cylinder wall with oil.

CAUTION
Use extreme care in Step 5 to prevent the connecting rod from nicking the crankshaft journal.

5. Install the piston/connecting rod assembly in its cylinder with a piston ring compressor as shown in **Figure 74**. Tap lightly with a wooden hammer handle to insert the piston. Make sure that the piston number (painted on top before removal) corresponds to the cylinder number, counting from the front of the engine. The notch on the piston crown must face the front of the engine (**Figure 75**).

6. Clean the connecting rod bearings carefully, including the back sides. Coat the journals and bearings with clean engine oil. Place the bearings in the connecting rod and cap.

7. Pull the connecting rod and bearing into position against the crankpin. Remove the protective hose or tape and lightly lubricate the connecting rod bolt threads with SAE 30 engine oil.

8. Install the connecting rod cap (**Figure 76**). Make sure the rod and cap marks align. Install the cap nuts finger-tight.

9. Repeat Steps 4-8 for each remaining piston/connecting rod assembly.

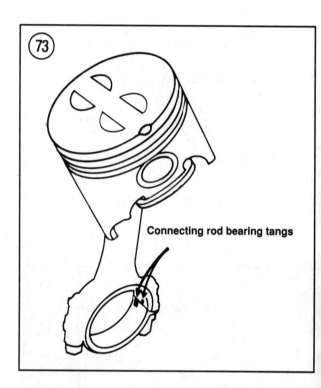

Connecting rod bearing tangs

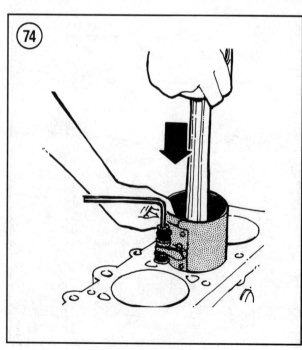

10. Tighten the cap nut to specifications (**Table 2**).

11. Check the connecting rod big-end play as described under *Piston/Connecting Rod Removal* in this chapter.

REAR MAIN OIL SEAL

Replacement (2-Piece Seal)

If seal kit comes with an installation tool, follow the instructions provided in the kit.

1. Remove the engine from the boat as described in this chapter.

2. Remove the oil pan and oil pump as described in this chapter.

3. Remove the rear main bearing cap. Pry the oil seal from the bottom of the cap with a small screwdriver.

4. Remove the upper half of the seal from the block with a brass pin punch. Tap the punch on one end of the seal until its other end protrudes far enough to be removed with pliers.

5. Clean all sealant from the bearing cap and crankshaft with a non-abrasive cleaner.

6. Coat the lips and head of a new seal with light engine oil. Do not let oil touch seal mating ends or parting line surface.

7. Install the new seal half into the rear main bearing cap, taking care that the sharp edge of the cap ridge does not cut the bead in the center of the outer seal surface.

8. Wipe the crankshaft seal surface clean. Position seal half on the crankshaft and roll into place by rotating the crankshaft gradually while pushing on the seal with a hammer handle. Make sure that the seal tangs at the parting line do not cut the bead on the back of the seal.

9. Coat the seal area of the block with Quicksilver Perfect Seal. See **Figure 77**.

10. Install the rear main bearing cap and tighten cap bolts to specification (**Table 2**).

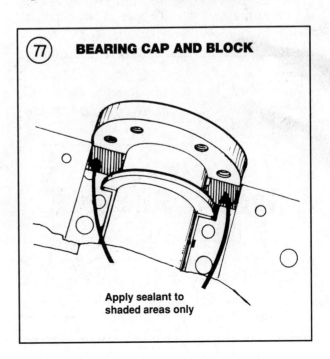

BEARING CAP AND BLOCK

Apply sealant to shaded areas only

11. Install the oil pump and oil pan as described in this chapter.

12. Install the engine in the boat as described in this chapter.

Replacement (1-Piece Seal)

On 3.0L models serial No. OC856451-on and 3.0LX models serial No. OC868143-on, a 1-piece rear main seal is used. The 1-piece rear seal can be removed and replaced without removing the oil pan or the rear main bearing cap from the engine.

Replace the seal as follows:

1. Remove the engine from the boat as described in this chapter.

2. Remove the engine coupler and flywheel from the engine.

3. Using a screwdriver or pry bar, carefully pry the rear main seal from the seal retainer. Pry the seal evenly at the 3 pry slots provided. See **Figure 78**.

4. Thoroughly clean the seal bore in the retainer and the sealing surface of the crankshaft.

5. Lubricate the seal lip with engine oil or grease. Apply Quicksilver Perfect Seal to the outer diameter of the seal.

6. Place the seal into its bore in the retainer. Using Kent Moore seal installer (part No. J-26817-A), drive the seal into its bore until fully seated.

7. Install the flywheel, engine coupler and install the engine into the boat as described in this chapter.

CRANKSHAFT

End Play Measurement

1. Pry the crankshaft to the front of the engine with a large screwdriver.

2. Measure the crankshaft end play at the front of the rear main bearing with a flat feeler gauge. See **Figure 79**. Compare to specification in **Table 1**.

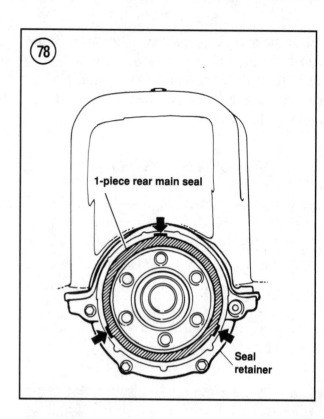

(78)

1-piece rear main seal

Seal retainer

CRANKSHAFT END PLAY MEASUREMENT

(79)

3. If the end play is excessive, replace the rear main bearing. If less than specified, check the bearing faces for imperfections.

Removal

1. Remove the engine from the boat as described in this chapter.

2. Remove the flywheel as described in this chapter.

3. Mount the engine on an engine stand, if available.

4. Remove the starter motor. See Chapter Eleven.

5. Invert the engine to bring the oil pan to an upright position.

6. Remove the oil pan and oil pump as described in this chapter.

7. Remove the timing gear cover as described in this chapter.

8. Remove the spark plugs to permit easy rotation of the crankshaft.

9. Measure crankshaft end play as described in this chapter.

10. Rotate the crankshaft to position one connecting rod at the bottom of its stroke.

11. Remove the connecting rod bearing cap and bearing (**Figure 76**). Move the piston/rod assembly away from the crankshaft.

12. Repeat Step 10 and Step 11 for each remaining piston/rod assembly.

13. Check the caps for identification numbers or marks. If none are visible, clean the caps with a wire brush. If marks still cannot be seen, make your own with an indelible marker.

14. Unbolt and remove the main bearing caps and bearing inserts (**Figure 80**).

NOTE
If the caps are difficult to remove, lift the bolts partway out, then use the bolts to lever the caps from side to side.

15. Carefully lift the crankshaft from the engine block and place it on a clean workbench.

16. Remove the bearing inserts from the block. Place the bearing caps and inserts in order on a clean workbench.

17. Remove the main bearing oil seal from the cylinder block and rear bearing cap.

Inspection

1. Clean the crankshaft thoroughly with solvent. Blow out the oil passages with compressed air.

2. Check the main and connecting rod journals for wear, scratches, grooves, scoring or cracks. Check oil seal surface for burrs, nicks or other sharp edges which might damage a seal during installation.

NOTE
Unless you have precision measuring equipment and know how to use it, have a machine shop perform Step 3.

3. Check all journals against specifications (**Table 1**) for out-of-roundness and taper. See **Figure 81**. Have the crankshaft reground, if necessary and install new undersize bearings.

Main Bearing Clearance Measurement

Main bearing clearance is measured with Plastigage in the same manner as the connecting rod bearing clearance, described in this chapter. Ex-

cessive clearance requires that the bearings be replaced, the crankshaft be reground or both.

Installation

1. Install a new rear main bearing oil seal as described in this chapter.

2. Install the main bearing inserts in the cylinder block. Bearing oil holes must align with block oil holes and bearing tabs must seat in the block tab slots.

> *NOTE*
> *Check cap bolts for thread damage before reuse. If damaged, replace the bolts.*

3. Lubricate the bolt threads with SAE 30 engine oil.

4. Install the bearing inserts in each cap.

5. Carefully lower the crankshaft into position in the block.

6. Install the bearing caps in their marked positions with the arrows pointing toward the front of the engine (**Figure 82**) and the number mark aligned with the corresponding mark on the journals.

7. Install and tighten all bolts except the rear main to 10-12 ft.-lb. Tighten rear main cap to specification (**Table 2**). Tap front of crankshaft with a hammer to drive it rearward, then tap the rear to drive it forward. This aligns the rear main bearing and crankshaft thrust surfaces.

8. Retighten all main bearing caps to specification (**Table 2**).

9. Rotate the crankshaft to make sure it turns smoothly at the flywheel rim. If not, remove the bearing caps and crankshaft and check that the bearings are clean and properly installed.

10. Reverse Steps 1-12 of *Removal* in this chapter.

FLYWHEEL

Removal/Installation

1. Remove the engine from the boat as described in this chapter.

2. Remove the bell housing.

3. Remove the coupler retaining fasteners. Remove the coupler.

4. Gradually loosen and remove the flywheel bolts, working in a diagonal pattern.

5. To install, align the dowel hole in the flywheel with dowel in crankshaft flange and position the flywheel on the studs. Install and tighten bolts to specifications (**Table 2**).

6. Fit the coupler on the studs. Install the washers and locknuts. Tighten nuts to specification (**Table 2**).

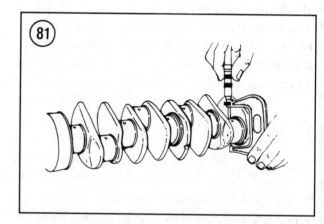

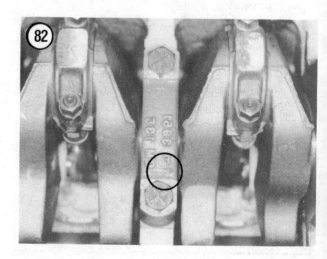

7. Install a dial indicator on the machined surface of the flywheel and check runout. If runout exceeds 0.008 in., remove the flywheel and check for burrs. If none are found, replace the flywheel.

8. Reinstall the bell housing.

9. Lubricate coupler splines with Quicksilver Engine Coupler Grease and reinstall the engine in the boat as described in this chapter.

Inspection

1. Visually check the flywheel surface for cracks, deep scoring, excessive wear, heat discoloration and checking. If the surface is glazed or slightly scratched, have the flywheel resurfaced by a machine shop.

2. Check the surface flatness with a straightedge and feeler gauge.

3. Inspect the ring gear for cracks, broken teeth or excessive wear. If severely worn, check the starter motor drive teeth for similar wear or damage. Replace as required.

CYLINDER BLOCK

Cleaning and Inspection

1. Clean the block thoroughly with solvent. Remove any gasket or RTV sealant residue from the

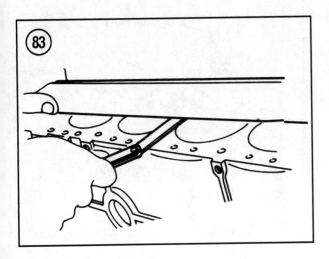

machined surfaces. Check all core plugs for leaks and replace any that are suspect. See *Core Plug Replacement* in this chapter. Remove any plugs that seal oil passages. Check oil and coolant passages for sludge, dirt and corrosion while cleaning. If the passages are very dirty, have the block boiled out by a machine shop. Blow out all passages with compressed air. Check the threads in the head bolt holes to be sure they are clean. If dirty, use a tap to true up the threads and remove any deposits.

2. Examine the block for cracks. To confirm suspicions about possible leaks areas, use a mixture of 1 part kerosene and 2 parts engine oil. Coat the suspected area with this solution, then wipe dry and immediately apply a solution of zinc oxide dissolved in wood alcohol. If any discoloration appears in the treated area, the block is cracked and should be replaced.

3. Check flatness of the cylinder block deck or top surface. Place an accurate straightedge on the block. If there is any gap between the block and straightedge, measure it with a flat feeler gauge (**Figure 83**). Measure from end to end and from corner to corner. Have the block resurfaced if it is warped more than 0.004 in. (0.102 mm).

4. Measure cylinder bores with a bore gauge (**Figure 84**) for out-of-roundness or excessive wear as described in *Piston Clearance Check* in this chapter. If the cylinders exceed maximum tolerances, they must be rebored. Reboring is also necessary if the cylinder walls are badly scuffed or scored.

NOTE
Before boring, install all main bearing caps and tighten the cap bolts to specification in **Table 2***.*

CORE PLUG REPLACEMENT

The condition of all core plugs in the block (**Figure 85**) and cylinder head should be checked whenever the engine is out of the boat for service. If any signs of leakage or corrosion are found around one core plug, replace them all.

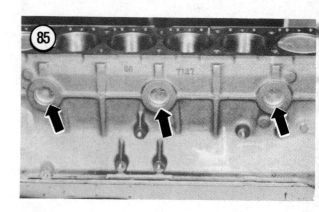

> *NOTE*
> *Core plugs can be replaced inexpensively by a machine shop. If you are having machine work done on the engine, have the core plugs replaced at the same time.*

Removal/Installation

> *CAUTION*
> *Do not drive core plugs into the engine casting. It will be impossible to retrieve them and they can restrict coolant circulation, resulting in serious engine damage.*

1. Tap the bottom edge of the core plug with a hammer and drift. Use several sharp blows to push the bottom of the plug inward, tilting the top out (**Figure 86**).

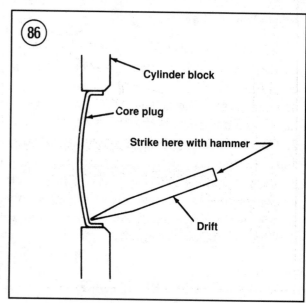

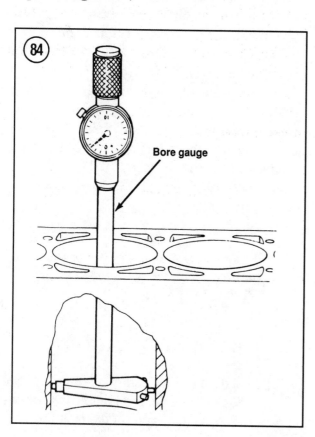

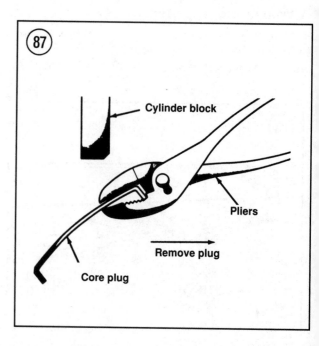

2. Grip the top of the plug firmly with pliers. Pull the plug from its bore (**Figure 87**) and discard.

NOTE
Core plugs can also be removed by drilling a hole in the center of the plug and

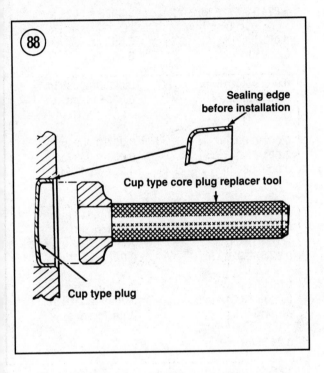

3. Clean the plug bore thoroughly to remove all traces of the old sealer. Inspect the bore for any damage that might interfere with proper sealing of the new plug. If damage is evident, true the surface by boring for the next oversize plug.

prying them out with an appropriate size drift or pin punch. On large core plugs, the use of a universal impact slide hammer is recommended.

NOTE
Oversize plugs can be identified by an "OS" stamped in the flat on the cup side of the plug.

4. Coat the inside diameter of the plug bore and the outer diameter of the new plug with sealer. Use an oil-resistant sealer if the plug is to be installed in an oil gallery or a water-resistant sealer for plugs installed in the water jacket.

5. Install the new core plug with an appropriate size core plug replacer tool (**Figure 88**), driver or socket. The sharp edge of the plug should be at least 0.02 in. (0.5 mm) inside the lead-in chamfer.

6. Repeat Steps 1-5 to replace each remaining core plug.

Tables 1-3 are on the following pages.

6

Table 1 GM INLINE 4-CYLINDER ENGINE SPECIFICATIONS

	2.5L	120 & 3.0L (Early*)	140 & 3.0L (Late*)
Bore	3.875 in.	4.00 in.	4.00 in.
Stroke	3.25 in.	3.60 in.	3.60 in.
Displacement	151 cid	181 cid	181 cid
Firing order	1-3-4-2	1-3-4-2	1-3-4-2
Cylinder bore diameter	3.8745-3.8775 in.	3.8745-3.8775 in.	3.9995-4.0025 in.
Max. out-of-round	0.002 in.	0.002 in.	0.002 in.
Max. taper	0.0005 in.	0.0005 in.	0.001 in.
Piston clearance			
Production	0.0005-0.0015 in.	0.0005-0.0015 in.	0.0025-0.0035 in.
Wear limit	0.0025 in. max.	0.0025 in. max.	0.0035 in. max.
Piston ring			
Side clearance			
Top ring	0.001-0.003 in.	0.001-0.003 in.	0.001-0.003 in.
Second ring	0.001-0.004 in.	0.001-0.004 in.	0.001-0.003 in.
Oil ring	0.00-0.006 in.	0.00-0.006 in.	0.001-0.007 in.
End gap			
Compression rings	0.010-0.030 in.	0.010-0.030 in.	0.010-0.040 in.
Oil ring	0.015-0.065 in.	0.015-0.065 in.	0.040 in. max.
Piston pin			
Diameter	0.9270-0.9273 in.	0.9270-0.9273 in.	0.9270-0.9273 in.
Pin-to piston clearance	0.001 in. max.	0.001 in. max	0.001 in. max.
Fit in rod	0.0008-0.0016 in. (interference)	0.0008-0.0016 in. (interference)	0.0008-0.0019 in. (interference)
Camshaft			
Lobe lift	0.2325 in.	0.2525 in.	0.2529 in.
Journal diameter	1.8682-0.8692 in.	1.8682-1.8692 in.	1.8677-1.8697 in.
End play	0.003-0.008 in.	0.003-0.008 in.	0.003-0.008 in.
Runout	0.0015 in. max.	0.0015 in. max.	0.0015 in. max.
Crankshaft			
Main journal diameter	2.2983-2.2993 in.	2.2983-2.2993 in.	2.2979-2.2994 in. in.
Max. journal taper	0.001 in.	0.001 in.	0.001 in.
Max. journal out-of-round	0.001 in.	0.001 in.	0.001 in.
End play	0.002-0.006 in.	0.002-0.006 in.	0.002-0.006 in.
Main bearing clearance			
Nos. 1-4	0.0003-0.004 in.	0.0003-0.004 in.	0.001-0.0025 in.
No. 5	0.0003-0.004 in.	0.0003-0.004 in.	0.002-0.0035 in.
Crankpin diameter	1.999-2.000 in.	2.099-2.100 in.	2.0998-2.099 in.
Max. taper	0.001 in.	0.001 in.	0.001 in.
Max. out-of-round	0.001 in.	0.001 in.	0.001 in.
Crankpin bearing clearance	0.0007-0.004 in.	0.0007-0.004 in.	0.0017-0.0027 in.

(continued)

Table 1 GM INLINE 4-CYLINDER ENGINE SPECIFICATIONS (continued)

	2.5L	120 & 3.0L (Early*)	140 & 3.0L (Late*)
Connecting rod side clearance	0.009-0.013 in.	0.009-0.013 in.	0.006-0.017 in.
Valve lifter	Hydraulic	Hydraulic	Hydraulic
Rocker arm ratio	1.75:1	1.75:1	1.75:1
Valve lash	3/4 to 1 turn down from zero lash	3/4 to 1 turn down from zero lash	1/2 to 1 turn down from zero lash
Valve face angle	45°	45°	45°
Valve seat angle	46°	46°	46°
Seat width			
Intake	1/32 to 1/16 in.	1/32 to 1/16 in.	1/16 in. max.
Exhaust	1/16 to 3/32 in.	1/16 to 3/32 in.	1/16 to 5/64 in.
Max. valve seat runout	0.002 in.	0.002 in.	0.002 in.
Valve stem clearance			
Intake	0.0010-0.0037 in.	0.0010-0.0037 in.	0.0010-0.003 in.
Exhaust	0.0015-0.0052 in.	0.0015-0.0052 in.	0.0007-0.004 in.
Valve spring			
Free length	2-5/16 in.	2-5/16 in.	2-1/6 in.
Installed height	1-21/32 in.	1-21/32 in.	1-21/32 in.
Load			
Closed	78-86 lb. @ 1-21/32 in.	83 lb. @ 1-21/32 in.	100-110 lb. @ 1-19/32 in.
Open	170-180 lb. @ 1-17/64 in.	175 lb. @ 1-17/64 in.	208-220 lb. @ 1-7/32 in.

*Early 3.0L models are prior to serial No. OC770947; late models are serial No. OC770947-on.

6

Table 2 GM INLINE 4-CYLINDER ENGINE TIGHTENING TORQUES

Fastener	in.-lb.	ft.-lb.
Camshaft sprocket bolts	80	
Connecting rod cap bolts		45
Cylinder head bolts		90
Distributor clamp bolt		20
Engine coupler-to-flywheel bolts		35
Flywheel housing bolts		21
Flywheel bolts		65
Front cover bolts	30	
Front mount-to-block		21
Main bearing cap bolts		65
Intake manifold bolts		23
Oil pan bolts		
Side	80	
End	45	

(continued)

Table 2 GM INLINE 4-CYLINDER ENGINE TIGHTENING TORQUES (continued)

Fastener	in.-lb.	ft.-lb.
Oil pump cover	72	
Oil pump-to-block bolt	120	
Oil pump pickup	60	
Rocker arm cover bolts	40	
Rear main seal retainer nuts (1-Piece seal)	135	
Spark plugs		22
Starter motor mounting bolts		37
Timing gear cover bolts	72	
Torsional damper bolts		50
Water pump mounting bolts		15

Table 3 STANDARD TORQUE VALUES

Fastener	ft.-lb.	N·m
Grade 5		
1/4-20	8	11
1/4-28	8	11
5/16-18	17	23
5/16-24	20	27
3/8-16	30	40
3/8-24	35	47
7/16-14	50	68
7/16-20	55	75
1/2-13	75	100
1/2-20	85	115
9/16-12	105	142
9/16-18	115	156
Grade 6		
1/4-20	10.5	14
1/4-28	12.5	17
5/16-18	22.5	31
5/16-24	25	54
3/8-16	40	34
3/8-24	45	61
7/16-14	65	88
7/16-20	70	95
1/2-13	100	136
1/2-20	110	149
9/16-12	135	183
9/16-18	150	203

Chapter Seven

Mercruiser Inline Engines

This chapter covers the MerCruiser 224 cid 4-cylinder engine variously designated as Models 165, 170, 3.7L, 180, 190 and 3.7LX. The Models 165, 170 and 3.7LX are improved versions of the older MerCruiser 470; the Models 180, 190 and 3.7LX are improved versions of the older MerCruiser 488. All models of this engine are essentially the same, differing primarily in the carburetor used. Models 165, 170 and 3.7L are equipped with a 2-barrel carburetor while Models 180, 190 and 3.7LX are equipped with a 4-barrel carburetor.

The cylinders are numbered 1-2-3-4 from front to rear. Engine firing order is 1-3-4-2.

Rocker arms are retained by individual threaded bolts. A simple ball-pivot valve train is used, with camshaft motion transferred through the hydraulic lifters to the rocker arms by pushrods.

The chain-driven camshaft is located above the crankshaft in the engine block and rotates in aluminum bores (no bearings).

The oil pump is located on the bottom front of the block on the starboard side and is driven by the distributor shaft.

The crankshaft is supported by 5 main bearings, with the No. 3 bearing providing the crankshaft thrust surfaces. Crankshaft rotation is counterclockwise when seen from the drive unit end of the engine.

The cylinder block is cast aluminum with full length water jackets around each cylinder.

Engine specifications (**Table 1**) and tightening torques (**Table 2** and **Table 3**) are at the end of the chapter.

ENGINE SERIAL NUMBER AND CODE

The engine serial number and model designation may be stamped on a plate mounted on the front port side of the engine block next to the heat exchanger (**Figure 1**) or located on a decal on the engine block. This information identifies the engine and indicates if there are unique parts or if internal changes have been made during the model run. It is important when ordering replacement parts for the engine.

SPECIAL TOOLS

Where special tools are required or recommended for engine overhaul, the tool numbers are provided. While these tools can sometimes be rented from rental dealers, those carrying a "J" prefix can be purchased from Kent-Moore Tool & Equipment Division, 29784 Little Mack, Roseville, MI 48066. Tools carrying a "T" prefix can be purchased from Owatonna Tools, Inc., Attn: Ford Order Desk, Owatonna, MN 55060. Tools carrying a "C" prefix are available directly from Mercury Marine or MerCruiser dealers.

GASKET SEALANT

Gasket sealant is used instead of pre-formed gaskets between some mating surfaces on the engines covered in this chapter. See *Gasket Sealant,* Chapter Six.

REPLACEMENT PARTS

Various changes are made to automotive engine blocks used for marine applications. Numerous part changes are required due to operation in fresh and saltwater. For example, the cylinder head gaskets must be corrosion resistant. Marine engines use head gaskets of copper or stainless steel instead of the standard steel used in automotive applications. Brass expansion or core plugs must be used instead of the steel plugs found in automotive blocks.

Since marine engine are run at or near maximum rpm most of the time, the use of special valve lifters, springs, pistons, bearings, camshafts and other heavy-duty moving components is necessary for maximum life and performance.

For these reasons, automotive-type parts should not be substituted for marine components. In addition, Mercury Marine recommends that only Quicksilver parts be used. Parts offered by other manufacturers may look alike, but may not be manufactured to MerCruiser's specifications. Any damage resulting from the use of other than Quicksilver parts is not covered by the Mercury Marine warranty.

ENGINE REMOVAL

Some service procedures can be performed with the engine in the boat; others require removal. The boat design and service procedure to

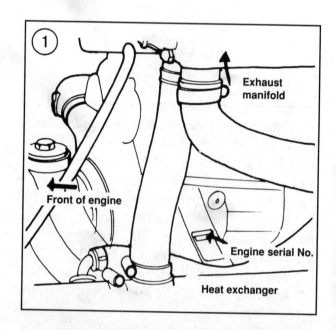

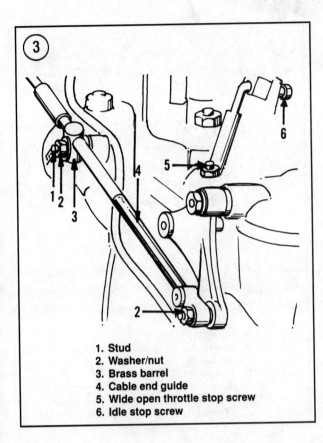

1. Stud
2. Washer/nut
3. Brass barrel
4. Cable end guide
5. Wide open throttle stop screw
6. Idle stop screw

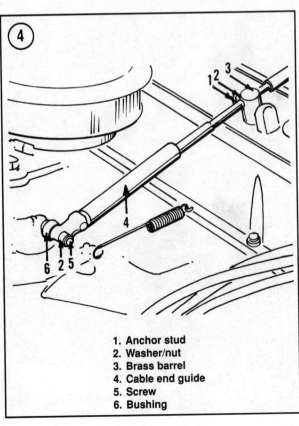

1. Anchor stud
2. Washer/nut
3. Brass barrel
4. Cable end guide
5. Screw
6. Bushing

be performed will determine whether the engine must be removed.

The stern drive unit *must* be removed to disengage the drive shaft from the engine coupler.

WARNING
The engine is heavy, awkward to handle and has sharp edges. It may shift or drop suddenly during removal. To prevent serious injury, always observe the following precautions.

1. Never place any part of your body where a moving or falling engine may trap, cut or crush you.

2. If you must push the engine during removal, use a board or similar tool to keep your hands out of danger.

3. Be sure the hoist is designed to lift engines and has enough load capacity for your engine.

4. Be sure the hoist is securely attached to safe lifting points on the engine.

5. The engine should not be difficult to lift with a proper hoist. If it is, stop lifting, lower the engine back onto its mounts and make sure the engine has been completely separated from the vessel.

1. Remove the stern drive unit. See Chapter Twelve.

2. Remove the engine hood cover and all panels that interfere with engine removal. Place the cover and panels to one side out of the way.

3. Disconnect the negative battery cable, then the positive battery cable. As a precaution, remove the battery from the boat.

4. Unplug the instrument harness connector from the engine harness receptacle.

5. Disconnect the fuel inlet line from the fuel pump (**Figure 2**). Cap the line and plug the fuel pump fitting to prevent leakage and the entry of contamination.

6. Disconnect the throttle cable from the carburetor. If necessary, remove the cable from the anchor plate. See **Figure 3** (165/170/3.7L) or **Figure 4** and **Figure 5** (180/190/3.7LX).

7

7. Disconnect the brown and black shift inter-lock wires from the shift plate terminal block, if so equipped.

8. Disconnect the trim position sender wires from the terminal block, if so equipped. See **Figure 6**, typical.

9. Disconnect the red and black power trim pump wires from the engine, if so equipped.

10. Disconnect the water inlet hose. Open the engine drain valve(s) and drain all water from the block.

11. Unclamp and disconnect the exhaust elbow bellows. See **Figure 7**, typical.

12. Unbolt and remove the upper exhaust pipe (**Figure 8**).

13. Remove both shift cables from the shift plate located on the exhaust manifold. See **Figure 9**, typical.

14. Disconnect any ground leads or accessories connected to the engine that will interfere with engine removal.

15. If equipped with power steering, use a flare nut wrench to loosen and disconnect both power steering hydraulic lines from the control valve (**Figure 10**). Cap the lines and plug the control valve fittings to prevent leakage and the entry of contamination. Secure the lines at a point higher than the engine power steering pump during the

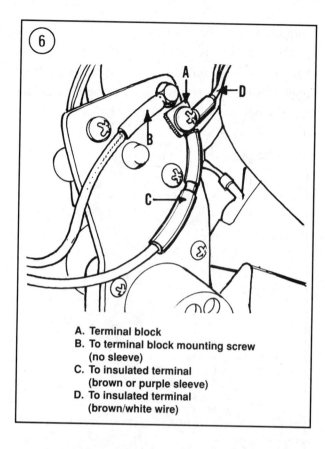

A. Terminal block
B. To terminal block mounting screw (no sleeve)
C. To insulated terminal (brown or purple sleeve)
D. To insulated terminal (brown/white wire)

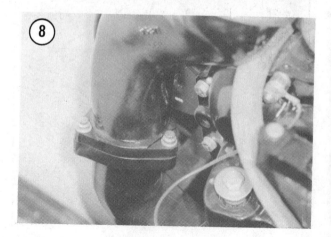

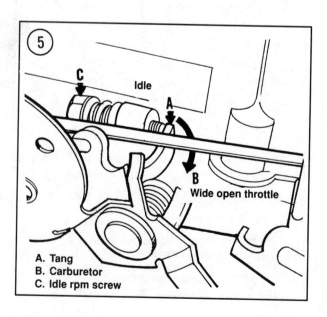

A. Tang
B. Carburetor
C. Idle rpm screw

remainder of this procedure to prevent damage or the loss of fluid.

16. Attach a suitable hoist to the engine lifting eyes. The hoist must have a minimum lift capacity of 1,500 lb. Raise the hoist enough to remove all slack.

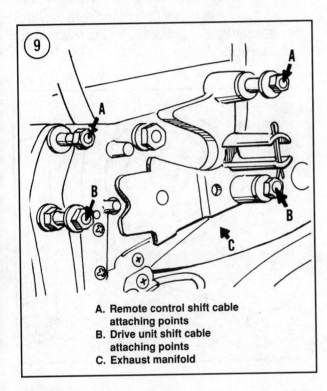

A. Remote control shift cable attaching points
B. Drive unit shift cable attaching points
C. Exhaust manifold

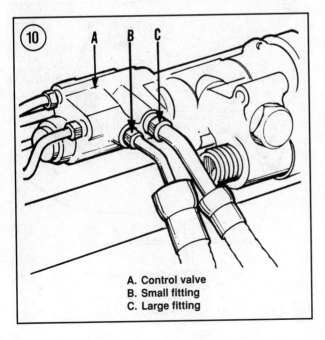

A. Control valve
B. Small fitting
C. Large fitting

NOTE
At this point, there should be no hoses, wires or linkage connecting the engine to the boat or stern drive unit. Recheck this to make sure nothing will hamper engine removal.

17. Unbolt the rear (**Figure 11**) and front (**Figure 12**) engine mounts from the boat.

18. Remove the engine from the boat with the hoist.

ENGINE INSTALLATION

1. Wipe the engine coupler splines with Quicksilver Engine Coupler Spline Grease.

7

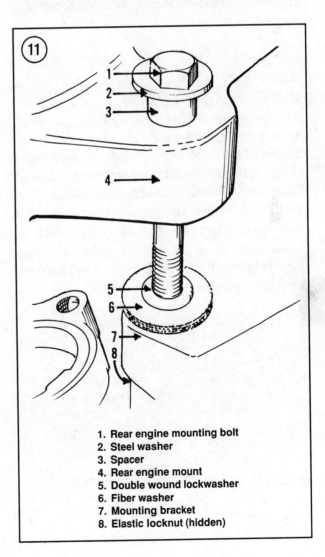

1. Rear engine mounting bolt
2. Steel washer
3. Spacer
4. Rear engine mount
5. Double wound lockwasher
6. Fiber washer
7. Mounting bracket
8. Elastic locknut (hidden)

2. Use guide bolts to align the engine to the bell housing. It may be necessary to rotate the crankshaft slightly to align the engine coupler spines with the drive shaft. You may also rotate the drive shaft by placing the outdrive in forward gear and rotating the propeller.

3. Fit a large fiber washer on top of each transom plate engine support, then install a double wound lockwasher inside each fiber washer. See **Figure 13**.

4. Install hose clamps on the rubber exhaust elbow bellows and position bellows over the exhaust manifold outlet. Lower the engine over the transom plate mounting brackets. Let rear engine mounts rest on the transom plate engine supports but do not remove the hoist tension.

> *CAUTION*
> *Elastic stop nuts should never be used more than twice. It is a good idea to replace such nuts with new ones each time they are removed. Never use worn-out stop nuts or non-locking nuts.*

5. Install one steel washer and spacer on each rear mount bolt. Install bolts downward through the engine mounts, washers and brackets. See **Figure 12**. Thread a new elastic stop nut on each bolt and tighten to 35-40 ft.-lb. (47-54 N•m).

6. Reinstall upper exhaust pipe to lower exhaust pipe (**Figure 8**). Reattach exhaust bellows and tighten clamps securely (**Figure 7**).

7. Install front engine mount fasteners (**Figure 12**) and tighten securely.

> *CAUTION*
> *If the alignment tool specified in Step 8 is not available, take the boat to a MerCruiser dealer for proper alignment. Drive shaft/coupling spline misalignment can cause serious damage.*

8. Check engine and drive unit alignment as follows:

  a. Modify alignment tool part No. C-91-57797A3 as shown in **Figure 14**.

  b. Coat the solid end of the tool with Quicksilver 2-4-C Multi-Lube and insert it from outside the boat through the U-joint bellows into the gimbal bearing (**Figure 15**).

  c. Index the bearing and drive shaft with the engine coupler splines. If indexing is difficult, raise or lower the engine with the hoist as required to permit indexing with no resistance.

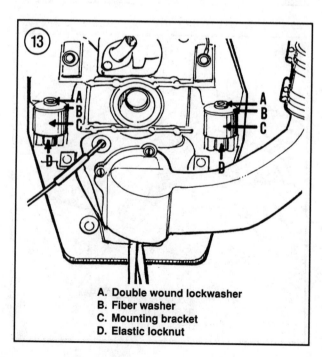

A. Double wound lockwasher
B. Fiber washer
C. Mounting bracket
D. Elastic locknut

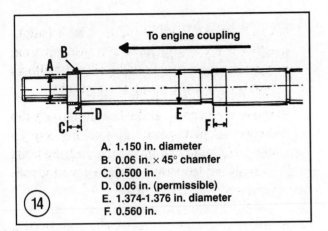

To engine coupling

A. 1.150 in. diameter
B. 0.06 in. × 45° chamfer
C. 0.500 in.
D. 0.06 in. (permissible)
E. 1.374-1.376 in. diameter
F. 0.560 in.

(14)

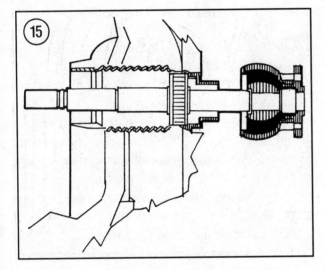

(15)

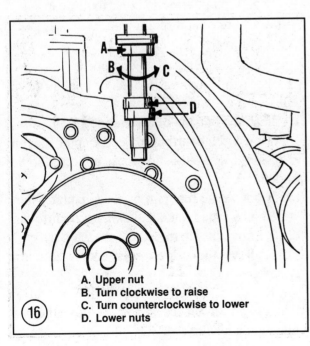

A. Upper nut
B. Turn clockwise to raise
C. Turn counterclockwise to lower
D. Lower nuts

(16)

d. Loosen the locknuts on the front engine mount (**Figure 16**) and thread the adjusting nut up or down as required to properly position the front of the engine to maintain the desired alignment.

e. Tighten the locknuts securely, then recheck alignment by repeating sub-step b.

9. Install water inlet hose to water inlet tube and tighten hose clamp securely.

10. Reconnect shift interlock wires, trim position sender wires and power trim pump leads, if so equipped. Reconnect instrument harness to engine harness.

11. Uncap and reconnect the fuel line to the fuel pump (**Figure 2**).

12. Reconnect drive unit and remote control shift cables (**Figure 9**).

13. Attach and adjust the throttle cable as follows:

a. With the remote control in NEUTRAL (idle position), fasten the cable end guide as shown in **Figure 3** (165/170/3.7L) or **Figure 4** (180/190/3.7LX).

b. Hold the throttle cable brass barrel and push the cable toward the throttle lever adjusting the barrel to align with the anchor stud. Tighten the fasteners securely (do not overtighten) to hold the barrel in place. See **Figure 3** (165/170/3.7L) or **Figure 4** (180/190/3.7LX).

c. Place the remote control in the full throttle position and make sure the throttle valves are completely open. The lever tang should rest against the stop as shown in **Figure 3** (165/170/3.7L) or **Figure 5** (180/190/3.7LX).

d. Model 165/170—Check wide-open throttle stop screw with throttle valves completely open. Loosen the set nut and rotate the screw until it barely contacts the stop, then rotate it another 1/4 turn and tighten the set nut.

e. Place the remote control back in NEUTRAL (idle position) and make sure the idle

7

stop screw rests against the stop. See **Figure 3** (165/170/3.7L) or **Figure 5** (180/190/3.7LX). If it does not, repeat this procedure.

CAUTION
In the next step, the small fitting is tightened to inch-pounds, not foot-pounds.

14. Tighten large power steering fitting to 20-25 ft.-lb. (27-34 N·m). Tighten small fitting to 96-108 in.-lb. (11-12 N·m). Bleed the power steering system. See Chapter Seventeen.

15. Connect any ground leads or accessories that were disconnected during removal.

16. Fill the engine with an oil recommended in Chapter Four.

17. Fill the cooling system, if equipped with a closed system. See Chapter Five.

18. Adjust the drive belts. See Chapter Ten.

19. Adjust the timing as required. See Chapter Four.

DISASSEMBLY CHECKLISTS

To use the checklists, remove and inspect each part in the order mentioned. To reassemble, go through the checklists backwards, installing the parts in order. Each major part is covered in its own section in this chapter, unless otherwise noted.

Decarbonizing or Valve Service

1. Remove the valve cover.
2. Remove the intake and exhaust manifolds.
3. Remove the rocker arm assemblies.
4. Remove the cylinder head.
5. Remove and inspect the valves. Inspect the valve guides and seats, repairing or replacing as required.
6. Assemble by reversing Steps 1-5.

Valve and Ring Service

1. Perform Steps 1-5 of *Decarbonizing or Valve Service*.
2. Remove the oil pan and oil pump.
3. Remove the pistons and connecting rods.
4. Remove the piston rings. It is not necessary to separate the pistons from the connecting rods unless a piston, connecting rod or piston pin needs repair or replacement.
5. Assemble by reversing Steps 1-4.

General Overhaul

1. Remove the engine from the boat.
2. Remove the flywheel.
3. Remove the mount brackets and oil pressure sending unit from the engine.
4. If available, mount the engine on an engine stand. These can be rented from equipment rental dealers. The stand is not absolutely necessary, but it will make the job much easier.
5. Remove the following accessories or components from the engine, if present:
    a. Alternator and mounting bracket
    b. Power steering pump and mounting bracket
    c. Spark plug wires and distributor cap
    d. Carburetor and fuel lines
    e. Oil dipstick and tube
    f. Seawater pump, if so equipped
6. Check the engine for signs of coolant or oil leaks.
7. Clean the outside of the engine.
8. Remove the distributor. See Chapter Eleven.
9. Remove all hoses and tubes connected to the engine.
10. Remove the fuel pump. See Chapter Nine.
11. Remove the intake and exhaust manifolds.
12. Remove the thermostat. See Chapter Ten.
13. Remove the valve cover and rocker arm assemblies.
14. Remove the crankshaft pulley/vibration damper and timing case cover. Remove the timing chain and sprockets.

15. Remove the camshaft.

16. Remove the cylinder head.

17. Remove the oil pan and oil pump.

18. Remove the pistons and connecting rods.

19. Remove the crankshaft.

20. Inspect the cylinder block.

21. Assemble by reversing Steps 1-19.

VALVE COVER

Removal/Installation

It may be necessary to remove the throttle cable on some models to provide sufficient clearance for valve cover removal.

1. Disconnect the crankcase ventilation hose at the valve cover.

2. Disconnect the spark plug cables at the plugs. Unclip or detach any wires or wire looms attached to the valve cover.

3. Remove any other accessory unit that might interfere with valve cover removal.

4. Remove the cover attaching fasteners and load spreaders, if used.

5. Rap the valve cover with a soft-faced mallet to break the gasket seal. Remove the valve cover. Discard the gasket.

6. Clean any gasket residue from the cylinder head and valve cover with degreaser and a putty knife.

7. Coat one side of a new gasket with an oil-resistant sealer. Install the gasket sealer-side down in the valve cover. Make sure the gasket tabs engage the cover notches.

8. Position the valve cover on the cylinder head.

9. Install the attaching fasteners (with load spreaders, if used) and tighten to specifications (**Table 2**).

10. Install the spark plug cable retainers on the valve cover brackets. Connect the wires to the appropriate spark plugs. See Chapter Four.

11. Install the crankcase ventilation hose in the valve cover.

INTAKE MANIFOLD

Removal/Installation

Refer to **Figure 17**, typical for this procedure.

1. Disconnect the negative battery cable.

2. Disconnect the crankcase ventilation hose from the valve cover.

3. Remove the flame arrestor.

4. Open the cylinder block water drains and allow all water to drain. Disconnect the water hoses from the manifold.

5. Disconnect the throttle cable linkage from the carburetor.

6. Disconnect the choke cover wire and fuel pump vent tube from the carburetor.

7. Disconnect the fuel line from the carburetor. Plug the line and fitting to prevent leakage and the entry of contamination.

8. Loosen and remove the intake manifold fasteners. Pry the manifold loose and remove it from the engine block. Remove and discard the intake manifold gasket.

9. Remove the carburetor as required. If carburetor is removed, use a new gasket when reinstalled.

10. Clean all gasket residue from the cylinder head and intake manifold with degreaser and a putty knife.

11. If the intake manifold is being replaced, transfer the carburetor and other hardware as required.

12. Coat both sides of a new intake manifold gasket with Quicksilver Perfect Seal. Install gasket on the cylinder head.

13. Position the intake manifold on the cylinder head.

14. Install the manifold attaching fasteners with flat washers. Tighten the manifold fasteners to specification (**Table 2**) working from the center to the ends.

15. The remainder of installation is the reverse of removal. Coat all electrical connections with Quicksilver Neoprene Dip. Pressure test the cooling system (Chapter Ten).

7

Inspection

1. Check the intake manifold for cracks or distortion. Replace if distorted or if cracks are found.

2. Check the mating surfaces for nicks or burrs. Small burrs may be removed with an oilstone.

3. Place a straightedge across the manifold flange/mating surfaces. If there is any gap between the straightedge and surface, measure it with a flat feeler gauge. Measure each manifold from end to end and from corner to corner. If the mating surface is not flat within 0.006 in. (0.15 mm) per foot of manifold length, replace the manifold.

4. Check manifold for stripped or damaged studs, drain plug and stud hole threads. Repair or replace as required.

5. Check for proper head/block alignment on the intake manifold side. There should be no more than a 0.020 in. (0.05 mm) gap between the face of the block and the face of the cylinder head. If the gap is excessive, either replace the head gasket and reposition the head to bring the

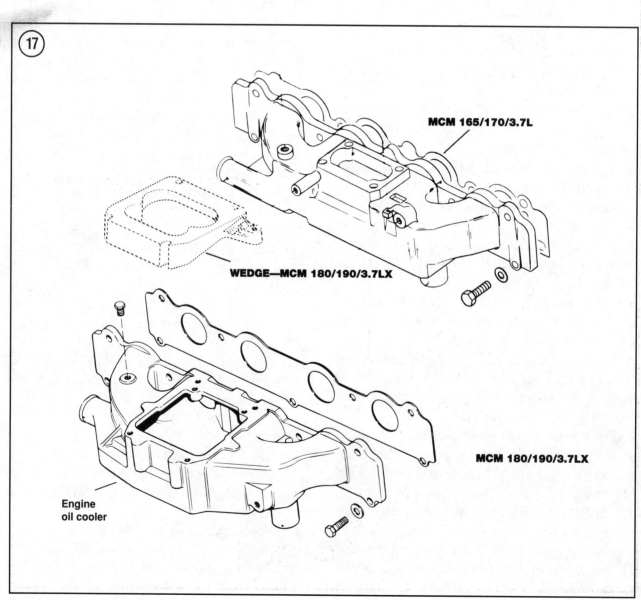

(17)

MCM 165/170/3.7L

WEDGE—MCM 180/190/3.7LX

MCM 180/190/3.7LX

Engine oil cooler

gap within specification or apply RTV sealant on the low surface and install a new intake manifold gasket.

EXHAUST MANIFOLD

Removal/Installation

All 1989-on models with thru transom exhaust are equipped with mufflers as standard equip-ment to reduce exhaust noise. The mufflers are installed between the exhaust elbows and tran-som and are easily disassembled for replacement or cleaning of the internal element.

Refer to **Figure 18**, typical for this procedure.

1. Disconnect the negative battery cable.
2. Drain both engine coolant systems. See Chapter Five.

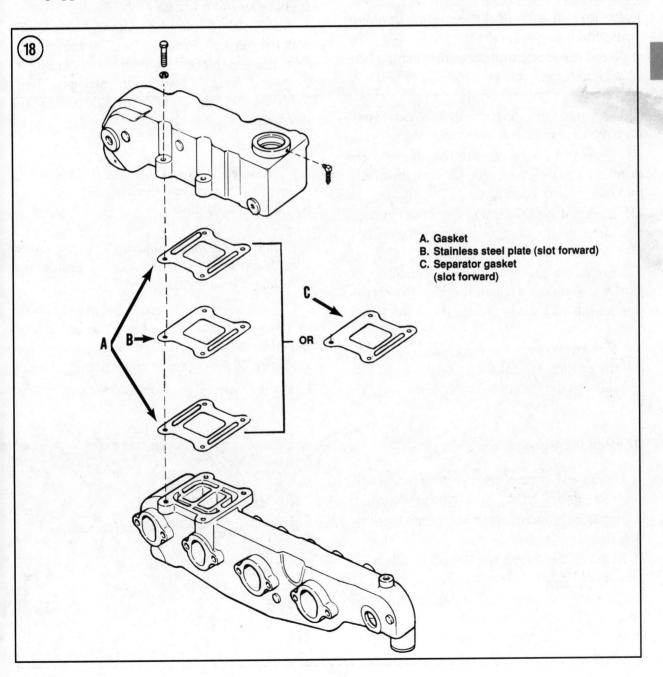

A. Gasket
B. Stainless steel plate (slot forward)
C. Separator gasket
   (slot forward)

3. Disconnect the temperature sending unit lead at the thermostat housing.

4. Disconnect all hoses and exhaust bellows from the manifold.

5. Drain the engine crankcase. See Chapter Four.

6. Unscrew the oil dipstick tube at the oil pan fitting. Remove the bracket attaching bolt. Remove the oil dipstick tube.

7. Remove all wiring harness clamps from the manifold.

8. Remove both shift cables from the shift plate located on the exhaust manifold. See **Figure 9**, typical.

9. Disconnect the shift interlock switch wires from the terminal block, if so equipped.

10. Support the exhaust manifold. Remove the manifold attaching fasteners. Remove the manifold and discard the gasket.

11. Clean all gasket residue from the cylinder head and manifold mating surfaces with degreaser and a putty knife.

12. Install the manifold on the cylinder head with a new gasket. Tighten fasteners to specification (**Table 2**), working from the center to the ends.

13. Reverse Steps 1-9 to complete installation. Fill the cooling system to the proper level and pressure test the system (Chapter Ten).

Disassembly/Reassembly

1. Unbolt and separate the exhaust elbow from the reservoir assembly. Discard the gasket(s).

2. Remove the thermostat housing and thermostat. Discard the gasket.

3. Remove the temperature sender and brass plug from the distribution housing.

4. Assembly is the reverse of disassembly. Use new gaskets and wipe the temperature sender/brass plug threads with Quicksilver Perfect Seal.

Inspection/Cleaning

1. Inspect the engine exhaust ports for excessive rust or corrosion. Replace manifold if excessive corrosion is present.

2. Check water passage from exhaust elbow for clogging.

3. Remove pipe plugs from the manifold and exhaust elbow, if so equipped. Check for sand, silt or other foreign matter.

4. Install elbow/reservoir assembly to manifold with new gaskets. Plug or seal all openings (except seawater inlet/outlet) with hoses, clamps or plugs and pressure test the unit (Chapter Ten) following the pressure tester manufacturer's instructions.

ROCKER ARM ASSEMBLIES

Removal/Installation

Each rocker arm (A, **Figure 19**) moves on its own fulcrum (B). The rocker arm and fulcrum are retained by a bolt (C).

It is not necessary to remove the rocker arm for pushrod replacement; simply loosen the bolt and move the arm away from the pushrod. Refer to **Figure 20** for complete removal procedure.

1. Remove the valve cover as described in this chapter.

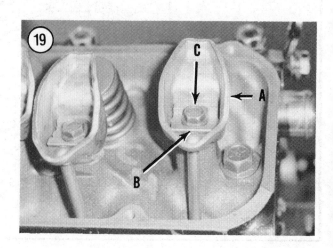

2. Remove each rocker arm/pushrod assembly. Place each assembly in a separate container or use as a rack to keep them separated for reinstallation in the same position from which they were removed.

NOTE
When installing new valve lifters, rocker arms or rocker arm fulcrums, coat the contact surfaces with engine oil, Molykote or GM EOS (engine oil supplement).

4. Lubricate the rocker arms and pivot balls with engine oil.

5. Install the pushrods, making sure that each fits into its lifter socket.

6. Install the rocker arms, fulcrums and bolts.

NOTE
Rocker arm bolt tightening and valve clearance checking both require the valve to be in the closed position. Both can be performed at the same time to reduce the time and effort required.

7

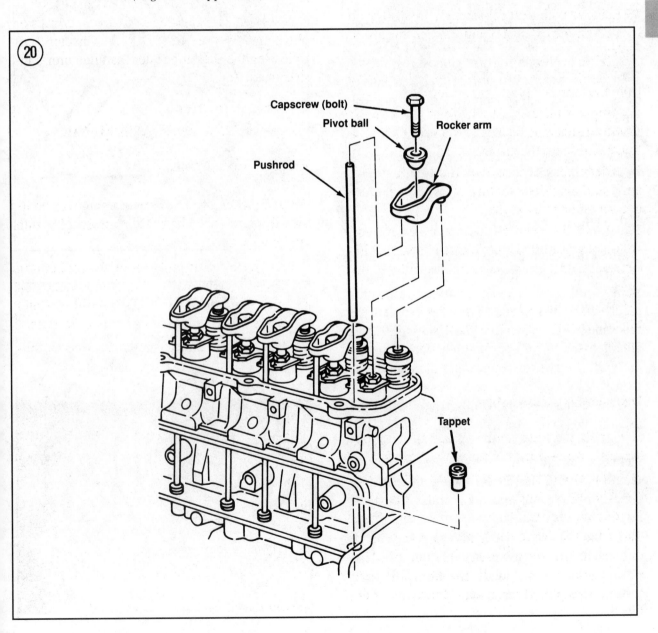

7. Check valve clearance as described in this chapter.

8. Install the rocker arm cover as described in this chapter.

Inspection

1. Clean all parts with solvent and use compressed air to blow out the oil passages in the pushrods.

2. Check each rocker arm, fulcrum, bolt and pushrod for scuffing, pitting or excessive wear; replace as required. If one component is worn, replace all components servicing that valve.

3. Check pushrods for straightness by rolling them across a flat, even surface such as a pane of glass. Replace any pushrods that do not roll smoothly.

4. If a pushrod is worn from lack of lubrication, replace the corresponding lifter and rocker arm as well.

Valve Clearance Check

Stem-to-rocker arm clearance must be within specification when the hydraulic lifter is completely collapsed. If valve clearance is insufficient, the valve opens early and closes late, resulting in a rough engine idle. Excessive clearance lets the valve open too late and close too early, causing valve bounce and damage to the camshaft lobe.

Valve adjustment is required only when the cylinder head valve train has been disassembled. Valves are not adjustable, but proper clearance can be maintained by installing the appropriate length pushrod. Use the following procedure to check valve clearance and determine if pushrod replacement is required.

1. Rotate the crankshaft until the pulley notch aligns with the zero mark on the timing tab. This positions the No. 1 cylinder at TDC. This position can be verified by placing a finger on the No. 1 rocker arms as the pulley notch nears the

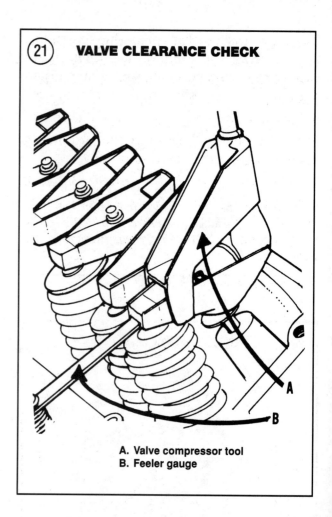

(21) **VALVE CLEARANCE CHECK**

A. Valve compressor tool
B. Feeler gauge

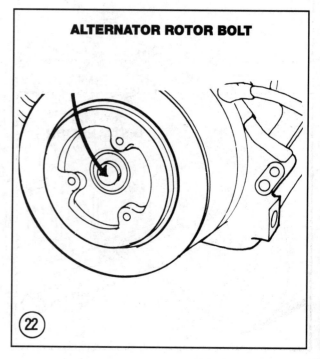

ALTERNATOR ROTOR BOLT

(22)

zero mark. If the valves are moving, the engine is in the No. 4 firing position; rotate the crankshaft pulley one full turn to reach the No. 1 firing position.

2. Install valve lifter collapsing tool T711P-6513A as shown in **Figure 21** and push firmly on tool handle until lifter is fully collapsed.

3. With valve closed and lifter fully collapsed, check clearance between valve stem and rocker arm with a flat feeler gauge and compare to specification in **Table 1** *Check the following valves:*

a. No. 1, 2 and 4 intake

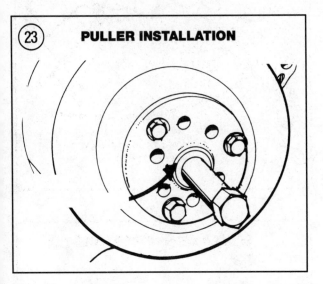

PULLER INSTALLATION

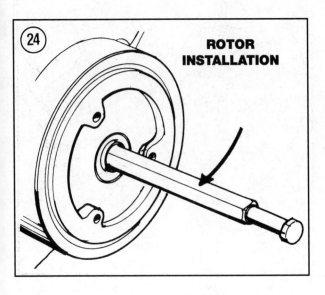

ROTOR INSTALLATION

b. No. 1 and 3 exhaust

4. Rotate the crankshaft one full revolution and repeat Step 2 and Step 3 to check the following valves:

a. No. 2 and 4 exhaust

b. No. 3 intake

5. If clearance of any valve is not within specification, check for worn valve train components. If worn components are not present, install a pushrod of the length required to bring valve clearance within specification (**Table 1**). If clearance is excessive, install a longer pushrod. If clearance is insufficient, install a shorter pushrod. See your dealer for pushrod selection.

6. Install the valve cover as described in this chapter.

ALTERNATOR ROTOR/STATOR

Rotor Removal/Installation

On some installations, it may be necessary to remove the front engine mount assembly before attempting to remove the rotor.

1. Remove the drive belt (Chapter Ten).

2. Remove the bolt and washer from the center of the rotor (**Figure 22**).

3. Apply grease to the end of puller part No. J-6978-04 or equivalent. Install puller to rotor hub as shown in **Figure 23** and remove the rotor.

4. Lubricate the seal lip and inside of rotor surface where seal rides with engine oil.

5. Make sure rotor locating key is properly installed in the crankshaft groove.

6. Lubricate the end of the crankshaft and ID of the rotor with Chicago Manufacturing and Distribution Company antiscoring, extreme pressure Lubricant No. 3, or equivalent.

7. Position rotor on crankshaft end and align rotor key slot with the crankshaft key.

8. Install tool part No. J-21058-20 on end of crankshaft (**Figure 24**). Hold center shaft of tool with a wrench and turn outer shaft with a second

7

wrench until the rotor bottoms out on the crankshaft.

9. Install the bolt with washer in the center of
the rotor and tighten to specifications (**Table 2**).

10. Reinstall and adjust the alternator drive belt.
See Chapter Ten.

Stator Removal/Installation

1. Remove the alternator rotor as described in
this chapter.

2. Disconnect the stator electrical leads from the
regulator.

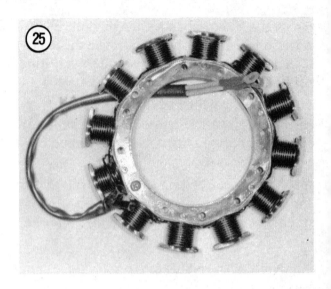

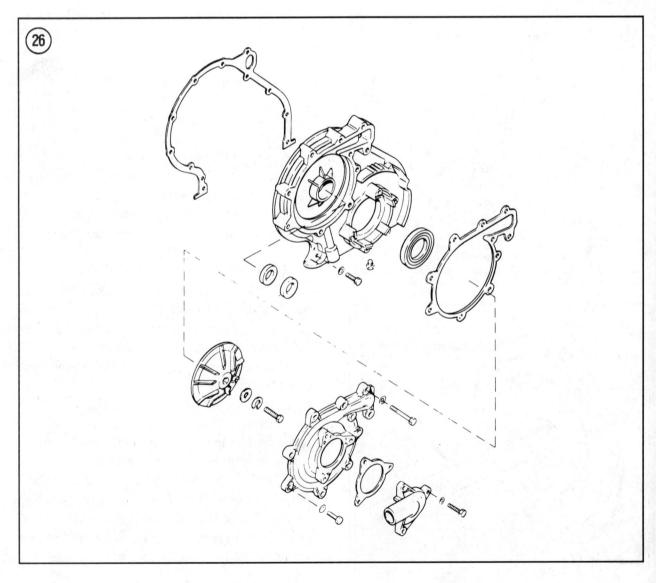

3. Remove the stator wire harness from the clamp.

4. Remove the stator attaching screws. Remove the stator (**Figure 25**).

5. Installation is the reverse of removal. Output wires must face toward cover recess. Wipe at-

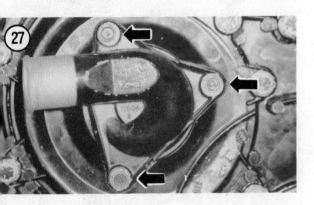

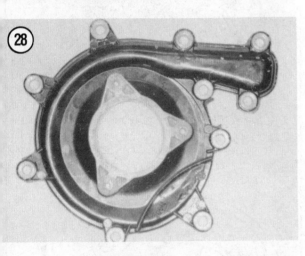

taching screw threads with Quicksilver Perfect Seal and tighten to specification (**Table 2**).

FRONT COVER, SEALS AND CIRCULATING PUMP

Removal/Installation

It is possible in many cases to perform this procedure without removing the engine from the boat, providing there is sufficient access and you are careful in cutting the oil pan gasket in Step 6. If the engine is out of the boat, remove the oil pan as described in this chapter as a first step and omit those steps describing oil pan gasket cutting and replacement.

Refer to **Figure 26** for this procedure.

1 Remove the alternator rotor and stator as described in this chapter.

2. Remove the 2 screws holding the front of the oil pan to the front cover.

3. Remove the water inlet housing (**Figure 27**).

4. Remove the pump impeller cover (**Figure 28**).

5. Remove the pump impeller fastener (**Figure 29**) or unscrew the impeller (left-hand threads) from the impeller stud. Remove the impeller assembly.

NOTE
*On late models, water pump impeller screws onto a stud that is screwed into the camshaft. Impeller, stud and camshaft have **left-hand** threads. Remove the impeller by placing the appropriate size wrench onto the hub of the impeller and turning in a clockwise direction. If removed, impeller stud should be secured to camshaft using Loctite type 271 and tightened to specification in **Table 2**.*

6. Use a sharp X-acto knife to cut the oil pan seal flush with the cylinder block face.

7. Remove the front cover bolts. Remove the cover (**Figure 30**), cover gasket and cut portion of the oil pan gasket. Discard the cover gasket. Retain the pan gasket segment for use as a template in Step 13.

7

8. Support the cover and drive out the crankshaft oil seal and both water pump shaft seals (arrows, **Figure 30**).

9. Clean the gasket mounting surfaces on the block and cover with degreaser and a putty knife.

10. Coat the OD of new water pump shaft and front cover oil seals with Loctite Type 242, taking care that it does not touch the seal lips.

11. Support the underside of the cover and install each seal with its lips facing away from engine block and toward the impeller. Press the first water pump seal in the cover until it bottoms; press the second seal in until it is flush with the cover surface. Fill the cavity between the seals with Quicksilver 2-4-C Multi-Lube.

13. Use the cut portion of the oil pan gasket as a template and cut a matching section from a new gasket for use in Step 14.

14. Coat the exposed surface of the oil pan flange with Perfect Seal and install the gasket portion cut in Step 13. Coat the exposed gasket surface with Perfect Seal.

15. Apply a 1/8 in. (3.2 mm) bead of Quicksilver RTV sealant along the joint on each side where the oil pan meets the block.

16. Position a new front cover gasket on the cylinder block dowel pins.

17. Position the front cover on the engine block. Work carefully to prevent damage to the gasket or movements of the oil pan gasket segment.

18. Wipe front cover bolt threads with Perfect Seal and install bolts. Tighten to specification (**Table 2**).

19. Apply downward pressure on the cover and install the oil pan attaching screws finger-tight.

20. Coat the attaching bolt threads with Perfect Seal and install the bolts. Tighten bolts and oil pan screws to specification (**Table 2**).

21A. *Early models*—Install the water pump impeller on the shaft. Tighten the attaching bolt to specification (**Table 2**).

21B. *Late models*—Screw impeller onto impeller stud and tighten to specification (**Table 2**). Note that impeller has *left-hand* threads.

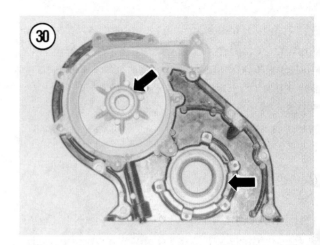

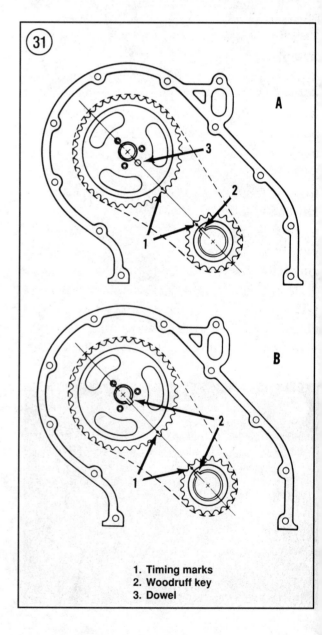

1. Timing marks
2. Woodruff key
3. Dowel

22. Install the water pump cover with a new gasket. Coat bolt threads with Perfect Seal and tighten bolts to specifications (**Table 2**).

23. Install the alternator stator and rotor as described in this chapter.

TIMING CHAIN AND SPROCKETS

Removal/Installation

1. Drain the cooling system. See Chapter Five.

2. Drain the crankcase oil and remove the spark plugs. See Chapter Four.

3. Remove the alternator rotor, stator and front cover as described in this chapter.

4. Temporarily reinstall the rotor bolt and washer in the end of the crankshaft. Place a wrench on the bolt and rotate the crankshaft to position the camshaft and crankshaft sprocket marks as shown in **Figure 31**.

5. Rotate the crankshaft clockwise (as seen from front of engine) to take up the slack on the left-hand side of the chain.

6. Pick a convenient reference point on the engine block and measure from that point to the chain. Record your measurement.

7. Rotate the crankshaft counterclockwise to take up the slack on the right-hand side of the chain. Force the left-hand side of the chain outward with your fingers, then measure the distance between the reference point and the chain. Remove the rotor bolt and washer.

8. Subtract the smaller measurement from the larger one. If the difference or deflection exceeds 1 in. (25.4 mm), replace the chain.

9. Remove the chain tensioner (A, **Figure 32**).

10. Remove the 3 camshaft sprocket screws (B, **Figure 32**).

11. Pull sprockets and chain forward as an assembly and remove from the camshaft and crankshaft. Disassemble the chain and sprockets.

12. Assemble the chain and sprockets with the sprocket timing marks aligned (**Figure 31**).

13. Install the sprocket/chain assembly to the crankshaft and camshaft. Use a straightedge to make sure the timing marks are properly aligned, then install the camshaft sprocket screws and tighten to specification (**Table 2**).

14. Install chain tensioner, then lubricate the chain, tensioner and sprockets with engine oil.

15. Reverse Steps 1-3 to complete installation.

Cleaning and Inspection

1. Clean all components in fresh solvent and blow dry with compressed air, if available.

2. Check chain for worn or broken links.

3. Check sprockets for cracks, scoring, nicks or worn/damaged teeth.

4. Check tensioner for excessive wear or damage. If chain deflection is within specification in Step 8 of *Removal/Installation* but tensioner does not touch the chain, replace the tensioner.

5. Inspect tensioner grooves for excessive wear and replace as required.

6. Place tensioner on a flat surface and measure to the highest point on its top. If not at least 1 1/4 in. (32 mm), replace the tensioner.

CAMSHAFT

Removal/Installation

1. Crank the engine over until the No. 1 piston is at the top of its compression stroke. The timing

mark on the pulley/damper will align with the TDC mark on the timing chain cover and the distributor rotor will point to the No. 1 spark plug terminal in the distributor cap.

2. Remove the valve cover as described in this chapter.

3. Remove the alternator rotor, stator and front cover as described in this chapter.

4. Remove the fuel pump. See Chapter Nine.

5. Remove the pushrod cover (**Figure 33**) and discard the gasket. Remove and discard the O-rings from the pushrod cover bolts.

6. Loosen the rocker arm bolts enough to swivel the arms off the pushrods and remove the pushrods. Identify each pushrod for reinstallation in its original location.

7. Remove the valve lifters with a pencil-type magnet. Place them in a rack in order of removal for reinstallation in their original locations.

8. Remove the timing chain and sprockets as described in this chapter.

9. Remove the camshaft thrust plate.

> *CAUTION*
> *Do not cock the camshaft during re-moval. This can damage the camshaft or its bearing bores in the block.*

10. Carefully withdraw the camshaft from the front of the engine with a rotating motion to avoid damage to the bearing bores.

11. Installation is the reverse of removal. Coat the camshaft lobes with General Motors Engine Oil Supplement (or equivalent) and the journals with heavy engine oil before reinstalling in the block. Use a new pushrod cover gasket and new O-rings on the cover bolts. Check camshaft end play as described in this chapter.

Inspection

1. Check the journals and lobes for signs of wear or scoring. Lobe pitting in the toe area is not sufficient reason for replacement unless the lobe lift loss exceeds specification.

> *NOTE*
> *If you do not have precision measuring equipment, have Step 2 done by a machine shop.*

2. Measure the camshaft journal diameters with a micrometer (**Figure 34**) and compare to specifications (**Table 1**). Replace the camshaft if any journal exceeds 0.001 in. (0.025 mm) out-of-round.

3. Suspend the camshaft between V-blocks and check for warpage with a dial indicator. See **Figure 35**. Replace camshaft if the runout is greater than 0.002 in. (0.051 mm).

4. Check the distributor drive gear for excessive wear or damage.

5. Check the camshaft gear and thrust plate for wear or damage.

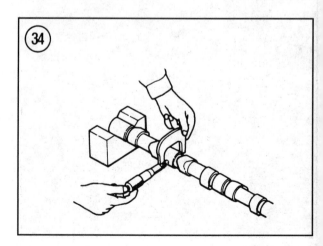

Lobe Lift Measurement

Camshaft lobe lift can be measured with the camshaft in the block and the cylinder head in place. The lifters must be bled down slowly in Step 6 or the readings will be incorrect.

1. Remove the valve cover as described in this chapter.

2. Remove the rocker arm assemblies as described in this chapter.

3. Remove the spark plugs. See Chapter Four.

4. Install a dial indicator on the end of a pushrod. A piece of rubber tubing will hold the dial indicator plunger in place on the center of the pushrod. See **Figure 36**, typical.

5. Rotate the crankshaft in the normal direction of rotation until the valve lifter seats on the heel or base of the cam lobe (**Figure 37**). This positions the pushrod at its lowest point.

6. Set the dial indicator at zero, then slowly rotate the crankshaft until the pushrod reaches its

7

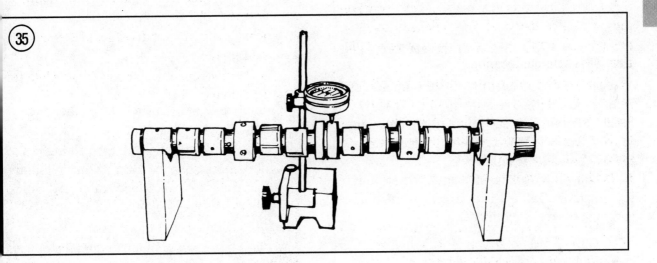

(35)

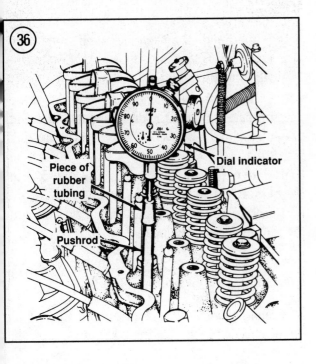

(36)

Dial indicator

Piece of rubber tubing

Pushrod

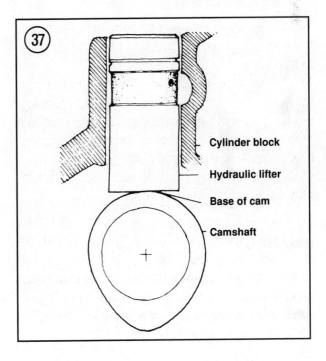

(37)

Cylinder block

Hydraulic lifter

Base of cam

Camshaft

maximum travel. Note the indicator reading and compare to specification (**Table 1**).

7. Repeat Steps 4-6 for each pushrod. If all lobes are within specification in Step 6, reinstall the rocker arm assemblies as described in this chapter.

8. If one or more lobes are worn beyond specification, replace the camshaft as described in this chapter.

9. Remove the dial indicator and reverse Steps 1-3.

End Play Measurement

End play is checked with the sprockets and timing chain installed.

1. Install a dial indicator with its plunger contacting the camshaft gear face.

2. Pry the camshaft back and forth using a large screwdriver behind the camshaft sprocket. Note the dial indicator reading.

3. If end play reading in Step 2 is not within specification (**Table 1**), replace the thrust plate and/or sprocket as required.

Bearing Replacement

This procedure requires special tools and skills. If you don't have them, have it done by a dealer or machine shop.

The camshaft rotates directly in its bores in the aluminum cylinder block. Bearings are not normally used, but if one or more bore surfaces become scratched or damaged, all bores can be enlarged to 2.2495-2.2510 in. diameter and bearings installed (**Figure 38**).

Bearing installation tool kit (part No. T65L-6250-A) and service bearings can be obtained from your MerCruiser dealer. Align bore the block and install the bearings according to the procedure included with the tool kit instructions. Make sure the bearing oil holes align with the oil holes in the block. After installation, have the ID of all bearings bored to 2.1258-2.1268 in.

OIL PAN

Ease of oil pan removal will depend upon the installation within a given boat. In some cases, the oil pan can be removed without removing the engine. In others, engine removal will be required to provide sufficient working space and clearance for oil pan removal.

A modification kit is available from marine dealers to assist in draining the oil when the engine is in the boat. This kit can be installed on any engine oil pan when the engine is removed for service.

Removal

1A. If the engine is in the boat:
   a. Remove the oil dipstick and siphon the oil from the crankcase. See Chapter Four.
   b. Unscrew the oil dipstick tube fitting at the oil pan. Remove the dipstick tube retaining clamp at the block. Remove the oil dipstick tube.

1B. If the engine is out of the boat:
   a. Place a suitable container under the oil pan drain plug. Remove the plug and let the crankcase drain. Reinstall the drain plug.
   b. If mounted in an engine stand, rotate the engine 180° to place the oil pan in an upright position.
   c. Unscrew the oil dipstick tube fitting at the oil pan. Remove the dipstick tube retaining clamp at the block. Remove the oil dipstick tube.

2. Remove the oil pan attaching screws and washers. Remove the oil pan.

3. Remove and discard the oil pan gasket and the rear main cap seals.

Inspection and Cleaning

1. Clean any gasket residue from the oil pan rail on the engine block, rear main bearing cap, front

cover and the oil pan sealing flange with de-greaser and a putty knife.

2. Clean the pan thoroughly in solvent and check for dents or warped gasket surfaces. Straighten or replace the pan as required.

Installation

If timing chain cover is removed for other service, it must be reinstalled before installing the oil pan.

1. Install the rear seals on the rear main bearing cap.

2. Coat the block side rails and oil pan flange with Quicksilver Perfect Seal. Apply additional sealer on the rear main cap seals and area where the timing cover mates with the block.

3. Position a new gasket on the cylinder block gasket surface.

4. Carefully place the oil pan in position. Make sure the gasket and seals are not misaligned and install a pan attaching screw with washer finger-tight on each side of the block.

7

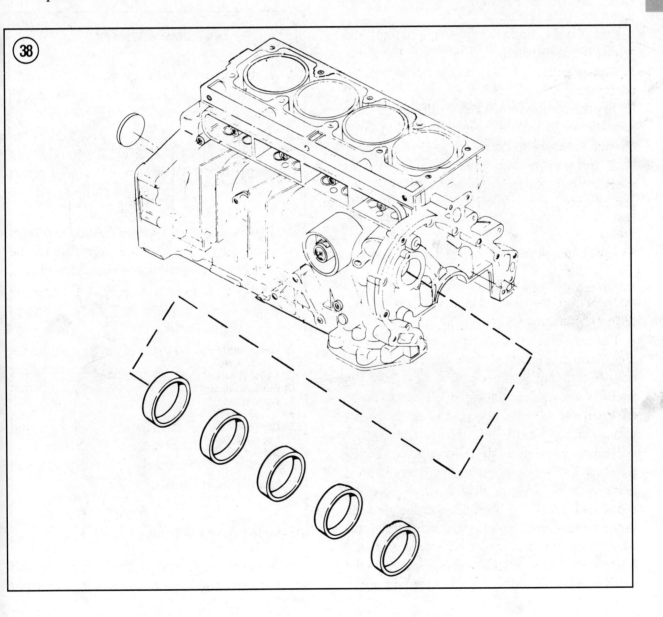

(38)

5. Install the remaining screws with washers and tighten all to specification (**Table 2**). Work from the center outward in each direction. When all pan screws are tightened, retorque a second time.

6. Install the engine in the boat as described in this chapter and fill the crankcase with an oil recommended in Chapter Four.

7. Reinstall the oil dipstick tube.

8. If engine was removed from the boat, reinstall as described in this chapter and fill the crankcase with an oil recommended in Chapter Four.

OIL PUMP

Removal/Installation

1. Remove the oil pan as described in this chapter.

2. Remove the nut and stud/nut holding the oil pump pickup brackets in place (**Figure 39**).

3. Remove the oil pump attaching bolts (**Figure 40**). Remove the oil pump.

4. To install, align the pump gear shaft slot with the distributor drive shaft.

5. Install the pump to the block. Tighten pump and bracket attaching bolts to specification (**Table 2**).

6. Install the oil pan as described in this chapter.

Disassembly/Assembly

Refer to **Figure 41** for this procedure.

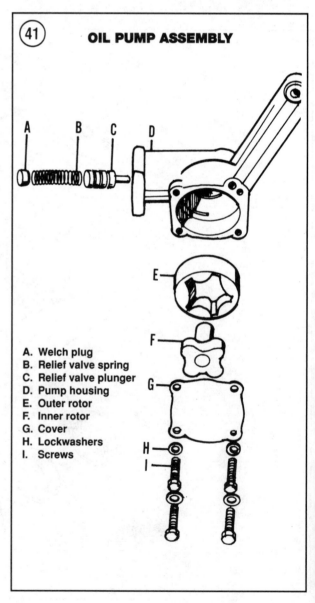

OIL PUMP ASSEMBLY

A. Welch plug
B. Relief valve spring
C. Relief valve plunger
D. Pump housing
E. Outer rotor
F. Inner rotor
G. Cover
H. Lockwashers
I. Screws

1. Remove the 2 bolts holding the pickup tube to the pump body. Remove the pickup tube, retaining flange and O-ring.

2. Remove the cover screws, lockwashers, cover and gasket. Discard the gasket.

3. Remove the inner and outer rotors from the body.

4. Remove the pressure regulator welch plug, spring and valve.

5. Lubricate all parts thoroughly with engine oil before reassembly.

6. Assembly is the reverse of disassembly. Index the gear identification marks, install a new cover gasket and rotate the pump drive shaft by hand to check for smooth operation.

Inspection

NOTE
The pump assembly and gears are serviced as an assembly. If one or the other

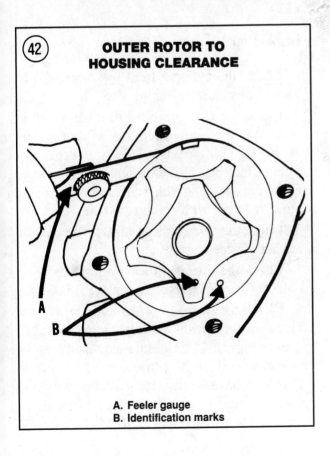

(42) **OUTER ROTOR TO HOUSING CLEARANCE**

A. Feeler gauge
B. Identification marks

is worn or damaged, replace the entire pump.

1. Clean all parts thoroughly in solvent. Brush the inside of the body and the pressure regulator chamber to remove all dirt and metal particles. Dry with compressed air, if available.

2. Check the pump body and cover for cracks or excessive wear.

3. Check the pump gears for damage or excessive wear.

4. Check the drive gear shaft-to-body fit for excessive looseness.

5. Check the inside of the pump cover for wear that could allow oil to leak around the ends of the gears.

6. Check the pressure regulator valve for a proper fit.

7. Install inner and outer rotors in pump body. Measure outer rotor race to housing clearance (**Figure 42**). Replace the pump body if the clearance exceeds 0.0125 in.(0.32 mm).

8. Place a straightedge across the pump rotors and measure any gap with a flat feeler gauge (**Figure 43**). If clearance exceeds 0.005 in. (0.13 mm), replace the pump body.

CYLINDER HEAD

Removal

Perform Steps 1-8 if engine is in boat. If engine has been removed from the boat, begin with Step 9.

1. Open the engine block drain valves and drain all water from the block.

2. Remove the intake and exhaust manifolds as described in this chapter.

3. Disconnect the fuel line support clamps. Remove the fuel line.

4. Disconnect the cooling hoses from the water distribution housing.

5. Disconnect the temperature sending lead and remove the water distribution housing.

6. Disconnect and remove the ignition coil.

7. Remove the circuit breaker bracket and engine lifting eye.

8. Disconnect all spark plug cables. Remove the spark plugs.

9. Remove the valve cover as described in this chapter.

10. Loosen the rocker arms and rotate them to one side. Remove the pushrods and identify each for reinstallation in its original position.

11. Loosen the cylinder head bolts, working from the center of the head to the end in each direction.

12. Remove the head bolts. Rap the end of the head with a soft-faced hammer to break the gasket seal. Remove the head from the engine.

> *CAUTION*
> *Place the head on its side to prevent damage to the spark plugs or head gasket surface.*

13. Remove and discard the head gasket. Clean all gasket residue from the head and block mating surfaces.

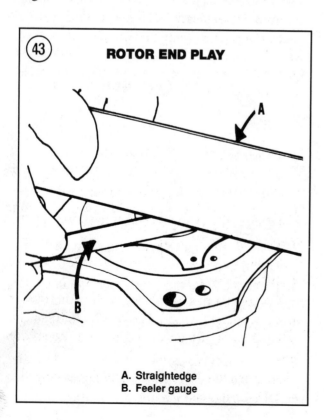

ROTOR END PLAY

A. Straightedge
B. Feeler gauge

Decarbonizing

1. Without removing the valves, remove all deposits from the combustion chambers, intake ports and exhaust ports. Use a fine wire brush dipped in solvent or make a scraper from hardwood. Be careful not to scratch or gouge the combustion chambers.

2. After all carbon is removed from the combustion chambers and ports, clean the entire head in solvent.

3. Clean all carbon from the piston tops. Do not remove the carbon ridge at the top of each cylinder bore.

4. Remove the valves as described in this chapter.

5. Clean the pushrod guides, valve guide bores and all bolt holes. Use a cleaning solvent to remove dirt and grease.

6. Clean the valves with a fine wire brush or buffing wheel.

Inspection

1. Check the cylinder head for signs of oil or water leaks before cleaning.

2. Clean the cylinder head thoroughly in solvent. While cleaning, look for cracks or other visible signs of damage. Look for corrosion or foreign material in the oil and water passages. Clean the passages with a stiff spiral brush, then blow them out with compressed air.

3. Check the cylinder head studs for damage and replace if necessary.

4. Check the threaded rocker arm studs or bolt holes for damaged threads; replace if necessary.

5. Check for warpage of the cylinder head-to-block surface with a straightedge and feeler gauge (**Figure 44**). Measure diagonally, as well as end to end. If the gap exceeds specification (**Table 2**), have the head resurfaced by a machine shop. If head resurfacing is necessary, do not remove more than 0.010 in. (0.25 mm). Replace

the head if a greater amount must be removed to correct warpage.

Installation

1. Make sure the cylinder head and block gasket surfaces and bolts holes are clean. Dirt in the block bolt holes or on the head bolt thread will affect bolt torque.

2. Recheck all visible oil and water passages for cleanliness.

3. Position a new head gasket over the cylinder dowels on the block with the stamped word FRONT facing down at the front of the block.

4. Carefully lower the head onto the cylinder block, engaging the dowel pins.

5. Wipe all head bolt threads and the underside of the bolt heads with Quicksilver Perfect Seal. Install and tighten the head bolts finger-tight.

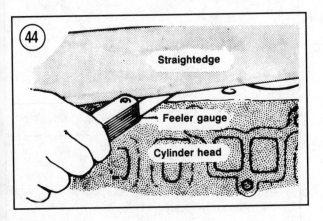

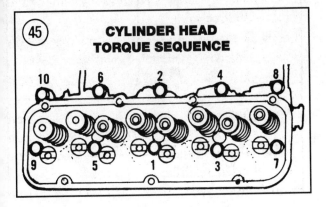

6. Tighten the head bolts to 55 ft.-lb (75 N·m) one at a time following the sequence shown in **Figure 45**.

7. Repeat Step 6 to tighten the head bolts to 90 ft.-lb. (122 N·m), then to 130 ft.-lb (176 N·m).

8. If engine is in boat, reverse Steps 1-10 of *Removal* in this chapter. If engine is out of boat, reverse Step 9 and Step 10 of *Removal* to complete installation.

VALVES AND VALVE SEATS

Some of the following procedures must be done by a dealer or machine shop, since they require special knowledge and expensive machine tools. Others, while possible for the home mechanic, are difficult or time-consuming. A general practice among those who do their own service is to remove the cylinder head, perform all disassembly except valve removal and take the head to a dealer or machine shop for inspection and service. Since the cost is low relative to the required effort and equipment, this is usually the best approach, even for experienced mechanics. The following procedures are given to acquaint the home mechanic with what the dealer or machine shop will do.

Valve Removal

Refer to **Figure 46** for this procedure.

1. Remove the cylinder head as described in this chapter.

2. Remove the rocker arm assemblies as described in this chapter.

3. Compress the valve spring with a compressor like the one shown in **Figure 47**. Remove the valve keys or cap locks and release the spring tension.

4. Remove the valve spring retainer, spring and seal. Discard the seal.

CAUTION
Remove any burrs from the valve stem lock grooves before removing the valves or the valve guides will be damaged.

5. Remove the valve and repeat Step 3 and Step 4 on each remaining valve.

6. Arrange the parts in order so they can be returned to their original positions when reassembled.

Inspection

1. Clean the valves with a fine wire brush or buffing wheel. Discard any cracked, warped or burned valves.

2. Measure valve stems at the top, center and bottom for wear. A machine shop can do this when the valves are ground. Also measure the length of each valve and the diameter of each valve head.

NOTE
*Check the thickness of the valve edge or margin after the valves have been ground. See **Figure 48**. Any valve with a margin of less than 1/32 in. (0.79 mm) should be discarded.*

3. Remove all carbon and varnish from the valve guides with a stiff spiral wire brush.

NOTE
*Check the thickness of the valve edge or margin after the valves have been ground. See **Figure 48**. Any valve with a margin of less than 1/32 in. (0.79 mm) should be discarded.*

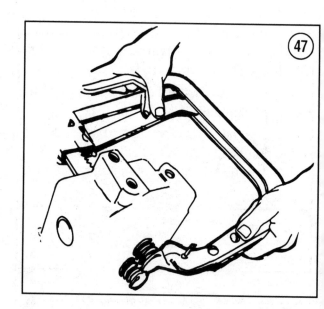

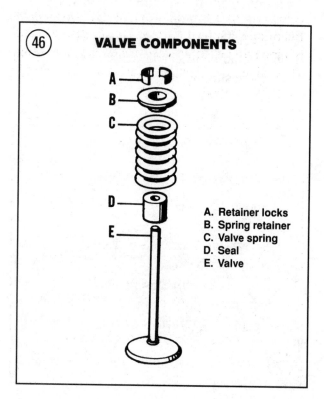

VALVE COMPONENTS

A. Retainer locks
B. Spring retainer
C. Valve spring
D. Seal
E. Valve

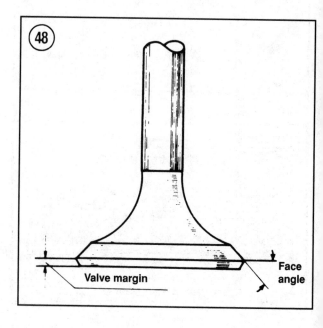

Valve margin

Face angle

4. Insert each valve into the guide from which it was removed. Holding the valve just slightly off its seat, rock it back and forth in a direction parallel with the rocker arms. This is the direction in which the greatest wear normally occurs. If the valve stem rocks more than slightly, the valve guide is probably worn.

5. If there is any doubt about valve guide condition after performing Step 4, have the valve guide measured with a valve stem clearance checking tool. Compare the results with specification in **Table 1**. Worn guides must be reamed for the next oversize valve stem.

6. Test the valve springs under load on a spring tester (**Figure 49**). Replace any weak spring.

7. Inspect the valve seat inserts. If worn or burned, they must be reconditioned. This is a job for a dealer or machine shop, although the procedure is described in this chapter.

8. Check each spring on a flat surface with a steel square. See **Figure 50**. Slowly revolve the spring 360° and note the space between the top of the coil and the square. If it exceeds 5/64 in. (1.98 mm) at any point, replace the spring.

9. Check each valve lifter to make sure it fits freely in the block and that the end that contacts the camshaft lobe is smooth and not worn excessively.

Valve Guide Reaming

Worn valve guides must be reamed to accept a valve with an oversize stem. These are available in 3 sizes for both intake and exhaust valves. Reaming must be done by hand (**Figure 51**) and is a job best left to an experienced machine shop. The valve seat must be refaced after the guide has been reamed.

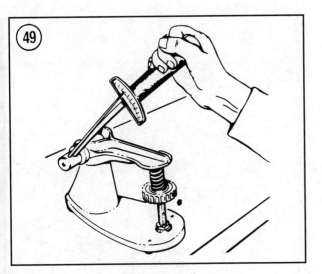

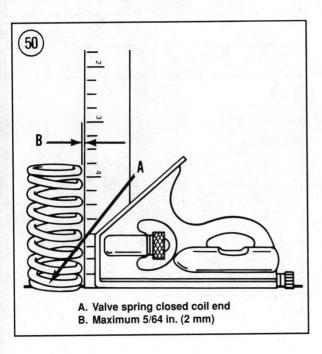

A. Valve spring closed coil end
B. Maximum 5/64 in. (2 mm)

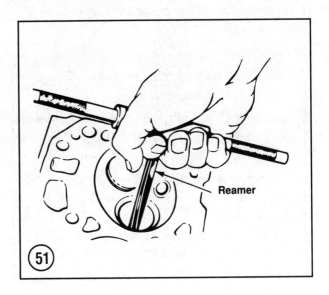

Reamer

Valve Seat Reconditioning

1. Cut the valve seats to the specified angle (**Table 1**) with a dressing stone. Remove only enough metal to obtain a good finish.

2. Use tapered stones to obtain the specified seat width when necessary.

3. Coat the corresponding valve face with Prussian blue dye.

4. Insert the valve into the valve guide.

5. Apply light pressure to the valve and rotate it approximately 1/4 turn.

6. Lift the valve out. If it seats properly, the dye will transfer evenly to the valve face.

7. If the dye transfers to the top of the valve face, lower the seat. If it transfers to the bottom of the valve face, raise the seat.

Valve Installation

> *NOTE*
> *Install all parts in the same positions from which they were removed.*

1. Lubricate the valve stems and guides with engine oil.

2. Install each valve in the port from which it was removed.

3. Install new oil seals on each valve stem.

4. Install the valve spring over the valve, then install the spring retainer.

5. Compress the spring and install the locks. Make sure both locks seat properly in the upper groove of the valve stem.

6. Measure the installed spring height between the top of the valve seat and the underside of the spring retainer, as shown in **Figure 52**. If height is greater than specifications, install an extra spring seat shim about 1/16 in. (1.58 mm) thick and remeasure the height.

VALVE LIFTERS

Removal/Installation

1. Remove the rocker arm assemblies and pushrods as described in this chapter.

2. Remove the pushrod cover. Discard the gasket.

3. Remove the valve lifters. This can be done without special tools, although an awl will make the job easier and faster.

4. Installation is the reverse of removal. Use a new pushrod cover gasket and O-rings on the cover bolts.

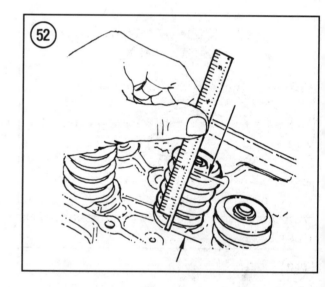

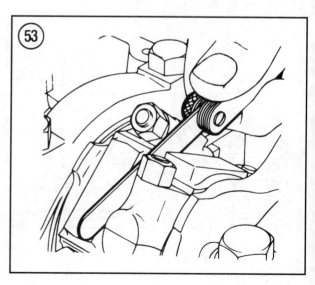

Inspection

Keep the lifter in proper sequence for installation in their original position in the head. Clean lifters in solvent and wipe dry with a clean, lint-free cloth. Inspect and test the lifters separately to prevent intermixing of their internal parts. If any part requires replacement, replace the entire lifter.

Inspect all parts. If any lifter shows signs of pitting, scoring, galling, non-rotation or excessive wear, discard it. Check the lifter plunger. It should drop to the bottom of the body by its own weight when dry and assembled.

PISTON/CONNECTING ROD ASSEMBLY

Piston/Connecting Rod Removal

1. Remove the engine as described in this chapter.
2. Place a suitable container under the oil pan and remove the drain plug. Let the crankcase oil drain, then reinstall the drain plug.
3. Remove the intake and exhaust manifolds as described in this chapter.

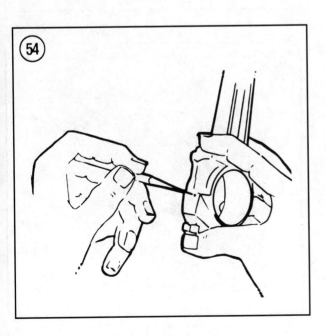

4. Remove the cylinder head as described in this chapter.
5. Remove the oil pan and oil pump as described in this chapter.
6. Rotate the crankshaft until one piston is at bottom dead center. Pack the cylinder bore with clean shop rags. Remove the carbon ridge at the top of each cylinder bore with a ridge reamer. These can be rented for use. Vacuum out the shavings, then remove the shop rags.
7. Rotate the crankshaft until the connecting rod is centered in the bore. Measure the clearance between the connecting rod and the crankshaft journal flange with a flat feeler gauge (**Figure 53**). If the clearance exceeds specifications (**Table 1**), replace the connecting rod during reassembly.

NOTE
*Mark the cylinder number on the top of each piston with quick-drying paint. Check the cylinder numbers or identification marks on the connecting rod and cap. If they are not visible, make your own (**Figure 54**).*

8. Remove the nuts holding the connecting rod cap. Lift off the cap, together with the lower bearing insert.

NOTE
If the connecting rod caps are difficult to remove, tap the studs with a wooden hammer handle.

9. Use the wooden hammer handle to push the piston and connecting rod from the bore.
10. Remove the piston rings with a ring remover (**Figure 55**).
11. Repeat Steps 6-10 for all remaining connecting rods.

Piston Pin Removal/Installation

The piston pins are press-fitted to the connecting rods and hand-fitted to the pistons. Removal requires the use of a press and support stand. This is a job for a dealer or machine shop equipped to fit the pistons to the pins, ream the pin bushings to the correct diameter and install the pistons and pins on the connecting rods.

Piston Clearance Check

> *NOTE*
> *Five different pistons have been used in the 224 cid (3.7L) engines. Three forged-aluminum pistons (part Nos. 759-5920, 759-6610 and 759-8312) and 2 cast-aluminum pistons (part No. 778-9015 and 778-9441) have been used. The 3 forged pistons may be mixed within the same engine; however, the forged pistons must not be mixed with the cast pistons. In addition, the 2 cast pistons must not be mixed within the same engine due to weight differences.*

Five different pistons have been used on 224 cid (3.7L) engines. The various pistons can be identified by the oil ring groove configuration as follows:

   a. Forged piston part No. 759-5920—2 long slots and 1 round hole in the oil ring groove.

   b. Forged piston part No. 759-6610—2 long slots and 2 round holes in the oil ring groove.

   c. Forged piston part No. 759-8312—8 square and 2 round holes in the oil ring groove.

   d. Cast piston part No. 778-9015—4 round holes in the oil ring groove.

   e. Cast piston part No. 778-9441—6 round holes in the oil ring groove.

Unless you have precision measuring equipment and know how to use it properly, have this procedure performed by a MerCruiser dealer or an experienced machine shop.

1. Using a micrometer, measure all pistons at a right angle to the piston pin bore (**Figure 56**) and at the approximate center of the skirt on forged pistons or 13/16 in. (20.6 mm) up from the bottom of the skirt on cast pistons.

2. Measure the cylinder bore diameter with a suitable bore gauge (**Figure 57**). **Figure 58** shows the points of normal cylinder wear. If dimension A exceeds dimension B by more than 0.003 in. (0.08 mm), the cylinders must be bored and oversize pistons and rings installed.

3. Subtract the piston diameter from the largest cylinder bore reading to determine piston clearance. Piston-to-cylinder clearance should be as follows:

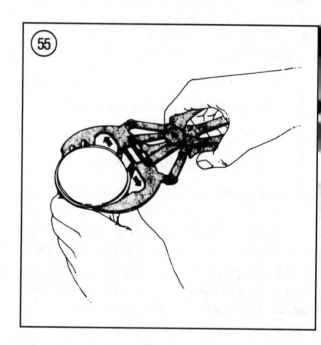

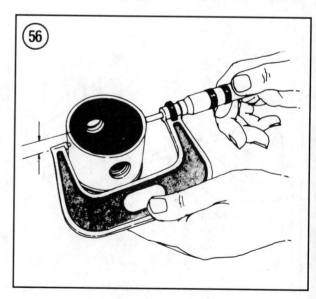

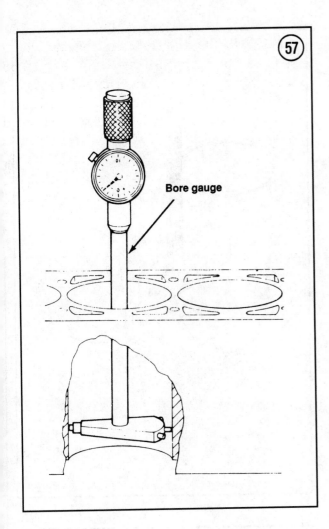

a. Forged pistons part No. 759-5920 and 759-6610—0.002-0.0037 in. (0.05-0.094 mm).

b. Forged piston part No. 759-8312—0.004-0.0057 in. (0.10-0.145 mm).

c. Cast pistons part Nos. 778-9015 and 778-9441—0.001-0.0027 in. (0.025-0.069 mm).

4. If piston-to-cylinder clearance exceeds specification, the cylinders must be bored and oversize pistons and rings installed.

Piston Ring Fit/Installation

1. Check the ring gap of each piston ring. To do this, position the ring at the bottom of the ring travel area and square it by tapping gently with an inverted piston. See **Figure 59**.

NOTE
If the cylinders have not been rebored, check the gap at the bottom of the ring travel, where the cylinder is least worn.

2. Measure the ring gap with a feeler gauge as shown in **Figure 60**. Compare with specifications in **Table 1**. If the measurement is not within specification, the rings must be replaced as a set. Check gap of new rings as well. If the gap is too

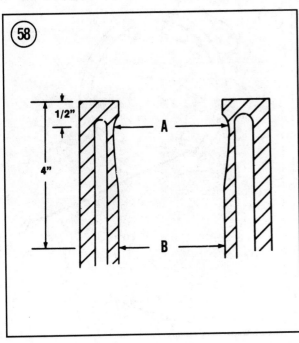

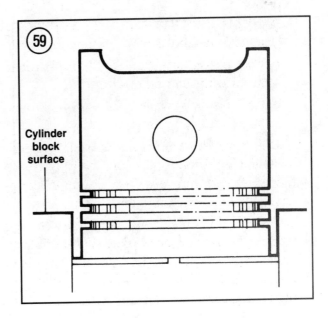

small, file the ends of the ring to correct it (**Figure 61**).

3. Check the side clearance of the rings as shown in **Figure 62**. Place the feeler gauge alongside the ring all the way into the groove. If the measurement is not within specification (**Table 1**), either the rings or the ring grooves are worn. Inspect and replace as required.

4. Using a ring expander tool (**Figure 63**), carefully install the oil control ring, then the compression rings. Oil rings consist of 3 segments. The wavy segment goes between the flat segments to act as a spacer. Upper and lower flat segments are interchangeable. The top ring has a bevel on the inner diameter; the second ring has a groove on the outer diameter. See **Figure 64**.

5. Position the ring gaps as shown in **Figure 65**.

Connecting Rod Inspection

Have the connecting rods checked for straightness by a dealer or machine shop. When installing new connecting rods, have them checked for misalignment before installing the piston and piston pin. Connecting rods can spring out of alignment during shipping or handling.

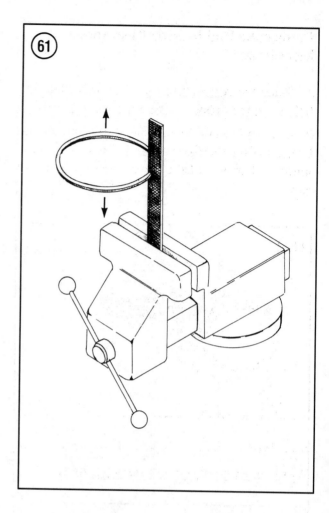

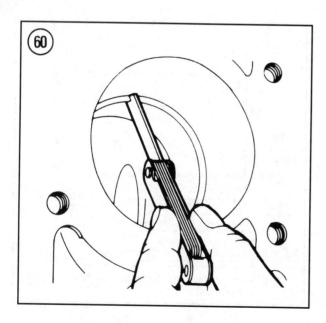

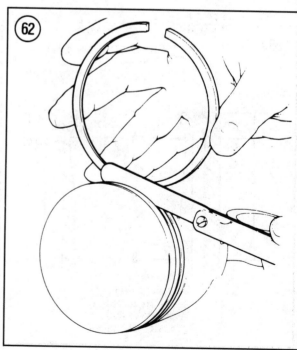

Connecting Rod Bearing Clearance Measurement

1. Place the connecting rods and upper bearing halves on the proper connecting rod journals.

2. Cut a piece of Plastigage the width of the bearing (**Figure 66**). Place the Plastigage on the journal, then install the lower bearing half end cap.

NOTE
Do not place Plastigage over the journal oil hole.

3. Tighten the connecting rod cap to specification (**Table 2**). Do not rotate the crankshaft while the Plastigage is in place.

4. Remove the connecting rod caps. Bearing clearance is determined by comparing the width of the flattened Plastigage to the markings on the envelope (**Figure 67**). If the clearance is excessive, the crankshaft must be reground and new undersize bearings installed.

7

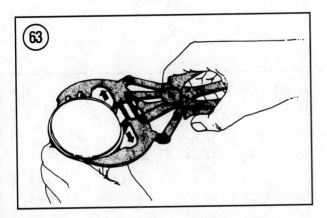

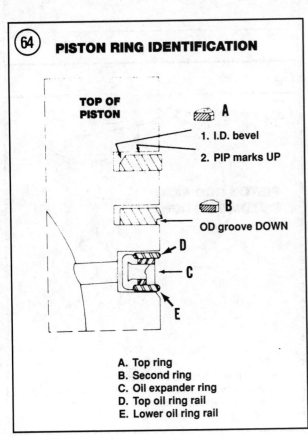

PISTON RING IDENTIFICATION

TOP OF PISTON

A
1. I.D. bevel
2. PIP marks UP

B
OD groove DOWN

D
C
E

A. Top ring
B. Second ring
C. Oil expander ring
D. Top oil ring rail
E. Lower oil ring rail

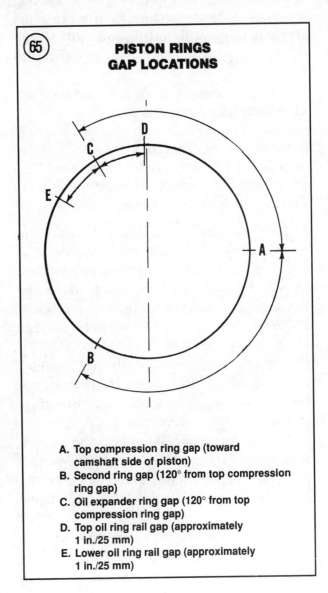

PISTON RINGS GAP LOCATIONS

A. Top compression ring gap (toward camshaft side of piston)
B. Second ring gap (120° from top compression ring gap)
C. Oil expander ring gap (120° from top compression ring gap)
D. Top oil ring rail gap (approximately 1 in./25 mm)
E. Lower oil ring rail gap (approximately 1 in./25 mm)

Piston/Connecting Rod Installation

1. Make sure the pistons are correctly installed on the connecting rods, if they were separated. On pistons with a cast notch (**Figure 68**), the notch must face the front of the engine with the rod and cap numbers facing the camshaft. If the piston has no cast notch, it can be installed either way on the connecting rod, but the rod and cap numbers must face the camshaft when the assembly is installed in the block.

2. Make sure the ring gaps are positioned as shown in **Figure 65**.

3. Slip short pieces of hose over the connecting rod studs to prevent them from nicking the crankshaft. Tape will work if you do not have the right diameter hose, but it is more difficult to remove.

4. Immerse the entire piston in clean engine oil. Coat the cylinder wall with oil.

CAUTION
Use extreme care in Step 5 to prevent the connecting rod from nicking the crankshaft journal.

5. Install the piston/connecting rod assembly in its cylinder with a piston ring compressor as shown in **Figure 69**. Tap lightly with a wooden hammer handle to insert the piston. Make sure that the piston number (painted on top before removal) corresponds to the cylinder number, counting from the front of the engine.

6. Clean the connecting rod bearings carefully, including the back sides. Coat the journals and bearings with clean engine oil. Place the bearings in the connecting rod and cap.

7. Pull the connecting rod and bearing into position against the crankpin. Remove the protective hose or tape and lightly lubricate the connecting rod bolt threads with SAE 30 engine oil.

8. Install the connecting rod cap. Make sure the rod and cap marks align. Install the cap nuts finger-tight.

9. Repeat Steps 4-8 for each remaining piston/connecting rod assembly.

10. Tighten the cap nuts to specification (**Table 2**).

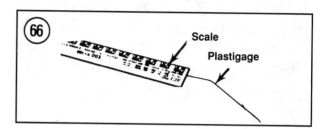

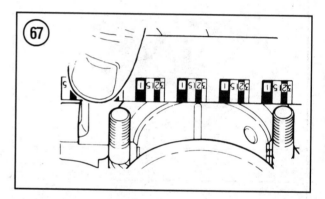

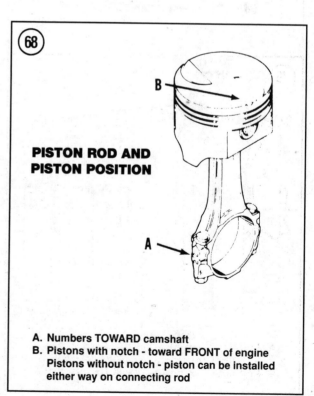

PISTON ROD AND PISTON POSITION

A. Numbers TOWARD camshaft
B. Pistons with notch - toward FRONT of engine
   Pistons without notch - piston can be installed either way on connecting rod

11. Check the connecting rod big-end play as described under *Piston/Connecting Rod Removal* in this chapter.

CRANKSHAFT

End Play Measurement

1. Pry the crankshaft toward the front of the engine with a large screwdriver.

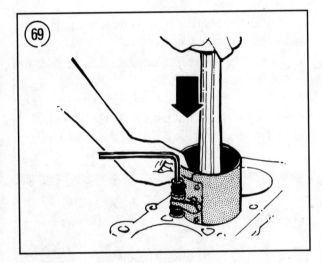

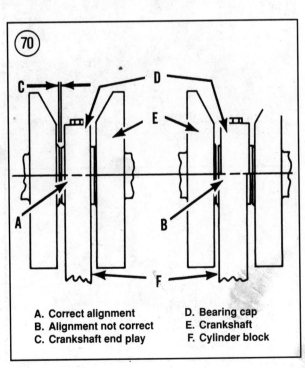

A. Correct alignment
B. Alignment not correct
C. Crankshaft end play
D. Bearing cap
E. Crankshaft
F. Cylinder block

2. Measure the crankshaft end play between the front of the No. 3 main bearing and the crankshaft thrust surface with a flat feeler gauge. See **Figure 70**. Compare to specification in **Table 1**.

3. If end play is excessive, replace the No. 3 main bearing. If less than specified, check the bearing faces for imperfections.

Removal

1. Remove the engine from the boat as described in this chapter.

2. Remove the flywheel as described in this chapter.

3. Mount the engine on an engine stand, if available.

4. Invert the engine to bring the oil pan to an upright position.

5. Remove the oil pan and oil pump as described in this chapter.

6. Remove the alternator rotor, stator, front cover and timing chain as described in this chapter.

7. Remove the spark plugs to permit easy rotation of the crankshaft.

8. Measure crankshaft end play as described in this chapter.

9. Rotate the crankshaft to position one connecting rod at the bottom of its stroke.

10. Remove the connecting rod bearing cap and bearing. Move the piston/rod assembly away from the crankshaft.

11. Repeat Step 9 and Step 10 for each remaining piston/rod assembly.

12. Check the caps for identification numbers or marks. If none are visible, clean the caps with a wire brush. If marks still cannot be seen, make your own with quick-drying paint.

13. Unbolt and remove the main bearing caps and bearing inserts (B, **Figure 71**).

14. Carefully lift the crankshaft from the engine block and place it on a clean workbench.

15. Remove the bearing inserts from the block. Place the bearing caps and inserts in order on a clean workbench.

16. Remove the side seals and pins from the rear bearing cap.

Inspection

When a production crankshaft cannot be precision-fit, all main journals are ground undersize and the front counterweight is stamped with a ".0-."

1. Clean the crankshaft thoroughly with solvent. Blow out the oil passages with compressed air.

2. Check the main and connecting rod journals for wear, scratches, grooves, scoring or cracks. Check oil seal surface for burrs, nicks or other sharp edges which might damage a seal during installation.

NOTE
Unless you have precision measuring equipment and know how to use it, have a machine shop perform Step 3.

3. Check all journals against specifications (**Table 1**) for out-of-roundness and taper. See **Figure 72**. Have the crankshaft reground, if necessary.

Main Bearing Clearance Measurement

Main bearing clearance is measured with Plastigage in the same manner as the connecting rod bearing clearance described in this chapter. Excessive clearance requires that the bearings be replaced, the crankshaft be reground or both.

Installation

1. Install the main bearing inserts in the cylinder block. Bearing oil holes must align with block oil holes and bearing tabs must seat in the block tab slots.

NOTE
Check cap bolts for thread damage before reuse. If damaged, replace the bolts.

2. Lubricate the bolt threads with SAE 30 engine oil.

3. Install the bearing inserts in each cap. Bearing tabs must engage cap slots.

4. Carefully lower the crankshaft into position in the block.

5. Slightly stretch new rear main bearing side oil seals and apply Quicksilver Perfect Seal, then install in groove at each side of the rear main cap.

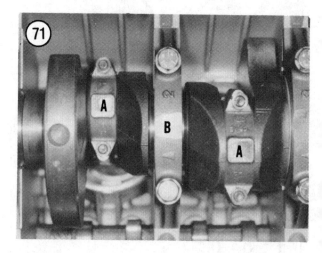

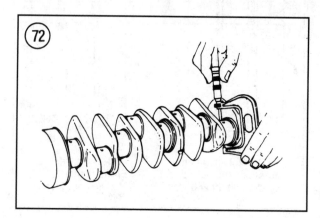

Seal end should protrude 0.015 in. (0.38 mm) from the block side of the cap. See **Figure 73**.

6. Apply Perfect Seal to area on cylinder block where rear main cap fits, as shown in **Figure 74**. Do *not* apply it beyond the centerline of the bolt holes toward the crankshaft. See **Figure 74**.

7. Apply Perfect Seal to outside face of side seals on the rear main cap.

8. Install the rear cap, making sure that the side seal does not move upward in the cap groove. When cap is fully installed, the end of the seal should still protrude from the block side of the cap.

9. Install, but do not tighten, the rear cap bolts. Install the pins with a hammer until they are flush with the cap top (**Figure 75**).

10. Tighten rear cap bolts to specifications (**Table 2**). Use a 0.025 in. (0.64 mm) flat feeler gauge as shown in **Figure 76** and cut each side

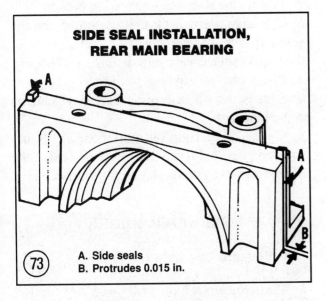

SIDE SEAL INSTALLATION, REAR MAIN BEARING

(73)
A. Side seals
B. Protrudes 0.015 in.

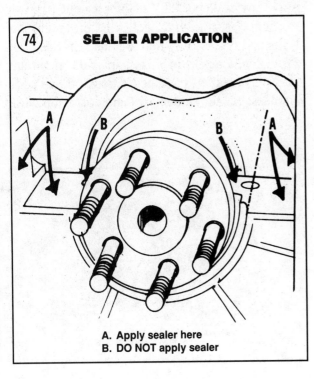

(74) **SEALER APPLICATION**

A. Apply sealer here
B. DO NOT apply sealer

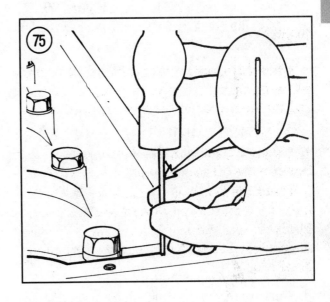

(75)

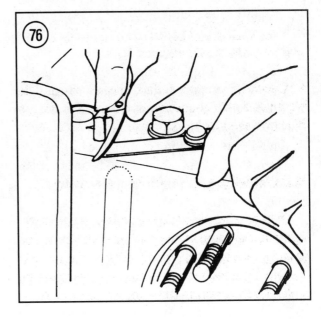

(76)

7

seal so that it will protrude 0.025 in. (0.64 mm) above the bottom of the cap.

11. Install the remaining main bearing caps with their arrows pointing toward the front of the engine. See **Figure 77**.

12. Tighten all except the No. 3 bearing cap to specification (**Table 2**).

13. Pry the crankshaft toward the front of the engine, then toward the rear to align the thrust bearing and crankshaft thrust surfaces. Hold crankshaft in this position and tighten the No. 3 cap bolts to specification (**Table 2**). Correct No. 3 bearing alignment as shown in **Figure 70**.

14. Measure crankshaft end play as described in this chapter.

15. Reverse Steps 1-10 of *Removal* in this chapter.

FLYWHEEL HOUSING, COUPLER AND FLYWHEEL

Removal/Installation

1. Remove the engine from the boat as described in this chapter.

2. Remove attaching parts from the flywheel housing. Remove the housing.

3. Remove the coupler retaining nuts and washers. Remove the coupler.

4. Loosen the flywheel bolts gradually in a diagonal pattern. Remove the flywheel.

5. To install, align the offset holes in the flywheel with the crankshaft studs and position the flywheel on the studs. Tighten flywheel bolts to specification (**Table 2**).

6. Fit the drive coupling on the studs. Install the washers and locknuts. Tighten nuts to specification (**Table 2**) with tool part No. C-91-35547 and torque wrench.

7. Install flywheel housing. Install attaching parts to housing.

8. Lubricate coupler splines with Quicksilver 2-4-C Multi-Lube and reinstall the engine in the boat as described in this chapter.

Inspection

1. Visually check the flywheel surface for cracks, deep scoring, excessive wear, heat discoloration and checking. If the surface is glazed or slightly scratched, have the flywheel resurfaced by a machine shop.

2. Check the surface flatness with a straightedge and feeler gauge.

3. Inspect the ring gear for cracks, broken teeth or excessive wear. If severely worn, check the starter motor drive teeth for similar wear or damage. Replace as required.

4. Check drive coupling splines for excessive wear caused by a lack of sufficient lubrication when installed.

5. Check drive coupling hub bond. If it has sheared or pulled loose from the hub center, the engine and stern drive unit are misaligned.

CYLINDER BLOCK

Cleaning and Inspection

1. Clean the block thoroughly with solvent. Remove any gasket or RTV sealant residue from the machined surfaces. Check all core plugs for leaks and replace any that are suspect. See *Core Plug Replacement* in this chapter. Remove any plugs that seal oil passages. Check oil and coolant passages for sludge, dirt and corrosion while

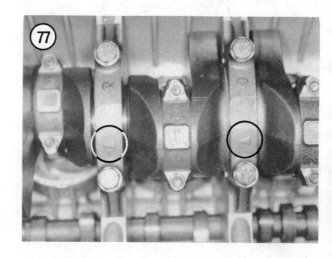

cleaning. If the passages are very dirty, have the block boiled out by a machine shop. Blow out all passages with compressed air. Check the threads in the head bolt holes to be sure they are clean. If dirty, use a tap to true up the threads and remove any deposits.

2. Examine the block for cracks. To confirm suspicions about possible leak areas, use a mixture of 1 part kerosene and 2 parts engine oil. Coat the suspected area with this solution, then wipe dry and immediately apply a solution of

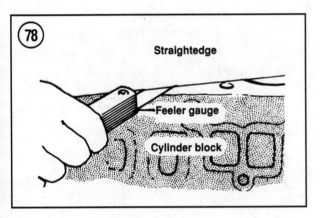

zinc oxide dissolved in wood alcohol. If any discoloration appears in the treated area, the block is cracked and should be replaced.

3. Check flatness of the cylinder block deck or top surface. Place an accurate straightedge on the block. If there is any gap between the block and straightedge, measure it with a flat feeler gauge (**Figure 78**). Measure from end to end and from corner to corner.

4. Measure cylinder bores with a bore gauge (**Figure 79**) for out-of-roundness or excessive wear as described in *Piston Clearance Check* in this chapter. If the cylinders exceed maximum tolerance, they must be rebored. Reboring is also necessary if the cylinder walls are badly scuffed or scored.

> *NOTE*
> *Before boring, install all main bearing caps and tighten the cap bolts to specification in* **Table 2**.

CORE PLUG REPLACEMENT

The condition of all core plugs in the block and cylinder head should be checked whenever the engine is out of the boat for service. If any leakage or corrosion are found around one core plug, replace them all.

> *NOTE*
> *Core plugs can be replaced inexpensively by a machine shop. If you are having machine work done on the engine, have the core plugs replaced at the same time.*

Removal/Installation

> *CAUTION*
> *Do not drive core plugs into the engine casting. It will be impossible to retrieve them and they can restrict coolant circulation, resulting in serious engine damage.*

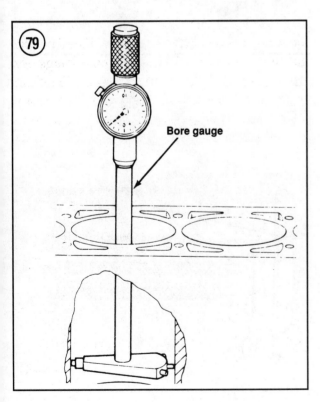

1. Tap the bottom edge of the core plug with a hammer and drift. Use several sharp blows to push the bottom of the plug inward, tilting the top out (**Figure 80**).

2. Grip the top of the plug firmly with pliers. Pull the plug from its bore (**Figure 81**) and discard.

> *NOTE*
> *Core plugs can also be removed by drilling a hole in the center of the plug and prying them out with an appropriate size drift or pin punch. On large core plugs, the use of a universal impact slide hammer is recommended.*

3. Clean the plug bore thoroughly to remove all traces of the old sealer. Inspect the bore for any damage that might interfere with proper sealing of the new plug. If damage is evident, true the surface by boring for the next oversize plug.

> *NOTE*
> *Oversize plugs can be identified by an "OS" stamped in the flat on the cup side of the plug.*

4. Coat the inside diameter of the plug bore and the outer diameter of the new plug with sealer. Use an oil-resistant sealer if the plug is to be installed in an oil gallery or a water-resistant sealer for plugs installed in the water jacket.

5. Install the new core plug with an appropriate size core plug replace tool (**Figure 82**), driver or socket. The sharp edge of the plug should be at least 0.02 in. (0.5 mm) inside the lead-in chamfer.

6. Repeat Steps 1-5 to replace each remaining core plug.

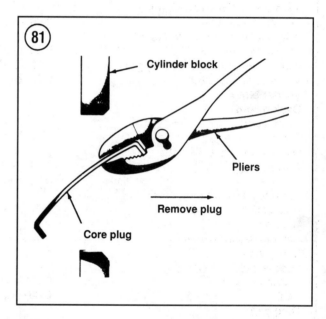

(81)

Cylinder block

Pliers

Remove plug

Core plug

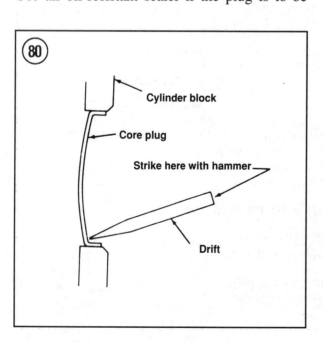

(80)

Cylinder block

Core plug

Strike here with hammer

Drift

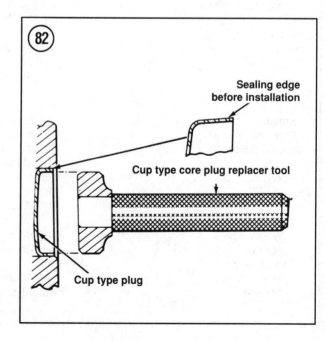

(82)

Sealing edge before installation

Cup type core plug replacer tool

Cup type plug

Table 1 MERCRUISER INLINE ENGINE SPECIFICATIONS

Engine type	Inline 4-cylinder
Displacement	224 cid (3.7 liter)
Firing order	1-3-4-2
Cylinder arrangement	1-2-3-4
Diameter	4.3602-4.3609 in. (110.749-110.767 mm)
Out-of-round	
Production	0.0005 in. (0.0127 mm) max.
Service	0.0015 in. (0.0381 mm) mzx.
Taper	
Production	0.0005 in. (0.0127 mm) max.
Service	0.003 in. (0.076 mm) max.
Piston clearance	
2 slots and 1 or 2 round holes in oil ring groove	0.002-0.0037 in. (0.05-0.94 mm)
8 square and 2 round holes in oil ring groove	0.004-0.0057 in. (0.10-0.145 mm)
4 or 6 round holes in oil ring groove	0.001-0.0027 in. (0.025-0.069 mm)
Cylinder head flatness	0.005 in. (0.1 mm) max.
Cylinder block	
Deck height[1]	
Production	10.255-10.265 in. (260.477-260.731 mm)
Service	10.240 in. (260.096 mm) min.
Main bearing bore diameter	
Production	2.9417-2.9429 in. (74.7191-74.7497 mm)
Service	2.9345 in. (74.7649 mm) mzx.
Hydraulic lifter bore diameter	
Production	0.875-0.876 in. (22.225-22.250 mm)
Service	0.878 in. (22.301 mm) max.
Camshaft bore diameter	2.1258-2.1278 in. (53.995-54.046 mm)
Piston rings	
Groove side clearance	
Compression	0.0025-0.0040 in. (0.07-0.10 mm)
Oil	0.0011-0.0054 in. (0.03-0.15 mm)
Ring gap	
Compression	0.010-0.020 in. (0.25-0.50 mm)
Oil	0.010-0.025 in. (0.25-0.60 mm)
Piston pin	
Diameter	1.0399-1.0402 in. (26.413-26.421 mm)
Clearance	0.0004-0.0006 in (0.0102-0.0152 mm)
Fit in rod	0.0006-0.0016 in. (0.0152-0.0406 mm) interference
Camshaft	
Lobe lift	
Intake	0.286 in. (7.2644 mm)
Exhaust	0.298 in. (7.5692 mm)
Journal diameter	2.1242-2.1248 in. (53.955-53.967 mm)
End play	0.002-0.005 in. (0.06-0.10 mm)
Runout	0.001 in. (0.0254 mm) max.
Crankshaft	
Main journal diameter	2.7472-2.7482 in. (69.779-69.804 mm)
Taper	
Production	0.0002 in. (0.0051 mm) max.
Service	0.0005 in. (0.0127 mm) max.
Out-of-round	
Production	0.0002 in. (0.0051 mm) max.
Service	0.0005 in. (0.0127 mm) max.

(continued)

7

Table 1 MERCRUISER INLINE ENGINE SPECIFICATIONS (continued)

Crankshaft (continued)	
Main bearing clearance	
Production	0.0009-0.0031 in. (0.0229-0.0787 mm)
Service	0.001-0.0035 in. (0.0254-0.0889 mm)
Rear seal area diameter	
Production	3.748-3.752 in. (95.1992-95.3008 mm)
Service	3.745 in. (95.123 mm) min.
Timing sprocket ID[2]	
Production	1.380-4.381 in. (35.052-35.077 mm)
Service	1.379 in. (35.026 mm) min.
End play	0.006-0.010 in. (0.15-0.25 mm)
Connecting rod journal	
Diameter	2.4979-2.4989 in. (63.477-63.472 mm)
Taper	
Production	0.0002 in. (0.051 mm) max.
Service	0.0005 in. (0.0127 mm) max.
Out-of-round	
Production	0.0002 in. (0.051 mm) max.
Service	0.0005 in. (0.0127 mm) max.
Rod bearing clearance	
Production	0.0009-0.0031 in. (0.0228-0.0787 mm)
Service	0.001-0.003 in. (0.03-0.07 mm)
Rod side clearance	0.005-0.012 in. (0.15-0.30 mm)
Alternator rotor front	
Oil seal diameter	
Production	1.873-1.877 in. (47.5742-47.6758 mm)
Service	1.871 in. (47.5234 mm) min.
Valve train	
Lifter	Hydraulic
Rocker arm ratio	1.73:1
Valve lash	0.110-0.210 in. (2.8-5.3 mm)
Face angle	44°
Seat angle	45°
Seat runout	0.002 in. (0.051 mm) max.
Seat width	0.060-0.080 in. (1.524-2.032 mm)
Stem clearance	
Production	0.0010-0.0027 in. (0.0254-0.0686 mm)
Service	
Intake	0.0037 in. (0.940 mm)
Exhaust	0.0052 in. (0.1321 mm)
Valve spring	
Free length	2.18 in. (55 mm)
Installed height	1.86 in. (47 mm)
Load[3]	
Closed	90-100 lb. @ 1.86 in. (122-136 N @ 47 mm)
Open	255-275 lb. @ 1.36 in. (346-372 N @ 35 mm)

1. Measure from center of main bearing bore to top of cylinder block.
2. Crankshaft is tapered; take measurement @ rear half of sprocket area on crankshaft.
3. Test springs with damper installed.

Table 2 MERCRUISER INLINE ENGINE TIGHTENING TORQUES

Fastener	in.-lb.	ft.-lb.	N·m
Alternator rotor		75	102
Camshaft			
Impeller bolt[1]		60	81
Thrust plate	115		13
Sprocket screws	150		17
Chain tightener bolt		20	27
Connecting rod cap		40	54
Coupler/flywheel		30	41
Cylinder head bolts[2]		130	176
Distributor clamp		15	20
Exhaust manifold		25	34
Flywheel housing-to-block		30	41
Front mount-to-block		50	68
Intake manifold		25	34
Impeller and cover		15	20
Main bearing cap		55	75
Oil pan			
Attaching screws	130		15
Drain plug		20	27
Oil pump			
Cover	120		14
Pickup		20	27
To block		25	34
Oil tube-to-block		20	27
Rocker arm bolt[3]		20	27
Side cover		15	20
Starter motor		60	81
Stator-to-front cover	45		5
Timing chain cover		15	20
Valve cover	90		10
Water pump cover		15	20

1. On late models, tighten camshaft impeller stud to 15 ft.-lb. (11 N·m).
2. Torque in 3 stages. Retorque after first start-up.
3. Torque with valves closed.

Table 3 STANDARD TORQUE VALUES

Fastener	ft.-lb.	N·m
Grade 5		
1/4-20	8	11
1/4-28	8	11
5/16-18	17	23
5/16-24	20	27
3/8-16	30	40
3/8-24	35	47
7/16-14	50	68
7/16-20	55	75
1/2-13	75	100
1/2-20	85	115

(continued)

Table 3 STANDARD TORQUE VALUES (continued)

Fastener	ft.-lb.	N·m
Grade 5 (continued)		
9/16-12	105	142
9/16-18	115	156
Grade 6		
1/4-20	10.5	14
1/4-28	12.5	17
5/16-18	22.5	31
5/16-24	25	54
3/8-16	40	34
3/8-24	45	61
7/16-14	65	88
7/16-20	70	95
1/2-13	100	136
1/2-20	110	149
9/16-12	135	183
9/16-18	150	203

Chapter Eight

Gm V6 And V8 Engines

MerCruiser drive installations may use one of several marine V6 and V8 engines. All current 6-and 8-cylinder MerCruiser engines are based on blocks sourced from the Chevrolet Division of General Motors. Engines are available in one of 3 small block displacements: a 262 cid (4.3 liter) V6, a 305 cid (5.0 liter) V8 or a 350 cid (5.7 liter) V8. The 454 cid (7.4 liter) is used in the 7.4L and 454 Magnum model and 502 cid (8.2 liter) V8 is used in the 502 Magnum models.

During March of the 1991 model year, MerCruiser introduced its 7.4L "Mark V" big block engine. In 1992, MerCruiser introduced the 454 and 502 Magnum Mark V models. Some of the more significant upgrades in the Mark V engine include nonadjustable, "torque to spec" rocker arms, O-ring sealed cylinder heads, a 1-piece rear main crankshaft seal and the elimination of the fuel pump mounting pad. Mark V engines can be easily identified by their fuel pump mounted on the belt-driven seawater pump.

For the 1993 model year (serial No. OF000001-on), MerCruiser introduced the "Generation II" 262 cid V6 engine. Some significant upgrades include roller valve lifters, 1-piece rear main seal and a balance shaft. The balance shaft eliminates much of the dynamic vibration in the 1,700-2,000 rpm range that is common to 90° V6 engines. The balance shaft is positioned in the engine block valley area, located directly above, and driven by, the camshaft. The shaft is supported at each end with a bearing.

The Chevrolet V6 and V8 engines are very similar in design and construction; there is little difference in the repair and service procedures for these engines. The procedures given in this chapter are typical and apply to all engines, except where specifically noted.

The V6 engine cylinders are numbered from front to rear: 1-3-5 on the port side and 2-4-6 on the starboard side. The firing order is 1-6-5-4-3-2. The V8 engine cylinders are also numbered from front to rear: 1-3-5-7 on the port side and 2-4-6-8 on the starboard side. The firing order is 1-8-4-3-6-5-7-2.

The cast iron cylinder head contains intake and exhaust valves with integral valve guides. Rocker arms, on all models except the Mark V

7.4L, 454 and 502 Magnum models, are retained on individual threaded shoulder studs. On Mark V big block models, the rocker arms are retained by individual shoulder bolts and the valve lash is not adjustable. Camshaft motion is transferred through hydraulic lifters to the rocker arms by pushrods. No lash adjustment is necessary in service or during assembly unless some component in the valve train has been removed or replaced.

The chain-driven camshaft is located above the crankshaft between the 2 cylinder banks and supported by 4 (V6) or 5 (V8) bearings. The oil pump, mounted at the bottom of the engine block, is driven by the camshaft via the distributor.

The crankshaft is supported by 4 (V6) or 5 (V8) main bearings, with the rear bearing providing the crankshaft thrust control. Crankshaft rotation is counterclockwise when seen from the drive unit end of the engine.

Engine specifications (**Table 1** and **Table 2**) and tightening torques (**Tables 3-5**) are located at the end of this chapter.

The intake manifold on V8 engines is the double level design. The upper manifold passages distribute fuel-air to cylinders 2,3,5 and 8 while the lower passages distribute fuel-air to cylinders 1,4,6 and 7. The intake manifold on V6 engines is a single level design, with all passages approximately the same length to ensure even fuel-air distribution.

ENGINE SERIAL NUMBER AND CODE

The engine serial number and model designation is stamped on a plate mounted at the rear of the engine on the flywheel housing or located on a decal on the engine. If the plate or decal is missing, you can determine the model by checking the last 2 letters of the engine code stamped on the front of the cylinder block. This code number is found on all factory engines and re-

placement partial engines, but not on replacement block assemblies.

The number is found on the starboard side near the cylinder head mating surfaces on small block engines (**Figure 1**). On big block V8 engines, the number is found just above the timing chain cover (**Figure 2**). This information indicates if there are unique parts or if internal changes have been made during the model year. It is important when ordering replacement parts for the engine.

SPECIAL TOOLS

Where special tools are required or recommended for engine overhaul, the tool numbers are provided. Mercury Marine tool part numbers have a "C" prefix. GM tool part numbers have a "J" prefix. While GM tools can sometimes be rented from rental dealers, they can be purchased from Kent-Moore Tool & Equipment Division, 29784 Little Mack, Roseville, MI 48066.

GASKET SEALANT

Gasket sealant is used instead of pre-formed gaskets between some mating surfaces on the engines covered in this chapter. See *Gasket Sealant,* Chapter Six.

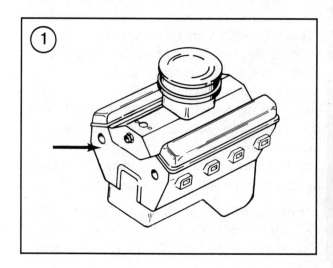

REPLACEMENT PARTS

Various changes are made to automotive engine blocks used for marine applications. Numerous part changes are required due to operation in fresh and salt water. For example, the cylinder head gasket must be corrosion-resistant. Marine engines use head gaskets of copper or stainless steel instead of the standard steel used in automotive applications. Brass expansion or core plugs must be used instead of the steel plugs found in automotive blocks.

Since marine engines are run at or near maximum rpm most of the time, the use of special valve lifters, springs, pistons, bearings, camshafts and other heavy-duty moving components is necessary for maximum life and performance.

For these reasons, automotive-type parts should not be substituted for marine components. In addition, Mercury Marine recommends that only Quicksilver parts be used. Parts offered by other manufacturers may look alike, but may not be manufactured to Mercury's specifications. Any damage resulting from the use of other than Quicksilver parts is not covered by the Mercury Marine warranty.

ENGINE REMOVAL

Some service procedures can be performed with the engine in the boat; others require removal. The boat design and service procedure to be performed will determine whether the engine must be removed.

If the installation uses a drive shaft extension, the stern drive does *not* have to be removed from the boat for engine removal. On all models without the drive shaft extension, however, the stern drive unit *must* be removed in order to disengage the drive shaft from the engine coupler.

> *WARNING*
> *The engine is heavy, awkward to handle and has sharp edges. It may shift or drop suddenly during removal. To prevent serious injury, always observe the following precautions.*

1. Never place any part of your body where a moving or falling engine may trap, cut or crush you.
2. If you must push the engine during removal, use a board or similar tool to keep your hands out of danger.
3. Be sure the hoist is designed to lift engines and has enough load capacity for your engine.
4. Be sure the hoist is securely attached to safe lifting points on the engine.
5. The engine should not be difficult to lift with a proper hoist. If it is, stop lifting, lower the engine back onto its mounts and make sure the engine has been completely separated from the vessel.

Without Drive Shaft Extension

1. Remove the stern drive unit. See Chapter Twelve.
2. Remove the engine hood cover and all panels that interfere with engine removal. Place the cover and panels to one side out of the way.
3. Disconnect the negative battery cable, then the positive battery cable. As a precaution, remove the battery from the boat.
4. Unplug the instrument harness connector from the engine harness receptacle.

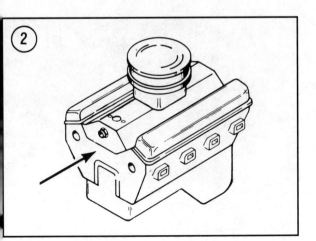

8

5. Disconnect the fuel inlet line from the tank to the fuel filter canister at the filter canister. Cap the line and plug the canister fittings to prevent leakage and the entry of contamination.

6. Disconnect the throttle cable from the carburetor. See A, **Figure 3**, typical. If necessary, remove the cable from the anchor plate. See B, **Figure 3**, typical.

7. Locate the trim sender wires at the circuit breaker/solenoid mounting bracket terminal block. Disconnect the trim sender wires from the terminal block and remove the hoses from the clamps holding the power steering hoses.

8. Disconnect the power trim pump wires (red and black) from the engine, if so equipped.

9. Disconnect the water inlet hose.

10. Disconnect the exhaust elbow bellows.

11. Disconnect both shift cables from the shift plate. See **Figure 4**, typical.

12. Disconnect any ground leads or accessories connected to the engine. If equipped with power steering, use a flare nut wrench to loosen and disconnect both power steering hydraulic lines from the control valve. Cap the lines and plug the control valve fittings to prevent leakage and the entry of contamination. Secure the lines at a point higher than the engine power steering pump during the remainder of this procedure to prevent damage or the loss of fluid.

13. Attach a suitable hoist to the engine lifting brackets. The hoist must have a minimum lift capacity of 1,500 lb. Raise the hoist enough to remove all slack.

NOTE
At this point, there should be no hoses, wires or linkage connecting the engine to the boat or stern drive unit. Recheck this to make sure nothing will hamper engine removal.

14. Unbolt the rear (**Figure 5**) and front (**Figure 6**) engine mounts from the boat. Do not loosen or move the mounts at the engine attaching points or a complete realignment will be required when the engine is reinstalled.

NOTE
Fluid-filled engine mounts are used on early V6 Alpha One models. The fluid-filled mount acts as a shock absorber and decreases vibration in the 1,700-2,200 rpm range by as much as 50 percent. Heavy-duty front engine mounts are used on 1989-on 350 Magnum Alpha One and 1989-on Bravo One models. The steel stud uses a larger bottom nut with Loctite on its threads and an elastic locknut on the top.

15. Remove the engine from the boat with the hoist.

With Drive Shaft Extension

1. Remove the engine hood cover and all panels that interfere with engine removal. Place the cover and panels to one side out of the way.

. Disconnect the negative battery cable, then he positive battery cable. As a precaution, remove the battery from the boat.

. Unplug the instrument harness connector rom the engine harness receptacle.

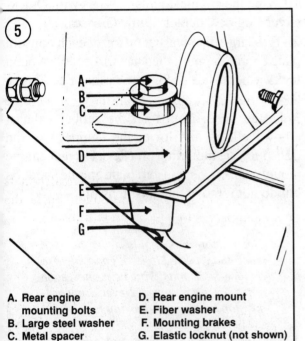

A. Rear engine
   mounting bolts
B. Large steel washer
C. Metal spacer
D. Rear engine mount
E. Fiber washer
F. Mounting brakes
G. Elastic locknut (not shown)

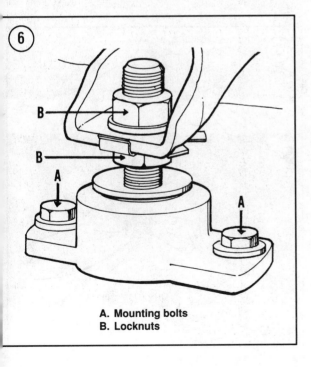

A. Mounting bolts
B. Locknuts

4. Disconnect the fuel inlet line from the fuel filter canister. Cap the line and plug the canister fittings to prevent leakage and the entry of contamination.

5. Disconnect the throttle cable from the carburetor. See A, **Figure 3**, typical. If necessary, remove the cable from the anchor plate. See B, **Figure 3**, typical.

6. Locate the trim sender brown and white wires at the circuit breaker/solenoid mounting bracket terminal block. Disconnect the trim sender wires from the terminal block and remove the hoses from the clamps holding the power steering hoses.

7. Disconnect the black and white/green (or gray) shift cut-out switch wires from the engine harness.

8. Disconnect the water inlet hose from the engine seawater pump.

9. Disconnect the exhaust pipes from the exhaust hoses.

10. Remove the top shield, then the bottom shield. See **Figure 7**.

11. Unbolt and disconnect the drive shaft from the output flange. See **Figure 8**.

12. Disconnect both shift cables from the shift plate. See **Figure 4**, typical.

8

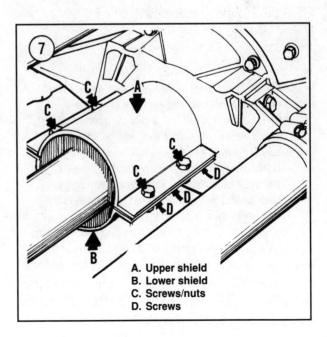

A. Upper shield
B. Lower shield
C. Screws/nuts
D. Screws

13. Disconnect any ground leads or accessories connected to the engine. If equipped with power steering, use a flare nut wrench to loosen and disconnect both power steering hydraulic lines from the control valve. Cap the lines and plug the control valve fittings to prevent leakage and the entry of contamination. Secure the lines at a point higher than the engine power steering pump during the remainder of this procedure to prevent damage or the loss of fluid.

14. Attach a suitable hoist to the engine lifting brackets. The hoist must have a minimum lift capacity of 1,500 lb. Raise the hoist enough to remove all slack.

NOTE
At this point, there should be no hoses, wires or linkage connecting the engine to the boat or stern drive unit. Recheck this to make sure nothing will hamper engine removal.

15. Unbolt the rear (**Figure 5**) and front (**Figure 6**) engine mounts from the boat. Do not loosen or move the mounts at the engine attaching points or a complete realignment will be required when the engine is reinstalled.

NOTE
Fluid-filled engine mounts are used on early V6 Alpha One models. The fluid-filled mount acts as a shock absorber and decreases vibration in the 1,700-2,200 rpm range by as much as 50 percent. Heavy-duty front engine mounts are used on 1989-on 350 Magnum Alpha One and 1989-on Bravo One models. The steel stud uses a larger bottom nut with Loctite on its threads and an elastic locknut on the top.

16. Remove the engine from the boat with the hoist.

ENGINE INSTALLATION

Without Drive Shaft Extension

Engine installation is the reverse of removal, plus the following:

1. Wipe the engine coupler splines with Quicksilver Engine Coupler Spline Grease

2. Fit a large fiber washer on top of each transom plate engine support, then install a double wound lockwasher inside each fiber washer. See **Figure 9**.

3. Install hose clamps on the rubber exhaust elbow bellows and lower the engine over the transom plate mounting brackets. Let rear engine mounts rest on the transom plate engine supports but do not remove the hoist tension.

CAUTION
Elastic stop nuts should never be used more than twice. It is a good idea to replace such nuts with new ones each time they are removed. Never use worn-out stop nuts or non-locking nuts.

4. Install one steel washer and spacer on each rear mount bolt. Install bolts downward through

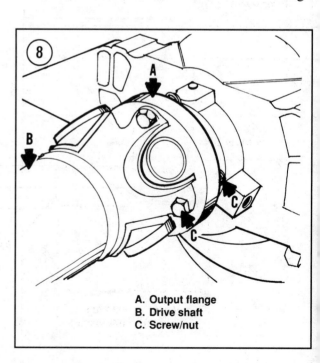

A. Output flange
B. Drive shaft
C. Screw/nut

the engine mounts, washers and brackets. See **Figure 5**. Thread a new elastic stop nut on each bolt and tighten to 35-40 ft.-lb. (47-54 N·m).

. Install front engine mount fasteners and tighten securely.

. Use guide bolts to align the engine to the bell housing. It may be necessary to rotate the crankshaft slightly to align the engine coupler splines with the drive shaft. You may also rotate the drive shaft by placing the outdrive in forward gear and rotating the propeller.

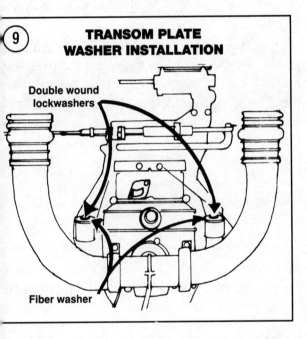

TRANSOM PLATE WASHER INSTALLATION

Double wound lockwashers

Fiber washer

> *CAUTION*
> *If the alignment tool specified in Step 7 is not available, take the boat to a Mer-Cruiser dealer for proper alignment. Drive shaft/coupling spline misalignment can cause serious damage.*

7. Using alignment tool part No. 91-805475A1 (Alpha One Generation II) or part No. 91-57797A3 (all others), check engine alignment as follows:

> *NOTE*
> *A new alignment tool (part No. 91-805475A1) is necessary to align the engine on Alpha One Generation II models. However, if the new alignment tool is not available, alignment tool (part No. 91-57797A3) can be modified to the dimensions shown in **Figure 10** and used on Alpha One Generation II engines. The new tool (part No. 91-805475A1) or the modified tool (part No. 91-57797A3) can be used to align the engine on ALL current models and ALL older models that used alignment tool (part No. 91-57797A3).*

8

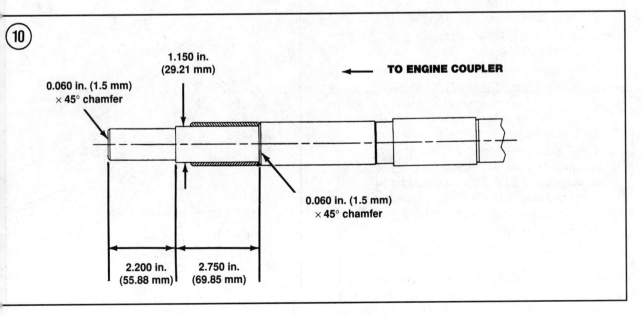

1.150 in. (29.21 mm)

0.060 in. (1.5 mm) × 45° chamfer

TO ENGINE COUPLER

0.060 in. (1.5 mm) × 45° chamfer

2.200 in. (55.88 mm)

2.750 in. (69.85 mm)

a. Coat the solid end of the tool with Quick-silver 2-4-C Multi-Lube and insert it from outside the boat through the U-joint bellows into the gimbal bearing (**Figure 11**).

b. Index the bearing and drive shaft with the engine coupler splines. If indexing is difficult, raise or lower the engine with the hoist as required to permit indexing with no resistance.

c. Loosen the locknut on both front engine mounts (**Figure 6**) and thread the adjusting nut up or down as required to properly position the front of the engine to maintain the desired alignment. Make sure that each side of the engine is raised or lowered the same amount to prevent cocking the front of the engine.

d. Tighten the locknuts securely, then recheck alignment by repeating sub-step a.

8. Attach and adjust the throttle cable as follows:

a. With the remote control in NEUTRAL (idle position), fasten the cable end guide as shown in **Figure 12** (2-barrel carburetor) or **Figure 13** (4-barrel carburetor).

b. Hold the throttle cable brass barrel and push the cable toward the throttle lever, adjusting the barrel to align with the anchor stud. Tighten the fasteners securely (do not overtighten) to hold the barrel in place, then back off 1/2 turn.

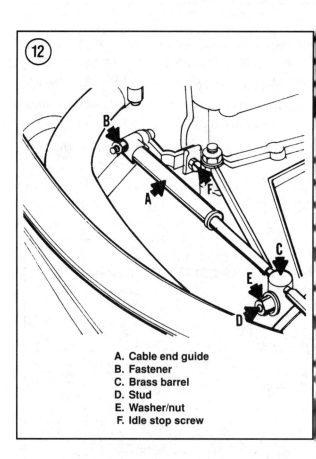

A. Cable end guide
B. Fastener
C. Brass barrel
D. Stud
E. Washer/nut
F. Idle stop screw

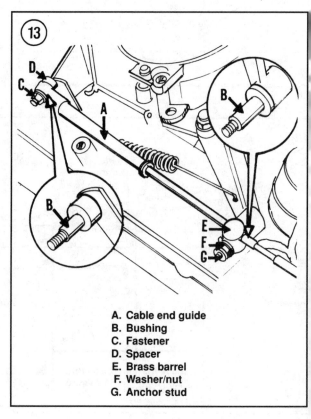

A. Cable end guide
B. Bushing
C. Fastener
D. Spacer
E. Brass barrel
F. Washer/nut
G. Anchor stud

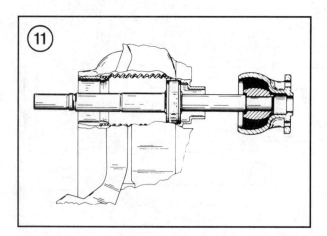

c. Place the remote control in the full-throttle position and make sure the throttle valves are completely open (vertical). The throttle lever tang should rest against the stop as shown in **Figure 14** (2-barrel carburetor) or **Figure 15** (4-barrel carburetor).

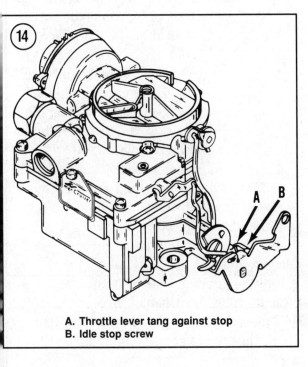

A. Throttle lever tang against stop
B. Idle stop screw

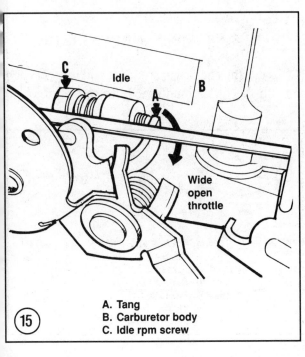

A. Tang
B. Carburetor body
C. Idle rpm screw

15

d. Place the remote control back in NEUTRAL (idle position) and make sure the idle stop screw rests against the stop. If it does not, repeat this procedure.

9. Tighten the large power steering fitting to 20-25 ft.-lb. (27-34 N•m). Tighten small fitting to 96-108 in.-lb. (11-12 N•m). Bleed the power steering system. See Chapter Seventeen.

10. Fill the engine with an oil recommended in Chapter Four.

11. Fill the cooling system, if equipped with a closed system. See Chapter Five.

12. Adjust the drive belts. See Chapter Ten.

13. Adjust the timing as required. See Chapter Four.

With Drive Shaft Extension

Engine installation is the reverse of removal, plus the following:

1. After connecting the drive shaft to the output flange, tighten fasteners to 50 ft.-lb. (68 N•m). Relieve the hoist tension and slide the engine fore or aft as necessary to provide a 1/4 in. (6.4 mm) clearance between the flange shoulder and extension shaft housing bearing. See **Figure 16**.

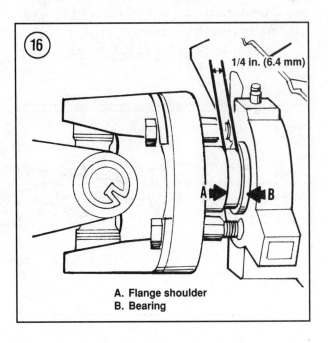

A. Flange shoulder
B. Bearing

2. To obtain correct engine/drive shaft lateral alignment:

   a. Measure the distance between the center of the bearing support attaching bolts on the inner transom plate and shaft extension housing grease fitting. See A, **Figure 17**. If the distances are not equal, slide the aft end of the engine in the direction required to equalize the distance measurements.

   b. Measure the distance between the center of the bearing support bolts and the rear engine mount adjusting bolt. See B, **Figure 17**. If the distances are not equal, slide the front end of the engine in the direction required to equalize the distance measurements.

3. After engine alignment is correct, secure the front and rear mounts to the stringers, then install the top and bottom shield. See **Figure 7**. Wipe the shield screws with Loctite Type A and tighten to 30 ft.-lb. (41 N•m).

4. Bleed the power steering system. See Chapter Seventeen.

5. Take the boat to a MerCruiser dealer for proper drive unit alignment with the engine. The procedure is complicated, requires various special tools and must be done correctly or damage will result to the engine, drive shaft and drive unit.

6. Attach and adjust the throttle cable as follows:

   a. With the remote control in NEUTRAL (idle position), fasten the cable end guide as shown in **Figure 12** (200) or **Figure 13** (all others).

   b. Hold the throttle cable brass barrel and push the cable toward the throttle lever, adjusting the barrel to align with the anchor stud. Tighten the fasteners securely (do not over-tighten) to hold the barrel in place, then back off 1/2 turn.

   c. Place the remote control in the full-throttle position and make sure the throttle valves are completely open. The lever tang should rest against the stop as shown in **Figure 14** (200) or **Figure 15** (all others).

   d. Place the remote control back in NEUTRAL (idle position) and make sure the idle stop screw rests against the stop. If it does not, repeat this procedure.

7. Fill the engine with an oil recommended in Chapter Four.

8. Fill the cooling system, if equipped with a closed system. See Chapter Five.

9. Adjust the drive belts. See Chapter Ten.

10. Adjust the timing as required. See Chapter Four.

DISASSEMBLY CHECKLISTS

To use the checklists, remove and inspect each part in the order mentioned. To reassemble, go

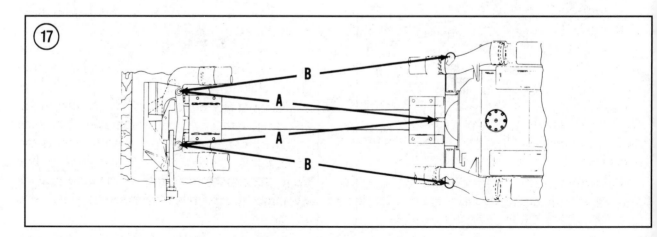

through the checklists backwards, installing the parts in order. Each major part is covered in its own section in this chapter, unless otherwise noted.

Decarbonizing or Valve Service

1. Remove the valve covers.
2. Remove the intake and exhaust manifolds.
3. Remove the rocker arms.
4. Remove the cylinder heads.
5. Remove and inspect the valves. Inspect the valve guides and seats, repairing or replacing as required.
6. Assemble by reversing Steps 1-5.

Valve and Ring Service

1. Perform Steps 1-5 of *Decarbonizing or Valve Service*.
2. Remove the oil pan and oil pump.
3. Remove the pistons and connecting rods.
4. Remove the piston rings. It is not necessary to separate the pistons from the connecting rods unless a piston, connecting rod or piston pin needs repair or replacement.
5. Assemble by reversing Steps 1-4.

General Overhaul

1. Remove the engine from the boat.
2. Remove the flywheel.
3. Remove the mount brackets and oil pressure sending unit from the engine.
4. If available, mount the engine on an engine stand. These can be rented from equipment rental dealers. The stand is not absolutely necessary, but it will make the job much easier.
5. Remove the following accessories or components from the engine, if present:
    a. Alternator and mounting bracket
    b. Power steering pump and mounting bracket
    c. Spark plug wires and distributor cap
    d. Carburetor and fuel lines
    e. Oil dipstick and tube
    f. Seawater pump, if so equipped
6. Check the engine for signs of coolant or oil leaks.
7. Clean the outside of the engine.
8. Remove the distributor. See Chapter Ten.
9. Remove all hoses and tubes connected to the engine.
10. Remove the fuel pump. See Chapter Nine.
11. Remove the intake and exhaust manifolds.
12. Remove the thermostat. See Chapter Ten.
13. Remove the valve cover and rocker arms.
14. Remove the crankshaft pulley, harmonic balancer, timing case cover and water pump. Remove the timing chain and sprockets.
15. Remove the camshaft.
16. Remove the cylinder heads.
17. Remove the oil pan and oil pump.
18. Remove the pistons and connecting rods.
19. Remove the crankshaft.
20. Inspect the cylinder block.
21. Assemble by reversing Steps 1-19.

VALVE COVERS

Removal/Installation

It may be necessary to remove the center exhaust outlet manifold on installations so equipped to provide sufficient clearance for valve cover removal.

1. Disconnect the crankcase ventilation hose from the valve cover.
2. Disconnect the spark plug cables from the plugs and remove the plug cable retainers from their brackets on the cover.
3. Remove any other accessory unit that might interfere with valve cover removal. On some installations, it will be necessary to unbolt and remove the Thunderbolt IV ignition module from the exhaust manifold in order to provide clearance for removal of the port side valve cover.

4. Remove the cover attaching fasteners and load spreaders, if used.

5. Rap the valve cover with a soft-faced mallet to break the gasket or RTV seal. Remove the valve cover. Discard the gasket, if used.

6. Clean any gasket or RTV sealant residue from the cylinder head and valve cover with degreaser and a putty knife.

7A. If valve cover uses a gasket, coat one side of a new gasket with an oil-resistant sealer. Install the gasket sealer-side down on the cylinder head.

7B. If valve cover uses RTV sealant, run a 3/16 in. (4.8 mm) bead of RTV sealant along the valve cover mating surface on the cylinder head rail. Make sure to run the bead on the inner side of fastener holes.

8. Position the valve cover on the cylinder head.

9. Install the attaching fasteners (with load spreaders, if used) and tighten to specification (**Table 3** or **Table 4**).

10. Install the spark plug cable retainers on the valve cover brackets. Connect the wires to the appropriate spark plugs. See Chapter Four.

11. Install the crankcase ventilation hose in the valve cover.

INTAKE MANIFOLD

Removal/Installation

Refer to **Figure 18**, typical for this procedure.

1. Disconnect the negative battery cable.

2. Disconnect the crankcase ventilation hose from each valve cover.

3. Remove the flame arrestor.

4. Open the cylinder block water drains and allow all water to drain. Disconnect the water hoses from the manifold, thermostat housing and water pump.

5. Disconnect the throttle cable linkage from the carburetor.

6. Disconnect the water temperature sending unit lead. On some 7.4L engines, it may be necessary to remove the sending unit to provide sufficient access for manifold fastener removal.

7. Disconnect and remove the fuel line between the carburetor and fuel pump.

8. Disconnect the spark plug cables. Remove the cable retainers from the valve covers.

9. Remove the distributor cap and place it (with plug cables attached) to one side out of the way.

10. Mark the position of the distributor rotor relative to the intake manifold. Loosen the hold-down clamp and remove the distributor. See Chapter Eleven.

11. Disconnect the oil pressure sending unit lead. On some small block engines, it may be necessary to remove the sending unit to provide sufficient access for manifold fastener removal.

12. Disconnect the electric choke lead and any other electrical wires that will interfere with manifold removal.

13. Loosen and remove the intake manifold fasteners. Pry the manifold loose and remove it from the engine block.

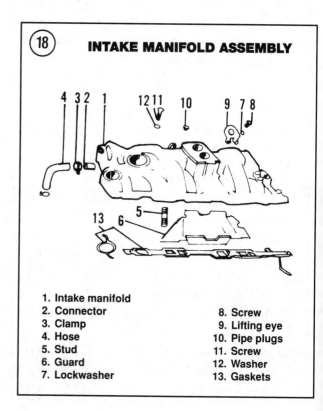

(18) **INTAKE MANIFOLD ASSEMBLY**

1. Intake manifold
2. Connector
3. Clamp
4. Hose
5. Stud
6. Guard
7. Lockwasher
8. Screw
9. Lifting eye
10. Pipe plugs
11. Screw
12. Washer
13. Gaskets

14. Remove and discard the intake manifold gaskets and seals. Discard the attaching bolt sealing washers.

15. Clean all gasket residue from the block, cylinder heads and intake manifold with degreaser and a putty knife.

16. If the intake manifold is being replaced, transfer the carburetor, thermostat and housing, throttle cable anchor block unit, distributor clamp, temperature sending unit and any other hardware that might be installed on the manifold.

NOTE
Remove the metal insert from the starboard cylinder head manifold gasket on 305 cid engines with a 2-bbl. carburetor. This is required to provide sufficient clearance for the intake manifold heat pipe. Make sure that the intake manifold gasket has an opening for the manifold exhaust crossover port. If it does not, the

automatic choke will not function properly.

17. Coat both sides of new intake manifold side gaskets with Quicksilver Perfect Seal. Install gaskets on the cylinder head(s). On 7.4L engines, install the unmarked gasket on the port cylinder head.

18A. *Except big block engines*—Run a 3/16 in. (4.8 mm) bead of Quicksilver RTV sealant on the front and rear of the cylinder block (between the cylinder heads). Extend the sealant 1/2 in. (12.7 mm) up each end of the manifold side gaskets. See **Figure 19**.

18B. *Big block engines*—Using Quicksilver Bellows Adhesive, glue the rubber end gaskets to the cylinder block (between the cylinder heads). Follow the instructions on the adhesive container. Then, apply a small amount of Quicksilver RTV sealant to each end of the end gaskets to provide a good seal between the side and end gaskets.

19. Lower the intake manifold into position on the cylinder block. Check the seal area to make sure the seals are in their proper positions. If not, remove the manifold, correct the seal position and reinstall the manifold.

20. Install the manifold attaching fasteners. Tighten the manifold fasteners to specification (**Table 3** or **Table 4**) in the sequence shown in **Figure 20** (V6 and small block) or **Figure 21** (big block).

21. Reverse Steps 1-13 to complete installation. Coat all electrical connections with Quicksilver Neoprene Dip.

Inspection

1. Check the intake manifold for cracks or distortion. Replace manifold if distorted or if cracks are found.

2. Check the mating surfaces for nicks or burrs. Small burrs may be removed with an oilstone.

3. Place a straightedge across the manifold flange/mating surfaces. If there is any gap be-

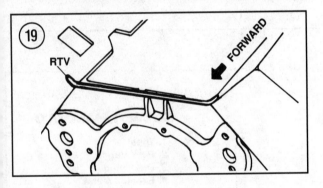

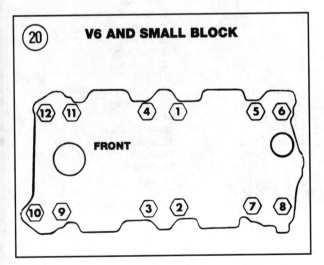

8

tween the straightedge and surface, measure it with a flat feeler gauge. Measure the manifold from end to end and from corner to corner. If the mating surface is not flat within 0.006 in. (0.15 mm) per foot of manifold length, replace the manifold.

EXHAUST MANIFOLDS

Figure 22 shows the typical exhaust manifold used on MerCruiser models through 1986. A new through-the-prop PlusPower ™ exhaust system was introduced on all 1987 V6 and V8 models (**Figure 23**). The PlusPower system provides near-equivalent performance to the through-the-transom exhaust system while reducing exhaust noise levels. The cast iron PlusPower manifold is more corrosion resistant and uses larger water passages to prevent salt accumulation and resulting clogging.

Exhaust elbow riser kits are available for al PlusPower exhaust systems (**Figure 24**). These kits are desirable with installations where the stern of the boat rests low in the water, and are

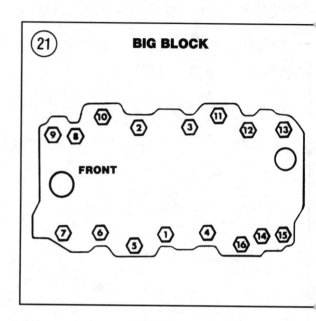

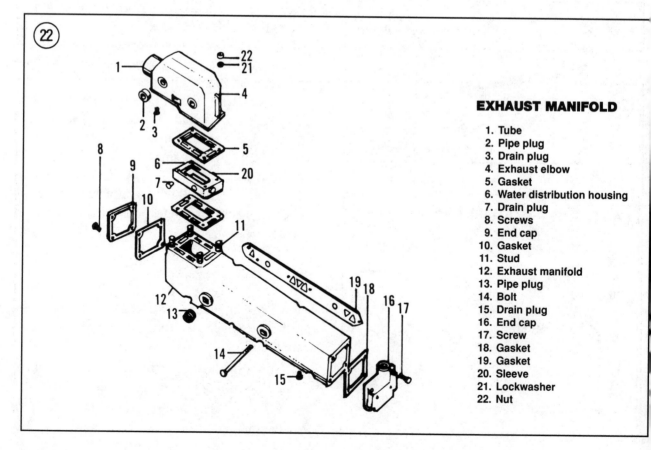

EXHAUST MANIFOLD

1. Tube
2. Pipe plug
3. Drain plug
4. Exhaust elbow
5. Gasket
6. Water distribution housing
7. Drain plug
8. Screws
9. End cap
10. Gasket
11. Stud
12. Exhaust manifold
13. Pipe plug
14. Bolt
15. Drain plug
16. End cap
17. Screw
18. Gasket
19. Gasket
20. Sleeve
21. Lockwasher
22. Nut

recommended in cases where the distance between the waterline and the top of the elbows is less than 13 in. (33 cm). See your MerCruiser dealer to determine the appropriate kit for your installation.

A muffler kit (part No. 42-17705A3) to reduce exhaust noise is available for all V8 Alpha and Bravo models with thru transom exhaust. The mufflers are installed between the exhaust elbows and transom and are easily disassembled

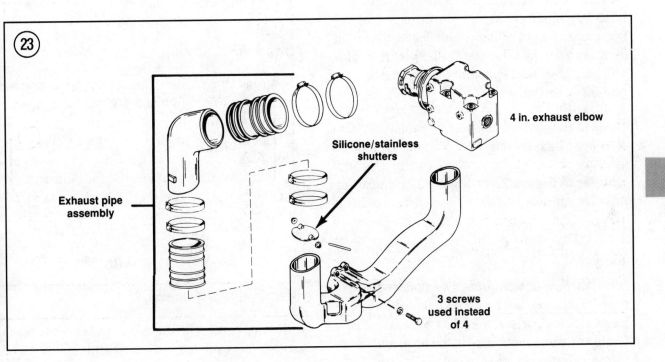

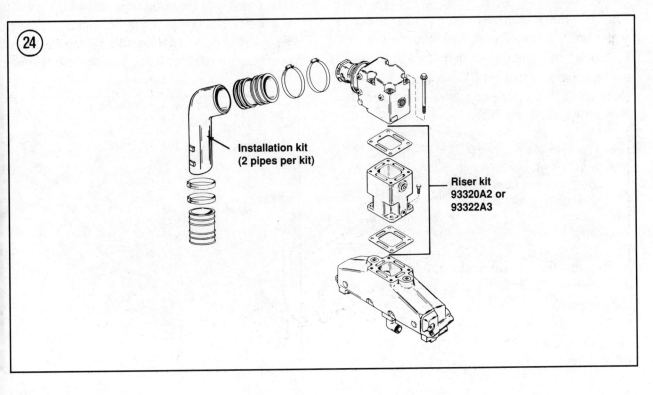

for replacement or cleaning of the internal element. The compact design can be installed directly in the exhaust system easily, requiring no modification to the transom exhaust holes on models with through-the-transom exhaust. Since exhaust noise varies considerably according to boat design, see your local MerCruiser dealer if noise abatement regulations or legislation is in effect in your area. He can advise you if this kit will help your boat to comply with local regulations.

Removal/Installation

Refer to **Figure 22** or **Figure 23**, typical for this procedure.

1. Disconnect the negative battery cable.

2. Open the cylinder block water drains and allow all water to drain.

3A. *PlusPower manifold*—Disconnect the exhaust pipe assembly from the manifold and exhaust elbow (or riser, if kit has been installed). Drain any water remaining in the manifold housing and elbow.

3B. *All others*—Remove the exhaust tube and water hoses from the manifold. Drain any water remaining in the manifold housing and elbow.

4. Starboard manifold—Disconnect the fuel lines from the water-separating fuel filter. Remove the filter assembly.

NOTE
The crankcase dipstick tube support bracket is retained by one starboard manifold attaching bolt. Remove the support bracket with the manifold in Step 5.

5. Remove the manifold attaching nuts or bolts and washers. Remove the manifold and discard the gasket(s).

6. Clean all gasket residue from the cylinder head, manifold and high-rise elbow mating surfaces with degreaser and a putty knife.

7. Install the manifold on the cylinder head with a new gasket. Tighten fasteners to specification (**Table 3** or **Table 4**), working from the center to the ends.

8. Reconnect the exhaust hose and reverse Steps 1-4 to complete installation.

Inspection/Cleaning

1. Inspect the engine exhaust ports for excessive rust or corrosion. Replace manifold if excessive corrosion is found.

2. Check water passage in exhaust elbow for clogging.

3. Remove pipe plugs from manifold and exhaust elbow, if so equipped. Check for sand, silt or other foreign matter.

ROCKER ARMS

Removal (All Engines)

On engines without roller rocker arms, each rocker arm moves on its own pivot ball. The rocker arm and pivot ball are retained by a nut on all models except Mark V engines (**Figure 25**). On Mark V engines, the rocker arm and pivot ball are retained by a shoulder bolt (**Figure**

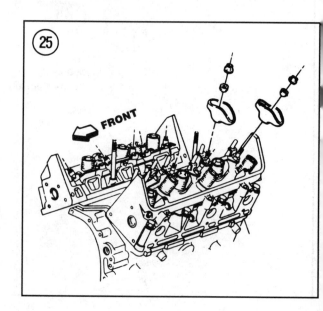

26). It is not necessary to remove the rocker arm for pushrod replacement; simply loosen the nut and move the arm away from the pushrod. To remove the entire assembly, refer to **Figure 25** (except Mark V) or **Figure 26** (Mark V) and proceed as follows:

1. Remove the valve cover(s) as described in this chapter.

2A. Except Mark V engines:

   a. Remove the rocker arm nut and pivot ball.

   b. Remove the rocker arm.

   c. Remove the pushrod from the cylinder block if necessary.

2B. Mark V engines:

   a. Remove the shoulder bolt, then lift the rocker arm and pivot ball off the cylinder head.

   b. Remove the pushrod from the cylinder block if necessary.

3. Repeat Step 2A or 2B for each remaining rocker arm. Place each rocker arm and pushrod assembly in a separate container or use a rack to keep them separated for reinstallation in the same position from which they were removed.

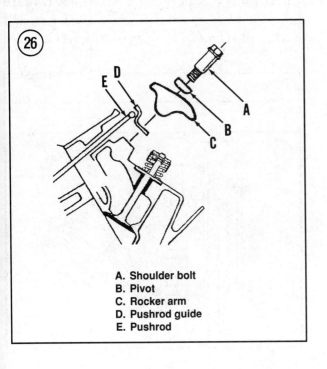

A. Shoulder bolt
B. Pivot
C. Rocker arm
D. Pushrod guide
E. Pushrod

Installation (Without Roller Rocker Arms)

1. Lubricate the rocker arms and pivot balls with engine oil.

2. Install the pushrods, making sure that each fits into its lifter socket. The tip on all pushrods should be marked with a blue stripe to indicate the end that must face the rocker arm.

3. Install the rocker arms, pivot balls and nuts or shoulder bolts. If new rocker arms or pivot balls are being installed, coat the contact surfaces with engine oil or Molykote.

4A. Except Mark V engines—Adjust the valve clearance as described in this chapter.

4B. Mark V engines—Tighten the rocker arm shoulder bolts to 45 ft.-lb. (61 N•m).

5. Install the valve cover(s) as described in this chapter.

Installation (With Roller Rocker Arms)

1. Lubricate rocker arms and pushrods with engine oil.

2. Install the pushrods, making sure that each fits into its lifter socket. The long pushrods are for exhaust valves; the short ones are for intake valves.

3. Install the rocker arms with the flat side of the pivot shaft facing upwards (**Figure 27**). If new rocker arms are installed on the No. 1 and No. 8 intake valves, you must remove 3/16 in. (4.8 mm) from the left-hand corner to clear the valve cover. See **Figure 28**.

4. Lubricate the ends of the rocker arm studs and valve stem ends with Quicksilver Needle Bearing Lubricant. Install the nuts.

5. Adjust the valve clearance as described in this chapter.

6. Install the rocker arm cover as described in this chapter.

8

Inspection

1. Clean all parts with solvent and use compressed air to blow out the oil passages in the pushrods.

2. Check each rocker arm, ball, nut or shoulder bolt and pushrod for scuffing, pitting or excessive wear; replace as required. If one component is worn, replace all components servicing that valve.

3. Check pushrods for straightness by rolling them across a flat, even surface such as a pane of glass. Replace any pushrods that do not roll smoothly.

4. If a pushrod is worn from lack of lubrication, replace the corresponding lifter and rocker arm as well.

VALVE LASH ADJUSTMENT (EXCEPT MARK V BIG BLOCKS AND GENERATION II V6 ENGINES)

Valve lash should be adjusted so the lifter plunger is positioned in the approximate center of its travel within the lifter body. Valve adjustment is required only when valve train components are replaced or the valve train has been disassembled. Adjust the valves with the lifter on the base circle of the camshaft lobe.

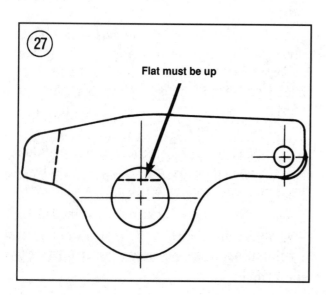

(27)

Flat must be up

Valve adjustment is not necessary on Mark V (454 and 502 cid) and Generation II V6 (262 cid) engines. On these models, valve lash is correctly set when the rocker arm fasteners are tightened to specification.

Engine Off (Without Roller Rocker Arms)

1. Rotate the crankshaft until the pulley notch aligns with the zero mark on the timing tab. This positions the No. 1 cylinder at TDC (**Figure 29**). This position can be verified by placing a finger on the No. 1 rocker arms as the pulley notch nears

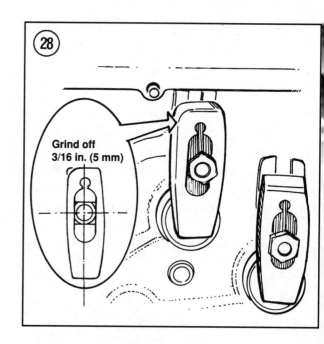

(28)

Grind off
3/16 in. (5 mm)

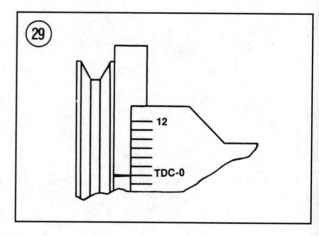

(29)

12

TDC-0

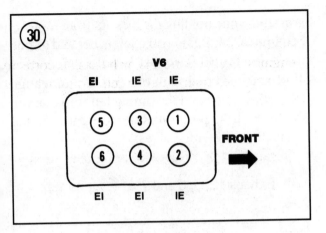

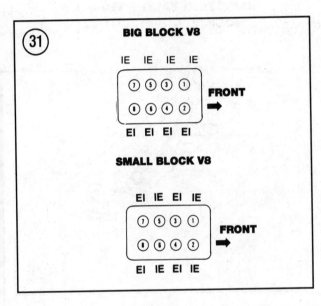

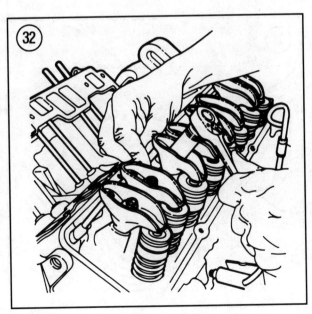

the zero mark. If the valves are moving, the engine is in the No. 4 (V6) or No. 6 (V8) firing position; rotate the crankshaft pulley one full turn to reach the No. 1 firing position.

NOTE
The intake valves are those closer to the intake manifold. Exhaust valves are closer to the exhaust manifold.

2. With the engine in the No. 1 firing position, refer to **Figure 30** (V6) or **Figure 31** (V8) and adjust the following valves:

    a. Intake: 1, 2, 3 (V6) or 1, 2, 5, 7 (V8.

    b. Exhaust: 1, 5, 6 (V6) or 1, 3, 4, 8 (V8).

3. To adjust each valve, back off the adjusting nut until lash is felt at the pushrod, then turn the nut to remove all lash. When lash has been removed, the pushrod will not rotate. Turn the nut in another 3/4 or full turn as specified in **Table 1** to center the lifter plunger. See **Figure 32**.

4. Rotate the crankshaft one full turn to realign the pulley notch and the timing tab zero mark in the No. 4 (V6) or No. 6 (V8) firing position. Refer to **Figure 30** (V6) or **Figure 31** (V8) and adjust the following valves:

    a. Intake: 4, 5, 6 (V6) or 3, 4, 6, 8 (V8).

    b. Exhaust: 2, 3, 4 (V6) or 2, 5, 6, 7 (V8).

5. Install the valve cover as described in this chapter.

**Engine Running
(Without Roller Rocker Arms)**

To prevent oil from splashing out of the cylinder heads while performing this procedure, cut the top out of a used valve cover. See **Figure 33**. Tape or file the cut edges of the reworked valve cover to prevent injury to yourself while working.

1. Warm the engine to normal operating temperature with the reworked cover temporarily installed.

2. With the engine idling, back off one rocker arm nut until the rocker arm starts to clatter.

3. Tighten the rocker arm nut until the clatter stops. This will remove all lash (zero lash position).

4. Tighten the nut another 1/4 turn. Wait 10 seconds to let the engine stabilize.

5. Repeat Step 4 two more times. This will tighten the nut an additional 3/4 turn from zero lash position.

6. Repeat steps 3-5 for each valve.

7. Stop the engine. Remove the reworked valve cover. Install the original valve cover as described in this chapter.

Engine Off (With Roller Rocker Arms)

1. Rotate the crankshaft until the pulley notch aligns with the zero mark on the timing tab. This positions the No. 1 cylinder at TDC (**Figure 29**). This position can be verified by placing a finger on the No. 1 rocker arms as the pulley notch nears the zero mark. If the valves are moving, the engine is in the No. 6 firing position; rotate the crankshaft pulley one full turn to reach the No. 1 firing position.

> *NOTE*
> *The intake valves are those closer to the intake manifold. Exhaust valves are closer to the exhaust manifold.*

2. With the engine in the No. 1 firing position, refer to **Figure 31** and adjust the following valves:

    a. Intake: 1, 2, 5 and 7.

    b. Exhaust: 1, 3, 4 and 8.

3. To adjust each valve, make sure that the pushrod is properly centered in the rocker arm socket, then tighten the 9/16 in. locknut on the rocker arm until there is no lash (zero clearance) between the valve stem and rocker arm. Without lash, the pushrod will not rotate. Tighten the locknut to specifications in **Table 2**, and then tighten the Allen head screw on top of the rocker

arm stud while holding the locknut from turning. See **Figure 34**. Remove the wrenches and torque the locknut to 30 ft.-lb. (41 N•m).

4. Rotate the crankshaft one full turn to realign the pulley notch and the timing tab zero mark in the No. 6 firing position. Refer to **Figure 31** and adjust the following valves:

    a. Intake: 3, 4, 6 and 8.

    b. Exhaust: 2, 5, 6 and 7.

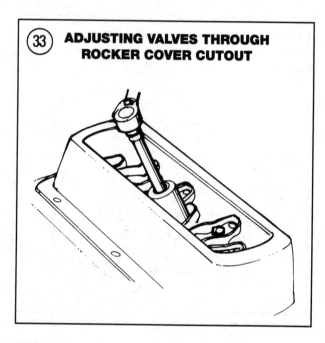

(33) **ADJUSTING VALVES THROUGH ROCKER COVER CUTOUT**

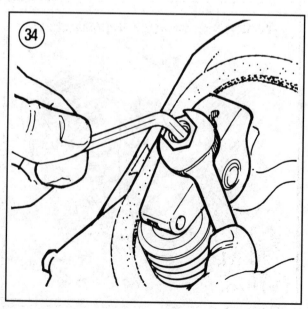

(34)

5. Install the valve cover as described in this chapter.

CRANKSHAFT PULLEY AND TORSIONAL DAMPER

Removal/Installation

1. Remove the alternator drive belt. See Chapter Ten.

㉟ TORSIONAL DAMPER REMOVAL

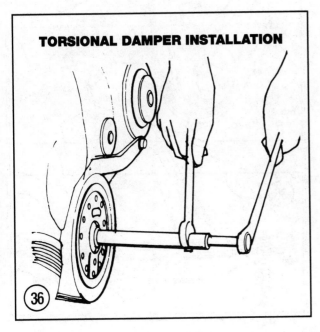

TORSIONAL DAMPER INSTALLATION

㊱

2, Remove the pulley attaching bolts. Remove the pulley.

3. Remove the torsional damper retaining bolt.

4. Install puller part No. J-23523E or equivalent to the damper with the pulley attaching bolts and remove the torsional damper from the crankshaft. See **Figure 35**, typical.

5. Lubricate the front cover seal lip and the contact areas on the torsional damper and crankshaft with clean engine oil.

NOTE
If tool part No. J-23523E is not available for use in Step 6, pull the balancer onto the crankshaft with a thick flat washer, a full-threaded 7/16-20 × 4 in. bolt and 7/16-20 nut.

6. Position the torsional damper over the crankshaft key and install the threaded end of tool part No. J-23523E in the crankshaft so that at least 1/2 in. (12.7 mm) of the tool threads are engaged. Install plate, thrust bearing and nut to complete tool installation.

7. Pull damper into position as shown in **Figure 36**, typical.

8. Remove the tool, install the damper retaining bolt and tighten to specifications (**Table 3** or **Table 4**).

9. Install pulley and tighten attaching bolts to specifications (**Table 3** or **Table 4**).

10. Install and adjust the alternator drive belt. See Chapter Ten.

CRANKCASE FRONT COVER AND OIL SEAL

Front Cover Removal/Installation (Small Block Engines)

1. Remove the engine from the boat as described in this chapter.

2. Remove the torsional damper as described in this chapter.

3. Remove the oil pan as described in this chapter.

8

4. Remove the engine water (circulating) pump. See Chapter Ten.

5. Unbolt and remove the front cover from the engine block. Remove and discard the gasket.

6. Installation is the reverse of removal. Use a new front cover gasket coated on both sides with Quicksilver Perfect Seal.

Front Cover Removal/Installation (7.4L and 8.2L Engines)

1. Open the engine drain valve(s) and drain all the water from the block.

2. Drain the crankcase oil. See Chapter Four.

3. Remove the seawater pump. See Chapter Ten.

4. Remove any accessory brackets attached to the engine water (circulating) pump. Remove the pump pulley and drive belt. See Chapter Ten.

5. Remove the crankshaft pulley and torsional damper as described in this chapter.

6. Remove the 2 screws holding the front of the oil pan to the front cover.

7. Use a sharp X-acto knife to cut the oil pan seal flush with the cylinder block face. See **Figure 37**.

8. Unbolt and remove the front cover. Discard the gasket.

9. Clean the block and front cover sealing surfaces of all oil, grease and gasket residue with degreaser and a putty knife.

10. Lubricate the timing chain and gears with engine oil.

11. Coat the gasket surfaces of the block and front cover with Quicksilver Perfect Seal and install a new gasket over the dowel pins on the engine block.

12. Use the cut portion of the oil pan seal as a template and cut a matching section from a new seal for use in Step 13. See **Figure 38**.

13. Coat the exposed surface of the oil pan flange with Perfect Seal and install the seal portion cut in Step 12. Make sure the seal tips fit into the cover holes. Coat the exposed seal surface with Perfect Seal.

14. Apply a 1/8 in. (3.2 mm) bead of Quicksilver RTV sealant along the joint on each side where the oil pan meets the block. See **Figure 39**.

15. Position the front cover on the engine block. Work carefully to prevent damage to the oil seal or movement of the gasket and oil pan seal.

16. Apply downward pressure on the cover and install the oil pan attaching screws finger-tight.

17. Coat the attaching bolt threads with Perfect Seal and install the bolts. Tighten bolts and oil pan screws to specifications (**Table 4**).

18. Reverse Steps 1-5 to complete installation.

Front Cover Seal Replacement

The seal can be replaced without removing the front cover. If the cover has been removed and seal replacement is necessary, support the cover on a clean workbench and perform Steps 2-4.

1. Remove the torsional damper as described in this chapter.

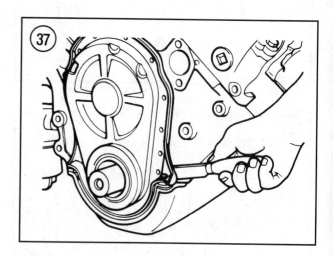

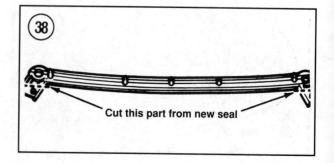

Cut this part from new seal

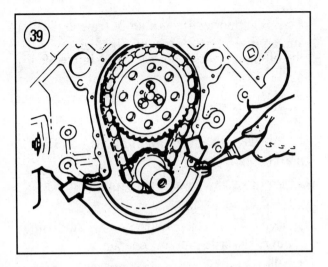

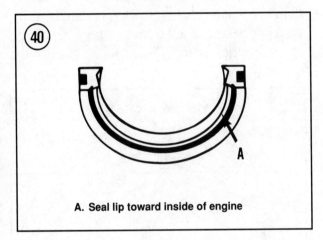

A. Seal lip toward inside of engine

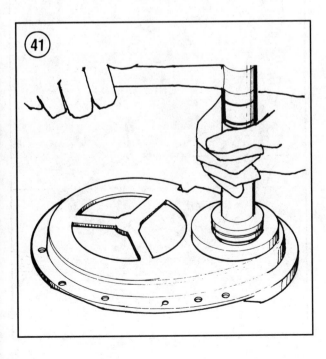

2. Pry the oil seal from the cover with a large screwdriver. Work carefully to prevent damage to the cover seal surface.

3. Clean the seal recess in the cover with solvent and blow dry with compressed air.

4. Position a new seal in the cover recess with its lip facing the inside of the engine (**Figure 40**). Drive seal into place with installer part No. J-22102 (7.4L and 8.2L) or part No. J-23042 (all others). See **Figure 41**.

5. Install the torsional damper as described in this chapter.

TIMING CHAIN AND SPROCKETS

Removal

1. Remove the spark plugs. See Chapter Four.

2. Remove the torsional damper as described in this chapter.

3. Remove the front cover as described in this chapter.

4. Temporarily reinstall the damper bolt and washer in the end of the crankshaft. Place a wrench on the bolt and rotate the crankshaft to position the camshaft and crankshaft sprocket marks as shown in **Figure 42**. Remove the damper bolt and washer.

5. Remove the camshaft sprocket bolts. The sprocket is a snug fit but should come off easily. If not, lightly tap the lower edge of the sprocket with a plastic hammer to dislodge it from the camshaft. Remove the sprocket and timing chain as an assembly.

6. If the crankshaft sprocket requires removal, pull it off the crankshaft using puller part No. J5825-A (V6 and small block) or J24420-B (big block).

Installation

Some engines were equipped with a link-type timing chain and aluminum/nylon camshaft sprocket. If either component requires replace-

8

ment, a new timing chain assembly (part No. 35378A1) must be used. This assembly includes a roller-type timing chain, an all-metal camshaft sprocket and a new crankshaft sprocket. Original components *cannot* be used in combination with the service replacement parts.

1. Install the crankshaft sprocket, if removed, with sprocket installer part No. J-21058-20 (7.4L and 8.2L) or part No. J-5590 (all others).

2. Install the timing chain on the camshaft sprocket. With chain hanging freely, align camshaft sprocket timing mark with crankshaft sprocket timing mark. See **Figure 43**.

3. Align the dowel hole in the camshaft sprocket with the dowel on the camshaft and press the sprocket onto the shaft.

NOTE
Do not drive the camshaft sprocket into place in Step 3 or you may dislodge the welch plug behind the camshaft in the rear of the block.

4. Install the camshaft sprocket mounting bolts. Tighten bolts to draw the sprocket onto the camshaft, then tighten to specification (**Table 3** or **Table 4**).

5. Lubricate the timing chain liberally with SAE 30 engine oil.

6. Install the front cover and torsional damper as described in this chapter.

7. Reinstall the spark plugs. See Chapter Four.

BALANCE SHAFT (V6 MODELS SERIAL NO. OF000001-ON)

V6 models serial No. OF000001-on are equipped with a balance shaft. The balance shaft is designed to eliminate much of the dynamic vibration in the 1,700-2,000 rpm range that is common to the 90° V6 engine. The balance shaft is positioned in the engine block valley area, located directly above the camshaft. The balance shaft is driven by a drive gear located behind the camshaft sprocket. See **Figure 44**. The balance

shaft is supported by a roller bearing at the front and an insert type bearing at the rear.

Removal/Inspection/Installation

1. Remove the intake manifold as described in this chapter.

2. Remove the crankcase front cover as described in this chapter.

3. Remove the camshaft sprocket and timing chain as described in this chapter.

4. Place a hardwood wedge between the balance shaft drive and driven gears to prevent the camshaft and balance shaft from turning. Then, using the appropriate size TORX socket, remove the

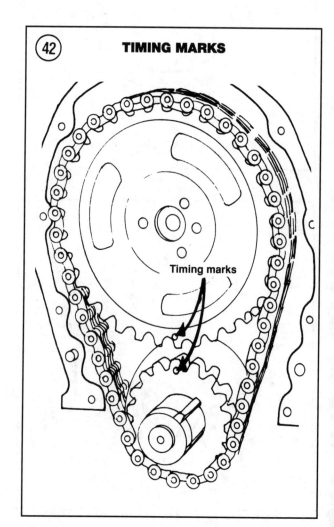

42 **TIMING MARKS**

Timing marks

driven gear retaining bolt. See 3, **Figure 45**. Remove the driven gear (4, **Figure 45**).

5. Remove the stud bolt (1, **Figure 45**) and remove the drive gear (2) from the camshaft.

6. Next, remove the 2 TORX bolts securing the balance shaft thrust plate.

CAUTION
Use caution when prying out the balance shaft in Step 7 to prevent damage to the shaft or cylinder block.

7. Place a suitable pry bar between the rear of the balance shaft counter weight and cylinder block. Carefully, pry the balance shaft straight forward to dislodge the shaft front bearing from

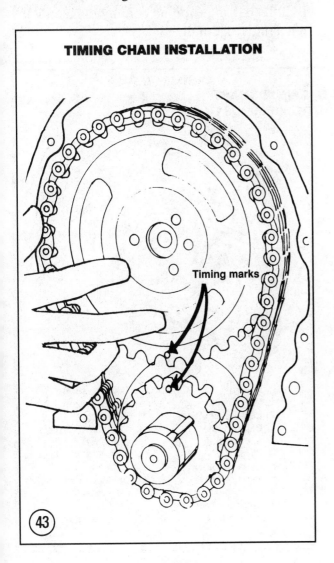

TIMING CHAIN INSTALLATION

Timing marks

⊙43

its bore in the block. Slide the shaft and front bearing out of the cylinder block.

8. Thoroughly clean the balance shaft and front bearing. Dry with compressed air.

9. Inspect the balance shaft rear bearing for excessive wear or damage. Refer to **Table 1** for bearing specifications.

10. Inspect the front bearing for scoring, roughness or excessive wear. The front bearing is not available separately from the balance shaft. If the bearing requires replacement, replace the balance shaft assembly.

11. Inspect the balance shaft front bearing bore in the cylinder block for wear or evidence of the bearing spinning in the bore.

12. Inspect the balance shaft driven gear for chipped teeth or excessive wear. Replace the gear as necessary.

13. To install the balance shaft, first lubricate the front and rear bearings with clean engine oil.

14. Install the balance shaft into the cylinder block. Make sure the front bearing correctly enters its bore. Then, using a soft-face mallet, tap the balance shaft until the snap ring around the front bearing is firmly seated against the cylinder block.

15. Install the balance shaft thrust plate and 2 TORX bolts. Tighten the bolts to 120 in.-lb. (13.5 N·m).

16. Install the balance shaft driven gear on the balance shaft. Install the gear retaining bolt and tighten it snug. Then, rotate the balance shaft until the timing mark on the driven gear (**Figure 46**) is facing DOWN.

17. Install the balance shaft drive gear on the camshaft, making sure the timing marks on the gears are aligned as shown in **Figure 46**. Rotate the camshaft and balance shaft as necessary to align the marks. Install the stud bolt (1, **Figure 45**) and tighten to 120 in.-lb. (13.5 N·m).

18. Install the camshaft sprocket and timing chain as described in this chapter.

19. Next, remove the balance shaft driven gear bolt (3, **Figure 45**) and apply Loctite 271 to its

8

threads. Reinstall the bolt. Place a hardwood wedge between the balance shaft drive and driven gears to prevent the camshaft and balance shaft from turning. Then tighten the driven gear bolt to 15 ft.-lb. (20 N·m), then an additional 35°.

20. Install the crankcase front cover and intake manifold as described in this chapter.

Balance Shaft Bearings Replacement

The front of the balance shaft is supported with a roller bearing pressed on the shaft. The rear of the shaft is supported in an insert-type bearing, similar to a camshaft bearing. The front balance shaft bearing is not available separately from the shaft. Should the bearing require replacement, replace the balance shaft assembly.

Bearing remover/installer kit part No. J38834 and bearing remover part No. J26941 are required to remove and install the rear balance shaft bearing.

1. Remove the balance shaft as described in this chapter.

2. Using a suitable punch, drive the core plug (1, **Figure 44**) from its bore at the rear of the cylinder block. Remove the balance shaft seal (2, **Figure 44**).

3. Cover the lifters and valley area of the cylinder block to prevent debris from entering the crankcase.

4. Assemble the bearing remover tool into the cylinder block and rear bearing. See **Figure 47**. Pull the bearing from its bore by tightening the nut at the front of the tool.

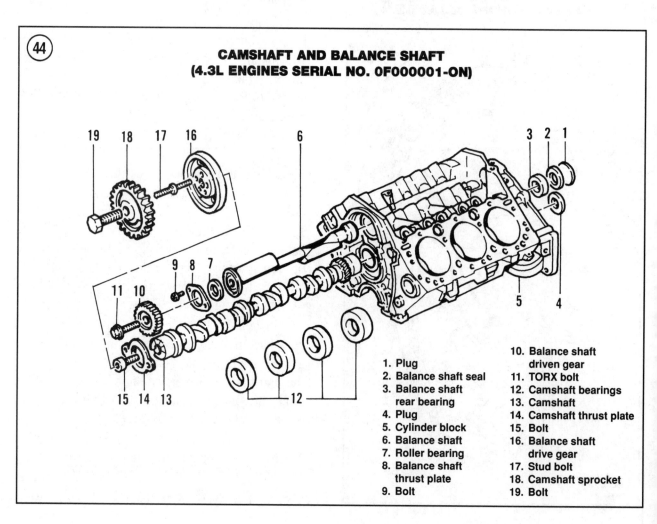

44

**CAMSHAFT AND BALANCE SHAFT
(4.3L ENGINES SERIAL NO. 0F000001-ON)**

1. Plug
2. Balance shaft seal
3. Balance shaft rear bearing
4. Plug
5. Cylinder block
6. Balance shaft
7. Roller bearing
8. Balance shaft thrust plate
9. Bolt
10. Balance shaft driven gear
11. TORX bolt
12. Camshaft bearings
13. Camshaft
14. Camshaft thrust plate
15. Bolt
16. Balance shaft drive gear
17. Stud bolt
18. Camshaft sprocket
19. Bolt

5. Install the rear bearing using bearing remover/installer tool (part No. 38834) and shim (GM part No. 10229872). The shim is installed on the tool before the rear bearing to ensure the bearing is installed to the proper depth.

6. Install a new seal (3, **Figure 44**) and core plug (1). See *Core Plug Replacement* in this chapter.

Coat the outer diameter of the core plug with Loctite 271 prior to installation.

7. Install the balance shaft as described in this chapter.

CAMSHAFT

Removal/Installation

1. Remove the valve covers as described in this chapter.

2. Remove the intake manifold as described in this chapter.

3. Loosen the rocker arm adjusting nuts, swivel the arms off the pushrods and remove the pushrods.

4. Identify each pushrod for reinstallation in its original location.

5. Remove the valve lifters with a pencil-type magnet. Place them in a rack in order of removal for reinstallation in their original locations.

6. Remove the fuel pump and pushrod. See Chapter Nine.

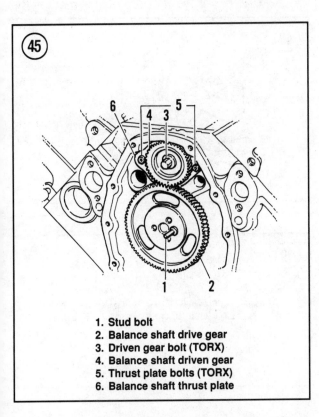

1. Stud bolt
2. Balance shaft drive gear
3. Driven gear bolt (TORX)
4. Balance shaft driven gear
5. Thrust plate bolts (TORX)
6. Balance shaft thrust plate

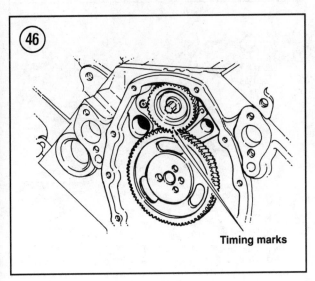

Timing marks

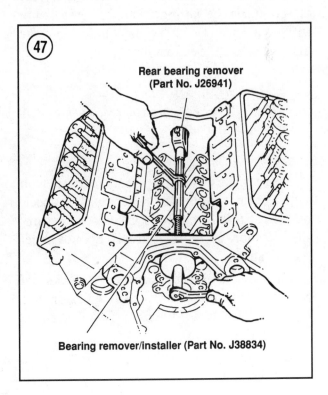

Rear bearing remover
(Part No. J26941)

Bearing remover/installer (Part No. J38834)

7. Remove the front cover, timing chain, camshaft sprocket and balance shaft drive gear as described in this chapter. Install two 5/16-18 × 4 in. bolts in the camshaft bolt holes at the end of the camshaft.

> *CAUTION*
> *Do not cock the camshaft during removal. This can damage the camshaft or its bearing thrust surfaces.*

8. Carefully withdraw the camshaft from the front of the engine with a rotating motion to avoid damage to the bearings.

9. Installation is the reverse of removal. Coat the camshaft lobes with GM cam and lifter prelube lubricant (or equivalent) and the journals with heavy engine oil before reinstalling in the block. Check and adjust ignition timing (Chapter Four).

Inspection

1. Check the journals and lobes for signs of wear or scoring. Lobe pitting in the toe area is not sufficient reason for replacement unless the lobe lift loss exceeds specifications.

> *NOTE*
> *If you do not have precision measuring equipment, have Step 2 done by a machine shop.*

2. Measure the camshaft journal diameters with a micrometer (**Figure 48**) and compare to specification (**Table 1** or **Table 2**). Replace the camshaft if one or more journals do not meet specification.

3. Suspend the camshaft between V-blocks and check for warpage with a dial indicator. See **Figure 49**. Replace if the runout is greater than 0.002 in. (0.051 mm).

4. Check the distributor drive gear for excessive wear or damage.

Lobe Lift Measurement

Camshaft lobe lift can be measured with the camshaft in the block and the cylinder head in place.

1. Remove the valve cover as described in this chapter.

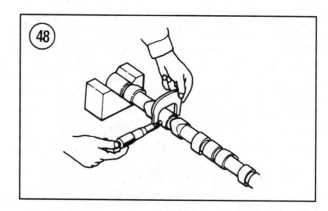

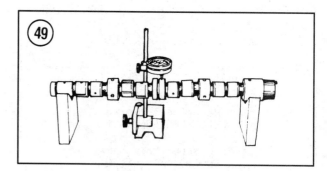

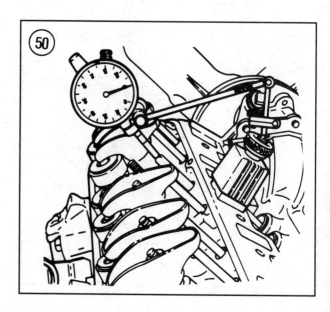

2. Remove the rocker arms and pivot assemblies as described in this chapter.

3. Remove the spark plugs. See Chapter Four.

4. Install a dial indicator on the end of a pushrod. A piece of rubber tubing will hold the dial indicator plunger in place on the center of the pushrod. See **Figure 50**, typical.

5. Rotate the crankshaft in the normal direction of rotation until the valve lifter seats on the heel or base of the cam lobe (**Figure 51**). This positions the pushrod at its lowest point.

6. Set the dial indicator at zero, then slowly rotate the crankshaft until the pushrod reaches its maximum travel. Note the indicator reading and compare to specifications (**Table 1** or **Table 2**).

7. Repeat Steps 4-6 for each pushrod. If all lobes are within specifications in Step 6, reinstall the rocker arm assemblies and adjust the valves as described in this chapter.

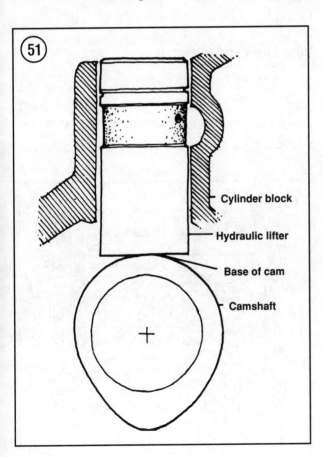

Cylinder block

Hydraulic lifter

Base of cam

Camshaft

8. If one or more lobes are worn beyond specification, replace the camshaft as described in this chapter.

9. Remove the dial indicator and reverse Steps 1-3.

Bearing Replacement

Camshaft bearings can be replaced without complete engine disassembly. Replace bearings in complete sets. Camshaft bearing and installer tool part No. J-6098 is required for bearing replacement.

1. Remove the camshaft as described in this chapter.

2. Remove the crankshaft as described in this chapter. Leave pistons in cylinder bores.

3. Drive the camshaft welch plug from the rear of the cylinder block.

4. Secure the connecting rods to the side of the engine to keep them out of the way while replacing the cam bearings.

5. Install the nut and thrust washer to tool part No. J-6098. Index the tool pilot in the front cam bearing. Install the puller screw through the pilot.

6. Install tool part No. J-6098 with its shoulder facing the front intermediate bearing and the threads engaging the bearing.

7. Hold the puller screw with one wrench. Turn the nut with a second wrench until the bearing has been pulled from its bore. See **Figure 52**.

8. When bearing has been removed from bore, remove tool and bearing from puller screw.

9. Repeat Steps 5-8 to remove the center bearing.

10. Remove the tool and index it to the rear bearing to remove the rear intermediate bearing from the block.

11. Remove the front and rear bearings by driving them toward the center of the block.

8

CAUTION
Improper alignment of the rear bearing during Step 12 will restrict oil pressure reaching the valve train.

12. Installation is the reverse of removal. Use the same tool to pull the new bearings into their bores. Bearing oil holes must align with those in the block. Since the oil hole is on the top of the bearings, and cannot be seen during installation, align bearing oil hole with hole in bore and mark opposite side of bearing and block at bore to assist in positioning the oil hole during installation as follows. Position the No. 1 bearing oil holes at an equal distance from the 6 o'clock position. Align No. 5 bearing oil hole with the 12 o'clock position.

13. Wipe a new camshaft welch plug with Quicksilver Perfect Seal and install it flush to 1/32 in. (0.8 mm) deep to maintain a level surface on the rear of the block.

OIL PAN

Ease of oil pan removal will depend upon the installation within a given boat. In some cases, the oil pan can be removed without removing the engine. In others, engine removal is required to provide sufficient working space and clearance for oil pan removal.

A modification kit is available from marine dealers to assist in draining the oil when the engine is in the boat. This kit can be installed on any engine oil pan when the engine is removed for service.

A 1-piece soft silicone rubber gasket is used with 1986 and later engines. The 1-piece gasket contains spacer around each oil pan screw hole to prevent gasket damage from excessive torque. Earlier engines use a 2-piece cork gasket with front and rear seals. The silicone rubber gasket (part No. 27-14901A1) can be used as a service replacement for the 2-piece gasket/seal arrangement.

Removal

1A. If the engine is in the boat:
  a. Remove the oil dipstick and siphon the oil from the crankcase. See Chapter Four.
  b. Remove the oil dipstick tube.

1B. If the engine is out of the boat:
  a. Place a suitable container under the oil pan drain plug. Remove the plug and let the crankcase drain. Reinstall the drain plug.
  b. If mounted in an engine stand, rotate the engine 180° to place the oil pan in an upright position.
  c. Remove the oil dipstick and dipstick tube.

2. Remove the oil pan attaching screws. Remove the oil pan.

3. Remove and discard the 2-piece pan gasket and the front/rear seals (1985) or the 1-piece silicone rubber gasket (1986-on).

Inspection and Cleaning

1. Clean any gasket residue from the oil pan rail on the engine block, rear main bearing cap, front cover and the oil pan sealing flange with degreaser and a putty knife.

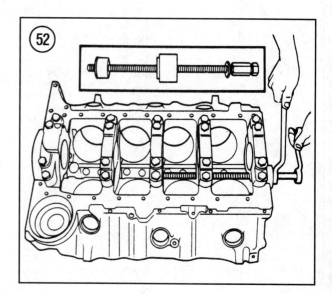

2. Clean the pan thoroughly in solvent and check for dents or warped gasket surfaces. Straighten or replace the pan as required.

Installation

1A. Two-piece gasket:
    a. Coat both sides of new oil pan gaskets with Quicksilver Perfect Seal and position on the cylinder block side rails. See A, **Figure 53**.
    b. Run a 1/8 in. (3.2 mm) bead of Quicksilver RTV sealant on the front and rear seal mating surfaces of the cylinder block rear main bearing cap, front cover and gasket. See B, **Figure 53**.
    c. Install new front and rear seals. Make sure the seal ends butt properly against the side gaskets.
    d. Run a 1/8 in. (3.2 mm) bead of RTV sealant on the outer surface of the seals. See C, **Figure 53**.

1B. One-piece silicone rubber gasket:
    a. Install gasket on oil pan rails.
    b. Insert an oil pan screw at each corner of the pan to hold the gasket in place.

2. Carefully position the oil pan in place. Make sure the gasket is not misaligned and then install

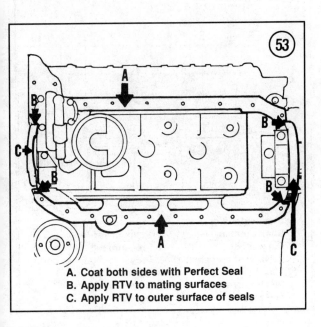

A. Coat both sides with Perfect Seal
B. Apply RTV to mating surfaces
C. Apply RTV to outer surface of seals

the attaching screws with lockwashers and tighten to specifications (**Table 3** or **Table 4**). Work from the center outward in each direction.

3. Reinstall the dipstick and guide tube.

4. Install the engine in the boat as described in this chapter and fill the crankcase with an oil recommended in Chapter Four.

OIL PUMP

Removal/Installation

A baffle is used on the pickup screen of all engines except Model 200. This eliminates pressure loss. To accommodate the baffle, the pickup screen tube is bent at special angles. The Model 200 has the baffle in the oil pan.

1. Remove the oil pan as described in this chapter.

> *NOTE*
> *The oil pump pickup tube and screen are a press fit in the pump housing of V6 and small block V8 engines and should not be removed unless replacement is required. The pickup screen and pipe assembly used with 7.4L and 8.2L engines cannot be removed from the pump.*

2. Remove the nut holding the pump to the rear main bearing cap.

3. Remove the pump, gasket (if used) and extension drive shaft.

4. To install, align the slot on the extension shaft top with the drive tang on the lower end of the distributor drive shaft.

> *NOTE*
> *The bottom edge of the oil pump pickup screen should be parallel to the oil pan rails when pump is installed in Step 5.*

5. Install pump to rear main bearing cap with a new gasket, if used. Tighten pump nut to specifications (**Table 3** or **Table 4**).

6. Reinstall the oil pan as described in this chapter.

Disassembly/Assembly

Refer to **Figure 54** or **Figure 55** as appropriate for this procedure.

1. Remove the cover screws, cover and gasket. Discard the gasket.

2. Mark the gear teeth to reassure reassembly with identical gear indexing and then remove the idler and drive gear with shaft from the body.

3. Remove the pressure regulator valve pin, regulator, spring and valve.

4. On V6 and small block V8, remove the pickup tube/screen assembly *only* if it needs replacement. Secure the pump body in a soft-jawed vise and separate the tube from the cover.

CAUTION
Do not twist, shear or collapse the tube when installing it in Step 5.

5. On V6 and small block V8, if the pickup tube/screen assembly was removed, install a new one. Secure the pump body in a soft-jawed vise. Apply sealer to the new tube and gently tap in place with a soft-faced mallet. See **Figure 56**.

6. Lubricate all parts thoroughly with clean engine oil before reassembly.

7. Assembly is the reverse of disassembly. Index the gear marks, install a new cover gasket and rotate the pump drive shaft by hand to check for smooth operation. Tighten cover bolts to specifications (**Table 3** or **Table 4**).

Inspection

NOTE
The pump assembly and gears are services as an assembly. If one or the other is worn or damaged, replace the entire pump. No wear specifications are provided by the manufacturer.

1. Clean all parts thoroughly in solvent. Brush the inside of the body and the pressure regulator chamber to remove all dirt and metal particles. Dry with compressed air, if available.

2. Check the pump body and cover for cracks or excessive wear.

3. Check the pump gears for damage or excessive wear.

4. Check the drive gear shaft-to-body fit for excessive looseness.

5. Check the inside of the pump cover for wear that could allow oil to leak around the ends of the gears.

6. Check the pressure regulator valve for a proper fit.

CYLINDER HEAD

Removal

Perform Steps 1-4 if engine is in boat. If engine has been removed from the boat, begin with Step 5.

1. Open the engine block drain valves and drain all water from the block.

2. Remove the intake and exhaust manifolds as described in this chapter.

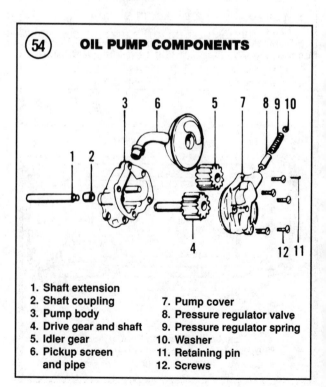

54   **OIL PUMP COMPONENTS**

1. Shaft extension
2. Shaft coupling
3. Pump body
4. Drive gear and shaft
5. Idler gear
6. Pickup screen and pipe
7. Pump cover
8. Pressure regulator valve
9. Pressure regulator spring
10. Washer
11. Retaining pin
12. Screws

3. Remove the alternator and oil filter mounting brackets.

4. Disconnect the spark plug wires and remove the wire looms from the cylinder head.

5. Remove the valve cover as described in this chapter.

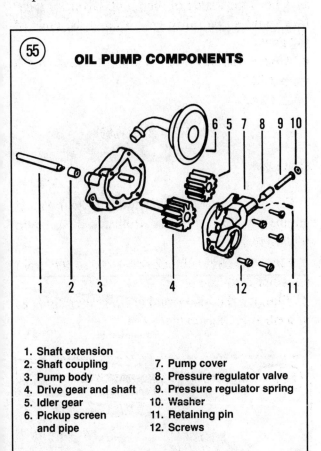

OIL PUMP COMPONENTS

1. Shaft extension
2. Shaft coupling
3. Pump body
4. Drive gear and shaft
5. Idler gear
6. Pickup screen and pipe
7. Pump cover
8. Pressure regulator valve
9. Pressure regulator spring
10. Washer
11. Retaining pin
12. Screws

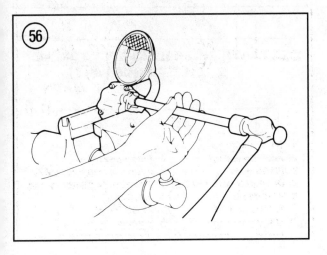

6. Loosen the rocker arms and rotate them to one side. Remove the pushrods and identify each for reinstallation in its original position.

7. Loosen the cylinder head bolts, working from the center of the head to the end in each direction.

8. Remove the head bolts. Rap the end of the head with a soft-faced hammer to break the gasket seal. Remove the head from the engine.

CAUTION
Place the head on its side to prevent damage to the spark plugs or head gasket surface.

9. Remove and discard the head gasket. Clean all gasket residue from the head and block mating surfaces.

Decarbonizing

1. Without removing the valves, remove all deposits from the combustion chambers, intake ports and exhaust ports. Use a fine wire brush dipped in solvent or make a scraper from hardwood. Be careful not to scratch or gouge the combustion chambers.

2. After all carbon is removed from the combustion chambers and ports, clean the entire head in solvent.

3. Clean all carbon from the piston tops. Do not remove the carbon ridge at the top of each cylinder bore.

4. Remove the valves as described in this chapter.

5. Clean the pushrod guides, valve guide bores and all bolt holes. Use a cleaning solvent to remove dirt and grease.

6. Clean the valves with a fine wire brush or buffing wheel.

Inspection

1. Check the cylinder head for signs of oil or water leaks before cleaning.

2. Clean the cylinder head thoroughly in solvent. While cleaning, look for cracks or other visible signs of damage. Look for corrosion or foreign material in the oil and water passages (**Figure 57**). Clean the passages with a stiff spiral brush, then blow them out with compressed air.

3. Check the cylinder head studs for damage and replace if necessary.

4. Check the threaded rocker arm studs or bolt holes for damaged threads; replace if necessary.

5. Check for warpage of the cylinder head-to-block surface with a straightedge and feeler gauge (**Figure 58**). Measure diagonally, as well as end-to-end. If the gap exceeds specification (**Table 1** or **Table 2**), have the head resurfaced by a machine shop. If head resurfacing is necessary, do not remove more than 0.010 in. (0.25 mm). Replace the head if a greater amount must be removed to correct warpage.

Installation

1. Make sure the cylinder head and block gasket surfaces and bolts holes are clean. Dirt in the block bolt holes or on the head bolt threads will affect bolt torque.

2. Recheck all visible oil and water passages for cleanliness.

> *CAUTION*
> *If a steel gasket is used, apply a thin coat of Quicksilver Perfect Seal to both sides of the gasket (excessive sealer may hold the gasket away from the head or block). Do **not** use sealer on graphite composition gaskets.*

3. Fit a new head gasket over the cylinder dowels on the block.

4. Carefully lower the head onto the cylinder block, engaging the dowel pins.

5. Wipe all head bolt threads with Quicksilver Perfect Seal or equivalent. Install and tighten the head bolts finger-tight.

6. Tighten the head bolts 1/2 turn at a time following the sequence shown in **Figure 59** (V6), **Figure 60** (small block V8) or **Figure 61** (big block V8) until the specified torque is reached. See **Table 3** or **Table 4**.

7. If engine is in the boat, reverse Steps 1-6 of *Removal* in this chapter to complete installation. If engine is out of the boat, reverse Step 5 and

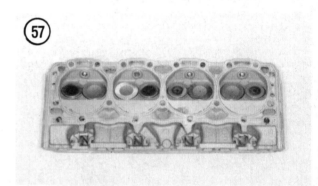

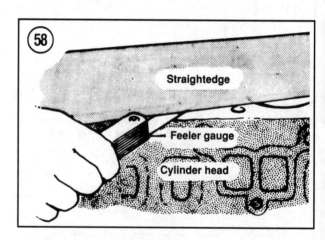

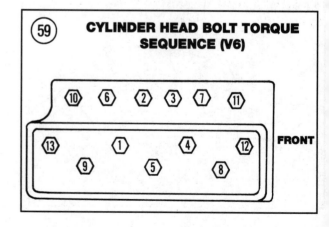

Step 6 of *Removal* in this chapter. Adjust the valves as described in this chapter. Check and adjust ignition timing as required. See Chapter Four.

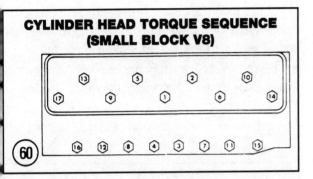

CYLINDER HEAD TORQUE SEQUENCE (SMALL BLOCK V8)

60

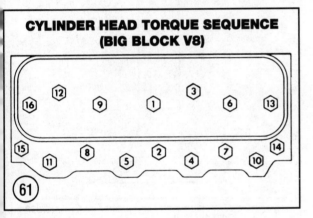

CYLINDER HEAD TORQUE SEQUENCE (BIG BLOCK V8)

61

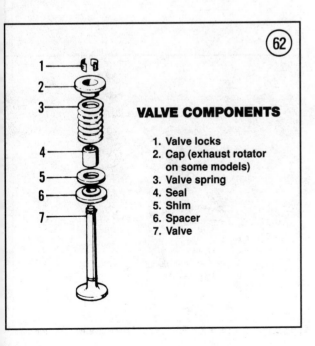

62

VALVE COMPONENTS

1. Valve locks
2. Cap (exhaust rotator on some models)
3. Valve spring
4. Seal
5. Shim
6. Spacer
7. Valve

VALVES AND VALVE SEATS

Servicing the valves, guides and valve seats must be done by a dealer or machine shop, since they require special knowledge and expensive machine tools. A general practice among those who do their own service is to remove the cylinder head, perform all disassembly except valve removal and take the head to a dealer or machine shop for inspection and service. Since the cost is low relative to the required effort and equipment, this is usually the best approach, even for experienced mechanics. The following procedures are given to acquaint the home mechanic with what the dealer or machine shop will do.

8

Valve Removal

Refer to **Figure 62** for this procedure.
1. Remove the cylinder head as described in this chapter.
2. Remove the rocker arm assemblies as described in this chapter.
3. Compress the valve spring with a compressor like the one shown in **Figure 63**. Remove the valve keys or cap locks and release the spring tension.
4. Remove the valve spring cap or exhaust valve rotator and valve spring.

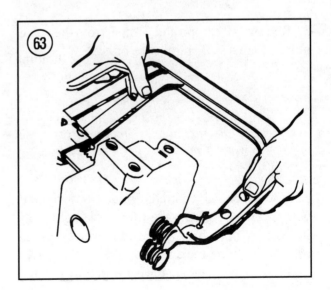

63

5. Remove the valve stem seal with a pair of pliers. Discard the seal. Remove the shim and spacer, if used. Remove the valve.

> *CAUTION*
> *Remove any burrs from the valve stem lock grooves before removing the valves or the valve guides will be damaged.*

6. Rrepeat Steps 3-5 on each remaining valve.

7. Arrange the parts in order so they can be returned to their original positions when reassembled.

Inspection

1. Clean the valves with a fine wire brush or buffing wheel. Discard any cracked, warped or burned valves.

2. Measure valve stems at the top, center and bottom for wear. A machine shop can do this when the valves are ground. Also measure the length of each valve and the diameter of each valve head.

> *NOTE*
> *Check the thickness of the valve edge or margin, after the valves have been ground. See Figure 64. Any valve with a margin of less than 1/32 in. (0.8 mm) should be discarded.*

3. Remove all carbon and varnish from the valve guides with a stiff spiral wire brush.

> *NOTE*
> *The next step assumes that all valve stems have been measured and are within specifications. Replace valves with worn stems before performing this step.*

4. Insert each valve into the guide from which it was removed. Holding the valve just slightly off its seat, rock it back and forth in a direction parallel with the rocker arms. This is the direction in which the greatest wear normally occurs.

If the valve stem rocks more than slightly, the valve guide is probably worn.

5. If there is any doubt about valve guide condition after performing Step 4, have the valve guide measured with a valve stem clearance checking tool. Compare the results with specifications in **Table 1** or **Table 2**. Worn guides must be reamed for the next oversize valve stem.

6. Test the valve springs under load on a spring tester (**Figure 65**). Replace any weak springs.

7. Inspect the valve seat inserts. If worn or burned, they must be reconditioned. This is a job

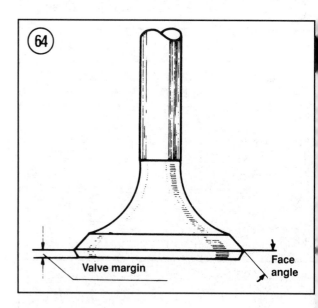

Valve margin   Face angle

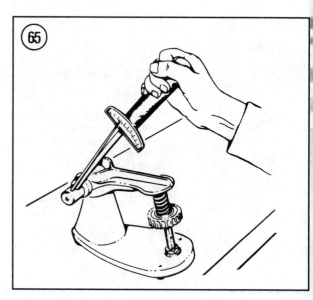

for a dealer or machine shop, although the procedure is described in this chapter.

8. Check each spring on a flat surface with a steel square. See **Figure 66**. Slowly revolve the spring 360° and note the space between the top of the coil and the square. If it exceeds 5/16 in. (8 mm) at any point, replace the spring

9. Check each valve lifter to make sure it fits freely in the block and that the end that contacts

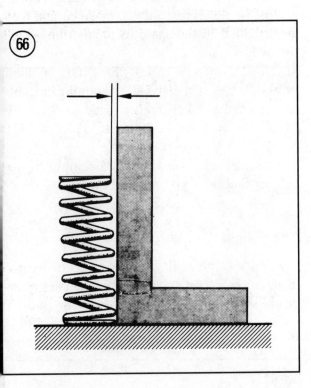

(66)

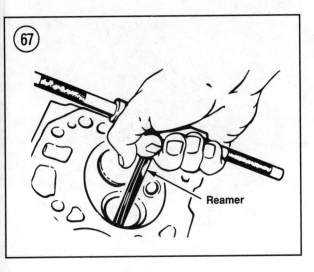

(67)

Reamer

the camshaft lobe is smooth and not worn excessively.

Valve Guide Reaming

Worn valve guides must be reamed to accept a valve with an oversize stem. These are available in 3 sizes for both intake and exhaust valves. Reaming must be done by hand (**Figure 67**) and is a job best left to an experienced machine shop. The valve seat must be refaced after the guide has been reamed.

Valve Seat Reconditioning

1. Cut the valve seats to the specified angle (**Table 1** or **Table 2**) with a dressing stone. Remove only enough metal to obtain a good finish.
2. Use tapered stones to obtain the specified seat width when necessary.
3. Coat the corresponding valve face with Prussian blue dye.
4. Insert the valve into the valve guide.
5. Apply light pressure to the valve and rotate it approximately 1/4 turn.
6. Lift the valve out. If it seats properly, the dye will transfer evenly to the valve face.
7. If the dye transfers to the top of the valve face, lower the seat. If it transfers to the bottom of the valve face, raise the seat.

Valve Installation

NOTE
Install all parts in the same position from which they were removed.

1. Coat the valves with engine oil and install them in the cylinder head.
2. Install new oil seals on each valve. Seal should be flat and not twisted in the valve stem groove.

8

3. Drop the valve spring shim/spacer around the valve guide boss. Install the valve spring over the valve, then install the cap or rotator.

4. Compress the springs and install the locks. Make sure both locks seat properly in the upper groove of the valve stem.

5. Measure the installed spring height between the top of the valve seat and the underside of the cap or rotator, as shown in **Figure 68**. If height is greater than specifications, install an extra spring seat shim about 1/16 in. thick and remeasure the height.

VALVE LIFTERS

The Generation II V6 and 350 Magnum models are equipped with roller lifters. Other models are equipped with conventional flat lifters.

On roller lifter models, 2 retaining brackets are used to hold the lifters in position and prevent them from rotating in their bores.

CAUTION
During disassembly, always arrange lifters, rocker arm assemblies and pushrods so they can be reinstalled in their original locations.

Removal/Installation

1. Remove the rocker arm assemblies, pushrods and intake manifold as described in this chapter.

2A. *Flat lifters*—Remove the lifters from their bores. Lifter remover tool (part No. J3049) can be used to remove lifters that are difficult to remove.

2B. *Roller lifters*—Place match marks on the lifters and lifter retaining brackets so the lifters can be reinstalled in their original bores, facing the same direction. See **Figure 69**. If reused, the lifter rollers should roll in the same direction from which removed. Remove the fasteners securing the lifter retaining brackets. Remove the brackets and lifters.

NOTE
Always use new lifters if a new camshaft is installed.

3. Coat the entire lifter assembly with clean engine oil prior to installation. If a new camshaft and lifters are being installed, lubricate the lifters and camshaft lobes with General Motors Cam and Lifter Prelube or a suitable equivalent containing an extreme pressure (EP) additive.

4A. *Flat lifters*—Install the lifters in their bores. If reusing the original lifters, make certain they are installed in the same location from which removed.

4B. *Roller lifters*—Install the lifters in their original bores. Install the lifter retaining brackets and align the match marks made in Step 2B. Install the retainer fasteners to 12 ft.-lb. (16 N•m).

5. Complete the remaining reassembly by reversing Step 1.

Inspection

Keep the lifters in the proper sequence for installation in their original location in the cylinder block. Clean the lifters in solvent and dry with compressed air. Inspect and test the lifters

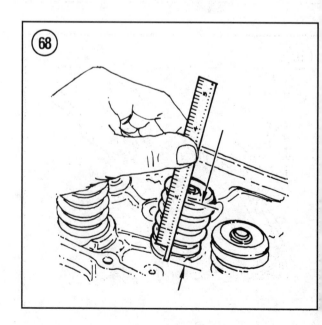

separately to prevent mixing of their internal components. If any part requires replacement, replace the entire lifter assembly.

Inspect all parts. Discard any lifter with pitting, scoring, galling or excessive wear. If the lifter bottom (flat lifters) or roller (roller lifters) shows excessive wear, the camshaft is probably

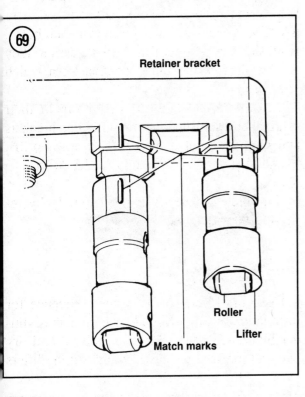

damaged. On roller lifters, make sure the roller turns freely without any noticeable roughness.

PISTON/CONNECTING ROD ASSEMBLY

Piston/Connecting Rod Removal

1. Remove the engine as described in this chapter.

2. Place a suitable container under the oil pan and remove the drain plug. Let the crankcase oil drain, then reinstall the drain plug.

3. Remove the intake and exhaust manifolds as described in this chapter.

4. Remove the cylinder heads as described in this chapter.

5. Remove the oil pan and oil pump as described in this chapter.

6. Rotate the crankshaft until one piston is at bottom dead center. Pack the cylinder bore with clean shop rags. Remove the carbon ridge at the top of the cylinder bore with a ridge reamer. These can be rented for use. Vacuum out the shavings, then remove the shop rags.

7. Rotate the crankshaft until the connecting rod is centered in the bore. Measure the clearance between the connecting rod and the crankshaft journal flange with a flat feeler gauge (**Figure 70**). If the clearance exceeds specification (**Table 1** or **Table 2**), replace the connecting rod during reassembly.

NOTE
*Mark the cylinder number on the top of each piston with quick-drying paint. Check the cylinder numbers or identification marks on the connecting rod and cap. If they are not visible, make your own (**Figure 71**).*

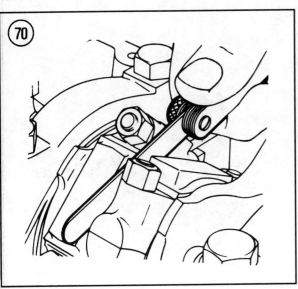

8. Remove the nuts holding the connecting rod cap. Lift off the cap, together with the lower bearing insert.

8

NOTE
If the connecting rod caps are difficult to remove, tap the stud with a wooden hammer handle.

9. Use the wooden hammer handle to push the piston and connecting rod from the bore.

10. Remove the piston rings with a ring remover (**Figure 72**).

11. Repeat Steps 6-10 for all remaining piston/connecting rods.

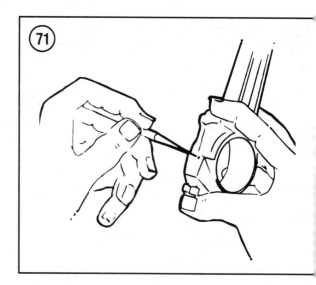

Piston Pin Removal/Installation

The piston pins are press-fitted to the connecting rods and hand fitted to the pistons. Removal requires the use of a press and support stand. This is a job for a dealer or machine shop equipped to fit the pistons to the pins, ream the pin bushings to the correct diameter and install the pistons and pins on the connecting rods.

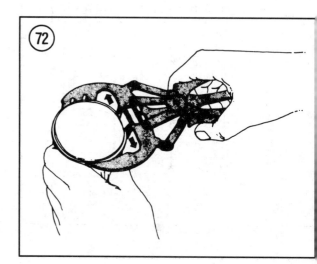

Piston Clearance Check

Unless you have precision measuring equipment and know how to use it properly, have this procedure done by a machine shop.

1. Measure the piston diameter with a micrometer (**Figure 73**) just below the rings at right angles to the piston pin bore.

2. Measure the cylinder bore diameter with a bore gauge (**Figure 74**). **Figure 75** shows the points of normal cylinder wear. If dimension A exceeds dimension B by more than 0.003 in. (0.076 mm), they cylinder must be rebored and a new piston/ring assembly installed.

3. Subtract the piston diameter from the largest cylinder bore reading. If it exceeds the specification in **Table 1** or **Table 2**, the cylinder must be rebored and an oversized piston installed.

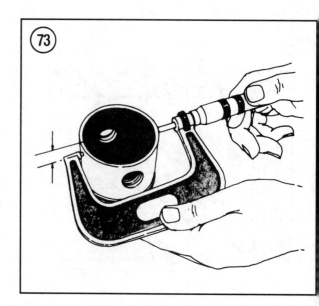

NOTE
Obtain the new piston and measure it to determine the correct cylinder bore oversize dimension.

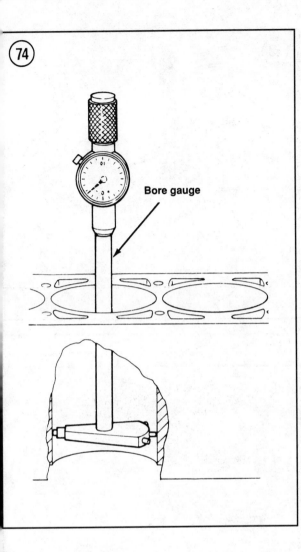

Bore gauge

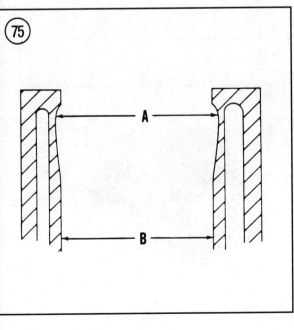

A

B

Piston Ring Fit/Installation

1. Check the ring gap of each piston ring. To do this, position the ring at the bottom of the ring travel area and square it by tapping gently with an inverted piston. See **Figure 76**.

NOTE
If the cylinders have not been rebored, check the gap at the bottom of the ring travel, where the cylinder is least worn.

2. Measure the ring gap with a feeler gauge as shown in **Figure 77**. Compare with specification in **Table 1** or **Table 2**. If the measurement is not within specification, the rings must be replaced as a set. Check gap of new rings as well. If the gap is too small, file the ends of the ring to correct it (**Figure 78**).

3. Check the side clearance of the rings as shown in **Figure 79**. Place the feeler gauge alongside the ring all the way into the groove. If the measurement is not within specification (**Table 1** or **Table 2**), either the rings or the ring grooves are worn. Inspect and replace as required.

8

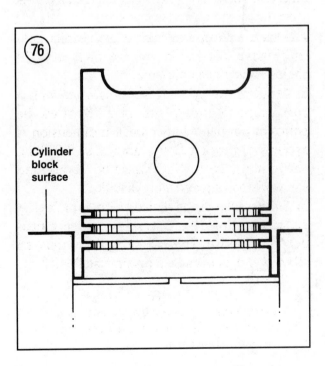

Cylinder block surface

4. Using a ring expander tool (**Figure 80**), carefully install the oil control ring, then the compression rings. Oil rings consist of 3 segments. The wavy segment goes between the flat segments to act as a spacer. Upper and lower flat segments are interchangeable. The second compression ring is tapered. The top of each compression ring is marked and must face upward.

5. Position the ring gaps as shown in **Figure 81**.

Connecting Rod Inspection

Have the connecting rods checked for straightness by a dealer or machine shop. When installing new connecting rods, have them checked for misalignment before installing the piston and piston pin. Connecting rods can spring out of alignment during shipping or handling.

Connecting Rod Bearing Clearance Measurement

1. Place the connecting rods and upper bearing halves on the proper connecting rod journals.

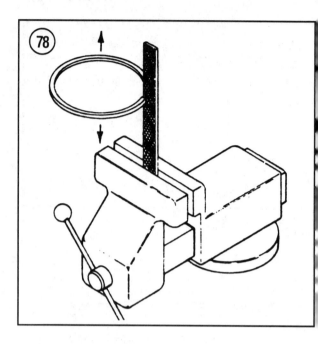

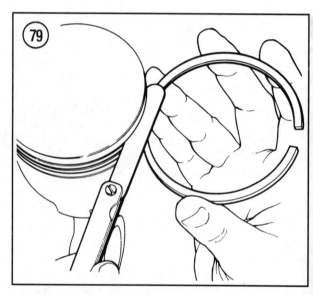

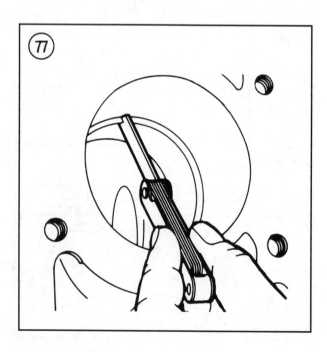

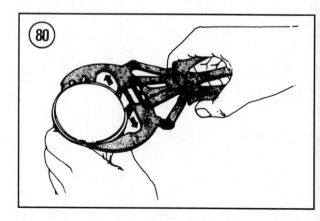

2. Cut a piece of Plastigage the width of the bearing (**Figure 82**). Place the Plastigage on the journal, then install the lower bearing half and cap.

NOTE
Do not place Plastigage over the journal oil hole.

3. Tighten the connecting rod cap to specification (**Table 3** or **Table 4**). Do not rotate the crankshaft while the Plastigage is in place.

4. Remove the connecting rod caps. Bearing clearance is determined by comparing the width of the flattened Plastigage to the markings on the envelope (**Figure 83**). If the clearance is excessive, the crankshaft must be reground and undersize bearings installed.

Piston/Connecting Rod Installation

1. Make sure the pistons are correctly installed on the connecting rods if they were separated. The cast notch on the top of the piston (**Figure 84**) must face the front of the engine. On 7.4L sumped pistons, the valve relief must face toward the center of the engine (**Figure 85**). On 7.4L pistons with a reference hole, the hole in the pistons must face the outside of the block on No. 2, 4, 6 and 8 cylinders. The hole in the pistons must face the center of the block on No. 1, 3, 5 and 7 cylinders. See **Figure 86**. On all engines, the connecting rod bearing tangs must face toward the outside of the engine (**Figure 86**).

2. Make sure the ring gaps are positioned as shown in **Figure 81**.

3. Slip short pieces of hose over the connecting rod studs to prevent them from nicking the crankshaft. Tape will work if you do not have the right diameter hose, but it is more difficult to remove.

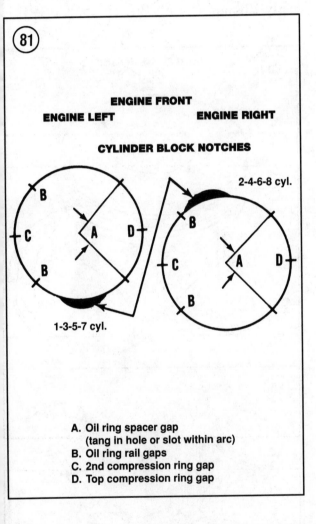

(81)

ENGINE FRONT
ENGINE LEFT   ENGINE RIGHT

CYLINDER BLOCK NOTCHES

2-4-6-8 cyl.

1-3-5-7 cyl.

A. Oil ring spacer gap
   (tang in hole or slot within arc)
B. Oil ring rail gaps
C. 2nd compression ring gap
D. Top compression ring gap

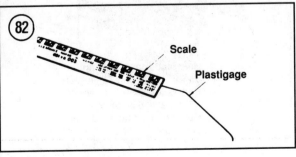

(82)

Scale

Plastigage

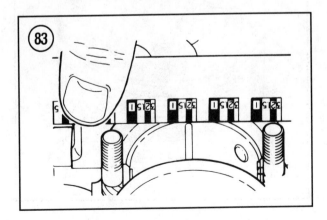

(83)

8

4. Immerse the entire piston in clean engine oil. Coat the cylinder wall with oil.

CAUTION
Use extreme care in Step 5 to prevent the connecting rod from nicking the crankshaft journal.

5. Install the piston/connecting rod assembly in its cylinder with a piston ring compressor as shown in **Figure 87**. Tap lightly with a wooden hammer handle to insert the piston. Make sure that the piston number (painted on top before removal) corresponds to the cylinder number, counting from the front of the engine.

6. Clean the connecting rod bearings carefully, including the back sides. Coat the journals and bearings with clean engine oil. Place the bearings in the connecting rod and cap.

7. Pull the connecting rod and bearing into position against the crankpin. Remove the protective hose or tape and lightly lubricate the connecting rod bolt threads with SAE 30 engine oil.

8. Install the connecting rod cap. Make sure the rod and cap marks align. Install the cap nuts finger-tight.

9. Repeat Steps 4-8 for each remaining piston/connecting rod assembly.

10. Tighten the cap nuts to specification (**Table 3** or **Table 4**).

11. Check the connecting rod big-end play as described under *Piston/Connecting Rod Removal* in this chapter.

REAR MAIN OIL SEAL

A 2-piece rear main crankshaft seal is used on early V6 models, early 305 cid (5.0L), 350 cid

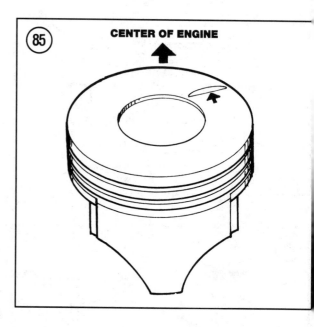

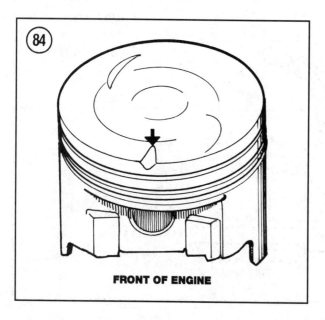

FRONT OF ENGINE

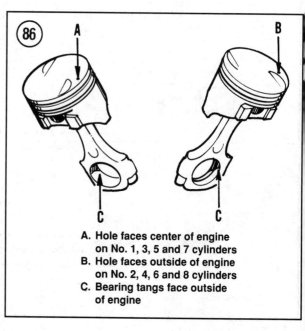

A. Hole faces center of engine on No. 1, 3, 5 and 7 cylinders
B. Hole faces outside of engine on No. 2, 4, 6 and 8 cylinders
C. Bearing tangs face outside of engine

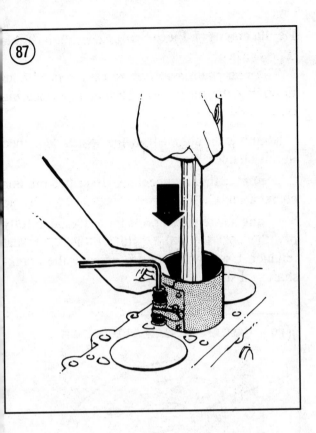

(5.7L) models and 7.4L, 454 and 502 Magnum models prior to the Mark V engine. The seal is located under the rear main bearing cap and can be replaced without crankshaft removal.

On Generation II V6 models, late 305 cid (5.0L) and 350 cid (5.7L) models, a 1-piece rear main crankshaft seal is pressed into a seal retainer which bolts to the rear of the engine. On 1991 7.4L models and 1992-on 454 and 502 Magnum models (Mark V engines), a 1-piece rear main seal is pressed into the cylinder block/rear main bearing cap counterbore. The 1-piece seal is pressed into place after the crankshaft is installed and can be replaced without removing the oil pan or rear main bearing cap.

8

Replacement (2-Piece Seal)

Refer to **Figure 88** for this procedure.

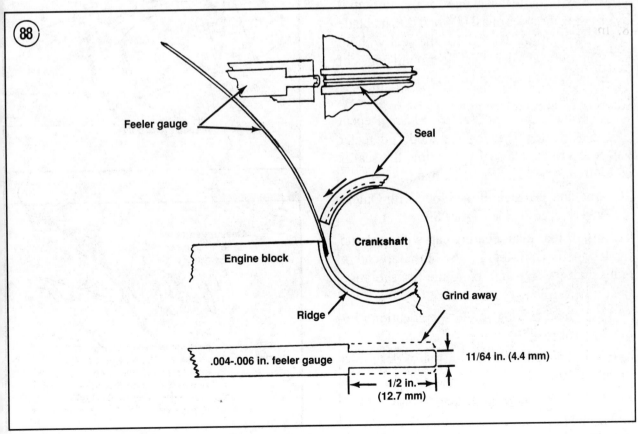

1. Remove the engine from the boat as described in this chapter.

2. Remove the oil pan and oil pump as described in this chapter.

3. Remove the rear main bearing cap. Pry the oil seal from the bottom of the cap with a small screwdriver.

4. Remove the upper half of the seal with a brass pin punch. Tap the punch on one end of the seal until its other end protrudes far enough to be removed with pliers.

5. Clean all sealant from the bearing cap and crankshaft with a non-abrasive cleaner.

6. Coat the lips and bead of a new seal with light engine oil. Do not let oil touch seal mating ends or parting line surface.

7. Install the new seal half into the rear main bearing cap, taking care that the sharp edge of the cap ridge does not cut the bead in the center of the outer seal surface.

8. Modify a flat feeler gauge for use in Step 9 by grinding the sides of a 0.004 or 0.006 in. blade until it will fit into the "U" of the seal without scraping the seal sides. File the ground edges of the feeler gauge to prevent them from scratching the seal.

9. Wipe the crankshaft surface clean. Repeat Step 6 and Step 7, using the modified feeler gauge to protect the seal bead while the seal is carefully fed into its groove by hand.

10. Coat the seal area of the block with Quicksilver Perfect Seal. See **Figure 89**.

11. Install rear main bearing cap with seal and tighten to 10-12 ft.-lb. (14-16 N.m). Tap end of crankshaft to the rear, then to the front to align the thrust surfaces.

12. Retighten bearing cap to specification (**Table 3** or **Table 4**).

13. Install the oil pump and oil pan as described in this chapter.

14. Install the engine in the boat as described in this chapter.

Replacement (1-Piece Seal)

The rear main seal can be replaced without removing the oil pan or the rear main bearing cap.

1. Remove the engine from the boat as described in this chapter.

2. Remove the flywheel as described in this chapter.

3. Using a screwdriver or similar tool, carefully pry the seal from the cylinder block or seal retainer. Use caution not to damage the crankshaft seal surface.

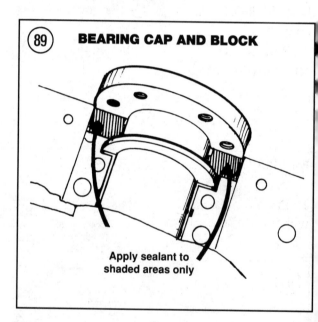

BEARING CAP AND BLOCK

Apply sealant to shaded areas only

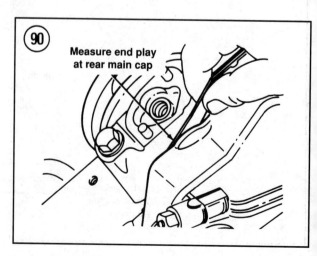

Measure end play at rear main cap

4. Thoroughly clean the crankshaft seal surface and the cylinder block/bearing cap counterbore or seal retainer. Inspect the crankshaft seal surface for corrosion, nicks or burrs.

5. Apply Quicksilver Perfect Seal to the outer diameter of a new seal. *Do not* allow the sealant to contact the sealing surface of the seal or crankshaft. Lubricate the sealing surface of the crankshaft and seal with clean engine oil.

6. Position the seal with the lip facing toward the engine (inward). Using seal installer part No. J26817-A (305 cid [5.0L] and 350 cid [5.7L]) or part No. J-38841 (Mark V), carefully drive the seal into the cylinder block/bearing cap counterbore. Make certain the seal is not cocked in the counterbore.

7. Reinstall the flywheel and engine as described in this chapter.

CRANKSHAFT

End Play Measurement

1. Pry the crankshaft to the front of the engine with a large screwdriver.

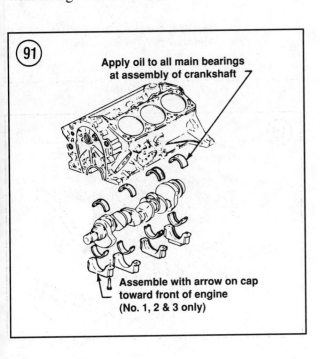

(91)

Apply oil to all main bearings
at assembly of crankshaft

Assemble with arrow on cap
toward front of engine
(No. 1, 2 & 3 only)

2. Measure the crankshaft end play at the front of the rear main bearing with a flat feeler gauge. See **Figure 90**. Compare to specifications in **Table 1** or **Table 2**.

3. If the end play is excessive, replace the rear main bearing. If less than specified, check the bearing faces for imperfections.

Removal

Refer to **Figure 91**, typical for this procedure.

1. Remove the engine from the boat as described in this chapter.

2. Remove the flywheel as described in this chapter.

3. Mount the engine on an engine stand, if available.

4. Remove the starter motor. See Chapter Eleven.

5. Invert the engine to bring the oil pan to an upright position.

6. Remove the oil pan and oil pump as described in this chapter.

7. Remove the torsional damper, front cover and timing chain as described in this chapter.

8. Remove the spark plugs to permit easy rotation of the crankshaft.

9. Measure crankshaft end play as described in this chapter.

10. Rotate the crankshaft to position one connecting rod at the bottom of its stroke.

11. Remove the connecting rod bearing cap and bearing. Move the piston/rod assembly away from the crankshaft.

12. Repeat Step 10 and Step 11 for each remaining piston/rod assembly.

13. Check the caps for identification numbers or marks. If none are visible, clean the caps with a wire brush. If marks still cannot be seen, make your own with quick-drying paint.

14. Unbolt and remove the main bearing caps and bearing inserts.

8

NOTE
If the caps are difficult to remove, lift the bolts partway out, then lever the bolts from side to side.

15. Carefully lift the crankshaft from the engine block and place it on a clean workbench.

16. Remove the bearing inserts from the block. Place the bearing caps and inserts from the block. Place the bearing caps and inserts in order on a clean workbench.

17. Remove the main bearing oil seal from the cylinder block and rear bearing cap.

Inspection

1. Clean the crankshaft thoroughly with solvent. Blow out the oil passages with compressed air.

2. Check the main and connecting rod journals for wear, scratches, grooves, scoring or cracks. Check oil seal surface for burrs, nicks or other sharp edges which might damage a seal during installation.

NOTE
Unless you have precision measuring equipment and know how to use it, have a machine shop perform Step 3.

3. Check all journals against specifications (**Table 1** or **Table 2**) for out-of-roundness and taper. See **Figure 92**. Have the crankshaft reground, if necessary, and install new underside bearings.

Main Bearing Clearance Measurement

Main bearing clearance is measured with Plastigage in the same manner as the connecting rod bearing clearance described in this chapter. Excessive clearance requires that the bearings be replaced, the crankshaft be reground or both.

Sprocket Removal/Installation

1. Remove the torsional damper as described in this chapter.

2. Remove the front cover as described in this chapter.

3. Remove the camshaft sprocket and timing chain as described in this chapter.

4. Install tool part No. J-1619 or equivalent and remove the crankshaft sprocket.

5. Installation is the reverse of removal. Use tool part No. J-21058 (7.4L and 8.2L) or part No. J-5590 (all others) to install the sprocket to the crankshaft.

Installation

1. Install a new rear main bearing oil seal as described in this chapter.

2. Install the main bearing inserts in the cylinder block. Bearing oil holes must align with block oil holes and bearing tabs must seat in the block tab slots.

NOTE
Check cap bolts for threads damage before reuse. If damaged, replace the bolts.

3. Lubricate the bolt threads with SAE 30 engine oil.

4. Install the bearing inserts in each cap.

5. Carefully lower the crankshaft into position in the block.

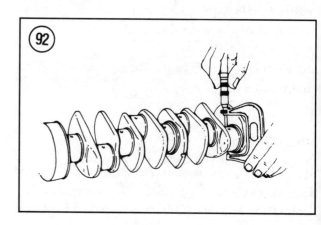

6. Install the bearing caps in their marked positions with the arrows pointing toward the front of the engine and the number mark aligned with the corresponding mark on the journals.

7. Install and tighten all bolts finger-tight. Recheck end play as described in this chapter, then tighten all bolts to specification (**Table 3** or **Table 4**).

8. Rotate the crankshaft to make sure it turns smoothly at the flywheel rim. If not, remove the bearing caps and crankshaft and check that the bearings are clean and properly installed.

9. Reverse Steps 1-12 of *Removal* in this chapter.

FLYWHEEL

Removal/Installation

1. Remove the engine from the boat as described in this chapter.

2. Unbolt the flywheel and coupler from the crankshaft. Remove the bolts gradually in a diagonal pattern.

3. To install, align the dowel hole in the flywheel with dowel in crankshaft flange and position the flywheel on studs.

4. Fit the coupler on the studs. Install the washers and locknuts. Tighten nuts to specification (**Table 3** or **Table 4**).

5. Install a dial indicator on the machined surface of the flywheel and check runout. If runout exceeds 0.008 in. (0.20 mm), remove the flywheel and check for burrs. If none are found, replace the flywheel.

6. Reinstall the engine in the boat as described in this chapter.

Inspection

1. Visually check the flywheel surface for cracks, deep scoring, excessive wear, heat discoloration and checking. If the surface is glazed or slightly scratched, have the flywheel resurfaced by a machine shop.

2. Check the surface flatness with a straightedge and feeler gauge.

3. Inspect the ring gear for cracks, broken teeth or excessive wear. If severely worn, check the starter motor drive teeth for similar wear or damage; replace as required.

CYLINDER BLOCK

Cleaning and Inspection

1. Clean the block thoroughly with solvent. Remove any gasket or RTV sealant residue from the machined surfaces. Check all core plugs for leaks and replace any that are suspect. See *Core Plug Replacement* in this chapter. Remove any plugs that seal oil passages. Check oil and coolant passages for sludge, dirt and corrosion while cleaning. If the passages are very dirty, have the block boiled out by a machine shop. Blow out all passages with compressed air. Check the threads in the head bolts holes to be sure they are clean. If dirty, use a tap to true up the threads and remove any deposits.

2. Examine the block for cracks. To confirm suspicions about possible leak areas, use a mixture of 1 part kerosene and 2 parts engine oil. Coat the suspected area with this solution, then wipe dry and immediately apply a solution of zinc oxide dissolved in wood alcohol. If any discoloration appears in the treated area, the block is cracked and should be replaced.

3. Check flatness of the cylinder block deck or top surface. Place an accurate straightedge on the block. If there is any gap between the block and straightedge, measure it with a flat feeler gauge (**Figure 93**). Measure from end to end and from corner to corner. Have the block resurfaced if it is warped more than 0.004 in. (0.102 mm).

4. Measure cylinder bores with a bore gauge (**Figure 94**) for out-of-roundness or excessive wear as described in *Piston Clearance Check* in

this chapter. If the cylinders exceed maximum tolerances, they must be rebored. Reboring is also necessary if the cylinder walls are badly scuffed or scored.

> *NOTE*
> *Before reboring, install all main bearing caps and tighten the cap bolts to specifications in **Table 3** or **Table 4**).*

CORE PLUG REPLACEMENT

The condition of all core plugs in the block and cylinder head should be checked whenever the engine is out of the boat for service. If any signs of leakage or corrosion are found around one core plug, replace them all.

> *NOTE*
> *Core plugs can be replaced inexpensively by a machine shop. If you are having machine work done on the engine, have the core plugs replaced at the same time.*

Removal/Installation

> *CAUTION*
> *Do not drive core plugs into the engine casting. It will be impossible to retrieve them and they can restrict coolant circulation, resulting in serious engine damage.*

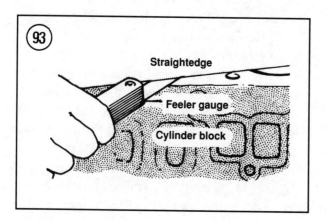

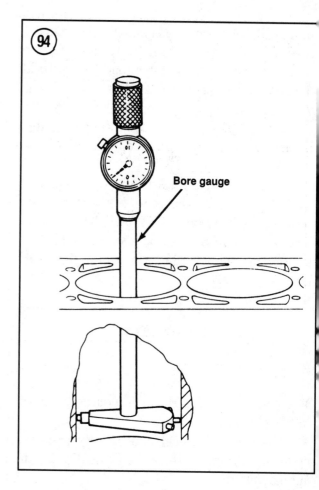

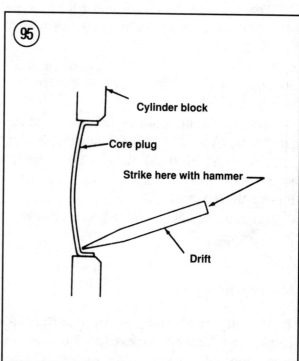

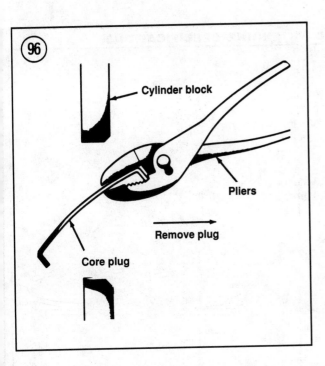

Cylinder block

Pliers

Remove plug

Core plug

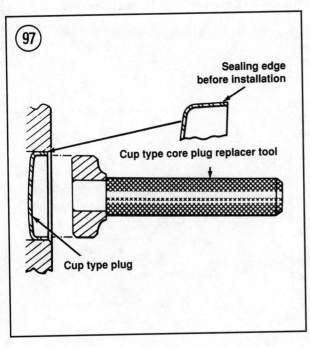

Sealing edge
before installation

Cup type core plug replacer tool

Cup type plug

1. Tap the bottom edge of the core plug with a hammer and drift. Use several sharp blows to push the bottom of the plug inward, tilting the top out (**Figure 95**).

2. Grip the top of the plug firmly with pliers. Pull the plug from its bore (**Figure 96**) and discard.

> *NOTE*
> *Core plugs can also be removed by drilling a hole in the center of the plug and prying them out with an appropriate size drift or pin punch. On large core plugs, the use of a universal impact slide hammer is recommended.*

3. Clean the plug bore thoroughly to remove all traces of the old sealer. Inspect the bore for any damage that might interfere with proper sealing of the new plug. If damage is evident, true the surface by boring for the next oversize plug.

> *NOTE*
> *Oversize plugs can be identified by an "OS" stamped in the flat on the cup side of the plug.*

4. Coat the inside diameter of the plug bore and the outer diameter of the new plug with sealer. Use an oil-resistant sealer if the plug is to be installed in an oil gallery or a water-resistant sealer for plugs installed in the water jacket.

5. Install the new core plug with an appropriate size core plug replacer tool (**Figure 97**), driver or socket. The sharp edge of the plug should be at least 0.02 in. (0.5 mm) inside the lead-in chamfer.

6. Repeat Steps 1-5 to replace each remaining core plug.

8

Table 1 SMALL BLOCK V6 AND V8 ENGINE SPECIFICATIONS

Engine type	90° V6 or V8
Bore	
Model 175/185/205/4.3L/4.3LX	
Prior to Serial No. OF000001	3.9995-4.0025 in.
Serial No. OF000001-on	4.0007-4.0017 in.
Model 200/230/5.0L/5.0LX	3.7350-3.7385 in.
Model 260/350 Magnum/5.7L	3.9995-4.0025 in.
Stroke	3.48 in.
Displacement	
Model 175/185/205/4.3L/4.3LX	262 cid (4.3 liter)
Model 200/230/5.0L/5.0LX	305 cid (5.0 liter)
Model 260/350 Magnum/5.7L	350 cid (5.7 liter)
Firing order	
V6	1-6-5-4-3-2
V8	1-8-4-3-6-5-7-2
Cylinder arrangement	
V6	
Port bank	1-3-5
Starboard bank	2-4-6
V8	
Port bank	1-3-5-7
Starboard bank	2-4-6-8
Cylinder head flatness	0.003 in. (max.) any 6 in. span or 0.007 in. (max.) overall
Cylinder bore	
Out-of-round	
Production	0.001 in. max.
Service	0.002 in. max.
Taper	
Production	
Thrust side	0.0005 in. max.
Relief side	0.001 in. max.
Service	0.001 in. max.
Piston clearance	
Production	0.0007-0.0017 in.
Service	0.0027 in. max.
Piston ring	
Groove side clearance	
Compression	0.0012-0.0032 in.
Oil	0.002-0.007 in.
Ring gap	
Top	0.010-0.020 in.
2nd	0.010-0.025 in.
Oil	0.015-0.055 in.
Piston pin	
Diameter	0.9270-0.9273 in.
Clearance	
In piston	0.001 in. max.
Fit in rod	0.0008-0.0016 in. (interference)
Camshaft	
Lobe lift	
Generation II V6	
Intake	0.269 in.
Exhaust	0.273 in.

(continued)

Table 1 SMALL BLOCK V6 AND V8 ENGINE SPECIFICATIONS (continued)

Camshaft (continued)	
Lobe lift (continued)	
350 Magnum	
Intake	0.287 in.
Exhaust	0.300 in.
All others	
Intake	0.263 in.
Exhaust	0.269 in.
Journal diameter	1.8682-1.8692 in.
Out-of-round	0.001 in. max.
Runout	0.002 in. max.
End play	0.004-0.012 in.
Crankshaft	
Main journal diameter	
No. 1	2.4484-2.4493 in.
No. 2, 3 and 4 (V8) or No. 2 and 3 (V6)	2.4481-2.4490 in.
No. 5 (V8) or No. 4 (V6)	2.4479-2.4488 in.
Taper	
Production	0.0002 in. max.
Service	0.001 in. max.
Out-of-round	
Production	0.0002 in. max.
Service	0.001 in. max.
Runout	0.0015 in. max.
Main bearing clearance	
Production	
No. 1	0.0008-0.0020 in.
No. 2, 3 and 4 (V8) or No. 2 and 3 (V6)	0.0011-0.0023 in.
No. 5 (V8) or No. 4 (V6)	0.0017-0.0032 in.
Service	
No. 1	0.001-0.0015 in.
No. 2, 3 and 4 (V8) or No. 2 and 3 (V6)	0.001-0.0025 in.
No. 5 (V8) or No. 4 (V6)	0.0025-0.0035 in.
End play	0.002-0.006 in.
Crankpin	
Diameter	
V6	2.2487-2.2497 in.
V8	2.0988-2.0998 in.
Taper	
Production	0.0005 in. max.
Service	0.001 in. max.
Out-of-round	
Production	0.0005 in. max.
Service	0.001 in. max.
Connecting rod	
Bearing clearance	
Production	0.0013-0.0035 in.
Service	0.003 in. max.
Side clearance	0.008-0.014 in.
Valve train	
Lifter	Hydraulic
Rocker arm ratio	1.5:1
Valve lash	
Except Generation II V6	1 turn down from zero lash
Generation II V6	Not adjustable

(continued)

8

Table 1 SMALL BLOCK V6 AND V8 ENGINE SPECIFICATIONS (continued)

Valve train (continued)	
Face angle	45°
Seat angle	46°
Seat width	
Intake	1/32-1/16 in.
Exhaust	1/16-3/32 in.
Stem clearance	
Production (intake & exhaust)	0.0010-0.0027 in.
Service	
Intake	0.0037 in. max.
Exhaust	0.0047 in. max.
Valve springs	
Free length	
V6 & 350 Magnum	2.03 in.
All others	1.91 in.
Installed height	
350 Magnum & Generation II V6	1.70 in.
All others	1.72 in.
Damper free length	1.86 in.
Valve spring load (with damper removed)	
Closed	76-84 lb. @ 1.70 in.
Open	194-206 lb. @ 1.25 in.
Balance shaft (Generation II V6)	
Front bearing journal diameter	1.1812-1.1815 in.
Rear bearing journal diameter	1.4209-1.4215 in.
Rear bearing inside diameter (installed)	1.5014-1.5030 in.
Rear bearing outside diameter	1.875-1.876 in.

Table 2 7.4L, 454 MAGNUM AND 502 MAGNUM ENGINE SPECIFICATIONS[1]

Engine type	90° V8
Bore	
7.4L and 454 Magnum	4.25 in.
502 Magnum	4.47 in.
Stroke	4.00 in.
Displacement	
7.4L and 454 Magnum	454 cid (7.4L)
502 Magnum	502 cid (8.2L)
Firing order	1-8-4-3-6-5-7-2
Cylinder arrangement	
Port bank	1-3-5-7
Starboard bank	2-4-6-8
Cylinder head flatness	0.003 in. (max.) over any 6 in. span or 0.007 in. overall
Cylinder bore diameter	
7.4L, 454 Magnum (prior to Mark V)	4.2495-4.2525 in.
502 Magnum (prior to Mark V)	4.4650-4.4725 in.
7.4L (after 1991)	4.2500-4.2507 in.
454 Magnum (Mark V)	4.2451-4.2525 in.
502 Magnum (Mark V)	4.4655-4.4662 in.

(continued)

8

Table 2 7.4L, 454 MAGNUM AND 502 MAGNUM ENGINE SPECIFICATIONS[1] (continued)

Out-of-round	
Production	0.001 in. max.
Service	0.002 in. max
Taper	
Production	
Thrust side	0.0005 in. max.
Relief side	0.001 in. max.
Service	0.001 in. max.
Piston clearance	
Prior to Mark V	
7.4L, 454 Magnum	
Production	0.0014-0.0024 in.
Service	0.0035 in. max.
502 Magnum	
Production	0.0040-0.0057 in.
Service	0.0065 in. max.
Mark V	
7.4L	
Production	0.0030-0.0042 in.
Service	0.005 in. max.
454 Magnum	
Production	0.0025-0.0037 in.
Service	0.0075 in. max.
502 Magnum	
Production	0.0040-0.0057 in.
Service	0.006 in. max.
Piston rings	
Side clearance	
Compression rings	
Production	0.0017-0.0032 in.
Service	0.0042 in. max.
Oil ring	
Production	0.0050-0.0065 in.
Service	0.0075 in. max.
End gap	
Prior to Mark V	
Compression rings	
Production	0.010-0.020 in.
Service	0.030 in. max.
Oil ring	
7.4L, 454 Magnum	
Production	0.010-0.018 in.
Service	0.028 in. max.
502 Magnum	
Production	0.020-0.035 in.
Service	0.045 in. max.
Mark V	
Top compression ring	
7.4L, 454 Magnum	
Production	0.010-0.018 in.
Service	0.028 in. max.
502 Magnum	
Production	0.011-0.021 in.
Service	0.031 in. max.

(continued)

Table 2 7.4L, 454 MAGNUM AND 502 MAGNUM ENGINE SPECIFICATIONS[1] (continued)

Piston rings (continued)	
End gap (continued)	
Mark V (continued)	
Second compression ring	
7.4L, 454 Magnum	
Production	0.016-0.024 in.
Service	0.034 in. max.
502 Magnum	
Production	0.016-0.026 in.
Service	0.036 in. max.
Oil ring	
7.4L	
Production	0.010-0.030 in.
Service	0.040 in. max.
454 Magnum	
Production	0.020-0.035 in.
Service	0.045 in. max.
502 Magnum	
Production	0.010-0.030 in.
Service	0.040 in. max.
Piston pin	
Diameter	0.9895-0.9898 in.
Clearance in piston	
Prior to Mark V	
Production	0.00025-0.00035 in.
Service	0.00135 in. max.
Mark V	
7.4L	
Production	0.0002-0.0007 in.
Service	0.0017 in. max.
454 Magnum, 502 Magnum	
Production	0.00025-0.00035 in.
Service	0.00135 in. max.
Fit in rod	0.0008-0.0016 in. interference
Camshaft	
Lobe lift	
7.4L, 454 Magnum (Alpha One)	
Intake	0.269-0.273 in.
Exhaust	0.280-0.284 in.
454 Magnum (Bravo One), 502 Magnum	
Intake and exhaust	0.298-0.302 in.
Journal diameter	1.9482-1.9492 in.
Out-of-round	0.001 in. max.
Runout	0.002 in. max.
Crankshaft	
Main journal diameter	
Prior to Mark V	
No. 1	2.7485-2.7494 in.
No. 2, 3 and 4	2.7481-2.7490 in.
No. 5	2.7478-2.7488 in.
Mark V	
No. 1-5	2.7482-2.7489 in.
Taper	
Production	0.0002 in. max.
Service	0.001 in. max.

(continued)

Table 2 7.4L, 454 MAGNUM AND 502 MAGNUM ENGINE SPECIFICATIONS[1] (continued)

Crankshaft (continued)	
Out-of-round	
Production	0.0002 in. max.
Service	0.001 in. max
Runout	
502 Magnum (Mark V)	0.0035 in. max.
All others	0.0015 in. max.
Main bearing clearance	
All models (prior to Mark V)	
Production	
No. 1-4	0.0013-0.0025 in.
No. 5	0.0024-0.0040 in.
Service	
No. 1	0.001-0.0015 in.
No. 2-4	0.001-0.0025 in.
No. 5	0.0025-0.0035 in.
7.4L, 454 Magnum (Mark V)	
Production	
No. 1-4	0.0017-0.0030 in.
No. 5	0.0025-0.0038 in.
Service	
No. 1-4	0.001-0.003 in.
No. 5	0.0025-0.0040 in.
502 Magnum (after 1991)	
Production	
No. 1-4	0.0017-0.0030 in.
No. 5	0.0025-0.0038 in.
Service	
No. 1	0.001-0.0015 in.
No. 2-4	0.001-0.0025 in.
No. 5	0.0025-0.0035 in.
End play	0.006-0.010 in.
Crankpin journal	
Diameter	
All models prior to Mark V	2.1985-2.1995 in.
All Mark V models	2.1990-2.1996 in.
Taper	
Production	0.005 in. max.
Service	0.001 in. max.
Out-of-round	
Production	0.0005 in. max.
Service	0.001 in. max.
Crankpin bearing clearance	
All models prior to Mark V	
Production	0.0009-0.0025 in.
Service	0.003 in. max.
All Mark V	
Production	0.0011-0.0029 in.
Service	0.003 in. max.
Connecting rod side clearance	
All models prior to Mark V	0.013-0.023 in.
7.4L, 454 Magnum (Mark V)	0.002-0.023 in.
502 Magnum (Mark V)	0.013-0.023 in.

(continued)

8

Table 2 7.4L, 454 MAGNUM AND 502 MAGNUM ENGINE SPECIFICATIONS[1] (continued)

Valve train	
Lifters	Hydraulic
Rocker arm ratio	1.7:1
Valve lash	
All models prior to Mark V	1 turn down from zero lash
All Mark V models	Not adjustable
Valve face angle	45°
Valve seat angle	46°
Valve seat width	
Intake	1/32 to 1/16 in.
Exhaust	1/16 to 3/32 in.
Valve seat runout	0.002 in. max.
Valve stem clearance	
All models prior to Mark V	
Production	
Intake	0.001-0.0027 in.
Exhaust	0.0012-0.0029 in.
Service	
Intake	0.0037 in. max.
Exhaust	0.0049 in. max.
7.4L (Mark V)	
Production	
Intake	0.001-0.0027 in.
Exhaust	0.0012-0.0029 in.
Service	
Intake	0.001 in. max.
Exhaust	0.002 in. max.
454 Magnum (Mark V)	
Production	
Intake	0.001-0.0027 in.
Exhaust	0.0012-0.0029 in.
Service	
Intake	0.003 in. max.
Exhaust	0.004 in. max.
502 Magnum (Mark V)	
Production	
Intake	0.001-0.0027 in.
Exhaust	0.0012-0.0029 in.
Service	
Intake	0.0037 in. max.
Exhaust	0.0049 in. max.
Valve spring	
Free length	
All models prior to Mark V	2.12 in.
All Mark V models	2.15 in.
Valve spring installed height	1.875 in.
Damper free length	1.86 in.
Load	
7.4L, 454 Magnum (prior to Mark V)[2]	
Closed	74-86 lb. @ 1.88 in.
Open	288-312 lb. @ 1.38 in.
502 Magnum (prior to Mark V)[3]	
Closed	110 lb. @ 1.88 in.
Open	316 lb. @ 1.34 in.

(continued)

Table 2 7.4L, 454 MAGNUM AND 502 MAGNUM ENGINE SPECIFICATIONS[1] (continued)

Valve spring (continued)	
Load (continued)	
7.4L (Mark V)[3]	
Closed	74-86 lb. @ 1.80 in.
Open	195-215 lb. @ 1.40 in.
454 Magnum, 502 Magnum (Mark V)3	
Closed	110 lb. @ 1.88 in.
Open	316 lb. @ 1.34 in.
Flywheel runout	0.008 in. max.

1. The 1991 7.4L models and 1992-on 454 and 502 Magnum models are Mark V engines. Mark V engines can be identified by the fuel pump mounted on the belt-driven sea water pump.
2. Check load with valve spring damper removed.
3. Check load with valve spring damper installed.

Table 3 SMALL BLOCK V6 AND V8 TIGHTENING TORQUES

Fastener	ft.-lb.	N·m
Alternator		
Brace-to-alternator	21	28
Brace-to-block	30	41
To mounting bracket	35	47
Mounting bracket	30	41
Balance shaft		
Drive gear retaining stud	10	13.5
Driven gear retaining bolt	15	20.3
	plus additional 35°	
Thrust plate bolts	10	13.5
Camshaft sprocket	20	27
Connecting rod caps	45	61
Coupler-to-flywheel	35	47
Crankshaft damper		
Stamped steel crankshaft		
pulley (1-1/4 in. bolt)	60	81
Cast aluminum crankshaft		
pulley (1-1/2 in. bolt)	40	54
Crankshaft pulley	35	47
Cylinder head	65	88
Distributor clamp	25	34
Exhaust manifold	20	27
Exhaust elbow/riser	20-25	27-34
Flywheel-to-crankshaft	70	95
Front cover	7	9
Intake manifold	30	41
Main bearing caps	80	109
Oil filter bypass valve	7	9
Oil pan		
1/4-20	7	9
5/16-18	14	19
Oil pump		
Attaching bolts	65	88
Cover screws	7	9
Power steering pump	30	41

(continued)

8

Table 3 SMALL BLOCK V6 AND V8 TIGHTENING TORQUES (continued)

Fastener	ft.-lb.	N·m
Rear mount	40	54
Remote oil filter adaptor		
1/2-13	25	34
5/16-18	20	27
Seawater pump	30	41
Starter motor	50	68
Temperature sending unit	20	27
Thermostat housing	30	41
Valve cover	5	6.8
Water pump	30	41

Table 4 7.4L, 454 MAGNUM AND 502 MAGNUM TIGHTENING TORQUES

Fastener	ft.-lb.	N·m
Alternator		
Brace-to-alternator	21	28
Brace-to-block	30	41
To mounting bracket	35	47
Mounting bracket	30	41
Camshaft sprocket	25	34
Connecting rod caps		
7.4L	50	68
454 Magnum, 502 Magnum	73	99
Coupler-to-flywheel	35	47
Crankshaft damper (7.4L)	85	115
Crankshaft pulley	35	47
Cylinder head bolts	85	115
Distributor clamp	25	34
Exhaust manifold		
Bolts	30	41
Nuts	25	34
Exhaust elbow/riser	20-35	27-34
Flywheel-to-crankshaft	70	95
Flywheel housing	30	41
Front cover	10	14
Intake manifold		
Prior to Mark V	30	41
Mark V	35	47
Main bearing caps	110	149
Oil filter bypass valve	7	9
Oil pan screws		
7.4L, 454 Magnum (prior to Mark V)		
1/4-20	7	9
5/16-18	14	19
502 Magnum (prior to Mark V)		
1/4-20	7	9
5/16-18	17	23
All Mark V	17	23
Oil pan drain plug	20	27

(continued)

Table 4 7.4L, 454 MAGNUM AND 502 MAGNUM TIGHTENING TORQUES (continued)

Fastener	ft.-lb.	N·m
Oil pump		
Mounting bolts		
All models prior to Mark V	65	88
All Mark V models	70	95
Cover screws	7	9
Power steering pump	30	41
Rear mount	40	54
Seawater pump	30	41
Starter motor	50	68
Temperature sending unit	20	27
Thermostat housing	30	41
Valve cover		
7.4L, 454 Magnum (prior to Mark V)	4.2	5.6
7.4L, 454 Magnum (Mark V) and		
all 502 Magnum	6	8
Water circulating pump		
All models prior to Mark V	30	41
All Mark V	35	47

Table 5 STANDARD TORQUE VALUES

Fastener	ft.-lb.	N·m
Grade 5		
1/4-20	8	11
1/4-28	8	11
5/16-18	17	23
5/16-24	20	27
3/8-16	30	40
3/8-24	35	47
7/16-14	50	68
7/16-20	55	75
1/2-13	75	100
1/2-20	85	115
9/16-12	105	142
9/16-18	115	156
Grade 6		
1/4-20	10.5	14
1/4-28	12.5	17
5/16-18	22.5	31
5/16-24	25	54
3/8-16	40	34
3/8-24	45	61
7/16-14	65	88
7/16-20	70	95
1/2-13	100	136
1/2-20	110	149
9/16-12	135	183
9/16-18	150	203

8

Chapter Nine

Fuel Delivery System

The fuel delivery system consists of the fuel tank(s), a water-separating fuel filter (some models), a fuel pump, the carburetor, carburetor filter and connecting lines. Fuel stored in the tank(s) is drawn through the line by a fuel pump. The fuel passes through the water-separating filter (if so equipped) into the fuel pump, which pushes it into the carburetor where it is metered, mixed with air and sent into the intake manifold.

This chapter includes service procedures for the flame arrestor, carburetor, fuel pump and connecting lines. Regular maintenance to the fuel system is limited to replacing the fuel filter, cleaning the flame arrestor and adjusting the carburetor, as described in Chapter Four. **Table 1** and **Table 2** are at the end of the chapter.

FLAME ARRESTOR

All MerCruiser engines are equipped with a flame arrestor cover (**Figure 1**). The cover is used to prevent water from leaking through the engine compartment seams and into the carburetor. On many V6 and V8 models, the flame

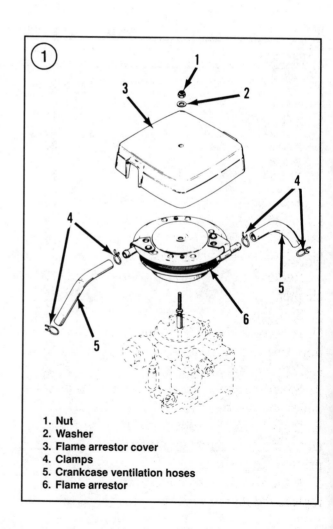

1. Nut
2. Washer
3. Flame arrestor cover
4. Clamps
5. Crankcase ventilation hoses
6. Flame arrestor

arrestor cover also protects the distributor from water.

Starting with 1989 models, an engine specification decal is affixed on the flame arrestor cover. The decal includes the engine, drive unit and transom serial numbers for quick reference. Each component continues to be marked with its own serial number, but the flame arrestor cover decal provides all the information in one place.

Removal/Installation

Refer to **Figure 1**, typical for this procedure.
1. Remove the engine compartment cover or hatch and place to one side out of the way.
2. Disconnect the crankcase vent hose(s) from the flame arrestor.
3. Remove the nut holding the flame arrestor and cover, if so equipped, to the carburetor air horn.
4. Remove the cover (if so equipped), flame arrestor and gasket (if used) from the carburetor air horn.
5. Installation is the reverse of removal.

Cleaning

Clean the flame arrestor in kerosene, carburetor cleaner or other commercial solvent. Do *not* use gasoline as a solvent—it is an extreme fire hazard in an open container.
1. Remove the flame arrestor as described in this chapter.
2. Submerge the flame arrestor in a container of clean solvent for several minutes to let the solution penetrate accumulated deposits of dirt, dust and other contaminants.
3. Slosh the flame arrestor in the solvent container and resubmerge for a few minutes.
4. Remove the flame arrestor from the solvent and allow it to drain, then blow dry with compressed air.
5. If the air inlet screen is deformed in any way, replace the flame arrestor.

6. Reinstall the flame arrestor as described in this chapter.

Gasoline Requirements

CAUTION
If gasoline containing alcohol must be used, the entire fuel system must be frequently inspected for leakage, deterioration or other damage. Do not store fuel in fuel tanks for extended periods.

On all models, the recommended fuel is regular or premium unleaded gasoline, containing no alcohol, with a minimum pump octane rating of 87. On 1986-1989 models and 1990 4.3L, 4.3LX, 5.0L and 5.0LX models, the manufacturer recommends adding Quicksilver Valve Lubricant to the fuel to prevent premature exhaust valve seat recession.

On all models, use a propeller that allows the engine to operate at or near its full throttle speed range at wide-open throttle. Prolonged wide-open throttle operation, however, should be avoided.

Sour Fuel

The fuel used plays a large role in satisfactory engine performance. In most temperate climates, fuel will start to break down after it has been in the fuel tank a few months. When this happens, it forms a gum-like substance that settles at the bottom of the tank where it can clog the in-tank filter. If drawn out of the tank by the fuel pump, this substance will affect the fuel filters. It will also start to clog the jets and other small passages inside the carburetor.

You should drain the fuel tank whenever the boat will not be in service for a period of time. The gasoline can be used in an automobile without harm, since it will be burned within a few days. If it is not possible or desirable to drain the tank, the use of Quicksilver Gasoline Stabilizer (or equivalent) is recommended to prevent the

9

fuel from spoiling. Regular use of this additive is also recommended to prevent corrosion and gum formation in the fuel system.

Gasohol

As mentioned in Chapter Three, some gasolines sold for marine use may contain alcohol, although this fact may not be advertised. Using such fuels is not recommended, unless you can determine the nature of the blend. Mercury Marine suggests that the following precautions be observed if gasohol must be used.

1. Buy fuel only as needed and use it as soon as possible.
2. Do not spill gasohol on painted surfaces.
3. Expect a slight decrease in power, stalling at lower speeds and somewhat greater fuel consumption.
4. Alternate the use of gasohol with regular unleaded gasoline. If it is necessary to operate an engine on gasohol, do not store such fuel in the tank(s) for more than a few days, especially in climates with high humidity.

Numerous problems have been identified with the use of misblended alcohol/gasoline fuels. Some of the most important are:

 a. Corrosion formation on the inside of fuel tanks and steel fuel lines
 b. Corrosion formation inside carburetor (zinc and aluminum alloys are especially susceptible)
 c. Deterioration and failure of synthetic rubber or plastic materials such as O-ring seals, diaphragms, accelerator pump cups and gaskets
 d. Premature failure of fuel line hoses

CARBURETOR FUNDAMENTALS

A gasoline engine must receive fuel and air mixed in precise proportions to operate efficiently at various speeds. Under normal conditions at sea level, the ratio is 14.7:1 at high speed and 12:1 at low speeds. Carburetors are designed to maintain these ratios while providing for sudden acceleration or increased loads.

A mixture with too much fuel is said to be "rich." One with too little fuel is said to be "lean." Incorrect mixture proportions can result from a variety of factors such as a dirty flame arrestor, defective choke, improperly adjusted idle mixture or speed screws, a leaking needle valve or a float that has absorbed fuel.

The choke valve in a carburetor provides a richer than normal mixture of fuel and air until the engine warms up. If the choke valve sticks in an open position, the engine will not start properly. A choke that sticks in a closed position will cause a flooding condition.

The throat of a carburetor is often called a "barrel." A single-barrel (1-bbl.) carburetor has only one throat. Two-barrel carburetors have 2 throats and 2 complete sets of metering devices. A 4-barrel carburetor has 4 throats and 4 complete sets of metering devices.

CARBURETORS

During the years covered by this manual, the following carburetors have been used:

 a. Rochester 2GC/2GV 2-bbl.

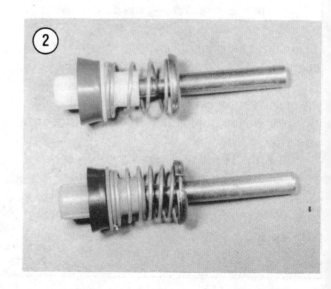

b. MerCarb 2-bbl.

c. Rochester 4MV 4-bbl.

d. Weber 4-bbl.

Removal, overhaul and installation procedures are provided for all models.

Carburetors used on MerCruiser marine engines are designed for marine use. Although they may appear to be identical to automotive carburetors, their internal components are *not* the same. **Figure 2** shows the difference between the accelerator pump plungers used in given carburetor models. The pump at the top is designed for marine use; the bottom pump is an automotive application. Automotive carburetors are externally vented and will allow fuel vapors to enter the bilge. Marine carburetors are internally vented to prevent this dangerous situation from occurring. Even the gaskets used in marine carburetor differ from those used in automotive applications.

> *WARNING*
> *Do not substitute an automotive carburetor or automotive carburetor parts for marine-grade components. Fuel vapors escaping from such carburetors or as a result of incorrect parts usage can create a fire or explosion hazard.*

Carburetor specifications vary with type, application and model year. The necessary specifications are provided on instruction sheets accompanying overhaul kits, along with any specific procedures required for adjustment. The specifications provided in **Table 1** should be used only if the overhaul kit instruction sheet is not available.

The carburetor model identification may be stamped on the carburetor main body or air horn casting, or on a tag attached to the carburetor by one of the air horn screws. See **Figure 3**. This information is necessary to obtain the proper overhaul kit from your MerCruiser dealer.

Vapor Lock (4-Cylinder Models)

A high-flow fuel pump kit (part No. 42725A5) is offered as a means of reducing vapor lock problems. See **Figure 4**. This fuel pump is factory-installed on models manufactured after August, 1986. A water-cooled fuel line assembly is also available from the manufacturer to combat

9

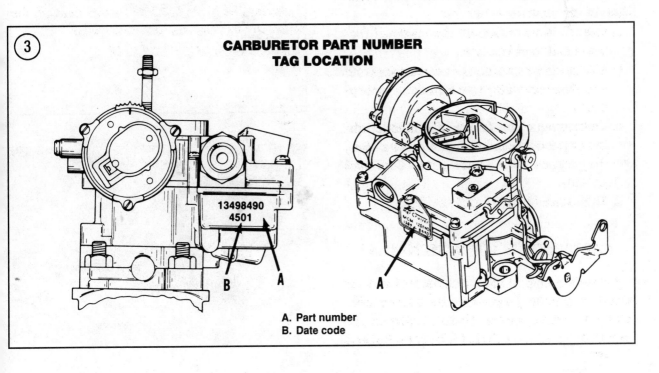

③ **CARBURETOR PART NUMBER TAG LOCATION**

13498490
4501

B   A

A

A. Part number
B. Date code

vapor lock on 4-cylinder engines. The water-cooled fuel line must be used in combination with the high-flow fuel pump.

The high-flow fuel pump and water-cooled fuel line may not be a totally satisfactory solution. Vapor lock problems are on the rise due to the increased use of alcohol and butane fuel additives, which result in lower fuel vaporization points. Mercury Marine offers the following pointers as steps in reducing the vapor lock problem.

1. Let the engine idle for several minutes after a hard run before shutting it down.
2. Let the engine idle 1-2 minutes after starting.
3. Operate the bilge blower (if so equipped) at idle and during shutdown.
4. Make sure there are sufficient vents to provide a good flow of air through the engine compartment.

Carburetor Removal/Installation

1. Remove the flame arrestor as described in this chapter. If the carburetor uses a spacer on the flame arrestor mounting stud, remove and place it where it will not be lost.
2. Close the fuel tank supply valve.
3. Place a container under the fuel line connection to catch any spillage. Disconnect the fuel line at the carburetor. See A, **Figure 5**, typical. Use one wrench to hold the fuel inlet nut while you loosen the fuel line fitting nut with a second wrench. Cap the line and fitting to prevent leakage and the entry of contamination.
4. Disconnect the transparent fuel pump sight hose from the carburetor.
5. Remove and discard any tie straps holding hoses, vacuum lines or electrical wiring to the carburetor.
6. Disconnect the electrical choke heater connection. If equipped with a well-type or remote choke, disconnect the choke coil rod from the carburetor.

7. Disconnect the crankcase ventilation hose, if so equipped, from the carburetor.
8. Disconnect the throttle cable (and swivel link assembly, if so equipped). See **Figure 6**, typical.
9. Remove the carburetor flange-to-manifold fasteners and lockwashers. Remove the carburetor from the manifold.
10. Stuff a clean cloth in the intake manifold opening to prevent small parts and contaminants from falling inside.

NOTE
For ease in starting, fill the carburetor bowl with fuel before installing the carburetor. Operate the throttle lever several times and verify that fuel discharges from the pump jets before installation.

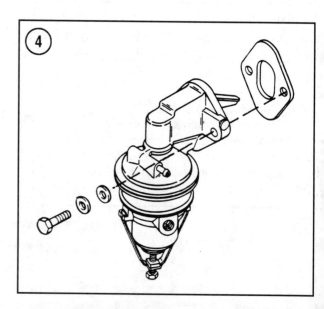

11. Installation is the reverse of removal. Clean all gasket residue from the intake manifold mating surface and install a new carburetor gasket. To prevent warpage of the carburetor base, snug the flange fasteners, then tighten the fasteners in a crisscross pattern until snug. Tighten Rochester 2-bbl. and MerCarb fasteners to 20 ft.-lb. (27 N·m). Tighten Rochester and Weber 4-bbl. fasteners to 132 in.-lb. (15 N·m).

Preparations for Overhaul

Before removing and disassembling any carburetor, be sure you have the proper marine carburetor overhaul kit, a sufficient quantity of fresh carburetor cleaner and the proper tools. Work slowly and carefully. Follow the disassembly and assembly procedures. Refer to the exploded drawing of your carburetor when necessary. Do not apply excessive force at any time.

It is not necessary to disassemble the carburetor linkage or remove linkage adjusting screws when overhauling a carburetor. Solenoids, dashpots and other diaphragm-operated assist devices attached to the carburetor body should be removed, as carburetor cleaner will damage them. Clean such parts using a suitable aerosol carburetor cleaner and dry with compressed air or wipe dry with a cloth.

Use carburetor legs to prevent throttle plate damage while working on the carburetor. If legs

are not available, thread a nut on each of four 2-1/4 in. bolts. Install each bolt in a flange hole and thread another nut on the bolt. These will hold the bolts securely to the carburetor and serve the same purpose as legs.

> *CAUTION*
> *Do not use the carburetor-to-manifold gasket supplied in any overhaul, gasket or repair kit unless it is specifically designed for marine application. Current MerCruiser carburetor kits contain the correct gasket. When using kits provided by other manufacturers, it is necessary to order the correct mounting gasket from your MerCruiser dealer.*

Cleaning and Inspection

Dirt, varnish, gum, water, carbon or other contamination in or on the carburetor are often the cause of unsatisfactory performance. Gaskets and accelerating pump cups may swell or leak, resulting in carburetion problems. Efficient carburetion depends upon careful cleaning, inspection and proper installation of new parts.

The new gaskets and parts provided in a marine carburetor overhaul kit should be installed when overhauling the carburetor and the old parts discarded. Automotive carburetor kits should not be used. The gaskets included in automotive overhaul kits will allow the carburetor to vent fuel vapors directly into the engine compartment. This venting of vapors presents a fire and explosion hazard.

Carburetors used on MerCruiser engines are painted Phantom Black, as are the engine and all other external components. The inside of the carburetor is coated with a greenish-yellow substance designed to reduce porosity of the carburetor castings and prevent corrosion. If this internal coating is removed, the carburetor will be prone to corrosion which will clog the passages. Any cleaner used should not be strong enough to remove either the external black paint or the internal greenish-yellow coating. If it

9

⑦ **ROCHESTER TWO-BARREL**

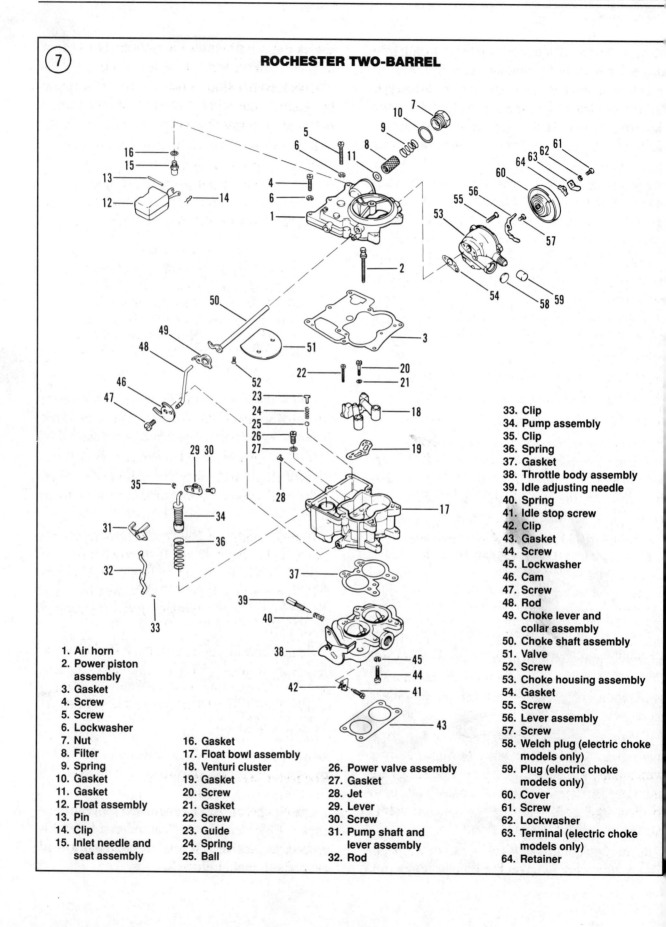

1. Air horn
2. Power piston
   assembly
3. Gasket
4. Screw
5. Screw
6. Lockwasher
7. Nut
8. Filter
9. Spring
10. Gasket
11. Gasket
12. Float assembly
13. Pin
14. Clip
15. Inlet needle and
    seat assembly

16. Gasket
17. Float bowl assembly
18. Venturi cluster
19. Gasket
20. Screw
21. Gasket
22. Screw
23. Guide
24. Spring
25. Ball

26. Power valve assembly
27. Gasket
28. Jet
29. Lever
30. Screw
31. Pump shaft and
    lever assembly
32. Rod

33. Clip
34. Pump assembly
35. Clip
36. Spring
37. Gasket
38. Throttle body assembly
39. Idle adjusting needle
40. Spring
41. Idle stop screw
42. Clip
43. Gasket
44. Screw
45. Lockwasher
46. Cam
47. Screw
48. Rod
49. Choke lever and
    collar assembly
50. Choke shaft assembly
51. Valve
52. Screw
53. Choke housing assembly
54. Gasket
55. Screw
56. Lever assembly
57. Screw
58. Welch plug (electric choke
    models only)
59. Plug (electric choke
    models only)
60. Cover
61. Screw
62. Lockwasher
63. Terminal (electric choke
    models only)
64. Retainer

does, carburetor performance will be unsatisfactory when reinstalled on the engine.

The best advice is to use and aerosol type carburetor cleaner or kerosene and a carburetor cleaning brush. If a commercial carburetor cleaning solvent is used and the parts are to be submerged in the solution, it should be weak enough so that it will not remove the external paint or internal coating. If parts are submerged, do not leave them in the carburetor cleaner longer than necessary to loosen the gum and dirt.

Rinse parts cleaned in solvent with kerosene. Blow all parts dry with compressed air. Wipe all parts which cannot be immersed in solvent (such as diaphragms, solenoids, dashpots, etc.) with a soft cloth slightly moistened with solvent, then with a clean, dry cloth.

Force compressed air through all passages in the carburetor.

CAUTION
Do not use a wire brush to clean any part. Do not use a drill or wire to clean out any opening or passage in the carburetor. A drill or wire may enlarge the hole or passage and change the calibration. If the carburetor passages are so clogged that cleaning as described with solvent will not clear them, the carburetor should be replaced.

Check the choke and throttle plate shafts for grooves, wear or excessive looseness or binding. Inspect the choke and throttle plates for nicked edges or burrs which prevent proper closure. Choke and throttle plates are positioned during production and should not be removed unless damaged.

Clean all gasket residue from the air horn, main body and throttle body sealing surfaces with a putty knife. Since carburetor castings are aluminum, a sharp instrument should not be used to clean the gasket residue or damage to the carburetor assemblies may result.

Inspect all components for cracks or warpage. Check floats for wear on the lip and hinge pin.

Check hinge pin holes in the air horn, bowl cover or float bowl for wear and elongation.

Check composition floats for fuel absorption by gently squeezing and applying fingernail pressure. If moisture appears, replace the float.

Replace the float if the arm needle contact surface is grooved. If the float or floats are serviceable, gently polish the needle contact surface of the arm with crocus cloth or steel wool. Replace the float if the shaft is worn.

NOTE
Some gasolines contain additives that will cause the viton tip of the fuel inlet needle to swell. This problem is also caused by gasoline and alcohol blends. If carburetor problems are traced to a deformed inlet needle tip, change brands of gasoline used.

Check the viton tip of the fuel inlet needle for swelling or distortion. Discard the needle if the overhaul kit contains a new needle for assembly.

Replace all screws and nuts that have stripped threads. Replace all distorted or broken springs. Inspect all gasket mating surfaces for nicks or burrs.

If main body on Rochester carburetors requires replacement, check float bowl casting. If marked "MW," be sure to replace the main body with one marked "MW." This stands for "machined pump well" and determines the type of pump used.

Reassemble all parts carefully. It should not be necessary to apply force to any parts. If force seems to be required, you are doing something wrong. Stop and refer to the exploded drawing for your carburetor.

Rochester 2GC Disassembly

The Rochester 2GC uses and integral cap-type choke. Refer to **Figure 7** as required for this procedure. Not all 2GC carburetors will use all the parts show in **Figure 7**.

1. Use carburetor legs to prevent throttle plate damage while working on the carburetor. If legs are not available, thread a nut on each of four 2-1/4 in. bolts. Install each bolt in a flange hole and thread another nut on the bolt. These will hold the bolts securely to the carburetor and serve the same purpose as legs.

2. Remove the choke cap retaining screws and retainers. See **Figure 8**, typical. Remove the cap cover, gasket and insulator baffle plate from the choke housing.

3. Remove the screw holding the choke piston and lever assembly to the choke shaft. Remove the piston and lever assembly. Remove the 2 screws holding the choke housing to the bowl cover. Remove the choke housing and gasket. See **Figure 9**. Discard the gasket.

4. Remove the hairpin retainers from each end of the pump rod with needlenose pliers. See **Figure 10**, typical. Rotate the upper rod end out of the pump lever hole and remove the pump rod.

5. Remove the fast idle cam screw from the floa bowl. See **Figure 11**.

6. Remove the bowl cover attaching screws and lockwashers. Rap the bowl cover, if necessary with a soft-faced hammer to break the gasket sea (do not pry loose) and lift the assembly straigh up and off the float bowl to prevent damage to the accelerator pump and power piston assembly See **Figure 12**.

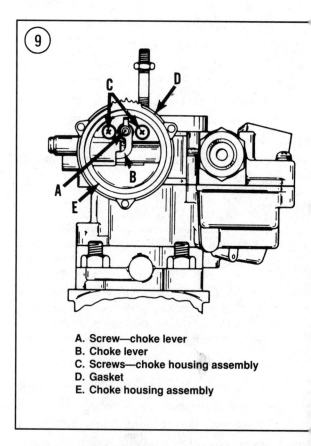

A. Screw—choke lever
B. Choke lever
C. Screws—choke housing assembly
D. Gasket
E. Choke housing assembly

A. Screws
B. Retainers
C. Choke cover

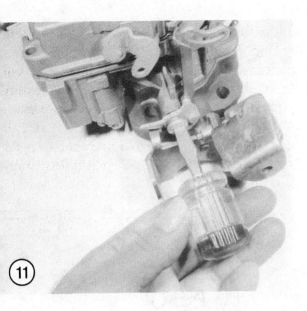

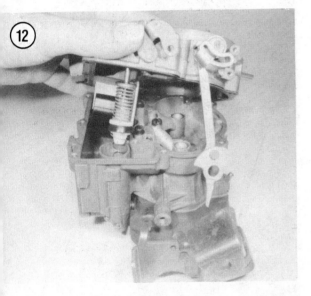

7. Invert the bowl cover and slide the float hinge pin from the retainer (**Figure 13**). Remove the float assembly from the bowl cover.

NOTE
Some models will use a pull clip on the float assembly. This will automatically remove the needle from the inlet valve. If no pull clip is used, remove the needle from its seat with needlenose pliers.

8. Remove and discard the bowl cover gasket.

9. Remove the inlet needle valve seat (**Figure 14**) with a wide-blade screwdriver. Remove and discard the gasket.

10. Unstake the power piston retaining washer. Depress and release the power piston stem—it should snap free. If it does not, repeat the depress/release sequence until it does. See A, **Figure 15**.

11. Remove the accelerator pump plunger only if it is damaged. To do so, loosen the setscrew (B, **Figure 15**) on the plunger inner lever and break the swaged end (C, **Figure 15**). Disengage pump assembly from inner pump arm.

12. Remove the fuel inlet fitting from the bowl cover. Remove the inlet gasket, fuel filter and gasket and spring. Discard the gaskets and filter.

13. Remove the accelerator pump plunger return from the pump well. Invert the float bowl and catch the check ball as it falls out of the pump well (**Figure 16**).

9

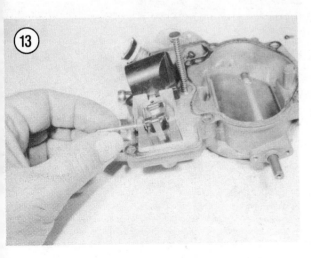

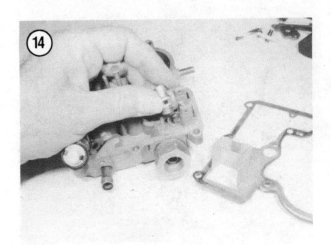

14. Remove the pump inlet screen from the bottom of the float bowl.

15. Remove the main metering jets and power piston check valve with a wide-blade screwdriver.

16. Remove the venturi cluster attaching screws. Remove the cluster and gasket (**Figure 17**). Discard the gasket.

17. Remove the staking around the T-shaped retainer holding the discharge spring and ball in the float bow. Remove the retainer with needlenose pliers. Invert the float bowl and remove the spring and ball.

18. Invert the float bowl and remove the throttle body attaching screws (**Figure 18**). Separate the throttle body from the float bowl and discard the gasket.

19. Turn each mixture screw clockwise until it seats lightly, counting the number of turns required. Write this information down for reference during reassembly. Back out and remove the idle mixture screws.

20. Clean and inspect the carburetor as described in this chapter.

Rochester 2GC Assembly

Refer to **Figure 7** as required for this procedure. Check replacement gaskets for proper punching by comparing them with old gaskets.

1. Install each idle mixture screw and spring assembly in the throttle body. Turn the screws clockwise until they seat lightly, then back out the number of turns recorded during disassembly to provide a temporary idle adjustment setting

> *WARNING*
> *Make sure a non-vented gasket is used in Step 1. An automotive-type gasket will vent fuel vapors to the atmosphere during hot engine operation which can result in a dangerous potential for an explosion or fire.*

2. Invert the float bowl and install a new gasket, aligning the gasket holes with those in the casting.

3. Install the throttle body to the float bowl and tighten the attaching screws securely (**Figure 18**).

4. Drop the pump discharge check ball into the discharge well in the float bow. Install the spring and T-shaped retainer. Stake the retainer in place flush with the top of the discharge well.

5. Fit a new gasket on the bottom of the venturi cluster and install the cluster. Tighten screws evenly and securely.

6. Reinstall the main metering jets with a wide-blade screwdriver. Fit a new gasket on the power piston check valve and install with the screwdriver.

7. Install the pump inlet check ball in the pump well (**Figure 16**). Install and center the pump return spring in the well.

8. If choke housing was removed, reinstall with a new gasket and tighten the attaching screws securely. Assemble choke piston to shaft/link assembly.

9. Install the pump inlet screen in the bottom of the float bowl.

10. If pump plunger assembly was removed, install outer pump lever and inner pump arm to bowl cover. Tighten setscrew. Connect plunger assembly to inner arm with shaft point inward and install the horseshoe retainer.

11. Install inlet needle valve seat with a new gasket (**Figure 14**). Tighten securely with a wide-blade screwdriver.

12. Install a new gasket on the bowl cover.

13. Install the power piston assembly in the bowl cover and stake housing slightly to hold piston in place.

NOTE
On models without a float assembly pull clip, insert the inlet needle in the needle seat before installing the float in Step 14. See Figure 19.

14. Connect inlet needle to float assembly and carefully reinstall bowl cover, then insert hinge pin (**Figure 13**). Check float operation.

15. Adjust float level and drop to specifications provided with the adjustment procedure in the overhaul kit. If not available, refer to **Table 1**.

16. Install bowl cover to float bowl (**Figure 12**), making sure that the accelerator pump plunger fits into the pump well properly. Hold air horn on float bowl and check pump operation to see that the plunger operates freely.

17. Install the bowl cover screws with lockwashers, tightening evenly and securely.

18. Install the fast idle cam and tighten the screw securely (**Figure 11**).

19. Attach the accelerator pump rod and install the hairpin retainers (**Figure 10**).

20. Position the baffle plate and cover gasket on the choke housing. Install cover and rotate until index marks are aligned as specified in overhaul

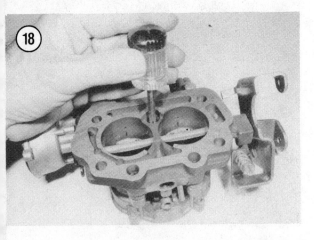

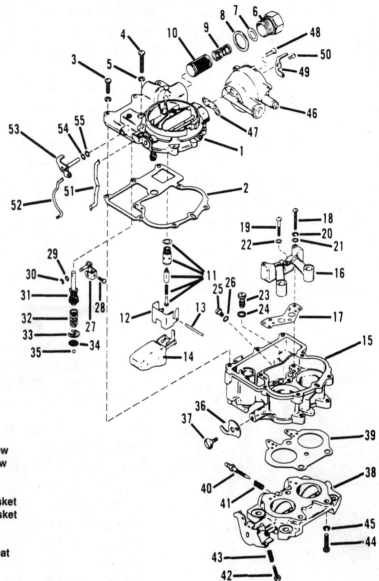

MERCARB 2-BBL. CARBURETOR

1. Air horn
2. Gasket
3. Short air horn screw
4. Long air horn screw
5. Lockwasher
6. Fuel inlet nut
7. Small fuel inlet gasket
8. Large fuel inlet gasket
9. Spring
10. Filter
11. Inlet needle and seat
12. Baffle plate
13. Float hinge pin
14. Float
15. Float bowl assembly
16. Venturi cluster
17. Gasket
18. Outer cluster screw
19. Inner cluster screw
20. Lockwasher
21. Gasket
22. Gasket
23. Power valve assembly
24. Gasket
25. Float bowl jet
26. Jet gasket
27. Pump shaft and lever assembly
28. Screw
29. Washer

30. Pump rod retainer clip
31. Accelerator pump assembly
32. Pump return spring
33. Check ball retainer clip
34. Strainer
35. Check ball
36. Fast idle cam
37. Screw
38. Throttle body assembly
39. Gasket
40. Idle mixture screw
41. Spring
42. Idle speed screw

43. Spring
44. Throttle body screw
45. Lockwasher
46. Choke housing assembly
47. Gasket
48. Screw
49. Choke lever
50. Screw
51. Choke rod
52. Accelerator pump rod
53. Accelerator pump shaft and lever
54. Washer
55. Washer

kit instructions (or **Table 1**). Install retainers/screws and tighten securely.

21. Install choke rod in idle cam and counterweight lever. Install idle cam to float bowl. Install choke lever to bowl cover.

MerCarb 2-bbl. Disassembly

The MerCarb 2-bbl. is similar in many respects to the Rochester 2GC, but uses a single idle mixture screw and a separate fuel feed for each venturi. The removable venturi cluster attached to the fuel bowl contains built-in calibrated main well tubes and pump jets. The venturi cluster is serviced as an assembly. The fixed orifice main metering jets work in conjunction with fixed air bleeds to meter the correct air/fuel mixture to the engine.

MerCarb 2-bbl. Carburetors installed on 1987 and later models have a larger accelerator pump to provide a 100 percent increase in fuel output.

The oversize pump uses an alcohol-resistant viton seal to reduce pump deterioration from misblended fuel. The new pump requires slotting the fuel inlet system and use of a heavier pump/throttle return spring to assure a consistent idle speed. This MerCarb version can be installed as a replacement for the previous model.

Refer to **Figure 20** as required for this procedure. Not all MerCarb 2-bbl. carburetors will use all the parts shown in **Figure 20**.

1. Use carburetor legs to prevent throttle plate damage while working on the carburetor. If legs are not available, thread a nut on each of four 2-1/4 in. bolts. Install each bolt in a flange hole and thread another nut on the bolt. These will hold the bolts securely to the carburetor and serve the same purpose as legs.

2. Remove the choke cap retaining screws and retainers. See **Figure 8**, typical. Remove the cap cover, gasket and insulator baffle plate from the choke housing.

3. Remove the screw holding the choke piston and lever assembly to the choke shaft. Remove the piston and lever assembly. Remove the 2 screws holding the choke housing to the bowl cover. Remove the choke housing and gasket. See **Figure 9**. Discard the gasket.

4. Remove the fuel inlet fitting from the bowl cover. Remove the inlet gasket, fuel filter and gasket and spring. Discard the gaskets and filter.

5. Remove the hairpin retainer from the end of the pump rod with needlenose pliers. See **Figure 21**. Rotate the upper rod end out of the pump lever hole and remove the pump rod.

6. Remove the fast idle cam screw from the float bowl. Pivot choke rod and disconnect from choke lever slot. See **Figure 22**.

7. Remove the air horn attaching screws and lockwashers. See **Figure 23**.

8. Rap the air horn, if necessary, with a soft-faced hammer to break the gasket seal (do not pry loose) and lift the assembly straight up and off the float bowl to prevent damage to the

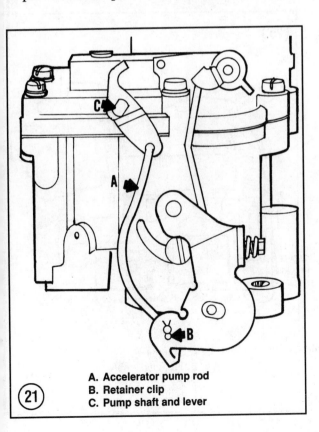

A. Accelerator pump rod
B. Retainer clip
C. Pump shaft and lever

(21)

9

accelerator pump and power piston assembly. See **Figure 24**.

9. Invert the float bowl and slide the float hinge pin from the retainer (**Figure 25**). Remove the float assembly from the bowl cover. Remove and discard the bowl cover gasket.

10. Remove the inlet needle baffle, then remove the inlet needle valve seat (**Figure 26**) with a wide-blade screwdriver. Remove and discard the gasket.

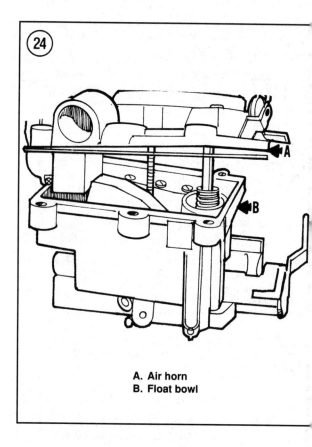

A. Air horn
B. Float bowl

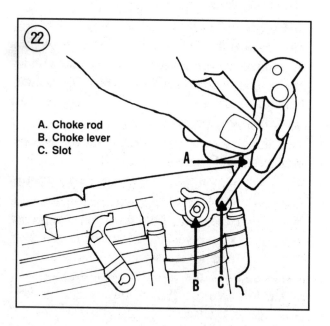

A. Choke rod
B. Choke lever
C. Slot

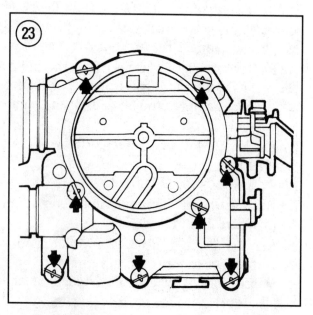

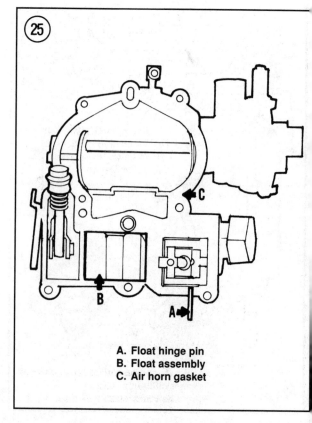

A. Float hinge pin
B. Float assembly
C. Air horn gasket

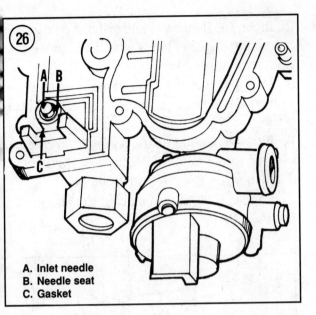

A. Inlet needle
B. Needle seat
C. Gasket

11. Loosen the accelerator pump plunger set-screw on the plunger inner lever. Slide pump shaft and lever assembly from bowl cover, then remove the pump assembly and lever. See **Figure 27**.

12. Remove retainer clip and washer from the pump shaft/lever assembly. Remove pump from shaft and lever assembly. See **Figure 28**.

13. Refer to **Figure 29** and remove the accelerator pump return spring, retainer clip, strainer and check ball from the pump well.

14. Remove the power valve assembly and gasket (**Figure 30**). Discard the gasket.

15. Remove the main metering jets with a wide-blade screwdriver. See **Figure 31**. Discard the gaskets.

16. Remove the venturi cluster attaching screws. Remove the cluster and gasket (**Figure 32**). Discard the gasket.

17. Invert the float bowl and remove the throttle body attaching screws (**Figure 33**). Separate the throttle body from the float bowl and discard the gasket.

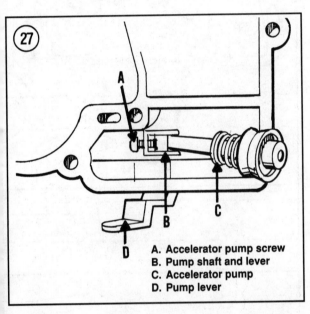

A. Accelerator pump screw
B. Pump shaft and lever
C. Accelerator pump
D. Pump lever

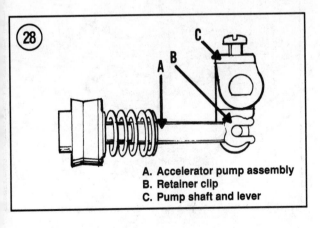

A. Accelerator pump assembly
B. Retainer clip
C. Pump shaft and lever

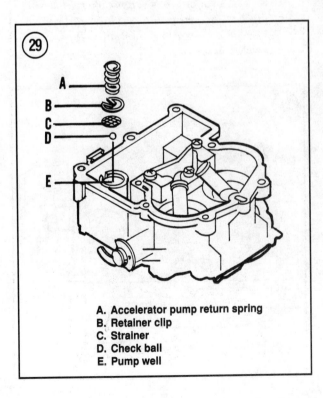

A. Accelerator pump return spring
B. Retainer clip
C. Strainer
D. Check ball
E. Pump well

9

18. Turn the mixture screw clockwise until it seats *lightly,* counting the number of turns required. Write this information down for reference during reassembly. Back out and remove the idle mixture screw.

19. Clean and inspect the carburetor as described in this chapter.

MerCarb 2-bbl. Assembly

Refer to **Figure 20** as required for this procedure. Check replacement gaskets for proper punching by comparing them with old gaskets.

1. Install the idle mixture screw and spring assembly in the throttle body. Turn the screw clockwise until it seats *lightly,* then back out the number of turns recorded during disassembly to provide a temporary idle adjustment setting.

> *WARNING*
> *Make sure a non-vented gasket is used in Step 2. An automotive-type gasket will vent fuel vapors to the atmosphere during hot engine operation which can result in a dangerous potential for an explosion or fire.*

2. Invert the float bowl and install a new gasket, aligning the gasket holes with those in the casting. See **Figure 34**.

3. Install the throttle body to the float bowl and tighten the attaching screws securely (**Figure 33**).

4. Fit a new gasket on the bottom of the venturi cluster and install the cluster (**Figure 32**). Tighten screws evenly and securely.

5. Reinstall the main metering jets and gaskets with a wide-blade screwdriver. See **Figure 31**.

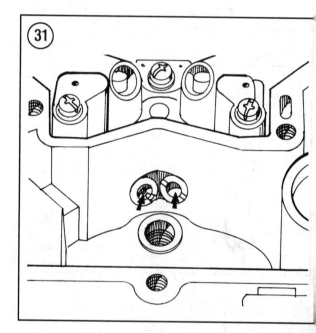

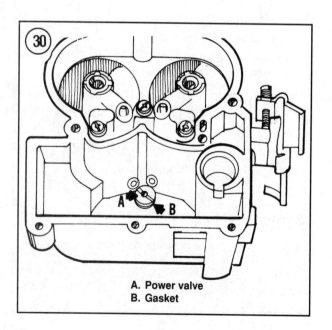

A. Power valve
B. Gasket

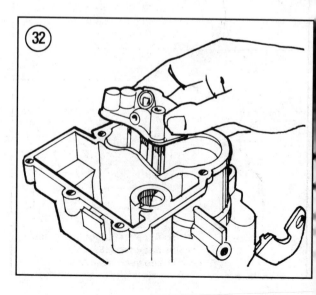

6. Fit a new gasket on the power valve and install with the screwdriver (**Figure 30**).

7. Install the check ball in the pump well, then install the retainer clip and pump return spring. See **Figure 29**. Mercury Marine currently recommends that the strainer not be reinstalled.

8. If pump plunger assembly was removed from pump lever, reattach and secure with pump

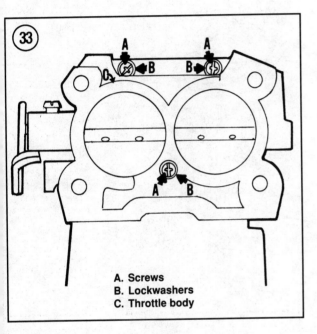

A. Screws
B. Lockwashers
C. Throttle body

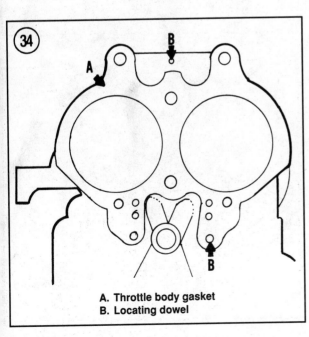

A. Throttle body gasket
B. Locating dowel

shaft/lever assembly with washer into bowl cover. Align pump lever indexed hole with shaft/lever assembly. Slide shaft into lever until shaft shoulder touches lever. Tighten setscrew snugly.

9. Install inlet needle valve seat with a new gasket. Tighten securely with a wide-blade screwdriver. Install inlet needle in seat assembly, then install the baffle.

10. Install a new gasket on the air horn.

11. Install float on the air horn, then insert hinge pin and check float operation.

12. Adjust float level and drop to specifications provided with the adjustment procedure in the overhaul kit. If not available, refer to **Table 1**.

13. Install air horn to float bowl (**Figure 12**), making sure that the accelerator pump plunger fits into the pump well properly. Hold air horn on float bowl and check pump operation to see that the plunger operates freely.

14. Install the air horn screws with lockwashers, tightening evenly and securely.

15. Connect choke rod to fast idle cam. Install the fast idle cam and tighten the screw securely.

16. Attach the accelerator pump rod to the pump shaft/lever assembly, then install the other end of the rod in the throttle lever and install the hairpin retainer.

17. If choke housing was removed, reinstall with a new gasket (if used) and tighten the attaching screws securely. Assemble choke piston to shaft/link assembly.

18. Position the baffle plate and cover gasket on the choke housing. Install cover and rotate until index marks are aligned as specified in overhaul kit instructions (or **Table 1**). Install retainers/screws and tighten securely.

Rochester 4MV Disassembly

The Rochester 4MV is a 2-stage carburetor. Primary fuel metering is controlled by tapered metering rods operated by engine vacuum. The secondaries are larger than the primaries, with

9

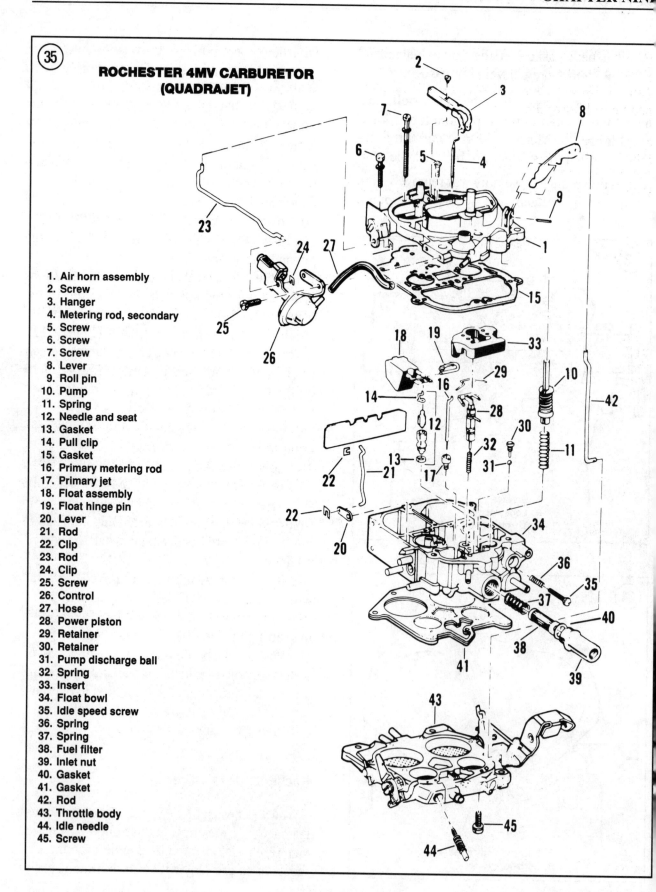

③⑤

ROCHESTER 4MV CARBURETOR
(QUADRAJET)

1. Air horn assembly
2. Screw
3. Hanger
4. Metering rod, secondary
5. Screw
6. Screw
7. Screw
8. Lever
9. Roll pin
10. Pump
11. Spring
12. Needle and seat
13. Gasket
14. Pull clip
15. Gasket
16. Primary metering rod
17. Primary jet
18. Float assembly
19. Float hinge pin
20. Lever
21. Rod
22. Clip
23. Rod
24. Clip
25. Screw
26. Control
27. Hose
28. Power piston
29. Retainer
30. Retainer
31. Pump discharge ball
32. Spring
33. Insert
34. Float bowl
35. Idle speed screw
36. Spring
37. Spring
38. Fuel filter
39. Inlet nut
40. Gasket
41. Gasket
42. Rod
43. Throttle body
44. Idle needle
45. Screw

secondary metering controlled by an air valve. Refer to **Figure 35** as required for this procedure. Not all 4MV carburetors will use all the parts shown in **Figure 35**.

1. Use carburetor legs to prevent throttle plate damage while working on the carburetor. If legs are not available, thread a nut on each of four 2-1/4 in. bolts. Install each bolt in a flange hole

and thread another nut on the bolt. These will hold the bolts securely to the carburetor and serve the same purpose as legs.

2. Remove the retaining clip/screw from the upper choke rod end. Disconnect rod from upper choke shaft lever and remove from the carburetor (**Figure 36**). If rod drops into main body, it can be removed later.

3. Drive the accelerator pump lever roll pin through the air horn boss just enough to disengage the pump lever. Remove the rod and pump lever from the carburetor.

4. Remove the small screw from the secondary metering rod hanger. Lift up on hanger and withdraw from air horn with metering rods attached (**Figure 37**). Leave rods on hanger unless they are to be replaced.

5. Disconnect and remove the vacuum break diaphragm assembly.

6. Remove the air horn attaching screws. Two of the screws are countersunk next to the venturi. See **Figure 38**.

7. If necessary, rap the air horn lightly with a soft-faced hammer to break the gasket seal—do not pry free. Lift the air horn straight up and off the main body to prevent bending the main air well air bleed tubes pressed into the casting. Angle the air horn slightly to disconnect the pump rod (**Figure 39**), if not disconnected in Step 3.

8. Remove the accelerating pump plunger and spring from the pump well (**Figure 40**).

9

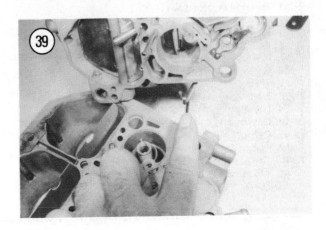

9. Remove and discard the air horn-to-float bowl gasket.

10. Remove the plastic filler block installed over the float assembly (**Figure 41**).

11. Pull up slightly on the float retaining pin and slide it toward the pump well. Lift the float and inlet needle from the float bowl (**Figure 42**).

12. Remove the inlet needle valve seat with a wide-blade screwdriver. Remove the gasket from the seat and discard.

13. Remove the pump discharge check ball retainer with a wide-blade screwdriver. Tilt body to remove check ball.

14. Remove power valve and primary metering rods assembly (**Figure 47**) by depressing power valve and allowing it to snap free. If it does not, repeat the depress/release sequence until it does. Be sure to retrieve spring under power valve/metering rods assembly.

15. Remove primary metering jets from the front of the fuel bowl with a wide-blade screwdriver. The secondary jets at the rear of the fuel bowl cannot be removed.

16. Remove the baffle from the secondary side of the main body.

17. Remove the fuel inlet fitting from the float bowl. Remove the inlet gasket, fuel filter and spring. Discard the gaskets and filter.

18. Invert the float bowl and remove the throttle body attaching screws. Leave throttle shaft linkage attached. Separate the throttle body from the float bowl and discard the gasket.

19. Turn the mixture screws clockwise until they *lightly* seat, counting number of turns re-

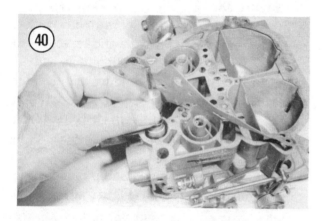

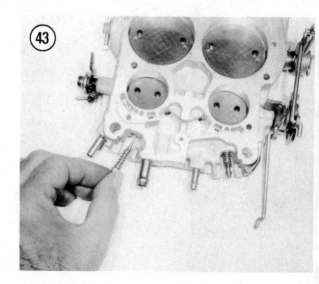

quired. Write this information down for reference during reassembly. Back out and remove the screw and spring assemblies (**Figure 43**).

20. Clean and inspect the carburetor as described in this chapter.

Rochester 4MV Assembly

Refer to **Figure 35** as required for this procedure. Check replacement gaskets for proper punching by comparing them with old gaskets.

1. Install each idle mixture screw and spring assembly in the throttle body. Turn the screws clockwise until they seat *lightly*, then back out

the number of turns recorded during disassembly to provide a temporary idle adjustment setting (**Figure 43**).

2. Position a new gasket over the throttle body dowels, then invert the float bowl and install the throttle body. Tighten the attaching screws snugly.

3. Install fuel filter spring, a new filter and the inlet nut with a new gasket. Tighten inlet nut securely.

4. Install the lower pump rod end in the throttle lever.

5. Install the inlet needle seat with a new gasket using a wide-blade screwdriver.

6. Drop the pump discharge check ball in the discharge well and install the ball retaining screw (**Figure 44**) with a wide-blade screwdriver.

7. Install the primary metering jets with a wide-blade screwdriver. Install the secondary baffle.

> *NOTE*
> *In Step 8, pull clip must be placed over edge of float arm as shown in **Figure 45**. DO NOT hook pull clip through either hole in float arm or inlet valve will not seat properly and severe flooding will result.*

8. Clip fuel inlet needle over float lever arm (**Figure 45**) and lower both into the fuel bowl (**Figure 46**). Make sure the needle seats in the valve properly, then press the float retaining pin into the casting cutouts.

9. Adjust float level to specifications provided with adjustment procedure in overhaul kit. If not available, refer to **Table 1**.

10. Press the plastic filler block (**Figure 41**) over the float assembly until it is fully seated.

11. Install the power piston sprin ginto the float bowl. Then, install the power piston/primary metering rods assembly into the float bowl. Using a small screwdriver, press the plastic power piston retainer into its bore until firmly seated. See **Figure 47**.

12. Drop the accelerator pump plunger spring into the pump well.

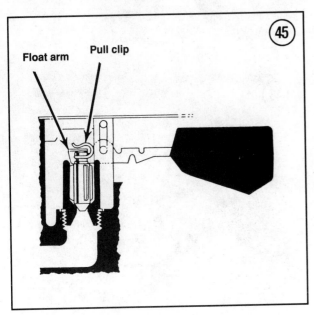

Float arm   Pull clip

13. Install a new air horn gasket on the main body. Make sure the tab slides under the power piston hanger.

14. Install the accelerator pump plunger in the pump well (**Figure 48**).

15. Carefully position air horn over main body and lower into place, making sure that the vent tubes, well tubes and pump plunger fit properly through the gasket.

16. Carefully install the 2 countersunk air horn screws first (**Figure 38**). Use of a magnetic screwdriver or needlenose pliers is recommended to position these screws. If they are accidentally dropped inside the venturi, the air horn will have to be removed to retrieve them.

17. Install and tighten the remaining air horn screws.

18. Install the secondary metering rods (**Figure 37**). They should drop freely into place as the hanger is lowered into the air horn. Install the hanger retaining screw snugly.

19. Install and connect the vacuum break diaphragm assembly.

20. Fit the choke rod into the bowl and connect its lower end to the lower choke lever inside. Fit the upper end in the choke shaft lever and install the retaining screw (**Figure 49**).

21. Connect the pump rod to the pump lever and pry the roll pin in place with a screwdriver blade.

Weber 4-bbl. Disassembly

Refer to **Figure 50** for this procedure. Not all Weber carburetors use all components shown in **Figure 50**.

1. Use carburetor legs to prevent throttle plate damage while servicing the carburetor. If legs are not available, thread a nut onto each of four 1 1/4 in. bolts. Insert each bolt into a carburetor flange hole, then thread another nut onto the bolt. These will hold the bolts securely to the carburetor.

2. Disconnect the choke linkage from the choke arm.

3. Remove the retaining clip holding the accelerator pump linkage rod to the pump arm.

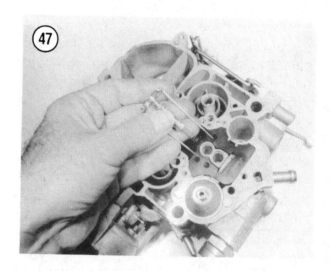

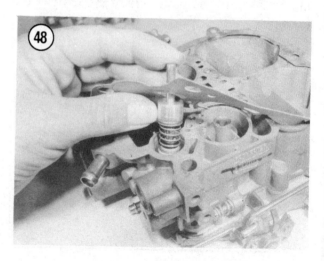

4. Disconnect the vacuum hose from the vacuum choke pull-off diaphragm. Remove the choke pull-off mounting screws. Disengage the pull-off linkage and remove the pull-off.

NOTE
Mark the metering rod assemblies for reassembly into the same position from which removed. The metering rods must not be interchanged.

5. Remove the metering rod cover screws. Remove the covers and lift the metering rods, pistons and springs from the air horn.

6. Remove 9 air horn screws. Carefully separate the air horn from the main body. Lift the air horn assembly straight up to prevent damage to the air horn components. See **Figure 51**.

7. Mark the floats and casting as left and right for correct reinstallation. Remove the float hinge pin and lift the float from the air horn. Repeat the procedure to remove the remaining float.

8. Remove the inlet valve needles from their seats. If the inlet valves are to be reused, mark the needles and seats for reference during reassembly, then remove the seats using a wide-blade screwdriver. Discard the gaskets under the seats.

9. Angle the bowl vent lever to one side and pry the rubber vent seal out of the casting.

10. Remove the screw holding the accelerator pump arm (A, **Figure 52**) to the air horn. Note the position of the pump link, then remove the

link from the pump plunger. Remove the pump plunger (B, **Figure 52**) from the air horn.

11. Unscrew and remove the fuel inlet fitting. Remove the filter screw and gasket from the fitting. See **Figure 53**.

12. Remove the accelerator pump plunger return spring from the carburetor body.

13. Remove the accelerator pump discharge housing (**Figure 54**). Remove and discard the housing gasket. Remove the pump discharge check ball and weight located under the discharge housing by inverting the carburetor body and catching the ball and weight.

14. Remove the hot idle compensator if so equipped.

15. Mark the primary and secondary venturi clusters for reinstallation in the same location from which removed.

16. Remove 2 screws securing each primary venturi cluster, then remove the clusters. See **Figure 55**. Remove and discard the venturi gaskets.

17. Remove 2 screws securing each secondary venturi cluster, then remove the clusters. See **Figure 56**. Remove and discard the gaskets.

18. Lift the air valve and weight assembly up and out of the carburetor body.

19. Remove the accelerator pump intake check valve from the fuel bowl (**Figure 57**).

NOTE
It is not necessary to remove the primary and secondary metering jets for routine carburetor cleaning. If jet removal is necessary, be certain the jets are identified for reinstallation in the same location from which removed.

20. If necessary, remove the primary and secondary metering jets from the fuel bowl using a suitable jet wrench or wide-blade screwdriver.

21. Turning the idle mixture screws clockwise, record the number of turns required to lightly seat each screws. Then remove the idle mixture screws and springs.

9

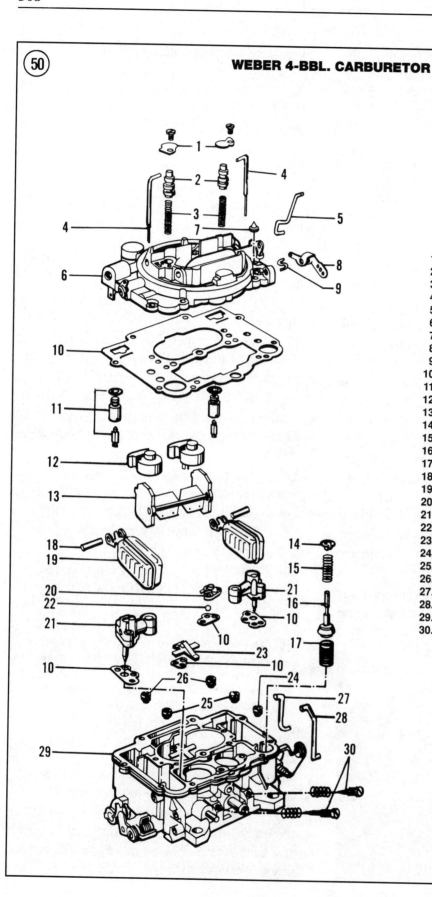

WEBER 4-BBL. CARBURETOR

1. Metering rod covers
2. Pistons
3. Springs
4. Metering rods
5. Linkage rod
6. Air horn
7. Vent valve
8. Pump arm
9. Pump link
10. Gasket
11. Inlet valve assembly
12. Secondary venturi
13. Air valve and weight assembly
14. Retainer
15. Spring
16. Pump plunger
17. Pump return spring
18. Float pin
19. Float
20. Accelerator pump discharge housing
21. Primary venturi
22. Pump discharge check ball
23. Hot idle compensator
24. Pump intake check valve
25. Primary main jet
26. Secondary main jet
27. Fast idle linkage rod
28. Pump linkage rod
29. Float bowl/throttle body assembly
30. Mixture screws

(51)

Weber 4-bbl. Adjustments

The following adjustments are necessary to ensure proper carburetor operation.

Float adjustments

1. With the inlet valve assembly and the float properly assembled to the air horn, hold the air

(55)

(52)

(56)

(53)

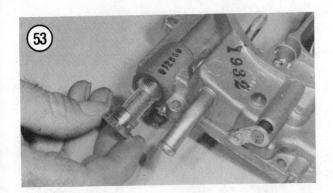

(54)

(57)

9

horn upright as shown in **Figure 58**. Allow the float to hang by its own weight.

2. Measure the distance between the bottom of the air horn mating surface to the bottom of the float as shown. The distance should be 2 in. (51 mm). If necessary, carefully bend the float tang to adjust.

3. Next, invert the air horn and measure the distance between the air horn mating surface and the bottom of the float as shown in **Figure 59**. The distance should be 1-9/32 in. (33 mm). If necessary, carefully bend the float arm where shown (**Figure 59**) to adjust.

Choke pull-off adjustment

1. While lightly holding the choke valve in the fully closed position, push the choke pull-off plunger into the diaphragm housing until the plunger is fully seated.

2. Measure the distance between the edge of the choke valve and inside of the air horn as shown in **Figure 60**. The distance should be 1/8 in. (3.2 mm).

3. Bend the pull-off linkage where shown (**Figure 60**) to adjust.

Accelerator pump adjustment

1. Make sure the accelerator pump linkage rod is positioned in the third hole from the end of the pump arm (**Figure 61**).

2. Back out the idle speed screw (**Figure 61**) until it is not contacting the throttle lever.

3. Measure the distance between the top of the air horn and the bottom of the pump link as shown in **Figure 61**. The distance should be 7/16 in. (11 mm).

4. Bend the pump linkage rod where shown (**Figure 61**) to adjust.

Weber 4-bbl. Assembly

Refer to **Figure 50** for this procedure. Check replacement gaskets for the proper punching by comparing them with the old gaskets.

1. Install the idle mixture screws and springs into the carburetor body. Turn each screw clock-

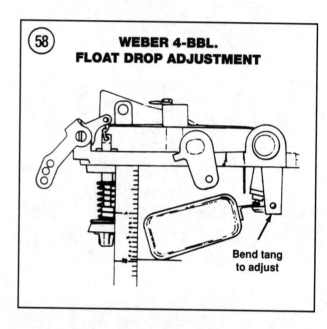

(58) WEBER 4-BBL. FLOAT DROP ADJUSTMENT

Bend tang to adjust

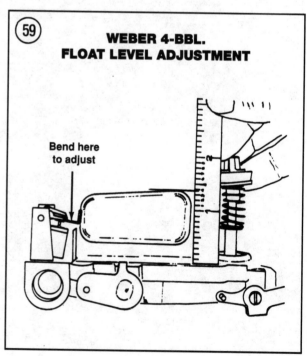

(59) WEBER 4-BBL. FLOAT LEVEL ADJUSTMENT

Bend here to adjust

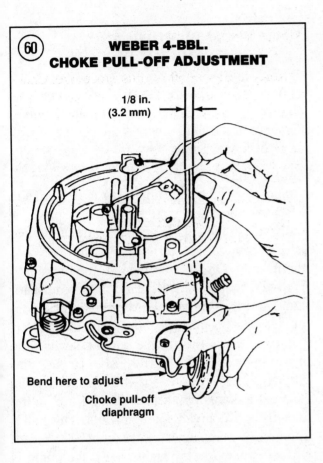

60 **WEBER 4-BBL.
CHOKE PULL-OFF ADJUSTMENT**

1/8 in.
(3.2 mm)

Bend here to adjust

Choke pull-off
diaphragm

wise until *lightly* seated, then back the screws out the number of turns recorded during disassembly.

2. Install the primary and secondary jets making certain the jets are installed into their original locations. Tighten the jets securely.

3. Install the accelerator pump inlet check valve into the fuel bowl.

4. Insert the accelerator pump discharge check ball into its correct passage, then insert the check ball weight on top of the ball. Install the pump discharge housing with a new gasket. See **Figure 62**. Tighten the housing screws securely.

5. Install the air valve and weight assembly into the carburetor body.

6. Using new gaskets, install the primary and secondary venturi clusters. Be certain the clusters are installed in their original locations. Tighten the venturi cluster screws securely.

7. Install the accelerator pump return spring into the pump well.

9

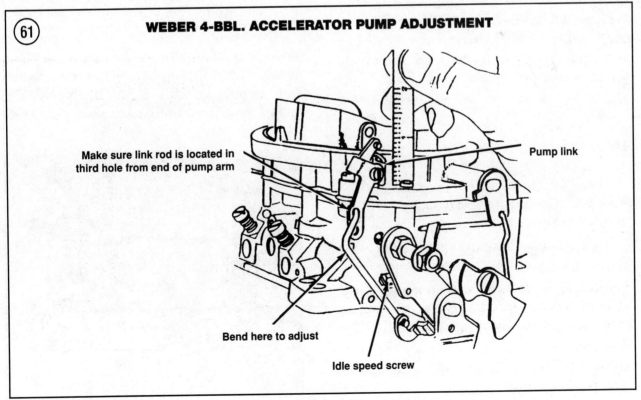

61 **WEBER 4-BBL. ACCELERATOR PUMP ADJUSTMENT**

Make sure link rod is located in
third hole from end of pump arm

Pump link

Bend here to adjust

Idle speed screw

8. Install the accelerator pump plunger (B, **Figure 52**) into the air horn. Connect the pump link rod to the plunger and into the third hole from the end of the pump arm (A, **Figure 52**). Secure the pump arm to the air horn with its screw. See **Figure 52**. Tighten the screw securely.

9. Place a new gasket onto the air horn.

10. Install the inlet filter screens (if so equipped) into the air inlet valve seats. Place new gaskets on the inlet valve seats then install the seats into the air horn. Tighten the seats securely using a wide-blade screwdriver.

11. Install the rubber fuel bowl vent. Install the hod idle compensator, if so equipped.

12. Place the inlet valve needles into their seats. Install the floats and float pins. Make sure the floats are installed in their original positions.

13. Carefully install the air horn onto the carburetor body. See **Figure 51**. Make sure the air horn gasket is properly positioned, then lower the air horn straight down onto the body.

14. Install 9 air horn screws. Using a crossing pattern, tighten the air horn screws securely.

15. Install the metering rod springs into the air horn. Place the metering rods and pistons into their respective holes. Make sure the rods and pistons are installed into their original locations.

NOTE
Some models are equipped with air deflectors attached to the metering rod cover screws. Be sure to reinstall the deflectors on models so equipped.

16. Install the metering rod covers and screws. Tighten the screws securely.

17. Reconnect the choke pull-off linkage to the carburetor. Install the pull-off diaphragm assembly to the carburetor body. Connect the pull-off vacuum hose.

18. Reconnect the choke and accelerator pump linkage using new retainer clips.

FUEL PUMP AND ANTI-SIPHON DEVICES

A mechanically-operated fuel pump is used on all models except Generation II 4.3 liter engines. Generation II 4.3 liter models are equipped with an electric fuel pump.

Mechanically-operated fuel pumps may be single-action or dual-diaphragm design. On Mark V big-block engines, the fuel pump is mounted on the belt-driven seawater pump and is driven by an eccentric cam on the seawater pump shaft. On all other models, the fuel pump is driven by an eccentric cam on the camshaft. Dual-diaphragm mechanically-driven fuel pumps can be identified by a sight gauge attached to the outside of the pump housing. The housing contains 2 differently shaped diaphragms manufactured of different materials. The extra diaphragm serves as a backup in the event the primary diaphragm fails. The pump requires no maintenance and cannot be serviced. If fuel is noted in the sight gauge, the pump is defective and must be replaced.

Single-action fuel pumps have a sight bowl containing a filter element mounted on the pump housing and held in place by a screw-pressure wire bale retainer. See **Figure 63**, typical. The pump is equipped with a transparent sight hose.

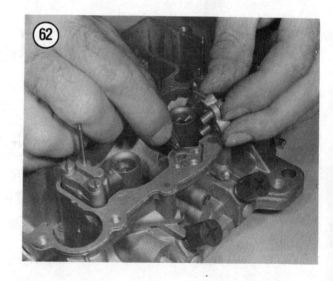

Normally, no oil or fuel should be present in the sight hose. If there is, the pump diaphragm has ruptured and the pump should be replaced immediately.

The electric fuel pump (Generation II 4.3 liter engines) is connected inline, between the fuel filter/water separator assembly and the carburetor. The electric pump and water separating fuel filter are designed to function correctly as a set; do not install additional fuel filters between the fuel tank and engine or pump failure or other runability problems will result. The fuel pump is activated when the ignition switch is turned ON. The pump is not serviceable and must be replaced if it fails.

In accordance with industry safety standards, all boats in which MerCruiser stern drives are used have some form of anti-siphon device installed between the fuel tank outlet and engine fuel inlet. This device is designed to shut the fuel supply off in case the boat capsizes or is involved in an accident. Quite often, the malfunction of such devices leads the owner to replace a good fuel pump in the belief that it is defective.

Anti-siphon devices malfunction in one of the following ways:

a. Anti-siphon valve: orifice in valve is too small or clogs easily; valve sticks in closed or partially closed position; valve fluctuates between open and closed position; thread

sealer, metal filing or debris clogs the orifice or lodges in the relief spring.

b. Solenoid-operated fuel shut-off valve: solenoid fails with valve in closed position; solenoid malfunctions, leaving valve in partially closed position.

c. Manually-operated fuel shut-off valve: valve is left in completely closed position; valve is not fully opened.

The easiest way to determine if the anti-siphon valve is defective is to bypass it by operating the engine with a remote fuel supply, such as an outboard fuel tank.

The two most common fuel pump problems are incorrect pressure and low volume. Low pressure results in a too-lean mixture and too little fuel at high speeds. High pressure will cause carburetor flooding and result in poor economy. Low volume also results in too little fuel at high speeds.

If a fuel system problem is suspected, check the fuel filter first. See Chapter Four. If the filter is not clogged or dirty, test the fuel pump for pressure and flow. If the pump fails either test, bypass the anti-siphon device and repeat the tests. If the pump fails a second time, replace it. If the pump passes both tests with the anti-siphon device bypassed, contact the boat manufacturer for replacement of the anti-siphon device.

**Pressure Test
(Mechanically-Operated Pump)**

Refer to **Figure 64** for this procedure.

1. Connect a tachometer according to its manufacturer's instructions.

2. Install a tee fitting in the fuel line between the fuel pump and carburetor. Connect a fuel pressure gauge to the fitting with a short hose.

3. Start the engine and run at idle. Record the pressure and compare to specifications in **Table 2**.

4. Gradually increase engine speed to 1,800 rpm while observing the pressure gauge. Pressure

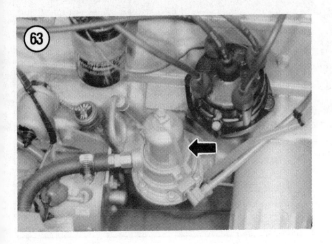

should remain constant and within specification during the entire range between idle and 1,800 rpm.

5. If pressure is too low, check the fuel lines for kinks, leaks or restrictions. Correct as required.

6. If pressure varies from specifications or changes at a higher engine speed, replace the fuel pump.

7. Shut the engine off. The pressure should drop off very slowly. If it drops off rapidly, the outlet valve in the pump is leaking and the pump should be replaced.

8. Remove the tachometer and pressure gauge. Reconnect the fuel line to the carburetor. Start the engine and check for leaks.

Flow Test

Refer to **Figure 64** for this procedure.

1. Disconnect the fuel inlet line at the carburetor and connect a length of flexible hose to the disconnected line.

2. Place the end of the flexible hose in a clean quart-size container.

3. Start the engine and let it run for 30 seconds (it should run this long on the fuel in the carburetor fuel bowl). Shut the engine off and check the container. It should be approximately 1/2 full within the 30 second interval. If not, check the fuel line for kinks. If none are found, disconnect the inlet line at the pump and fuel tank. Blow compressed air through the line.

4. Reconnect the inlet line and repeat the procedure. If pump volume is still too low, replace the pump.

Pressure Test (Electric Pump)

1. Disconnect the battery cables from the battery.

2. Disconnect the fuel line from the carburetor inlet. Install a tee fitting in the fuel line between the fuel pump and carburetor. Then, connect a fuel pressure gauge to the fitting with a short

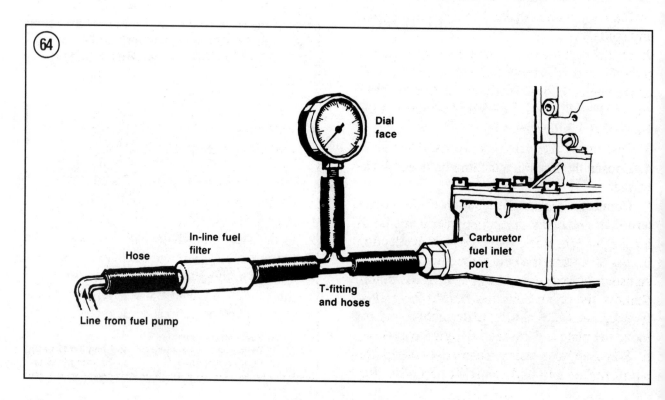

(64)

Dial face

In-line fuel filter

Hose

Carburetor fuel inlet port

T-fitting and hoses

Line from fuel pump

hose. See **Figure 64**, typical. Securely clamp all connections to prevent fuel leakage.

3. Reconnect the battery cables. Start the engine and allow it to run at idle speed while noting the pressure gauge.

4. Compare the fuel pressure reading to the specification in **Table 2**.

5. If the fuel pressure is less than specified, check the water separating fuel filter for plugging or excessive contamination. Also check all fuel lines and hoses for kinks, leakage or other damage. If no faults are noted, replace the fuel pump assembly as described in this chapter.

Removal/Installation (Mechanically-Operated Pump)

> *NOTE*
> *On Mark V big block engines, the fuel pump is mounted on the belt-driven seawater pump.*

Removal/Installation

1. Place a container under the fuel pump to catch any spillage.

2. Disconnect the inlet and outlet lines from the pump. Use one wrench to hold the pump fitting and the other to loosen the line nut. Cap the lines and plug the fittings to prevent leakage and the entry of contamination.

3. Disconnect the sight tube from the pump.

4. Loosen the 2 pump attaching bolts and lockwashers.

5. Connect a remote start button to the starter terminals and crank the engine over while holding the pump in place. When you feel a reduction in tension against the pump, the low point of the camshaft eccentric is resting against the pump. Remove the pump bolts and discard the gasket. If pump uses a mounting plate, unbolt and remove the plate and gasket. Discard the gasket.

6. Some engines use a pushrod between the pump rocker arm and camshaft eccentric. Re-

move the pushrod (if so equipped) and check it for wear or bending.

7. Clean the pump mounting pad on the engine block to remove all gasket residue.

8. Coat both sides of a new pump gasket with Quicksilver Perfect Seal and install it on the pump flange.

9. If the pump uses a pushrod, apply a heavy coat of grease to one end of the pushrod and insert that end into the engine.

10. If pump uses a mounting plate, coat both sides of plate with Quicksilver Perfect Seal, then install it on the block mounting pad.

11. Install the pump and new gasket on the engine. Make sure the pump rocker arm rides on the camshaft eccentric or pushrod, then tighten the attaching bolts to 20 ft.-lb. (27 N·m).

12. Uncap and connect the fuel inlet/outlet lines and sight tube to the fuel pump.

13. Start the engine and check for leaks.

Removal/Installation (Electric Pump)

Refer to **Figure 65** for this procedure.

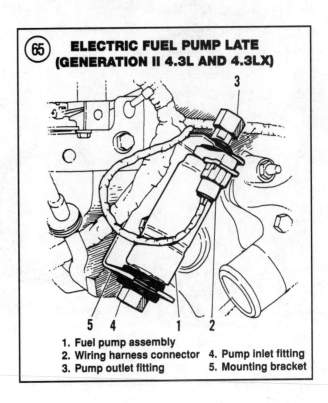

65 **ELECTRIC FUEL PUMP LATE (GENERATION II 4.3L AND 4.3LX)**

1. Fuel pump assembly
2. Wiring harness connector
3. Pump outlet fitting
4. Pump inlet fitting
5. Mounting bracket

1. Disconnect the negative battery cable from the battery.

2. While securely holding the pump outlet fitting with a wrench, loosen and remove the pump outlet line from the fitting. Then, repeat this procedure to remove the inlet line from the pump. Plug the lines to prevent fuel leakage.

3. Disconnect the wiring harness connector from the pump.

4. Pull the fuel pump out of its mounting bracket.

5. Place an appropriate size wrench on the flat area of the fuel pump next to the outlet fitting. See **Figure 66**. While holding the pump, loosen and remove the outlet fitting. Repeat to remove the inlet fitting. If necessary, remove the large and small grommets from the pump.

6. To install the pump, first inspect the O-rings located on the inlet and outlet fittings. Replace the O-rings if cracked, flattened, deteriorated or damaged.

7. If removed, install the small grommet on the outlet end of the pump. Install the large grommet on the inlet end.

8. Apply Loctite 592 Pipe Sealant with Teflon to the threads of the inlet and outlet fittings. Install the fittings finger tight.

9. Place a wrench on the flat of the pump at the outlet end. Hold the pump securely and tighten the outlet fitting to 84 in.-lb. (9.5 N.m). Next, place the wrench on the flat at the inlet end of the pump. Hold the pump and tighten the inlet fitting to 96 in.-lb. (10.8 N.m).

10. Slide the pump into its mounting bracket.

11. Connect the pump inlet and outlet lines to the pump. Hold the pump fittings using a suitable wrench and securely tighten the fuel lines.

12. Reconnect the battery cables, start the engine and check for fuel leakage.

FUEL LINES

Fuel lines must be Coast Guard approved (USCG Type A) and their inside diameter must be at least 3/8 in. (9.5 mm). If long lines or numerous fittings are involved in the fuel delivery system, larger ID lines should be used.

Fuel lines are usually a combination of rigid steel lines and flexible hoses. Flexible hoses are used to connect the fuel line to the engine and absorb deflection and vibration when the engine is running. Hoses are subject to extreme temperature changes and chemical deterioration from the fuel. In areas where fuel quality is poor or gasohol is used, even the rigid steel lines can deteriorate.

Damaged or leaking fuel lines and hoses must be replaced as soon as possible, and in a safe manner. While it is tempting to cut out a bad section of fuel line and insert a short length of hose as a replacement, this is not recommended

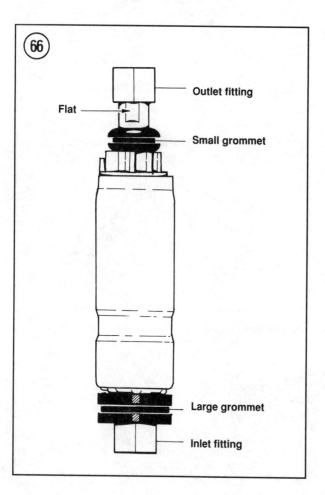

(66)

Outlet fitting

Flat

Small grommet

Large grommet

Inlet fitting

except as a means of temporary repair allowing you to reach port or a marina where the line can be properly replaced. Other portions of the line may be just as weak and will fail sooner or later. Since the dangers of fire or explosion are always present when a fuel line fails, it is safer, more economical and less time consuming to do the job right in the beginning.

Double-wrap brazed steel tubing should always be used to replace steel fuel lines. This is available from marine dealers. Do *not* use copper or aluminum tubing as neither will withstand normal engine and boat vibration. Rubber hose made specifically for fuel systems should be used. Other hose materials are not formulated to withstand chemical deterioration from gasoline.

To temporarily replace a fuel line, carry a length of fuel line hose, several worm-screw clamps and a tubing cutter with you. If it is necessary to make on-the-spot repairs, the damaged section of the line can be cut out and replaced by a length of fuel hose secured at each end with a clamp. This temporary repair should be replaced at the first available opportunity.

1. Obtain a suitable length of steel fuel line of the correct diameter.

2. Disconnect the negative battery cable.

3. Remove the damaged or deteriorated fuel line.

4. Slip a spring-type tubing bender over the tubing and carefully bend to match the old line. See **Figure 67**.

5. Remove the fittings, if any, from the old line and install on the new line.

6. Use a flaring tool to make a double lap flare on each end of the line. See **Figure 68**. This will provide a good seal and prevent the flare from cracking.

7. Install the new line and tighten the fittings securely.

8. Reconnect the negative battery cable. Start the engine and check for leaks.

9

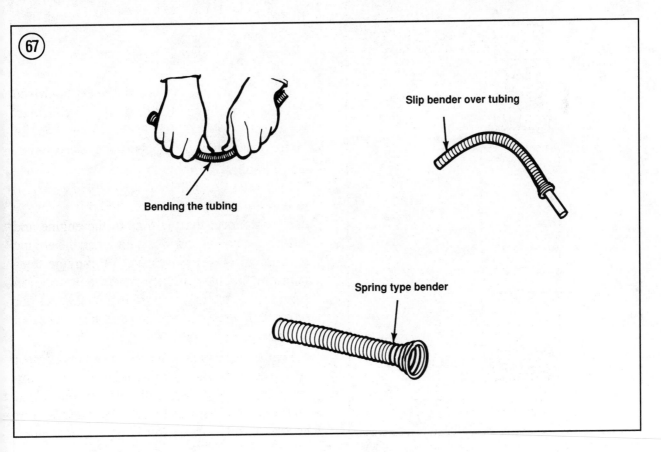

67

Bending the tubing

Slip bender over tubing

Spring type bender

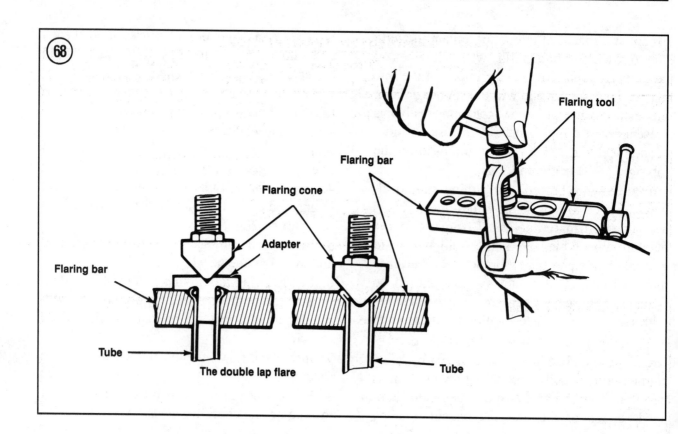

Table 1 CARBUERTOR SPECIFICATIONS

Carb model	Float level (in.)	Float drop (in.)	Choke setting	Initial idle mixture setting
Rochester 2GC 17081060	5/8	1 7/16	Index	1/25 turns out
MerCarb 1389-8490, 1389-8488A2	(See note 1)	1 3/32	1 notch lean (clockwise)	1.25 turns out
Rochester 4MV 17089112				
502 Magnum	1/4	—	(See note 2)	3 turns out
All others	15/64	—	(See note 2)	2-3 turns out
Weber WFB	1 9/32	2	(See note 2)	2 turns out

1. With spring-loaded inlet needle—9/16 in.; with solid inlet needle—3/8 in.
2. Top of rod even with bottom of hole.

Table 2 FUEL PUMP SPECIFICATIONS

Pump pressure @ 1,800 rpm	
Carter	3.0-7.0 psi
AC	5.25-6.5 psi
Airtex	5.5-7.0 psi
Electric pump	3.0-7.0 psi
Pushrod length	
Carter (V6 except electric pump)	5 in.
All others	5.76 in.
Pushrod movement	0.34 in.

9

Chapter Ten

Cooling System

This chapter covers service procedures for the thermostat, engine and stern drive water pumps, seawater pumps, drive belts and connecting hoses in both standard and closed cooling systems.

Cooling system flushing procedures are provided in Chapter Four. Drain and refill procedures are given in Chapter Five.

Tightening torques (**Table 1**) are at the end of the chapter.

Standard Cooling System

All MerCruier marine engines are equipped with a standard cooling system. The water in which the boat is being operated is used as a coolant to absorb engine heat. Water from outside the boat is picked up at the water intake on each side of the Alpha One lower gearcase by an impeller-type pump located in the upper portion of the lower gear housing (**Figure 1**, typical). The second generation Alpha One models are equipped with a new floppy-vane type impeller and a stainless steel water pump body. The pump sends the water to the engine's water pump (also called a circulating pump) for circulation

through the engine block, head(s) and manifold(s).

An internal water pump is not used on Bravo stern drive units. Water from outside the boat is picked up at the water intake on each side of the gearcase housing and drawn through the drive unit and cooling system passages by a belt-driven seawater pump attached to the front of the engine (**Figure 2**).

Because the fuel pump mounting pad on Mark V engines (1991-on 7.4L, 1992-on 454 and 502 Magnum models) has been eliminated, the fuel pump is mounted on the belt-driven seawater pump as shown in **Figure 3**.

NOTE
Mark V engines can quickly be identified by the fuel pump mounted on the belt-driven seawater pump.

On some models, the water may be circulated through one or more oil coolers before reaching the engine's water pump. The water absorbs the heat created by engine operation and then enters the exhaust elbow, where it mixes with exhaust gases before being expelled from the boat.

A. Fuel pump
B. Seawater pump
C. Idler pulley

A thermostat controls water circulation to provide quick engine warmup and maintain a constant operating temperature.

Closed Cooling System

MerCruiser marine engines may also be equipped with a closed cooling system. This cooling system is divided into two separate subsystems: one uses seawater and the other uses a coolant mixture of distilled water and ethylene glycol antifreeze. The sub-system containing the coolant is referred to as the "freshwater" system.

Various configurations of the closed cooling system are used, but all function essentially the same. The seawater system operation is similar to the standard cooling system previously described, except as follows:

a. V8 engine exhaust manifolds are cooled by the coolant in the closed cooling system; all others are cooled by seawater.

b. A belt-driven seawater pump (**Figure 2**) is located at the front of V8 engines to transmit seawater to the heat exchanger; all others use the stern drive pump (**Figure 1**).

c. Water from outside the boat drawn into the system by the stern drive pump is used to cool the stern drive, then dumped overboard.

Instead of passing directly into the engine, however, the seawater circulates through the power steering and oil coolers, if so equipped. After removing heat from the cooler(s), the water travels through a series of parallel copper tubes in the heat exchanger where it absorbs engine heat before returning to the exhaust elbows for discharge from the boat. **Figure 4** shows a typical heat exchanger design with a cross-section of its interior.

The "freshwater" system circulates the coolant mixture inside the engine to absorb engine heat. This coolant is then routed to the heat exchanger, where the heat absorbed from engine

10

operation is transferred through the parallel copper tubes to the water in the seawater system.

Engine cooling is thus accomplished without seawater entering the engine. This eliminates the corrosion, deposit buildup and debris accumulation which occurs in a standard cooling system, resulting in longer engine life—especially if the boat is used in saltwater.

Like an automotive cooling system, the freshwater section is pressurized at 14 psi. This raises the boiling point of the coolant to permit higher operating temperatures for increased engine efficiency.

A thermostat controls coolant circulation. When the thermostat is closed, it prevents coolant from entering the heat exchanger, rerouting it back to the engine circulating pump. Once the thermostat opens, it closes off the passage to the circulating pump and sends the coolant through the heat exchanger before returning it to the engine pump. This provides quick engine warmup and maintains a constant operating temperature.

THERMOSTAT

The thermostat blocks coolant flow to the exhaust manifold (standard cooling) or heat exchanger (closed cooling) when the engine is cold. As the engine warms up, the thermostat gradually opens, allowing coolant to circulate through the system.

> *CAUTION*
> *Do not operate the engine without a thermostat. This can lead to overheating and serious engine damage.*

Thermostats are rated according to their opening temperature. The opening temperature value is stamped in the thermostat flange or other area. The thermostat should start to open at the tem-

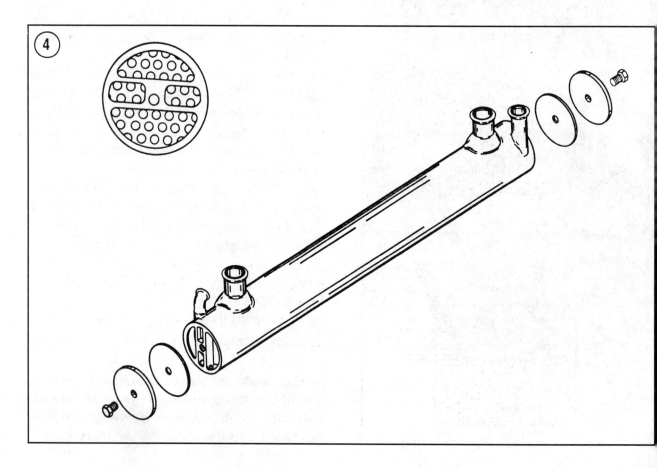

...erature stamped on the thermostat and should ...e fully open at 25° above that temperature. ...heck the thermostat rating after removing the ...hermostat. It should generally be as specified in **Table 2**.

During prolonged cold-water operation at low engine speed (such as trolling), it may be necessary to install a 160° F thermostat in models normally equipped with a 140 or 143° F thermostat. This may be necessary to maintain normal engine operating temperature, improve low-speed operation and prevent excessive crankcase condensation. You should, however, avoid wide-open throttle operation when using a hotter thermostat and always reinstall the recommended thermostat (**Table 2**) when resuming operation in warmer waters.

> *CAUTION*
> *Do **not** substitute an automotive-type thermostat. Its higher rating will cause the engine to run hotter than normal and could cause engine damage.*

Removal

1. Drain the engine coolant or water from the block and exhaust manifold(s). See Chapter Five.

2. Loosen the hose clamps and disconnect the hoses from the thermostat cover or coolant reservoir.

3A. *MerCruiser 165/170/3.7L and 180/190/3.7LX models*—Remove the thermostat reservoir attaching bolts and lockwashers from the exhaust manifold, elbow or water distribution block. Remove reservoir with gaskets. Discard the gaskets.

3B. *All others*—Remove the thermostat cover attaching bolts and lockwashers. Remove cover with gasket. Discard the gasket. See **Figure 5** (inline) or **Figure 6** (V6 and V8), typical.

4. *V8 block with closed cooling system*—Remove the thermostat retaining sleeve with gasket. Discard the gasket.

5. Remove the thermostat.

Testing (Out of Engine)

1. Pour some tap water (not distilled water or coolant) into a container that can be heated. Submerge the thermostat in the water and suspend a thermometer as shown in **Figure 7**.

10

NOTE
Suspend the thermostat with wire so it does not touch the sides or bottom of the pan.

2. Heat the water until the thermostat starts to open. Check the water temperature on the thermometer. It should be approximately the same as the temperature value stamped on the thermostat. If the thermostat has not started to open at this temperature, replace it.

3. Heat the water another 25° F above the temperature value stamped on thermostat. The thermostat should now be fully open (5/32 in.). If it is not, replace it.

4. Allow the water to cool to 10° F *under* the thermostat's rated opening temperature. If the thermostat valve is not fully closed at this temperature, replace it.

5. Remove the thermostat from the water and let it cool to room temperature. Hold it close to a light bulb and check for leakage. If light can be seen at more than 1 or 2 tiny points around the edge of the valve, the thermostat is defective and should be replaced. See **Figure 8**, typical.

Testing (In Engine)

Thermostat operation can be tested without removing it from the engine or reservoir. This procedure requires the use of 2 thermomelt sticks (**Figure 9**) available from marine supply or automotive parts stores. A thermomelt stick looks like a carpenter's pencil and is made of a chemically impregnated wax material which melts at a specific temperature.

This technique can be used to check thermostat opening by marking the thermostat housing or reservoir with a 140° F or 170° F thermomelt stick, depending upon the problem. As the coolant or water reaches the first temperature, the mark made by that stick will melt. The mark made by the second stick will not melt until the coolant or water increases to that temperature.

WARNING
Do not remove the pressure fill cap from closed cooling systems when the engine is warm. Coolant may blow out of the heat exchanger and cause serious personal injury.

Overheated engine

1. Relieve the freshwater cooling system pressure on closed cooling systems by carefully re-

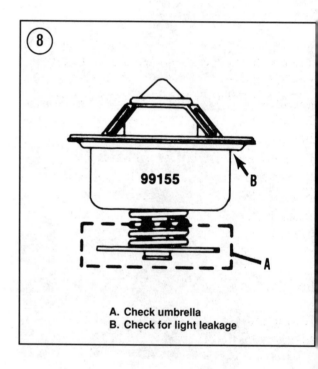

A. Check umbrella
B. Check for light leakage

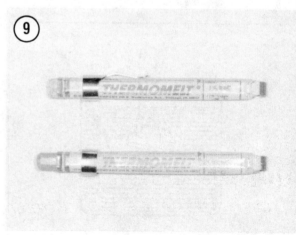

moving the pressure fill cap from the heat exchanger. See **Figure 10**, typical.

2. Rub the 170° F thermomelt stick on the thermostat cover or reservoir.

3. Start the engine and run at a fast idle.

4. If no coolant or water flows through the housing-to-manifold or housing-to-exhaust elbow hoses by the time the mark starts to melt, either the thermostat is stuck closed or the water pump is failing. Remove the thermostat and test it as described in this chapter. If satisfactory, replace the water pump.

Slow engine warmup

1. Relieve the freshwater cooling system pressure on closed cooling systems by carefully removing the pressure fill cap from the heat exchanger. See **Figure 10**, typical.

2. Rub the 140° F thermomelt stick on the thermostat cover or reservoir.

3. Start the engine and run at a fast idle.

4. If coolant or water flows through the housing-to-manifold or housing-to-exhaust elbow hoses before the mark starts to melt, the thermostat is stuck open and should be replaced.

Installation

1. If a new thermostat is being installed, test it as described in this chapter.

2. Clean the thermostat cover or reservoir and housing or manifold mating surfaces of all gasket residue.

3A. Standard cooling systems:

   a. Install the thermostat in the housing with its thermostatic element facing the engine. The thermostat flange must fit into the housing recess.

NOTE
*On late models equipped with audio warning system, continuity rivets are installed in the thermostat gasket. **Do not** use sealer on gasket with continuity rivets or audio warning system may not function.*

   b. Coat both sides of a new gasket with Quicksilver Perfect Seal and install the gasket to the thermostat cover.

   c. Install the cover and tighten the bolts to specification (**Table 1**).

3B. V8 block, closed cooling systems:

   a. Coat both sides of a new thermostat housing gasket with Quicksilver Perfect Seal.

   b. Position gasket on intake manifold, then install thermostat housing.

   c. Install thermostat in housing with thermostatic element facing the engine.

   d. Position a new cork gasket, then install the retaining sleeve with its rolled-over edge facing downward.

NOTE
*On late models, equipped with audio warning system, continuity rivets are installed in the thermostat gasket. **Do not** use sealer on gasket with continuity rivets or audio warning system may not function.*

   e. Coat both sides of a new cover gasket with Quicksilver Perfect Seal. Position gasket on housing and install cover.

   f. Tighten cover bolts to specification (**Table 1**).

3C. All other engines, closed cooling systems:

a. Install the thermostat in the housing with the thermostatic element facing the engine or manifold. The thermostat flange must fit into the housing recess.

b. Coat both sides of a new gasket with Quicksilver Perfect Seal and install gasket to reservoir.

c. Install reservoir and tighten bolts to specification (**Table 1**).

4. Reverse Steps 1-3 of *Removal* to complete installation.

HOSE REPLACEMENT

Replace any hoses that are cracked, brittle, mildewed or very soft and spongy. If a hose is in doubtful condition but not definitely bad, replace it to be on the safe side. Hoses in some installations are extremely difficult to change; attention to hose condition can prevent a failure while you are off-shore.

Hose manufacturers generally rate cooling system hose life at 2 years. How long the hoses will last depends a great deal on how much you use your boat and how well you maintain the system; however, it is a good ideal to change all hoses every 2 years. Always replace a cooling system hose with the same type as removed. Pleated rubber hoses do not have the same strength as reinforced molded hoses. Check the hose clamp condition and install new worm screw-type clamps with a new hose, if necessary.

Partially drain the seawater section of closed cooling systems when replacing upper hoses. Completely drain it when replacing lower hoses.

1. Loosen the clamp at each end of the hose to be removed. Grasp the hose and twist it off the fitting with a pulling motion.

2. If the hose is corroded to the fitting and will not twist free, cut it off with a sharp knife about one inch beyond the fitting. Remove the clamp and slit the remaining piece of hose lengthwise, then peel it off the fitting.

3. Clean any rust or corrosion from the fitting by wrapping a piece of medium grit sandpaper around it and rotating until the fitting surface is relatively clean and smooth.

4. Wipe the inside diameter of the hose with liquid detergent and install the hose ends on the fittings with a twisting motion.

5. Position the new clamps at least 1/4 in. from the end of the hose. Make sure the clamp screw is positioned for easy access with a screwdriver or nut driver. Tighten each clamp snugly.

6. Refill the cooling system. Start the engine and check for leaks. Recheck clamps for tightness after operating the engine for a few hours.

ENGINE CIRCULATING PUMP

The circulating pump may warn of impending failure by making noise. If the seal is defective, coolant or water may leak from behind the pump pulley. The pump is serviced as an assembly and can be replaced on all model with the engine in the boat. MerCruiser marine engine water pumps contain stainless steel components and use a special marine shaft seal assembly. Do *not* replace with an automotive-type water pump.

The pump used on 165, 170, 180, 190, 3.7L and 3.7LX models is a 2-piece unit, with a replaceable cover attached to the front cover. The pump shaft and impeller are available as separate

eplacement items if the pump fails. On all other models, the pump is serviced as an assembly.

Removal/Installation (Except MerCruiser 165/170/3.7L and 180/190/3.7LX)

. Disconnect the negative battery cable.

. Drain the cylinder block. See Chapter Five.

. Loosen, but do not remove, the pump pulley asteners.

. Loosen the alternator adjusting and pivot olts (**Figure 11**, typical). Swivel the alternator oward the engine and remove the drive belt. If quipped with power steering, repeat this step to emove the power steering drive belt.

.. Remove any accessory brackets attached to he water pump or those which will interfere with ts removal.

. Remove the pump pulley fasteners. Remove he pulley.

'. Unclamp and disconnect the hoses from the irculating pump.

.. Remove the pump-to-cylinder block bolts. Remove the pump and gasket. Discard the gas-et.

). Clean all gasket residue from the pump and ngine block mounting surfaces.

10. Installation is the reverse of removal. Tighten water pump fasteners to specifications (**Table 1**). Adjust drive belts as described in this chapter. Fill freshwater section of closed cooling systems with coolant. See Chapter Five. Start the engine and check for leaks.

Removal/Installation (MerCruiser 165/170/3.7L and 180/190/3.7LX)

Refer to **Figure 12** for this procedure.

1. Drain the freshwater section of closed cooling system. See Chapter Five.

> *NOTE*
> *If a pyramid-type front engine mount is used, support the engine with an overhead hoist. Remove the front engine mount/bracket assembly to provide access for Step 2.*

2. Remove the alternator rotor and stator. See Chapter Seven.

3. Disconnect the inlet hose from the pump inlet cover. Remove the pump inlet cover (**Figure 13**).

4. Remove the impeller cover fasteners (**Figure 14**). Remove the cover and gasket. Discard the gasket.

> *NOTE*
> *On late models, water pump impeller screws onto a stud that is screwed into the camshaft. Impeller, stud and camshaft have **left-hand** threads. Remove*

10

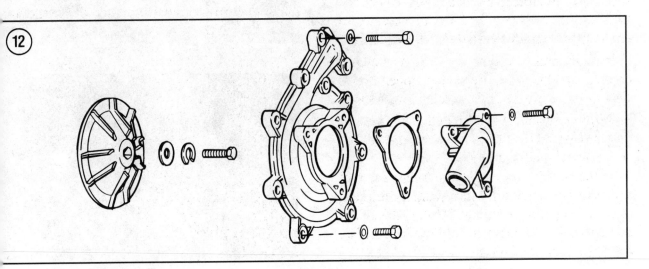

(12)

*the impeller by placing the appropriate size wrench onto the hub of the impeller and turning in a clockwise direction. If removed, impeller stud should be secured to camshaft using Loctite type 635 and tightened to specification in **Table 2**.*

5A. Early models:

a. Loosen and remove the impeller bolt (**Figure 15**). Remove the washer, shim and impeller.

b. Turn the pump shaft clockwise and remove it from the front cover.

5B. Late models: Place the appropriate size wrench or socket on the hub of the impeller, loosen impeller by turning clockwise, then unscrew impeller from camshaft stud.

6. If seal replacement is required, remove old seals with a slide hammer puller and install new seals with a suitable driver. The seal lips must face away from the engine block.

7A. Early models:

a. Insert pump shaft through the seals and turn counterclockwise until securely tightened.

b. Install the impeller, shim washer, cup washer and bolt onto the shaft. The shim washer fits on the large diameter of the shaft; the hollow side of the cup washer faces the impeller. Tighten the bolt to specification in **Table 1**.

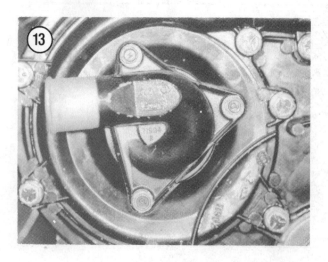

7B. Late models: Screw the impeller onto the camshaft stud in a counterclockwise direction. Tighten impeller to specifications in **Table 1**.

8. Coat both sides of a new gasket and wipe the cover bolt threads with Quicksilver Perfect Seal. Position the gasket to the front cover and install

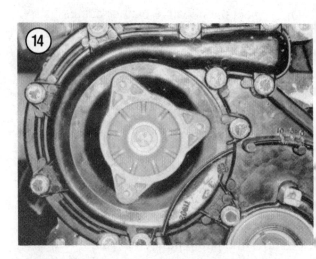

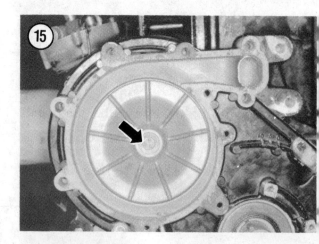

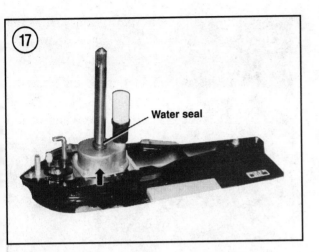

Water seal

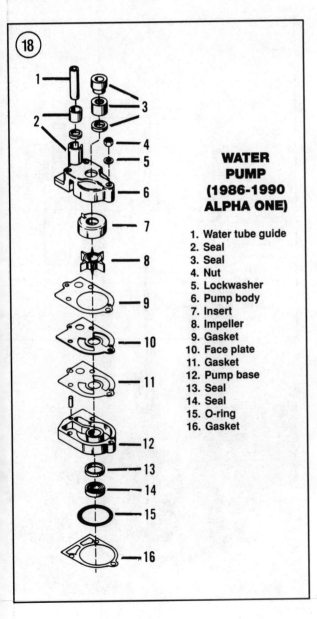

**WATER
PUMP
(1986-1990
ALPHA ONE)**

1. Water tube guide
2. Seal
3. Seal
4. Nut
5. Lockwasher
6. Pump body
7. Insert
8. Impeller
9. Gasket
10. Face plate
11. Gasket
12. Pump base
13. Seal
14. Seal
15. O-ring
16. Gasket

the impeller cover. Tighten the cover bolts to specification in **Table 1**.

9. Reverse Steps 1-3 to complete installation. Fill the freshwater section of closed cooling systems with coolant. See Chapter Five. Start engine and check for leaks.

STERN DRIVE WATER PUMP

A stern drive water pump is used on all Alpha One models. The water pump is mounted on top of the gearcase housing as shown in **Figure 16** (1986-1990 Alpha One) or **Figure 17** (1991-on Alpha One Generation II). The pump impeller is driven by the gearcase drive shaft.

> *CAUTION*
> *Whenever the engine is operated, water must circulate through the stern drive or the water pump will be damaged.*

Removal (1986-1990 Alpha One)

Refer to **Figure 18** and **Figure 19**, typical for this procedure.

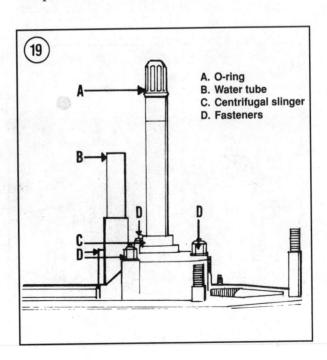

A. O-ring
B. Water tube
C. Centrifugal slinger
D. Fasteners

10

1. Remove the stern drive lower unit. See Chapter Fourteen.

2. Secure the lower unit upright in a vise with protective jaws. If protective jaws are not available, clamp the housing between soft wooden blocks.

3. Remove the O-ring from the top of the drive shaft. If O-ring is missing, check upper drive shaft housing and remove it.

4. Remove the centrifugal slinger above the water pump housing (arrow, **Figure 16**). Remove the water pump housing fasteners.

5. Insert 2 screwdrivers in the pry slots provided in the pump housing (**Figure 20**) and pry housing from base. Slide housing off shaft (**Figure 21**).

NOTE
In extreme cases, it may be necessary to split the impeller hub with a hammer and chisel to remove it in Step 6.

6. Remove impeller drive key and impeller (**Figure 22**). If necessary, drive impeller upward on shaft with a punch and hammer.

7. Remove the face plate and gaskets (one on each side). See **Figure 23**) Discard the gaskets.

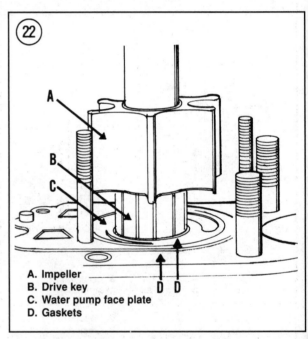

A. Impeller
B. Drive key
C. Water pump face plate
D. Gaskets

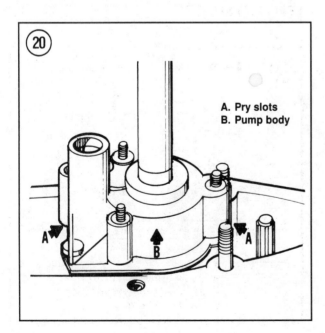

A. Pry slots
B. Pump body

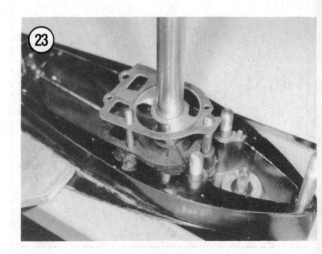

CAUTION
Work carefully with pry tool in Step 8 to avoid damage to the gear housing mating surface.

8. Use 2 screwdrivers as in Step 5 to pry the pump base loose, then remove it from the drive shaft. See **Figure 24**.

9. Remove and discard the base-to-gear housing gasket and water pump base O-ring. See **Figure 25**).

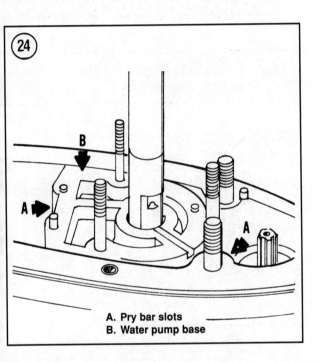

A. Pry bar slots
B. Water pump base

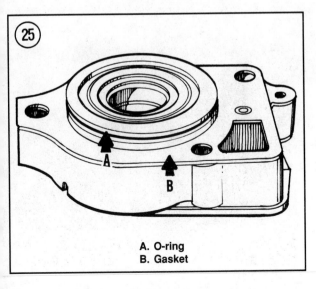

A. O-ring
B. Gasket

Inspection
(1986-1990 Alpha One)

1. Clean all metal parts in solvent and blow dry with compressed air, if available.

2. Inspect the pump face plate for grooving or other defects. Replace if any defects are found.

3. Check the pump impeller blades for wear. Check impeller and hub for proper bonding. An impeller blade with excessively curved blades has taken a "set" and must be replaced.

4. Check the area on the drive shaft where it contacts the pump oil seal lips. If grooves or other defects are noted, replace the drive shaft.

Disassembly/Reassembly
(1986-1990 Alpha One)

1. Clamp the pump base in a vise with protective jaws. If protective jaws are not available, clamp the pump base between soft wooden blocks.

2. Carefully pry all oil seals from the pump base. Wipe OD of new seals with Loctite Type 242 and install with tool part No. 91-44110 or equivalent. Lip of small seal faces impeller side of base (**Figure 26**); large seal lip faces gear housing side of base (**Figure 27**).

10

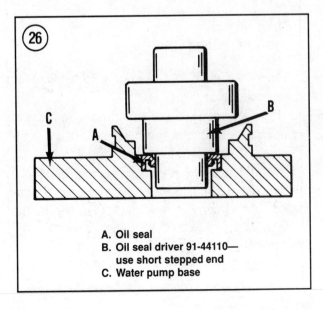

A. Oil seal
B. Oil seal driver 91-44110—
   use short stepped end
C. Water pump base

3. If water pump insert is worn, grooved or damaged, replace as follows:

    a. Hold the pump body firmly and rap it sharply on a hard surface. If impeller cannot be removed in this manner:

    b. Drill two 3/16 in. (4.8 mm) holes through the plastic body—do *not* drill through the insert. See **Figure 28**.

    c. Insert a suitable punch in the holes and carefully drive the insert from the pump body.

    d. Lubricate the OD of a new insert with Quicksilver Special Lubricant 101, 2-4-C Multi-Lube or Perfect Seal (listed in order of effectiveness).

    e. Position the new insert so its locating tab aligns with the recess in the pump body, then carefully rap insert into place.

    f. Remove any excess lubricant. If the inside of the insert is not perfectly clean, it will cause premature damage to the impeller.

4. Remove and discard the pump body water tube seal. Lubricate the ID of a new seal with Quicksilver 2-4-C Multi-Lube and install in pump body water tube.

5. Install a new water pump base gasket (A, **Figure 29**) and O-ring (B). Lubricate the O-ring with Quicksilver 2-4-C Multi-Lube.

Installation
(1986-1990 Alpha One)

Refer to **Figure 18** and **Figure 19**, typical for this procedure.

1. Tape the drive shaft O-ring groove to prevent seal damage. Slide pump base over drive shaft (**Figure 30**) and into housing.

2. Install a new lower gasket on the pump base. Install the face plate with its lip facing downward. Install another new gasket on top of the face plate. See **Figure 31**.

3. Remove the tape applied in Step 1.

4. Install impeller drive key in shaft slot with Quicksilver 2-4-C Multi-Lube to keep it in place.

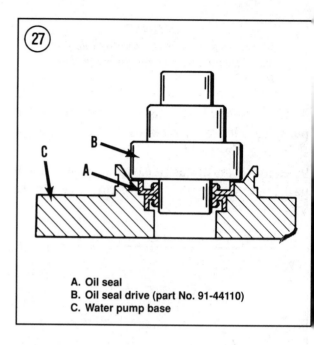

A. Oil seal
B. Oil seal drive (part No. 91-44110)
C. Water pump base

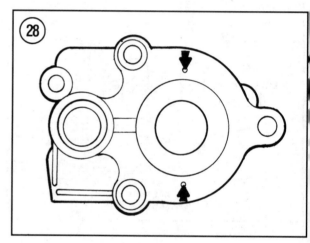

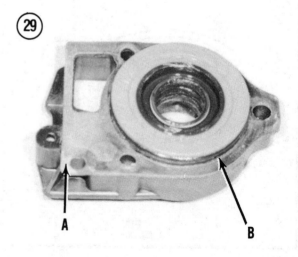

CAUTION
*Mercury Marine recommends that the water pump impeller be replaced if removal was required. If the original impeller must be reused, install it in the same rotational direction to avoid premature failure. The curl of the blades should be positioned in a counterclockwise direction, as seen from the top of the unit. See **Figure 32**.*

5. Slide the impeller over the drive shaft, align impeller key slot with shaft key and seat impeller on face plate. See **Figure 33**.

6. Lubricate water pump insert with soapy water. Position pump body over drive shaft and seat on pump studs.

7. Push downward on pump body while rotating drive shaft clockwise to assist impeller in entering the cover. See **Figure 34**.

CAUTION
Proper torque is required in Step 8 or the water pump may fail prematurely.

8. Install pump body fasteners. Tighten aft bolt and nuts, then the forward nut to specifications (**Table 1**).

9. Install the centrifugal slinger and a new drive shaft O-ring.

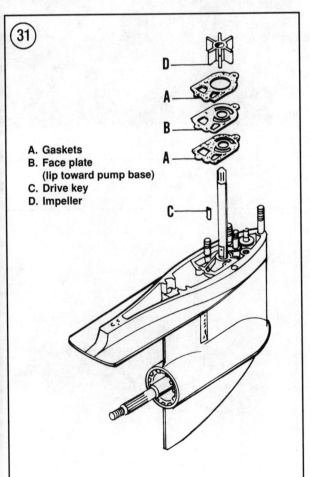

A. Gaskets
B. Face plate
   (lip toward pump base)
C. Drive key
D. Impeller

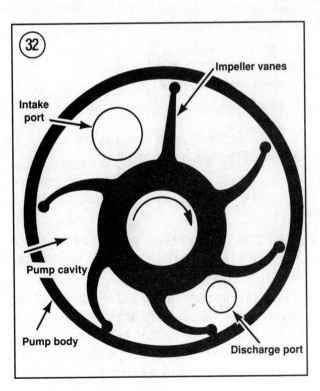

Impeller vanes
Intake port
Pump cavity
Pump body
Discharge port

10

Removal (1991-on Alpha One [Generation II])

Refer to **Figure 35** and **Figure 36** for this procedure.

1. Remove the stern drive gearcase as described in Chapter Fourteen.

2. Secure the gearcase upright in a suitable holding fixture. If a holding fixture is not available, clamp the gearcase skeg into a vise with wooden blocks on each side of the skeg.

3. Slide the water seal (**Figure 35**) up and off the drive shaft.

4. Remove the 4 screws securing the pump body to the gearcase. Lift the body straight up and off the drive shaft. If necessary, dislodge the pump body by carefully prying at each side using screwdrivers. Do not distort the body mounting flange.

5. Remove the impeller, impeller drive key, face plate and gaskets. Remove and discard the gaskets.

6. Remove the drive shaft seal carrier from the gearcase by carefully prying with 2 screwdrivers positioned on each side of the carrier.

Inspection (1991-on Alpha One [Generation II])

1. Thoroughly clean all components using clean solvent. Dry with compressed air.

2. Inspect the pump face plate for grooves, roughness or other damage. Replace the plate as necessary.

3. Inspect the inner diameter of the pump body for grooves, excessive wear or other damage. Replace the body as necessary.

4. Inspect the pump impeller for excessive wear (especially at the blade tips), cracks, hardness or other damage. Inspect the impeller for proper bonding between the impeller and hub. Replace the impeller if any defects are noted.

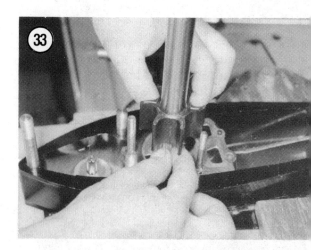

Water seal

NOTE
The manufacturer recommends replacing the water pump impeller anytime the pump is disassembled. If the original impeller is reused, be sure to install it in the same rotational direction from which removed.

5. Inspect the water tube coupling for excessive wear or damage. Remove and discard the 2 O-rings inside the coupler.

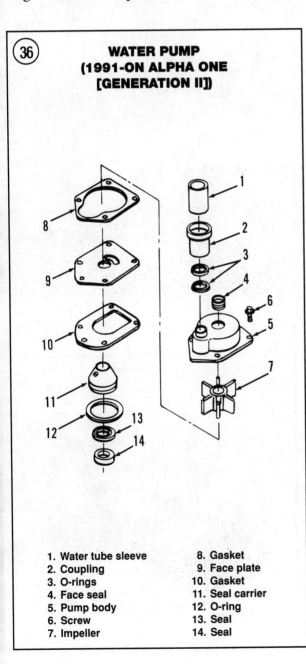

(36)

**WATER PUMP
(1991-ON ALPHA ONE
[GENERATION II])**

1
8
2
3
9
4
6
10
5
7
11
13
12
14

1. Water tube sleeve
2. Coupling
3. O-rings
4. Face seal
5. Pump body
6. Screw
7. Impeller
8. Gasket
9. Face plate
10. Gasket
11. Seal carrier
12. O-ring
13. Seal
14. Seal

6. Inspect the seal carrier, O-ring and seals for excessive wear or other damage. Replace the seals and O-ring as necessary.

Seal Carrier Disassembly/Reassembly (1991-on Alpha One [Generation II])

NOTE
Do not remove the drive shaft seals from the seal carrier unless seal replacement is necessary

1. Remove the O-ring from the outer diameter of the seal carrier.
2. Clamp the carrier assembly into a vise with protective jaws.
3. Using a suitable tool, pry the seals from the carrier. Discard the seals.
4. Thoroughly clean the carrier using clean solvent, then dry with compressed air.
5. Apply a thin coat of Quicksilver Perfect Seal to the seal bore of the carrier.
6. Invert the seal carrier. Place the small carrier seal onto the long end of seal driver part No. 91-817569. Make sure the seal lip is facing the shoulder of the driver. Press the seal into the carrier until the driver contacts the carrier. See A, **Figure 37**.
7. Place the large carrier seal onto the short end of the seal driver (part No. 91-817569). Make sure the seal lip is facing the shoulder of the driver. Press the seal into the carrier until the driver contacts the carrier. See B, **Figure 37**.

Installation (1991-on Alpha One [Generation II])

Refer to **Figure 35** and **Figure 36** for this procedure.

1. Lubricate the lips of both carrier seals and O-ring with Quicksilver 2-4-C Marine Lubricant. Place the seal carrier assembly over the drive shaft and into the gearcase. Seat the carrier by hand.

10

NOTE
The water pump face plate gaskets are not symmetrical. Be sure all holes in the gaskets, face plate and gearcase are aligned.

2. Place the face plate gasket with the small center hole onto the gearcase first, followed by the face plate and gasket with the large hole.

3. Install the impeller drive key into position on the drive shaft. Hold the key in place using a small amount of Quicksilver 2-4 C Marine Lubricant.

CAUTION
The manufacturer recommends replacing the impeller anytime the water pump is disassembled. If the original impeller must be used, be sure to install it in the same rotational direction from which removed to prevent premature impeller failure.

4. Slide the impeller onto the drive shaft and into position over the drive key.

5. Install the pump body over the drive shaft and onto the impeller. While pushing downward on the pump body, rotate the drive shaft *clockwise* until the body is properly seated over the impeller.

6. Install the pump body attaching screws. Tighten the screws evenly until snug, then tighten in a crossing pattern to 60 in.-lb. (6.8 N.m).

CAUTION
The water pump face seal must be properly installed or premature failure may result

7. Apply a light coat of Quicksilver 2-4-C Marine Lubricant to the drive shaft. Slide the face seal approximately 1/2 way down onto the drive shaft. Be certain the seal is positioned as shown in **Figure 38**.

8. Place the face seal setting tool (part No. 91-818769) over the drive shaft. Using the setting tool, push the face seal downward onto the water

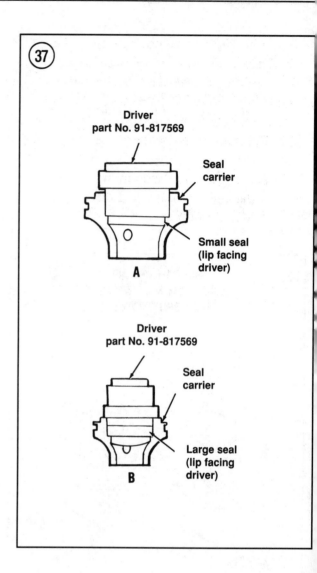

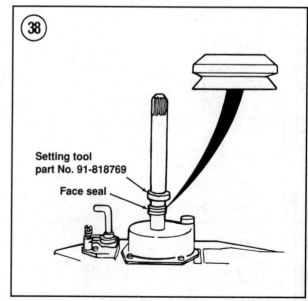

pump body. Remove the setting tool from the drive shaft.

9. Lubricate the water tube coupling O-rings with Quicksilver 2-4-C Marine Lubricant. Insert the water tube coupling onto the pump body.

10. Reinstall the gearcase as described in Chapter Fourteen.

Engine Mounted Seawater Pump Removal/Installation

A belt-driven seawater pump is used on V8 Alpha One models equipped with closed cooling systems and all Bravo models. See **Figure 39**,

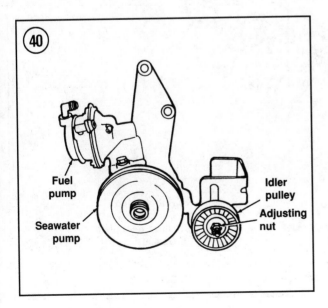

Fuel pump
Seawater pump
Idler pulley
Adjusting nut

typical. On Mark V engines (1991-on 7.4L and 1992-on 454 and 502 Magnum models), the fuel pump is mounted on and operated by the belt-driven seawater pump. See **Figure 40**.

1. Loosen the hose clamps and remove the inlet and outlet hoses from the aft side of the seawater pump.

2A. Mark V engine—Loosen the idler pulley adjusting nut (**Figure 40**). Slide the pulley in its slot to loosen the tension on the pump drive belt. Remove the belt.

2B. All others—Loosen, but do not remove, the bolts holding the pump pulley to the pulley hub. Loosen the pump brace bolts and mounting bracket bolt(s). Swivel the pump toward the engine and remove the drive belt. On some models equipped with power steering, it is necessary to remove the power steering pump belt to remove the water pump belt.

> *WARNING*
> *Use extreme caution when working around gasoline. Immediately wipe up any spilled fuel during Step 3.*

3. Mark V—Disconnect the fuel lines from the fuel pump (**Figure 40**) using an appropriate size wrench.

4. Remove the pump assembly fasteners. Remove the pump from the engine.

5. Reverse the removal procedure to reinstall the pump. Hand tighten all fasteners until the pump is properly mounted and positioned. Adjust the drive belt as described in this chapter.

Disassembly/reassembly (except Mark V engines)

Refer to **Figure 41**, typical, for this procedure.

1. Remove the 5 screws securing the pump cover to the body.

2. Remove the cover, gasket, outer wear plate and gasket. Discard the gaskets.

3. Slide the pump body off the shaft and remove the impeller from the pump body. Remove the

10

rubber plug from the impeller. Remove and discard the O-ring (9, **Figure 41**).

NOTE
It is recommended to replace the pump assembly if the bearings and seals require replacement.

4. Rotate the pump shaft to check bearings for roughness, excessive wear or other damage. Do not remove the shaft from the housing unless bearing replacement is necessary.

5. If necessary, press the pulley hub from the shaft using a universal puller plate and arbor press. Remove the front seal (2, **Figure 41**) by puncturing a hole into the seal, then prying out using a suitable tool. After removing the front seal, remove the snap ring (3, **Figure 41**), then press the shaft and bearings from the housing. If

necessary, drive the rear seals (8, **Figure 41**) from the pump housing.

6. Press the bearings from the pump shaft using a universal press plate and arbor press.

7. Clean all metal components using clean solvent, then dry with compressed air.

8. Thoroughly clean all gasket material from all mating surfaces.

9. Inspect pump shaft for grooves in the seal contact area.

10. Inspect the impeller for cracked blades or excessive wear at the tips of the blades. Replace the impeller if any defects are noted.

11. Apply Loctite 242 to the outer diameter of the rear housing seals (8, **Figure 41**). With the seal lips facing the impeller end of the pump, press the first seal into the housing until fully

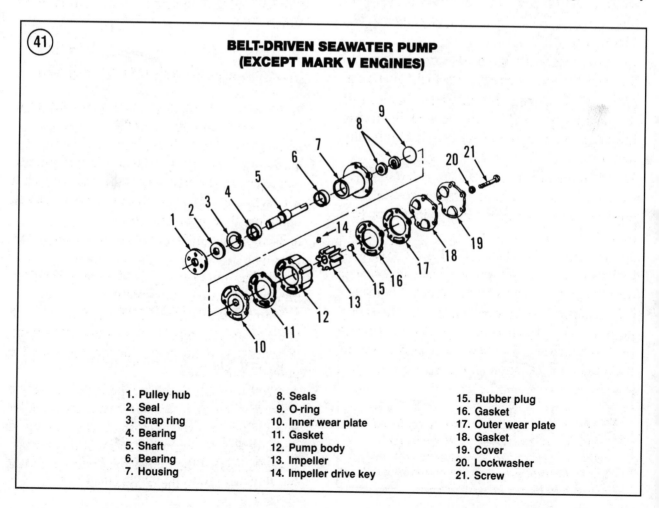

**BELT-DRIVEN SEAWATER PUMP
(EXCEPT MARK V ENGINES)**

1. Pulley hub	8. Seals	15. Rubber plug
2. Seal	9. O-ring	16. Gasket
3. Snap ring	10. Inner wear plate	17. Outer wear plate
4. Bearing	11. Gasket	18. Gasket
5. Shaft	12. Pump body	19. Cover
6. Bearing	13. Impeller	20. Lockwasher
7. Housing	14. Impeller drive key	21. Screw

bottomed, then the second seal until flush with the housing.

NOTE
The manufacturer recommends packing the area between the pump seals and bearings with Shell Alvania No. 2 Grease. If Shell Alvania Grease is not available, substitute Quicksilver 2-4-C Marine Lubricant. However, 2-4-C Marine Lubricant should not be used if prolonged high-speed or heavy-duty operation is anticipated.

12. Pack the cavity between the seals and bearings with Shell Alvania No. 2 Grease or Quicksilver 2-4-C Marine Lubricant.

13. Press the shaft bearings onto the pump shaft until fully seated. Press only on the bearing inner races. Pack the area between the bearings with Shell Alvania No. 2 Grease or Quicksilver 2-4-C Marine Lubricant.

14. Install the shaft and bearings assembly into the pump housing then secure with the snap ring.

15. Apply Loctite 242 to the outer diameter of the pump front seal. With the seal lip facing inward, press the seal into the housing until fully bottomed.

16. With the impeller end of the pump securely supported, press the pulley hub onto the shaft until the front face of the hub is 0.260 in. (6.6 mm) past the end of the shaft.

17. Lubricate the O-ring (9, **Figure 41**) with Quicksilver 2-4-C Marine Lubricant, then install the O-ring into its groove in the pump housing.

18. Install the inner wear plate onto the pump housing. Apply a thin coat of Quicksilver Perfect Seal to both sides of a new inner gasket. Install the gasket into position on the wear plate.

NOTE
The pump impeller should be replaced anytime it is removed from the pump. If the original impeller must be reused, be sure to install it in the same rotational direction from which removed.

19. Install the impeller into the pump body by rotating the impeller in the direction it will rotate during operation. Be certain all impeller blades are facing the same direction.

20. Install the impeller drive key onto the pump shaft. Hold the key in place with a small amount of grease.

21. Align the impeller drive key groove with the drive key, then install the impeller and pump body onto the shaft. Rotate the pump body as necessary to align all passages and bolt holes. Install the rubber plug into the end of the impeller.

22. Apply Quicksilver Perfect Seal to both sides of a new cover gasket and outer wear plate gasket. Install the new gaskets on both sides of the outer wear plate. Install the wear plate onto the pump body. Install the cover and 5 attaching screws. Tighten the screws to 120 in.-lb. (13.6 N•m).

Disassembly/reassembly (Mark V engines)

1. Remove the seawater pump assembly from the mounting bracket.

2. Remove the 5 through-bolts securing the pump cover (7, **Figure 42**) to the pump body. Note that one through-bolt is secured with a nut and lockwasher. Remove the cover, cover gasket, separator plate and plate gasket.

3. Remove the rubber plug from the end of the impeller.

4. Lift the pump body off the base. Push the impeller out of the pump body.

5. Remove the drain and fill plugs from the side of the pump housing. Allow all lubricant to drain. If necessary, remove the fuel pump from the pump housing.

6. To reassemble, lubricate the impeller using a water and detergent solution. Install the impeller into the pump body by pushing and turning in the direction the pump will rotate during normal operation. Place the rubber plug into the end of the impeller facing the pump cover.

10

7. Apply Quicksilver Perfect Seal to both sides of new pump gasket (4 and 6, **Figure 42**). Place the gasket with small center hole (6) onto the pump cover, then assemble the separator plate and gasket (4) to the cover. Place the cover onto the pump body, then insert the 5 pump through-bolts.

8. Install the body assembly onto the pump housing. Rotate the pump shaft as necessary to align the impeller and shaft. Install and tighten the through-bolts to 10-15 ft.-lb. (13.6-20 N.m).

9. Complete reassembly by reversing the disassembly procedure.

10. Place the pump assembly in the upright position. Install the drain plug into the pump housing. Fill the housing with Quicksilver High-Performance Gear Lube until the lubricant is even with the fill screw hole. Install the fill plug and tighten both plugs to 18 in.-lb. (2 N.m).

DRIVE BELTS

All drive belts should be inspected at regular intervals to make sure they are in good condition and are properly tensioned. Worn, frayed, cracked or glazed belts should be replaced immediately. The components to which they direct power are essential to the safe and reliable operation of the boat. If correct adjustment is maintained on each belt, all will usually give the same service life. For this reason and because of the cost involved in replacing an inner belt (requiring the removal of the outer belt), it is a good idea to replace all belts as a set. The added expense is small compared to the cost of replacing the belts individually and eliminates the possibility of a breakdown on the water which could cost far more in time and money.

Drive belts should be properly tensioned at all times. If loose, the belt(s) will not permit the driven components to operate at maximum efficiency. The belt(s) will also wear rapidly because of the increased friction caused by slippage. Belts that are too tight will be overstressed and

prone to premature failure. An excessively tight belt will also overstress the accessory unit's bearings, resulting in premature failure.

Drive belts used on MerCruiser marine engines are heavy-duty belts and should not be

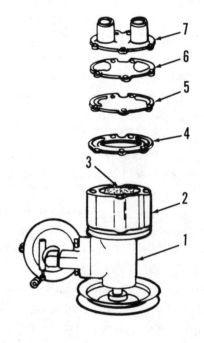

BELT-DRIVEN SEAWATER PUMP (MARK V ENGINES [1991 7.4I, 1992 454 MAGNUM AND 502 MAGNUM])

1. Housing assembly
2. Pump body
3. Impeller
4. Gasket (large center hole)
5. Separator plate
6. Gasket (small center hole)
7. Cover

replace with drive belts designed for use with automobiles.

Figure 43 (4-cylinder) and **Figure 44** (V6 and V8) show typical drive belt routing.

Drive belt tension can be checked and adjusted according to belt deflection, but Mercury Marine recommends the use of a drive belt tension gauge. If the deflection method is used, depress the belt firmly at a point midway between the pulleys. See B, **Figure 45**. The belt should deflect approximately 1/2 in. (12.7 mm) if properly tensioned. If it does not, perform Steps 2-4 of the procedure below.

Adjustment

Adjust drive belt tension with a tension gauge as follows:

1. Install the belt tension gauge and take a reading. Tension should be 65-95 lb.

2. Loosen the alternator bracket and pivot bolts. See **Figure 46**, typical.

3. Move the alternator toward the engine to loosen the belt or away from the engine to tighten the belt, as required.

4. Tighten the bracket bolt, then tighten the pivot bolt.

5. Recheck belt tension. If necessary, repeat the procedure to obtain the correct tension.

Replacement

Replace the drive belt as follows:

1. Loosen the alternator bracket and pivot bolts. See **Figure 46**, typical.

2. Move the alternator toward the engine and slip the belt off the crankshaft and alternator pulleys.

3. Install a new belt over the pulleys and move the alternator away from the engine until the correct deflection or tension is obtained.

10

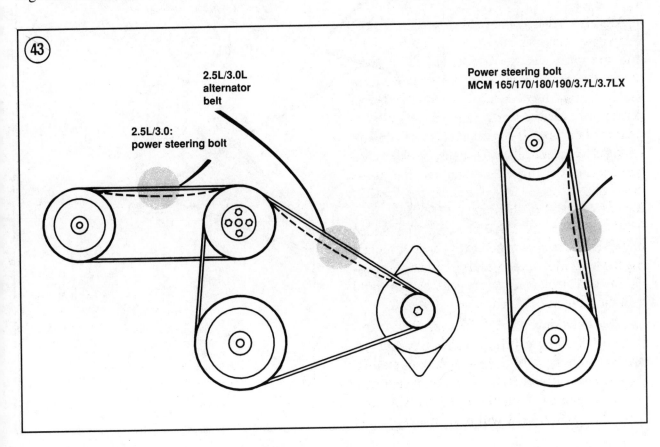

4. Tighten the bracket and pivot bolts securely.

CLOSED COOLING SYSTEM MAINTENANCE

Pressure Testing the Freshwater Section

If the freshwater section of a closed cooling system requires frequent topping up, it probably has a leak. Small leaks in a cooling system are not easy to locate; the hot coolant evaporates as fast as it leaks out, preventing the formation of tell-tale rusty or grayish-white stains.

A pressure test of the freshwater section will usually help to pinpoint the source of the leak. The procedure is very similar to that used in pressure testing automotive cooling systems and requires the same type of pressure tester.

1. Remove the pressure fill cap from the heat exchanger or reservoir. See **Figure 47**, typical.

2. Wash the cap with clean water to remove any debris or deposits from its sealing surfaces.

3. Check the gasket, if so equipped, and rubber seal on the cap for cuts, cracks, tears or deterioration. See **Figure 48**. Replace the cap if the seal

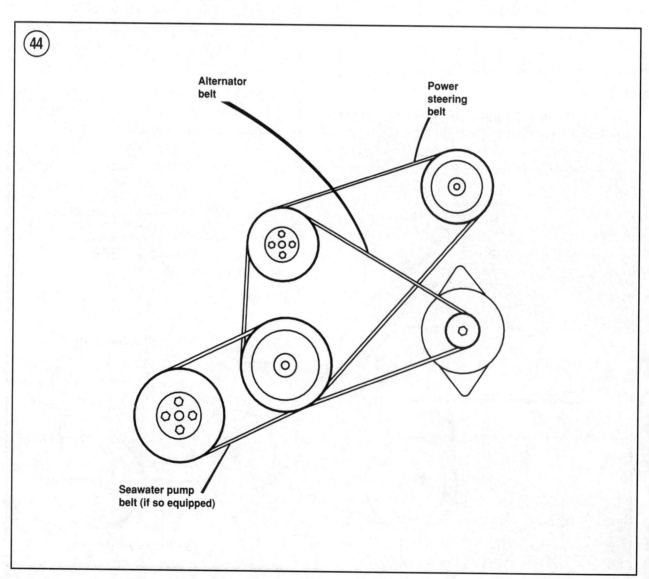

(44)

Alternator belt

Power steering belt

Seawater pump belt (if so equipped)

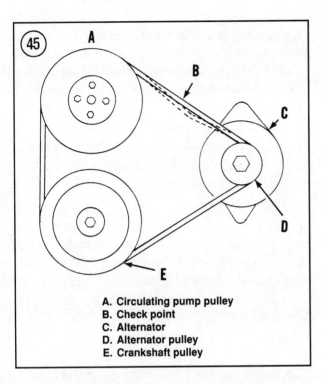

A. Circulating pump pulley
B. Check point
C. Alternator
D. Alternator pulley
E. Crankshaft pulley

is damaged. Make sure the locking tabs on the cap are not damaged or bent.

4. Dip the cap in water and attach to a cooling system pressure tester, using the adapters supplied with the tester. See **Figure 49**.

5. Pump the pressure to 14 psi (96 kPa). If the cap fails to hold pressure for 30 seconds without dropping under 11 psi (76 kPa), replace it.

6. Inspect the filler neck seat and sealing surface (**Figure 48**) for nicks, dents, distortion or contamination. Wipe the sealing surface with a clean cloth to remove any rust or dirt. Make sure the locking cams are not bent or damaged.

7. Check coolant level. It should be within 1 in. of the filler neck. Top up if necessary.

8. Connect the cooling system pressure tester to the filler neck and pressurize the freshwater section to 17 psi (116 kPa). If pressure does not hold

10

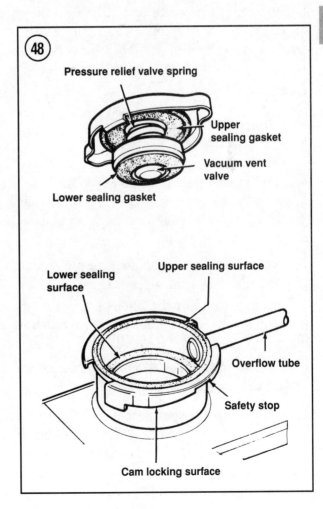

Pressure relief valve spring
Upper sealing gasket
Vacuum vent valve
Lower sealing gasket

Lower sealing surface
Upper sealing surface
Overflow tube
Safety stop
Cam locking surface

constant for at least 2 minutes, check all hoses, gaskets, drain plugs, drain valves, core plugs and other potential leak points for leakage. Listen for a hissing or bubbling sound while the system is under pressure.

9. If no leaks are found, refer to the appropriate cooling system flow diagram (**Figures 50-55**) and disconnect the seawater outlet hose from the heat exchanger. Repressurize the system to 17 psi (16 kPa) and note the outlet connection on the heat exchanger. If water flows from the connection, air bubbles are seen in the water or a bubbling or hissing noise is heard, there is probably a leak between the fresh and seawater sections within the heat exchanger.

10. If no signs of leakage can be found in Step 8 or Step 9, yet the coolant level continues to require frequent topping up, there is probably an internal leak. This could be caused by a blown head gasket; loose cylinder head, intake manifold, exhaust elbow or distributor block bolts; or a cracked or porous head, block or manifold.

Alkalinity Test

The coolant used in the freshwater section of a closed cooling system should be replaced every 2 years. After a year's service, test the coolant for alkalinity with pink litmus paper obtained from a local drug store.

1. With the engine cold, remove the pressure fill cap from the heat exchanger or reservoir.

2. Insert one end of the litmus paper into the coolant, wait a few seconds and then withdraw it.

   a. If the pink litmus paper has turned blue, the coolant alkalinity is satisfactory.

   b. If the litmus paper does not change color, the coolant has lost its alkalinity and should be replaced. Drain and refill the freshwater section of the cooling system. See Chapter Five.

Cleaning the Freshwater Section

The freshwater section should be flushed and cleaned every other season or 200 hours of operation. Any high quality automotive cooling system cleaning solution can be used to remove scale, rust, mineral deposits or other contamination. Use the cleaning solution according to the manufacturer's directions.

If extremely dirty or corroded, remaining deposits may be flushed out with a pressure flushing device. Refer to the appropriate cooling system flow diagram (**Figures 50-55**) and follow the manufacturer's instructions regarding the connection of the pressure flushing device and procedure to be followed.

Cleaning the Seawater Section of the Heat Exchanger

Contaminants and minerals collect inside the copper tubes in the seawater section of the heat exchanger during engine operation. Such foreign material reduces the ability of the heat exchanger to operate efficiently and, if not removed periodically, will eventually lead to engine overheating. It is a good idea to remove and clean the heat exchanger whenever the coolant is changed.

1A. On all except V8 engines with front mounted system and MerCruiser 165/170/3.7L and 180/190/3.7LX models, drain both sections of the closed cooling system. See Chapter Five.

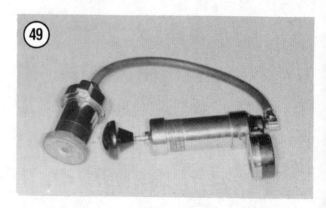

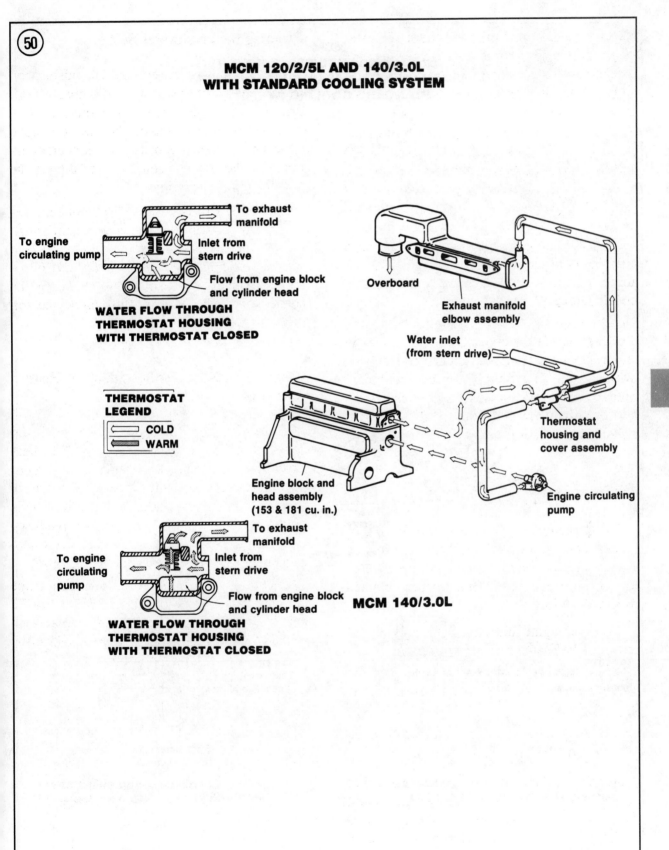

50

MCM 120/2/5L AND 140/3.0L
WITH STANDARD COOLING SYSTEM

To exhaust manifold

To engine circulating pump

Inlet from stern drive

Flow from engine block and cylinder head

WATER FLOW THROUGH THERMOSTAT HOUSING WITH THERMOSTAT CLOSED

Overboard

Exhaust manifold elbow assembly

Water inlet (from stern drive)

Thermostat housing and cover assembly

THERMOSTAT LEGEND

COLD
WARM

Engine block and head assembly (153 & 181 cu. in.)

Engine circulating pump

To exhaust manifold

To engine circulating pump

Inlet from stern drive

Flow from engine block and cylinder head

MCM 140/3.0L

WATER FLOW THROUGH THERMOSTAT HOUSING WITH THERMOSTAT CLOSED

10

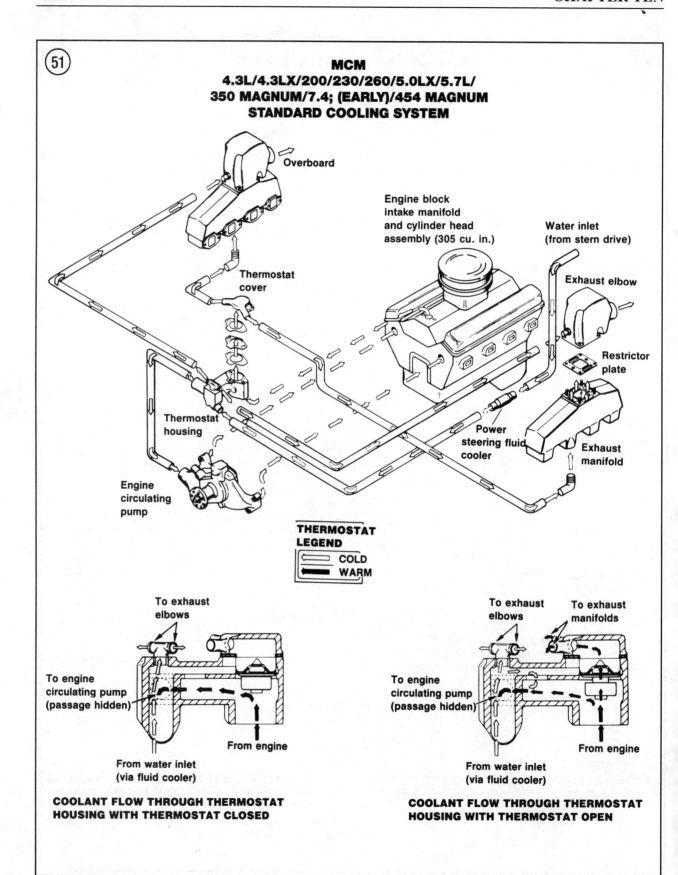

51

**MCM
4.3L/4.3LX/200/230/260/5.0LX/5.7L/
350 MAGNUM/7.4; (EARLY)/454 MAGNUM
STANDARD COOLING SYSTEM**

Overboard

Engine block
intake manifold
and cylinder head
assembly (305 cu. in.)

Water inlet
(from stern drive)

Exhaust elbow

Thermostat
cover

Restrictor
plate

Thermostat
housing

Power
steering fluid
cooler

Exhaust
manifold

Engine
circulating
pump

**THERMOSTAT
LEGEND**

⟱ COLD
⟱ WARM

To exhaust
elbows

To engine
circulating pump
(passage hidden)

From engine

From water inlet
(via fluid cooler)

**COOLANT FLOW THROUGH THERMOSTAT
HOUSING WITH THERMOSTAT CLOSED**

To exhaust
elbows

To exhaust
manifolds

To engine
circulating pump
(passage hidden)

From engine

From water inlet
(via fluid cooler)

**COOLANT FLOW THROUGH THERMOSTAT
HOUSING WITH THERMOSTAT OPEN**

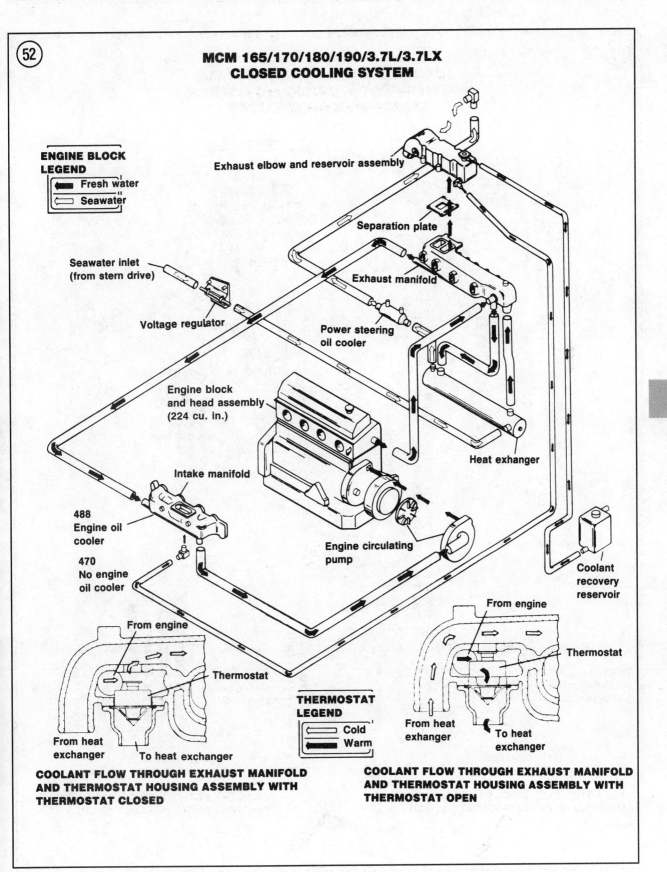

52

MCM 165/170/180/190/3.7L/3.7LX CLOSED COOLING SYSTEM

ENGINE BLOCK LEGEND
- Fresh water
- Seawater

Exhaust elbow and reservoir assembly

Separation plate

Seawater inlet (from stern drive)

Exhaust manifold

Voltage regulator

Power steering oil cooler

Engine block and head assembly (224 cu. in.)

Intake manifold

Heat exhanger

488 Engine oil cooler

470 No engine oil cooler

Engine circulating pump

Coolant recovery reservoir

From engine

Thermostat

From engine

Thermostat

From heat exchanger

To heat exchanger

From heat exchanger

To heat exchanger

THERMOSTAT LEGEND
- Cold
- Warm

COOLANT FLOW THROUGH EXHAUST MANIFOLD AND THERMOSTAT HOUSING ASSEMBLY WITH THERMOSTAT CLOSED

COOLANT FLOW THROUGH EXHAUST MANIFOLD AND THERMOSTAT HOUSING ASSEMBLY WITH THERMOSTAT OPEN

10

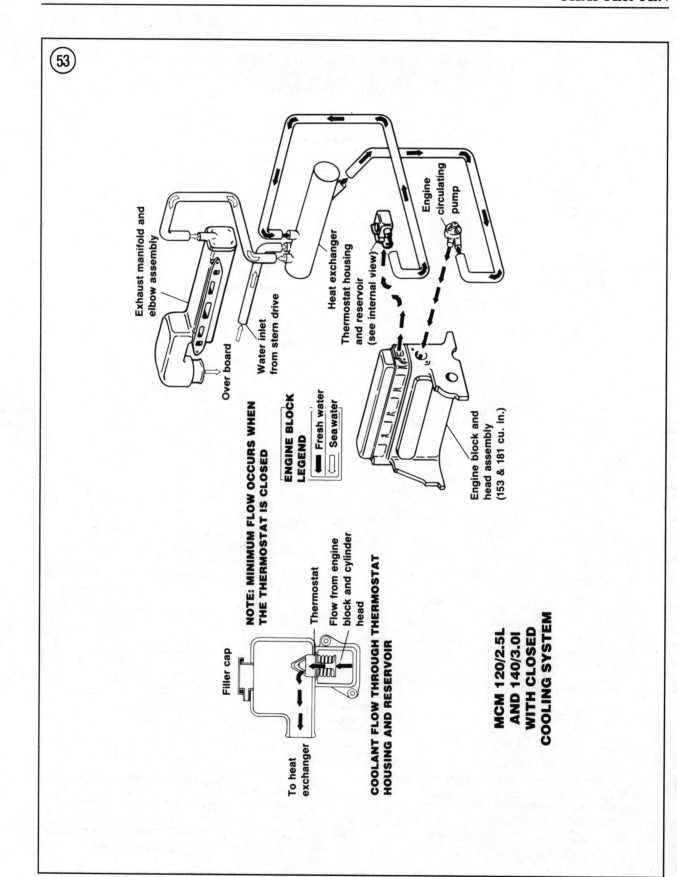

53

Exhaust manifold and elbow assembly

Over board

Water inlet from stern drive

Heat exchanger

Thermostat housing and reservoir (see internal view)

Engine circulating pump

Engine block and head assembly (153 & 181 cu. in.)

ENGINE BLOCK LEGEND
◀━ Fresh water
◀▭ Sea water

NOTE: MINIMUM FLOW OCCURS WHEN THE THERMOSTAT IS CLOSED

Filler cap

Thermostat

Flow from engine block and cylinder head

To heat exchanger

COOLANT FLOW THROUGH THERMOSTAT HOUSING AND RESERVOIR

MCM 120/2.5L AND 140/3.0I WITH CLOSED COOLING SYSTEM

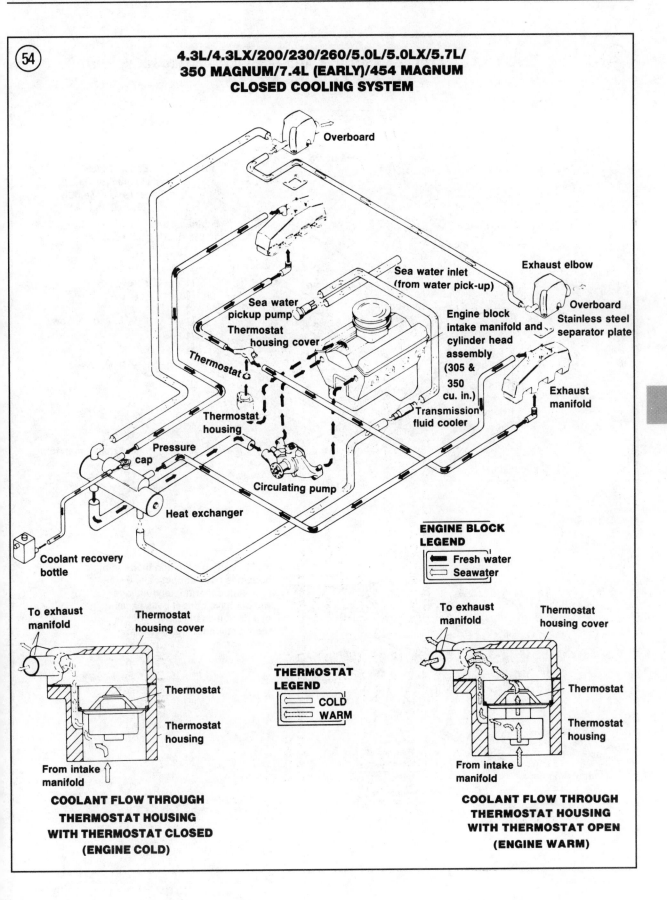

54

**4.3L/4.3LX/200/230/260/5.0L/5.0LX/5.7L/
350 MAGNUM/7.4L (EARLY)/454 MAGNUM
CLOSED COOLING SYSTEM**

Overboard

Sea water inlet
(from water pick-up)

Exhaust elbow

Sea water
pickup pump

Overboard

Stainless steel
separator plate

Thermostat
housing cover

Engine block
intake manifold and
cylinder head
assembly
(305 &
350
cu. in.)

Thermostat

Exhaust
manifold

Thermostat
housing

Transmission
fluid cooler

Pressure
cap

Circulating pump

Heat exchanger

**ENGINE BLOCK
LEGEND**

◄■■■ Fresh water
◁▭▭ Seawater

Coolant recovery
bottle

10

To exhaust
manifold

Thermostat
housing cover

**THERMOSTAT
LEGEND**

▭▭▭ COLD
▭▭▭ WARM

To exhaust
manifold

Thermostat
housing cover

Thermostat

Thermostat

Thermostat
housing

Thermostat
housing

From intake
manifold

From intake
manifold

**COOLANT FLOW THROUGH
THERMOSTAT HOUSING
WITH THERMOSTAT CLOSED
(ENGINE COLD)**

**COOLANT FLOW THROUGH
THERMOSTAT HOUSING
WITH THERMOSTAT OPEN
(ENGINE WARM)**

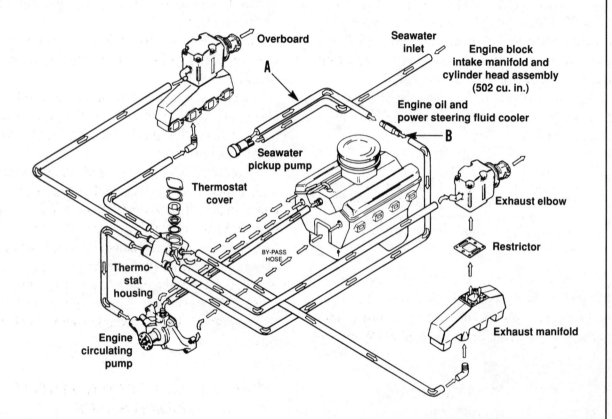

55

MCM 7.4L (LATE) 454 MAGNUM AND 502 MAGNUM (MARK V) STANDARD COOLING SYSTEM

Overboard

Seawater inlet

Engine block intake manifold and cylinder head assembly (502 cu. in.)

A

Engine oil and power steering fluid cooler

B

Seawater pickup pump

Thermostat cover

Exhaust elbow

Restrictor

Thermo-stat housing

BY-PASS HOSE

Engine circulating pump

Exhaust manifold

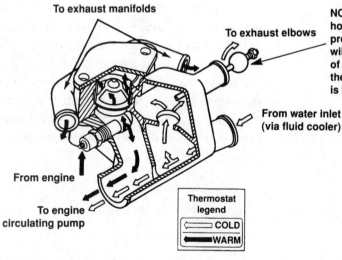

To exhaust manifolds

To exhaust elbows

From water inlet (via fluid cooler)

From engine

To engine circulating pump

Thermostat legend

⟸ COLD

➡ WARM

NOTE: Early production thermostat housings have poppet balls. Later production thermostat housings will not have poppet balls because of a design change inside of the thermostat housing. Water flow is the same.

Loosen the hose clamps and disconnect all hoses at the heat exchanger. Remove the attaching bolts. Remove the heat exchanger.

1B. On V8 engines with front mounted system and MerCruiser 165/170/3.7L and 180/190/3.7LX models, remove the drain plug from the bottom of the heat exchanger. Allow the water to drain, then coat the plug threads with Quicksilver Perfect Seal and reinstall.

2. Unbolt and remove the heat exchanger end plate(s). Remove and discard the seal washer(s) and gasket(s).

> *NOTE*
> *If the heat exchanger is plugged or contains heavy scale deposits, take it to an automotive radiator repair shop for proper cleaning to avoid potential damage to the unit.*

3. Clean all gasket residue from the end plate(s) and heat exchanger sealing surfaces.

4. Insert an appropriate-size wire brush into each passage in the heat exchanger. Work the brush back and forth with a vigorous motion, but work carefully to avoid damage to the soldered joints.

5. Remove the brush, hold the heat exchanger vertically and blow loosened particles out with compressed air.

6. Repeat Step 4 and Step 5 as necessary to remove as much of the accumulated deposits as possible.

7. Remove the zinc anode, if so equipped, and check for erosion. If more than 25% gone, install a new anode. Coat anode threads with Quicksilver Perfect Seal.

8. Coat both sides of new end plate gasket(s) with Quicksilver Perfect Seal and reinstall the end plate(s) with a new seal washer. Tighten end plate bolts to 16 ft.-lb. (21 N·m).

9. Install the heat exchanger. Check hoses and clamps. Replace any that have deteriorated. Connect hoses and tighten hose clamps securely.

10. Fill the freshwater section with coolant. See Chapter Five. Start the engine and check for leaks.

STANDARD COOLING SYSTEM MAINTENANCE

The only maintenance required for the standard cooling system is a periodic cleaning of the exhaust manifold. See the appropriate chapter for your engine. However, if the water pump is the cause of an overheating condition, be sure to disassemble the exhaust system and check the condition of the exhaust shutters. See **Figure 56**, typical. If burned or otherwise damaged, they should be replaced.

(56)

10

Table 1 TIGHTENING TORQUES

Fastener	in.-lb.	ft.-lb.	N·m
Alternator			
Mounting brace		30	41
To mounting brace		35	48
Alternator brace			
To alternator		16	22
To cylinder block		30	41
Alternator rotor-to-crankshaft			
165, 170, 180, 190, 3.7L, 3.7LX		50	68
Camshaft impeller stud			
165, 175, 180, 190, 3.7L, 3.7LX		15	20
Circulating pump			
165, 170, 180, 190, 3.7L, 3.7LX			
Cover		15	20
Impeller nut		40	54
Impeller-to-stud		15	20
All V6 and V8 (except Mark V)		30	41
All Mark V		35	47
Seawater pump			
Except Mark V			
Bracket/brace-to-cylinder block		30	41
Clamp bolt		20	27
Mark V			
Fill/drain screws	18		2.0
Fuel pump-to-housing		25-28	34-38
Idler pulley bracket-to-housing		30-35	41-47
Idler pulley locknut		30	41
Pump-to-engine		30	41
Through-bolts		10-15	14-20
Water pump body (stern drve)			
Prior to 1991			
Nuts	90		10
Screw	20-30		2-3
1991-on	60		6.8
Water temperature sender		20	27
Thermostat housing/cover		30	41
Standard screws			
1/4 in.	60		6.8
5/16		12-14	16-19
3/8		20-25	27-34
7/16		32-40	43-54

Table 2 RECOMMENDED THERMOSTAT

Model	Thermostat rating
All 224 cid (3.7 liter)	160° F
262 cid (4.3 liter)	
Stainless steel thermostat	140° F
Brass thermostat	143° F
All others	143° F

Chapter Eleven

Electrical Systems

All engines covered in this manual are equipped with a 12-volt, negative-ground electrical system. Many electrical problems can be traced to a simple cause such as a blown fuse, a loose or corroded connection, a loose alternator drive belt or a frayed wire. While these are easily corrected problems which may not appear to be important, they can quickly lead to serious difficulty if allowed to go uncorrected.

Complete overhaul of electrical components such as the alternator, distributor or starter motor is neither practical nor economical. In some cases, the necessary bushings, bearings or other worn parts are not available for individual replacement.

If tests indicate a unit with problems other than those discussed in this chapter, replace it with a new or rebuilt marine unit. Make certain, however, that the new or rebuild part to be installed is an exact replacement for the defective one removed. Also make sure to isolate and correct the cause of the failure before installing a replacement. For example, an uncorrected short in an alternator circuit will most likely burn out a new alternator as quickly as it damaged the old one. If in doubt, always consult an expert.

This chapter provides service procedures for the battery, charging system, starting system, ignition system and switches. Wiring diagrams are included at the end of the book. **Tables 1-4** are at the end of the chapter.

BATTERY

Since batteries used in marine applications endure far more rigorous treatment than those used in an automotive charging system, they are constructed differently. Marine batteries have a thicker exterior case to cushion the plates inside during tight turns or on rough water. Thicker plates are also used, with each one individually fastened within the case to prevent failure. Spill-proof caps on the battery cells prevent electrolyte from spilling into the bilge. Automotive batteries should be used *only* in an emergency situation when a suitable marine battery is not available.

If used, the automotive battery should be replaced with a suitable marine battery as soon as possible.

To assure sufficient cranking power, Mercury Marine recommends the use of a 12-volt marine battery with a minimum cold cranking amperage rating of:

a. 2 amps per cu. in. displacement for 4-cylinder engines
b. 1 1/2 amps per cu. in. displacement for 6-cylinder engines
c. 1 amp per cu. in. displacement for 8-cylinder engines

The battery used should also have a reserve capacity of at least 100 minutes. **Table 1** provides the suggested cold cranking amperage for current MerCruiser engines. For engines not included in **Table 1**, refer to the recommended specifications provided above to calculate the minimum cold cranking amperage requirement.

NOTE
A "deep cycle" battery is not suitable for use with MerCruiser marine engines. Such batteries are designed to charge and discharge at moderate current levels. If the battery does not have a specified cold cranking amperage rating, it should not be used.

A good state of charge should be maintained in the battery. Any battery that cannot deliver at least 9.6 volts under a starting load should be recharged. If recharging does not bring it up to strength or if it does not hold the charge, replace the battery.

Care and Inspection

1. Disconnect both battery cables (negative first, then positive) and remove the battery hold-down or retainer clamp. See **Figure 1** for a typical open installation and **Figure 2** for a typical enclosed installation.

NOTE
*Some batteries have a carry strap built in for use in Step 2. See **Figure 3**.*

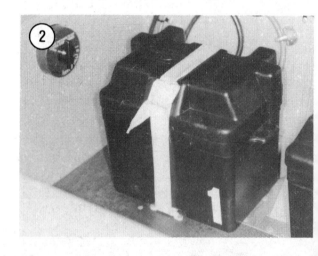

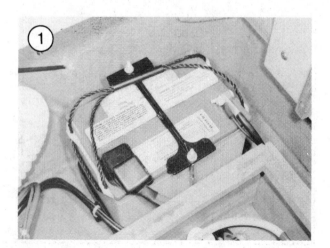

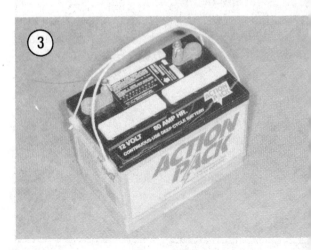

2. Attach a battery carrier or carrier strap to the terminal posts and lift the battery from the battery tray. Remove battery from the engine compartment.

3. Check the entire battery case for cracks or other damage.

4. If the battery has removable vent caps, cover the vent holes in each cap with small pieces of masking tape.

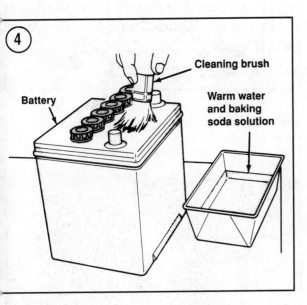

Figure 4

- Cleaning brush
- Battery
- Warm water and baking soda solution

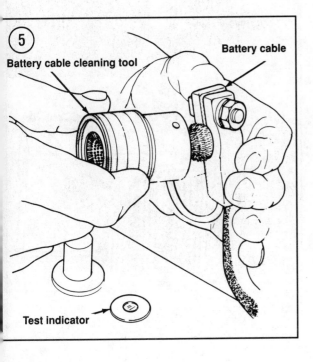

Figure 5

- Battery cable cleaning tool
- Battery cable
- Test indicator

NOTE
Keep cleaning solution out of the battery cells in Step 5 or the electrolyte will be seriously weakened.

5. Scrub the top of the battery with a stiff bristle brush, using a baking soda and water solution (**Figure 4**). Rinse the battery case with clear water and wipe dry with a clean cloth or paper towels. Remove the masking tape from the filler cap vent holes, if so equipped.

6. Inspect the battery tray or container in the engine compartment for corrosion. Remove and clean, if necessary, with the baking soda and water solution. Rinse with clear water and wipe dry, then reinstall.

7. Clean the battery cable clamps with a stiff wire brush or one of the many tools made for this purpose (**Figure 5**). The same tool is used for cleaning the battery posts (**Figure 6**).

8. Reposition the battery on the battery tray or container and remove the carrier or strap. Install and tighten the hold-down device.

11

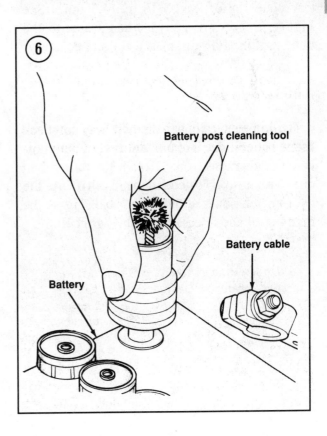

Figure 6

- Battery post cleaning tool
- Battery cable
- Battery

9. Reinstall the positive battery cable, then the negative battery cable.

CAUTION
Be sure the battery cables are connected to their proper terminals. Connecting the battery backwards will reverse the polarity and can damage the alternator.

10. Tighten the battery cable connections to 9 ft.-lb. (12 N•m). Tightening the connections more than this can cause damage to the battery case. Coat the connections with a petroleum jelly such as Vaseline or a light mineral grease. Aerosol anti-corrosion sprays can also be used.

NOTE
Do not overfill the battery cells in Step 11. The electrolyte expands due to heat from charging and may overflow if the level is more than 1/4 in. (6 mm) above the battery plates.

11. Remove the filler caps and check the electrolyte level. The electrolyte should cover the battery plates by at least 3/16 in. (4.8 mm). See **Figure 7**. Top up with distilled water to the bottom of the fill ring in each cell, if necessary.

Battery Testing

Hydrometer testing is the best way to check battery condition. Use a hydrometer with numbered graduations from 1.100-1.300 rather than one with just color-coded bands. To use the hydrometer, squeeze the rubber ball, insert the tip in a cell and release the ball (**Figure 8**).

NOTE
Do not attempt to test a battery with a hydrometer immediately after adding water to the cells. Run the engine or charge the battery for 15-20 minutes prior to testing.

Draw enough electrolyte to float the weighted float inside the hydrometer. When using a temperature-compensated hydrometer, release the

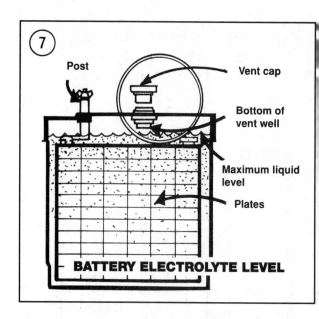

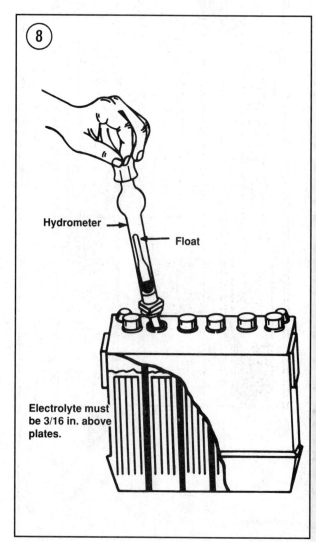

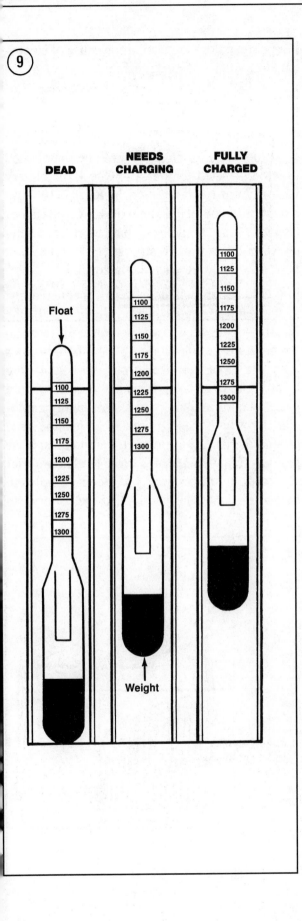

electrolyte and repeat this process several times to make sure the thermometer has adjusted to the electrolyte temperature before taking the reading.

Hold the hydrometer vertically and note the number aligned with the surface of the electrolyte (**Figure 9**). This is the specific gravity for the cell. Return the electrolyte to the cell from which it came.

The specific gravity of the electrolyte in each battery cell is an excellent indicator of that cell's condition. A fully charged cell will read 1.260 or more at 80° F (27° C). If the cells test below 1.220, the battery must be recharged. Charging is also necessary if the specific gravity varies more than 50 points from cell to cell.

> *NOTE*
> *If a temperature-compensated hydrometer is not used, add 0.004 to the specific gravity reading for every 10 degrees above 80° F (27° C). For every 10 degrees below 80° F (27° C), subtract 0.004.*

11

Safety Precautions

When working with batteries, use extreme care to avoid spilling or splashing the electrolyte. This solution contains sulfuric acid, which can ruin clothing and cause serious chemical burns. If any electrolyte is spilled or splashed on clothing or skin, immediately neutralize with a solution of baking soda and water, then flush with an abundance of clean water.

> *WARNING*
> *Electrolyte splashed into the eyes is extremely dangerous. Safety glasses should always be worn while working with batteries. If electrolyte is splashed into the eyes, call a physician immediately, force the eyes open and flood with cool, clean water for approximately 5 minutes.*

If electrolyte is spilled or splashed onto any surface, it should be immediately neutralized with baking soda and water solution and then rinsed with clean water.

While batteries are being charged, highly explosive hydrogen gas forms in each cell. Some of this gas escapes through filler cap openings and may form an explosive atmosphere in and around the battery. This condition can persist for several hours. Sparks, an open flame or a lighted cigarette can ignite this gas, causing an internal battery explosion and possible serious personal injury.

Take the following precautions to prevent injury.

1. Do not smoke or permit any open flame near any battery being charged or which has been recently charged.

2. Do not disconnect live circuits at battery terminals, since a spark usually occurs when a live circuit is broken.

3. Take care when connecting or disconnecting any battery charger. Be sure its power switch is off before making or breaking any connection.

Poor connections are a common cause of electrical arcs which cause explosions.

Charging

A good state of charge should be maintained in batteries used for starting. Check the battery with a voltmeter as shown in **Figure 10**. Any battery that cannot deliver at least 9.6 volts under a starting load should be recharged. If recharging does not bring it up to strength or if it does not hold the charge, replace the battery.

A cold battery will not accept a charge readily. If the temperature is below 40° F (5° C), the battery should be allowed to warm up to room temperature before charging. The battery does not have to be removed from the boat before charging but it is a recommended procedure since a charging battery gives off highly explosive hydrogen gas. In many boats, the area around the battery is not well ventilated and the gas may remain in the area for several hours after the charging procedure has been completed. Sparks or flames occurring near the battery can

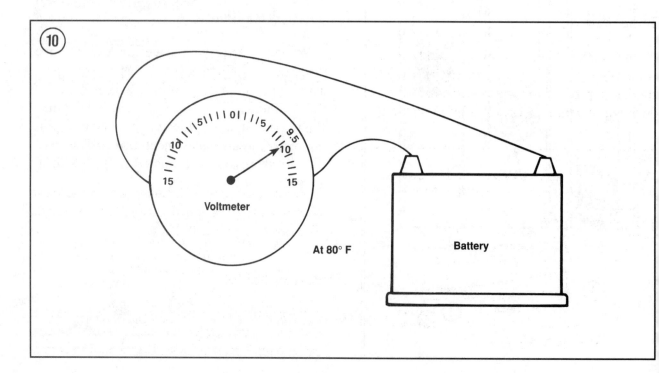

Voltmeter

At 80° F

Battery

cause it to explode, spraying battery acid over a wide area.

Disconnect the negative battery cable first, then the positive battery cable. Make sure the electrolyte is fully topped up. Remove the vent caps and place a folded paper towel over the vent openings to absorb any electrolyte that may spew as the battery charges.

Connect the charger to the battery; negative-to-negative, positive-to-positive. If the charger output is variable, select a 10-12 amp setting. Set the voltage selector to 12 volts and plug the charger in. Once the battery starts to accept a charge, the charge rate should be reduced to a level that will prevent excessive gassing and electrolyte spewing.

The length of time required to recharge a battery depends upon its size, state of charge and temperature. Generally speaking, the current input time should equal the battery amp-hour rating. For example, a 45 AH battery will require a 9-amp charging rate for 5 hours ($9 \times 5 = 45$) or a 15-amp charging rate for 3 hours ($15 \times 3 = 45$). Check charging progress with the hydrometer.

Jump Starting

If the battery becomes severely discharged, it is possible to start and run an engine by jump starting it from another battery. Mercury Marine does not recommend that you jump start a dis-charged battery due to the possible danger of explosion. Since many owners will disregard this warning, however, the following procedure is provided as the safest method to use.

Before jump starting a battery when temperatures are 32° F (0° C) or lower, check the condition of the electrolyte. If it is not visible or if it appears to be frozen, do *not* attempt to jump start the battery, as the battery may explode or rupture.

> *WARNING*
> *Use extreme caution when connecting a booster battery to one that is discharged to avoid personal injury or damage to the system.*

1. Connect the jumper cables in the order and sequence shown in figure 11.

> *WARNING*
> *An electrical arc may occur when the final connection is made. This could cause an explosion if it occurs near the battery. For this reason, the final connection should be made to the alternator mounting bracket or another good engine ground and not the battery itself.*

2. Check that all jumper cables are out of the way of moving parts on both engines.

3. Start the engine with the good battery and run at a moderate speed.

4. Start the engine with the discharged battery. Once it starts, run it at a moderate speed.

> *CAUTION*
> *Racing the engine may damage the electrical system.*

5. Remove the jumper cables in the exact reverse order shown in **Figure 11**. Begin at point 4, then disconnect at points 3, 2 and 1.

Battery Cables

Poor terminal connections will cause excessive resistance. Defective cable insulation can cause partial short circuits. Both conditions may

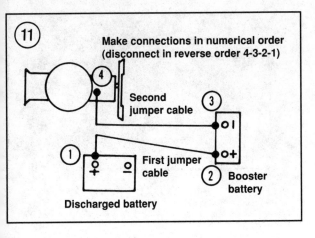

Make connections in numerical order (disconnect in reverse order 4-3-2-1)

Second jumper cable

First jumper cable

Booster battery

Discharged battery

result in an abnormal voltage drop in the starter motor cable. When this happens, the resulting hard-start condition will place further strain on the battery. Cable condition and terminal connections should be checked periodically.

CHARGING SYSTEM

The charging system consists of the battery, alternator, voltage regulator, ignition switch, ammeter and connecting wiring. A Motorola alternator with a rear-mounted voltage regulator is used on some inline engines; all others use a Mando alternator with a rear-mounted voltage regulator.

Preliminary Testing

The first indication of charging system trouble is usually a slow engine cranking speed during starting or running lights that dim as engine speed decreases. This will often occur long before the ammeter or voltmeter indicates that there is a potential problem. When charging system trouble is first suspected, perform the following checks.

1. Check the alternator drive belt for correct tension (Chapter Ten).
2. Check the battery to make sure it is in satisfactory condition and fully charged and that all connections are clean and tight.
3. Check all connections at the alternator to make sure they are clean and tight.

If there are still indications that the charging system is not performing as it should after each of the above points has been carefully checked and any unsatisfactory conditions corrected, refer to Chapter Three and perform the *Charging System Test*.

This section provides alternator replacement procedures. Complete alternator overhaul is not practical for the amateur mechanic. Rebuilt marine-approved alternators can be purchased quite inexpensively compared to the time and effort involved in disassembly, testing, repair and reassembly. In some cases, such overhaul is not even possible since replacement components are not available.

Alternator Removal/Installation

This procedure is generalized to cover all applications. Access to the alternator is quite limited in some engine compartments and care should be taken to avoid personal injury.

1. Disconnect the negative battery cable.
2. Disconnect all wiring harnesses and leads at the rear of the alternator. See **Figure 12** (typical).
3. Loosen the alternator adjusting and pivot bolts (**Figure 13**, typical).
4. Swivel the alternator toward the engine and remove the drive belt from the alternator pulley.
5. Support the alternator with one hand and remove the adjusting and pivot bolts, noting the position of any washers or spacers used. Remove the alternator.
6. Installation is the reverse of removal. Tighten fasteners securely and adjust drive belt tension (Chapter Ten) before reconnecting wiring harnesses and leads to the rear of the alternator.

DIRECT DRIVE ALTERNATOR CHARGING SYSTEM

Service to the direct drive charging system requires partial engine disassembly. Refer to Chapter Seven.

STARTING SYSTEM

The starting system consists of the starter motor, starter solenoid, assist solenoid, ignition switch, neutral safety or cut-out switch, battery and connecting wiring with one or more inline fuses. The neutral safety or cut-out switch is located inside the remote control box and allows starter operation only when the shift selector lever is in NEUTRAL.

MerCruiser marine engines may be equipped with a Delco-Remy or Prestolite starter motor. The Delco-Remy starter solenoid is enclosed in the drive housing to protect it from exposure to dirt and adverse weather conditions.

A Delco-Remy permanent magnet starter motor is used on 1989 V6 engines. This smaller and lightweight starter motor has no electromagnetic

field coils or pole shoes. The magnetic field is provided by a series of small permanent magnets. As a result, there is no motor field circuit and thus no potential field wire-to-frame shorts or other electrical problems related to the field. The motor uses only an armature circuit.

The permanent magnets mounted inside the starter frame (**Figure 14**) are made from an alloy of iron and rare-earth materials that deliver a magnetic field strong enough to operate the motor with the same cranking performance as a comparable starter motor with electromagnetic fields. A planetary gear train transmits power between the armature and the pinion shaft, resulting in a low-speed, high-torque starter motor.

Like any other permanent magnet motor, permanent magnet starts require care in handling. The permanent magnets are quite brittle, and the magnetic field can be destroyed by a sharp impact or by dropping the starter motor.

Starter service requires experience and special tools. Troubleshooting procedures are provided in Chapter Three. The procedures described below consist of removal, installation and brush replacement. Any repairs inside the unit itself (other than brush replacement) should be done by a dealer or certified electrical shop. Installation of a professionally rebuilt marine-type unit is generally less expensive and thus more practical.

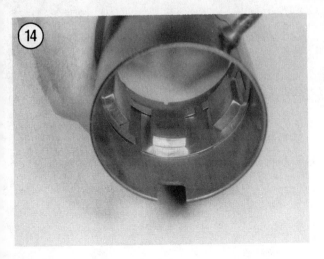

Delco-Remy Starter Solenoid Replacement

1. Remove the starter motor as described in this chapter.
2. Disconnect the field strap at the starter from the motor terminal.
3. Remove the solenoid-to-drive housing screws and the motor terminal bolt.
4. Rotate the solenoid 90° and remove it from the drive housing with the plunger return or torsion spring.
5. Installation is the reverse of removal.

11

Slave Solenoid Removal/Installation

1. Disconnect the negative battery cable.

2. Disconnect the cable connector wires from the solenoid terminals.

3. Remove the nuts holding the starter and battery cables to the solenoid. Disconnect the cables and reinstall the nuts to prevent their loss.

4. Remove the solenoid attaching screws. Remove the solenoid.

5. Installation is the reverse of removal.

Starter Removal/Installation

1. Disconnect the negative battery cable.

2A. *Delco-Remy starter*—Disconnect the solenoid terminal wires. See **Figure 15**.

2B. *Prestolite starter*—Disconnect the heavy starter cable at the starter terminal.

3. Remove the starter motor mounting bolts. Pull the starter motor away from the flywheel and remove it from the engine. Retrieve any mounting shims that may fall out.

4. Installation is the reverse of removal. Reinstall any shims that were removed to assure proper pinion-to-flywheel mesh. Tighten mounting bolts to 20-25 ft.-lb. (27-34 N·m). Apply Quicksilver Liquid Neoprene or equivalent to all terminal connections to prevent corrosion.

Starter Brush Replacement (Delco-Remy Permanent Magnet Starter)

Brushes cannot be replaced individually or in sets. Brush replacement requires replacement of the entire brush holder assembly (**Figure 16**). New brush holder assemblies come complete with new brushes. To disassemble the starter motor and check brush condition:

1. Remove the nut holding the brush terminal to the solenoid stud. Disconnect the terminal from the stud (**Figure 17**).

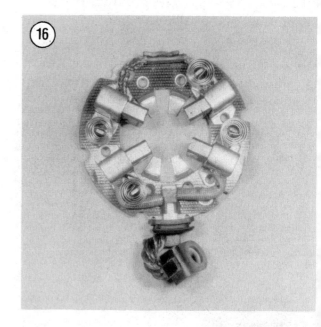

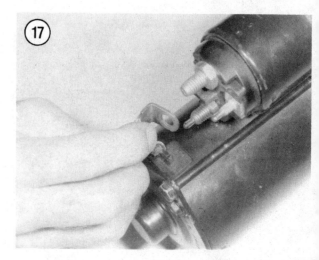

2. Remove the two through bolts holding the end cap to the field frame (**Figure 18**). If cap does not come off easily, tap on its ears with a soft-faced hammer.

3. Remove the end cap (**Figure 19**). Note that there are six locating dowels in the cap that must

align and engage the brush holder during reassembly.

4. Disengage the brush terminal insulator from the field frame; then slide the brush holder from the armature shaft and remove complete assembly (**Figure 20**). The brushes appear to be removable but they are not. If one or more brushes require replacement, the entire assembly must be replaced.

5. Check the brushes for length and condition. Replace the brush holder if any are oil-soaked or worn to 1/4 in. (6 mm) or less.

6. Make sure the brush holder is clean and that the brushes do not bind individual holders.

7. Check the brush springs; replace the entire assembly if distorted or discolored.

8. Installation is the reverse of removal.

Starter Brush Replacement (Delco-Remy Field Coil Starter)

Brush replacement requires special disassembly of the starter. Always replace brushes in complete sets. Refer to **Figure 21** for this procedure.

1. Remove the terminal nut and disconnect the field lead from the solenoid terminal. See **Figure 22**.

2. Remove the 2 through-bolts. Separate the end frame and field frame assembly from the solenoid and drive assembly. See **Figure 23**.

3. Remove the brush and lead attaching screws (**Figure 24**).

4. Remove the brush holder pivot pins.

5. Remove the 2 brush holder and spring assemblies from the field housing. See **Figure 25**.

6. Check the brushes for length and condition. Replace all if any are oil-soaked or worn to 1/4 in. (6 mm) or less in length.

7. Make sure the brush holders are clean and that the brushes do not bind in the holder.

8. Check the brush springs; replace if distorted or discolored.

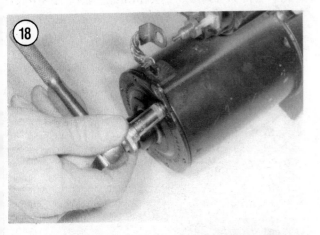

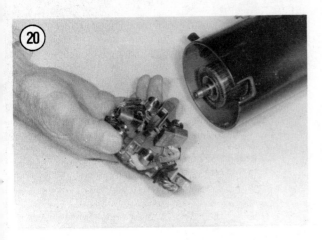

11

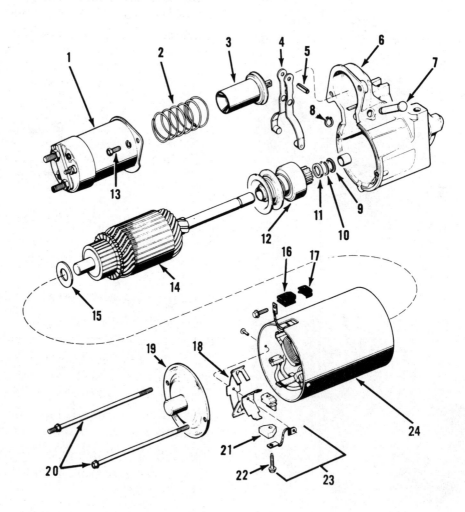

(21)

DELCO STARTER

1. Solenoid switch
2. Plunger return spring
3. Plunger
4. Shift lever
5. Plunger pin
6. Drive end housing
7. Shift lever shaft
8. Lever shaft retaining ring
9. Thurst collar
10. Pinion stop retainer ring
11. Pinion stop collar
12. Drive

13. Screw
14. Armature
15. Washer
16. Grommet
17. Grommet
18. Brush holder
19. Commutator end frame
20. Through bolt
21. Brush
22. Screw
23. Brush and holder assembly
24. Frame and field winding

9. Secure new brushes to the leads with the attaching screws.

10. Reverse Steps 1-3 to complete brush installation.

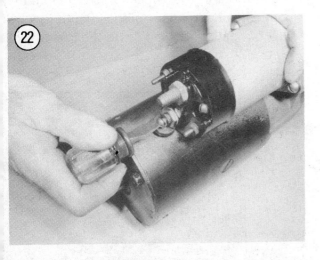

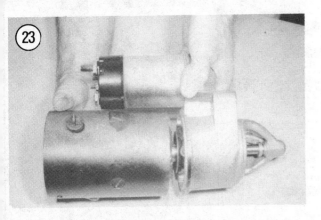

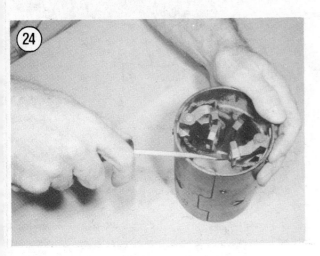

Starter Brush Replacement (Prestolite Starter)

Brush replacement requires partial disassembly of the starter. Always replace brushes in complete sets. Refer to **Figure 26** for this procedure.

1. Remove the 2 through-bolts. Remove the end plate, plug and thrust washer.

2. Note position of brushes in the brush holder. Pull back and hold the brush retaining clip with a wire hook, then remove the brush. Repeat this step to remove the remaining brushes from the holder.

3. Remove the brush holder from the frame.

4. Inspect the brushes. Replace all brushes if any are oil-soaked or worn to 1/4 in. (6 mm) or less in length.

5. To replace ground brushes, install a new brush plate.

6. To replace field coil brushes, cut the insulated brush leads as close as possible to the field coils. Attach new brush leads with the clips provided in the brush replacement kit. Solder the connections together with rosin core solder and a 300-watt soldering iron.

7. Install the brush holder. Pry the retaining springs open and insert the field brushes in their respective holders.

8. Install the thrust washer, plug and end plate. Install the 2 through-bolts.

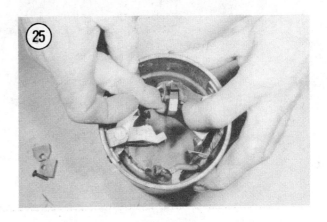

11

IGNITION SYSTEM

MerCruiser marine engines are equipped with either a breaker point ignition system, a Thunderbolt IV (breakerless) ignition system, a digital distributorless ignition system (DDIS) or electronic spark timing (EST) ignition system.

The breaker point system consists of a distributor (containing the breaker points and condenser), ignition coil, ignition switch, battery spark plugs and connecting wiring. See **Figure 27**, typical.

The Thunderbolt IV ignition system consists of a distributor (with trigger or sensor assembly) ignition coil, ignition amplifier, ignition switch battery, spark plugs and connecting wiring. See **Figure 28**, typical.

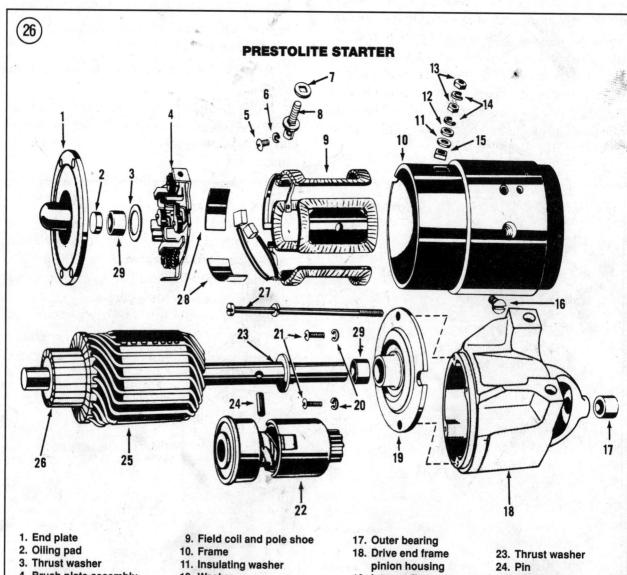

(26)

PRESTOLITE STARTER

1. End plate
2. Oiling pad
3. Thrust washer
4. Brush plate assembly
5. Screw
6. Lockwasher
7. Insulating washer
8. Terminal
9. Field coil and pole shoe
10. Frame
11. Insulating washer
12. Washer
13. Nut
14. Lockwasher
15. Insulating bushing
16. Pole shoe screw
17. Outer bearing
18. Drive end frame pinion housing
19. Intermediate bearing housing
20. Lockwasher
21. Screw
22. Bendix drive
23. Thrust washer
24. Pin
25. Armature
26. Commutator
27. Through bolt
28. Insulator
29. Intermediate bearing

The DDIS system consists of a crankshaft position sensor assembly, ignition coils, module assembly, ignition switch, battery, spark plugs and connecting wiring. The DDIS system eliminates the distributor, distributor cap, rotor and centrifugal spark advance. The direct-fire ignition coils (**Figure 29**) are connected directly to the spark plugs.

EST (electronic spark timing) is a breakerless, electronic ignition system consisting of a distributor, magnetic pickup coil, ignition module, ignition coil, battery, ignition switch and related circuitry. A centrifugal spark advance mechanism is not used—spark advance is controlled electronically by the ignition module. The ignition module and pickup coil are contained inside the distributor. See **Figure 30**.

BREAKER POINT DISTRIBUTOR

Servicing

MerCruiser marine distributors are heavy-duty units manufactured with special housings, caps, advance weights and other components. They are designed to withstand climatic and environmental abuse to which the typical automotive distributor is not subjected. For this reason, automotive parts should not be substituted. Periodic care, cleaning and lubrication of the breaker point distributor are recommended for long service life.

1. Remove the distributor as described in this chapter.
2. Clean the outside of the distributor with solvent and a brush to remove all dirt, grease and other contamination.

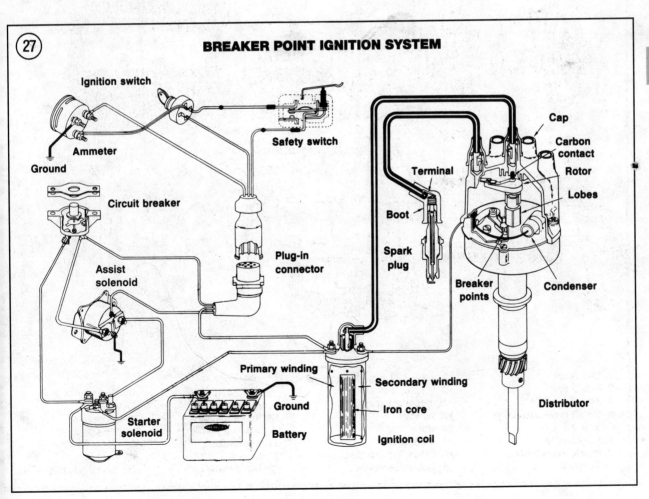

(27) BREAKER POINT IGNITION SYSTEM

11

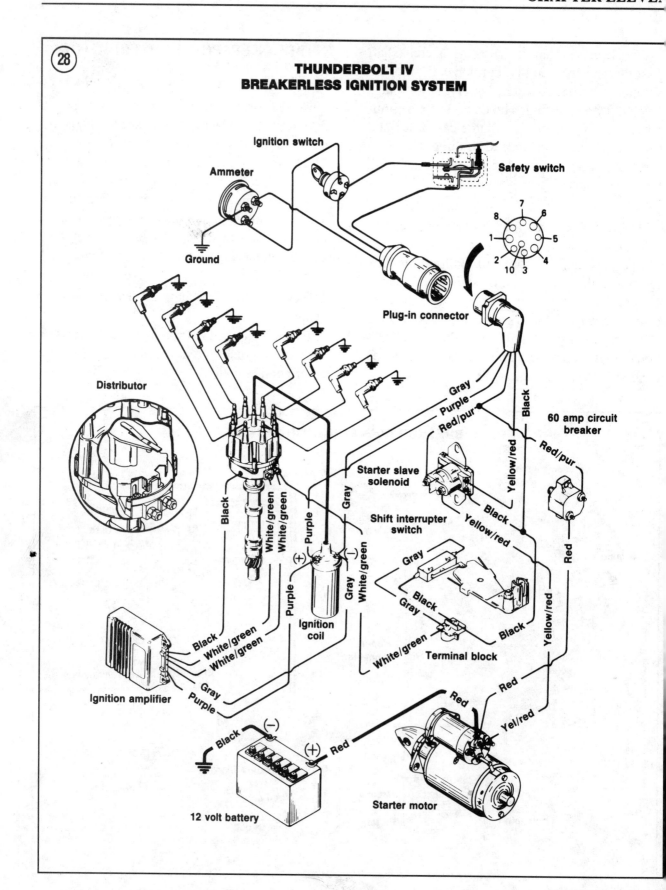

28

THUNDERBOLT IV
BREAKERLESS IGNITION SYSTEM

Ignition switch

Ammeter

Safety switch

Ground

Plug-in connector

Distributor

Gray
Purple
Red/pur

Black

60 amp circuit breaker

Red/pur

Black

White/green
White/green

Purple

Gray

Starter slave solenoid

Yellow/red

Black

Shift interrupter switch

Yellow/red

Gray

Purple

Gray
White/green

Gray

Black

Gray

Red

Ignition coil

Black
White/green
White/green

White/green

Black

Yellow/red

Terminal block

Gray
Purple

Ignition amplifier

Red

Red

Red

Yel/red

Black

Red

12 volt battery

Starter motor

3. Remove the distributor cap and rotor. Inspect both as described in Chapter Four. If the cap is vented, make sure the vent screen is not plugged and that it is properly installed.

4. Have a dealer or qualified electrical shop test distributor operation on a synchroscope or distributor test machine (**Figure 31**). Have worn parts replaced as necessary.

11

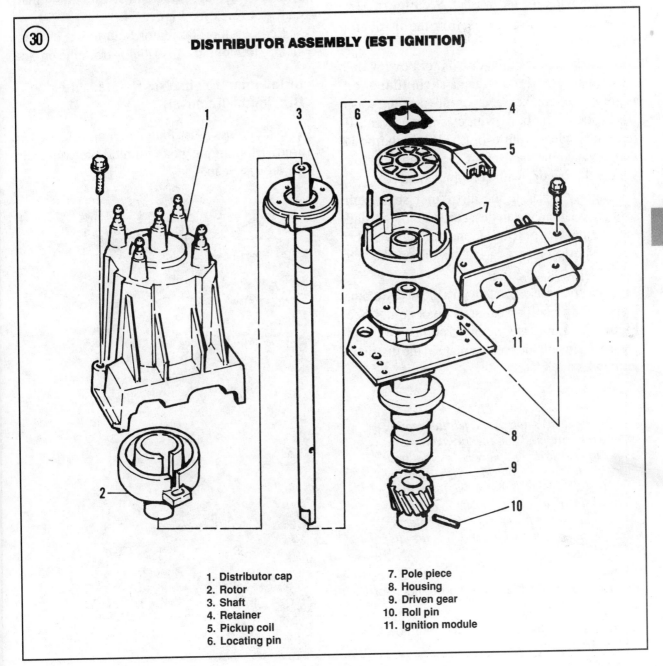

DISTRIBUTOR ASSEMBLY (EST IGNITION)

1. Distributor cap
2. Rotor
3. Shaft
4. Retainer
5. Pickup coil
6. Locating pin
7. Pole piece
8. Housing
9. Driven gear
10. Roll pin
11. Ignition module

5. Remove the breaker point and condenser assembly. See Chapter Four.

6. Remove the breaker plate attaching screws. Lift or carefully pry on breaker plate and remove from distributor bowl.

7. Remove the felt lubrication washer (if so equipped) from the center of the cam assembly. Some distributors use a tiny wire retaining clip inside the cam assembly that must be removed after removing the felt washer. See **Figure 32**.

8. Remove the cam assembly from the distributor shaft.

9. Wipe the inside of the distributor bowl with a clean dry cloth. If more than a slight film of oil is present, or crankcase vapors are present, wash the inside of the bowl with cleaning solvent. If necessary, clean with a brush. When the bowl and advance mechanism are clean, rinse in solvent and blow dry with compressed air.

10. Lightly lubricate the distributor shaft with cam grease, then install the cam assembly. Install the retaining clip, if used, and the felt washer. Place a drop or two of engine oil on the felt lubrication washer.

11. Wipe the breaker plate with a clean dry cloth. Inspect the plate for wear at its pivot points. See **Figure 33**. Lubricate the pivot points with cam grease. Reinstall the breaker plate in the distributor bowl.

> *NOTE*
> *Some distributors use a felt lubricating wick mounted on the breaker plate. Other distributors may have an oil cup located on the outside of the housing bowl. Always replace the lubricating wick with a new one or put 2-3 drops of engine oil in the oil cup when replacing points or otherwise servicing the distributor.*

12. Install the breaker point and condenser assembly. See Chapter Four.

13. Install the distributor in the engine as described in this chapter.

Removal

1. Remove the distributor cap retaining screws.
2. Remove the distributor cap with the spark plug wires attached and place to one side out of the way.
3. Disconnect the distributor primary wire at the coil.
4. Scribe a mark on the distributor housing in line with the rotor tip. Scribe a corresponding mark on the engine. See **Figure 34**.
5. Remove the distributor hold-down bolt and clamp. Remove the distributor from the engine.

Installation (Engine Not Rotated After Distributor Removal)

1. Install a new distributor mounting gasket (if used) in the engine block counterbore. Make sure the area is clean.

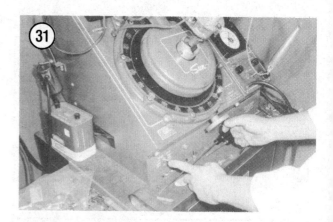

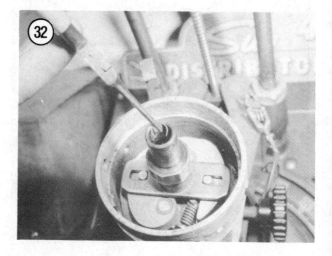

2. Align the rotor tip with the mark scribed on the distributor housing during removal. Turn the rotor about 1/8 turn counterclockwise past the scribed mark. Position the distributor to align the housing mark with the mark scribed on the engine prior to removal. Slide the distributor down into the engine.

> *NOTE*
> *The rotor and shaft might have to be moved slightly to engage the distributor and camshaft gears and oil pump drive tang. However, the rotor should align with the scribed mark when the distributor is in its final position.*

3. Install the distributor hold-down clamp and bolt. Do not tighten at this time.

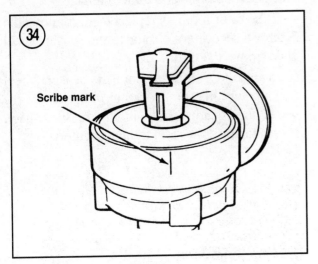

Scribe mark

4. Install the distributor cap on the housing. Be sure the tang on the housing engages the cap slot and that the cap fits snugly on the housing.

5. Connect the distributor lead and set ignition timing. See Chapter Four. When timing is correctly adjusted, tighten the distributor hold-down bolt snugly.

Installation (Engine Rotated After Distributor Removal)

1. Remove the No. 1 spark plug. See Chapter Four. Hold a finger over the plug hole and crank the engine over or rotate the crankshaft pulley until compression pressure is felt. Continue to rotate the engine slowly until the timing mark on the crankshaft pulley aligns with the TDC (zero) mark on the timing scale.

> *NOTE*
> *Always rotate the engine in the direction of normal rotation. Do not back up the engine to align the timing marks.*

2. Install a new distributor mounting gasket (if used) in the engine block counterbore. Make sure the area is clean.

3. Turn the distributor shaft until the rotor tip points in the direction of the No. 1 terminal in the distributor cap. Turn the rotor 1/8 turn counterclockwise past the No. 1 terminal position. Slide the distributor into the engine.

> *NOTE*
> *The rotor and shaft may have to be moved slightly to engage the distributor and camshaft gears and the oil pump drive tang. However, the rotor should align with the No. 1 terminal when the distributor is in place.*

4. Install the distributor hold-down clamp and bolt. Do not tighten bolt at this time.

5. Install the distributor cap on the housing. Be sure the tang on the housing engages the cap slot and that the cap fits snugly on the housing.

11

6. Connect the distributor lead and set ignition timing. See Chapter Four. When timing is correctly adjusted, tighten the distributor hold-down bolt snugly.

THUNDERBOLT IV IGNITION

The Thunderbolt distributor contains a trigger device which performs like a switch to make or break current flow when subjected to a magnetic field. Sensor switching is comparable to the points in a conventional breaker-point ignition system. The ignition amplifier or module provides ignition timing advance by controlling ignition coil primary current.

Distributor Removal/Installation

1. Disconnect the negative battery cable from the battery.
2. Disconnect the white/red and white/green wires from the distributor.
3. Scribe a mark on the distributor housing under the No. 1 spark plug terminal in the distributor cap.
4. Loosen the distributor cap retaining screws. Remove the cap with the spark plug leads attached.
5. Rotate the crankshaft until the rotor aligns with the mark scribed in Step 3. The timing mark on the harmonic balancer should align with the TDC mark on the timing scale.

NOTE
Always turn the engine in the normal direction of rotation. Do not turn the engine backward to align the timing marks or the water pump impeller can be damaged.

6. Remove the distributor ground wire screw at the intake manifold.
7. Remove the distributor hold-down screw and clamp. Remove the distributor from the engine. Remove and discard the distributor base gasket.

8. Installation is the reverse of removal. If the crankshaft is rotated while the distributor is out of the engine, perform Step 1 of *Breaker Point Distributor Installation (Engine Rotated After Distributor Removal)* in this chapter to set the No. 1 piston at TDC on its compression stroke.

Distributor Rotor and Sensor Wheel Removal/Installation

1. Remove the distributor cap from the distributor. Allow the spark plug leads to remain attached to the cap.

NOTE
The rotor/sensor wheel is affixed to the distributor shaft with thread locking compound. A torch lamp or heat gun (do not use open flame) will ease rotor removal from the shaft.

2. If necessary, heat the rotor using a torch lamp or heat gun. Position 2 screwdrivers on opposite sides of the rotor and carefully pry the rotor and sensor wheel assembly from the shaft.
3. Carefully inspect the rotor locating tab. The edges of the tab should be clean and sharp edged, 1/8 in. (3.2 mm) wide. The rotor should be replaced if material is shaved off the locating tab or if the tab is damaged. Inspect the rotor for cracks, carbon tracks or other damage.
4. If the rotor requires replacement, remove the 3 screws securing the rotor to the sensor wheel and remove the rotor.
5. Install the new rotor onto the sensor wheel making sure the rotor locating pin properly engages the locating hole in the sensor wheel. Install the 3 screws and tighten securely.

NOTE
The rotor must fit the distributor shaft very tightly. It may be necessary to heat the rotor using a torch lamp or heat gun to ease installation. Do not heat the rotor with open flame.

6. Apply Loctite 242 to the rotor locating tab and locating slot in the distributor shaft. Install the rotor onto the shaft making sure the tab properly engages the slot in the shaft.

7. Invert the distributor to prevent Loctite from draining down the shaft into the distributor bushing. Allow the Loctite to cure overnight before returning the distributor to service.

Ignition Sensor Removal/Installation

1. Disconnect the negative battery cable from the battery.

2. If necessary, remove the distributor as described in this chapter. If the sensor can be removed without distributor removal, disconnect the white/red and white/green wires from the sensor terminals on the side of the distributor.

3. Remove the rotor and sensor wheel as described in this chapter.

4. Remove the 2 screws securing the sensor to the distributor (**Figure 35**). Remove the sensor.

5. Reinstall the sensor by reversing the removal procedure. Tighten the sensor mounting screws securely.

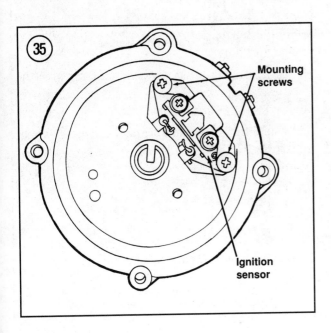

Ignition Module Removal/Installation

1. Disconnect the negative battery cable from the battery.

NOTE
*The early ignition amplifier has been superseded by a later design ignition module. See **Figure 36**. In addition, on serial No. OF000001-on, the ignition module is mounted on the distributor instead of the exhaust elbow. Although the part number is different between the exhaust elbow-mounted module and the distributor-mounted module, the spark advance curve is the same. Be sure the correct module is used according to engine type and timing advance. Installing the wrong amplifier/module assembly will result in poor engine performance and could cause engine damage.*

2A. *Early design amplifier*—Disconnect the amplifier ground wire, the white/red and white/green wires from the distributor and the purple and gray wires from the ignition coil.

2B. *Late design module*—Disconnect the 5-pin connector from the module.

3. Remove the amplifier/module mounting fasteners and remove the amplifier/module.

NOTE
On the late design distributor-mounted ignition module, a suitable thermal-conductive grease must be applied to the back of the module during installation. The grease is necessary to conduct heat away from the module.

4. Install the amplifier/module assembly by reversing the removal procedure while noting the following:

    a. On exhaust elbow-mounted module, be sure the spacers located between the module mounting plate and exhaust elbow are properly installed.

    b. On late, distributor-mounted module, apply an even coat of Quicksilver Thermal-conductive Grease (part No. 92-805701) to the

11

back of the module prior to installing on the distributor.

DDIS IGNITION

Motion Sensor Removal/Installation

The crankshaft motion sensor assembly is mounted where the distributor would normally be installed. The sensor provides crankshaft position information to the ignition module so the module can trigger the proper cylinder (spark plug) to fire.

1. Disconnect the negative battery cable from the battery.

2. Disconnect the 2-pin connector leading from the sensor assembly (**Figure 37**).

3. Remove the 2 screws securing the motion sensor cover. Remove the cover.

4. Scribe a mark onto the sensor housing in line with one tip of the reluctor (**Figure 37**). Scribe a corresponding mark onto the engine.

5. Remove the sensor housing hold-down bolt and clamp. Remove the sensor assembly from the engine.

6. Installation is the reverse of removal. If the crankshaft is rotated while the sensor is out of the engine, position the No. 1 piston at TDC. Make sure the timing mark on the crankshaft damper is aligned with the TDC mark on the timing scale.

7. Position the sensor shaft so one of the reluctor tips with double points will be aligned with the

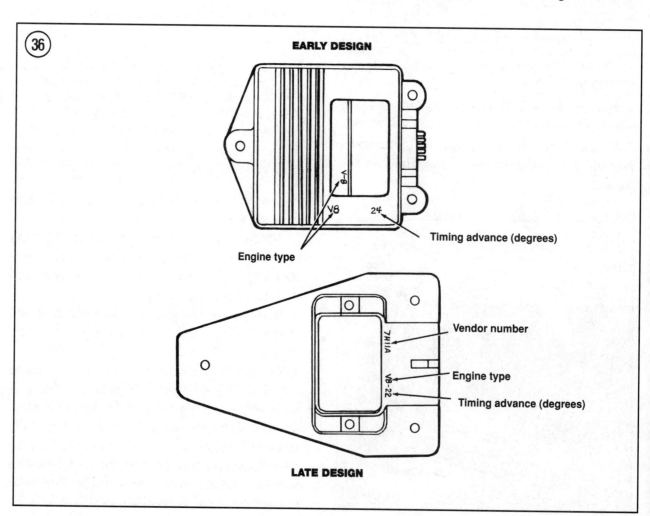

36 **EARLY DESIGN**

Engine type

Timing advance (degrees)

Vendor number

Engine type

Timing advance (degrees)

LATE DESIGN

sensor (**Figure 37**) when the sensor assembly is reinstalled.

> *NOTE*
> *The sensor shaft might have to be moved slightly to engage the camshaft gear and the oil pump drive tang. However, one of the double reluctor tips must be aligned with the sensor when the assembly is in place.*

8. Reconnect the 2-pin connector. Adjust the ignition timing as described in Chapter Four. Tighten the sensor hold-down bolt securely after adjusting the timing.

Ignition Amplifier Removal/Installation

1. Disconnect the negative battery cable from the battery.
2. Disconnect the 2-pin connector (red and white wires) between the amplifier and motion sensor. Disconnect the 3-pin connector (blue, yellow and red wires) between the amplifier and the ignition coil pack.
3. Remove the amplifier mounting fasteners and remove the amplifier.
4. Install by reversing the removal procedure. Tighten the amplifier mounting fasteners securely.

Ignition Coil Pack Removal/Installation

1. Disconnect the negative battery cable from the battery.

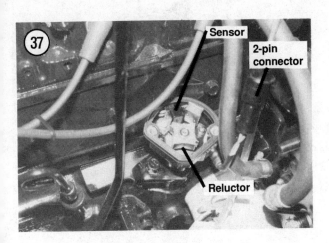

2. Disconnect the 3-pin connector between the coil pack and ignition amplifier.
3. Label the spark plug leads for correct reinstallation. Disconnect the spark plug leads from the coil pack.
4. Remove the coil pack fasteners and remove the coil pack.
5. Install by reversing the removal procedure. Tighten the coil pack mounting fasteners securely. Apply a small amount of Quicksilver Insulating Compound into the secondary lead nipples before installation onto the coil pack to waterproof the connection. Wipe off any excess compound after the lead is fully seated.

EST IGNITION

Distributor Removal/Installation

> *NOTE*
> *Do not turn the crankshaft after distributor removal. If the crankshaft is turned with the distributor removed, refer to **Installation (Engine Rotated After Distributor Removal)** in this chapter.*

1. Remove the distributor cap with the spark plug leads attached. Lay the cap aside.
2. Disconnect the 2-pin and 3-pin connectors from the distributor base.
3. Scribe a mark on the distributor housing aligned with the tip of the rotor. Place corresponding marks on the base of the distributor and the engine.
4. Remove the distributor hold-down bolt and clamp. Lift the distributor assembly from the engine.
5. To reinstall, first make sure the distributor bore area in the engine is clean. Install a new distributor base gasket (if used) onto the distributor.
6. Align the rotor tip with the reference mark made on the distributor during removal. Turn the rotor approximately 1/8 turn counterclockwise past the reference mark. Position the distributor to align the mark on the distributor base with the

match mark on the engine made during removal. Insert the distributor into the engine.

NOTE
The rotor and distributor shaft may have to be rotated slightly to engage the distributor gear with the camshaft drive gear and oil pump drive tang; however, the rotor tip should align with the reference mark on the housing when the distributor is fully seated.

7. Install the distributor hold-down clamp and bolt. Install the bolt snugly, but do not tighten.

8. Reinstall the distributor cap.

9. Reconnect the 2-pin and 3-pin connectors to the distributor base.

10. Adjust the ignition timing as described in Chapter Four. Securely tighten the distributor hold-down bolt after the timing is properly adjusted.

Pickup Coil Removal/Installation

1. Remove the distributor as described in this chapter.

2. Place match marks onto the distributor drive gear and shaft so the gear can be reinstalled on the shaft in the original position.

3. Carefully drive out the roll pin securing the gear to the shaft. Slide the shaft assembly out of the distributor housing.

4. Disconnect the pickup coil connector (A, **Figure 38**) from the ignition module.

5. Carefully pry off the pickup coil retainer (B, **Figure 38**). Lift the pickup coil off the distributor housing.

6. To reinstall the pickup coil, align the locating tab as shown in **Figure 39** and place the coil onto the pole piece. Make sure the pickup coil is properly seated on the pole piece.

7. Install the pickup coil retainer making sure the locking tabs are securely engaged in the groove.

8. Lubricate the distributor shaft with clean engine oil and insert the shaft into the distributor housing.

9. Install the drive gear onto the distributor shaft, aligning the match marks made in Step 2. Drive a *new* roll pin through the gear and shaft. The pin should be flush on both sides.

Distributor Shaft/Magnet Assembly Removal/Installation

Remove and reinstall the distributor shaft/magnet assembly as described under *Pickup Coil Removal/Installation* in this chapter.

Ignition Module Removal/Installation

The distributor does not normally require removal to replace the ignition module.

1. Remove the 2 screws securing the distributor cap. Remove the distributor cap and lay to one side. Remove the distributor rotor.

2. Remove the 4-pin and 2-pin connectors from the ignition module.

3. Remove the 2 module mounting screws (C, **Figure 38**) and lift the module off the distributor.

4. Thoroughly clean all silicone grease from the module and distributor mounting surfaces.

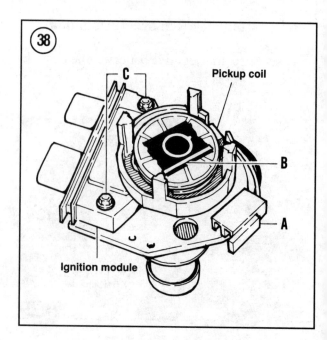

5. To install the module, apply an even coat of silicone grease or a suitable heat sink compound to the mounting surface of the module.

6. Place the module on the distributor, install the mounting screws and tighten securely.

7. Install the rotor and distributor cap.

IGNITION COIL

A conventional oil-filled ignition coil is used on models equipped with breaker-point and Thunderbolt IV ignition systems. **Figure 40** shows a typical installation. The Thunderbolt coil contains a special winding and core. Because of its low output, a standard breaker-point coil should not be used with a Thunderbolt IV system.

The ignition coil on DDIS systems is actually 2 coils with 4 high voltage towers. **Figure 29**

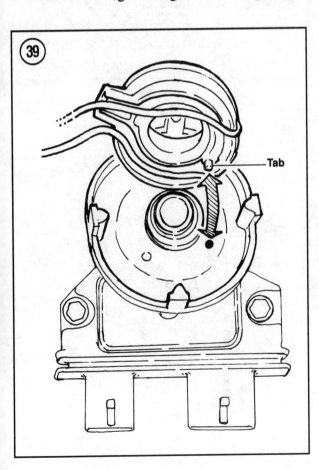

shows a typical installation. The coils fire on both compression and exhaust strokes. The ignition coil used on EST systems is a metal laminated design with epoxy-coated windings to prevent moisture from entering the coil.

Whenever the secondary lead(s) is removed from the ignition coil or distributor cap, pack a small amount of Quicksilver Insulating Compound (part No. 92-41669-1) into the secondary nipple to waterproof the connection. Wipe off any excess compound after the lead is fully seated.

Ignition coils can be tested using an ohmmeter. However, resistance tests generally only detect open or shorted windings. For this reason, do not fail a coil that is only slightly out of specification. Refer to Chapter Three for testing procedures. A more reliable test for ignition coils can be performed using a suitable ignition analyzer. Follow the instructions included with the analyzer. See **Table 3** for specifications.

Ignition Coil Removal/Installation

1. Disconnect the high tension lead from the coil.

2A. *Except EST ignition*—Disconnect the primary ignition wires from the coil. Reinstall the nuts onto the coil studs to prevent loss.

2B. *EST ignition*—Disconnect the distributor harness connector and engine harness connector from the coil.

3. Remove the coil mounting fasteners and remove the coil.

4. Reverse the removal procedure to install the coil. Tighten the mounting fasteners securely.

IGNITION RESISTOR WIRE (BREAKER POINT IGNITION)

A replacement ignition resistance wire (part No. 84-94227A2) is available and should be installed according to the instructions accompanying it if the old wire proves to be faulty. The test procedure used depends upon whether or not the engine is equipped with an electric choke heater element.

Testing (With Choke Heater Element)

1. Disconnect the positive coil lead at the coil.
2. Unplug the electric choke heater element connector at the carburetor.
3. Connect ohmmeter test leads between the 2 disconnected choke heater wires. If the reading is not within 1.8-2.0 ohms, replace the resistor wire.

Testing (Without Choke Heater Element)

1. Disconnect the positive coil lead at the coil.
2. Unplug the engine and instrumentation harness connectors.
3. Connect one ohmmeter lead to the disconnected coil lead.
4. Connect the other ohmmeter lead to the No. 5 terminal pin hole in the engine harness (**Figure 41**). If ohmmeter reading is not within 1.8-2.0 ohms, replace the resistor wire.

SWITCHES AND CONNECTORS

Switches can be tested with an ohmmeter or a self-powered test lamp. If a switch does not perform properly, replace it.

Many electrical problems encountered are due to poor connections in the waterproof connec-

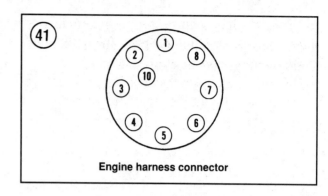

Engine harness connector

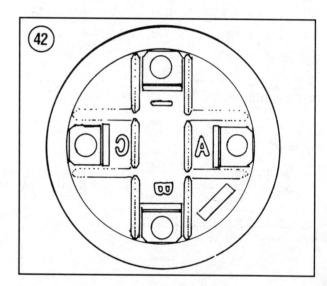

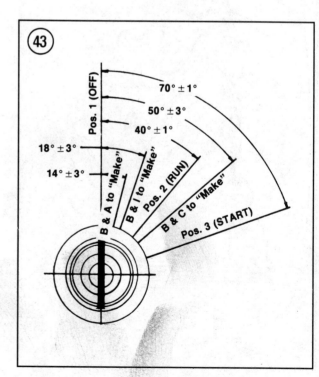

tors. If the pins and sockets are improperly seated in their connectors, the resulting electrical connection will be poor or non-existent.

Ignition Switch

Disconnect the negative battery cable when testing the ignition switch in the boat. Refer to **Figure 42** and **Figure 43** for this procedure.

1. Test all switch terminals (**Figure 42**) with an ohmmeter or self-powered test lamp and the ignition key in the OFF position. There should be no continuity between the switch terminals.

2. Turn the switch to the RUN position (No. 2) and test terminals. There should be no continuity between terminals B and A and between B and 1. There should be no continuity between the C terminal and any of the other terminals.
3. Turn the switch to the START position (No. 3) and test terminals. There should be continuity between terminals B and A, B and 1 and B and C.
4. Make sure the terminals make contact at the angles shown in **Figure 43**. They must remain in contact as the switch is rotated to the START position.
5. If any switch position does not check out as described, unsolder the wires and remove the switch. Repeat Steps 1-3 with the switch out of the instrument panel. If the switch now performs as specified, the problem is in the wiring. If the switch still fails the continuity check, replace it.

Power Trim 3-Button Control Panel Switch

Testing

Refer to **Figure 44** for this procedure.
1. Disconnect the trim pump wire harness.
2. Place one button in its free position and connect an ohmmeter between the corresponding terminals on the rear of the switch. There should be no continuity.
3. Depress button to place it in the ON position and repeat Step 2. There should be no continuity between the terminals.
4. Repeat Step 2 and Step 3 for each remaining button.

Removal/installation

1. Disconnect the power trim pump harness.
2. Remove the control panel from its mounting hole in the instrument panel.
3. Remove the retainer screws from the rear of the switch. Remove the retainer and switch from the control panel.

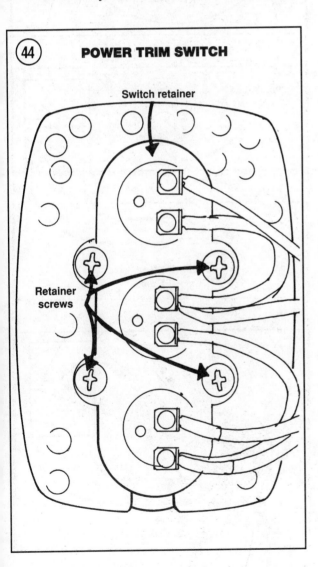

(44) POWER TRIM SWITCH

Switch retainer

Retainer screws

11

4. Unsolder the wire connections from the old switch. Solder the wires to the new switch terminals as shown in **Figure 44**.

5. Coat the wire terminals with Quicksilver Liquid Neoprene.

6. Reverse Steps 1-3 to install the switch.

Power Trim Indicator (Rotary Sender Switch)

Refer to **Figure 45** for this procedure.

1. Remove the sender unit and connect an ohmmeter to the sender leads.

2. Align sender housing and rotor shaft index marks. Sender resistance should be 0-160 ohms (single installation) or 0-80 ohms (dual installation).

3. If the meter needle does not move or if its movement is erratic, replace the sender.

Neutral Safety Switch

1. Disconnect the switch leads from the starter solenoid or slave solenoid and terminal block on the flywheel.

2. Connect an ohmmeter between the switch leads. Shift the remote control into NEUTRAL, FORWARD and REVERSE. The ohmmeter should indicate continuity only as the remote control unit is shifted into NEUTRAL.

3. If continuity is shown in FORWARD or REVERSE, or if there is no continuity in NEUTRAL, replace the switch.

Emergency Stop Switch

1. Remove switch leads from their connections. Tape the white lead back to the switch harness.

2. With the switch cap in place, connect the ohmmeter between the leads (**Figure 46**). There should be no continuity.

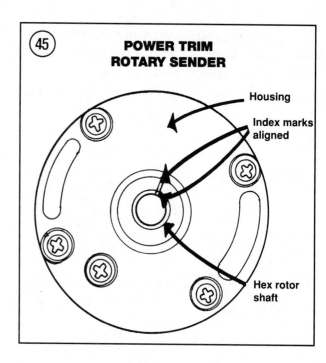

POWER TRIM ROTARY SENDER

- Housing
- Index marks aligned
- Hex rotor shaft

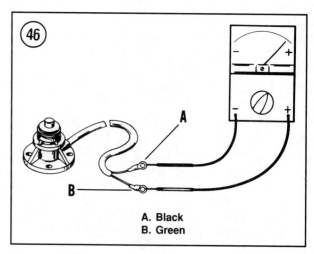

A. Black
B. Green

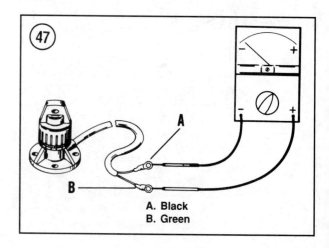

A. Black
B. Green

3. Remove the switch cap with the ohmmeter connected between the leads (**Figure 47**). There should be continuity.

4. If the switch does not perform as specified in Step 2 and Step 3, replace it.

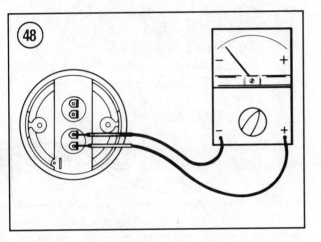

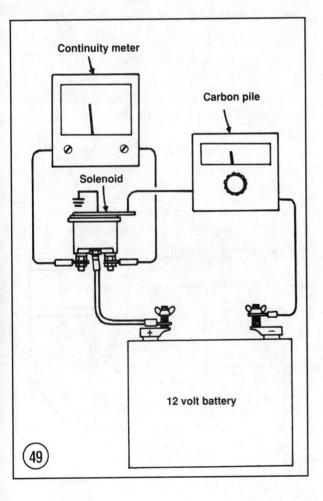

Stop/Start Switch Panel

Refer to **Figure 48** for this procedure.

1. Disconnect the negative battery cable.

2. Connect an ohmmeter between the start switch terminals. There should be no continuity.

3. Depress the switch button with the ohmmeter connected to the switch terminals. There should now be continuity.

4. Repeat Step 2 and Step 3 to check the stop switch.

5. If either switch does not perform as specified in Step 2 and Step 3, replace the panel button.

SOLENOIDS

Solenoids are used with the starter and tilt motors to carry the large amount of electrical current used by the motors. The solenoid is a completely sealed and non-serviceable unit. The 2 large terminals are the battery and motor terminals. The small terminal is the switch control. Ground is internal through the solenoid bracket. If a solenoid is suspected of faulty operation, test it as follows:

1. Connect a volt/ohmmeter between the 2 large solenoid terminals. See **Figure 49**.

2. Connect a carbon pile as shown in **Figure 49** and reduce the voltage to under 6 volts.

3. Adjust the carbon pile until the ohmmeter or test lamp shows a complete circuit. At this point, the voltmeter should show a reading of 6-8 volts. If more than 8 volts are required to complete the circuit, replace the solenoid.

OIL PRESSURE SWITCH/SENDER UNIT

All engines are equipped with an oil pressure switch or sender unit connected to the oil pressure gauge. The switch/sender designation is stamped on the unit hex. Test the operation of the sending unit as follows.

11

Switch 364-AF

1. Disconnect the wire at the sender terminal.
2. Connect an ohmmeter between the sender terminal and the hex on the base of the sender (**Figure 50**).
3. With the engine off, the meter should show continuity.
4. Start the engine. As the oil pressure builds above 6 psi, the meter should switch from continuity to no continuity. If it does not, replace the sender unit.

Sender 353-AM

1. Disconnect the wire at the sender terminal.
2. Connect an ohmmeter between the sender terminal and the hex on the base of the sender (**Figure 50**).
3. With the engine off, the meter should read 227-257 ohms (single station sender) or 113.5-128.5 ohms (dual station sender).
4. Start the engine. As the oil pressure builds above 6 psi, the meter reading should drop to 142-162.5 ohms at 20 psi, 91.7-113.6 ohms at 40 psi and 9-49 ohms at 89 psi. For dual station senders, the reading should be one-half of that specified for single station senders.

WATER TEMPERATURE SENDING UNIT

All engine are equipped with a temperature sending unit or water temperature switch connected to the temperature gauge or indicator light. The normally open switch should close at a specified temperature range and reopen as the temperature decreases. The two different switches used can be identified by the color of their mylar sleeve: the 48952 switch has a red sleeve; the 87-86080 switch has a black sleeve. Test the operation of the switch as follows:
1. Remove the switch from the engine.
2. Connect a digital ohmmeter to the switch.
3. Immerse the sending unit and a cooking thermometer in a container of oil.

4. Heat the container over a flameless source and note the ohmmeter reading. The switch should close as follows:
   a. 48952 switch—190-200° F
   b. 87-86080 switch—215-225° F
5. Remove the container from the heat and let it cool. The switch should reopen as follows:
   a. 48952 switch—150-170° F
   b. 87-86080 switch—175-195° F
6. Replace the switch if it does not function as specified at each temperature range.

ELECTRICAL PROTECTION

All engines are equipped with a 50- or 60-amp circuit breaker installed in the wiring harness between the ignition switch and starter motor. Individual circuits are fused. If additional electrical accessories are added to any installation, install individual fused circuits for each accessory with power takeoff at the terminal block.

Whenever a failure occurs in any part of the electrical system, always check the fuse first to see if it is blown. Usually, the trouble is a short circuit in the wiring. This may be caused by worn-through insulation or by a wire that has worked its way loose and shorted to ground. Occasionally, the electrical overload which causes a fuse to blow may occur in a switch or motor.

A blown fuse should be treated as more than a minor annoyance; it should serve as a warning that something is wrong in the electrical system.

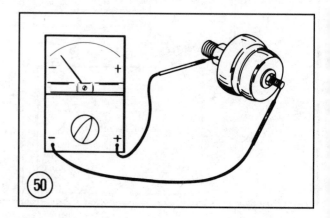

Before replacing a fuse, determine what caused it to blow and correct the problem. Always carry several spare fuses of the proper amperage values onboard. Never replace a fuse with one of higher amperage rating than that specified for use. Failure to follow these basic rules could result in heat or fire damage to major parts or even the loss of the entire vessel.

WIRING HARNESS WITH AUDIO WARNING SYSTEM

All 1989-on MerCruiser engines incorporate an audio warning circuit that sounds an alert to the operator whenever the oil pressure is too low or the engine temperature is too high. **Figure 51** shows a typical instrumentation wiring harness

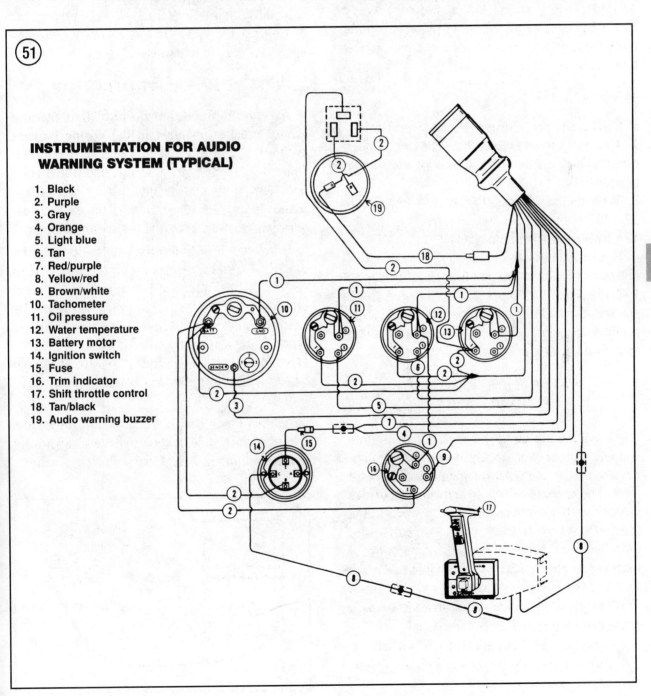

INSTRUMENTATION FOR AUDIO WARNING SYSTEM (TYPICAL)

1. Black
2. Purple
3. Gray
4. Orange
5. Light blue
6. Tan
7. Red/purple
8. Yellow/red
9. Brown/white
10. Tachometer
11. Oil pressure
12. Water temperature
13. Battery motor
14. Ignition switch
15. Fuse
16. Trim indicator
17. Shift throttle control
18. Tan/black
19. Audio warning buzzer

11

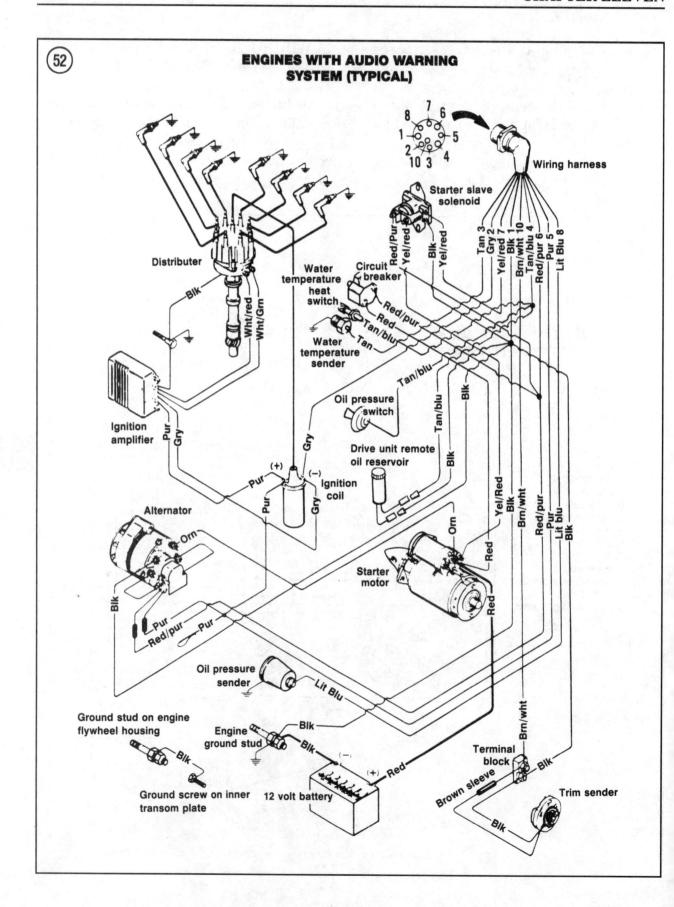

(52)

ENGINES WITH AUDIO WARNING SYSTEM (TYPICAL)

Wiring harness

Distributer

Blk

Wht/red

Wht/Grn

Ignition amplifier

Pur

Gry

Alternator

Orn

Blk

Pur

Red/pur

Pur

Water temperature heat switch

Water temperature sender

Oil pressure switch

Drive unit remote oil reservoir

Ignition coil

Pur (+)

Pur

Gry (−)

Gry

Circuit breaker

Red/pur

Red

Tan/blu

Tan

Starter slave solenoid

Red/Pur

Yel/red

Blk

Yel/red

Tan 3

Gry 2

Yel/red 7

Blk 1

Brn/wht 10

Tan/blu 4

Red/pur 6

Pur 5

Lit Blu 8

Tan/blu

Tan/blu

Blk

Blk

Red

Yel/Red

Blk

Brn/wht

Red/pur

Pur

Lit blu

Blk

Orn

Starter motor

Red

Oil pressure sender

Lit Blu

Ground stud on engine flywheel housing

Blk

Ground screw on inner transom plate

Engine ground stud

Blk

Blk

12 volt battery

(−)

(+) Red

Terminal block

Brn/wht

Blk

Brown sleeve

Trim sender

Blk

at incorporates the audio warning circuit. **Figure 52** shows a typical engine wiring harness that incorporates the audio warning circuit.

Replacement wiring harnesses have the lead or the audio warning system integrated into the harness, eliminating the need to route and connect a separate lead for this system. A bullet-type connector (**Figure 51**) permits fast and easy connection of the dash-mounted warning buzzer to the instrumentation harness.

The engine wiring harness is designed to permit the use of older instrumentation harness of the standard large 2-pin type with a separate lead for the audio warning system. The large 3-pin instrumentation harness cannot be used with the new engine wiring harness design.

Table 1 MERCRUISER BATTERY REQUIREMENTS

Engine	Cold cranking amperage
2.5L	375
3.0L	375
3.7L	450
4.3L	450
5.0L, 5.7L	450
7.4L/8.2L	550 (min.)

Table 2 BATTERY CHARGING GUIDE (6- AND 12-VOLT BATTERIES)

Twenty hour rating	Recommended rate* and time for fully discharged condition					
	5 amps	10 amps	20 amps	30 amps	40 amps	50 amps
50 amp-hrs. or less	10 hrs.	5 hrs.	2 1/2 hrs.	2 hrs.		
Above 50 to 75 amp-hrs.	15 hrs.	7 1/2 hrs.	3 1/4 hrs.	2 1/2 hrs.	2 hrs.	1 1/2 hrs.
Above 75 to 100 amp-hrs.	20 hrs.	10 hrs.	5 hrs.	3 hrs.	2 1/2 hrs.	2 hrs.
Above 100 to 150 amp-hrs.	30 hrs.	15 hrs.	7 1/2 hrs.	5 hrs.	3 1/2 hrs.	3 hrs.
Above 150 amp-hrs.		20 hrs.	10 hrs.	6 1/2 hrs.	5 hrs.	4 hrs.

* Initial rate for constant voltage taper rate charger.
To avoid damage, charging rate must be reduced or temporarily halted if:
1. Electrolyte temperature exceeds 125° F (52° C).
2. Violent gassing or spewing of electrolyte occurs.
Battery is fully charged when, over a two hour period @ a low charging rate in amps, all cells are gassing freely and no change in specific gravity occurs. For the most satisfactory charging, the lower charging rates in amps are recommended.
Full charge specific gravity is 1.250-1.280, corrected for temperature with electrolyte level @ split ring.

11

Table 3 IGNITION COIL SPECIFICATIONS

Coil number	Resistance (ohms @ 75° F)		Maximum operating amperage
	Primary	Secondary	
26433	0.9-1.2	7,500-10,500	0.9
32193	1.1-1.5	9,500-15,000	1.1
392-7803/ 392-7803A4	0.6-0.8	9,400-11,700	NA

Table 4 MERCRUISER WIRING COLOR CROSS-REFERENCE

Old color	NMMA (new) color	Application
Black	Black	All ground
Black	Brown	MerCathode reference electrode
Black	Orange	MerCathode anode electrode
Blue	Lt. blue/white	Trim up switch
Brown	Gray	Tachometer signal
Green	Green/white	Trim down switch
Green	Tan	Water temperature sender to gauge
Orange	Lt. blue	Oil pressure sender to gauge
Pink	Pink	Fuel gauge sender to gauge
Purple	Brown/white	Trim sender to trim gauge
Purple	Purple/white	Trim trailer switch
Red	Red	Unfused wires from battery
Red	Red/purple	Fused wires from battery
Red	Red/purple	Fused wires to trim panel
Red/white	Orange	Alternator output to ammeter or voltmeter
Tan	Purple/yellow	Ballast bypass
White	Purple	Ignition switch
Yellow	Yellow	Starter solenoid to stator motor (Model 470)
Yellow	Yellow/red	Starter switch to starter solenoid to neutral start switch

Chapter Twelve

Mercruiser Drive System

This chapter provides removal and installation procedures for all MerCruiser Alpha One, Bravo One, Bravo Two and Bravo Three stern drive models and inner transom plate assemblies. Repair procedures for individual subsections are given in the chapters that follow. Engine removal and installation procedures are described in the appropriate engine chapter. Refer to Chapter Six (GM inline engines), Chapter Seven (MerCruiser inline engines) or Chapter Eight (GM V6 and V8 engines).

Stern drive removal is generally a fairly simple procedure. However, if the unit has not been removed recently or if it has been subjected to considerable corrosion, it may be necessary to use some force in excess of that normally required. In some cases, it may even be necessary to heat components with a torch to free frozen bearings or shafts.

Installation of the stern drive is more complex than removal, requiring both time and patience. Components must be properly aligned and care

should be taken in mating them to prevent possible bearing, gasket or seal damage.

Table 1 at the end of the chapter contains a reference guide to engine/stern drive installations by model and year, as well as a list of the stern drive gear ratios by engine usage.

CAUTION
Stern drive removal and installation involves the use of elastic stop nuts. Such nuts should never be used more than twice. When elastic stop nuts are used, it is a good idea to replace them with new nuts during reinstallation. Never use worn-out nuts or non-locking nuts.

MERCRUISER ALPHA ONE DRIVE

The Alpha One gear housing was introduced on 1986 MerCruiser stern drives. The Alpha One gear housing is a completely redesigned version of the earlier Model I-MR drive and is intended to provide extended service life. It is fully interchangeable with the previous Model I-MR and can be installed as a replacement for any 1974 and later MerCruiser Model I drive with a short slot in the shift plate lever (**Figure 1**).

The Alpha One SS models are nearly identical to the MR and Alpha One units except the drive shaft is slightly shorter and the leading edge of the gearcase housing is crescent shaped. Service procedures on Alpha One SS models are identical to MR and Alpha One units.

Alpha One Generation II models were introduced on the 1991 MerCruiser models. Some of the significant changes in the second generation models include: a redesigned 2-piece shift shaft, a fitting to connect a gear lube monitor, an internal speedometer pickup and a volume-type water pump which uses a floppy-vane impeller designed for extended service life. Although most service on Generation II Alpha One units is the same as on earlier models, the Generation II is not interchangeable with earlier units (prior to 1991).

Stern Drive Removal

1. Shift the drive unit into FORWARD gear.
2. On Generation II models, raise the drive unit enough to gain access to the speedometer pickup fitting. The fitting is located at the top front of the antiventilation plate. Disconnect the speedometer pickup by turning the top half of the fitting counterclockwise, then pulling straight up.
3. Disconnect the aft end of each trim cylinder from the drive unit. See Chapter Sixteen.
4. On models prior to 1991 equipped with a lube oil monitor, disconnect the remote oil reservoir hole from the port side of the drive shaft housing. Plug the hose and the drive unit hole to prevent leakage.
5. Remove the 6 elastic stop nuts and washers from the stern drive-to-bell housing studs (**Figure 2**). If equipped with a continuity circuit, a ground plate will be used in place of 1 washer and should not be removed. See inset, **Figure 2**.

WARNING
Do not attempt to remove the stern drive unit from the boat in Step 6 without the aid of a suitable hoist for support. The unit is heavy and may slip from your grasp, causing damage to the stern drive and possible personal injury.

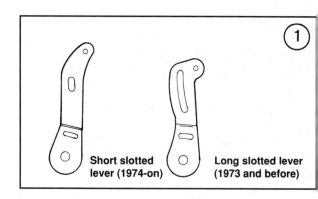

Short slotted lever (1974-on)   Long slotted lever (1973 and before)

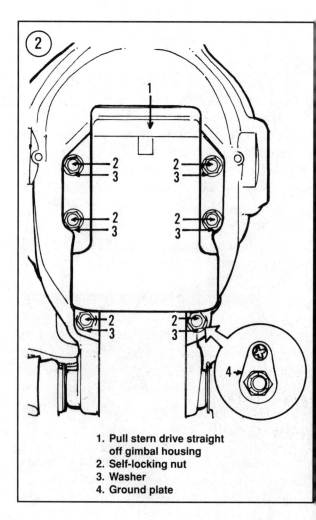

1. Pull stern drive straight off gimbal housing
2. Self-locking nut
3. Washer
4. Ground plate

. Attach an overhead hoist to the stern drive top cover with a suitable lifting eye and an appropriate sling. Support the unit with the hoist.

. Carefully guide the stern drive unit straight back and remove it from the boat.

. Lower stern drive to the ground and remove the hoist.

. Remove and discard the bell housing gasket. See **Figure 3**.

0. Support trim cylinders. This can be done by wiring them to the bell housing studs. If the drive

is going to be off the bell housing for any length of time, a better idea is to cut and drill a piece of wood to form a support as shown in **Figure 4**.

Stern Drive Installation

1. If engine was removed, reinstall and check alignment. See Chapters Six-Eight, as appropriate.

2. Remove trim cylinder supports and carefully lower cylinders to the ground.

3. If bell housing rubber gasket and O-ring were removed, install new ones. See **Figure 5**.

4. Lubricate the bell housing studs and the shifting slide assembly with Quicksilver 2-4-C Multi-Lube. See **Figure 5**. Make sure the shifting slide assembly is engaged with the shift shaft lever.

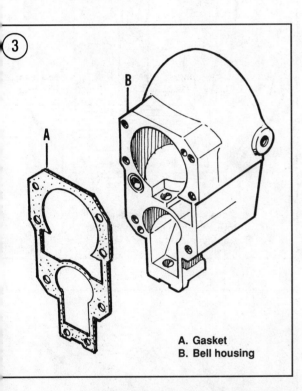

A. Gasket
B. Bell housing

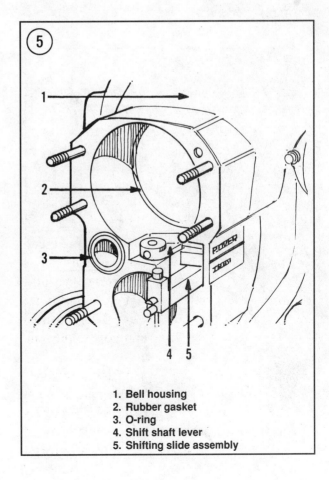

1. Bell housing
2. Rubber gasket
3. O-ring
4. Shift shaft lever
5. Shifting slide assembly

12

5. Lubricate the drive shaft and U-joint assembly with 2-4-C Multi-Lube at the points shown in **Figure 6**.

6. Correctly position the shift shaft coupler by moving the shifting slide assembly fore and aft. Make sure the shift shaft slot faces straight ahead. See **Figure 7**. Lubricate the coupler with 2-4-C Multi-Lube.

7. Make sure the stern drive is in FORWARD gear. The shift shaft coupler on the stern drive will face straight ahead as shown in **Figure 8**.

8. Install a new bell housing gasket. See **Figure 3**. If the unit is equipped with a gear lube monitor, the gasket must have a hole punched for the oil passages. Be sure to use the correct gasket.

9. If the unit has a wide splash plate (**Figure 9**), position the trim cylinders on top of the splash plate.

10. Align the drive unit U-joint with the gimbal bearing.

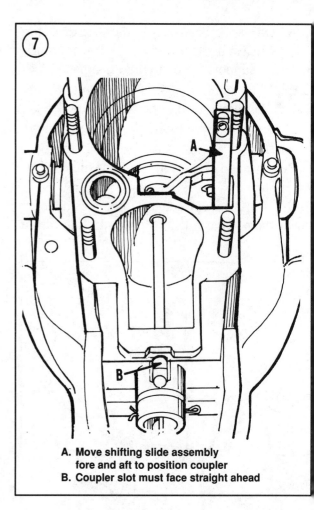

A. Move shifting slide assembly fore and aft to position coupler
B. Coupler slot must face straight ahead

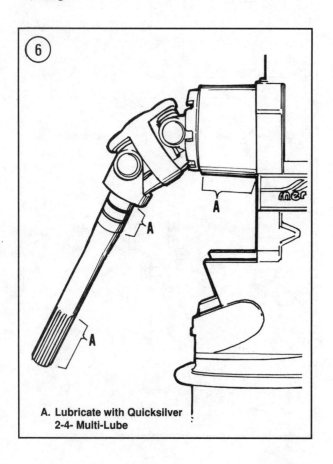

A. Lubricate with Quicksilver 2-4- Multi-Lube

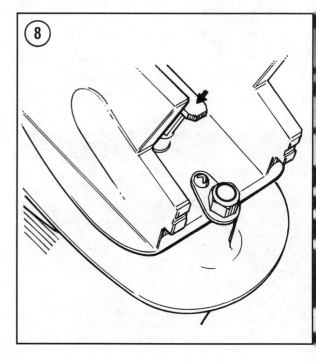

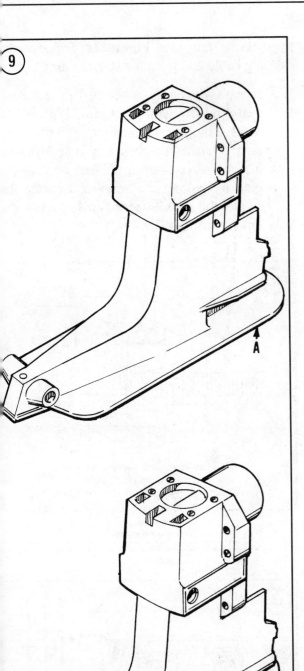

A. Wide splash plate
B. Narrow splash plate

Do not attempt to install the stern drive unit to the boat in Step 11 without the aid of a suitable hoist for support. The unit is heavy and may slip from your grasp, causing damage to the stern drive and possible personal injury.

11. Attach an overhead hoist to the stern drive top cover with a suitable lifting eye and an appropriate sling. Support the unit with the hoist.

NOTE
If the universal joint shaft splines do not engage with the engine coupling splines in Step 12, rotate the propeller shaft counterclockwise until the stern drive can be pushed into position.

12. Install the stern drive to the bell housing, guiding the universal joint shaft through the gimbal housing bearing and into the engine coupling. At the same time, guide the shift shaft into the drive shaft housing opening and into the coupler slot (**Figure 10**). Do not move the shift shaft assembly or coupler.

12

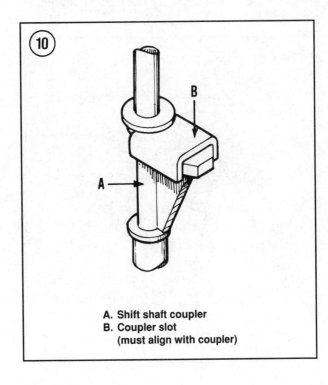

A. Shift shaft coupler
B. Coupler slot
(must align with coupler)

13. Install a flat washer and new elastic stop nut on each stern drive-to-bell housing stud (except a stud fitted with a ground plate). See **Figure 2**. Start with the center nuts and tighten to 50 ft.-lb. (68 N·m).

14. Raise the drive unit enough to gain access to the speedometer fitting located at the top front of the antiventilation plate. Reconnect the speedometer fitting by aligning the plastic fittings, then pushing down and turning the top half clockwise to engage the locking device.

15. On models prior to 1991 equipped with a lube oil monitor, reconnect the remote oil reservoir hose to the drive shaft housing.

16. Reinstall the aft end of each trim cylinder to the stern drive housing. See Chapter Sixteen.

Transom Plate Removal/Installation

1. Remove the stern drive as described in this chapter.

2. Remove the engine. See Chapters Six-Eight as appropriate.

3A. Manual steering—Remove the cotter pin from the clevis pin securing the steering cable to the steering arm. See **Figure 11**. Separate the steering cable end from the steering arm.

   a. If the swivel ring is secured to the inner transom plate with pivot pins (**Figure 12**), remove the 2 cotter pins securing the pivot pins. Thread appropriate size screws into the end of each pivot pin and remove the pins by pulling the screws. Separate the swivel ring and steering cable from the inner transom plate.

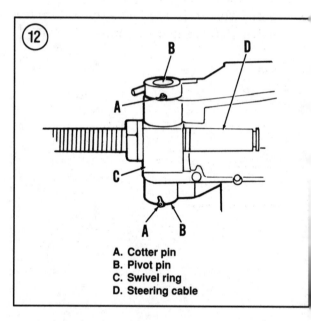

A. Cotter pin
B. Pivot pin
C. Swivel ring
D. Steering cable

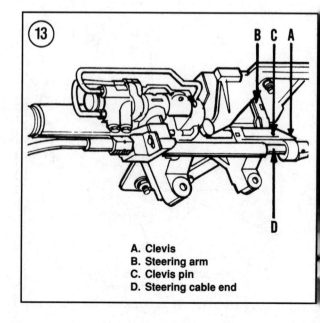

A. Clevis
B. Steering arm
C. Clevis pin
D. Steering cable end

A. Cotter pin
B. Clevis pin
C. Steering arm
D. Steering cable
E. Pivot balls
F. Swivel ring

b. If the swivel ring is secured to the inner transom plate with pivot bolts (**Figure 11**), bend the tab of the locking tab washer away from the pivot bolt head. Loosen the pivot bolts until the swivel ring can be separated from the inner transom plate.

3B. Power steering—Disconnect the clevis from the steering arm. Remove the clevis from the steering cable. See **Figure 13**.

a. Disconnect the power steering hydraulic hoses from the power steering unit control valve. Plug the hoses to prevent leakage.

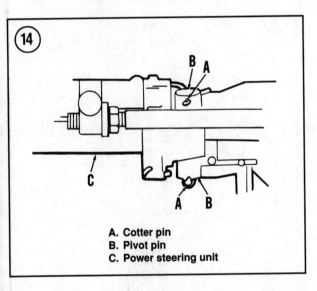

A. Cotter pin
B. Pivot pin
C. Power steering unit

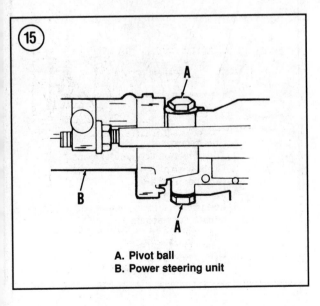

A. Pivot ball
B. Power steering unit

b. If the power steering unit is secured to the inner transom plate with pivot pins (**Figure 14**), remove the cotter pins securing the pivot pins. Thread appropriate size screws into the ends of each pivot pin, then remove the pins by pulling the screws. Separate the power steering unit from the inner transom plate.

c. If the power steering unit is secured to the inner transom plate with pivot bolts (**Figure 15**), bend the tabs of the locking tab washers away from the pivot bolt heads. Remove the pivot bolts and separate the power steering unit from the inner transom plate.

4. Disconnect the remote reservoir hose if equipped with a gear lube monitor.

5. Disconnect the speedometer pickup hose, if so equipped.

6. Disconnect the MerCathode wires, if so equipped.

7. Disconnect the trim limit switch wires. Disconnect and plug the power trim hoses from the pump assembly. See Chapter Sixteen.

8. Unbolt and remove the exhaust pipe assembly. See **Figure 16** (4-cylinder) or **Figure 17** (V6 and V8).

9. Disconnect the ground wire attached to the steering arm.

12

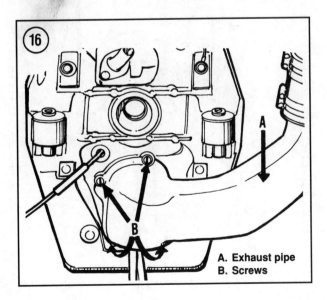

A. Exhaust pipe
B. Screws

10. Pull the hydraulic hoses, drive unit shift cable and trim sender leads through the inner transom plate.

NOTE
The gimbal housing must be secured or supported to prevent it from falling prior to removing the transom plate fasteners in Step 11.

11. Remove the transom plate fasteners. See **Figure 18**. Remove the inner transom plate from the transom gimbal housing.

12. During transom plate installation, make sure all anode head bolts have a new rubber seal to prevent water from leaking into the boat.

13. Install the inner transom plate assembly. Pull all cables and wires completely through the inner transom plate to prevent pinching.

14. Install the transom plate fasteners. Tighten the fasteners evenly to 20-25 ft.-lb. (27-34 N·m). Tighten the center fasteners first, and work outward.

15. Reconnect the remote reservoir hose, if equipped with a gear lube monitor.

16. Reconnect the speedometer pickup hose, if so equipped.

17. Reinstall the exhaust pipe. Make sure the exhaust pipe and gimbal housing mating surfaces are clean and free from nicks or scratches. Make sure the O-ring is properly seated or water and/or exhaust gasses can enter the boat. Tighten the exhaust pipe fasteners to 20-25 ft.-lb. (27-34 N·m).

18. Reconnect the power trim hydraulic hoses to the pump assembly. Use caution not to cross-thread the hose fittings.

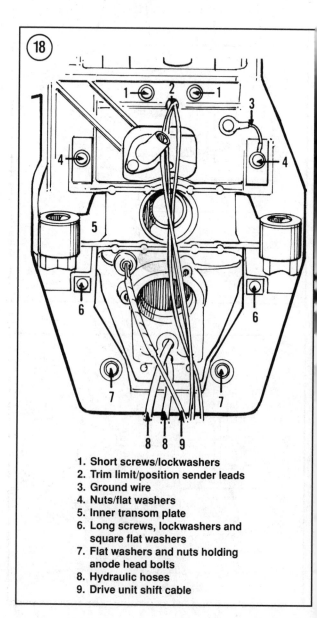

1. Short screws/lockwashers
2. Trim limit/position sender leads
3. Ground wire
4. Nuts/flat washers
5. Inner transom plate
6. Long screws, lockwashers and square flat washers
7. Flat washers and nuts holding anode head bolts
8. Hydraulic hoses
9. Drive unit shift cable

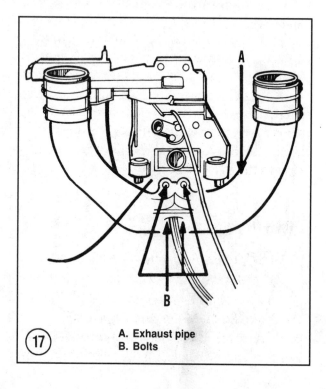

A. Exhaust pipe
B. Bolts

9. Lubricate the steering swivel ring, clevis pins, steering cable end and pivot pins or pivot bolts with Quicksilver Special Lube 101. Reconnect the swivel ring to the inner transom plate. Reconnect the steering cable end to the steering arm. Install the clevis pins and secure with new cotter pins. Tighten the pivot bolts (if so equipped) to 25 ft.-lb. (34 N.m). Bend the locking tab washers securely over against the pivot bolt heads.

20. Reinstall the engine. See Chapters Six-Eight as appropriate. Reinstall the stern drive unit as described in this chapter. Complete the remaining reinstallation by reversing the removal procedure.

MERCRUISER BRAVO ONE, BRAVO TWO AND BRAVO THREE DRIVE

The Bravo One stern drive was introduced in 1988 to provide the durability necessary for use with high-horsepower engines used in high-performance sport boats and fast cruisers. The Bravo Two stern drive was introduced in 1989 and was designed specifically for large cruiser applications, which require high propeller thrust to plane quickly and stay on plane at lower speeds. The gearcase housing used on the Bravo Two is physically larger than the Bravo One, and also uses larger shafts, bearings and gears to withstand the added load associated with higher propeller thrust. The Bravo Three stern drive was introduced for the 1993 model year. The Bravo Three has twin, counter-rotating propellers and is designed for use on fast cruisers and large runabouts which typically run in the 40-60 mph range. Except for the gearcase housings (lower units), the Bravo Two and Bravo Three are identical to the Bravo One unit.

Stern Drive Removal

1. Shift the remote control into NEUTRAL.
2. Tilt the drive unit to the fully UP position.
3. Disconnect the speedometer hose fitting at the drive shaft housing. See **Figure 19**.
4. Return the drive unit to the fully DOWN position and disconnect the aft end of each trim

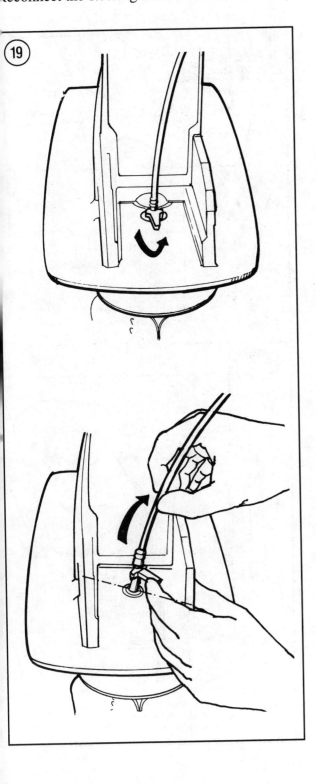

12

cylinder from the drive unit. See Chapter Sixteen.

5. Remove the 6 elastic stop nuts and washers from the stern drive-to-bell housing studs (**Figure 20**). If equipped with a continuity circuit, a ground plate is used in place of 2 washers and should not be removed. See **Figure 20**.

> *WARNING*
> *Do not attempt to remove the stern drive unit from the boat in Step 6 without the aid of a suitable hoist for support. The unit is heavy and may slip from your grasp, causing damage to the stern drive and possible personal injury.*

6. Attach an overhead hoist to the stern drive top cover with a suitable lifting eye and an appropriate sling. Support the unit with the hoist.

7. Carefully guide the stern drive unit straight back, making sure that the shift slide jaws open enough to release the end of the shift cable

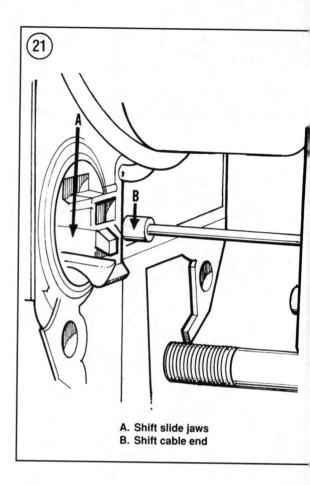

A. Shift slide jaws
B. Shift cable end

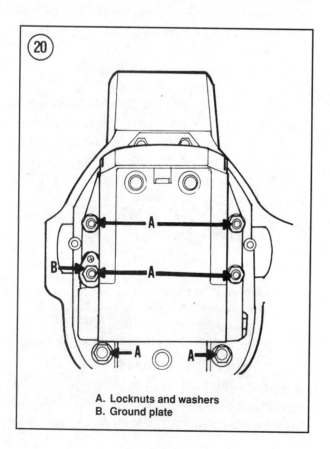

A. Locknuts and washers
B. Ground plate

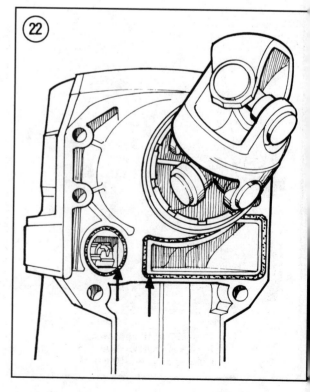

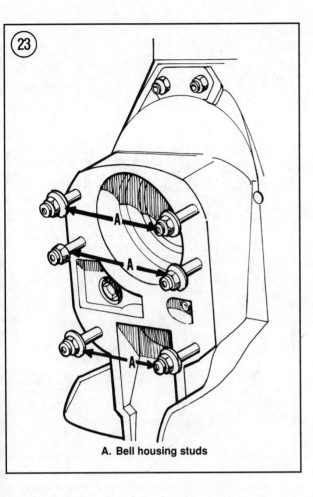

A. Bell housing studs

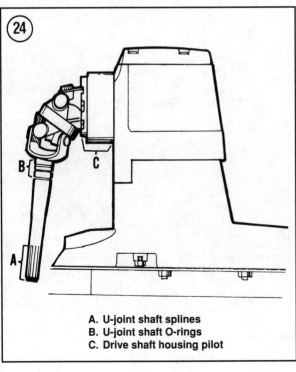

A. U-joint shaft splines
B. U-joint shaft O-rings
C. Drive shaft housing pilot

12

(**Figure 21**). Remove the stern drive from the boat.

8. Lower the stern drive to the ground and remove the hoist.

9. Support trim cylinders. This can be done by wiring them to the bell housing studs. If the drive is going to be off the bell housing for any length of time, a better idea is to cut and drill a piece of wood to form a support as shown in **Figure 4**.

Stern Drive Installation

1. If engine was removed, reinstall and check alignment. See Chapters Six-Eight, as appropriate. If shift cable was disconnected from engine, reinstall and adjust. See Chapter Fifteen.

2. Make sure the remote control is in NEUTRAL.

3. If drive shaft housing O-rings were removed, install new ones. See **Figure 22**. Lubricate O-rings with Quicksilver 2-4-C Multi-Lube.

4. Remove trim cylinder supports and carefully lower cylinders to the ground.

5. Lubricate the bell housing studs with Quicksilver 2-4-C Multi-Lube. See **Figure 23**.

6. Lubricate the drive shaft and U-joint assembly with 2-4-C Multi-Lube at the points shown in **Figure 24**.

7. Pull the shift linkage out as far as it will go using needlenose pliers. The jaws will open as shown in **Figure 25**.

8. Align the drive unit U-joint with the gimbal bearing.

> *WARNING*
> *Do not attempt to install the stern drive unit to the boat in Step 9 without the aid of a suitable hoist for support. The unit is heavy and may slip from your grasp, causing damage to the stern drive and possible personal injury.*

9. Attach an overhead hoist to the stern drive top cover with a suitable lifting eye and an appropriate sling. Support the unit with the hoist.

NOTE
If the universal joint shaft splines do not engage with the engine coupling splines in Step 10, rotate the propeller shaft clockwise or counterclockwise as required until the stern drive can be pushed into position.

10. Install the stern drive to the bell housing, guiding the universal joint shaft through the gimbal housing bearing and into the engine coupler. At the same time, guide the shift cable into the shift linkage assembly (**Figure 26**). As the cable enters the linkage assembly, it will push the assembly into the drive shaft housing. This closes the linkage jaws to hold the cable securely. See **Figure 27**.

11. Once the drive unit is mated to the bell housing, rotate the propeller shaft slightly to make sure that the drive unit is still in NEUTRAL gear.

12. Install a flat washer and new elastic stop nut on each stern drive-to-bell housing stud (except

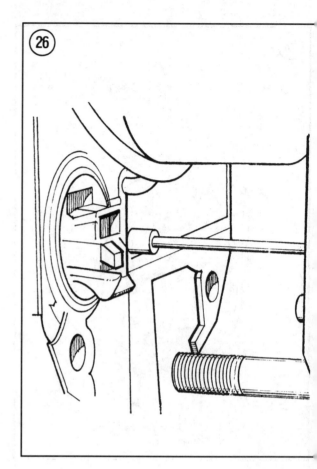

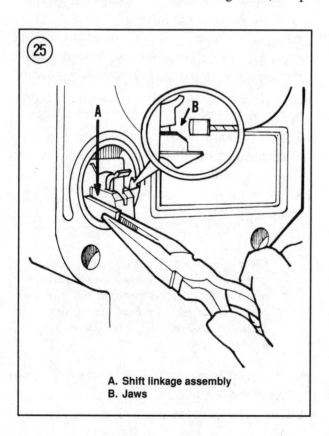

A. Shift linkage assembly
B. Jaws

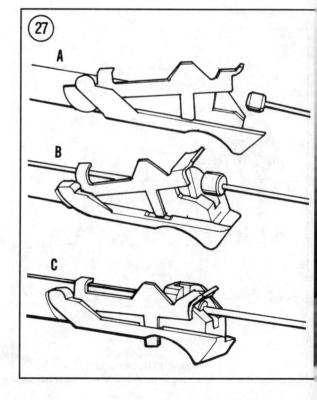

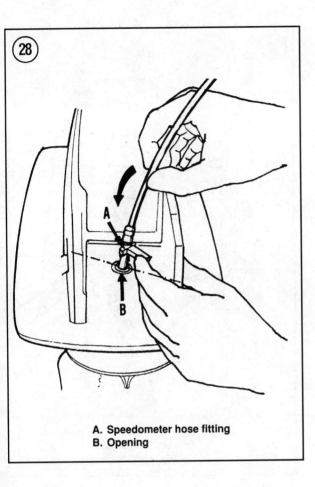

A. Speedometer hose fitting
B. Opening

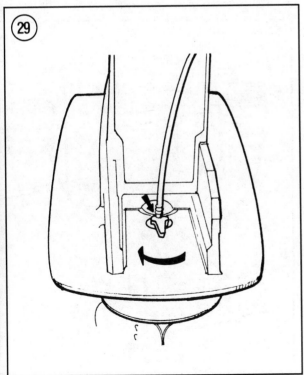

a stud fitted with a ground plate). See **Figure 20**. Start with the center nuts and tighten to 50 ft.-lb. (68 N•m).

13. Reinstall the aft end of each trim cylinder to the stern drive housing. See Chapter Sixteen.

14. Raise the drive unit up enough to provide access to connect the speedometer hose, install the hose fitting in the drive housing opening as shown in **Figure 20**.

15. Depress the fitting until it is fully seated, then rotate the fitting handle clockwise as far as possible to assure that the fitting is locked in place. See **Figure 29**.

Transom Plate Removal/Installation

It is not necessary to disconnect the hydraulic lines from the power steering control valve.

1. Remove the stern drive as described in this chapter.

2. Remove the engine. See Chapter Eight.

3. Remove the cotter pin from the clevis pin on the power steering control valve. Discard the cotter pin. Remove the clevis pin and separate the clevis from the steering lever. See **Figure 30**.

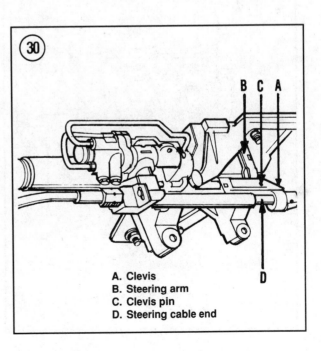

A. Clevis
B. Steering arm
C. Clevis pin
D. Steering cable end

12

4. Repeat Step 3 to disconnect the steering cable (**Figure 31**).

5. Remove the 2 pivot bolts holding the control valve and suspend the valve assembly out of the way with a suitable length of wire.

6. Cut the sta-strap holding the trim limit switch connection, then disconnect the wires at the bullet connectors. Loosen the hydraulic hoses at the power trim pump with a flare nut wrench. Disconnect the hoses from the pump. See **Figure 32**. Cap the hoses and pump fittings to prevent leakage and the entry of contamination.

7. If equipped with through-prop exhaust, unbolt and remove the exhaust pipe (**Figure 33**).

8. Remove the screws holding the ground wire to the steering lever. Remove the wire and reinstall the screws to prevent their being lost. See **Figure 34**.

9. Unclamp and remove the speedometer hoses (**Figure 35**).

10. Unbolt and remove the water hose fitting (**Figure 36**). Remove and discard the fitting gasket.

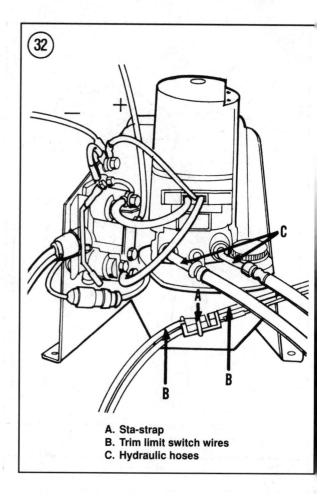

A. Sta-strap
B. Trim limit switch wires
C. Hydraulic hoses

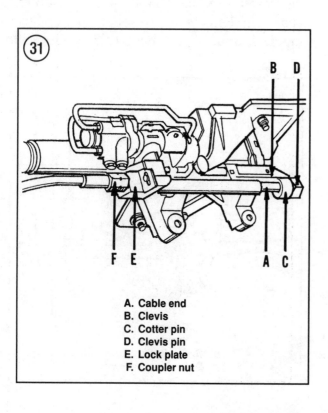

A. Cable end
B. Clevis
C. Cotter pin
D. Clevis pin
E. Lock plate
F. Coupler nut

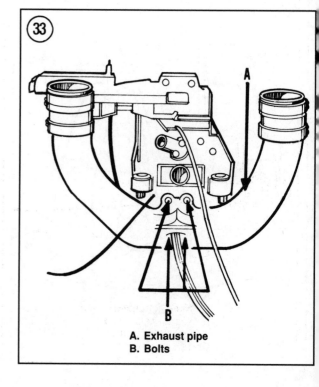

A. Exhaust pipe
B. Bolts

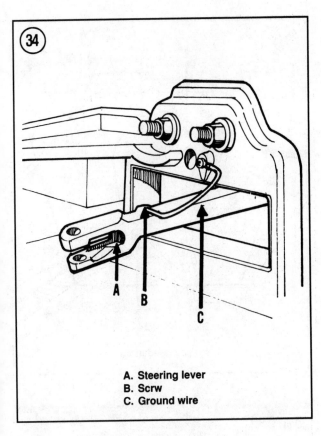

A. Steering lever
B. Scrw
C. Ground wire

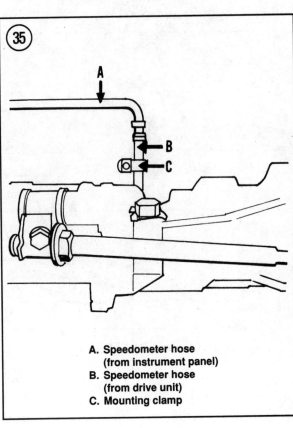

A. Speedometer hose
   (from instrument panel)
B. Speedometer hose
   (from drive unit)
C. Mounting clamp

11. Pull the hydraulic hoses, drive unit shift cable and trim sender leads through the inner transom plate.

12. Unbolt and separate the inner transom plate from the transom gimbal housing unit. See **Figure 37**.

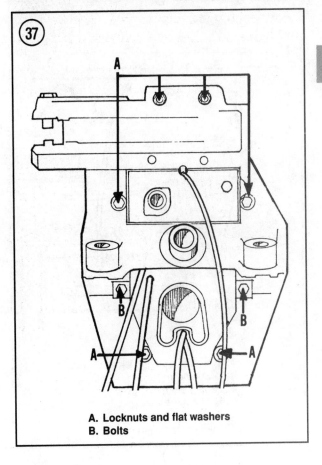

A. Locknuts and flat washers
B. Bolts

12

13. Installation is the reverse of removal, plus the following:

a. Position the inner transom plate and install the washers and locknuts (A, **Figure 37**) finger-tight, then install the carriage bolts (B, **Figure 37**). Make sure the rubber seal on each bolt is in good condition before reinstalling them. If not, water will leak into the boat. Tighten all fasteners to 20-25 ft.-lb. (27-34 N·m) starting from the center and working outward.

b. Route the power trim hoses, shift cable, trim sender and MerCathode leads (if so equipped) as shown in **Figure 38**. Make

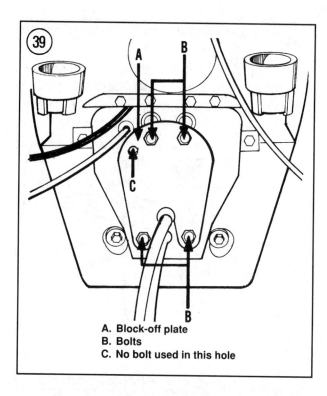

A. Block-off plate
B. Bolts
C. No bolt used in this hole

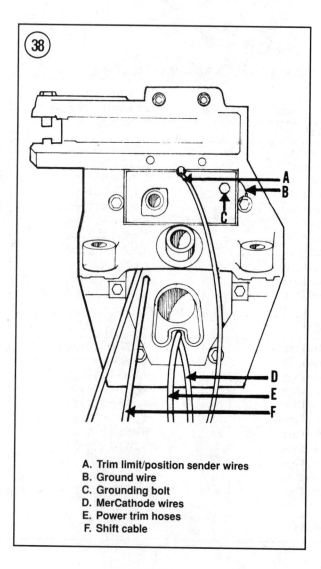

A. Trim limit/position sender wires
B. Ground wire
C. Grounding bolt
D. MerCathode wires
E. Power trim hoses
F. Shift cable

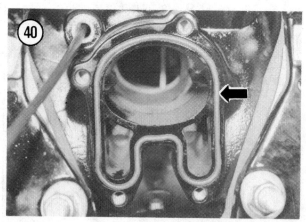

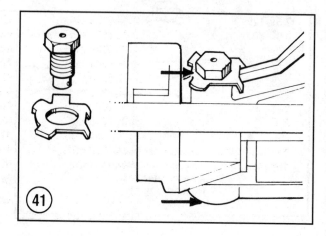

sure the ground wire is installed on the grounding bolt.

c. If equipped with through-transom exhaust, make sure the exhaust block-off plate is installed as shown in **Figure 39**. Tighten bolts to 20-25 ft.-lb. (27-34 N·m).

d. Install a new O-ring seal in the transom plate groove (**Figure 40**).

e. When reinstalling the power steering control valve pivot bolts, make sure the washer tangs fit over the inner transom plate ridges

as shown in **Figure 41**. Tighten the bolts to 25 ft.-lb. (34 N·m) and bend the washer tabs against the bolt head flats.

f. Tighten the water hose fittings to 135 in.-lb. (15 N·m). Tighten the steering coupler nut to 35 ft.-lb. (48 N·m). Tighten all other mounting fasteners to 20-25 ft.-lb. (27-34 N·m).

g. Install new cotter pins in the clevis pins. Spread the end of the pins.

Table 1 MERCRUISER MODEL, STERN DRIVE AND GEAR RATIO

Model/HP	Displacement	Drive unit	Gear ratio	Full throttle engine operating range
1986				
120	2.5L (153 cid)	Alpha One	1.98:1	4,200-4,600 rpm
140	3.0L (181 cid)	Alpha One	1.98:1	4,200-4,600 rpm
170	3.7L (224 cid)	Alpha One	1.84:1	4,200-4,600 rpm
185	4.3L (262 cid)	Alpha One	1.84:1	4,400-4,800 rpm
190	3.7L (224 cid)	Alpha One	1.84:1	4,400-4,800 rpm
200	5.0L (305 cid)	Alpha One	1.65:1	4,200-4,600 rpm
205	4.3L (262 cid)	Alpha One	1.84:1	4,400-4,800 rpm
230	5.0L (305 cid)	Alpha One	1.50:1	4,200-4,600 rpm
260	5.7L (350cid)	Alpha One	1.50:1	4,200-4,600 rpm
350 Magnum	5.7L (350 cid)	Alpha One	1.50:1	4,200-4,600 rpm
454 Magnum	7.4L (454 cid)	Alpha One	1.32:1	4,200-4,600 rpm
1987				
2.5L/120	2.5L (153 cid)	Alpha One	1.98:1	4,200-4,600 rpm
3.0L/130	3.0L (181 cid)	Alpha One	1.98:1	4,200-4,600 rpm
165	3.7L (224 cid)	Alpha One	1.84:1	4,400-4,800 rpm
175	4.3L (262 cid)	Alpha One	1.84:1	4,400-4,800 rpm
180	3.7L (224 cid)	Alpha One	1.84:1	4,400-4,800 rpm
200	5.0L (305 cid)	Alpha One	1.65:1	4,200-4,600 rpm
205	4.3L (262 cid)	Alpha One	1.84:1	4,400-4,800 rpm
230	5.0L (305 cid)	Alpha One	1.50:1	4,200-4,600 rpm
260	5.7L (350 cid)	Alpha One	1.50:1	4,200-4,600 rpm
350 Magnum	5.7L (350 cid)	Alpha One	1.50:1	4,200-4,600 rpm
454 Magnum	7.4L (454 cid)	Alpha One	1.32:1	4,200-4,600 rpm

(continued)

12

Table 1 MERCRUISER MODEL, STERN DRIVE AND GEAR RATIO (continued)

Model/HP	Displacement	Drive unit	Gear ratio	Full throttle engine operating range
1988-1989				
2.5L/120	2.5L (153 cid)	Alpha One	1.98:1	4,200-4,600 rpm
3.0L/130	3.0L (181 cid)	Alpha One	1.98:1	4,200-4,600 rpm
3.7L/165	3.7L (224 cid)	Alpha One	1.84:1	4,400-4,800 rpm
4.3L/175	4.3L (262 cid)	Alpha One	1.84:1	4,400-4,800 rpm
3.7LX/180	3.7L (224 cid)	Alpha One	1.84:1	4,400-4,800 rpm
5.0L/200	5.0L (305 cid)	Alpha One	1.65:1	4,200-4,600 rpm
4.3LX/205	4.3L (262 cid)	Alpha One	1.84:1	4,400-4,800 rpm
5.0LX/230	5.0L (305 cid)	Alpha One	1.50:1	4,200-4,600 rpm
5.7L/260	5.7L (350 cid)	Alpha One	1.50:1	4,200-4,600 rpm
350 Magnum/270	5.7L (350 cid)	Alpha One	1.50:1	4,200-4,600 rpm
7.4L/330	7.4L (454 cid)	Bravo One	1.50:1	4,200-4,600 rpm
454 Magnum/365	7.4L (454 cid)	Alpha One	1.32:1	4,600-5,000 rpm
454 Magnum/365	7.4L (454 cid)	Bravo One	1.50:1	4,600-5,000 rpm
1990[1]				
3.0L/115	3.0L (181 cid)	Alpha One	1.98:1	4,200-4,600 rpm
3.0LX/135	3.0L (181 cid)	Alpha One	1.98:1	4,400-4,800 rpm
4.3L/155	4.3L (262 cid)	Alpha One	1.84:1	4,400-4,800 rpm
4.3LX/175	4.3L (262 cid)	Alpha One	1.84:1	4,400-4,800 rpm
5.0L/180	5.0L (305 cid)	Alpha One	1.65:1	4,200-4,600 rpm
5.0LX/205	5.0L (305 cid)	Alpha One	1.50:1	4,200-4,600 rpm
5.7L/230	5.7L (350 cid)	Alpha One	1.50:1	4,200-4,600 rpm
350 Magnum/240	5.7L (350 cid)	Alpha One	1.50:1	4,200-4,600 rpm
7.4L/300	7.4L (454 cid)	Bravo One	1.50:1	4,200-4,600 rpm
454 Magnum/360	7.4L (454 cid)	Bravo One	1.50:1	4,600-5,000 rpm
502 Magnum/410	8.2L (502 cid)	Bravo One	1.36:1	4,400-4,800 rpm
1991[1]				
3.0L/115	3.0L (181 cid)	Alpha One	1.98:1	4,200-4,600 rpm
3.0LX/135	3.0L (181 cid)	Alpha One	1.98:1	4,400-4,800 rpm
4.3L/155	4.3L (262 cid)	Alpha One	1.84:1	4,400-4,800 rpm
4.3LX/175	4.3L (262 cid)	Alpha One	1.84:1	4,400-4,800 rpm
5.0L/180	5.0L (305 cid)	Alpha One	1.65:1	4,200-4,600 rpm
5.0LX/205	5.0L (305 cid)	Alpha One	1.50:1	4,200-4,600 rpm
5.7L/230	5.7L (350 cid)	Alpha One	1.50:1	4,200-4,600 rpm
5.7L/240	5.7L (350 cid)	Bravo Two	2:1	4,200-4,600 rpm
350 Magnum/240	5.7L (350 cid)	Alpha One	1.50:1	4,200-4,600 rpm
7.4L/300	7.4L (454 cid)	Bravo One	1.5:1	4,200-4,600 rpm
7.4L/300	7.4L (454 cid)	Bravo Two	2:1	4,200-4,600 rpm
454 Magnum/350	7.4L (454 cid)	Bravo One	1.5:1	4,600-5,000 rpm
502 Magnum/390	8.2L (502 cid)	Bravo One	1.36:1	4,600-5,000 rpm
1992[1]				
3.0L/115	3.0L (181 cid)	Alpha One	1.98:1	4,200-4,600 rpm
3.0LX/135	3.0L (181 cid)	Alpha One	1.98:1	4,400-4,800 rpm
4.3L/155	4.3: (262 cid)	Alpha One	1.84:1	4,400-4,800 rpm
4.3LX/175	4.3L (262 cid)	Alpha One	1.84:1	4,400-4,800 rpm
5.0L/180	5.0L (305 cid)	Alpha One	1.65:1	4,200-4,600 rpm

(continued)

Table 1 MERCRUISER MODEL, STERN DRIVE AND GEAR RATIO (continued)

Model/HP	Displacement	Drive unit	Gear ratio	Full throttle engine operating range
1992[1] (continued)				
5.0LX/205	5.0L (305 cid)	Alpha One	1.50:1	4,200-4,600 rpm
5.7L/230	5.7L (350 cid)	Alpha One	1.50:1	4,200-4,600 rpm
5.7L/250	5.7L (350 cid)	Bravo Two	2.2:1	4,400-4,800 rpm
350 Magnum/250	5.7L (350 cid)	Alpha One	1.50:1	4,400-4,800 rpm
7.4L/300	7.4L (454 cid)	Bravo One	1.5:1	4,200-4,600 rpm
7.4L/300	7.4L (454 cid)	Bravo Two	2:1	4,200-4,600 rpm
454 Magnum/350	7.4L (454 cid)	Bravo One	1.5:1	4,600-5,000 rpm
502 Magnum/390	8.2L (502 cid)	Bravo One	1.36:1[2]	4,600-5,000 rpm
1993[1]				
3.0L/115		Alpha One	1.98:1	4,200-4,600 rpm
3.0LX/135		Alpha One	1.98:1	4,400-4,800 rpm
4.3L/160		Alpha One	1.84:1	4,400-4,800 rpm
4.3LX/180		Alpha One	1.84:1	4,400-4,800 rpm
5.0L/190		Alpha One	1.65:1	4,200-4,600 rpm
5.0LX/205		Alpha One	1.50:1	4,200-4,600 rpm
5.7L/235		Alpha One	1.50:1	4,200-4,600 rpm
5.7L/250		Bravo Two	2.2:1	4,400-4,800 rpm
350 Magnum/250		Alpha One	1.5:1	4,400-4,800 rpm
7.4L/300		Bravo One	1.5:1	4,200-4,600 rpm
7.4L/300		Bravo Two	2.0:1	4,200-4,600 rpm
7.4L/300		Bravo Three	2.0:1	4,200-4,600 rpm
454 Magnum/350		Bravo One	1.5:1	4,600-5,000 rpm
502 Magnum/390		Bravo One	1.36:1[2]	4,600-5,000 rpm
1994[1]				
3.0L/115		Alpha One	1.98:1	4,200-4,600 rpm
3.0LX/135		Alpha One	1.98:1	4,200-4,600 rpm
4.3L/160		Alpha One	1.84:1	4,400-4,800 rpm
4.3LX/180		Alpha One	1.84:1	4,400-4,800 rpm
5.0L/190		Alpha One	1.65:1	4,200-4,600 rpm
5.0LX/205		Alpha One	1.50:1	4,200-4,600 rpm
5.7L/235		Alpha One	1.50:1	4,200-4,600 rpm
5.7L/250		Bravo Two	2.2:1	4,400-4,800 rpm
5.7L/250		Bravo Three	2.0:1	4,400-4,800 rpm
350 Magnum/250		Alpha One	1.5:1	4,400-4,800 rpm
7.4L/300		Bravo One	1.5:1	4,200-4,600 rpm
7.4L/300		Bravo Two	2.0:1	4,200-4,600 rpm
7.4L/300		Bravo Three	2.0:1	4,200-4,600 rpm
454 Magnum/350		Bravo One	1.5:1	4,600-5,000 rpm

1. Horsepower rated at the propeller shaft.
2. Also available in 1.5:1 gear ratio.

12

Chapter Thirteen

Drive Shaft Housing

Engine torque passes through a drive shaft/universal joint to a pinion and drive gear in the drive shaft (upper) housing, changing the horizontal power flow from the engine into a vertical power flow sent to the gearcase (lower) housing through a drive shaft. Power application is controlled by shifting the gearcase housing (Alpha One) or drive shaft housing (Bravo One, Bravo Two and Bravo Three).

Shifting is accomplished through a shift rod connected between the engine and drive shaft housing. The engine shift rod is connected by a shift cable to the remote control box, providing shift control at the helm.

In the Alpha One gearcase, a fitting in the drive shaft housing transmits horizontal motion of the engine shift rod to a vertical shift shaft which extends to the shift mechanism on the gearcase propeller shaft.

When the Alpha One unit is shifted into gear, a sliding clutch (dog clutch) in the gearcase engages a forward or reverse gear on the propeller shaft, creating a direct coupling between the selected gear and the pinion gear on the vertical

drive shaft. This direct coupling changes the power flow back to horizontal movement of the propeller shaft. When the shift mechanism is in NEUTRAL, the sliding clutch does not engage with either gear and the propeller shaft does not rotate.

Since the dog clutch and drive shaft pinion gear are the central components in the shift operation, they are prone to the greatest amount of wear. The forward gear also receives more wear than the reverse gear.

Shifting of the Bravo drive is done in the drive shaft housing. The universal joint assembly transmits horizontal motion of the engine to a vertical clutch assembly through a pinion gear.

When the Bravo unit is shifted into gear, a sliding clutch on the drive shaft clutch assembly engages the forward or reverse clutch gear as desired. This creates a direct coupling that sends the power flow to the gearcase drive shaft, where a pinion gear changes the power flow back to horizontal movement of the propeller shaft. When the shift mechanism is in NEUTRAL, the drive shaft clutch does not engage with either clutch gear and so the propeller shaft does not rotate.

The Alpha One, Bravo One, Bravo Two and Bravo Three gearcase housings can be removed from the drive shaft housing for service without removing the entire stern drive from the boat. This chapter covers the removal, overhaul and installation of the Alpha and Bravo drive shaft housings. Other MerCruiser drives are manufactured for heavy-duty use including high-performance models used for racing. Mercury Marine does not recommend service by amateur mechanics on such models. **Table 1** and **Table 2** are at the end of the chapter.

FASTENER REMOVAL

Elastic stop nuts should never be used more than twice. It is a good idea to replace such nuts with new ones each time they are removed. Never use worn-out stop nuts or non-locking nuts.

SERVICE PRECAUTIONS

Whenever you work on a stern drive unit, there are several precautions to keep in mind that will make your work easier, faster and more accurate.

1. Use special tools where noted. In some cases, it may be possible to perform the procedure with makeshift tools, but this is not recommended. The use of makeshift tools can damage the components and may cause serious personal injury.

2. Use a vise with protective jaws to hold housings or components. If protective jaws are not available, insert blocks of soft wood on either side of the part(s) before clamping them in the vise.

3. Remove and install pressed-on parts with an appropriate mandrel, support and hydraulic press. Do not try to pry, hammer or otherwise force them on or off.

4. Refer to the appropriate table and the end of the chapter for torque values, if not given in the text. Proper torque is vital to assure long life and service from stern drive components.

5. Apply Quicksilver Perfect Seal to the outer surfaces of all retainer and housing mating surfaces during reassembly. Do *not* allow Perfect Seal to touch O-rings or enter the bearings or gears.

6. Lubricate all O-rings and seal lips.

7. Apply Loctite 271 on the outside diameter of all metal-case oil seals.

8. Keep a record of all shims and where they came from. As soon as the shims are removed, inspect them for damage and write down their thickness and location. Wire the shims together for reassembly and put them in a safe place. Follow shimming instructions closely. If gear backlash is not properly set, the unit will be noisy and suffer premature gear failure. Incorrect bearing preload will result in premature bearing failure.

9. Work in a clean area where there is good lighting and sufficient space for components to be stored. Keep an ample number of containers available for storing small parts. Cover parts with clean shop cloths when you are not working with them.

ALPHA ONE AND ALPHA ONE GENERATION II DRIVE

Figure 1 is an exploded view of the first generation Alpha One drive shaft housing. On Alpha One Generation II models, O-ring (8, **Figure 1**) and water pocket assembly (41 and 42) are not used. In addition, the top cover (3, **Figure 1**) is equipped with a dipstick to check drive unit oil level on second generation models. **Figure 2** is a cross-sectional view of the drive shaft housing to provide component relationships inside the drive shaft housing.

13

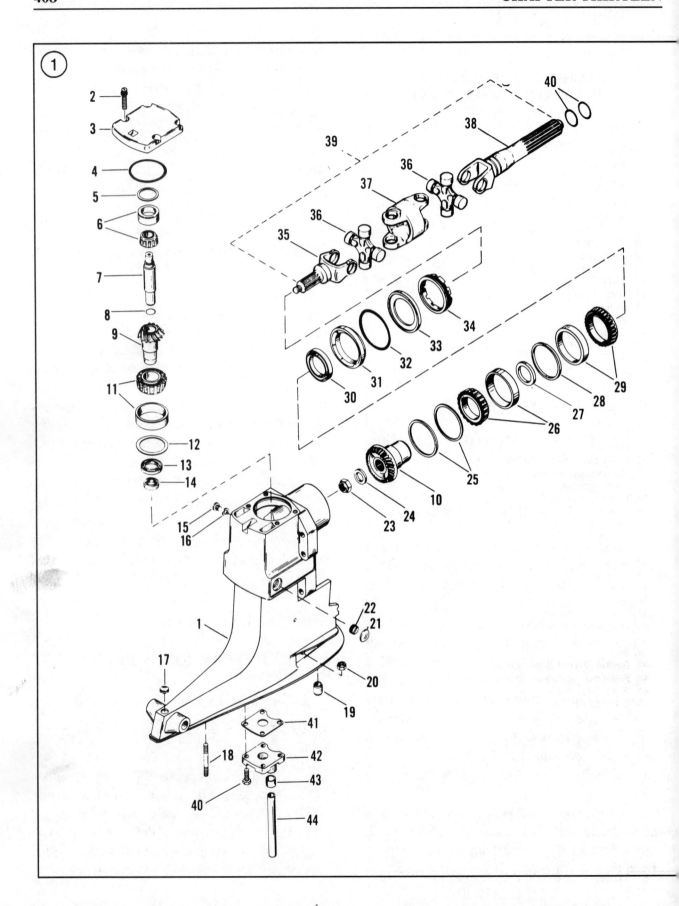

ALPHA ONE DRIVE SHAFT HOUSING (EXPLODED VIEW)

1. Drive shaft housing
2. Screw
3. Top cover
4. O-ring
5. Shim(s)
6. Drive shaft bearing assembly
7. Upper drive shaft
8. O-ring (except Generation II)
9. Driven gear
10. Drive gear
11. Driven gear bearing
12. Shim(s)
13. Seal
14. Seal
15. Vent screw
16. Gasket
17. Plug
18. Stud
19. Bushing
20. Nut
21. Plug
22. Pipe plug
23. Nut
24. Washer
25. Shim(s)
26. Drive gear bearing assembly
27. Bearing spacer (except after serial No. D492656)
28. Bearing cup spacer
29. Drive gear bearing assembly
30. Seal
31. Seal carrier
32. O-ring
33. Retaining ring
34. Retainer
35. Universal joint yoke
36. Universal joint cross and bearing assembly
37. Universal joint center socket
38. Universal joint yoke
39. Universal joint assembly
40. O-rings
41. Bolt
42. Gasket (except Generation II)
43. Water pocket cover (except Generation II)
44. Water tube seal
45. Water tube

Troubleshooting
Universal Joint Bellows Chafing

Excessive exhaust gas backpressure with MCM 230 and 260 models may cause the exhaust bellows to balloon. If this happens, the exhaust bellows pushes the universal joint bellows against the moving U-joints and results in excessive chafing and premature failure. The problem can be eliminated by replacing the exhaust bellows with exhaust tube part No. 78458A1. Models manufactured after July 1985 have this exhaust tube installed at the factory.

Universal Joint Knocking

Excessive side-to-side play in the U-joint cross and bearing assemblies can cause a knock or vibration during turning or trimming maneuvers. If the original cross and bearing assembly has not been replaced, the problem can be eliminated by installing C-ring kit part No. 53-12067A1. The C-rings are curved at the ends and must be installed as shown in **Figure 3** with the curve facing the yoke or center socket.

If the original assembly has been replaced, the C-ring kit cannot be installed. The bearing cap grooves in service replacement Spicer assemblies are too narrow to accept the new C-rings.

Drive Shaft Housing Removal

1. Remove the gearcase (lower unit). See Chapter Fourteen.
2. Remove the power trim cylinders. See Chapter Sixteen.
3. Remove the 6 elastic stop nuts and washers holding the drive shaft housing to the bell housing. See **Figure 4**.
4. Shift the drive unit into forward gear to allow the shift shafts to separate.

NOTE
If the drive shaft housing refuses to move in Step 5, the drive shaft splines may be

13

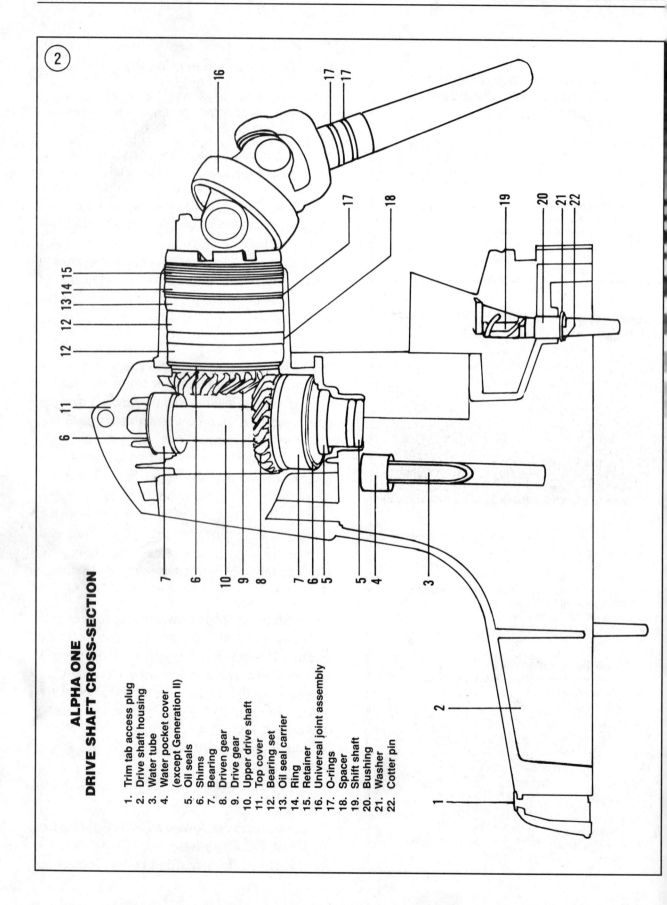

ALPHA ONE
DRIVE SHAFT CROSS-SECTION

1. Trim tab access plug
2. Drive shaft housing
3. Water tube
4. Water pocket cover
   (except Generation II)
5. Oil seals
6. Shims
7. Bearing
8. Driven gear
9. Drive gear
10. Upper drive shaft
11. Top cover
12. Bearing set
13. Oil seal carrier
14. Ring
15. Retainer
16. Universal joint assembly
17. O-rings
18. Spacer
19. Shift shaft
20. Bushing
21. Washer
22. Cotter pin

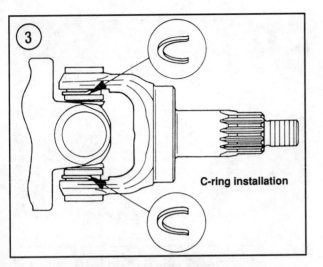

③ C-ring installation

④

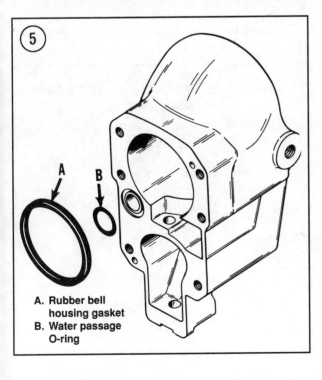

⑤

A. Rubber bell housing gasket
B. Water passage O-ring

frozen in the engine coupler or the drive shaft may be frozen to the gimbal bearing. To remove the unit in such cases, you must either disconnect the engine and move it forward or remove the drive shaft housing top cover and drive the U-joint nut off with a hammer and punch, leaving the frozen drive shaft in the bell housing.

5. Pull the drive shaft housing straight back from the bell housing, then mount the assembly in a suitable holding fixture.

6. Remove and discard the rubber bell housing gasket and water passage O-ring (**Figure 5**). Remove and discard the bell housing gasket, if used.

Drive Shaft Housing Installation

Engine alignment should be checked with engine coupler alignment shaft before reinstalling the drive shaft housing.

CAUTION
Engine alignment is a critical operation which requires good judgment and experience in addition to use of the special alignment tool. It is best to have your MerCruiser dealer perform any alignment procedures required to prevent premature failure of the drive shaft unit.

Check engine alignment to make sure there is no resistance to the alignment tool entering the engine. If there is, the engine must be aligned. This required raising or lowering the front of the engine until the alignment tool meets no resistance when installed. See the appropriate chapter for your engine.

1. Install a new O-ring in the water passage. See A, **Figure 6**.

2. Install a new rubber gasket in the bell housing (B, **Figure 6**).

3. Lubricate the shift slide assembly (C, **Figure 6**) with 2-4-C Multi-Lube.

4. Install a new bell housing gasket, if used.

13

5. Position the upper shift shaft as shown in **Figure 7**A (except Generation II) or **Figure 7**B (Generation II) to place the drive unit in forward gear.

6. Position the bell housing shift mechanism as shown in **Figure 8**. Lubricate the universal joint splines and O-rings with 2-4-C Multi-Lube.

> *NOTE*
> *If the shaft and coupling splines do not properly align in Step 7, rotate propeller shaft counterclockwise until they do.*

7. Guide universal joint shaft through gimbal housing bearing and into engine drive coupler. At the same time, guide the shift slide into the drive shaft housing opening.

8. Lubricate bell housing stud threads with 2-4-C Multi-Lube. Install flat washer and new elastic stop nut on each stud. Tighten nuts to specifications (**Table 1**).

9. Reinstall the trim cylinders (Chapter Sixteen).

10. Reinstall the gearcase (lower housing). See Chapter Fourteen.

Water Pocket Cover Removal/Installation (Except Generation II)

Water pocket screws may be very difficult to remove if the stern drive has been operated in salt-water or in water that is polluted or has a heavy mineral content. Be sure to use Quicksilver Perfect Seal on the screw threads during reinstallation.

1. Reach inside the drive shaft housing from underneath the unit and remove the copper water tube, if still in the water pocket cover. See **Figure 9**.

2. Remove the screws holding the water pocket cover in the housing. Remove cover and gasket. See **Figure 10**. Discard the gasket.

3. Clean and inspect the cover as described in this chapter.

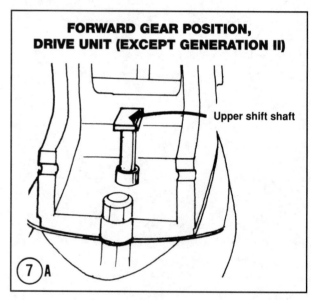

FORWARD GEAR POSITION, DRIVE UNIT (EXCEPT GENERATION II)

Upper shift shaft

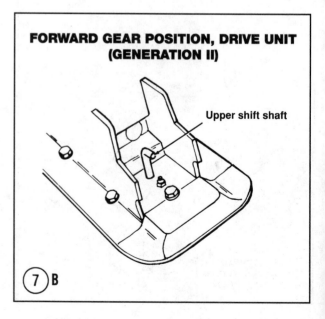

FORWARD GEAR POSITION, DRIVE UNIT (GENERATION II)

Upper shift shaft

⑧

FORWARD GEAR POSITION, BELL HOUSING

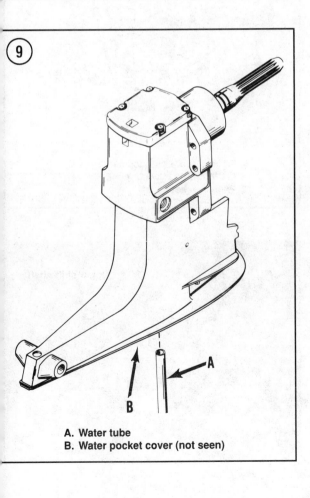

⑨

A. Water tube
B. Water pocket cover (not seen)

NOTE
On Alpha One SS models, a restrictor plate is installed between 2 water pocket cover gaskets. During reassembly, the side of the restrictor plate marked "G.C. SIDE-THIS SIDE ONLY" must be facing the gear housing (down).

4. Installation is the reverse of removal. Use a new gasket. Wipe cover screw threads with Quicksilver Perfect Seal and tighten to 30-40 in.-lb. (3-4 N•m).

Water Pocket Cover Cleaning and Inspection (Except Generation II)

1. Remove the rubber seal from the cover (**Figure 11**).

⑩

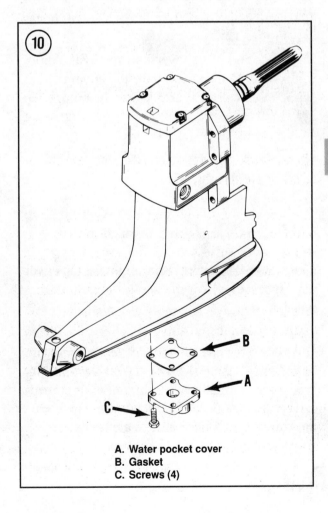

A. Water pocket cover
B. Gasket
C. Screws (4)

13

2. Clean the cover in solvent and blow dry with compressed air.

3. Check the cover for cracks, warpage or overheating.

4. Install a new rubber seal.

Top Cover Removal/Installation

1. On Generation II models, remove the dipstick and gasket from the top cover.

2. Unbolt and remove the 4 screws holding the top cover on the drive shaft housing. The screws require use of a 12-point socket.

3. Insert screwdriver blades in each of the 2 pry slots provided in the top cover and pry the cover free of the drive shaft housing.

4. Remove the cover from the drive shaft housing (**Figure 12**).

5. Installation is the reverse of removal. Apply Quicksilver Perfect Seal to the top cover mating surface in the shaded area shown in **Figure 13**. Tighten the cover screws evenly, in a crossing pattern, to 20 ft.-lb. (27 N·m). Correct torque is important as it affects upper drive shaft bearing preload.

Top Cover Cleaning and Inspection

1. Remove the rubber O-ring from the top cover (A, **Figure 13**).

2. Clean the cover assembly in solvent and blow dry with compressed air.

3. Check the upper drive shaft top bearing cup (B, **Figure 13**) inside the cover for pitting, grooving, scoring, heat discoloration or embedded metallic particles. Replace bearing and bearing cup if any of these defects are noted.

4. Check shim(s) for damage that may have occurred during removal. Replace with same thickness shim(s) if damaged.

Top Cover Disassembly/Assembly

It is not necessary to remove the top cover bearing cup unless the cup and bearing assembly requires replacement or the shim pack requires changing.

The top bearing on the upper drive shaft and the bearing cup in the top cover should be replaced as a set. If the bearing and cup are replaced, install shims of the same thickness as removed from the top cover. If the original shim thickness is not known, install a shim pack 0.015 in. (0.38 mm) thick into the top cover. Refer to *Upper Drive Shaft Preload Adjustment and Gear Clearance Adjustment* in this chapter for drive

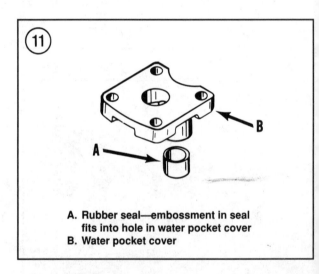

A. Rubber seal—embossment in seal fits into hole in water pocket cover
B. Water pocket cover

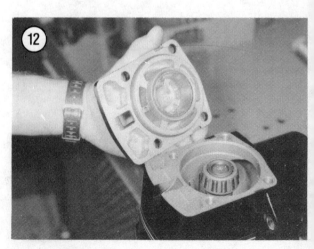

shaft preload and driven gear clearance adjustment procedure.

1. Remove the bearing cup from the top cover (B, **Figure 13**) with a suitable puller and slide hammer.

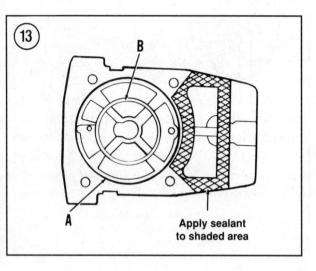

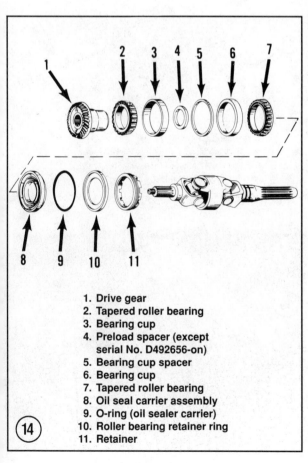

1. Drive gear
2. Tapered roller bearing
3. Bearing cup
4. Preload spacer (except serial No. D492656-on)
5. Bearing cup spacer
6. Bearing cup
7. Tapered roller bearing
8. Oil seal carrier assembly
9. O-ring (oil sealer carrier)
10. Roller bearing retainer ring
11. Retainer

2. Retrieve any shim(s) under the bearing cup and tag for reassembly reference.

3. Clean bearing cup bore with a cloth dampened in solvent and wipe dry.

4. Install shim(s) in top cover bearing cup bore.

5. Install a new bearing cup with a suitable installer.

6. Install a new top cover O-ring (A, **Figure 13**).

Universal Joint, Drive Gear and Bearing Assembly Removal

While the top cover may be removed for this procedure, it is not absolutely necessary. However, it must be removed for reinstallation. Refer to **Figure 14** for this procedure.

1. Install bearing retainer wrench (part No. 91-36235 or 91-17256) onto the bearing retainer. Rotate the wrench counterclockwise to remove the retainer. See **Figure 15**. If necessary, strike the wrench handle with a mallet to break the retainer loose. When the retainer is loose enough to remove by hand, remove the bearing retainer wrench.

2. Pull the universal joint with drive gear and bearing assembly from the drive shaft housing. See **Figure 16**.

3. Remove any shims and/or spacers which may remain inside the housing. Wire shims/spacer together and place to one side for reassembly reference.

13

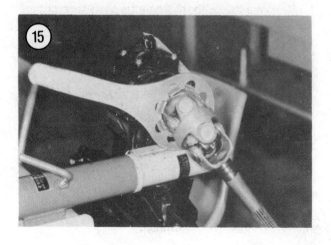

4. Clamp the bearing retainer wrench at a 45° angle in the vise with the handle facing at 10 o'clock or 2 o'clock. Fit the universal joint yoke over the wrench handle to hold the assembly and remove the drive gear nut with an appropriate socket and flex handle. See **Figure 17**.

5. Remove the drive gear (**Figure 18**) from the universal joint shaft.

> *CAUTION*
> *Mark the bearing location in Step 6 for reassembly reference. Bearings must be installed on the gear in the same order as removed. If replacement is necessary, replace both bearings, bearing cups, preload spacers and outer spacers as an assembly.*

6. Remove the bearing/cup assemblies with small preload spacer (if used) and large outer spacer. See **Figure 19**.

> *NOTE*
> *The small preload spacer (4, Figure 14) is not used to set the bearing preload on late models (serial No. D492656-on).*

7. Remove the oil seal carrier, O-ring and retainer ring (**Figure 20**).

8. Place the carrier across the vise jaws and remove the inner oil seal with a punch and hammer. See **Figure 21**.

9. Remove the 2 O-rings from the end of the universal joint shaft coupling (**Figure 22**).

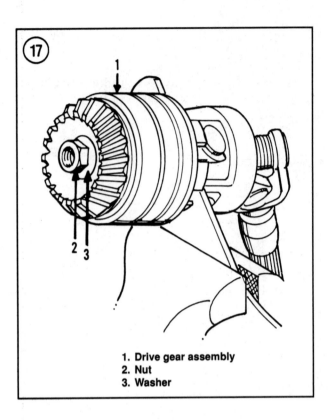

1. Drive gear assembly
2. Nut
3. Washer

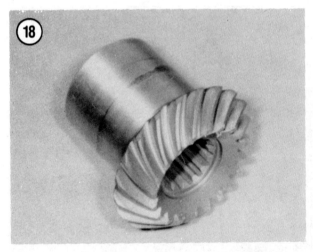

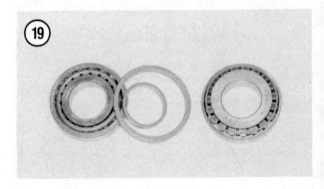

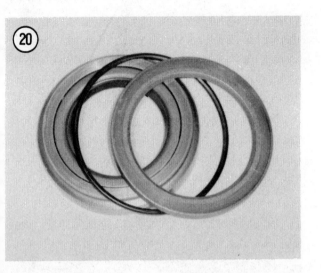

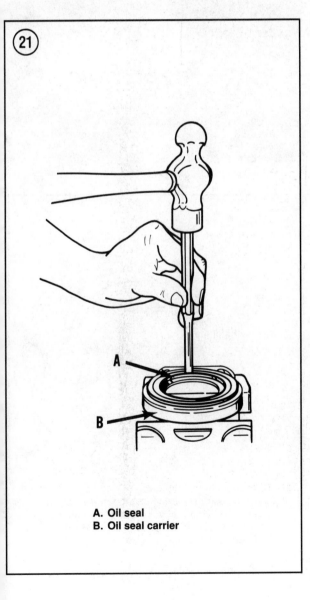

A. Oil seal
B. Oil seal carrier

Universal Joint, Drive Gear and Bearing Cleaning and Inspection

1. Clean all parts in fresh solvent. Blow dry with compressed air.

NOTE
If wear or corrosion is found in Step 2 or Step 3, also check engine coupling splines for the same defect.

2. Inspect coupling and gear end of U-joint for spline wear.

3. Clean all corrosion from the coupling. Replace coupling yoke if splines are partially corroded away.

4. Check the drive gear for pitting, excessive wear and chipped or broken teeth. See **Figure 18**. Replace gear if any of these defects are noted.

5. Inspect bearing cups for pitting, scoring, grooving, heat discoloration or embedded metallic particles. Replace bearing and cup if any defect is found.

6. Check condition of shim(s). Replace any that are damaged.

Universal Joint Disassembly/Assembly

While universal joint disassembly may not be absolutely necessary, it is always a good idea to replace the cross and bearings whenever the drive shaft is out of the housing. Refer to **Figure 23** for this procedure.

13

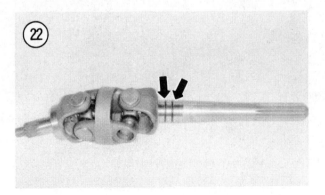

1. Place universal joint assembly over a suitable support (**Figure 24**) and remove the snap rings with a punch and hammer.

2. Install an automotive-type U-joint tool and adaptor part No. C-91-38756 as shown in **Figure 25** (large adaptor opening should face outward). Tighten the tool to apply pressure on one bearing cap and force the other one into the adaptor. If the tool is not available, support the yoke between a pair of appropriate size sockets. Apply pressure with a hydraulic press on one bearing cap until the opposite one is pressed into the socket, then remove the one free bearing cap.

3. Rotate the tool 180° and repeat Step 2 to press the 2nd bearing cap into the adaptor, then remove the yoke.

4. Repeat Steps 1-3 to remove the remaining bearings. Remove the spider.

5. Repeat Steps 1-4 to remove the second spider/yoke assembly.

6. Position the bearing caps, yoke and cross as shown in **Figure 26** (small adaptor opening should face outward). Make sure the cross is installed with its grease fitting facing the coupling end yoke.

7. Press both bearing caps into the yoke and onto the cross, then install new C-rings (**Figure 27**). If curved C-rings are used, they must be installed with the curve facing outward. See **Figure 3**.

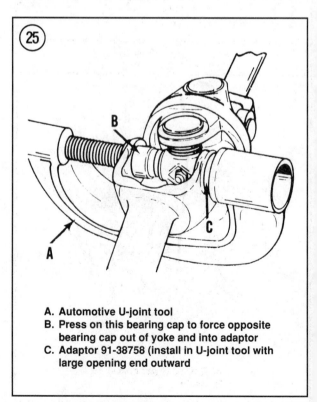

A. Automotive U-joint tool
B. Press on this bearing cap to force opposite bearing cap out of yoke and into adaptor
C. Adaptor 91-38758 (install in U-joint tool with large opening end outward

. Repeat Step 6 and Step 7 to install the remaining bearings.

. Repeat Steps 6-8 to install the second spider/yoke assembly.

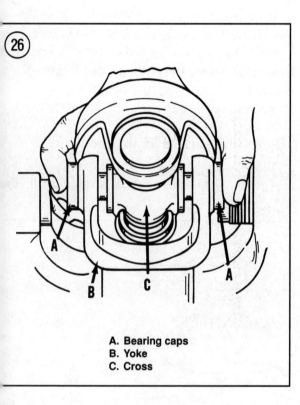

A. Bearing caps
B. Yoke
C. Cross

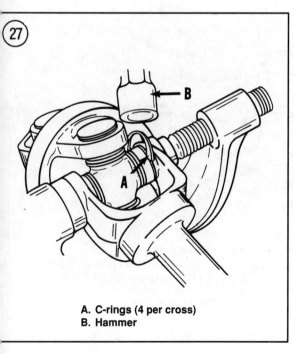

A. C-rings (4 per cross)
B. Hammer

10. Install new O-rings on the universal joint shaft coupling (**Figure 22**).

Universal Joint, Drive Gear and Bearing Assembly (Early Models [Prior to Serial No. D492656])

Refer to **Figure 28** for this procedure.

1. If oil seal in carrier was removed, position a new seal (lip side facing the concave side of the carrier) and press into place until flush with carrier. Wipe seal lip with Quicksilver 2-4-C Multi-Lube.

2. Clamp the bearing retainer wrench at a 45° angle in the vise with the handle facing at 10 o'clock or 2 o'clock. Fit the universal joint yoke over the wrench handle to hold the assembly.

3. Starting with the threaded cover nut, install the drive gear bearing assembly components on the drive shaft gear in the order shown in **Figure**

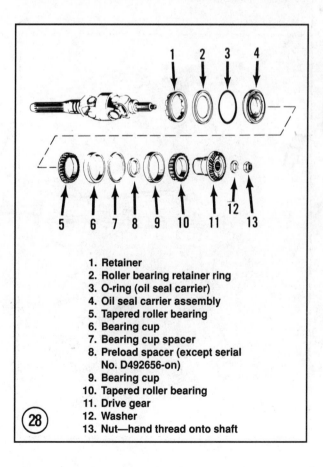

1. Retainer
2. Roller bearing retainer ring
3. O-ring (oil seal carrier)
4. Oil seal carrier assembly
5. Tapered roller bearing
6. Bearing cup
7. Bearing cup spacer
8. Preload spacer (except serial No. D492656-on)
9. Bearing cup
10. Tapered roller bearing
11. Drive gear
12. Washer
13. Nut—hand thread onto shaft

13

28. Make sure the original bearings are reinstalled in the same order in which they were removed.

4. Fit a large automotive worm-type hose clamp over the spacer (between the bearing cups) and tighten it securely. This will hold the preload spacer in position while the drive gear nut is being tightened and will assist in aligning the components properly for easy installation of the assembly in the drive shaft housing.

CAUTION
Correct torque is important in Step 5, as it applies preload on the drive gear assembly. Insufficient torque may result in damage to the drive and driven gears,

while excessive torque can damage the shaft.

5. Torque the drive gear nut to 70-80 ft.-lb (95-108 N•m) while rotating the bearing assembly.

6. Remove the hose clamp.

Universal Joint, Drive Gear and Bearing Assembly (Late Models [Serial No. D492656-on])

Refer to **Figure 28** for this procedure.

1. If the carrier oil seal was removed, position new seal in the carrier with its lip side facing th

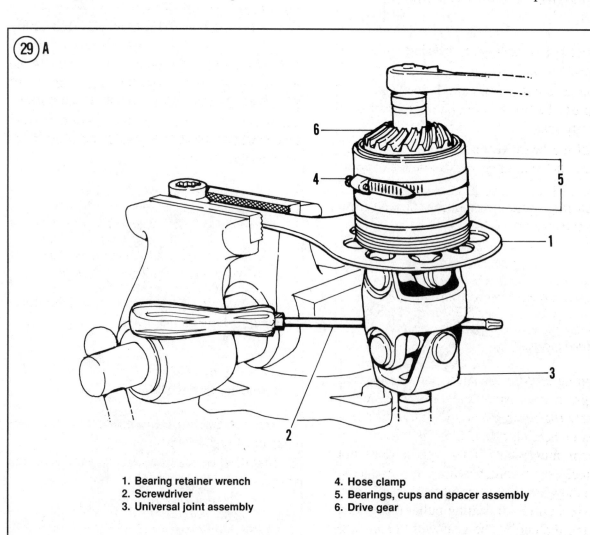

1. Bearing retainer wrench
2. Screwdriver
3. Universal joint assembly
4. Hose clamp
5. Bearings, cups and spacer assembly
6. Drive gear

concave side of the carrier. Press the seal into the carrier until flush with the carrier surface. Lubricate the seal lip with Quicksilver 2-4-C Marine Lube.

2. Clamp the bearing retainer wrench in a vise at a 45° angle. Position the wrench handle at either the 10 o'clock or 2 o'clock position. Place the universal joint yoke over the wrench handle to hold the assembly.

NOTE
On late Alpha One stern drives (serial No. D492656-on), the small cone spacer is no longer used to set the bearing preload. The bearings on these models are a slight interference fit on the drive gear hub.

3. Lubricate the drive gear bearings with the recommended gear lube.

4. Using an arbor press and a suitable bearing driver, press the first bearing onto the drive gear until firmly seated.

5. Install the bearing cup on the first bearing, then place the bearing cup spacer on the bearing cup.

6. Install the second bearing cup on top of the bearing cup spacer.

CAUTION
To prevent excessive bearing preload, do not press the second bearing too far onto the drive gear in Step 7. Press the bearing on the gear only until it contacts its bearing cup.

7. Using an arbor press and a suitable bearing driver, press the second bearing onto the drive gear. Press the bearing onto the gear until it *just contacts* its bearing cup. Check the bearing cup spacer for movement. If the spacer does not move freely, the second bearing was pressed too far onto the gear. If so, support the second bearing cup in a universal bearing puller plate, then lightly tap the end of the gear with a soft-face mallet.

8. Fit a large automotive hose clamp over the bearing and spacer assembly to keep the bearing cups and spacer properly aligned while adjusting bearing preload.

9. Install all remaining components on the drive gear in the order shown in **Figure 28**.

10. Next, install the drive gear and bearings onto the universal joint shaft. Install the washer and locknut. Tighten the locknut until it just contacts the washer.

11. Support the drive gear assembly as shown in **Figure 29**A. Insert a screwdriver or similar tool through the universal joint assembly to hold the assembly from turning (**Figure 29**A). Then tighten the retaining nut 1/16 turn. Next, hold the drive gear bearings and rotate the drive gear at least 2 full turns to seat the bearings. Then, using an in.-lb. torque wrench, check bearing preload by rotating the drive gear assembly. Continue tightening the nut in 1/16 turn increments until the rolling torque (preload) is 6-15 in.-lb. for new bearings or 3-7.5 in.-lb. for used bearings. Note that bearings should be considered used if rotated one turn under load.

CAUTION
If the nut is tightened excessively in Step 11, loosen the nut and strike the gear and bearing assembly with a soft-face mallet to loosen the preload. Excessive preload will result in premature bearing failure.

12. After obtaining the correct bearing preload, remove the hose clamp.

Universal Joint, Drive Gear and Bearing Installation

1. Remove the top cover as described in this chapter (if not already removed).

2. Install the bearing cup-to-gear housing shim(s) and spacer in drive shaft housing.

CAUTION
MerCruiser drive units with a 1.65:1 ratio have the same number of teeth on

13

*the drive and driven gears in the drive shaft housing. These gears have marks that must be aligned as shown in **Figure 29**.*

3. Align gear marks, if necessary, and install universal joint/drive gear assembly into drive shaft housing. See **Figure 29**B (1.65:1 ratio) or **Figure 30** (all others).

4. Wipe bearing retainer nut threads with Quick-silver Perfect Seal and hand start the nut in the housing threads.

NOTE
*To properly torque the bearing retainer in Step 5, it will be necessary to modify the retainer wrench by grinding off a 1/2 in. drive socket and welding the drive end to the wrench (**Figure 31**). Since this method of attachment will change the actual torque applied, it is necessary to measure the length of the wrench as shown in **Figure 31** and refer to **Table 2** to determine the torque wrench reading required to correctly torque the bearing retainer.*

5. Install bearing retainer wrench (part No. C-91-36235) (**Figure 15**) and tighten bearing retainer to 200 ft.-lb. (271 N•m).

6. Check drive-to-driven gear clearance as described under *Gear Clearance* in this chapter.

7. When clearance is correct, install top cover and tighten to specification (**Table 1**).

Upper Drive Shaft/Driven Gear Assembly Removal/Disassembly

1. Remove the top cover and water pocket cover (except Generation II) as described in this chapter.

2. Remove the universal joint, drive gear and bearing assembly as described in this chapter.

3. Reach into the drive shaft housing and remove the upper drive shaft and driven gear/bearing assembly.

NOTE
*If drive gear and bearing are both in good condition, they can be pressed off the shaft as a unit (**Figure 32**) instead of separately as in Step 4 and Step 6.*

4. Install a universal puller plate between the drive gear and tapered roller bearing. Press the bearing off the upper drive shaft.

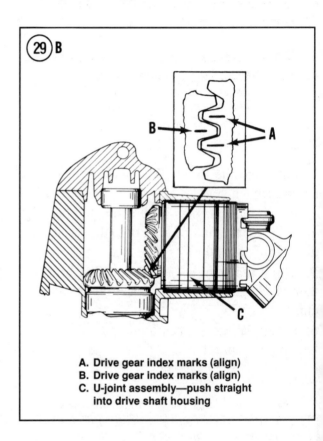

A. Drive gear index marks (align)
B. Drive gear index marks (align)
C. U-joint assembly—push straight into drive shaft housing

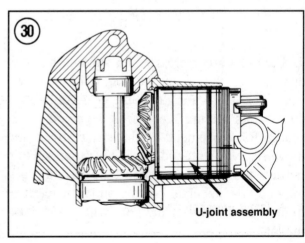

U-joint assembly

5. Reverse puller plate position to press small bearing off the other end of the drive shaft.

6. Press the drive gear from the upper drive shaft.

7. Remove and discard the upper drive shaft O-ring.

Upper Drive Shaft/Driven Gear Assembly Cleaning and Inspection

1. Check drive gear for pitting, worn, chipped or broken teeth. Replace as required.

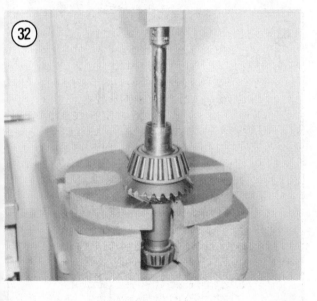

2. Check tapered roller bearing cup for scoring, pitting, grooving, heat discoloration or embedded metallic particles. Replace bearing and cup if any of these defects are noted.

3. Check driven gear shaft surface where oil seal lip rides. Replace gear/shaft assembly if grooves or scoring are noted.

Upper Drive Shaft/Driven Gear Assembly Assembly/Installation

1. Install a new O-ring on the upper drive shaft.

2. Wipe ID of driven gear with Quicksilver Premium Blend Gear Lube, then press upper drive shaft into driven gear.

3. Wipe ID of upper drive shaft small bearing and press into place.

4. Wipe ID of driven gear tapered roller bearing and press into place until it seats on the driven gear shoulder.

5. Install upper drive shaft and driven gear assembly into drive shaft housing.

6. Establish upper drive shaft bearing preload as described in this chapter.

7. Check drive and driven gear clearances as described in this chapter.

8. Install the universal joint, drive gear and bearing assembly as described in this chapter.

13

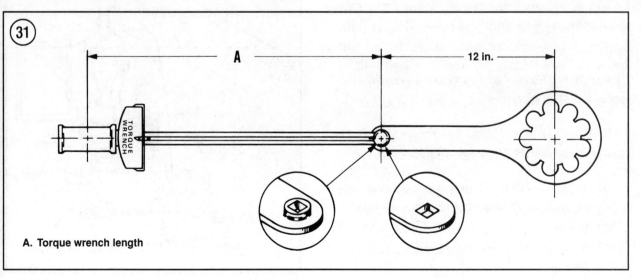

A. Torque wrench length

9. Install the top cover and water pocket cover (if so equipped) as described in this chapter.

Intermediate Shift Shaft/Bushing Removal/Installation

1. Remove the drive shaft housing as described in this chapter.
2. Invert the housing and install in a suitable holding fixture.
3. Remove the cotter pin holding the intermediate shift shaft in place. Remove the washer and shift shaft.
4. Drive the shift shaft bushing out with an appropriate size socket and hammer.
5. Installation is the reverse of removal. Install a new cotter pin.

Drive Shaft Housing Bearing Cup Replacement

Whenever the drive shaft housing is completely disassembled, wash the entire assembly in solvent and blow dry with compressed air. If one or more bearing cups and/or oil seals must be replaced, they can be removed with a standard 2-jaw puller and slide hammer (bearing cups) or screwdriver (oil seals). See **Figure 33** (bearing cup) or **Figure 34** (oil seal). New bearing cups and/or oil seals can be installed with appropriate size sockets or drivers. Be sure to retrieve any shims located under the bearing cup(s).

Wipe the OD of all metal-case oil seals with Loctite Type A before installation. Install the upper and lower drive shaft oil seals with their lip facing the driven gear. After installation, lubricate the seal lip with Quicksilver 2-4-C Multi-Lube.

Upper Drive Shaft Preload Adjustment

The upper drive shaft preload must be correctly established before the drive and driven gear clearances can be properly shimmed. The gearcase (lower unit) must be removed from the drive shaft housing for this check.

1. Remove the gearcase (lower unit) as described in Chapter Fourteen and mount it in a suitable holding fixture.
2. Lubricate all bearings and gears involved with a few drops of Quicksilver Premium Blend Gear Lube to prevent erratic results from dry bearings and gears.
3. Rotate the drive shaft several times in one direction to seat the bearings.
4. Install an in.-lb. torque wrench to the end of the drive shaft and slowly rotate the shaft in the same direction as in Step 3. Maintain a smooth rotational motion and note the torque reading. It

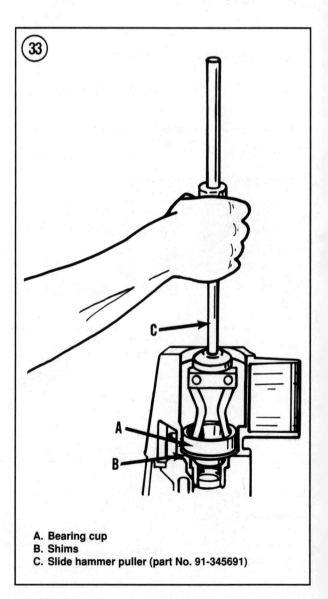

A. Bearing cup
B. Shims
C. Slide hammer puller (part No. 91-345691)

should be between 6-10 in.-lb. for new bearings and 2 1/2-4 in.-lb. for used bearings. Repeat this step 3-4 times to allow the bearings to seat and to obtain a correct reading.

NOTE
If the top cover bearing cup shimming is changed, the cover must be retorqued and drive shaft clearance rechecked.

5. If torque reading is greater than specified, remove shims from under the top cover bearing cup. If less than specified, add shims under the top cover bearing cup.

Gear Clearance Check/Adjustment

Whenever the universal joint, drive gear and bearing assembly is removed, drive and driven gear clearances must be checked and corrected as the unit is reassembled.

Driven gear shimming

This procedure requires the use of shimming tool part No. C-91-60526. Refer to **Figure 35** for this procedure.

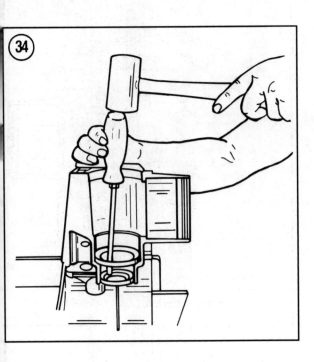

1. Check the upper drive shaft bearing preload as described in this chapter.
2. Make sure that the top cover is properly torqued in position.
3. Select the proper face of the shimming tool to be used according to your drive unit (**Figure 35**). Align that face with 3 teeth of the driven gear.
4. Insert a 0.025 in. flat feeler gauge as shown in **Figure 35** between one outer tooth of the aligned gear teeth and the shimming tool.
5. Rotate the shimming tool to provide a slight drag on the feeler gauge. Hold the shimming tool in position and move the feeler gauge between another outer tooth of the aligned gear teeth and the tool.
6. If clearance is greater or smaller than 0.025 in., repeat Step 4 and Step 5 with feeler gauges of varying thicknesses until the same clearance is felt between both outer teeth and the tool.
7. If clearance is less than 0.025 in., the gear is too high. Subtract your reading from 0.025 in. The difference is the shim thickness that must be *removed* from under the upper drive shaft bearing cup in the top cover to maintain upper drive shaft preload.
8. If clearance is greater than 0.025 in., the gear is too low. Subtract 0.025 in. from your reading. The difference is the shim thickness that must be added under the upper drive shaft bearing cup in the top cover to maintain upper drive shaft preload.
9. After making the necessary calculations and changing shims as required, check and readjust bearing preload as required, then repeat this procedure to make sure the driven gear clearance is still correct. When it is, continue unit reassembly.

Drive gear shimming

This procedure requires the use of shimming tool part No. C-91-60523. Refer to **Figure 36** as required for this procedure.

1. Select the proper face of the shimming tool to be used according to your drive unit (**Figure 36**).

13

Align that face with at least 2 full teeth of the drive gear.

2. Insert a 0.025 in. flat feeler gauge as shown in **Figure 36** between one outer tooth of the aligned gear teeth and the shimming tool.

3. Rotate the shimming tool to provide a slight drag on the feeler gauge. Hold the shimming tool in position and move the feeler gauge between the other outer tooth of the aligned gear teeth and the tool.

4. If clearance is greater or smaller than 0.025 in., repeat Step 2 and Step 3 with feeler gauges of varying thicknesses until the same clearance is felt between both outer teeth and the tool.

5. If clearance is less than 0.025 in., the gear is too far forward. Subtract your reading from 0.025 in. The difference is the shim thickness that must be *removed* from the driven gear bearing cup.

6. If clearance is greater than 0.025 in., the gear is too far aft. Subtract 0.025 in. from your reading. The difference is the shim thickness that must be *removed* from the U-joint front bearing cup. The same amount of shimming must be *added* behind the drive gear bearing cup.

7. After making the necessary calculations and changing shims as required, repeat this procedure to make sure the drive gear clearance is now correct. When it is, continue unit reassembly.

BRAVO ONE, BRAVO TWO AND BRAVO THREE DRIVE

Figure 37 is an exploded view of the Bravo drive shaft housing.

Drive Shaft Housing Removal

1. Remove the gearcase (lower unit). See Chapter Fourteen.

2. Remove the power trim cylinders. See Chapter Sixteen.

3. Disconnect the speedometer hose fitting at the drive shaft housing.

4. Remove the 6 elastic stop nuts and washer holding the drive shaft housing to the bell hous ing. See **Figure 38**. If equipped with a continuit circuit, a ground plate will be used in place of washer and should not be removed.

5. Shift the drive unit into NEUTRAL gear t allow the shift slide jaws to open and release th shift cable end.

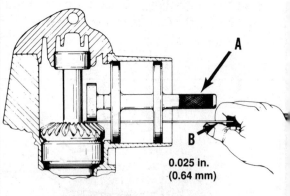

(35) **DRIVEN GEAR CLEARANCE**

SHIMMING TOOL 91-60526	
Overall Drive Unit Gear Ratio	Tool Position
1.32:1	Z
1.50:1	Z
1.65:1	X
1.84:1	Y
1.98:1	Y

0.025 in. (0.64 mm)

A. 0.025 in. (0.64 mm) feeler gauge
B. Rotate shimming tool until a slight tool drag is felt on feeler gauge

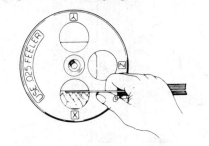

6. Pull the drive shaft housing straight back from the bell housing, then mount the assembly in a suitable holding fixture.

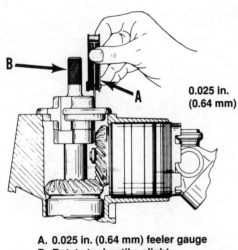

36 **DRIVE GEAR CLEARANCE**

SHIMMING TOOL 91-60523	
Overall Drive Unit Gear Ratio	Tool Position
1.32:1	Z
1.50:1	Z
1.65:1	X
1.84:1	Y
1.98:1	Y

0.025 in. (0.64 mm)

A. 0.025 in. (0.64 mm) feeler gauge
B. Rotate tool until a slight drag is felt on feeler gauge

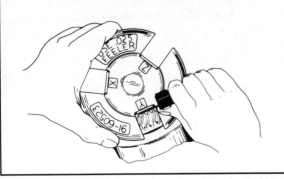

Drive Shaft Housing Installation

If engine was removed, reinstall and check alignment. See Chapter Eight. If shift cable was disconnected from engine, reinstall and adjust. See Chapter Fifteen.

CAUTION
Engine alignment is a critical operation which requires good judgment and experience in addition to use of the special alignment tool. It is best to have your MerCruiser dealer perform any alignment procedures required to prevent premature failure of the drive shaft unit.

Check engine alignment to make sure there is no resistance to the alignment tool entering the engine. If there is, the engine must be aligned. This requires raising or lowering the front of the engine until the alignment tool meets no resistance when installed. See Chapter Eight.

1. Make sure the remote control is in NEUTRAL.

2. Remove and discard the drive shaft housing O-rings (**Figure 39**). Clean O-ring grooves of all residue. Coat grooves with 3M Adhesive and install new O-rings. Wipe off any excess adhesive and lubricate the O-rings with Quicksilver 2-4-C Multi-Lube.

3. Lubricate the bell housing studs with Quicksilver 2-4-C Multi-Lube. See **Figure 40**.

4. Lubricate the drive shaft and U-joint assembly with 2-4-C Multi-Lube at the points shown in **Figure 41**.

5. Pull the shift linkage out as far as it will go using needlenose pliers. The jaws will open as shown in **Figure 42**.

6. Align the drive unit U-joint with the gimbal bearing.

NOTE
If the universal joint shaft splines do not engage with the engine coupling splines in Step 7, rotate the propeller shaft clockwise or counterclockwise as re-

13

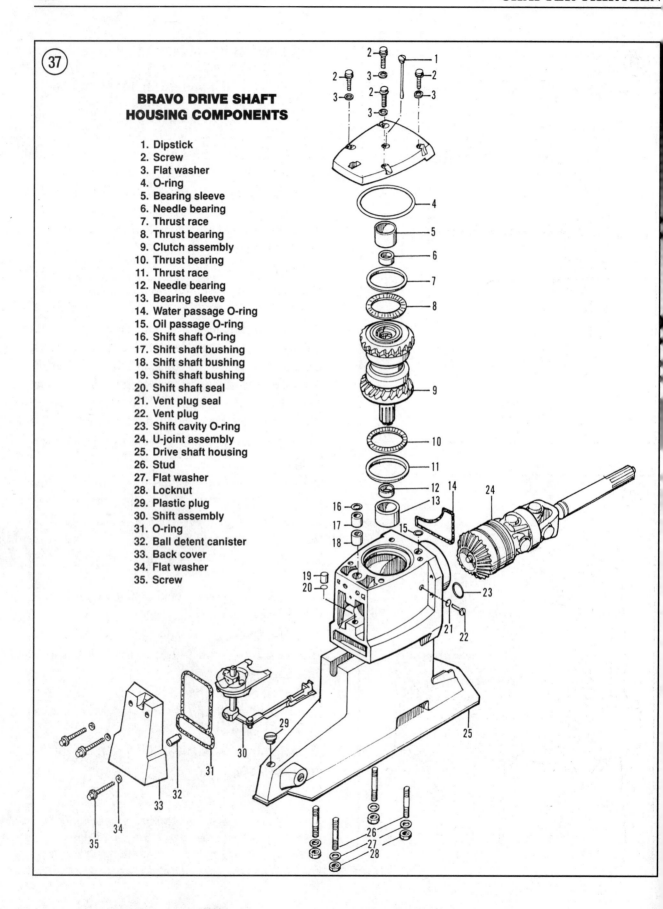

**BRAVO DRIVE SHAFT
HOUSING COMPONENTS**

1. Dipstick
2. Screw
3. Flat washer
4. O-ring
5. Bearing sleeve
6. Needle bearing
7. Thrust race
8. Thrust bearing
9. Clutch assembly
10. Thrust bearing
11. Thrust race
12. Needle bearing
13. Bearing sleeve
14. Water passage O-ring
15. Oil passage O-ring
16. Shift shaft O-ring
17. Shift shaft bushing
18. Shift shaft bushing
19. Shift shaft bushing
20. Shift shaft seal
21. Vent plug seal
22. Vent plug
23. Shift cavity O-ring
24. U-joint assembly
25. Drive shaft housing
26. Stud
27. Flat washer
28. Locknut
29. Plastic plug
30. Shift assembly
31. O-ring
32. Ball detent canister
33. Back cover
34. Flat washer
35. Screw

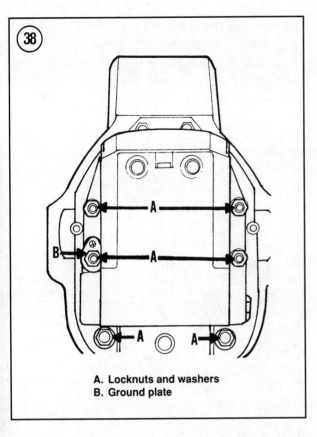

A. Locknuts and washers
B. Ground plate

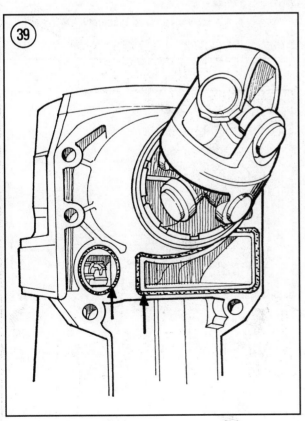

quired until the stern drive can be pushed into position.

7. Install the stern drive to the bell housing, guiding the universal joint shaft through the gimbal housing bearing and into the engine coupler. At the same time, guide the shift cable into the shift linkage assembly (**Figure 43**). As the cable enters the linkage assembly, it will push the assembly into the drive shaft housing. This closes the linkage jaws to hold the cable securely. See **Figure 44**.

8. Once the drive unit is mated to the bell housing, rotate the propeller shaft slightly to make sure that the drive unit is still in NEUTRAL gear.

9. Install a flat washer and new elastic stop nut on each stern drive-to-bell housing stud (except a stud fitted with a ground plate). See **Figure 38**. Start with the center nuts and tighten to 50 ft.-lb. (68 N·m).

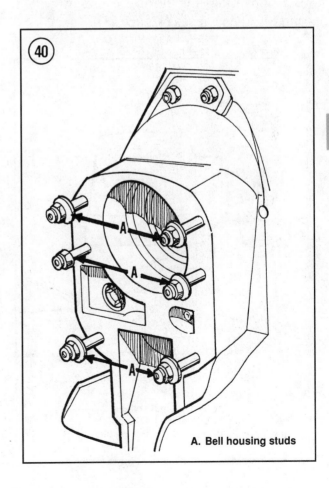

A. Bell housing studs

13

10. Raise the drive unit up enough to provide access to connect the speedometer hose. Install the hose fitting in the drive housing opening as shown in **Figure 45**.

11. Depress the fitting until it is fully seated, then rotate the fitting handle clockwise as far as possible to assure that the fitting is locked in place. See **Figure 46**.

12. Install the gearcase (lower unit). See Chapter Fourteen.

13. Install the power trim cylinders. See Chapter Sixteen.

Drive Shaft Housing Disassembly

1. Shift the drive shaft housing into its NEUTRAL detent position.

2. Use a 12-point socket to unbolt and remove the rear cover (**Figure 47**).

3. Remove the shift linkage capscrew with a suitable Allen wrench (**Figure 48**).

4. Remove the shift cam capscrew (**Figure 49**). If the capscrew cannot be removed easily, thread shift handle part No. 91-17302 into the shift lever/shift shaft to hold the assembly in place while loosening the capscrew (**Figure 50**).

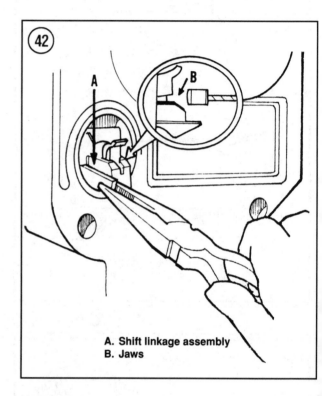

A. Shift linkage assembly
B. Jaws

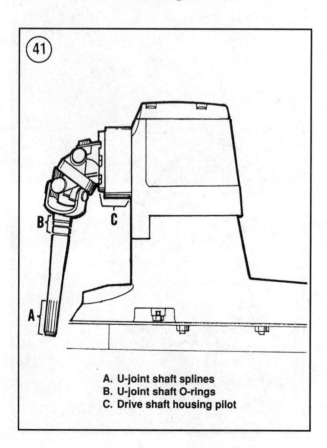

A. U-joint shaft splines
B. U-joint shaft O-rings
C. Drive shaft housing pilot

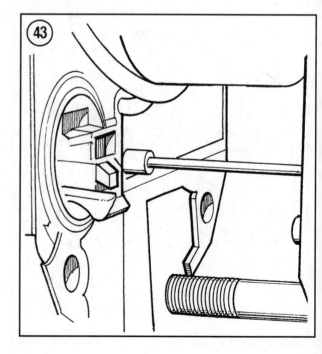

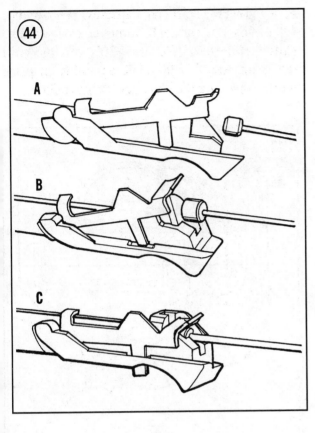

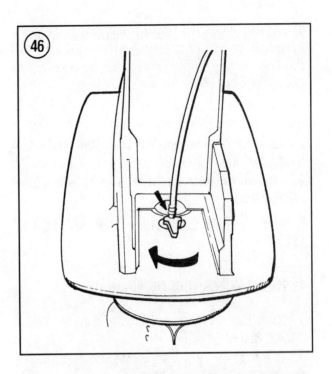

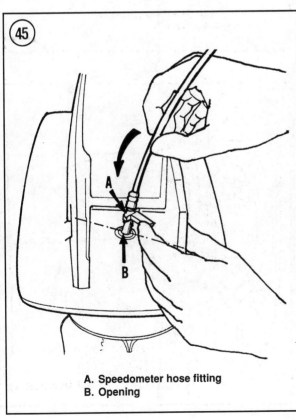

A. Speedometer hose fitting
B. Opening

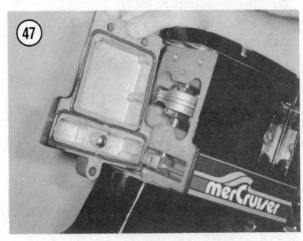

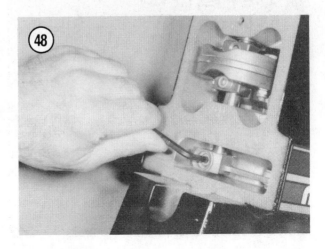

5. Use a 12-point socket to unbolt and remove the top cover (**Figure 51**).

6. Thread the shift handle tool (part No. 91-17302) in the shifter shaft and lift the shift shaft straight up and out of the housing (**Figure 52**).

7. Rotate the shift linkage link bar 1/4 turn clockwise and move assembly from side to side as required to pull it out of the housing. See **Figure 53**.

8. Remove the yoke and cam assembly (**Figure 54**).

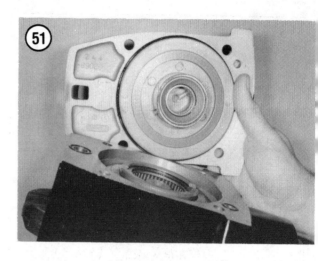

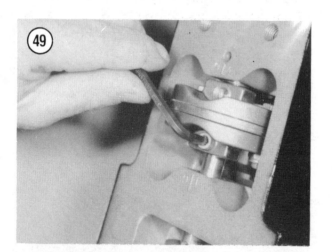

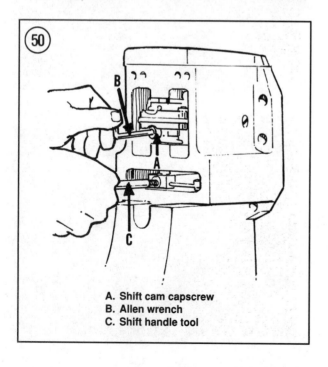

A. Shift cam capscrew
B. Allen wrench
C. Shift handle tool

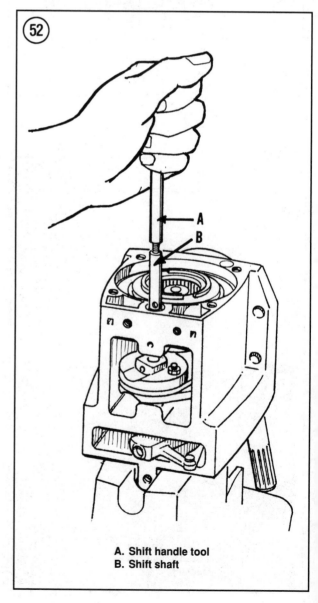

A. Shift handle tool
B. Shift shaft

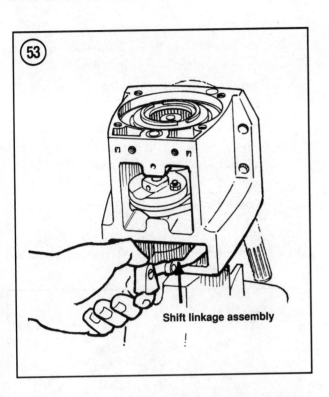

Shift linkage assembly

9. Install retainer wrench part No. 91-36235 (**Figure 55**) and loosen the retainer nut. Remove the wrench and unscrew the retainer nut. When it is free of the housing, remove the U-joint assembly by pulling it straight out (**Figure 56**).

10. Remove the upper thrust race and thrust bearing (**Figure 57**). The thrust race serves double duty as a shim. Label and tie these together to prevent mixing them up with similar components to be removed in Step 12.

11. Reach into the U-joint bore and lift the clutch assembly up far enough to grasp it with the other hand, then remove the clutch assembly from the housing. See **Figure 58**.

12. Reach into the clutch assembly bore and remove the lower thrust race and thrust bearing (**Figure 59**). The thrust race also serves double duty as a shim. Label and tie these together to

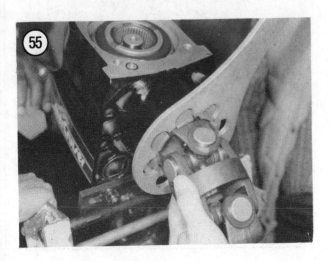

13

prevent mixing them up with the similar components removed in Step 10.

13. Remove the shift shaft upper O-ring (A, **Figure 60**) and oil passage O-ring (B) from the top of the housing. Discard the O-rings.

14. The shifter shaft bushings must be replaced whenever a new shifter shaft is installed or when the bushings are excessively worn. If shift shaft bushings require replacement:

   a. Use tool part No. 91-17273 and a hammer to drive out the upper bushing (**Figure 61**).

b. Use the same tools to drive out the lower bushing and oil seal (**Figure 62**).

c. Partially install a new lower bushing in the housing bore (**Figure 63**).

d. Fit a new seal on driver part No. 91-17275 with its lip facing upward. Wipe OD of seal with Loctite Type 271 (**Figure 64**).

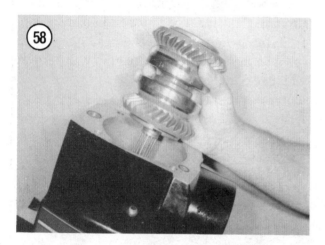

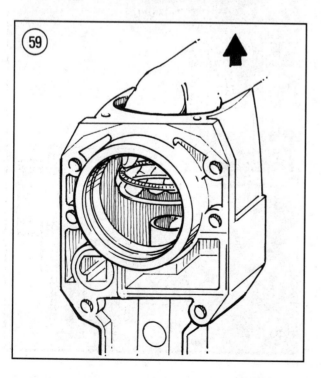

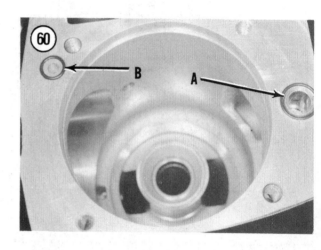

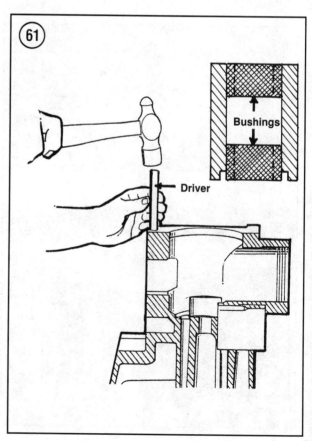

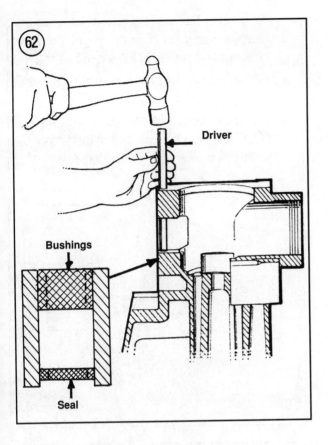

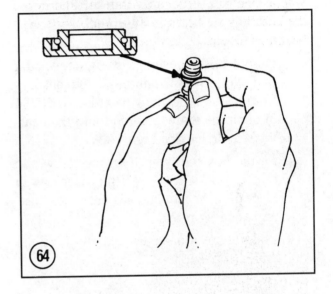

e. Insert driver with seal into the bottom of the bushing. Insert screw pilot part No. 91-17274 through the bushing from the top. Fit screw part No. 10-20784 through the screw pilot and into the bearing/seal driver. See **Figure 65**.

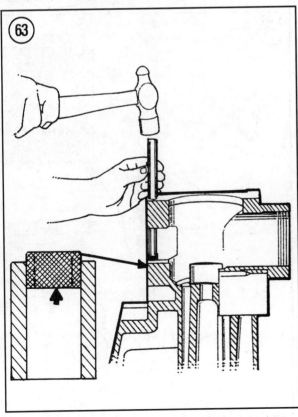

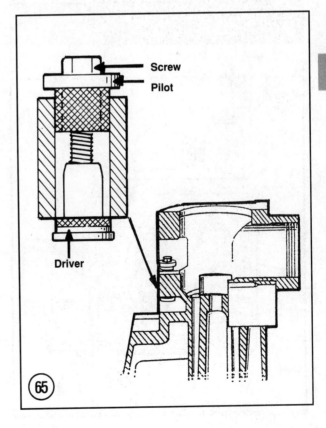

13

f. Fit a suitable box-end wrench on the screw and turn it clockwise until the tool bottoms out on the casting. See **Figure 66**.

g. Install a new upper bushing in its bore and drive into the bore until it protrudes from the bottom as shown in **Figure 67**.

h. Repeat sub-step g to install the 2nd upper bushing as shown in **Figure 68**.

i. Insert driver used in sub-step e into the bottom of the bushing. Insert screw pilot part No. 91-17274 through the bushing from the top. Fit screw part No. 10-20784 through the screw pilot and into the bearing/seal driver. See **Figure 69**.

j. Fit the box-end wrench on the screw and turn it clockwise to pull the bushings in place until the tool bottoms out on the casting. See **Figure 70**.

k. Loosen the tool screw and remove the driver, pilot and tool.

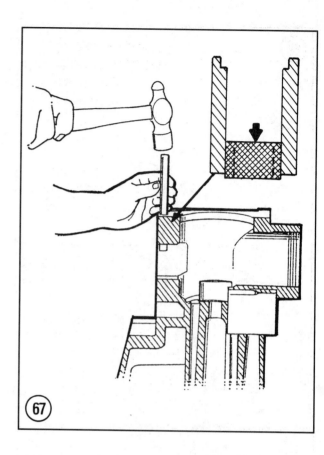

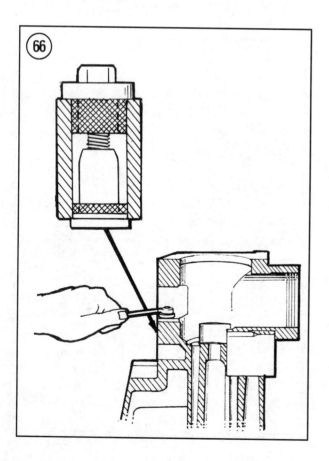

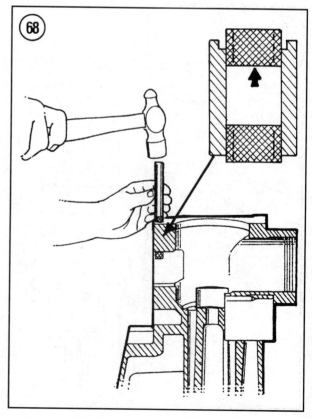

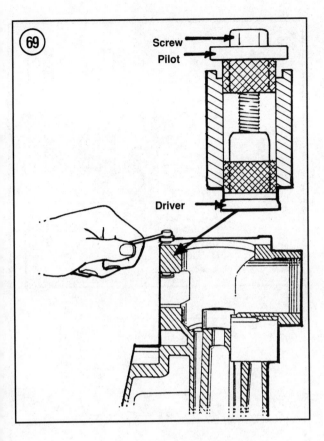

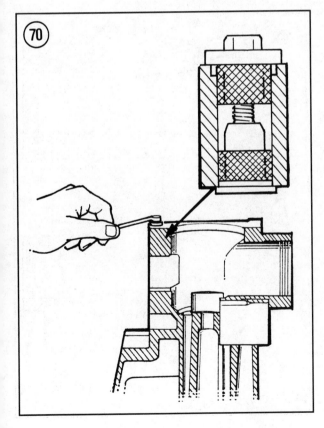

Shifter Mechanism Disassembly/Assembly

Refer to **Figure 71** for this procedure.

1. Remove and discard the clevis pin's cotter pin (**Figure 72**). Remove the clevis pin and separate the link bar from the shift lever.

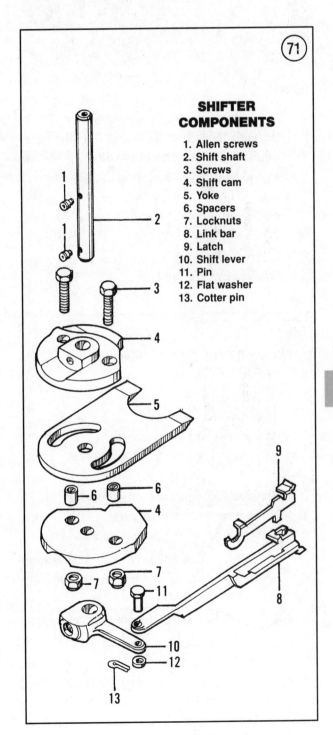

SHIFTER COMPONENTS

1. Allen screws
2. Shift shaft
3. Screws
4. Shift cam
5. Yoke
6. Spacers
7. Locknuts
8. Link bar
9. Latch
10. Shift lever
11. Pin
12. Flat washer
13. Cotter pin

13

2. Remove the latch from the link bar (**Figure 73**).

3. Remove the ball detent canister and compression spring from the rear cover (**Figure 74**).

4. Remove the fasteners (A, **Figure 75**) from the shift cam. Remove the shift cam (B, **Figure 75**) from the shift yoke (C).

5. Separate the shifter yoke from the shift cam. Do not lose the spacers installed over the cam bolts. See **Figure 76**.

6. Clean and inspect all components as described in this chapter.

7. Assembly is the reverse of disassembly. Install new shift cam locknuts and tighten to specification (**Table 1**). Lubricate the compression spring and ball detent canister with Quicksilver Special Lubricant 101 before reinstalling in the rear cover.

Cleaning and Inspection

1. Clean all parts in fresh solvent and blow dry with compressed air.

2. Check the shift link bar and lever for bending, distortion or other damage. Check the jaw area for excessive wear. Check the shift lever detent area for excessive wear. Replace parts as required.

3. Check the ball detent canister. Replace canister if ball is not secured in place. Check the spring. Replace if broken or distorted.

4. Inspect the yoke and cam assembly for damaged spacers or excessive wear on the cam surface.

5. Check the shift shaft for signs of excessive wear where the bushings ride. Replace the shaft and bushings if such wear is noted.

6. Check the shift shaft bushings for nicks, scratches or excessive wear. If such wear is found, replace the bushings and the shift shaft.

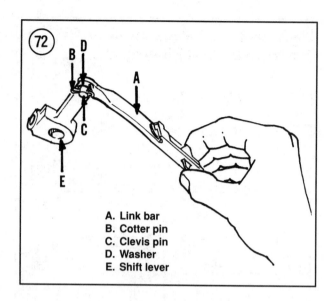

A. Link bar
B. Cotter pin
C. Clevis pin
D. Washer
E. Shift lever

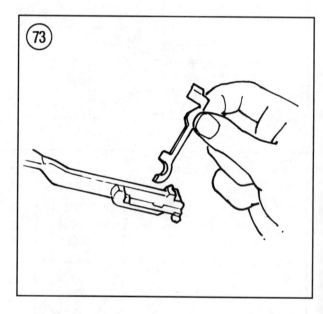

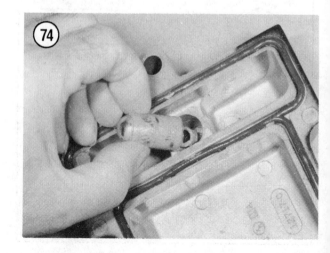

Universal Joint/Pinion Gear Assembly Pre-Inspection and Disassembly

Refer to **Figure 77** for this procedure.

1. Check the pinion gear for pitted, chipped or broken teeth. Look for uneven or excessive wear. See **Figure 78**. If any of these defects are found, replace the complete drive gear and bearing assembly.

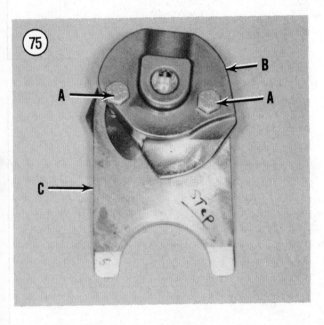

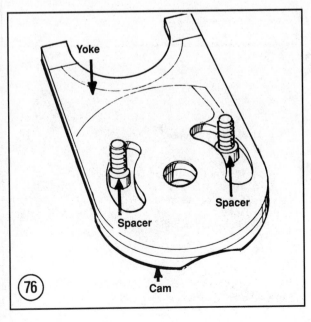

2. Rotate the pinion gear bearings manually. Check for rough or uneven movement or looseness. If bearings appear to be defective and drive gear assembly is satisfactory, only the bearings need be replaced.

3. Check for loose or rough movement in the U-joints. Replace components as required.

4. Clamp the bearing retainer wrench at a 45° angle in the vise with the handle facing at 10 o'clock or 2 o'clock. Fit the universal joint yoke over the wrench handle to hold the assembly and remove the drive gear nut with an appropriate socket and flex handle. See **Figure 79**.

5. Refer to **Figure 77** and remove the drive gear assembly and remaining components from the universal joint shaft.

6. If only the bearings require replacement, press them off the gear with a universal puller plate. Removal will damage the bearings; new ones must be installed on reassembly. Work carefully to avoid damaging the spacer while removing the first bearing from the pinion gear, as it must be reused during assembly.

7. If the oil seal requires replacement, drive the oil seal out of the carrier with a suitable punch and hammer.

8. Remove the 2 O-rings from the end of the universal joint shaft coupling (**Figure 80**).

9. Clean and inspect the universal joint and shaft assembly as described in this chapter.

Universal Joint Shaft Cleaning and Inspection

1. Clean all parts in fresh solvent. Blow dry with compressed air.

NOTE
If wear or corrosion is found in Step 2 or Step 3, also check engine coupler splines for the same defect.

2. Inspect coupler and gear end of U-joint for spline wear.

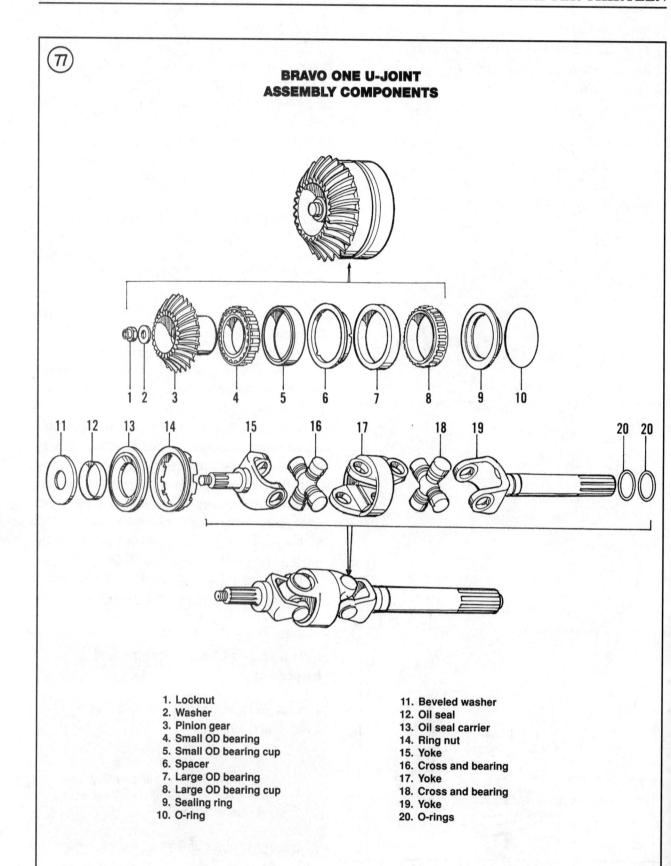

77

BRAVO ONE U-JOINT ASSEMBLY COMPONENTS

1. Locknut
2. Washer
3. Pinion gear
4. Small OD bearing
5. Small OD bearing cup
6. Spacer
7. Large OD bearing
8. Large OD bearing cup
9. Sealing ring
10. O-ring

11. Beveled washer
12. Oil seal
13. Oil seal carrier
14. Ring nut
15. Yoke
16. Cross and bearing
17. Yoke
18. Cross and bearing
19. Yoke
20. O-rings

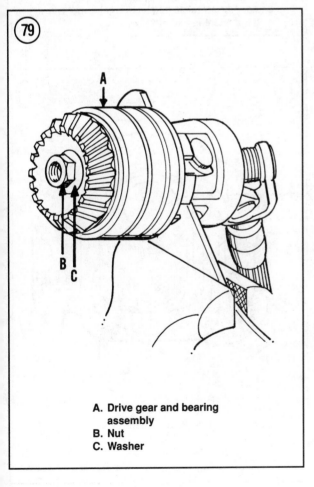

A. Drive gear and bearing
   assembly
B. Nut
C. Washer

3. Clean all corrosion from the coupling. Replace coupling yoke if splines are partially corroded away.

4. Service defective U-joints as described in this chapter.

Universal Joint Disassembly/Assembly

While universal joint disassembly may not be absolutely necessary, it is always a good idea to replace the spider and bearings whenever the drive shaft is out of the housing. Refer to **Figure 77** for this procedure.

1. Place universal joint assembly over a suitable support and note the location of the grease fittings (**Figure 81**). The spiders should be reinstalled with their grease fittings in the same location. Remove the snap rings with a punch and hammer.

2. Install an automotive-type U-joint tool and adaptor (part No. C-91-38756) as shown in **Figure 82** (large adaptor opening should face outward). Tighten the tool to apply pressure on one bearing cap and force the other one into the adaptor. If the tool is not available, support the yoke between a pair of appropriate size sockets. Apply pressure with a hydraulic press on one bearing cap until the opposite one is pressed into the socket, then remove the one free bearing cap.

13

3. Rotate the tool 180° and repeat Step 2 to press the 2nd bearing cap into the adaptor, then remove the yoke.

4. Repeat Steps 1-3 to remove the remaining bearings. Remove the spider.

5. Repeat Steps 1-4 to remove the second spider/yoke assembly.

6. Position the bearing caps, yoke and cross as shown in **Figure 83** (small adaptor opening should face outward). Make sure the cross is installed with its grease fitting facing the coupling end yoke.

7. Press both bearing caps into the yoke and onto the cross, then install new C-rings (**Figure 84**). The curved C-rings must be installed with the curve facing outward. See **Figure 85**.

8. Repeat Step 6 and Step 7 to install the remaining bearings.

9. Repeat Steps 6-8 to install the second spider/yoke assembly.

10. Install new O-rings on the universal joint shaft coupling (**Figure 80**).

Universal Joint, Drive Gear and Bearing Assembly

Refer to **Figure 28** for this procedure.

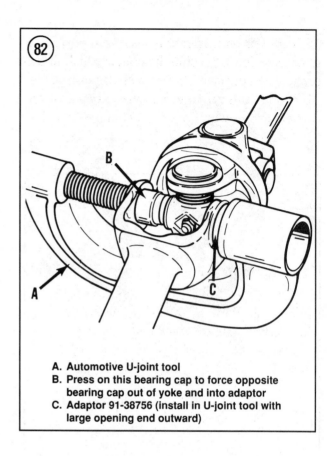

A. Automotive U-joint tool
B. Press on this bearing cap to force opposite bearing cap out of yoke and into adaptor
C. Adaptor 91-38756 (install in U-joint tool with large opening end outward)

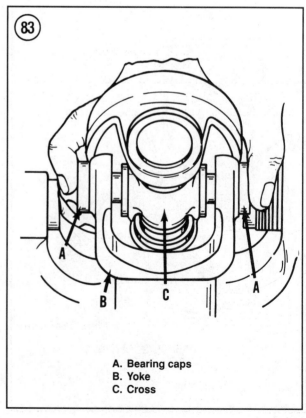

A. Bearing caps
B. Yoke
C. Cross

1. If oil seal in carrier was removed, position a new seal (lip side facing the concave side of the carrier) and press into place with driver part No. 91-89868 until the tool bottoms out against the carrier. Wipe seal lip with Quicksilver 2-4-C Multi-Lube.

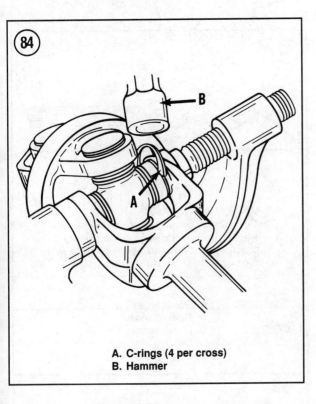

A. C-rings (4 per cross)
B. Hammer

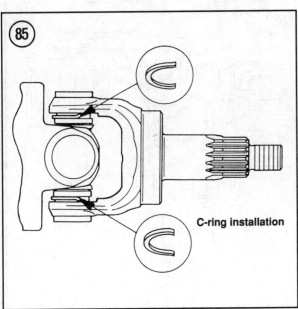

C-ring installation

2. If the tapered roller bearings were removed from the pinion gear, press the small diameter bearing onto the gear with tool part No. 91-90774.

3. Refer to **Figure 86** and place the smaller bearing cup over the bearing installed in Step 2, then install the spacer with its flat side facing the gear. If spacer is incorrectly positioned, it will cause serious damage to the gear during reassembly.

4. Install the larger bearing cup, then press the larger bearing onto the gear to a point where the rollers just contact the cup.

5. Make sure the spacer rotates freely between the bearing cups. If it does not, you have over-pressed the bearing, which will fail prematurely. To correct the condition, support the large bearing with a universal puller plate and gently tap the end of the gear with a soft-faced hammer until the spacer can rotate freely.

6. Starting with the threaded retainer nut, install the components shown in **Figure 87** in the order shown. The oil carrier seal lip should face the pinion gear. The washer and sealing ring tapers should face the U-joints. The O-ring is posi-

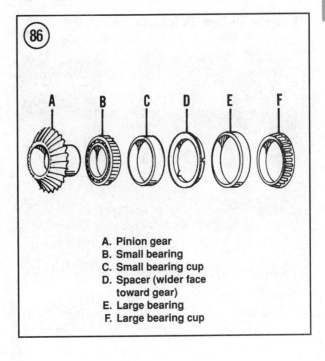

A. Pinion gear
B. Small bearing
C. Small bearing cup
D. Spacer (wider face toward gear)
E. Large bearing
F. Large bearing cup

13

tioned between the oil seal carrier and sealing ring.

7. Install the pinion gear assembly on the shaft splines. Install the washer and a new nut.

8. Refer to **Figure 87** and install the components in the order shown.

9. Fit the universal joint yoke over the bearing retainer wrench handle (**Figure 79**) and tighten the nut until the washer just contacts the gear.

10. Establish bearing preload as follows:

a. Install the U-joint/pinion gear assembly in the drive shaft housing.

b. Tighten the retaining nut finger-tight.

c. Reposition the drive shaft housing so that the U-joint coupling shaft points straight down.

d. Attach an appropriate size socket to an extension and an in.-lb. torque wrench. Fit over the pinion gear nut and tighten 1/16 of a turn at a time, checking the torque wrench indicator until a reading of 6-10 in.-lb. is obtained. See **Figure 88**.

e. If excessive torque is applied, preload will be excessive. To correct, loosen the nut several turns and lightly tap the end of the pinion gear with a soft bar and hammer. Repeat sub-step d.

f. When preload is correct, return the drive shaft housing to a horizontal position and remove the U-joint/pinion gear assembly.

Clutch Disassembly/Assembly

Refer to **Figure 89** for this procedure.

NOTE
*On late models, the lower thrust collar (2, **Figure 89**) is part of the drive shaft (4) and cannot be removed.*

1. Place the clutch assembly upright on a clean workbench.

2. Grasp the top gear with one hand, push down on the gear and hold it in that position. This will depress the thrust collar and allow you to pry the keepers out with an awl. See **Figure 90**.

3. Remove the keepers (**Figure 91**), the thrust collar (**Figure 92**) and the top gear (**Figure 93**).

4. Remove the thrust bearing and race (**Figure 94**).

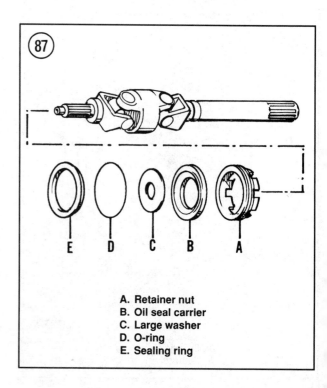

A. Retainer nut
B. Oil seal carrier
C. Large washer
D. O-ring
E. Sealing ring

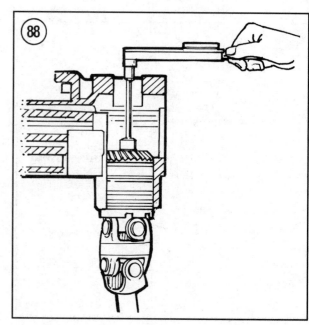

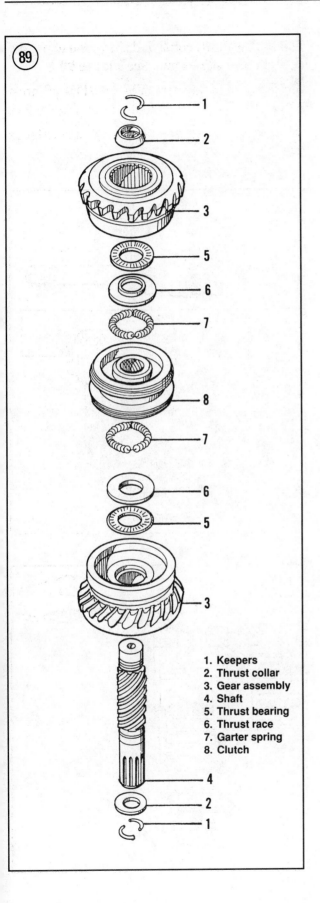

1. Keepers
2. Thrust collar
3. Gear assembly
4. Shaft
5. Thrust bearing
6. Thrust race
7. Garter spring
8. Clutch

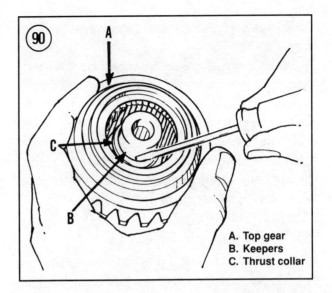

A. Top gear
B. Keepers
C. Thrust collar

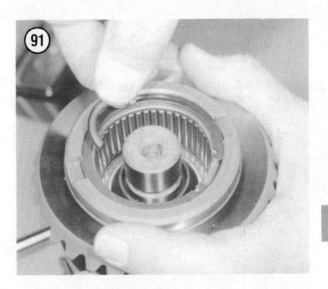

13

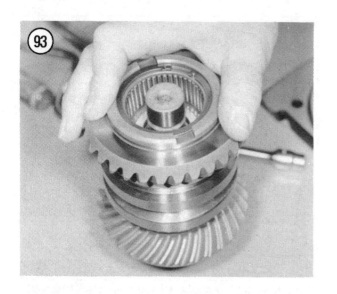

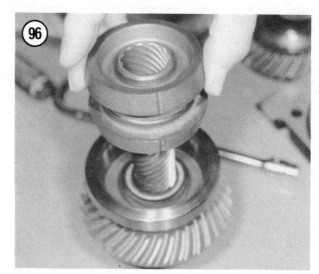

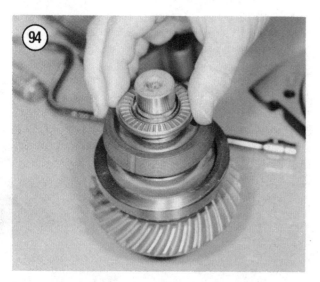

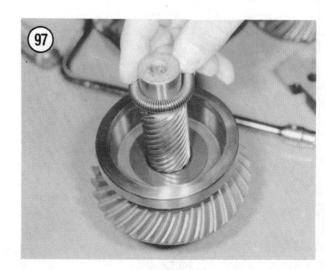

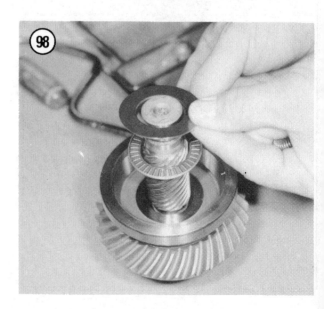

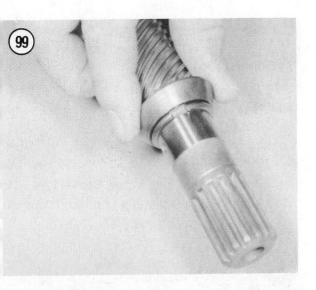

5. Remove the garter spring (**Figure 95**).

6. Rotate the clutch counterclockwise while pulling upward and disengage it from the shaft (**Figure 96**).

7. Remove the lower garter spring (**Figure 97**).

8. Remove the lower thrust race and bearing (**Figure 98**).

> *NOTE*
> *On late models, the lower thrust collar (**Figure 99**) is part of the drive shaft and cannot be removed.*

9. Remove the bottom gear, then pull the thrust collar back and remove the keepers (**Figure 99**).

10. Clean and inspect all parts as described in this chapter.

11. Fit a thrust collar on the splined end of the shaft. Fit the keepers in the groove and pull the collar over them. See **Figure 99**.

12. Lubricate the shaft splines with gear oil. Install the bottom gear on the shaft against the thrust collar (**Figure 100**).

13. Reverse Steps 1-8 to complete assembly. Installing the keepers can be a slow, frustrating task, especially if you have large hands. When properly installed, the keepers should be level with the top of the thrust collar as shown in **Figure 101**.

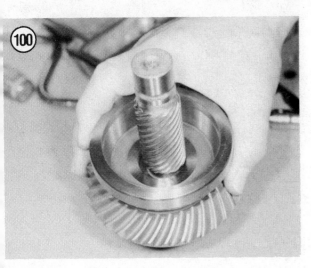

Cleaning and Inspection

1. Clean all parts in clean solvent and blow dry with compressed air.

2. Check the condition of the needle bearings inside the gears (A, **Figure 102**). Also check the bearing surfaces in the drive shaft housing and top cover. If the bearing surfaces are pitted, grooved, scored, unevenly worn or show signs of heat discoloration or embedded metallic particles, replace the gear and bearing (as well as the bearing sleeve) as an assembly.

3. Check the gear for excessively worn, pitted, chipped or broken teeth (B, **Figure 102**). Replace gear as required.

13

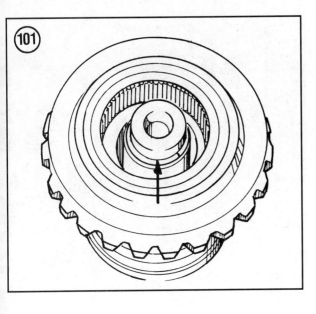

4. Check gear for heat discoloration or metallic particles. If either is found, clean the clutch grooves with a pick or bead blaster—do not use a wire wheel or wire brush. If grooves look flattened or nicked after cleaning, replace the clutch.

5. Check the clutch shaft splines for nicks or damage. Replace shaft as required.

6. Check the clutch shaft bearing surfaces for pitting, grooving, scoring or heat discoloration. Replace shaft and drive shaft housing/top cover bearings if any defect is found.

Drive Shaft Housing/Top Cover Bearings and Bearing Sleeve Replacement

The drive shaft housing and top cover bearings and sleeves should be replaced if any defects are found on the clutch shaft bearing surfaces.

1. Remove the top cover thrust bearing and race (A, **Figure 103**) and the O-ring (B).

2. To remove the top cover bearing sleeve:

   a. Clamp puller jaws part No. 91-90777A1 and 91-90778 around the sleeve (**Figure 104**).

   b. Install puller guide part No. 91-90774 and bolt part No. 90-90775 on the top cover as shown in **Figure 105**.

c. Install driver guide part No. 92-90244 and tighten the bolt to remove the sleeve. See **Figure 106**.

3. To remove the drive shaft housing bearing sleeve:

   a. Clamp puller jaws part No. 91-90777A1 and 91-90778 around the sleeve (**Figure 107**).

   b. Fit the puller guide part No. 91-90774 around the puller jaws and install bolt part No. 90-90775 (**Figure 108**).

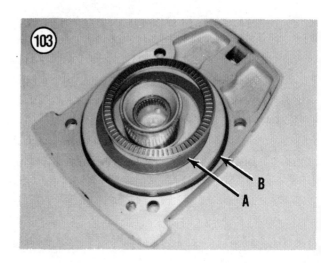

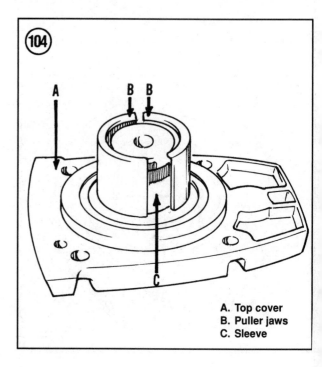

A. Top cover
B. Puller jaws
C. Sleeve

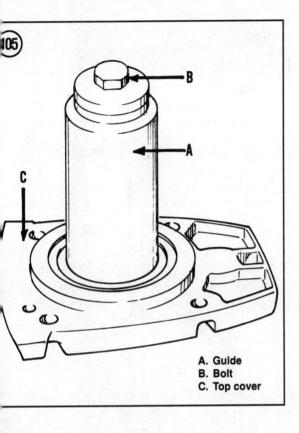

A. Guide
B. Bolt
C. Top cover

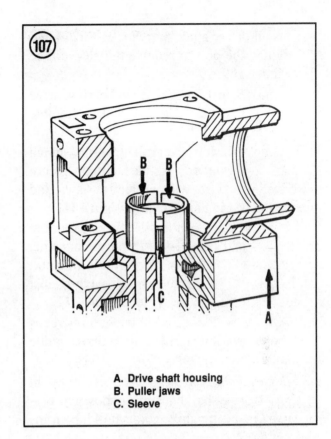

A. Drive shaft housing
B. Puller jaws
C. Sleeve

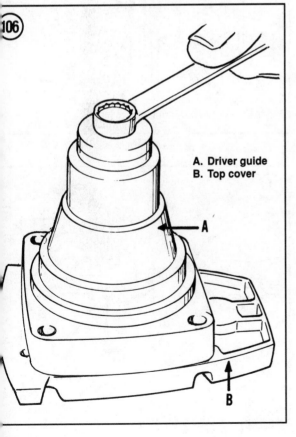

A. Driver guide
B. Top cover

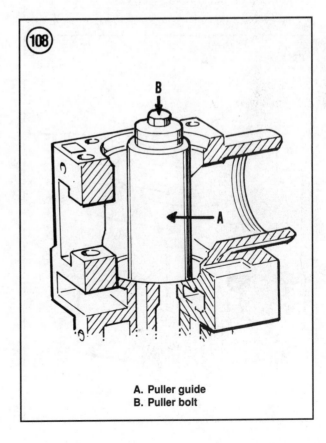

A. Puller guide
B. Puller bolt

13

c. Install driver guide part No. 91-90244 and tighten the bolt to remove the sleeve. See **Figure 109**.

4. To remove the drive shaft roller bearing, drive the bearing into the oil cavity with a suitable mandrel (**Figure 110**).

5. To remove the top cover roller bearing, attach a suitable 2-jaw puller to a slide hammer. Secure the cover in a vise with protective jaws and remove the bearing as shown in **Figure 111**.

6. To install new bearing sleeves, assemble driver head part No. 91-90773 on puller guide part No. 91-90774. Fasten the assembly with bolt part No. 90-90775. Fit the bearing sleeve against the edge of the driver head. See **Figure 112**.

   a. *Top cover*—Place assembly on top cover as shown in **Figure 113** and tap driver guide until it bottoms out.

   b. *Drive shaft housing*—Place assembly in top of drive shaft housing as shown in **Figure 114** and tap drive guide until it bottoms out.

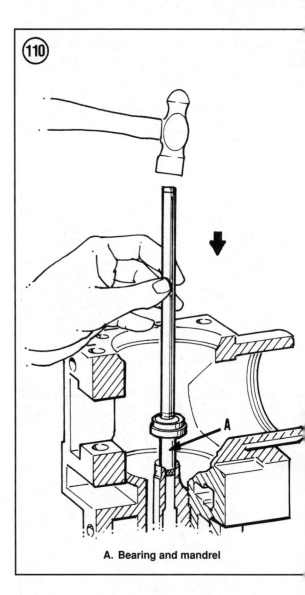

A. Bearing and mandrel

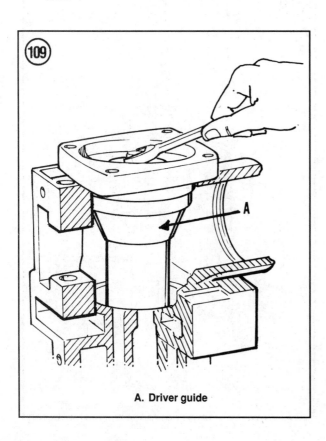

A. Driver guide

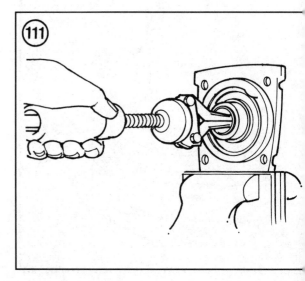

To install new roller bearings, assemble the iver components as in Step 6 and fit the roller aring on the driver head (instead of the sleeve).

a. *Top cover*—Place assembly on top cover as shown in **Figure 113** and tap driver guide until it bottoms out.

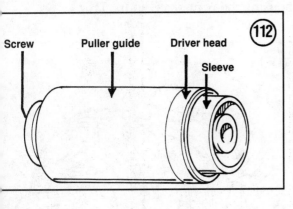

Screw   Puller guide   Driver head
                                    Sleeve

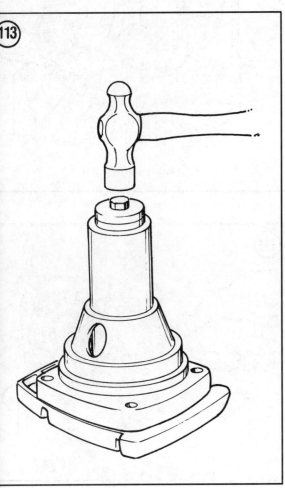

b. *Drive shaft housing*—Place assembly in top of drive shaft housing as shown in **Figure 114** and tap driver guide until it bottoms out.

Drive Shaft Housing Assembly

Refer to **Figure 37** as required for this procedure.

1. Check the shift cavity on the rear of the drive shaft housing and locate the 2 sets of numbers stamped in the casting (**Figure 115**). You may find a 91, 94 or 97 stamped in the casting. The number stamped indicates the thickness of the thrust race (shim) to be installed—0.091 in., 0.094 in. or 0.097 in.

2. Measure the thrust bearing races with a micrometer and make sure that their thickness cor-

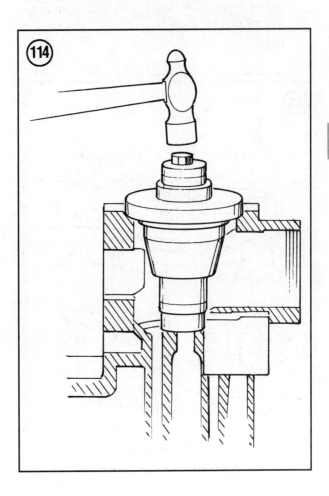

13

responds with the number stamped in the casting. In the example shown in **Figure 115**, the top race should measure 0.094 in. and the bottom race should measure 0.097 in.

3. If original races are to be reinstalled, they should be positioned so that the bearing contact side is the same as it was before they were removed. Install the lower thrust bearing race in the drive shaft housing.

4. Wipe the bottom face of the clutch lower gear with Quicksilver Special Lubricant 101 and press the thrust bearing in place (**Figure 116**). The grease will hold it during installation.

5. Carefully lower the clutch assembly into the drive shaft housing (**Figure 117**).

6. Wipe the face of the clutch top gear with Special Lubricant 101 and install the thrust bearing and bearing race on the gear.

CAUTION
Never align two negative (–) or two positive (+) marks with the housing index marks in Step 7. If like marks are aligned, the clutch will not disengage correctly.

7. Align the clutch gear timing marks. Each clutch gear has a negative (–) and a positive (+) mark stamped on it. Rotate the clutch gears to align one - and one + mark with the drive shaft housing index marks (**Figure 118**).

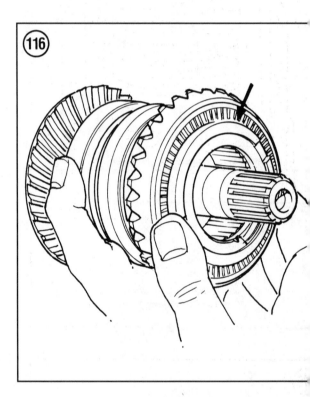

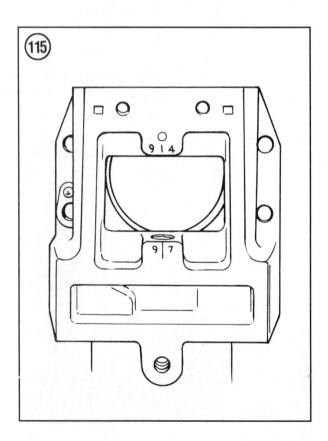

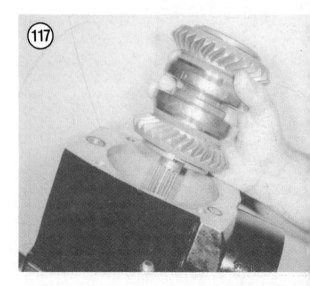

NOTE

To properly torque the retaining nut in Step 8, it is necessary to modify the retainer wrench by grinding off a 1/2 in. drive socket and welding the drive end

*to the wrench (**Figure 31**). Since this method of attachment will change the actual torque applied, it is necessary to measure the length of the wrench as shown in **Figure 31** and refer to **Table 2** to determine the torque wrench reading required to correctly torque the retaining nut.*

8. Carefully install the U-joint assembly in the drive shaft housing. This is a tight fit and may require several attempts as the unit must be inserted straight into the housing. Once in place, thread the retaining nut in finger-tight, then tighten to 150 ft.-lb. (203 N·m) with a modified bearing retainer wrench.

9. Check the alignment of the clutch gear timing marks with the drive shaft housing index marks. The timing marks must be within 1/8 in. (3.2 mm) from each other. If they are not properly aligned as in Step 7, remove the U-joint assembly and realign.

10. Install the shift cam assembly in the drive shaft housing shift cavity (**Figure 119**).

11. Insert the shift linkage assembly as shown in **Figure 120**, then rotate the assembly 1/4 turn clockwise and position as shown in **Figure 121**.

12. Install shift handle tool part No. 91-71302 in the shift shaft. Insert the shift shaft in the housing and engage the shift cam and shift lever. Rotate the shift shaft as required to align the shaft holes with the capscrew holes in the cam and lever.

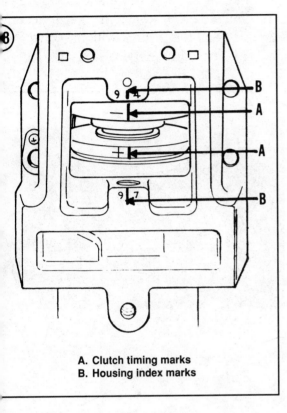

A. Clutch timing marks
B. Housing index marks

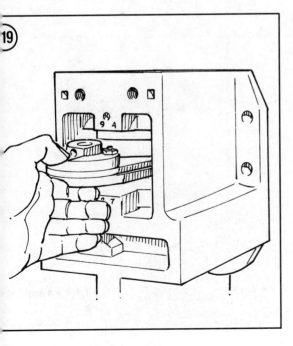

13

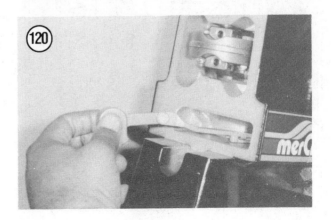

13. Install the shift cam capscrew and then the shift linkage capscrew (**Figure 122**). Tighten both capscrews to specification (**Table 1**).

14. Move the shift linkage to its neutral detent position. See **Figure 123**.

15. Install a new shift shaft O-ring (A, **Figure 124**) and oil passage O-ring (B).

16. Remove and discard rear cover O-rings. Clean grooves of all residue, then wipe new O-rings with 3M Adhesive and install in the rear cover. See **Figure 125**.

17. Install a new O-ring on the top cover. Install the top cover on the drive shaft housing. See **Figure 126**.

18. Install the cover screws with washers (**Figure 127**). If oil dipstick was removed from cover, reinstall it (**Figure 128**). Tighten fasteners to specifications (**Table 1**).

19. Install the rear cover (**Figure 129**) and tighten the screws to specifications (**Table 1**).

20. Reinstall drive shaft housing as described in this chapter.

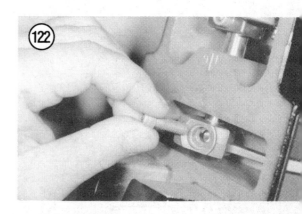

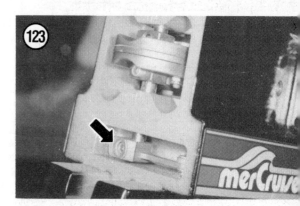

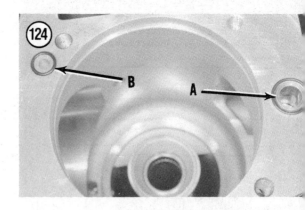

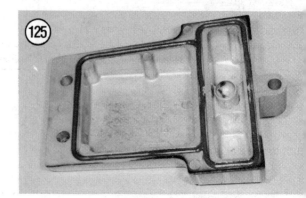

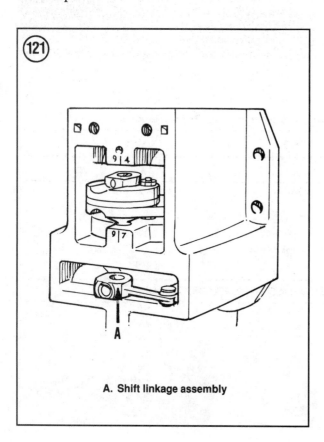

A. Shift linkage assembly

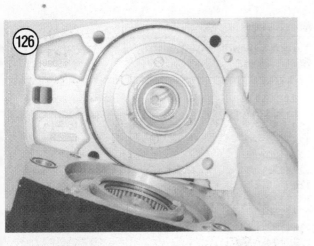

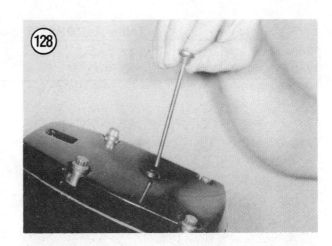

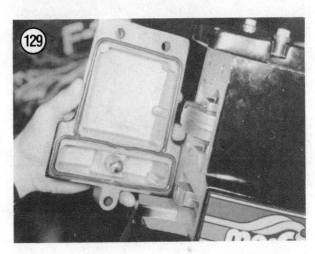

13

Table 1 DRIVE SHAFT HOUSING TIGHTENING TORQUES

	in-lb.	ft.-lb.	N·m
ALPHA ONE			
Drive shaft housing nuts		50	68
Universal joint			
Drive gear nut		70-80	95-108
Retainer nut		180-200	244-271
Top cover screws		17-23	23-31
Water pocket cover screws	30-40		3-4
BRAVO ONE, BRAVO TWO AND BRAVO THREE			
Back cover screws		20	27
Drive shaft housing fasteners		35	48
Shift cam			
Capscrew	110		13
Locknuts	103		12
Shift linkage capscrew	110		13
Top cover screws		20	27
Universal joint retainer nut		150	203

Table 2 TORQUE CONVERSION CHART

Torque wrench length in. (cm)	Torque wrench reading ft.-lb. (N·m)
15 (38)	111 (151)
16 (48)	114 (155)
17 (43)	117 (159)
18 (46)	120 (163)
19 (48)	123 (167)
20 (51)	125 (170)
21 (53)	127 (172)
22 (56)	129 (175)
23 (58)	131 (178)
24 (61)	133 (180)
25 (64)	135 (183)
26 (66)	136 (184)
27 (69)	138 (187)
28 (71)	140 (190)
29 (74)	141 (191)
30 (76)	143 (194)
31 (79)	144 (195)
32 (81)	145 (197)
33 (84)	147 (200)
34 (86)	148 (201)
35 (89)	149 (202)
36 (91)	150 (203)

Chapter Fourteen

Gearcase Housing (Lower Unit)

Engine torque passes through a drive shaft/universal joint to a pinion and drive gear in the drive shaft (upper) housing, changing the horizontal power flow from the engine into a vertical power flow sent to the gearcase (lower) housing through a drive shaft. Power application is controlled by shifting the gearcase housing (Alpha One) or drive shaft housing (Bravo One, Bravo Two and Bravo Three).

Shifting is accomplished through a shift rod connected between the engine and drive shaft housing. The engine shift rod is connected by a shift cable to the remote control box, providing shift control at the helm.

In the Alpha One gearcase, a fitting in the drive shaft housing transmits horizontal motion of the engine shift rod to a vertical shift shaft which extends to the shift mechanism on the gearcase propeller shaft.

When the Alpha One unit is shifted into gear, a sliding clutch (dog clutch) in the gearcase engages a FORWARD or REVERSE gear on the

propeller shaft. This creates a direct coupling that changes the power flow back to horizontal movement of the propeller shaft. When the shift mechanism is in NEUTRAL, the sliding clutch does not engage with either gear and the propeller shaft does not rotate.

Since the dog clutch and drive shaft pinion gear are the central components in the shift opertion, they are prone to the greatest amount of wear. The FORWARD gear also receives more wear than the REVERSE gear.

Shifting of the Bravo drive is done in the drive shaft housing. The universal joint assembly transmits horizontal motion of the engine to a vertical clutch assembly through a pinion gear.

When the Bravo unit is shifted into gear, a sliding clutch on the drive shaft clutch assembly engages the FORWARD or REVERSE clutch gear as desired. This creates a direct coupling that sends the power flow to the gearcase drive shaft, where a pinion gear changes the power flow back to horizontal movement of the propeller shaft. When the shift mechanism is in NEU-TRAL, the drive shaft clutch does not engage with either clutch gear and so the propeller shaft does not rotate.

The Alpha and Bravo gearcase housing can be removed from the drive shaft housing for service without removing the entire stern drive from the boat. This chapter covers the removal, overhaul and installation of the Alpha One, Bravo One, Bravo Two and Bravo Three gearcase housings. Other MerCruiser drives are manufactured for heavy-duty use including high-performance models used for racing. Mercury Marine does not recommend service by amateur mechanics on such models. **Table 1** is at the end of the chapter.

FASTENER REMOVAL

Elastic stop nuts should never be used more than twice. It is a good idea to replace such nuts with new ones each time they are removed. Never use worn-out stop nuts or non-locking nuts.

SERVICE PRECAUTIONS

Whenever you work on a stern drive unit, there are several precautions to keep in mind that will make your work easier, faster and more accurate.

1. Use special tools where noted. In some cases, it may be possible to perform the procedure with makeshift tools, but this is not recommended. The use of makeshift tools can damage the components and may cause serious personal injury.
2. Use a vise with protective jaws to hold housings or components. If protective jaws are not available, insert blocks of soft wood on either side of the part(s) before clamping them in the vise.
3. Remove and install pressed-on parts with an appropriate mandrel, support and hydraulic press. Do not try to pry, hammer or otherwise force them on or off.
4. Refer to the appropriate table at the end of the chapter for torque values, if not given in the text. Proper torque is vital to assure long life and service from stern drive components.
5. Apply Quicksilver Perfect Seal to the outer surfaces of all bearing carrier, retainer and housing mating surfaces during reassembly. Do not allow Perfect Seal to touch O-rings or enter the bearings or gears.
6. Lubricate all O-rings and seals.
7. Apply Loctite 271 on the outside diameter of all metal-case oil seals.
8. Keep a record of all shims and where they came from. As soon as the shims are removed, inspect them for damage and write down their thickness and location. Wire the shims together for reassembly and place them in a safe place. Follow shimming instructions closely. If gear backlash is not properly set, the unit will be noisy and suffer premature gear failure. Incorrect bearing preload will result in premature bearing failure.
9. Work in a clean area where there is good lighting and sufficient space for components to be stored. Keep an ample number of containers available for storing small parts. Cover parts with clean shop cloths when you are not working with them.

ALPHA ONE DRIVE

Figure 1 is an exploded view of the Alpha One gear housing prior to the Generation II models (1986-1990). **Figure 2** is an exploded view of the Alpha One Generation II gear housing (1991-on).

Identification and Description

The Alpha One (1986-1990) is a redesigned version of the earlier MR gear housing. Alpha One SS models are heavy-duty units designed for high-performance and racing applications.

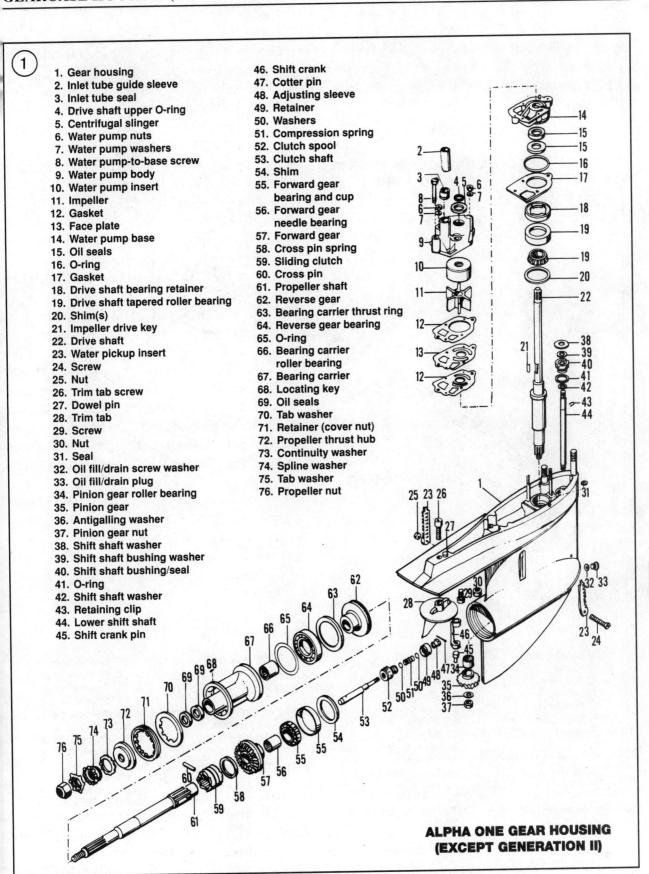

1. Gear housing
2. Inlet tube guide sleeve
3. Inlet tube seal
4. Drive shaft upper O-ring
5. Centrifugal slinger
6. Water pump nuts
7. Water pump washers
8. Water pump-to-base screw
9. Water pump body
10. Water pump insert
11. Impeller
12. Gasket
13. Face plate
14. Water pump base
15. Oil seals
16. O-ring
17. Gasket
18. Drive shaft bearing retainer
19. Drive shaft tapered roller bearing
20. Shim(s)
21. Impeller drive key
22. Drive shaft
23. Water pickup insert
24. Screw
25. Nut
26. Trim tab screw
27. Dowel pin
28. Trim tab
29. Screw
30. Nut
31. Seal
32. Oil fill/drain screw washer
33. Oil fill/drain plug
34. Pinion gear roller bearing
35. Pinion gear
36. Antigalling washer
37. Pinion gear nut
38. Shift shaft washer
39. Shift shaft bushing washer
40. Shift shaft bushing/seal
41. O-ring
42. Shift shaft washer
43. Retaining clip
44. Lower shift shaft
45. Shift crank pin

46. Shift crank
47. Cotter pin
48. Adjusting sleeve
49. Retainer
50. Washers
51. Compression spring
52. Clutch spool
53. Clutch shaft
54. Shim
55. Forward gear bearing and cup
56. Forward gear needle bearing
57. Forward gear
58. Cross pin spring
59. Sliding clutch
60. Cross pin
61. Propeller shaft
62. Reverse gear
63. Bearing carrier thrust ring
64. Reverse gear bearing
65. O-ring
66. Bearing carrier roller bearing
67. Bearing carrier
68. Locating key
69. Oil seals
70. Tab washer
71. Retainer (cover nut)
72. Propeller thrust hub
73. Continuity washer
74. Spline washer
75. Tab washer
76. Propeller nut

ALPHA ONE GEAR HOUSING (EXCEPT GENERATION II)

14

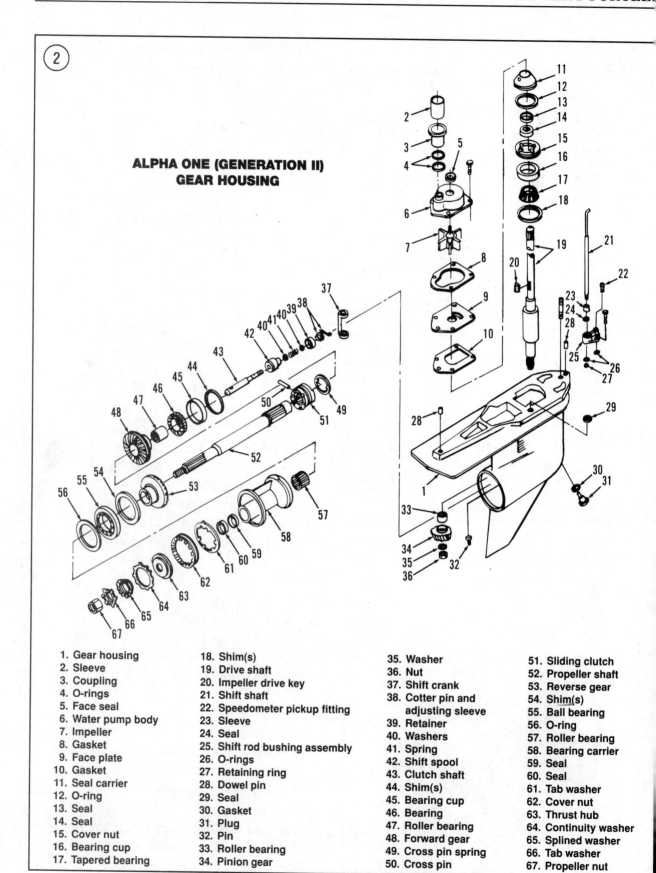

ALPHA ONE (GENERATION II)
GEAR HOUSING

1. Gear housing
2. Sleeve
3. Coupling
4. O-rings
5. Face seal
6. Water pump body
7. Impeller
8. Gasket
9. Face plate
10. Gasket
11. Seal carrier
12. O-ring
13. Seal
14. Seal
15. Cover nut
16. Bearing cup
17. Tapered bearing
18. Shim(s)
19. Drive shaft
20. Impeller drive key
21. Shift shaft
22. Speedometer pickup fitting
23. Sleeve
24. Seal
25. Shift rod bushing assembly
26. O-rings
27. Retaining ring
28. Dowel pin
29. Seal
30. Gasket
31. Plug
32. Pin
33. Roller bearing
34. Pinion gear
35. Washer
36. Nut
37. Shift crank
38. Cotter pin and adjusting sleeve
39. Retainer
40. Washers
41. Spring
42. Shift spool
43. Clutch shaft
44. Shim(s)
45. Bearing cup
46. Bearing
47. Roller bearing
48. Forward gear
49. Cross pin spring
50. Cross pin
51. Sliding clutch
52. Propeller shaft
53. Reverse gear
54. Shim(s)
55. Ball bearing
56. O-ring
57. Roller bearing
58. Bearing carrier
59. Seal
60. Seal
61. Tab washer
62. Cover nut
63. Thrust hub
64. Continuity washer
65. Splined washer
66. Tab washer
67. Propeller nut

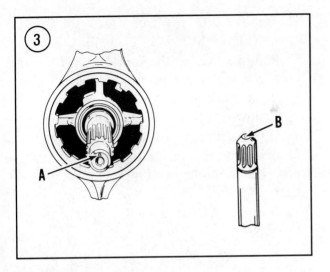

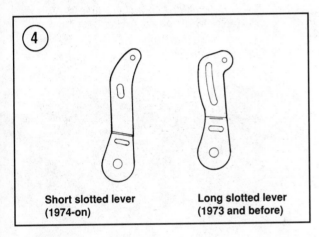

**Short slotted lever
(1974-on)**

**Long slotted lever
(1973 and before)**

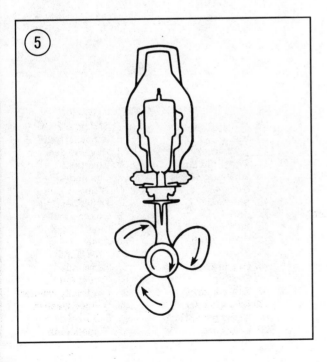

The Alpha One SS models are nearly identical to the MR and Alpha One units except the drive shaft is slightly shorter and the leading edge of the gear housing is crescent shaped. Service procedures on Alpha One SS models are identical to MR and Alpha One units.

During the first year of production, the Alpha One gear housing was identified by an "A" stamped in the end of the propeller shaft (A, **Figure 3**). This mark is not used on later models. The drive shaft preload pin used on earlier Model I drives is absent on all Alpha One models (B, **Figure 3**).

Early Alpha One drives (prior to Generation II) are interchangeable with previous Model I drives and can be installed as a replacement for any 1974 and later MerCruiser Model I drive equipped with a short slot in the shift plate lever (**Figure 4**).

Alpha One Generation II was introduced on the 1991 MerCruiser models. Some of the significant changes in the second generation models include: a redesigned shift shaft, a fitting to connect a gear lube monitor, an internal speedometer pickup and a volume-type water pump which uses a floppy-vane impeller designed for extended service life. Although most service on Generation II Alpha One units is the same as on earlier models, the Generation II is not interchangeable with earlier units (prior to 1991). Generation II models can be easily identified by the dipstick in the drive shaft housing top cover and the molded-in water intakes in the gear housing (earlier models had removable water intakes).

Propeller shaft rotation on all Alpha One drives in clockwise (right-hand rotation) while in FORWARD gear, as viewed from behind the propeller. See **Figure 5**.

The Alpha One gear housing contains the drive shaft, drive shaft bearing retainer, pinion gear and bearings, shift mechanism, sliding clutch, forward and reverse gears, reverse gear bearing carrier and propeller shaft. See **Figure 1**

14

(1986-1990 models) and **Figure 2** (1991-on models).

Gearcase Removal

1. Trim the stern drive to its full OUT position.
2. Place a suitable container under the drain plug. Remove the drain and vent plugs. Drain the lubricant from the unit.

> *NOTE*
> *If metallic particles are found in Step 3, remove and disassemble both the drive shaft and gearcase housings to inspect for damaged oil seals, O-rings and/or housing cracks. Clean all parts in solvent and blow dry with compressed air.*

3. Wipe a small amount of lubricant on a finger and rub the finger and thumb together. Check for the presence of metallic particles.
4. Note color of gear lubricant. If white or cream in color, there is water in the lubricant. Inspect the drain container for signs of water separation from the lubricant.
5. Place a mark on the gearcase and trim tab for reassembly reference. Remove the plastic plug (**Figure 6**) from the rear edge of the gearcase.
6. Remove the trim tab screw. Remove the trim tab (**Figure 7**).

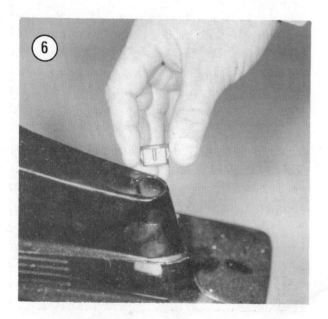

7. Remove the screw from inside the trim tab cavity (**Figure 8**).
8. Remove the two locknuts from the center bottom of the antiventilation plate (**Figure 9**).
9. Bend propeller washer tabs away from the splined washer. See A, **Figure 10**.
10. Fit a suitable wooden block between the propeller and antiventilation plate to prevent the propeller from rotating. Loosen the prop nut (B, **Figure 10**).
11. Remove the locknut at the front of the gear housing mounting stud.

> *CAUTION*
> *If it is necessary to pry the units apart in Step 12, pry only at the front and rear of the gearcase housing. Attempting to pry along the right-hand side of the unit may*

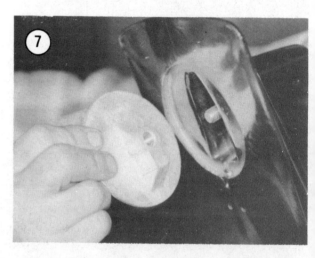

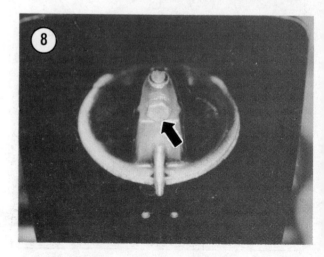

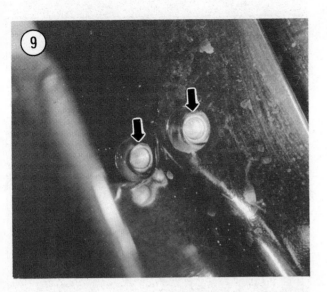

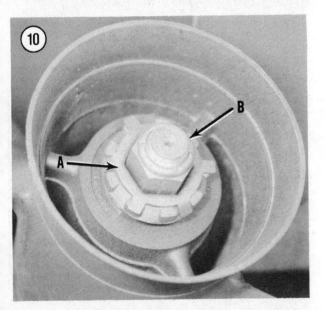

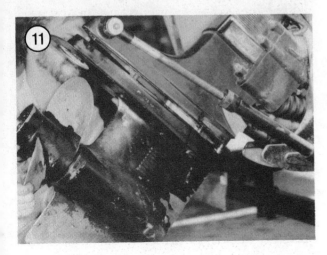

cause damage to the interconnecting oil passage in the gearcase housing.

12. Loosen the mounting locknuts on each side equally and drop the gearcase housing slightly. On badly corroded units, the water tubes and drive shaft may be frozen, making it necessary to pry the gearcase housing loose from the drive shaft housing.

13. Holding the gearcase housing firmly, remove the loosened nuts and separate the gearcase from the drive shaft housing (**Figure 11**).

14. Mount the gearcase housing in a suitable holding fixture.

15. Remove the prop nut, washers (tabbed, spline and continuity), propeller and thrust hub. See **Figure 12**.

Gearcase Installation

1. If the water inlet tube came free when gearcase housing was removed, coat the upper end

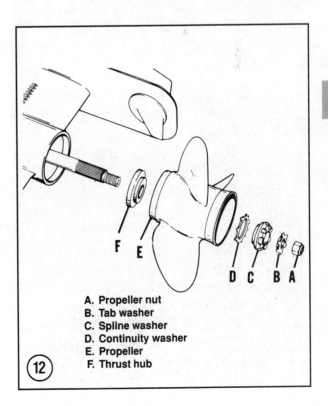

A. Propeller nut
B. Tab washer
C. Spline washer
D. Continuity washer
E. Propeller
F. Thrust hub

14

of the tube with Quicksilver 2-4-C Multi-Lube and reinsert in the upper housing.

2. Wipe the lower end of the water tube with a light coat of 2-4-C Multi-Lube. Apply a heavy coat of the same lubricant to the drive shaft splines.

3A. Prior to Generation II:

a. Make sure the alignment pins, centrifugal slinger and drive shaft O-ring are in position. See **Figure 13**. Wipe a new oil passage seal with Quicksilver Special Lube 101, Perfect Seal or 2-4-C Marine Lubricant. Install the seal into its groove (B, **Figure 13**).

b. Install a shift shaft wrench over the shift shaft. Rotate the wrench clockwise to shift the gear housing into FORWARD gear. Apply a light counterclockwise pressure onto the propeller shaft to hold the gear housing in gear.

3B. Generation II:

a. If the water pump dam is removed, apply a bead of Permatex Ultra Blue Silicone Sealant to both sides of the dam and reinstall it into the gear housing. Apply a bead of sealant to the top of the dam. See **Figure 14**. Be certain the drain hole in the water pump dam is not obstructed or the gear housing may be damaged from freezing.

b. Insert the trim tab bolt into its hole in the aft end of the gear housing.

c. Shift the gear housing into FORWARD gear. The shift shaft should be positioned as shown in **Figure 14**. Light counterclockwise pressure can be applied to the propeller shaft to hold the gear housing in gear.

d. Apply Quicksilver Special Lube 101, Perfect Seal or 2-4-C Marine Lubricant to a new oil passage seal. Install the seal into its groove (**Figure 15**, typical).

4. Make sure that the upper shift shaft in the drive shaft housing is also in its full FORWARD gear (straight-ahead) position. If it is not, shift the remote control unit into FORWARD gear.

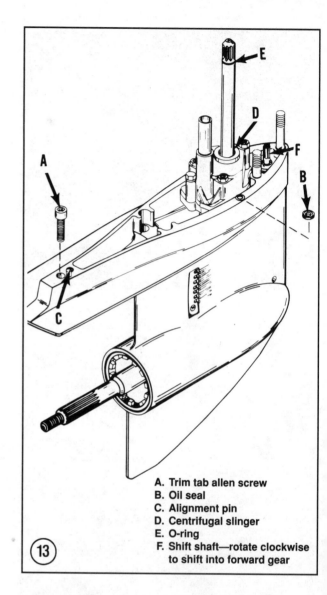

A. Trim tab allen screw
B. Oil seal
C. Alignment pin
D. Centrifugal slinger
E. O-ring
F. Shift shaft—rotate clockwise to shift into forward gear

(13)

(14)

Shift shaft

Water pump dam

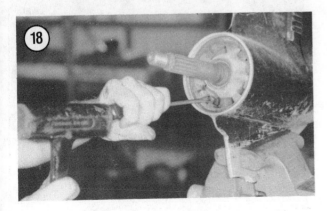

5. Align water inlet tube with water tube guide and drive shaft and shift shaft splines with upper drive shaft/shift shaft splines, then install the gearcase housing to the drive shaft housing (**Figure 11**). Once the shift shaft splines have engaged, rotate the propeller shaft counterclockwise as necessary to assist drive shaft splines in engaging the upper drive shaft splines.

6. Once the 2 housings are properly coupled, install new elastic stop nuts on the side and front mounting studs. Tighten the stop nuts to specification (**Table 1**).

7. Install the antiventilation plate locknuts (**Figure 9**).

8. Install the screw inside the trim tab cavity and tighten to specification (**Table 1**).

9. Install trim tab with the index marks (Step 5) aligned. Tighten the trim tab screw to specification (**Table 1**). Install plastic plug over the screw (**Figure 6**).

10. Install the thrust hub and lubricate the propeller shaft splines with Quicksilver 2-4-C Marine Lubricant (**Figure 16**).

11. Install propeller, continuity washer, spline washer and tab washer (**Figure 12**). Install prop nut finger-tight.

12. Bend propeller washer tabs toward from the splined washer.

13. Fit a suitable wooden block between the propeller and anti-cavitation plate to prevent the propeller from rotating. Tighten the prop nut securely (**Figure 17**).

Bearing Carrier/Reverse Gear Removal

1. Remove the water pump. See Chapter Ten.

2. Remove the propeller as described in *Gearcase Housing Removal* in this chapter.

3. Bend the bearing carrier retainer washer locktab away from the cover nut with a screwdriver and hammer (**Figure 18**).

14

NOTE
If the cover nut is frozen in place and cannot be removed in Step 4, use an electric drill to drill out one side of the nut for easier removal. Discard the cover nut if removed in this manner.

4. Install bearing carrier retainer wrench (part No. 91-61069) (**Figure 19**) and rotate counterclockwise with a socket and breaker bar to loosen and remove the cover nut.

5. Install puller jaws (part No. 91-46086A1) and puller bolt (part No. 91-85716). Bosses inside the bearing carrier should support the puller jaws.

NOTE
If the bearing carrier is corroded, you may have to apply heat to the housing while pulling on the assembly in Step 6. Be careful not to overheat the housing, as this will cause distortion.

6. Tighten the puller bolt until the bearing carrier comes loose. Remove puller jaws/bolt, then remove bearing carrier (**Figure 20**) and carrier-to-housing shims.

7. Wire the shims together and attach a tag indicating their location.

8. Remove and discard bearing carrier O-ring.

9. Disassemble bearing carrier/reverse gear and clean/inspect all components as described in this chapter.

Bearing Carrier/Reverse Gear Cleaning and Inspection

1. Remove and discard the bearing carrier O-ring (**Figure 21**).

2. Clean all parts in fresh solvent. Blow dry with compressed air.

3. Check the reverse gear for pitted, chipped or broken teeth (A, **Figure 22**). Replace gear as required.

4. Inspect reverse gear clutch jaws (B, **Figure 22**). If surface is chipped or rounded off, replace gear.

5. Clamp the bearing carrier in a vise with protective jaws (clamp on carrier reinforcing rib).

6. Remove reverse gear, the thrust ring and bearing as a unit with puller part No. 91-34569A1 or another suitable 2-jaw puller.

7. Apply a light coat of oil to the reverse gear ball bearing and rotate the bearing to check for rough spots. Push and pull on the bearing to check for side wear. If movement is excessive, replace bearing using an arbor press.

8. Check propeller shaft surface where oil seal lips touch shaft. If grooved, replace the propeller shaft as well as the bearing carrier oil seals (**Figure 23**).

9. Check needle bearing contact points on propeller shaft. If shaft shows signs of pitting, grooving, scoring, heat discoloration or embedded metallic particles, replace the propeller shaft and the bearing carrier oil seals and needle bearing (**Figure 23**).

10. Inspect cover nut for cracks or broken/corroded threads. Replace as required.

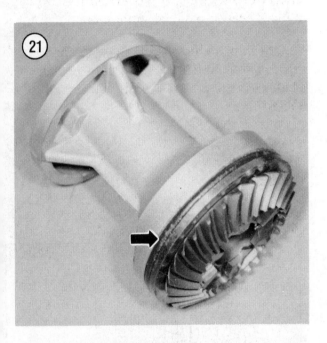

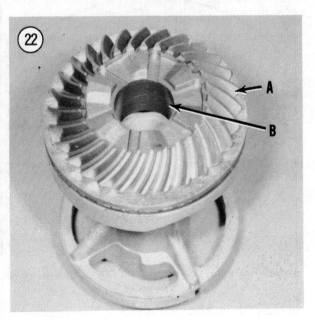

Bearing Carrier/Reverse Gear Installation

If bearing or oil seals do not require replacement, begin procedure with Step 9.

1. Position a new carrier roller bearing with its numbered side facing upward and press into the carrier with driver part No. 91-15755 or equivalent.

2. Wipe OD of new oil seals with Loctite 271.

3. Fit one seal on the long shoulder side of driver (part No. 91-31108) with lip facing *away* from shoulder to retain lubrication inside the housing. Install seal in carrier until driver bottoms.

4. Fit second seal on the short shoulder side of the driver with its lip facing *toward* the shoulder to keep water out of the housing. Install seal in carrier until driver bottoms.

5. Wipe off any excess Loctite and fill the cavity between the seals with Quicksilver 2-4-C Marine Lubricant.

6. Pressing only on the bearing inner race, install the reverse gear ball bearing and thrust washer on the reverse gear. Beveled side of thrust washer should face toward gear.

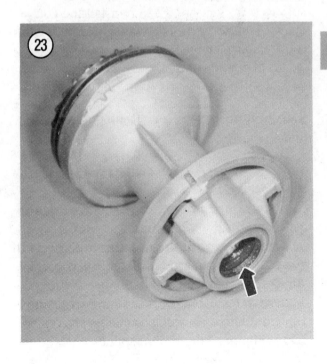

14

7. Wipe OD of reverse gear bearing with 2-4-C Marine Lubricant. Position bearing carrier over reverse gear/bearing and press into place.

8. Install a new O-ring over the bearing carrier between the thrust washer and carrier housing.

9. Install shim(s) that were removed during disassembly in gearcase housing. If shim(s) were lost or damaged, or if a new gear housing is being installed, start with a 0.020 in. thick shim.

10. Install the bearing carrier in the gearcase housing (**Figure 24**) with its keyway facing up. Push down on carrier to seat it on the shim(s). Install key in carrier keyway (**Figure 25**).

11. Install carrier retainer tab washer (**Figure 26**). Align "V" tab on washer with "V" notch on carrier.

12. Thread the cover nut into the gearcase housing. Tighten nut to specification, then check forward and reverse gear backlash as described under *Gearcase Shimming* in this chapter.

13. After backlash has been measured (and corrected, if necessary), remove the bearing carrier and apply a liberal quantity of Quicksilver Perfect Seal to its outer diameter as well as to the gearcase housing threads. Do *not* let sealer enter the ball bearing or reverse gear.

14. Repeat Steps 10-12 to reinstall the components. Tighten cover nut to specification (**Table 1**), then bend one tab on the tab washer into one of the cover nut slots (**Figure 27**).

Drive Shaft/Pinion Gear Removal

1. Remove the water pump. Remove the water pump base (prior to Generation II) or seal carrier (Generation II). See Chapter Ten.

2. Remove the bearing carrier/retainer and reverse gear as described in this chpater.

3. Loosen the drive shaft bearing retainer 2 full turns using bearing retainer tool (part No. 91-43506). Do not completely remove the bearing retainer yet.

4. Install drive shaft nut wrench (part No. 91-56775) onto the drive shaft splines.

5. Insert pinion nut adapter (part No. 91-61067A2) over the propeller shaft and into the gear cavity. Position the pinion nut adapter so the slot marked "MR" is facing up toward the pinion nut. It may be necessary to lift and/or rotate the drive shaft to engage the adapter with the pinion nut.

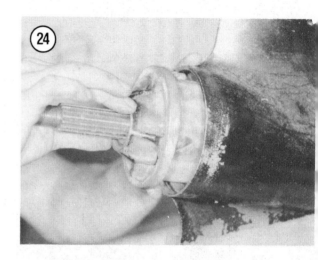

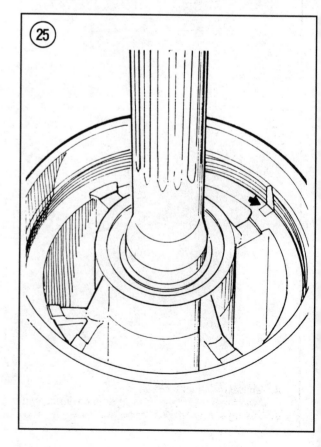

NOTE

*If the drive shaft is broken, install the pinion nut adapter (part No. 91-61067A2) over the propeller shaft and onto the pinion gear nut. Install the propeller shaft tool (part No. 91-61077) onto the propeller shaft splines. Shift the gear housing into **forward** gear and rotate the propeller shaft counterclockwise to remove the pinion nut from the broken drive shaft.*

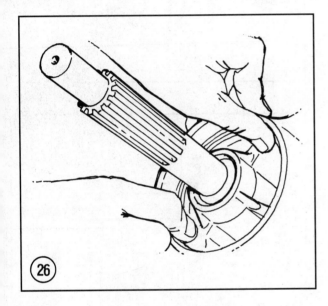

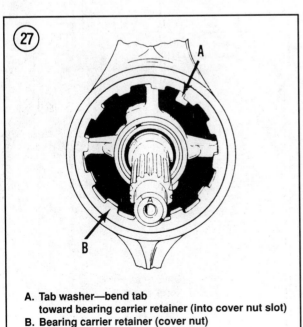

A. Tab washer—bend tab
  toward bearing carrier retainer (into cover nut slot)
B. Bearing carrier retainer (cover nut)

6. Install an appropriate size socket or wrench onto the drive shaft nut wrench and turn the drive shaft counterclockwise to loosen and remove the pinion nut. Continue turning the drive shaft until the pinion nut is removed.

7. Remove the pinion nut adapter, reach into the gear housing and remove the pinion nut and washer.

NOTE

The 18 pinion roller bearings may fall out of the outer bearing race in Step 8. If so, be sure to retrieve all 18 or a new set will have to be installed during reassembly. Do not substitute a roller bearing from another unit for one that is missing.

8. Remove the drive shaft bearing retainer loosened in Step 3. Lift the drive shaft with the bearing and bearing cup from the gearcase housing. Remove and tag the shims for reinstallation reference.

Drive Shaft/Pinion Gear Cleaning and Inspection

1. Clean all parts in fresh solvent. Blow dry with compressed air.

2. Check the pinion gear for pitting, excessive wear or broken or chipped teeth; replace as required.

3. Check drive shaft where roller bearing rides. Replace drive shaft and bearing if pitting, scoring, grooving, heat discoloration or embedded metallic particles are found.

4. Check drive shaft tapered roller bearing cup. Replace bearing and cup if pitting, scoring, grooving, heat discoloration or embedded metallic particles are found.

5. Check splines on each end of drive shaft for excessive wear, twisting or damage.

6. Suspend drive shaft between V-blocks and check straightness using a dial indicator. Replace the drive shaft if runout exceeds 0.005 in. (0.13 mm).

14

Drive Shaft/Pinion Gear Installation

The unit does not require reshimming if no new parts are installed.

1. If rollers (A, **Figure 28**) fell out of the drive shaft roller bearing race (B, **Figure 28**) during removal, coat all 18 rollers with Quicksilver Needle Bearing Assembly Lubricant and reinstall.

2. Reinstall any shim(s) removed from the drive shaft housing bore during disassembly. If shim(s) were lost or if the pinion gear, drive shaft, drive shaft roller bearing or gearcase housing were replaced, install a 0.015 in. shim as a starting point.

3. Grease the pinion gear washer and attach it to the pinion gear nut.

4. Position the pinion gear in the gearcase housing. Gear teeth must mesh with the forward gear teeth.

5. Hold pinion gear in place and insert the drive shaft in the housing bore. Rotate the drive shaft to align and engage its splines with those of the pinion gear. Install but do not tighten pinion gear washer and nut.

6. Install the drive shaft bearing cup over the tapered roller bearings, then thread the retainer in place until all threads are engaged.

7. Install drive shaft bearing retainer tool (part No. 91-43506) and tighten the pinion gear nut to specification (**Table 1**) using appropriate sockets, a breaker bar and a torque wrench. See **Figure 29**.

9. Check pinion gear height as described in this chapter.

> *CAUTION*
> *Loctite sets up in 3 hours, but does not dry completely for 24 hours. If the Loctite applied to the nut threads in Step 10 is not completely dry, the nut may back off during operation at a later date especially if the torque applied to the nut is incorrect.*

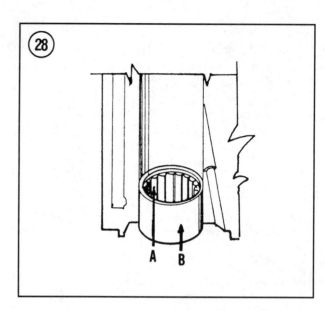

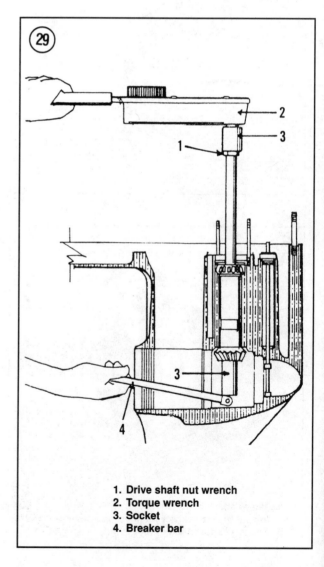

1. **Drive shaft nut wrench**
2. **Torque wrench**
3. **Socket**
4. **Breaker bar**

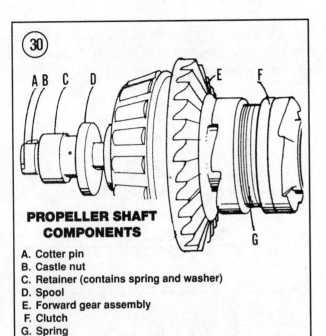

PROPELLER SHAFT COMPONENTS

A. Cotter pin
B. Castle nut
C. Retainer (contains spring and washer)
D. Spool
E. Forward gear assembly
F. Clutch
G. Spring

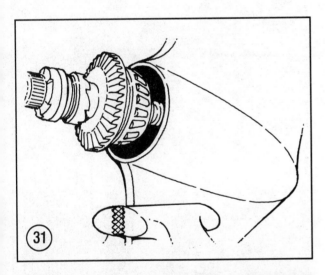

10. Remove pinion gear nut and washer. Wipe the nut threads with Loctite Type 271. Reinstall the washer and nut and tighten to specification (**Table 1**).

11. Reinstall the bearing carrier retainer/reverse gear as described in this chapter.

12. Reinstall the water pump base or seal carrier, and the water pump as described in Chapter Ten.

Propeller Shaft/Forward Gear Removal/Disassembly

Disassembly of the spool assembly can result in damage to the assembly and is not recommended unless its components show obvious signs of damage. The spool assembly can be cleaned satisfactorily without disassembly.

The forward gear needle bearing case is manufactured of a very high tensile strength steel and cannot be easily split with a chisel and hammer. If replacement is required, use a high-speed grinder to cut one or more notchs in the bearing case as required for removal.

Refer to **Figure 30** for this procedure.

1. Remove the bearing carrier retainer/reverse gear as described in this chapter.

2. Remove the drive shaft/pinion gear as described in this chapter.

3. Move outer end of propeller shaft to the port side of the gearcase housing to disengage the spool from the shift crank in the housing. Pull assembly from housing (**Figure 31**).

4. Slip a small screwdriver blade under one end of the sliding clutch cross pin retaining spring and feed spring up and over the clutch (**Figure 32**).

5. Remove the cross pin with an appropriate size punch or screwdriver blade (**Figure 33**).

6. Remove the spool assembly, forward gear, sliding clutch dog and actuating shaft from the propeller shaft.

7. If spool disassembly is required:

   a. Remove cotter pin from the end of the spool assembly.

b. Unscrew the adjusting castle nut.

c. Clamp spool in a vise with protective jaws.

d. Remove the retainer cap with channel lock pliers.

e. Remove the spring and washer.

8. If tapered roller bearing or forward gear is to be replaced, press bearing from gear with appropriate puller plate and mandrel. When bearing is replaced, remove and discard bearing cup from inside the gearcase housing. Retain the shim(s) under the cup for reassembly.

9. If the forward gear roller bearing is to be replaced, split the caes with a chisel and remove the broken bearing.

Propeller Shaft/Forward Gear Cleaning and Inspection

1. Clean all parts in fresh solvent. Blow dry with compressed air.

2. Check forward gear (**Figure 34**) for broken or chipped teeth, chipped or rounded-off clutch jaws, pitting or excessive wear.

3. Check the forward gear roller bearing (**Figure 35**) and drive shaft area where bearing rides. If any signs of pitting, grooving, scoring, heat discoloration or embedded metallic particles are noted, replace shaft and bearing.

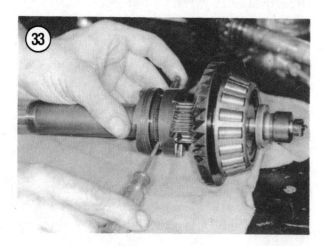

4. Check engaging jaws of sliding clutch (**Figure 36**) for chipped or rounded-off condition; replace as required.

5. Install propeller shaft on balance wheels and check for wobble at the propeller end of the shaft. Replace shaft if propeller end wobbles.

6. Install propeller shaft on V-blocks and rotate the shaft. Replace if shaft is bent.

7. Install propeller shaft between lathe centers and check needle bearing contact area with a dial indicator. Replace shaft if the indicator reading

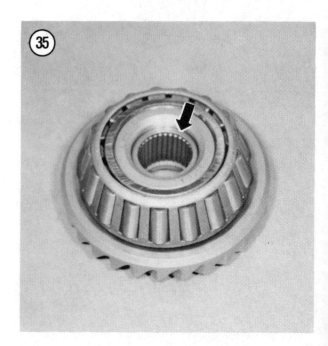

exceeds 0.005 in. during one complete shaft revolution.

8. Clean propeller shaft splines with a wire brush to remove any corrosion. If splines are partially corroded away, twisted or otherwise damaged, replace the shaft.

9. Check shift spool for excessive or uneven wear. **Figure 37** shows the spool assembled (top) and disassembled (bottom).

Propeller Shaft/Forward Gear Assembly/Installation

Refer to **Figure 30** for this procedure.

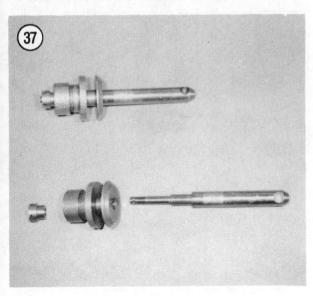

1. If forward gear tapered roller bearing was removed, wipe inner bore of new bearing with Quicksilver Premium Blend Gear Lube and press bearing onto the forward gear. Apply pressure against the center race only.

2. If forward gear needle bearing was removed, wipe forward gear bore with Premium Blend Gear Lube and press new bearing into bore with its lettered side facing upward. Bearing must seat against inner gear shoulder.

3. Install sliding clutch dog on propeller shaft. Grooved end of clutch should face *reverse* gear end of shaft. Align cross pin holes in clutch and shaft.

4. Install the cross pin through the sliding clutch dog, propeller shaft and actuating shaft.

CAUTION
Use care not to excessively stretch spring during installation in Step 5.

5. Install the cross pin retainer spring over the sliding clutch inside the retainer groove.

6. Install the forward gear/bearing assembly on the propeller shaft. Gear must face sliding clutch dog.

7. If shift actuating spool was disassembled, install the first washer, spring and second washer into the spool, then thread the retainer in place and tighten securely. See **Figure 38**.

8. Slip the spool assembly over the clutch actuating shaft. Thread the adjusting nut onto the shaft until it barely touches the washer, providing slight resistance to further turning.

NOTE
The spool must rotate freely on its shaft when installation is completed in Step 9. Do not over-tighten the adjusting nut or the spring becomes useless and excessive shaft shoulder wear will result.

9. Back sleeve off until the first cotter pin slot aligns with the shaft hole and install a new cotter pin.

10. Insert the propeller shaft into the gearcase housing and tilt the propeller end of the shaft

14

toward the oil fill hole side of the gearcase housing to engage the shift actuating shaft spool with the shift crank.

11. Straighten the propeller shaft in the housing and operate the shift shaft to make sure installation is correct. Only the sliding clutch should move when the shift shaft is turned in this step.

12. Install drive shaft and pinion gear as described in this chapter.

13. Install the bearing carrier retainer/reverse gear as described in this chapter.

Shift Shaft Removal (Prior to Generation II)

1. Remove the bearing carrier retainer/reverse gear as described in this chapter.

2. Remove the drive shaft/pinion gear as described in this chapter.

3. Remove the propeller shaft/forward gear as described in this chapter.

4. Remove the metal and rubber washers from the shift shaft.

5. Remove the shift shaft bushing with bushing remover part No. 91-31107.

6. Pull shift shaft from gearcase housing.

7. Reach inside gear housing and remove the shift crank from its locating pin.

Shift Shaft Cleaning and Inspection (Prior to Generation II)

Refer to **Figure 39** for this procedure.

1. Remove and discard the shift shaft O-ring. Remove the clip, washer and bushing from the shift shaft.

2. Clean all parts in fresh solvent. Blow dry with compressed air.

3. Check shift shaft splines for wear and/or corrosion.

4. Check shift shaft bushing for corrosion.

5. Check shift crank for excessive wear in shift spool contact areas.

6. Install a new O-ring on bushing.

Shift Shaft Installation (Prior to Generation II)

Refer to **Figure 40** for this procedure.

1. Drive oil seal through top of bushing and install a new seal with its lip facing upward.

2. Install the retaining clip in the shift shaft groove.

3. Reach all the way into the gearcase housing and position the shift crank on the locating pin.

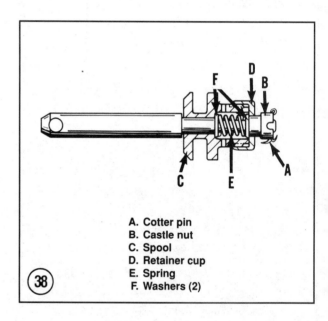

A. Cotter pin
B. Castle nut
C. Spool
D. Retainer cup
E. Spring
F. Washers (2)

(38)

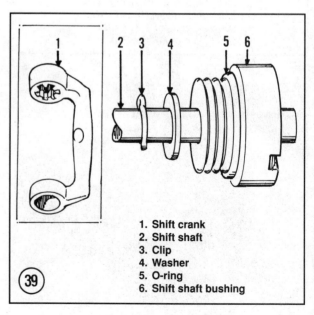

1. Shift crank
2. Shift shaft
3. Clip
4. Washer
5. O-ring
6. Shift shaft bushing

(39)

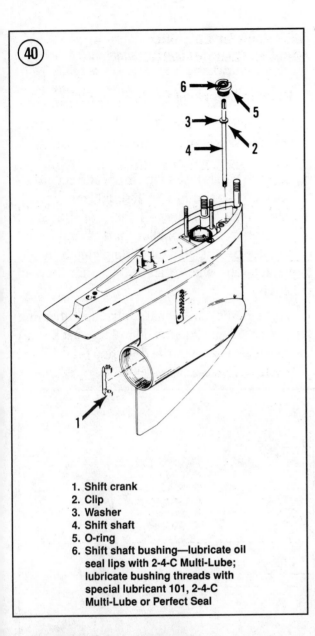

1. Shift crank
2. Clip
3. Washer
4. Shift shaft
5. O-ring
6. Shift shaft bushing—lubricate oil seal lips with 2-4-C Multi-Lube; lubricate bushing threads with special lubricant 101, 2-4-C Multi-Lube or Perfect Seal

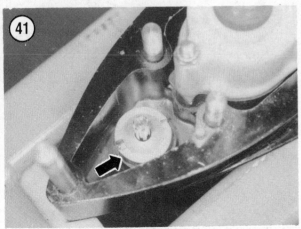

The "throw" side of the crank shold face the oil fill side of the gearcase housing.

4. Insert the shift shaft with retaining clip in gearcase housing and engage with shift actuating crank splines.

5. Position the retaining washer over the shift shaft on the top side of the retaining clip.

6. Thread the shift shaft into the gearcase housing.

7. Lubricate shift shaft bushing threads, oil seal lip and O-ring with Quicksilver 2-4-C Multi-Lube.

8. Install the shift shaft bushing in the gearcase housing (**Figure 41**) and tighten to 50 ft.-lb. (68 N.m) with shift shaft tool part No. 91-31107.

9. Install the rubber washer on the shift shaft, then install the stainless steel washer.

Shift Shaft Removal (Generation II)

The following procedure describes shift shaft and shift crank removal, cleaning, inspection and installation. However, if necessary, the shift shaft (but not the shift crank) can be removed from the gear housing without removing any gear housing internal components.

1. Remove the bearing carrier/retainer and reverse gear assembly as described in this chapter.

2. Remove the drive shaft/pinion gear assembly as described in this chapter.

3. Remove the propeller shaft/forward gear assembly as described in this chapter.

4. Remove the 2 screws securing the shift shaft bushing to the gear housing. Lift the shift shaft and bushing assembly straight up and out of the gear housing. See **Figure 42**.

5. Reach into the gear cavity and remove the shift crank.

6. Remove the E-ring from the shift shaft and slide the shaft out of the bushing. Remove the sleeve from the shaft. See **Figure 43**.

14

Shift Shaft Cleaning and Inspection (Generation II)

1. Remove and discard the bushing O-rings (**Figure 43**).

2. Clean all components in clean solvent and dry with compressed air.

3. Inspect the shift crank for excessive wear at the shift spool contact area. Inspect the shift crank splines for excessive wear, corrosion or other damage.

4. Inspect the shift shaft bushing for excessive wear, cracking or other damage. Inspect the seal located in the top side of the bushing for wear or damage. The seal and bushing are not available separately. Inspect the speedometer pickup fitting for restrictions or damage.

5. Inspect the shift shaft splines for excessive wear, corrosion or other damage.

6. Replace any defective shift components.

Shift Shaft Reassembly/Installation (Generation II)

1. If removed, apply Quicksilver Perfect Seal to the threads of the speedometer pickup fitting. Install the fitting and tighten to 4.5 in.-lb. (0.5 N.m).

2. Lubricate the bushing O-rings and seal with Quicksilver 2-4-C Marine Lubricant. Assemble the shift shaft assembly as shown in **Figure 43**.

3. Install the shift crank into the gear housing. Make sure the crank is positioned on the port side of the housing.

4. Install the shift shaft and bushing assembly into the gear housing. Be sure the shaft splines properly engage the shift crank, the O-rings are properly positioned and the bent end of the shift shaft is facing forward. Seat the bushing in the gear housing and install (but do not tighten) the bushing attaching screws. See **Figure 42**.

5. Install the propeller shaft assembly as described in this chapter.

NOTE
The bent end of the shift shaft must face forward when the shaft is rotated fully clockwise. If not, remove the bushing screws and lift the shaft upward enough to realign the shift shaft splines with the shift crank.

6. Operate the shift shaft to ensure correct installation. Only the sliding clutch should move when the shift shaft is rotated. If the propeller shaft moves, remove the propeller shaft assembly and repeat Step 5. Note that the sliding clutch should move forward when the shift shaft is turned clockwise.

7. Tighten the shift shaft bushing attaching screws to 60 in.-lb. (6.8 N.m). Recheck shift shaft operation as described in Step 6.

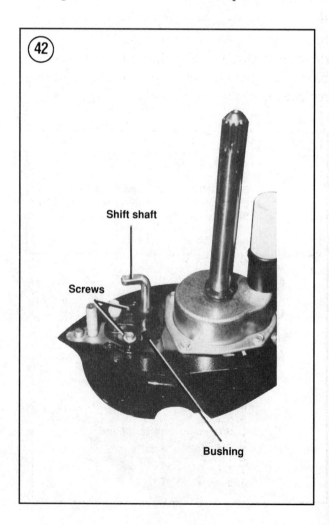

(42)

Shift shaft

Screws

Bushing

Gearcase Housing Inspection

1. Clean housing in fresh solvent. Blow dry with compressed air.

2. Check housing for signs of impact damage.

> *CAUTION*
> *If the drive shaft roller bearing has failed and the original bearing case has turned in the housing, replace the housing. Loose fitting roller bearings will move out of position and cause repeated premature failure.*

3. Check the bearings and cups for looseness or signs that they have spun in the housing.

4. Check the gearcase housing carrier retainer threads for corrosion or stripped threads. Do *not* wire brush the threads.

5. Check the 2 alignment pins on the gearcase housing mating surface. These should engage the drive shaft housing when the 2 units are assembled. If the pins are damaged, distorted or loose, replace the gearcase housing.

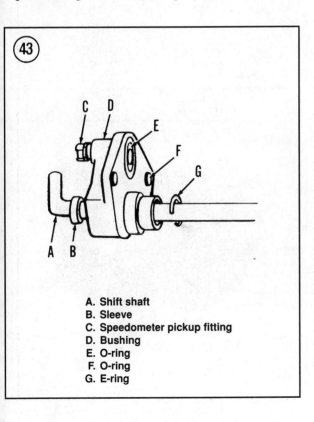

A. Shift shaft
B. Sleeve
C. Speedometer pickup fitting
D. Bushing
E. O-ring
F. O-ring
G. E-ring

Drive Shaft Roller Bearing, Drive Shaft and Forward Gear Bearing Cups

Gearcase housing bearings or cups should be removed only if they have failed. None should be reused after removal.

1. Remove the drive shaft roller bearing from the gearcase housing with special tool part No. 91-36569 and a suitable driver.

> *NOTE*
> *New bearings come with a cardboard shipping sleeve which holds the bearings in the race. Leave the shipping sleeve in place during bearing installation to prevent the rollers from falling out.*

2. Wipe a new bearing with Quicksilver 2-4-C Marine Lubricant and install in drive shaft bore with its numbered side facing upward.

3. Install and pull roller bearing place with puller rod and nut (part No. 91-31229), pilot (part No. 91-36571), plate (part No. 91-29310) and puller head (part No. 91-38628). See **Figure 44**. Pull bearing up into bore until it bottoms on the gearcase housing shoulder.

4. Install the forward gear bearing cup shim(s) in the gearcase housing.

5. Place the bearing cup in the housing and install with driver cup (part No. 91-36577), driver rod (part No. 91-37323) and adaptor (part No. 91-37263). See **Figure 45**.

Gearcase Shimming

Three shimming procedures must be performed to properly set up the gearcase housing components. The pinion gear height must be shimmed to a correct depth, the forward gear must be shimmed to the pinion gear for proper backlash and the reverse gear must be shimmed to the pinion gear for proper backlash.

14

Pinion gear height

1. Push inward on the propeller shaft and rotate it to seat the bearings.

2. Install bearing preload tool (part No. 91-44307A1) components over the drive shaft in the order shown in **Figure 46**.

3. Install and tighten the water pump screws or nuts until they just bottom (**Figure 47**).

4. Fit the collar from tool part No. 91-44307A1 over the drive shaft with setscrew facing downward (**Figure 48**). Align setscrew with water pump impeller keyway.

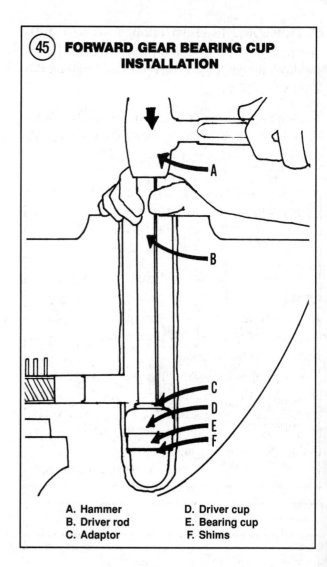

45 FORWARD GEAR BEARING CUP INSTALLATION

A. Hammer
B. Driver rod
C. Adaptor
D. Driver cup
E. Bearing cup
F. Shims

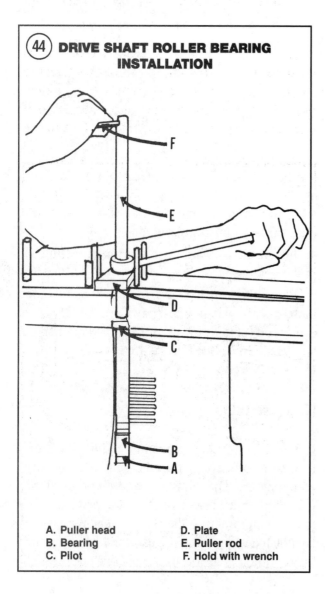

44 DRIVE SHAFT ROLLER BEARING INSTALLATION

A. Puller head
B. Bearing
C. Pilot
D. Plate
E. Puller rod
F. Hold with wrench

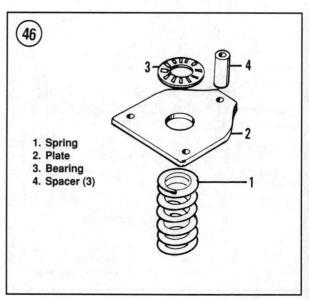

46

1. Spring
2. Plate
3. Bearing
4. Spacer (3)

5. Pull upward on the drive shaft and push downward on the collar at the same time. Holding both assemblies in this position, tighten the setscrew securely.

6. Back off the water pump stud nuts 3-4 turns, then rotate the drive shaft clockwise at least 2 full turns to seat its bearings (**Figure 49**).

7. Insert pinion gear shimming tool part No. 91-56048 in gearcase housing. See A, **Figure 50**.

8. Insert a 0.025 in. flat feeler guage between the high point of the shimming tool and one of the pinion gear geeth. See B, **Figure 50**. The feeler gauge should just fit.

9. Repeat Step 8 to take 2 more readings, rotating the drive shaft 120° between each reading. This will provide 3 readings taken at 120° intervals or one full turn of the drive shaft.

NOTE
Before removing the preload tool, tighten the water pump stud nuts until they bottom, then loosen the tool setscrew.

10. If the clearance is not exactly 0.025 in. at each reading, determine how much clearance exists, then remove the shimming tool, pinion gear, drive shaft and bearing cup. Add shims if clearance is too great; remove shims if clearance

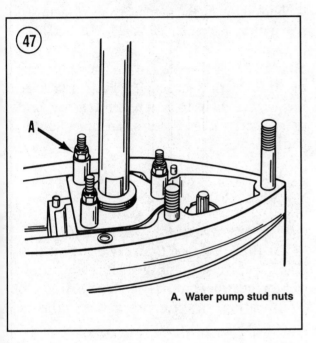

A. Water pump stud nuts

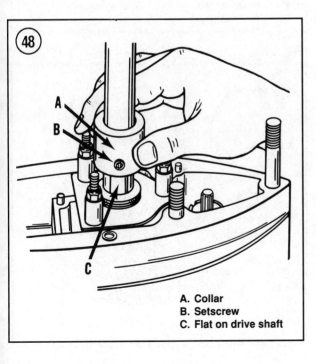

A. Collar
B. Setscrew
C. Flat on drive shaft

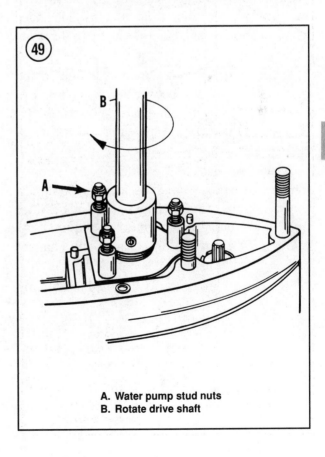

A. Water pump stud nuts
B. Rotate drive shaft

14

is insufficient. Reinstall bearing cup, drive shaft and pinion gear, then repeat procedure to recheck clearance.

Forward gear backlash

1. Perform Steps 1-6 of *Pinion Gear Height* in this chapter.

2. Thread the stud adaptor from tool (part No. 91-44307A1) onto the rear water pump stud (starboard side) and install a dial indicator to the adaptor.

3. Install backlash indicator rod (part No. 91-53459) to the drive shaft. See **Figure 51**.

4. Move the dial indicator plunger to the "I" line on the backlash indicator rod. Set indicator scale to zero.

5. Install puller jaws (part No. 46086A1) and puller bolts (part No. 91-85716) to the bearing carrier and propeller shaft. Tighten the puller bolt to 45 in.-lb. (5 N•m).

6. Rotate drive shaft back and forth lightly without allowing propeller shaft to turn. The dial indicator should read 0.017-0.028 in. (0.43-0.71 mm).

7. Repeat Step 6 to take 3 more readings, rotating the drive shaft 90° between each reading. Be sure to realign the dial indicator plunger to the "I" line on the backlash indicator rod for each reading.

8. If backlash readings are within specifications, continue with procedure. If backlash is too small, remove shim(s) from the forward gear bearing race; if too great, add shim(s) as required. A 0.001 in. (0.025 mm) shim change will change backlash approximately 0.0008 in. (0.020 mm).

9. Remove puller assembly installed in Step 5.

Reverse gear backlash

1. Perform Steps 1-6 of *Pinion Gear Height* in this chapter.

2. Shift the gearcase housing into full *reverse* position and rotate the drive shaft clockwise to make sure the sliding clutch dog engages fully.

3. Install pinion nut adapator (part No. 91-61067A2) over the propeller shaft. Next, install belleville washer (part No. 12-54048) on the propeller shaft. Make sure the concave side of the washer is facing away from the pinion nut adapter. Install the propeller shaft nut on the propeller shaft and tighten to 45 in.-lb. (5 N•m).

4. Rotate the drive shaft back and forth lightly without allowing the propeller shaft to turn. The dial indicator should read 0.028-0.052 in. (0.71-1.32 mm).

5. If backlash is correct, continue with assembly. If backlash is too small, add shims between the gearcase housing and bearing carrier; if too great, check for improper installation of bearing carrier.

BRAVO ONE AND BRAVO TWO DRIVE

The Bravo One and Bravo Two gearcase contains the drive shaft, drive shaft bearings, drive pinion gear/bearing, propeller shaft pinion gear/bearing, bearing carrier and propeller shaft/bearing. See **Figure 52** (Bravo One) or

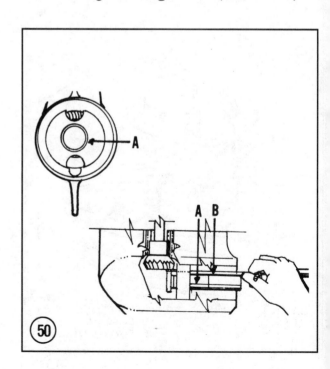

Figure 53 (Bravo Two) for components and relationships.

Gearcase Removal

1. On models prior to 1990, tilt the stern drive to a 45° angle. On 1990-on models, trim the stern drive to the fully down/in position.

2A. Prior to 1990—Place a suitable container under the drain plug. Remove the fill/drain plug from the gearcase and the vent screw or dipstick from the drain shaft housing. Drain the lubricant from the unit.

2B. 1990-on Models—Refer to **Figure 54** and remove the propeller and related hardware. Place a suitable container under the gear cavity opening and remove the drain plug located in the bearing carrier. Remove the dipstick and drain the lubricant from the unit.

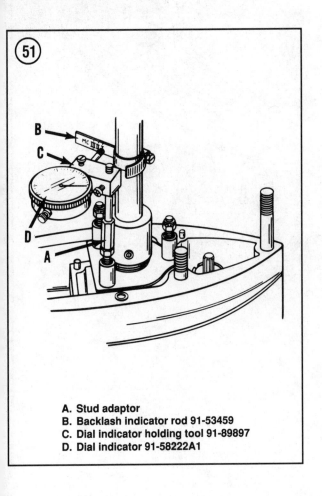

A. Stud adaptor
B. Backlash indicator rod 91-53459
C. Dial indicator holding tool 91-89897
D. Dial indicator 91-58222A1

NOTE
If metallic particles are found in Step 3, remove and disassemble both the drive shaft and gearcase housings to inspect for damaged oil seals, O-rings and/or housing cracks. Clean all parts in solvent and blow dry with compressed air.

3. Wipe a small amount of lubricant on a finger and rub the finger and thumb together. Check for the presence of metallic particles.

4. Note color of gear lubricant. If white or cream in color, there is water in the lubricant. Inspect the drain container for signs of water separating from the lubricant.

5. Place a mark on the gear housing and trim tab for reassembly reference.

6A. Bravo One—Remove the plastic plug (**Figure 55**) from the rear edge of the gear housing. Insert a 1/2 in. socket and extension into the plug hole (**Figure 56**). Unbolt and remove the trim tab (**Figure 57**). Remove the bolt from inside the trim tab cavity (A, **Figure 58**).

6B. Bravo Two—Remove the bolt from the upper side of the aft end of the gear housing and remove the trim tab. Remove the bolt from the bottom of the antiventilation plate just ahead of the trim tab.

7. Prior to 1990—Refer to **Figure 54** and remove the propeller as follows:

   a. Bend the propeller washer tabs away from the splined washer.

   b. Place a suitable wooden block between the propeller and the antiventilation plate to prevent the propeller from rotating. Loosen the propeller nut.

   c. Remove the propeller nut, tab washer, splined washer and continuity washer (if so equipped), propeller and thrust hub.

8. Loosen the 3 mounting locknuts on each side (B, **Figure 58**) equally and drop the gearcase housing slightly. On badly corroded units, the drive shaft may be frozen, making it necessary to pry the gearcase housing loose from the drive shaft housing.

14

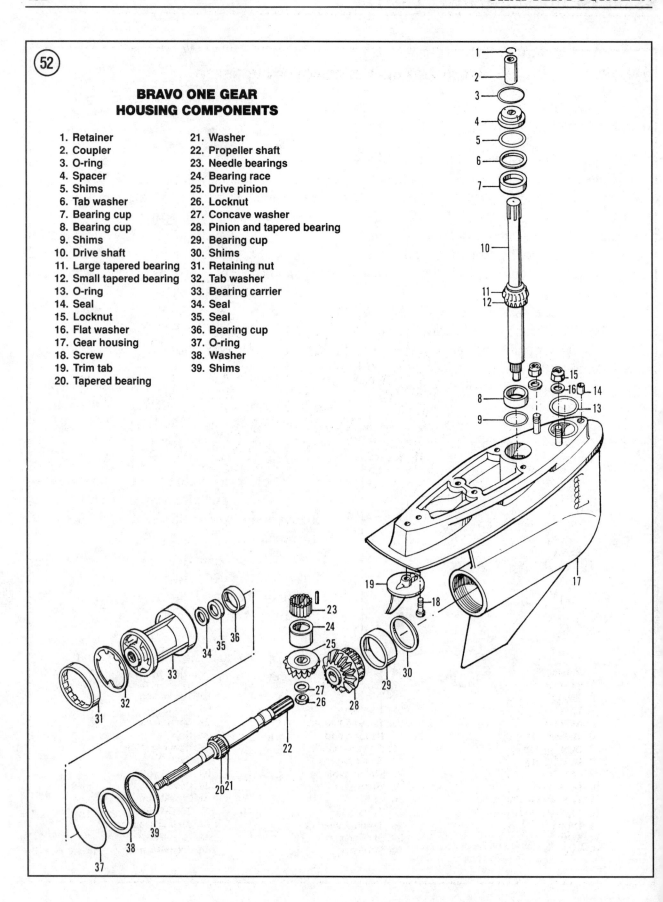

**BRAVO ONE GEAR
HOUSING COMPONENTS**

1. Retainer
2. Coupler
3. O-ring
4. Spacer
5. Shims
6. Tab washer
7. Bearing cup
8. Bearing cup
9. Shims
10. Drive shaft
11. Large tapered bearing
12. Small tapered bearing
13. O-ring
14. Seal
15. Locknut
16. Flat washer
17. Gear housing
18. Screw
19. Trim tab
20. Tapered bearing

21. Washer
22. Propeller shaft
23. Needle bearings
24. Bearing race
25. Drive pinion
26. Locknut
27. Concave washer
28. Pinion and tapered bearing
29. Bearing cup
30. Shims
31. Retaining nut
32. Tab washer
33. Bearing carrier
34. Seal
35. Seal
36. Bearing cup
37. O-ring
38. Washer
39. Shims

(53)

BRAVO TWO GEAR HOUSING COMPONENTS

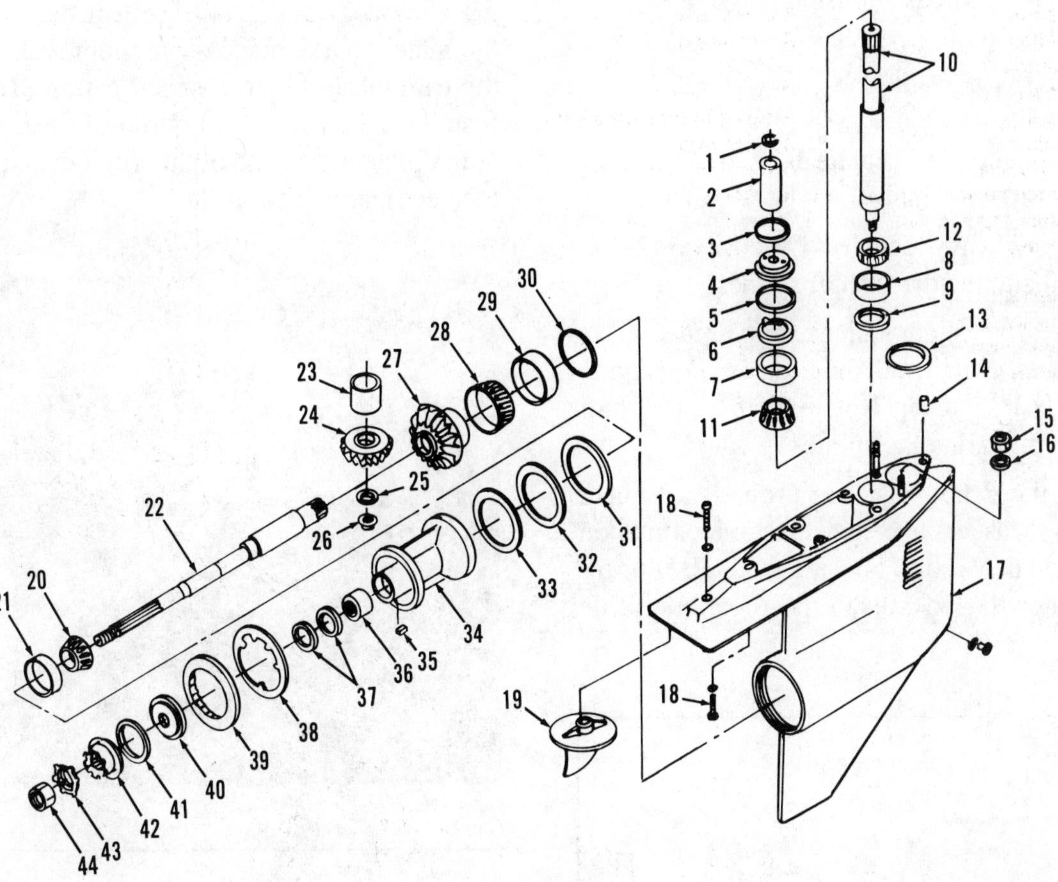

1. Retainer
2. Coupler
3. O-ring
4. Spacer
5. Shim(s)
6. Tab washer
7. Bearing cup
8. Bearing cup
9. Shim(s)
10. Drive shaft
11. Tapered bearing
12. Tapered bearing
13. O-ring
14. Seal
15. Nut
16. Flat washer
17. Gear housing
18. Screw
19. Trim tab
20. Tapered bearing
21. Bearing cup
22. Propeller shaft
23. Roller bearing
24. Pinion gear
25. Washer
26. Nut
27. Drive gear
28. Tapered bearing
29. Bearing cup
30. Shim(s)
31. Crush sleeve (load ring)
32. Thrust ring
33. O-ring
34. Bearing carrier
35. Key
36. Roller bearing
37. Seals
38. Tab washer
39. Cover nut
40. Thrust hub
41. Thrust washer
42. Splined washer
43. Tab washer
44. Propeller nut

14

9. Holding the gearcase housing firmly, remove the loosened nuts and separate the gearcase from the drive shaft housing.

10. Mount the gearcase housing in a suitable holding fixture.

11. Install clamp plate part No. 91-43559 securely on the gearcase housing (**Figure 59**).

Gearcase Installation

1. Remove the clamp plate from the gearcase housing (**Figure 59**).

2. Apply a heavy coat of Quicksilver 2-4-C Multi-Lube to the drive shaft splines.

3. Align drive shaft splines with upper drive shaft splines, then install the gearcase housing to the drive shaft housing. Rotate the propeller shaft as required to align the splines.

4. Once the 2 housings are properly coupled, install the washers and new elastic locknuts on each of the drive shaft housing studs (B, **Figure 58**). Tighten the locknuts to specification (**Table 1**).

5A. *Bravo One*—Install the bolt inside the trim tab cavity and tighten to specification (**Table 1**). Install the trim tab, aligning the match marks made during removal. Tighten the trim tab bolt to specification (**Table 1**). Install the plastic plug over the bolt. See **Figure 55**).

5B. *Bravo Two*—Install the trim tab, aligning the match marks made during removal. Tighten the trim tab fastener to specification (**Table 1**). Install the bolt into the bottom of the antiventilation plate just ahead of the trim tab and tighten to specification (**Table 1**).

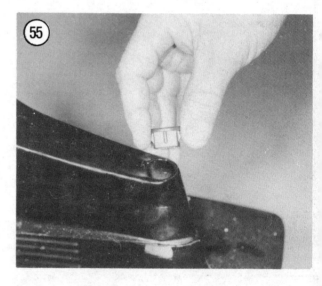

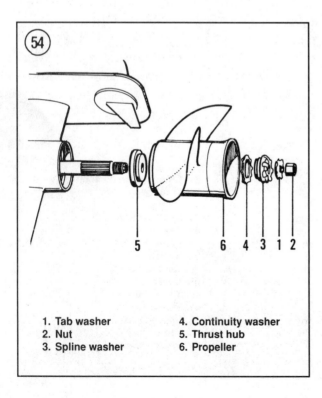

1. Tab washer
2. Nut
3. Spline washer
4. Continuity washer
5. Thrust hub
6. Propeller

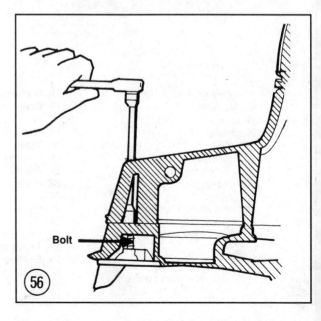

Bolt

6. Install the thrust hub and lubricate the propeller shaft splines with Quicksilver 2-4-C Marine Lubricant.

7. Install propeller, continuity washer, spline washer and tab washer (**Figure 54**). Install prop nut finger-tight.

8. Bend propeller washer tabs toward from the splined washer.

9. Fit a suitable wooden block between the propeller and antiventilation plate to prevent the propeller from rotating. Tighten the prop nut to minimum of 55 ft.-lb. (75 N•m).

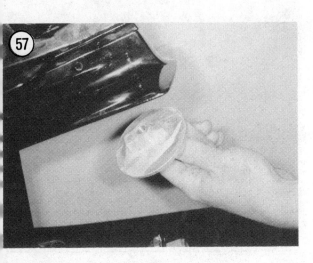

Gearcase Housing Disassembly

Refer to **Figure 52** (Bravo One) or **Figure 53** (Bravo Two) for this procedure.

1. Install a dial indicator on the side of the propeller shaft housing so that the indicator plunger will contact the propeller shaft. Move the shaft to one side as far as possible, hold in that position and set the indicator to zero. Move the shaft to the opposite side as far as possible and note the reading.

2. Reposition the dial indicator at the top of the housing bore and repeat Step 1 to check up/down deflection. Note the reading.

3. If the dial indicator shows a shaft deflection greater than 0.003 in. in Step 1 or Step 2, either the prop shaft bearings are worn or the prop shaft preload is incorrect.

4. With the dial indicator positioned on the propeller shaft housing as in Step 1 or Step 2, set the indicator to zero and rotate the propeller shaft 360°. If the indicator shows a shaft deflection greater than 0.005 in., the propeller shaft is bent.

5. Bend the tab washer tabs away from the retaining ring nut (**Figure 60**).

6. Install bearing carrier retainer wrench part No. 91-61069 (Bravo One) or part No. 91-17257 (Bravo Two) over the propeller shaft as shown in **Figure 61**. Remove the retaining ring (cover nut). See **Figure 62**.

14

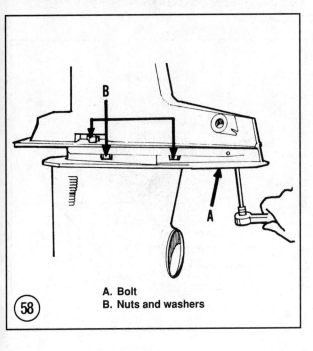

A. Bolt
B. Nuts and washers

7A. Bravo One—Install bearing carrier puller part No. 91-90338A1 as shown in **Figure 63**. Dislodge the bearing carrier from the gear housing by pulling down on the puller handle. Remove the bearing carrier (**Figure 64**).

7B. Bravo Two—Dislodge the bearing carrier from the gear housing using puller jaws part No. 91-45086A1 and slide hammer puller part No. 91-34569A1 (or equivalent). Remove the bearing carrier (**Figure 64**). Be careful not to lose the bearing carrier locating key.

NOTE
A new design bearing carrier is used on late Bravo One models (serial No. D782690-on). The length of the carrier has been changed to allow the use of a load ring and thrust ring in place of the shims and washer used on early models. See **Figure 65**, *typical. The late design bearing carrier can be identified by a "C-3" cast into the carrier directly after*

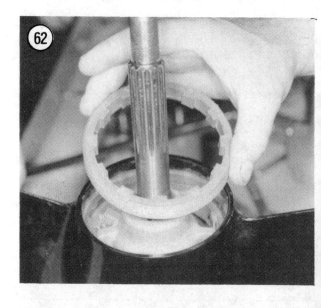

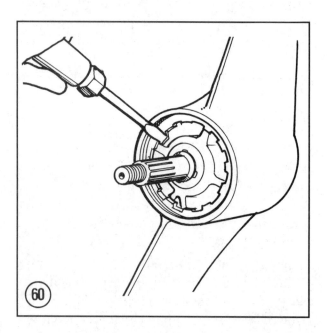

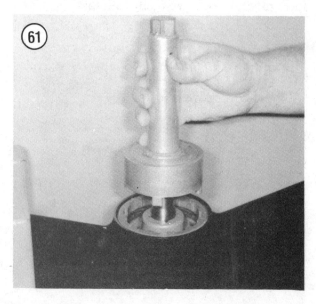

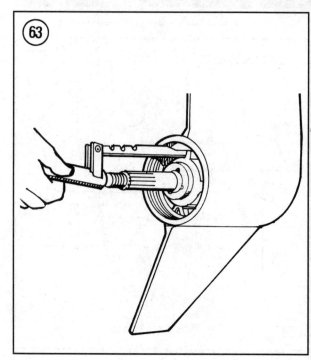

the part number. The early model carrier is identified by a "C-2" after the part number.

8. Reach into the propeller shaft bore and remove the O-ring, washer and shims (early Bravo One), O-ring, washer and load ring (late Bravo One) or O-ring, thrust ring and load ring (Bravo Two). See **Figure 65**, typical.

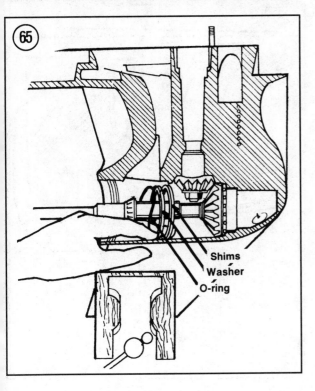

NOTE
Retain the O-ring, washer and shims or O-ring, thrust ring and load ring removed in Step 8 for use during the gear housing shim selection procedures.

9. Withdraw the propeller shaft and remove it from the housing bore.

10. Temporarily reinstall the retaining ring nut to protect the propeller shaft bore threads during Step 11.

11. Install drive shaft adaptor (part No. 91-61077) on the drive shaft. Hold the pinion gear nut with an appropriate socket and breaker bar as shown in **Figure 66** and rotate the drive shaft

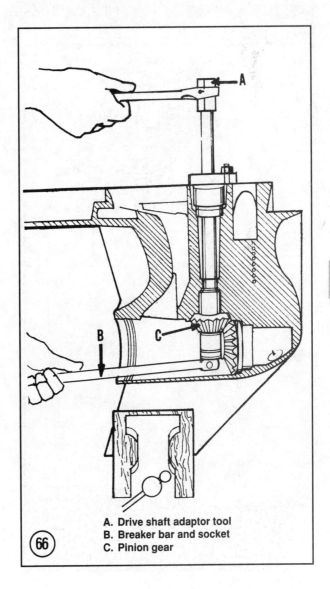

14

A. Drive shaft adaptor tool
B. Breaker bar and socket
C. Pinion gear

counterclockwise to break the pinion gear nut free. Remove the tools and then remove the retaining ring nut, pinion gear nut and washer from the housing bore.

12. Unbolt and remove the clamp plate (**Figure 59**).

13. Remove the O-ring, spacer, shims and tab washer (**Figure 67**).

14. Reach inside the propeller shaft bore with one hand and hold the pinion gear, then lift the drive shaft up enough to free the gear. Remove the gear and drive shaft from the gearcase. See **Figure 68**.

15. Reach inside the propeller shaft bore and remove the driven gear and bearing (**Figure 69**).

16. Remove and discard the water passage O-ring (**Figure 70**).

Drive Shaft/Pinion Bearing Service

The drive shaft and pinion bearings should not be removed unless replacement is required. To determine this, check the tapered bearing cups in the housing for signs of pitting, grooving, scoring, uneven wear, heat discoloration or embedded metallic particles. If any of these defects are found, replace the 2 tapered roller bearings on the drive shaft.

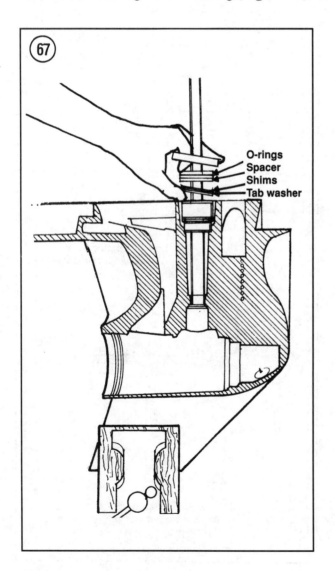

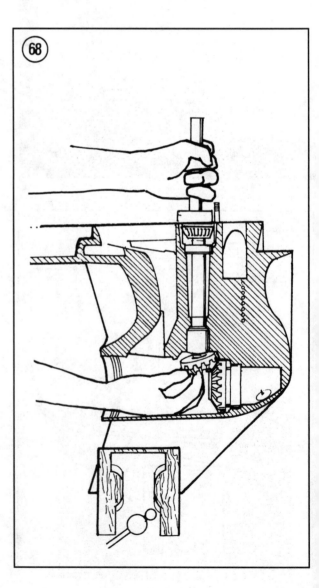

Check the surface of the drive shaft where the pinion bearing rides. If any of the defects listed above are found, replace the pinion bearing needles and sleeve.

Check the drive shaft splines for wear, twisting or distortion. If any of these defects are noted, replace the drive shaft.

Drive Shaft Bearing Replacement

Removal will damage the tapered roller bearings on the drive shaft. Be sure you have the correct replacement bearings before removing the old ones.

1. Install a universal puller plate as shown in **Figure 71** and press the large roller bearing from the shaft. Repeat this step to remove the small roller bearing.

2. Press a new small roller bearing on the drive shaft using the universal puller plate. Make sure the smaller outer diameter of the bearing faces the pinion end of the drive shaft.

3. Press a new large roller bearing on the drive shaft using a suitable mandrel as shown in **Figure 72**. Make sure the larger outer diameter of the bearing faces the pinion end of the drive shaft.

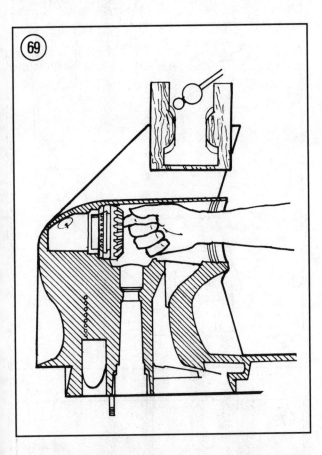

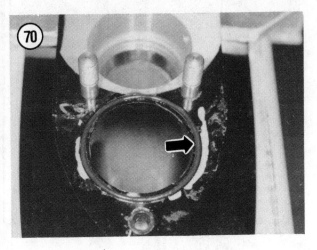

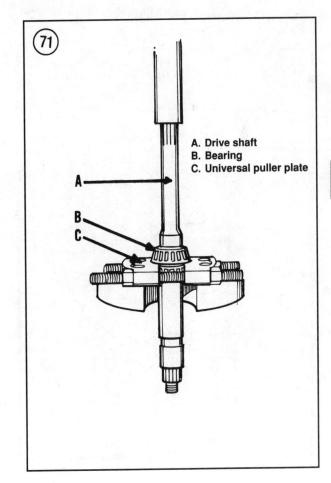

A. Drive shaft
B. Bearing
C. Universal puller plate

14

Drive Shaft Bearing Cup Replacement

1. Use a suitable 2-jaw puller as shown in **Figure 73** to remove the bearing cup and shims.
2. Install the shims and new bearing cup with driver part No. 91-67443 or equivalent.

Pinion Bearing Inner Race Replacement (Bravo Two)

The drive shaft is equipped with a removable pinion bearing inner race on Bravo Two models. Do not remove the pinion bearing inner race from the drive shaft unless the bearing and race require replacement.

1. Remove the pinion bearing inner race from the drive shaft using a universal puller plate and press as shown in **Figure 74**. Thread the pinion nut onto the drive shaft as shown to prevent damaging the drive shaft threads.

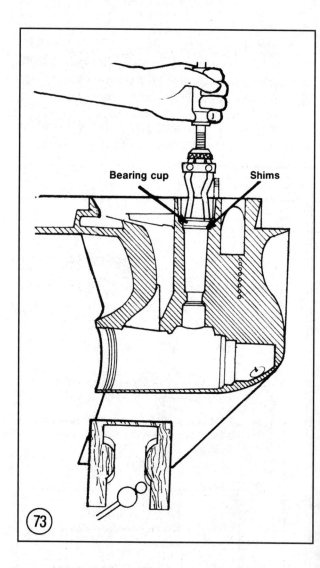

Bearing cup   Shims

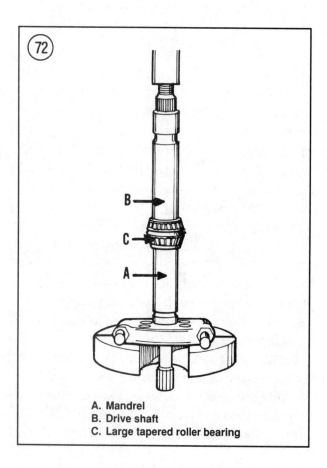

A. Mandrel
B. Drive shaft
C. Large tapered roller bearing

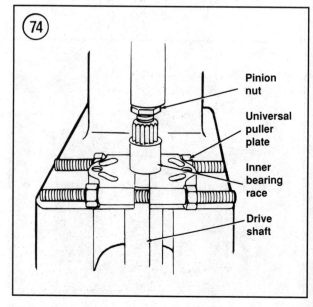

Pinion nut

Universal puller plate

Inner bearing race

Drive shaft

NOTE
The early design pinion bearing inner race used on Bravo Two models has a slightly larger inside diameter (1.473 in.) than the later bearing design (1.467 in.). The early style bearing and race must be used on units with gear housing

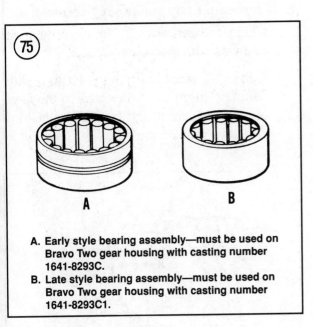

75

A. Early style bearing assembly—must be used on Bravo Two gear housing with casting number 1641-8293C.
B. Late style bearing assembly—must be used on Bravo Two gear housing with casting number 1641-8293C1.

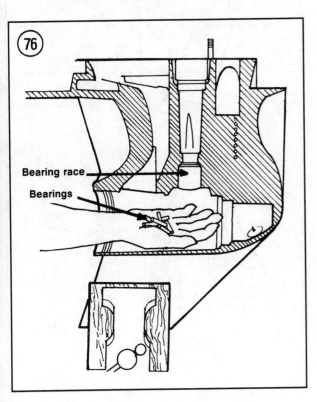

76

Bearing race

Bearings

casting number 1641-8293C. Be certain the correct pinion bearing and inner race are installed or bearing failure and drive unit damage will result.

2. Place a new inner bearing race onto the drive shaft. Using a press and universal puller plate, press the race onto the shaft until fully seated.

Drive Shaft Pinion Bearing Replacement (Bravo One and Bravo Two)

NOTE
*Bravo Two models may be equipped with an early or late design pinion bearing. The early style bearing and race must be used on units with gear housing casting number 1641-8293C. The later design bearing and race must be used on units with gear housing casting number 1641-8293C1. Be certain the correct pinion bearing and inner race are installed or bearing failure and drive unit damage will result. See **Figure 75** to identify early and late pinion bearings used on Bravo Two models.*

All the needle bearing rollers must be installed in the bearing race during bearing removal. If they are not, the bearing case may bend or break, making removal very difficult.

1. If the needle bearings fell out of the race during drive shaft removal (**Figure 76**), reinstall the rollers using Quicksilver Special Lube 101 to hold them in place.

2. Install driver rod (part No. 91-37323), driver (part No. 91-89868) and bearing remover (part No. 91-90337) as shown in **Figure 77**. Make sure bearing remover tabs align with the gearcase slots. Drive the bearing from the gearcase.

3. Install the new needle bearing assembly over bearing installer (part No. 91-89867) with the number stamped on the bearing casing facing up. Wipe outer diameter of casing with gear oil.

4. Install bearing installer tool along with bearing, threaded rod (part No. 91-31229), bearing driver (part No. 91-31229) and bearing driver

14

(part No. 91-89868) with a washer and nut as shown in **Figure 78**.

5. Tighten the nut to pull the bearing assembly into place, then remove the tools.

Propeller Shaft/Bearing Carrier Service

The propeller shaft bearing should not be removed unless replacement is required. To determine this, check the tapered bearing cup in the bearing carrier for pitting, grooving, scoring, uneven wear, heat discoloration or embedded metallic particles. If any of these defects are found, replace the tapered roller bearing on the propller shaft and the bearing cup in the carrier.

Check the surface of the carrier for corrosion. If excessive corrosion is present, replace the bearing carrier.

Check the surface of the propeller shaft where the bearing carrier oil seals ride (A, **Figure 79**) for signs of grooving. If grooves are noted, replace the bearing carrier oil seals.

Check the propeller shaft splines (B, **Figure 79**) for wear, twisting or distortion. If any of these defects are noted, replace the propeller shaft.

Propeller Shaft Bearing Replacement

1. Use a universal puller plate as a press plate and press the tapered roller bearing from the propeller shaft. Remove the washer and check its condition.

2. Reinstall the washer on the propeller shaft. Wipe the inner diameter of a new bearing with Quicksilver Special Lubricant 101.

3. Install bearing on shaft using a universal puller plate for support and a suitable mandrel to press the bearing in place.

Bearing Carrier Oil Seal/Bearing Cup Replacement (Bravo One)

The oil seals and the bearing cup can be serviced separately. It is not necessary to remove one to replace the other.

1. If the bearing cup requires replacement:

   a. Clamp the carrier by its reinforcement rib in a vise with protective jaws.

   b. Connect a suitable 2-jaw puller to a slide hammer. Insert the puller jaws in the large end of the carrier and behind the bearing cup, then remove the cup.

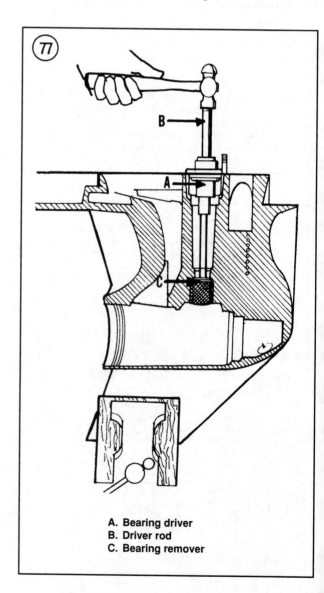

A. Bearing driver
B. Driver rod
C. Bearing remover

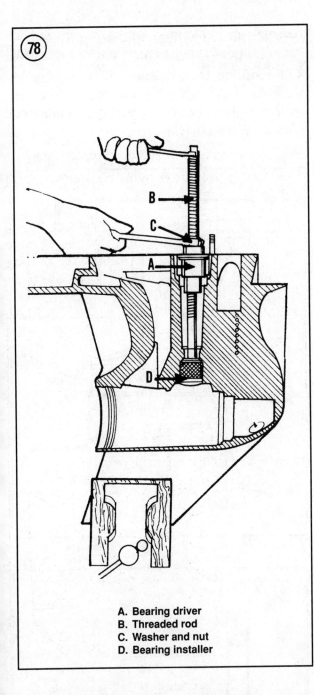

(78)

A. Bearing driver
B. Threaded rod
C. Washer and nut
D. Bearing installer

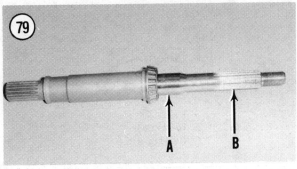

(79)

c. To install a new bearing cup, support the carrier in a press with the large end facing upward. Insert the new cup and press into place with driver part No. 91-89865 or equivalent.

2. If the oil seals require replacement:

a. Place the bearing carrier on a solid surface with the seal end facing up.

b. Drive both seals from the carrier with a suitable punch and hammer.

c. Coat the outer diameter of 2 new seals with Loctite 271.

d. Support the carrier in a press with the large end facing upward. Insert the first oil seal with its lip facing down and press into place with driver part No. 91-89865 or equivalent.

e. Insert the second oil seal with its lip facing up and press into place with driver part No. 91-89865 or equivalent.

f. Fill the cavity between the seals with Quicksilver Special Lubricant 101.

Bearing Carrier Oil Seal/Bearing Cup/Roller Bearing Replacement (Bravo Two Models)

The bearing carrier oil seals and bearing cup can be serviced separately. The oil seals must be removed first, however, if the bearing carrier roller bearing requires replacement.

1. If the bearing cup requires replacement:

a. Clamp the bearing carrier by its reinforcement rib in a vise with protective jaws.

b. Insert the puller jaws of slide hammer puller (part No. 91-34569A1) into the large end of the bearing carrier and behind the bearing cup. Remove the cup.

c. To install a new bearing cup, support the carrier in a press with the large end facing upward. Press the cup into the carrier until fully seated using driver part No. 91-63626 (or equivalent).

2. If the oil seals require replacement:

14

a. Place the bearing carrier on a solid surface with the seal end facing upward.

b. Pry the seals from the carrier using a suitable prying tool.

c. Apply Loctite 271 to the outer diamter of the new bearing carrier seals.

d. Install the inner seal with its lip facing down. Press the seal into the carrier until fully seated using the wide shoulder of seal driver part No. 91-55916 (or equivalent).

e. Install the outer seal with its lip facing up. Press the seal into the carrier until seated using the narrow shoulder of seal driver part No. 91-55916 (or equivalent).

f. Pack the area between the seals with Quicksilver 2-4-C Marine Lubricant.

3. If the roller bearing requires replacement:

a. Place the carrier on a solid surface with the seal end facing down

b. Drive the roller bearing and seals from the carrier using driver part No. 91-55919 (or equivalent) and a suitable driver rod.

c. To install a new roller bearing, place the carrier in a press with the seal end facing up. Place the bearing into the carrier. The numbered end of the bearing should face upward. Press the bearing into the carrier until fully seated using driver part No. 91-55918 (or equivalent) and driver rod part No. 91-37323 (or equivalent).

d. Install new carrier seals as previously described.

Driven Gear/Bearing/Bearing Cup Service

1. Use a universal puller plate and suitable mandrel to press the bearing from the driven gear.

2. Wipe the inner diameter of a new bearing with Quicksilver Special Lubricant 101. Support the driven gear on a wooden or metal block and press the new bearing into place with a suitable mandrel.

3. Attach puller part No. 91-34569A1 to a slide hammer. Insert puller jaws behind driven gear

bearing cup in the propeller shaft bore and remove the bearing cup and shims. See **Figure 80**.

4. Reposition the gearcase with the propeller shaft bore facing up. Install the shims, then wipe the outer diameter of the new bearing cup with gear oil and install with driver part No. 91-31106

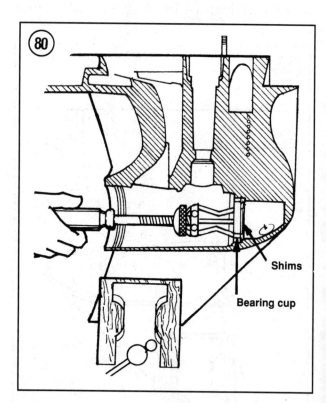

Shims

Bearing cup

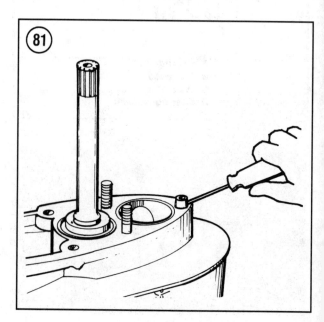

(Bravo One) or part No. 91-63626 (Bravo Two) and a suitable driver rod.

Water Tube Pickup and Seal Service

1. Check the small hole on the leading edge of the gearcase housing near the water intake. Insert

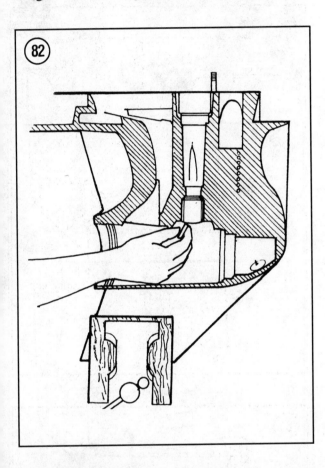

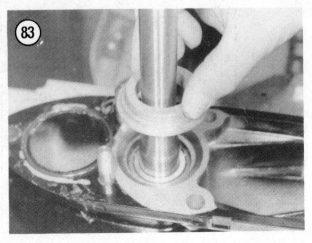

a length of stiff wire (straightened paper clip) and make sure the hole is clear.

2. Check the condition of the water tube seal at the top of the housing. If cut, nicked or distorted, pry seal out with an awl (**Figure 81**).

3. Wipe the outer diameter of a new seal with 3M Weatherstrip Adhesive and gently tap in place in the gearcase until the top edge is flush with the housing surface.

Gear Housing Assembly and Shimming

Refer to **Figure 52** (Bravo One) or **Figure 53** (Bravo Two) for this procedure.

1. Lubricate all bearings and gears with gear lube to assure accurate bearing preload readings.

2. Wipe water passage O-ring groove with 3M Weatherstrip Adhesive. Install a new O-ring (**Figure 70**).

3. If any rollers fell out of the lower pinion bearing during disassembly, reinstall with Quicksilver Special Lubricant 101 (**Figure 82**). This can be a slow, frustrating process, as it can be difficult to place the bearings upright and have them remain in that position for any length of time.

4. Install the driven gear assembly in the propeller shaft bore (**Figure 69**).

5. Position the pinion gear inside the propeller shaft bore and carefully insert the drive shaft to avoid disturbing the rollers in the pinion bearing.

6. Install the upper bearing cup, tab washer and original shim pack over the drive shaft and into the housing bore.

7. Install the spacer (**Figure 83**) and a new O-ring (**Figure 84**).

8. Install clamp plate (part No. 91-43559) securely on the gear housing (**Figure 59**).

9. Refer to **Figure 85**. Coat the pinion nuts threads with Loctite 271. Place the pinion nut washer on the nut with its concave side facing the gear. Insert the washer/nut assembly in the propeller shaft bore and under the drive shaft. Carefully lift the drive shaft just enough to slide the washer/nut in place, then rotate the drive

14

shaft to engage its threads with the nut. If the drive shaft is lifted too much or cocked while lifting, the pinion roller bearings may dislodge and require a return to Step 3. Thread the drive shaft into the pinion nut.

10. Temporarily reinstall the retaining ring nut to protect the propeller shaft bore threads during Step 11.

11. Install drive shaft adaptor (part No. 91-61077) on the drive shaft. Hold the pinion gear nut with an appropriate socket and breaker bar as shown in **Figure 66** and rotate the drive shaft to tighten the pinion nut to 113 ft.-lb. (150 N•m). Remove the tools and remaining ring nut.

12. Refer to **Figure 86** and check pinion height as follows:

   a. Install shimming tool part No. 91-42840 (Bravo One) or part No. 91-96512 (Bravo Two) in the propeller shaft bore.

   b. Measure the clearance between the gear and tool with a flat feeler gauge at 3 locations 120° apart.

   c. If clearance is less than 0.025 in., subtract the measurement from 0.025 in. The difference represents the shim thickness to be added under the lower tapered roller bearing cup. For exampe, if the measurement is 0.018 in., you must add 0.007 in. shimming.

   d. If clearance exceeds 0.025 in., subtract 0.025 in. from the measurement. The difference represents the shim thickness to be removed from under the lower tapered roller bearing cup. For example, if the measurement is 0.027 in., you must remove 0.002 in. shimming.

> *CAUTION*
> *Loctite sets up in 3 hours, but does not dry completely for 24 hours. If the Loctite applied to the nut threads in Step 13 is not dry, the nut may back off during operation at a later date, especially if the torque applied to the nut is incorrect.*

13. If shim changes are necessary to readjust pinion height, remove the drive shaft and refer

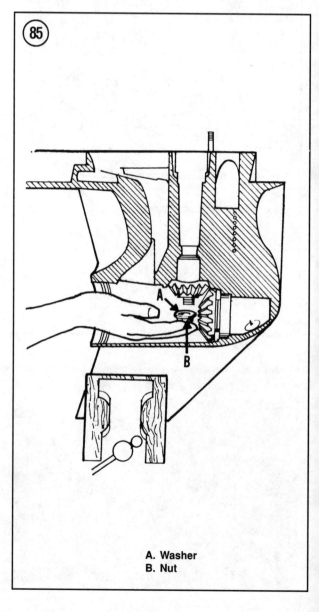

A. Washer
B. Nut

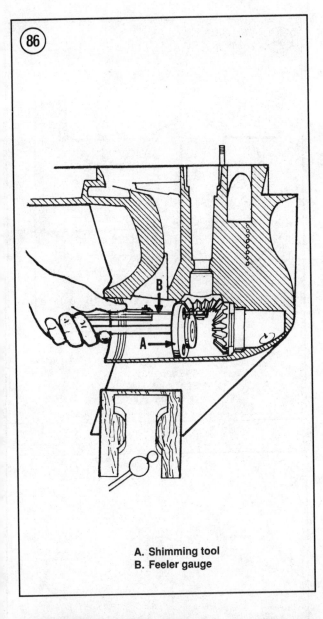

86

A. Shimming tool
B. Feeler gauge

to *Drive Shaft Bearing Cup Replacement* in this chapter. On final assembly, wipe the pinion nut threads with Loctite 271.

14. Once the correct pinion height has been established, remove the clamp plate (**Figure 59**).

15. Remove the O-ring (**Figure 84**), spacer (**Figure 83**) and the shims.

16. To determine the required shim pack thickness for correct drive shaft bearing preload:

  a. Measure the distance between the tab washer and top of the gearcase housing with a depth micrometer (**Figure 87**). Take three measurements and determine average (should be approximately 0.300 in.).

  b. Measure the thickness of the spacer's machined surface (**Figure 88**). Take three measurements and determine average (should be approximately 0.250 in.).

  c. Subtract the measurement obtained in Step 16a from that obtained in Step 16b, then add 0.001 in. This is the correct shim pack thickness.

17. Reinstall the correct shim pack, spacer and O-ring in the drive shaft bore.

18. Install the clamp plate part No. 91-43559 (**Figure 59**). Tighten the clamp plate screws securely.

19. Place drive shaft adapter (part No. 91-61077) onto the drive shaft splines. Install an in.-lb. torque wrench onto the drive shaft adapter

14

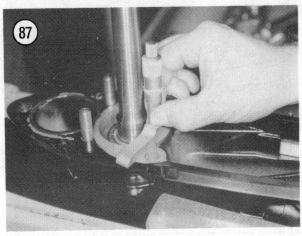

87

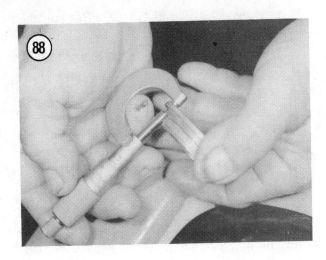

88

using an appropriate size socket. Rotate the drive shaft using the torque wrench to check the drive shaft rolling preload. The rolling preload should be 3-5 in.-lb.

NOTE
*A new design bearing carrier is used on late Bravo One models (serial No. D782690-on). The length of the carrier has been changed to allow the use of a load ring and thrust ring in place of the shims and washer used on early models (prior to serial No. D782690). See **Figure 65**, typical. The late design bearing carrier can be identified by a "C-3" cast into the carrier directly after the part number. The early model carrier is identified by a "C-2" after the part number. If installing a new design bearing carrier into an early model gearcase housing, discard shims located forward of the bearing carrier. Also, be sure to use a thrust ring (**Figure 89**) of 0.105 in. thickness (part No. 12-42256). Do not use the 0.200 in. thick thrust ring (part No. 12-41641A6).*

20A. Bravo One (prior to serial No. D782690):
  a. Install the propeller shaft, then insert the original shim pack, washer and O-ring into the propeller shaft bore (**Figure 65**).
  b. Reinstall the bearing carrier. Install the retaining nut and tighten to specification (**Table 1**) using retainer wrench part No. 91-61069.

20B. Bravo One (serial No. D782690-on) and Bravo Two:
  a. Install the propeller shaft, then insert the original load ring, thrust ring and O-ring into the gear housing. See **Figure 89**.
  b. Install the bearing carrier and retaining nut. Tighten the retaining nut until some resistance to rotation is noted in the propeller shaft.

21. Install dial indicator adapter (part No. 91-83155), backlash indicator rod (part No. 91-53459) and dial indicator (part No. 91-58222A1) onto the drive shaft as shown in **Figure 90**. Align

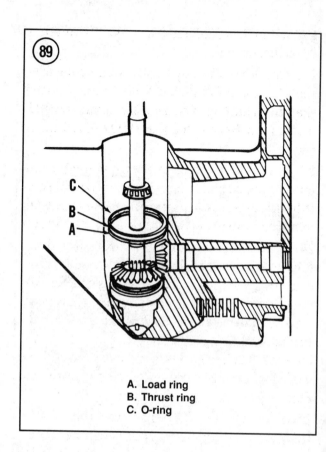

A. Load ring
B. Thrust ring
C. O-ring

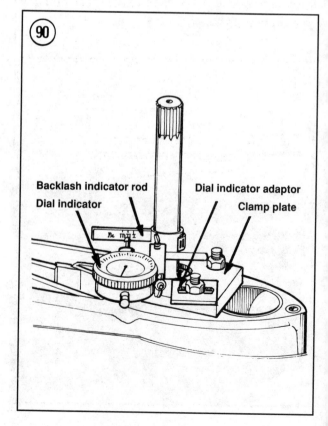

Backlash indicator rod
Dial indicator
Dial indicator adaptor
Clamp plate

the dial indicator plunger with the "II" mark on the indicator rod.

22. Check backlash by lightly rotating the drive shaft back and forth while holding the propeller shaft from turning. The backlash should be 0.12-0.15 in. on Bravo One and 0.009-0.018 in. on Bravo Two.

23. If backlash is greater than specified, shims must be added under the driven gear bearing cup. If backlash is less than specified, shims must be removed from under the driven gear bearing cup.

24. If backlash adjustment is necessary, disassemble the gear housing and remove the driven gear bearing cup as described in this chapter. Add or subtract shims as necessary, then reassemble the gear housing and recheck backlash. When the correct backlash is established, remove the dial indicator adapter, backlash indicator rod and dial indicator. Do not remove the clamp plate. See **Figure 90**.

25A. *Bravo One (prior to serial No. D782690)*—If backlash adjustment is not necessary, continue at Step 26 to check gear housing overall bearing preload.

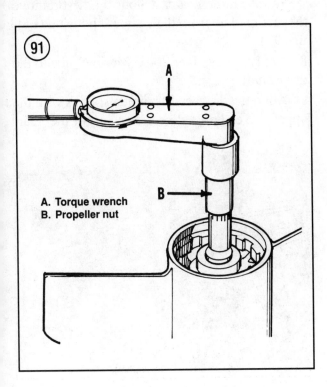

A. Torque wrench
B. Propeller nut

NOTE
*A new load ring (A, **Figure 89**) must be installed upon final assembly on Bravo Two models.*

25B. *Bravo One (serial No. D782690-on) and Bravo Two*—If backlash adjustment is not necessary, proceed as follows:

a. Remove the retainer, bearing carrier and tab washer from the gear housing. Remove the load ring, thrust ring and O-ring.

b. Install a new load ring, the original thrust ring and a new O-ring (**Figure 89**).

c. Apply Quicksilver Special Lubricant 101 or Perfect Seal to the outer diameter mating surfaces of the bearing carrier. Install the bearing carrier and locking tab washer. Be sure the locating key grooves in the carrier and gear housing are aligned, then install the locating key.

d. Lubricate the bearing carrier retainer threads with Quicksilver Special Lubricant 101 or Perfect Seal. Install the retainer into the gear housing. Using retainer wrench (part No. 91-17257), tighten the retainer until resistance to rotation is noted in the propeller shaft.

26. Position the gear housing so the propeller shaft is facing upward. Install the propeller nut onto the propeller shaft.

27. Using an appropriate size socket, attach an in.-lb. torque wrench to the propeller nut. See **Figure 91**.

28. Rotate the torque wrench in the normal direction of rotation, in a smooth, steady motion, while noting the reading to check bearing preload.

NOTE
Bearings can be considered used if spun once under load (power applied).

29. Bearing preload should be 8-12 in.-lb. for new bearings or 5-8 in.-lb. for used bearings.

14

30A. *Bravo One (prior to serial No. D782690)*—If shim changes are necessary to adjust preload:

    a. Remove the retainer and bearing carrier. Remove the O-ring, washer and shim pack (**Figure 65**). If preload is greater than specified, increase thickness of the shims (**Figure 65**). If preload is less than specified, decrease thickness of the shims (**Figure 65**).

    b. Install the correct shim pack, washer and a new carrier O-ring. Apply Quicksilver Special Lubricant 101 or Perfect Seal to the mating surfaces of the carrier outer diameter, then install the carrier, locking tab washer and retainer. Tighten the retainer to specification (**Table 1**). Make sure the special tab engages the "V" in the bearing carrier (**Figure 92**). Use a punch and hammer to bend one tab into the retaining ring nut, then bend the other tabs down into the bore.

30B. *Bravo One (serial No. D782690-on) and Bravo Two*—Tighten the bearing carrier retainer slowly, in small increments until the specified preload is obtained. When the specified preload is obtained, secure the retainer by bending one tab into place in the retainer, then bend the remaining tabs down into the gear housing.

31. Remove the clamp plate (**Figure 90**). Install the gear housing as described in this chapter.

BRAVO THREE

The Bravo Three stern drive was introduced for the 1993 model year. The Bravo Three has twin, counter-rotating propellers and is designed for use on fast cruisers and large runabouts which typically run in the 40-60 mph range. Except for the gearcase housing (lower unit), the Bravo Three is identical to Bravo One and Two stern drive units.

The Bravo Three gearcase contains the drive shaft, drive shaft bearings, drive pinion gear and bearings, inner and outer propeller shafts and bearings, bearing carrier and related seals and O-rings. Refer to **Figure 93**.

Gearcase Removal/Installation

1. On models equipped with a remote gear lube reservoir, remove, drain and thoroughly clean the reservoir.

2. Drain the gearcase housing as described in Chapter Four.

3. Remove the plastic plug at the top rear of the gearcase housing. Then insert a suitable socket into the hole and remove the anode mounting bolt (**Figure 94**) and anode (**Figure 95**).

4. Remove the bolt inside the anode cavity and remove the splash plate extension (**Figure 94**).

5. Remove the locknuts and washers (**Figure 96**) from each side of the gearcase. Lower the gearcase down and off the drive shaft housing. Mount the gearcase in a suitable holding fixture.

6. Install the clamp plate (part No. 91-43559) over the drive shaft and onto the gearcase housing. See **Figure 97**.

7. To install the gearcase housing, first remove the clamp plate from the gearcase housing (**Figure 97**).

8. Apply Quicksilver 2-4-C Marine Lube to the drive shaft splines.

9. Align the drive shaft coupler splines with the upper drive shaft splines, then install the gear-

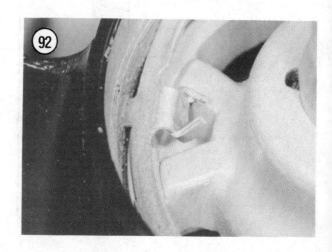

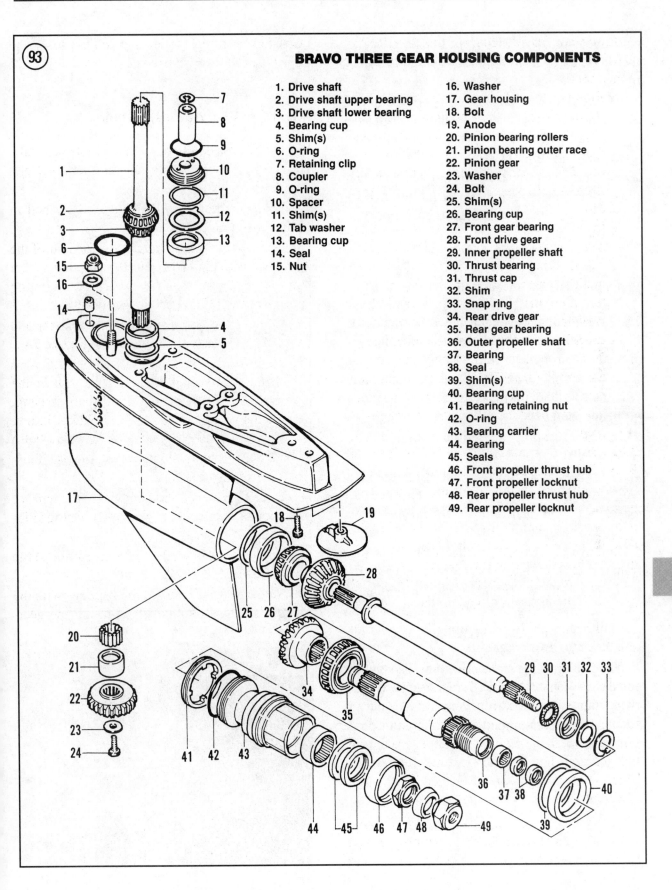

93

BRAVO THREE GEAR HOUSING COMPONENTS

1. Drive shaft
2. Drive shaft upper bearing
3. Drive shaft lower bearing
4. Bearing cup
5. Shim(s)
6. O-ring
7. Retaining clip
8. Coupler
9. O-ring
10. Spacer
11. Shim(s)
12. Tab washer
13. Bearing cup
14. Seal
15. Nut
16. Washer
17. Gear housing
18. Bolt
19. Anode
20. Pinion bearing rollers
21. Pinion bearing outer race
22. Pinion gear
23. Washer
24. Bolt
25. Shim(s)
26. Bearing cup
27. Front gear bearing
28. Front drive gear
29. Inner propeller shaft
30. Thrust bearing
31. Thrust cap
32. Shim
33. Snap ring
34. Rear drive gear
35. Rear gear bearing
36. Outer propeller shaft
37. Bearing
38. Seal
39. Shim(s)
40. Bearing cup
41. Bearing retaining nut
42. O-ring
43. Bearing carrier
44. Bearing
45. Seals
46. Front propeller thrust hub
47. Front propeller locknut
48. Rear propeller thrust hub
49. Rear propeller locknut

14

case housing to the drive shaft housing. Rotate the propeller shaft as required to align the splines.

10. Once the 2 housings are properly coupled, install the washers and new locknuts on each side of the unit (**Figure 96**). Tighten the nuts to specification (**Table 1**).

11. Reverse Steps 3 and 4 to complete installation. Fill the gearcase and remote reservoir (if so equipped) with the recommended gear lubricant (Chapter Four).

Propellers Remove/Reinstall

1. Place a suitable wooden block between the front propeller and the antiventilation plate to prevent the propellers from turning.

2. Loosen and remove the rear propeller nut (**Figure 98**). Slide the rear propeller off the inner propeller shaft.

3. Slide the rear propeller thrust hub off the shaft (**Figure 99**).

4. Loosen the front propeller nut using tool part No. 91-805457 (or equivalent). See **Figure 100**. Unscrew the nut and remove it from the outer propeller shaft (**Figure 101**).

5. Remove the front propeller then slide the front thrust hub (**Figure 102**) off the outer shaft.

6. To install the propellers, first coat the inner and outer propeller shafts with Quicksilver Special Lubricant 101, 2-4-C Marine Lubricant or a suitable anticorrosion grease.

7. Slide the front thrust hub (**Figure 102**) on the outer propeller shaft. Make sure the tapered side of the hub is facing rearward.

8. Install the front propeller over the outer propeller shaft.

> *NOTE*
> *After 20 hours of operation, remove the rear propeller and retighten the front propeller nut to at least 100 ft.-lb.(136 N•m). Never operate the boat with a loose propeller.*

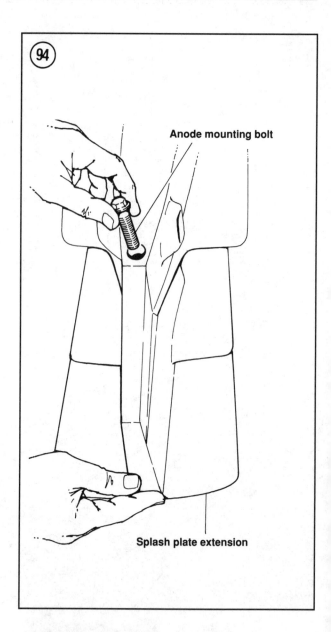

(94) Anode mounting bolt

Splash plate extension

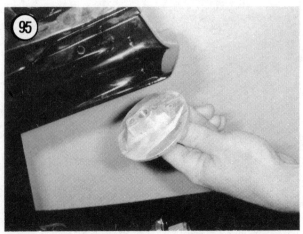

(95)

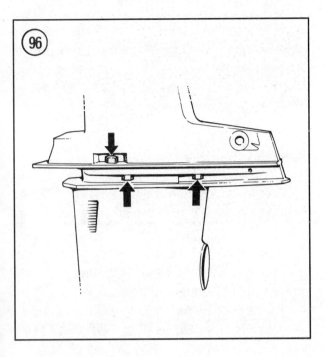

9. Install the front propeller nut (**Figure 101**). Tighten the nut to 100 ft.-lb. (136 N•m) (minimum) using tool part No. 91-805457. See **Figure 100**.

10. Slide the rear thrust hub onto the inner propeller shaft (**Figure 99**). Make sure the tapered side of the hub is facing rearward.

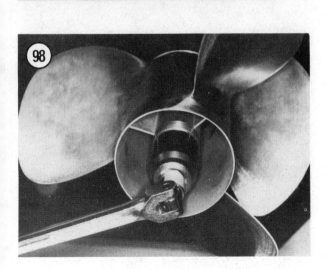

14

NOTE
Check propeller nut tightness after 20 hours of operation. Never operate the boat with a loose propeller.

11. Position the front propeller with one blade facing straight UP. Then install the rear propeller with one of its blades facing straight DOWN. See **Figure 103**. Install the rear propeller nut and tighten it to at least 60 ft.-lb. (81 N•m).

Pre-Disassembly Inspection

Prior to disassembling the gearcase, check the inner and outer propeller shafts for excessive runout or deflection using a dial indicator as follows.

1. Mount a dial indicator (part No. 91-58222A1) on the rear of the propeller shaft bearing carrier using a hose clamp as shown in **Figure 104**. Position the indicator plunger against the inner propeller shaft, at a right-angle to the shaft.

2. Rotate the inner shaft while observing the dial indicator.

3. If runout or deflection exceeds 0.005 in. (0.13 mm), the inner propeller shaft is bent and must be replaced. Do not attempt to straighten a bent shaft.

4. Next, position the dial indicator plunger against the outer propeller shaft. Make sure the indicator plunger is at a right-angle to the shaft. See **Figure 105**.

5. Rotate the outer propeller shaft while observing the dial indicator. If runout or deflection exceeds 0.010 in. (0.25 mm), the outer propeller shaft is bent and must be replaced. Do not attempt to straighten a bent shaft.

Gearcase Housing Disassembly

Record the location and thickness of all shims removed from the gearcase housing during disassembly.

1. If not previously done, drain the gearcase into a suitable container while watching for metal chips or water contamination.

2. Be sure the clamp plate (part No. 91-43559) is correctly installed as described under *Gearcase Removal/Installation* in this chapter.

NOTE
*The propeller shaft bearing carrier has left-hand threads. Turn the carrier **clockwise** to remove it.*

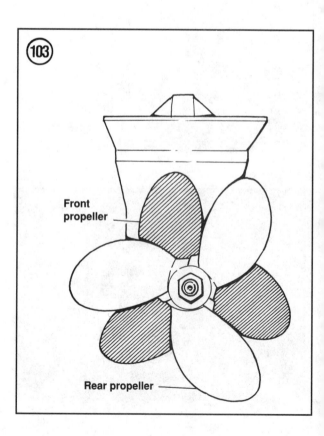

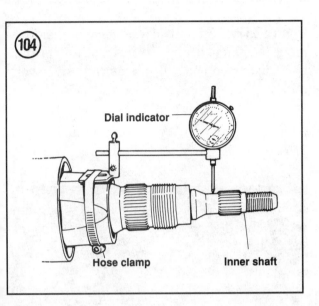

Dial indicator

Hose clamp   Inner shaft

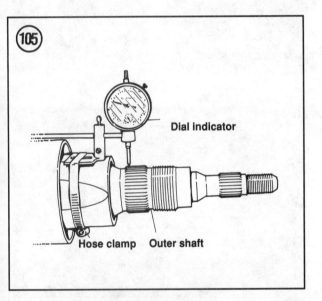

Dial indicator

Hose clamp   Outer shaft

3. Using a heat lamp or heat gun (not open flame), heat the gearcase housing where the bearing carrier enters the housing. Then, using bearing carrier removal/installation tool, part No. 91-805377, (**Figure 106**) and a suitable breaker bar, loosen the bearing carrier by turning it clockwise (left-hand threads). Unscrew the carrier and slide it off the outer propeller shaft.

NOTE
*The bearing retainer nut has left-hand threads. See **Figure 107**. Turn the retainer clockwise to loosen it.*

4. Next, install the bearing retainer nut removal/installation tool, part No. 91-805382, (**Figure 108**) over the outer propeller shaft, into the gearcase housing and engage it with the bearing retainer nut (**Figure 107**). Then, install bearing carrier tool, part No. 91-805374, over the bearing retainer nut tool as shown in **Figure 109**. Turn the tool clockwise (left-hand threads)

14

to loosen the bearing retainer nut. Unscrew the retainer nut and remove it (**Figure 110**) from the gearcase.

5. Pull the inner and outer propeller shafts along with the rear drive gear, bearing and bearing cup from the gearcase as an assembly. See **Figure 111**.

6. Reach into the gearcase and remove the shim(s) located forward of the rear drive gear bearing cup.

7. Temporarily reinstall the bearing retaining nut to protect the propeller shaft bore threads during Step 8.

8. Remove the drive shaft coupler (**Figure 122**) from the drive shaft. Install drive shaft adapter part No. 91-61077 (A, **Figure 113**) on the drive shaft. Hold the pinion gear bolt with an appropriate socket and breaker bar as shown in **Figure 113**. Rotate the drive shaft counterclockwise to loosen and remove the pinion gear bolt. Remove the tools, then remove the retaining nut, pinion gear bolt and washer from the gearcase housing bore.

9. Unbolt and remove the clamp plate (**Figure 97**). Remove the O-ring, spacer, shims and tab washer (**Figure 114**).

10. Reach inside the propeller shaft bore with one hand and hold the pinion gear, then lift the drive shaft up enough to free the gear. Remove the gear and drive shaft from the gearcase. See

Figure 115. Reach inside the gearcase and remove the pinion bearing rollers. The rollers may have dislodged and fell free during drive shaft removal.

11. Reach inside the propeller shaft bore and remove the front drive gear and bearing (**Figure 116**).

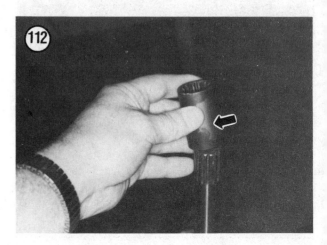

12. Remove and discard the water passage O-ring (**Figure 117**).

Drive Shaft/Pinion Bearing Service

The drive shaft and pinion bearings should not be removed unless replacement is required. To determine this, check the tapered bearings and cups for pitting, grooving, scoring, uneven wear, heat discoloration or embedded metallic particles. If any defects are noted, the bearings and cups must be replaced.

Inspect the surface of the drive shaft where the pinion bearing rides (**Figure 118**). This surface must be perfectly smooth without pits, scoring, galling, uneven wear, discoloration or other damage. If not in acceptable condition, replace the pinion bearing rollers, outer race and drive shaft.

Inspect the drive shaft splines for wear, twisting or distortion. If any defects replace the drive shaft.

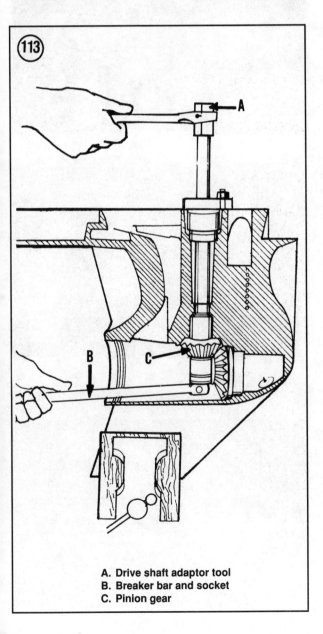

A. Drive shaft adaptor tool
B. Breaker bar and socket
C. Pinion gear

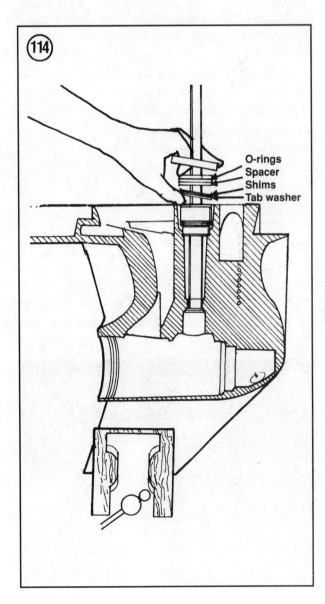

O-rings
Spacer
Shims
Tab washer

14

Drive shaft bearing replacement

Removal will damage the tapered roller bearings on the drive shaft. Only remove the bearings if replacement is necessary.

1. Install a universal bearing puller plate as shown in **Figure 119** and press the large roller bearing from the shaft. Repeat this step to remove the small bearing.

2. Lubricate the inner diameter of the new drive shaft bearings with gear lubricant.

3. Press a new small roller bearing on the drive shaft using the universal puller plate. Make sure the smaller outer diameter of the bearing faces the pinion end of the drive shaft.

4. Press the large tapered bearing on the drive shaft using a suitable mandrel as shown in **Figure 120**. Make sure the larger outer diameter of the bearing is facing the pinion end of the drive shaft.

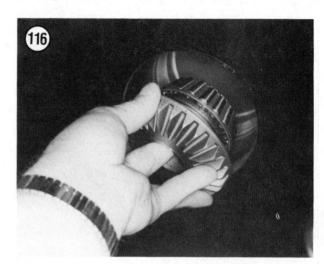

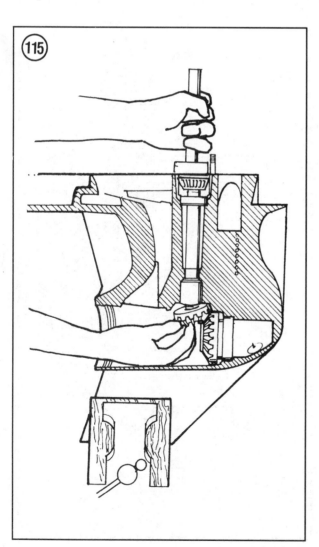

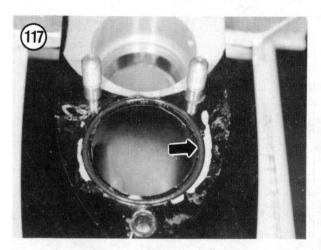

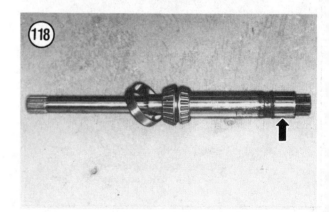

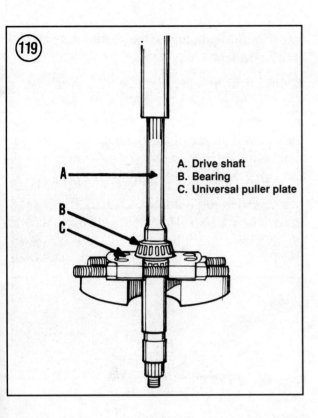

A. Drive shaft
B. Bearing
C. Universal puller plate

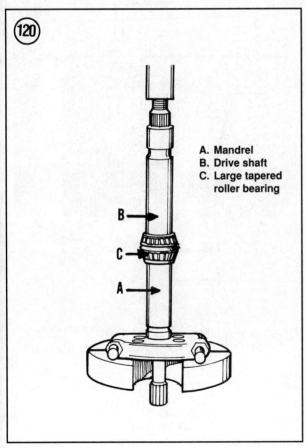

A. Mandrel
B. Drive shaft
C. Large tapered
   roller bearing

Drive shaft lower bearing cup replacement

1. Remove the drive shaft lower bearing cup using a suitable slide-hammer puller as shown in **Figure 121**.

2. Remove the shim(s) under the bearing cup.

3. To install the bearing cup, first place the original shims in the bearing cup bore. If the original shim thickness is not known, install a 0.050 in. thick shim pack.

4. Place the cup in position. Using bearing cup driver (part No. 91-67443), drive the cup into the gearcase until firmly seated.

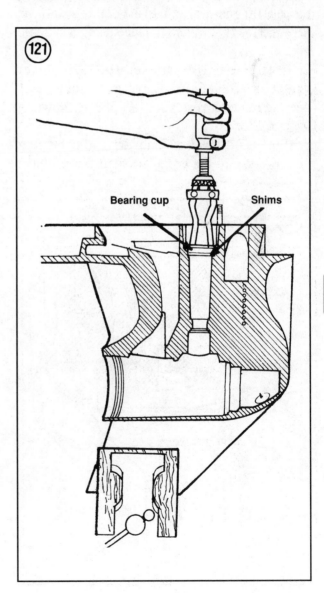

Bearing cup   Shims

14

Drive shaft pinion bearing replacement

The pinion bearing rollers must be installed in their outer race during bearing removal. If not, the bearing outer race may bend or break, making removal very difficult.

NOTE
To ease bearing removal, heat the gearcase housing in the area of the pinion bearing to approximately 200° F, using a heat lamp or heat gun. Do not use open flame to heat the housing.

1. If the bearing rollers fell out of the race during drive shaft removal (**Figure 122**), reinstall the rollers. Hold the rollers in place using a suitable grease.

2. Install driver rod part No. 91-37323, driver part No. 91-89868 (to serve as a guide) and bearing remover part No. 91-90337 as shown in **Figure 123**.

3. Tap the driver rod and drive the bearing downward into the propeller shaft bore. Reach into the bore and remove the bearing race and all bearing rollers.

4. Install the new bearing assembly over bearing installer (part No. 91-89867) with the number stamped on the outer race facing up. Lubricate the outer diameter of the bearing race with gear lubricant.

5. Install the bearing installer tool with the bearing, threaded rod (part No. 91-31229) and bearing driver (part No. 91-89868) with a washer and nut as shown in **Figure 124**.

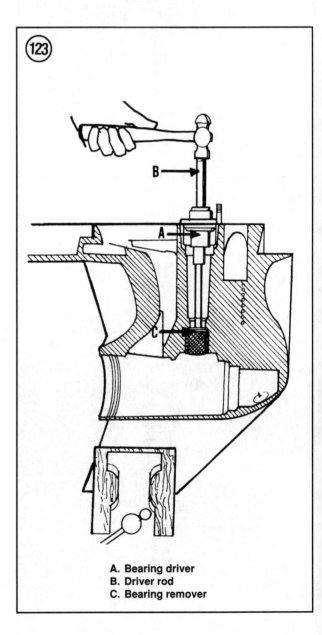

A. Bearing driver
B. Driver rod
C. Bearing remover

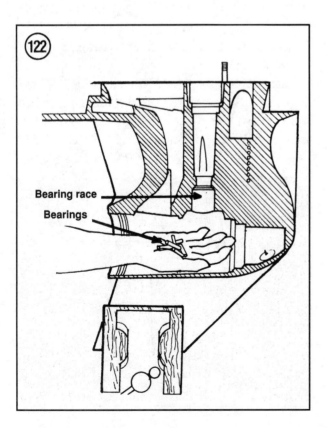

Bearing race
Bearings

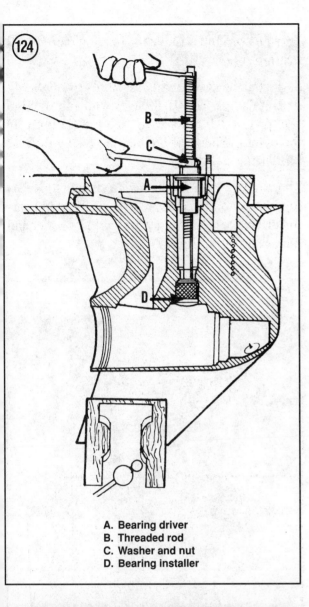

A. Bearing driver
B. Threaded rod
C. Washer and nut
D. Bearing installer

6. Tighten the nut to pull the bearing assembly into position, then remove the tools.

7. Apply Quicksilver Needle Bearing Assembly Grease to the bearing rollers to hold them in place.

Propeller Shaft/Bearing Carrier Service

All propeller shaft bearings and seals are damaged during removal. Therefore, do not remove the bearings and seals unless replacement is necessary.

The solid inner propeller shaft fits inside the hollow outer propeller shaft. The outer shaft contains a caged needle bearing and a pair of seals that the inner shaft rides in. The bearing carrier contains a caged needle bearing and a pair of seals that the outer shaft rides in.

Propeller shaft disassembly

1. Slide the inner propeller shaft (A, **Figure 125**) and thrust bearing (B) out of the outer shaft (C).

2. Remove the rear drive gear bearing cup from the outer shaft, if necessary.

3. Using a small punch and hammer, tap the thrust cap (**Figure 126**) off the outer propeller shaft. Align the punch with the end gap in the snap ring located behind the cap.

14

4. Remove the thrust cap (A, **Figure 127**) and shim (B) from the outer shaft. Note that the shim is used to control inner propeller shaft end play.

5. Remove the snap ring (**Figure 128**) using snap ring pliers.

6. Slide the rear drive gear off the outer propeller shaft (**Figure 129**) to complete propeller shaft disassembly.

Propeller shaft/bearing carrier inspection

1. Inspect the inner and outer propeller shafts for bent or twisted splines.

2. Inspect the outer shaft in the needle bearing contact area (A, **Figure 130**) for pitting, grooves, galling, discoloration, corrosion or other damage. The condition of this bearing surface is a good indicator of the condition of the needle bearing in the bearing carrier. Replace the bearing in the carrier and outer propeller shaft if any defects are noted.

3. Inspect the outer propeller shaft where the bearing carrier seals contact the shaft (B, **Figure 130**). Replace the bearing carrier seals if grooves are evident. Replace the outer shaft if the grooves are deep.

4. Inspect the inner propeller shaft in the needle bearing contact area (A, **Figure 131**) and seal contact area (B). If the bearing contact area shows pitting, galling, grooves, corrosion or

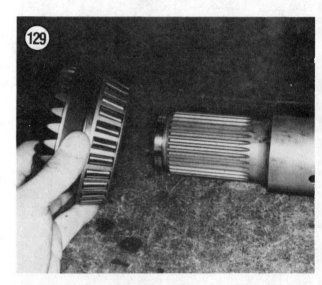

other damage, replace the inner propeller shaft and the needle bearing and seals in the outer shaft (**Figure 132**).

5. Remove and discard the bearing carrier O-ring (**Figure 133**).

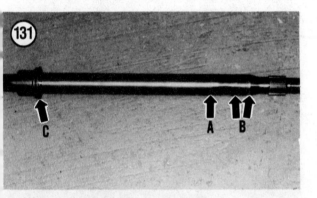

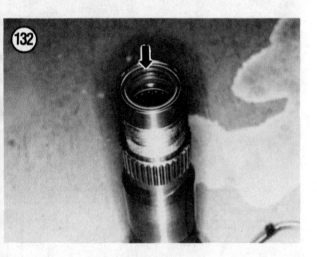

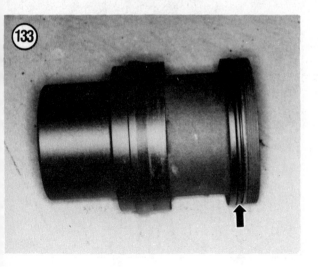

6. Inspect the carrier assembly for corrosion in the carrier-to-gearcase housing mating surface. Replace the carrier assembly if excessive corrosion is noted.

7. Inspect the carrier needle bearing (A, **Figure 134**) for excessive wear, pitting, grooves, corrosion, discoloration or other damage. Replace the bearing and seals (B, **Figure 134**) if defects are noted.

Outer propeller shaft bearing/seals replacement

1. Remove the outer propeller shaft bearing and seals (**Figure 132**) using a 3-jaw puller and a slide-hammer attachment (part No. 91-34569A1). Securely hold the shaft and remove the 2 seals, then the bearing.

2. Press a new bearing into the shaft using bearing installation tool (part No. 91-805352) and an arbor press. Press the bearing from its numbered side. Lubricate the bearing with Quicksilver Special Lubricant 101.

3. Apply Loctite 271 to the outer diameter of the outer propeller shaft seals.

4. Install the seals into the outer propeller shaft using seal installation tool (part No. 91-805358). Place both seals on the installation tool with their seal lips facing away from each other (inner lip facing center of shaft and outer lip facing away

14

from shaft). Press the seals into the shaft until the installation tool bottoms on the shaft.

5. Lubricate the seal lips and pack the area between the seals with Quicksilver Special Lube 101.

Bearing carrier bearing and seal replacement

1. Remove the bearing carrier seals (B, **Figure 134**) using a slide-hammer and 3-jaw puller. Then, if necessary, remove the bearing (A, **Figure 134**) using the same puller assembly.

2. Lubricate the outer diameter of a new bearing with gear lube. Position the bearing in the carrier. Make sure the numbered side of the bearing is facing up and that it is started squarely in the carrier.

3. Press the bearing into the carrier using bearing installation tool (part No. 91-805356) and an arbor press.

4. Apply Loctite 271 to the outer diameter of new bearing carrier seals.

5. Position the seals with their lips facing opposite each other (inner seal lip facing inward and outer seal lip facing outward).

6. Place both seals onto seal installation tool (part No. 91-805372). Press the seals into the carrier until the installation tool bottoms on the carrier.

7. Lubricate the seal lips and pack the area between the seals with Quicksilver Special Lube 101.

Drive Gear Bearing and Bearing Cup Service

> *NOTE*
> *The bearing cup for the front drive gear bearing is pressed into the gearcase housing. The rear drive gear bearing cup is loose once the propeller shafts are removed.*

Inspect the drive gears (A, **Figure 135**) for chipped or broken teeth, pitting, corrosion, excessive or uneven wear or other damage. If any

defects are present, replace the drive gear(s), tapered bearing and cup along with the pinion gear.

Inspect the drive gear tapered bearing (B, **Figure 135**) and bearing cup for pitting, grooves, excessive or uneven wear, corrosion, discoloration or other damage. Replace the bearing and cup as a set.

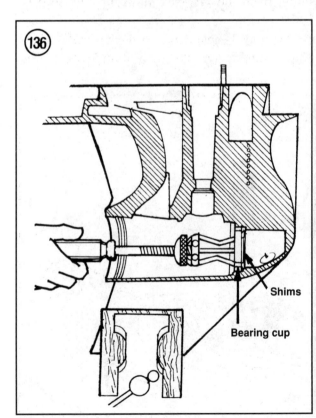

Shims

Bearing cup

Proceed as follows to replace the bearings/cups.

1. Use a universal puller plate, an arbor press and a suitable mandrel to remove the tapered bearings from the drive gears.

2. Lubricate the inner diameter of the new bearings with gear lube. Support the gear on a wooden or metal block and press the new bearing into place using a suitable mandrel. The inner race of the old bearing makes a good mandrel.

> *NOTE*
> *The shim(s) located behind the front drive gear bearing cup (**Figure 136**) is generally damaged during cup removal. If so, do not reuse the shim(s). Measure the thickness of the shims using a micrometer then replace them with a shim pack of equal thickness.*

3. Attach puller (part No. 91-34569A1) to a slide-hammer. Insert the puller jaws behind the front drive gear bearing cup. Pull the bearing and shims from the gearcase housing. See **Figure 136**.

4. Position the gearcase so the propeller shaft bore is facing up. Install a shim pack of the original thickness into the gearcase. If the original thickness is not known, install a 0.015 in. shim.

5. Lubricate the outer diameter of the new bearing cup with gear lube. Install the cup into the gearcase. Make sure the cup is positioned squarely in its bore.

6. Using driver (part No. 91-805454) and a suitable driver rod, drive the cup into its bore until fully seated.

Water Tube Pickup and Seal Service

1. Check the small hole on the leading edge of the gearcase housing, near the water intake, for restriction or plugging.

2. Insert a stiff wire (straightened paper clip) and make sure the hole is clear. If the hole cannot be cleaned, carefully drill it out using a 5/64 in. bit. Use caution not to drill deeper than 2-7/16 in. (62 mm) into the gearcase.

3. Check the condition of the water tube seal at the top of the housing. If cut, nicked or distorted, pry the seal out with an awl or similar tool. See **Figure 137**.

4. Coat the outer diameter of a new seal with 3M Adhesive (part No. 92-25234-1). Insert the seal into its bore and gently tap into place. The top edge of the seal should be flush with the housing surface.

Gearcase Housing Reassembly and Shim Selection

Refer to **Figure 93** during this procedure.

1. Lubricate all gears and bearings with gear lube.

2. Apply 3M Adhesive (part No. 92-25234-1) to the water passage O-ring groove. Install a new O-ring into the groove (**Figure 138**).

3. Install the rear drive gear and bearing assembly on the outer propeller shaft. Secure the gear/bearing assembly with the snap ring (**Fig-**

14

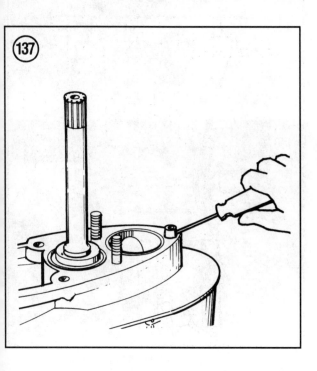

ure 139). Make sure the snap ring is fully seated in its groove.

NOTE
The shim installed in Step 4 is used to control propeller shaft end play. If the housing, all gears, shafts and bearings were reused (no components replaced), install the original thickness shim. If any components (housing, gears, bearings, shafts) were replaced, install a 0.020 in. shim as a starting point.

4. Apply a light coat of Loctite 242 to the inside diameter of the thrust cap. Do not allow Loctite to get on the shim. Install the shim and thrust cap. Make sure the thrust cap is square with the shaft and press it on until bottomed. See **Figure 126**.

5. Install all pinion bearing rollers into the pinion bearing outer race. Hold the rollers in place using Quicksilver Needle Bearing Assembly Grease.

6. Install the front drive gear and bearing assembly into the gearcase housing.

7. Position the pinion gear inside the propeller shaft bore and carefully insert the drive shaft. Make certain that all pinion bearing rollers are still correctly positioned. Install the pinion gear bolt and washer. Make sure the concave side of the washer is facing the gear. Tighten the bolt finger tight.

8. Before proceeding with reassembly, determine the shim thickness for setting drive shaft bearing preload. First, install the drive shaft upper bearing cup and tab washer. Make sure the bearing cup and washer are fully seated in the gearcase.

9. Next, using a depth micrometer, measure the distance from the top of the gearcase housing to the tab washer. See **Figure 140**. Take 3 measurements and record the average reading. The reading should be approximately 0.300 in.

10. Then, measure the thickness of the spacer from the top of the machined surface to the bottom of the machined surface. See **Figure 141**. Take 3 measurements and record the average reading. This reading should be approximately 0.250 in.

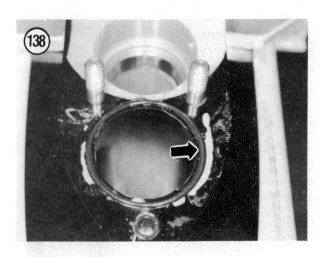

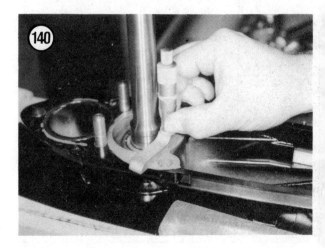

11. Determine shim thickness as follows: Subtract the depth reading obtained in Step 9 from the thickness of the spacer obtained in Step 10.

12. Then add 0.001 in. to the remainder (Step 10 minus Step 9) obtained in Step 11. This is the shim thickness required to correctly adjust drive shaft bearing preload.

13. Install the shims, spacer (**Figure 141**) and a new O-ring (**Figure 142**).

14. Install the clamp plate over the drive shaft and mount it to the gearcase (**Figure 143**). Tighten the nuts securely.

15. Install the drive shaft adapter (part No. 91-61077) on the drive shaft splines (**Figure 144**).

16. Rotate the drive shaft several turns to seat the bearings.

17. Next, check the drive shaft bearing preload. Install an in.-lb. torque wrench and socket on the drive shaft adapter (**Figure 144**). Turn the torque wrench while noting the rolling torque required to turn the drive shaft. It should be 3-10 in.-lb.

18. If necessary, remove the clamp plate (**Figure 143**) and spacer (**Figure 141**) and subtract shims under the spacer to decrease preload or add shims to increase the preload. Reinstall the spacer and clamp plate and recheck bearing preload as described in Step 17.

NOTE
Shimming tool (part No. 92-805462) is necessary to properly set pinion gear depth. Incorrect pinion gear depth will cause abnormal gear noise and premature failure.

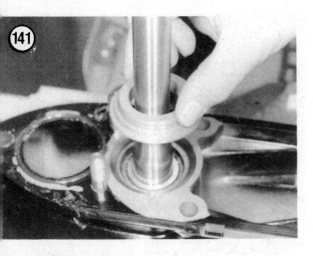

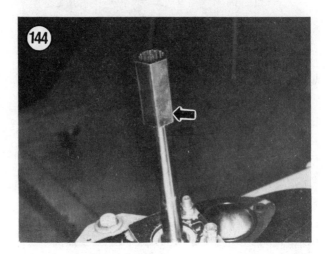

14

19. Once the correct drive shaft bearing preload is established, adjust the pinion gear depth. Make sure the clamp plate (**Figure 143**) is securely fastened to the gearcase, then temporarily tighten the pinion gear bolt to 35 ft.-lb. as shown in **Figure 145**.

20. Referring to **Figure 146**, install shimming tool (part No. 91-805462) into the propeller shaft bore.

21. Using a flat feeler gauge, measure the clearance between the shimming tool and the bottom surface of the pinion gear. Take measurements in 3 locations on the gear, 120° apart. The clearance should be 0.23-0.28 in.

22. If the clearance is not as specified, the drive shaft and drive shaft lower bearing cup must be removed from the gearcase.

    a. To increase the clearance, add shims under the drive shaft lower bearing cup.

NOTE
To maintain the correct drive shaft bearing preload, any shims added under the lower bearing cup must be subtracted equally from under the spacer.

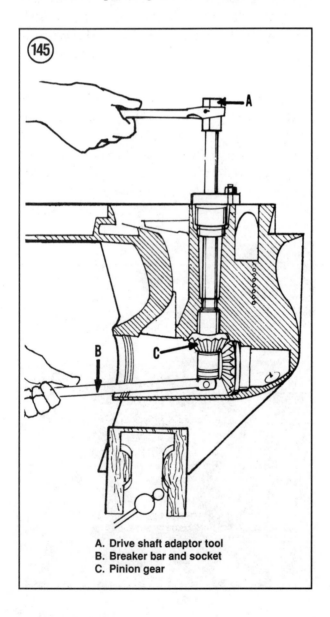

A. Drive shaft adaptor tool
B. Breaker bar and socket
C. Pinion gear

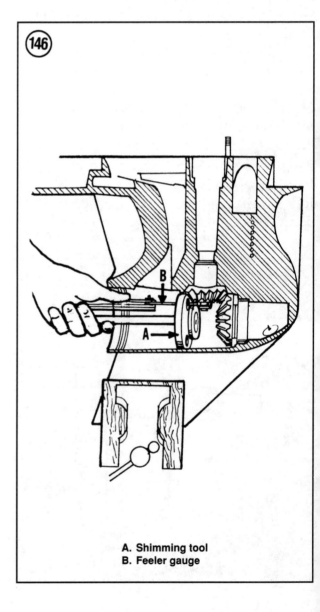

A. Shimming tool
B. Feeler gauge

b. To decrease the clearance, subtract shims from under the drive shaft lower bearing cup.

NOTE
To maintain the correct drive shaft bearing preload, any shims subtracted from under the lower bearing cup must be added equally to the shims under the spacer.

23. After changing shims, reinstall the drive shaft and related components. Tighten the pinion gear bolt to 35 ft.-lb. (**Figure 145**). Reinstall the clamp plate, then, repeat Step 21 to check adjustment.

24. Once the correct pinion gear depth is established, remove the pinion gear bolt (**Figure 145**). Apply Loctite 271 to the threads of the bolt. Make sure the concave side of the pinion gear washer is facing the gear, then install and tighten the bolt to 35 ft.-lb. as shown in **Figure 145**.

25. Before proceeding with reassembly, perform the propeller shaft spline lash check as follows. The propeller shaft spline lash must be determined to correctly adjust front and rear

drive gear backlash later in the reassembly process.

26. Refer to **Figure 147**. Place the inner propeller shaft on V-blocks. Install backlash indicator rod (part No. 91-805481) on the shaft, just behind the splines. Install the front drive gear and bearing assembly on the shaft. Mount a dial indicator to the gear using a large hose clamp and align the indicator plunger with the stamped mark on the backlash indicator rod. The plunger must be at a right angle to the indicator rod.

27. Rotate the drive gear back and forth without turning the inner propeller shaft while observing the dial indicator. This movement is the lash between the inner propeller shaft and drive gear splines. Record the measurement for later reference.

28. Next, place the outer propeller shaft on V-blocks. Refer to **Figure 148**. Mount backlash indicator rod (part No. 91-805482) on the outer shaft, just behind the splines. Then install the rear drive gear on the shaft and mount a dial indicator to the gear. Make sure the indicator plunger is at a right-angle to the indicator rod and aligned with the stamped mark on the rod.

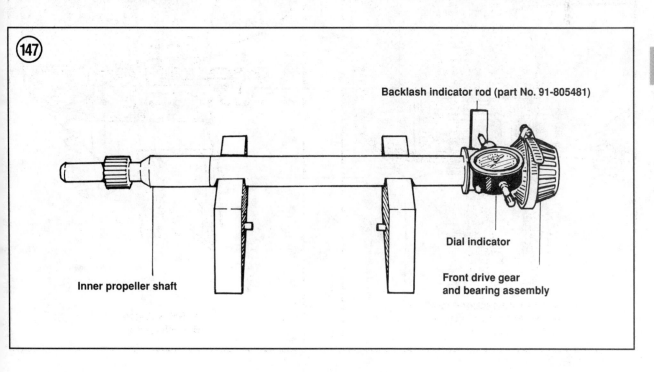

(147)

Backlash indicator rod (part No. 91-805481)

Dial indicator

Front drive gear
and bearing assembly

Inner propeller shaft

14

29. Rotate the drive gear back and forth without turning the outer propeller shaft while observing the dial indicator. This movement is the lash between the outer propeller shaft and drive gear splines. Record the measurement for later reference.

30. Install the inner propeller shaft thrust bearing. Install the shaft and bearing into the gearcase and into the front drive gear.

31. Install the outer propeller shaft over the inner shaft and into the gearcase.

32. Install the original shim pack (39, **Figure 93**) into the gearcase. If original shims are lost or damaged, install a 0.050 in. shim pack as a starting point.

33. Install the rear drive gear bearing cup into the gearcase. Firmly seat the bearing cup against the shim pack.

34. Lubricate the outer propeller shaft bearing retainer nut threads with Quicksilver Special Lube 101. Install the retainer nut into the gearcase (left-hand threads).

35. Using bearing retainer installation tool (part No. 91-805382), bearing carrier tool (part No. 91-805374) and a torque wrench, tighten the retainer nut to 200 ft.-lb. See **Figure 149**, typical.

36. Install a new O-ring into its groove in the bearing carrier.

37. Lubricate the bearing carrier threads and O-ring with Quicksilver Special Lube 101. Apply Quicksilver Perfect Seal to the tapered area of the bearing carrier that contacts the gearcase housing.

38. Install the bearing carrier into the gearcase (left-hand threads). Using bearing carrier installation tool (part No. 91-805374), tighten the carrier to 150 ft.-lb. See **Figure 150**, typical.

39. Remove the clamp plate (**Figure 143**), O-ring, spacer and shim(s). Do not remove the tab washer.

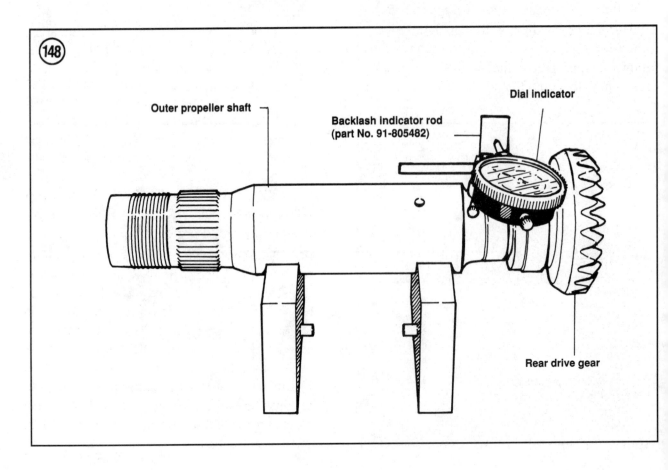

(148)

Outer propeller shaft

Dial indicator

Backlash indicator rod
(part No. 91-805482)

Rear drive gear

40. Slide drive shaft retaining tool (part No. 91-805381) down over the drive shaft, into the gearcase and against the tab washer. See **Figure 151**. Do not tighten the lock screw yet.

41. Position the gearcase housing so the propeller shafts are facing UP. Rotate the propeller shafts several turns to seat the bearings.

42. While turning the drive shaft, lightly push downward on the drive shaft retaining tool, then tighten the lock screw.

43. Refer to **Figure 152**. Install backlash indicator rod (part No. 91-805481) on the inner propeller shaft, just behind the splines. Mount a dial indicator to the bearing carrier. Align the indicator plunger with the stamped mark on the backlash indicator rod. The plunger must be at a right angle to the rod.

44. Check front drive gear backlash by rotating the inner propeller shaft back and forth while observing the dial indicator. Record the reading. This is the *total* front drive gear backlash. To establish the *actual* backlash, subtract the inner propeller shaft spline lash determined in Step 27 from the total backlash determined in this step. Actual front drive gear backlash should be 0.012-0.016 in. If backlash is not as specified, disassemble the gearcase and proceed as follows:

   a. If backlash is less than specified, subtract shims (25, **Figure 93**) from behind the front driven gear bearing cup (26).

   b. If backlash is more than specified, add shims (25, **Figure 93**) behind the front gear bearing cup (26).

45. Recheck front gear backlash after performing adjustments.

46. To adjust the rear drive gear backlash, position the gearcase housing so the propeller shafts are facing DOWN.

47. Loosen the lock screw on the drive shaft retaining tool (**Figure 151**) and rotate the drive shaft several turns to seat the bearings. Mount backlash indicator rod (part No. 91-805482) on the outer propeller shaft, just behind the splines. Mount a dial indicator to the bearing carrier. Align the indicator plunger with the stamped mark on the backlash indicator rod. The plunger must be at a right angle to the rod.

48. Check rear drive gear backlash by turning the outer propeller shaft back and forth while observing the dial indicator. Record the reading. This is the *total* rear drive gear backlash. To determine the *actual* rear drive gear backlash, subtract the outer propeller shaft spline lash established in Step 29 from the *total* backlash determined in this step. *Actual* rear drive gear backlash should be 0.012-0.016 in. If backlash is not as specified, disassemble the gearcase and proceed as follows:

14

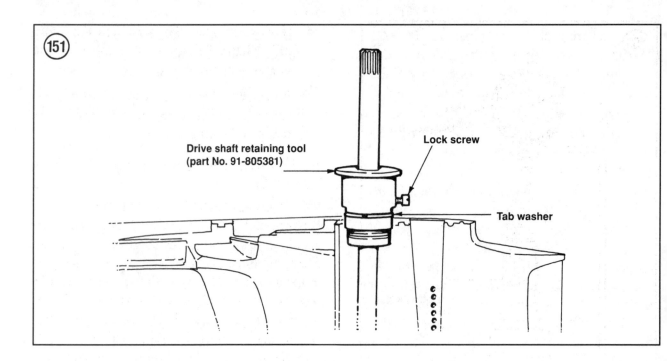

Drive shaft retaining tool
(part No. 91-805381)

Lock screw

Tab washer

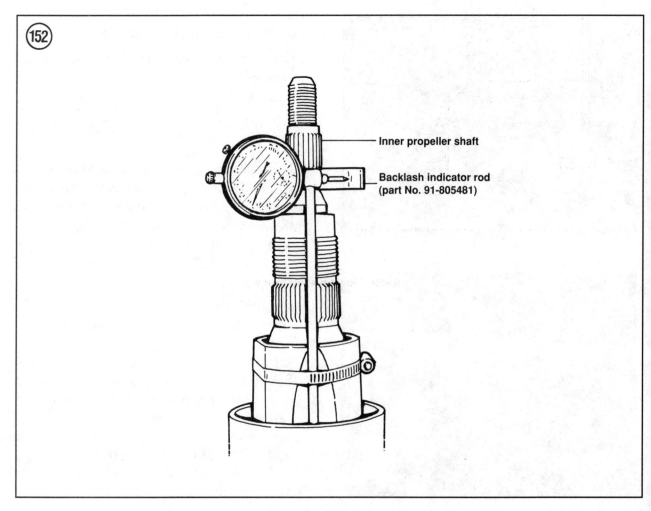

Inner propeller shaft

Backlash indicator rod
(part No. 91-805481)

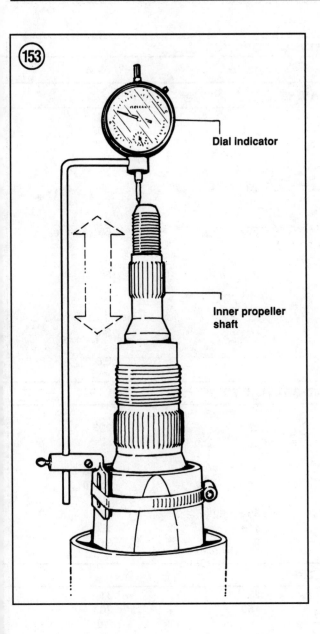

Dial indicator

Inner propeller shaft

a. If backlash is less than specified, add shims (39, **Figure 93**) in front of the rear gear bearing cup (40).

b. If backlash is more than specified, subtract shims (39, **Figure 93**) from in front of the rear gear bearing cup (40).

49. Recheck backlash after performing adjustments.

50. To complete the shim selection process, check propeller shaft end play. First, position the gearcase so the propeller shafts are facing up. Then, mount a dial indicator to measure inner propeller shaft end play as shown in **Figure 153**. Move the inner shaft up and down while observing the dial indicator. Make sure the outer shaft is lifted as the inner shaft is pulled up. The end play should be 0.001-0.005 in. If not, disassemble the gearcase and add or subtract from the shims (32, **Figure 93**) as necessary.

51. Recheck end play after performing the adjustments.

52. Remove all measuring equipment and the drive shaft retaining tool. Reinstall the shim(s), spacer and O-ring.

53. Install the gearcase as described in this chapter. Install the propellers as described in this chapter. Fill the gearcase with the recommended lubricant as described in Chapter Four.

14

Table 1 is on the next page.

Table 1 TIGHTENING TORQUES

Fastener	in.-lb.	ft.-lb.	N·m
ALPHA ONE			
Antiventilation plate nut		28	38
Bearing carrier retainer		210	285
Drive shaft bearing retainer		100	136
Gear housing fasteners			
Nuts		35	47
Screw		28	38
Pinion gear nut		70	95
Shift shaft bushing			
Prior to Generation II		50	68
Shift shaft bushing screws			
Generation II	60		6.8
Trim tab screw		23	31
Water pump body			
Prior to Generation II			
Nuts	60-90		7-10
Screw	30-40		3-5
Generation II			
Screws	60		6.8
BRAVO ONE AND BRAVO TWO			
Bearing carrier retaining nut			
Bravo One		150	203
Gear housing fasteners			
Bravo One			
Nuts		25-32	34-43
Trim tab cavity screw		30-37	41-50
Bravo Two			
Nuts and screw		35	47
Pinion gear nut		113	150
Trim tab screw		23	31
BRAVO THREE			
Anode (gearcase housing plug)		23	31
Bearing carrier		150	203
Drain/fill/vent plugs	17		2.0
Gearcase housing fasteners		35	47
Outer propeller shaft			
bearing retainer nut		200	271
Pinion gear bolt		35	47
Propeller nut			
Front propeller		100	136
Rear propeller		60	81

Chapter Fifteen

Bell Housing, Gimbal Bearing and Gimbal Ring

This chapter covers removal, overhaul and installation of the Alpha One, Bravo One, Bravo Two and Bravo Three transom assembly components, including the bell housing, gimbal bearing and gimbal ring.

Table 1 is at the end of the chapter.

EXHAUST BELLOWS/TUBE

Early V8 MerCruiser Alpha One models with a drive shaft extension used an exhaust bellows. This was replaced on later models by an exhaust tube. Mercury Marine has found that use of the bellows on such models results in excessive exhaust backpressure, which affects performance. In addition, it can cause the bellows to balloon and contact the U-joint bellows. If this happens, the U-joint bellows will rub against the U-joint. This will chafe and weaken the bellows enough to cause a water leak. If a unit fitted with an exhaust bellows requires bellows replacement, install a replacement tube (part No. 78458A1) instead.

Exhaust Bellows Removal/Installation

Refer to **Figure 1** for this procedure.
1. Remove the stern drive unit. See Chapter Twelve.
2. Check bellows for hardening, cuts, cracks or internal charring.

NOTE
If bellows is deteriorated and/or damaged, it is faster and easier to simply cut it off and then remove the residue in Step 3 than to spend the time removing it carefully.

3. Unclamp and remove the exhaust bellows. It may be necessary to work a flat tool around the inside diameter of the bellows to free it for removal without damage.

WARNING
The use of lacquer thinner and bellows adhesive will cause extremely flammable vapors in Steps 4-6. Be sure to perform these steps in a well-ventilated area, close the container after each use

and see that all possible causes of sparks or an open flame (such as motors, stoves, pilot lights, cigarettes, etc.) are removed or shut off until all vapors have dissipated. Avoid prolonged contact with skin or breathing of vapors.

4. Clean the gimbal housing and bell housing bellows mounting flanges with sandpaper and lacquer thinner.

5. If bellows is to be reused, repeat Step 4 to clean the bellows mounting surface.

6. Apply a coat of Quicksilver Bellows Adhesive to the mounting surfaces inside the bellows to be reinstalled. Let the adhesive dry for about 10 minutes or until it is no longer tacky.

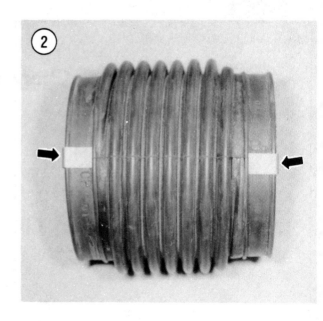

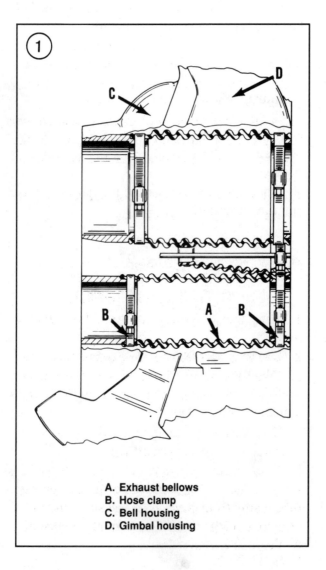

A. Exhaust bellows
B. Hose clamp
C. Bell housing
D. Gimbal housing

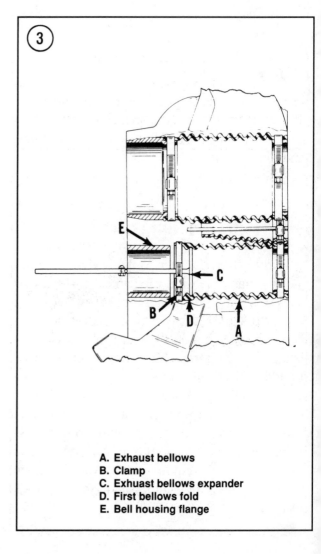

A. Exhaust bellows
B. Clamp
C. Exhuast bellows expander
D. First bellows fold
E. Bell housing flange

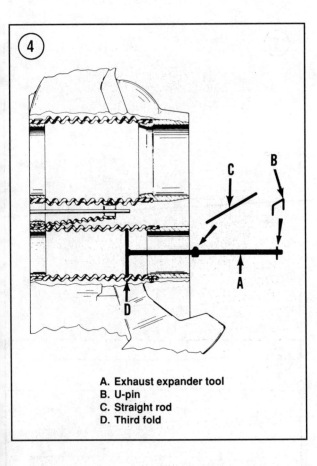

A. Exhaust expander tool
B. U-pin
C. Straight rod
D. Third fold

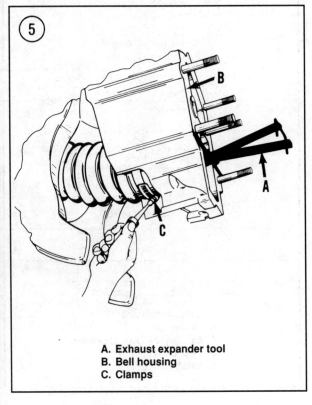

A. Exhaust expander tool
B. Bell housing
C. Clamps

7. Install new grounding clips on each end of the bellows. See **Figure 2**. The clips prevent the bellows clamps from corroding. The short end of the clip containing the 2 bumps should be installed on the inside of the bellows.

8. Slip the front hose clamp over the bellows. Install the bellows as shown in **Figure 1**. Make sure that the bead on the inside of the bellows engages the groove in the bell housing and gimbal housing. Position the front clamp with the worm screw facing downward and tighten screw securely.

9. Slip the rear hose clamp over the bellows. Fit exhaust extender tool (part No. 91-45497A1) into the first fold of the bellows (**Figure 3**). Pull outward on the tool until it contacts the bell housing flange, then release the tool.

10. Reposition the tool in the third fold of the bellows. Pull the bellows onto the bell housing flange (**Figure 4**), then insert the straight rod and U-pin in the tool.

11. With the extender tool in position as shown in **Figure 5**, tilt the bell housing up, position the clamp at the bottom and tighten the worm screw securely.

12. Remove the extender tool and reinstall the stern drive (Chapter Twelve).

Exhaust Tube Replacement

Refer to **Figure 6** for this procedure.

1. Raise the stern drive unit to its full UP position.

2. Unclamp and remove the exhaust tube.

3. Clean the gimbal housing and bell housing tube mounting flanges with sandpaper to remove any corrosion.

4. If exhaust tube is to be reused, repeat Step 3 to clean the tube flange surface.

5. Install a new grounding clip on the top of the front flange (B, **Figure 6**). The clip prevents the tube clamp from corroding. The short end of the clip containing the 2 bumps should be installed on the inside of the tube.

15

6. Install the tube with the stamped SIDE markings facing port and starboard. Tighten the clamp worm screw securely.

SHIFT CABLE SERVICE

Two styles of shift cables are used. The older style is attached to the front of the bell housing; the new style connects from the aft end (**Figure 7**). Installation and adjustment are the same for both cables; only the attachment method differs. The new style cable can be used with all Alpha One models covered in this manual.

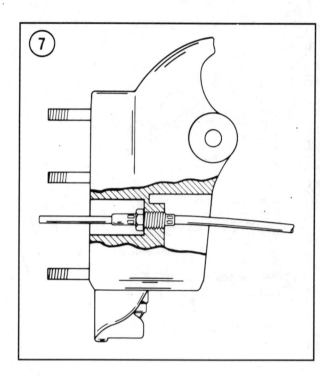

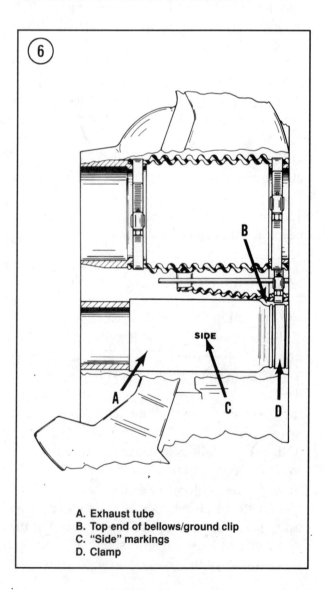

A. Exhaust tube
B. Top end of bellows/ground clip
C. "Side" markings
D. Clamp

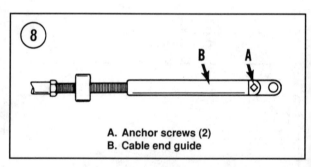

A. Anchor screws (2)
B. Cable end guide

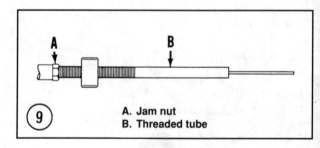

A. Jam nut
B. Threaded tube

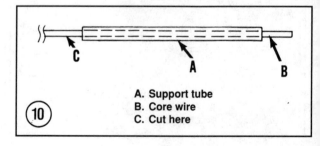

A. Support tube
B. Core wire
C. Cut here

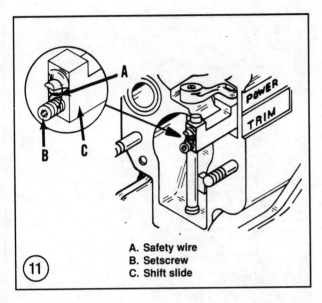

A. Safety wire
B. Setscrew
C. Shift slide

(11)

Shift Cable Removal
(Alpha One)

1. Remove the stern drive unit. See Chapter Twelve.

2. Remove the 2 anchor screws holding the shift cable. Remove the cable end guide. See **Figure 8**.

3. Loosen the jam nut and unscrew/remove the threaded tube (**Figure 9**).

4. Cut the support tube from the core wire (**Figure 10**).

5. Alpha One—Cut the setscrew safety wire (A, **Figure 11**) and remove the shift slide setscrew.

6. Pull the inner core wire from the shift cable, then remove the shift slide from the inner core wire.

7. Loosen the crimp clamp on the shift cable bellows (**Figure 12**).

8. Remove the shift cable wrapping, then pull the cable through the bellows (**Figure 13**).

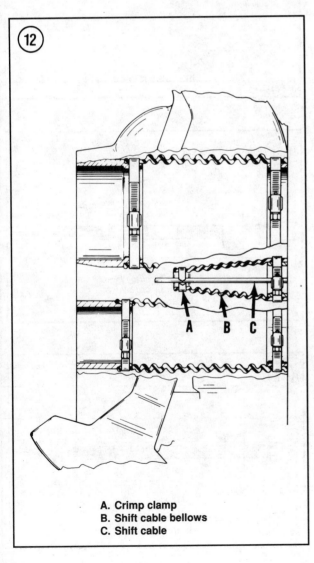

(12)

A. Crimp clamp
B. Shift cable bellows
C. Shift cable

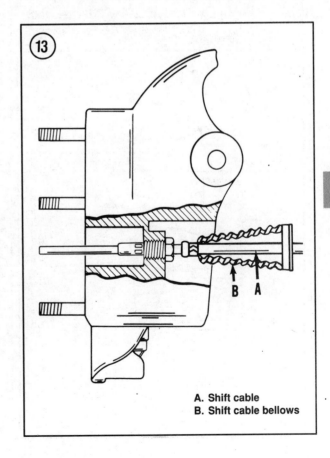

(13)

A. Shift cable
B. Shift cable bellows

15

9. Loosen the shift cable retainer nut with tool (part No. 91-12037). See **Figure 14** (old style cable) or **Figure 15** (new style cable). Pull the shift cable from the bell housing.

10. Disconnect the shift (lower) cable from the engine shift plate. Remove the cable.

Shift Cable Installation (Alpha One)

1. Wipe shift cable retainer nut threads with Quicksilver Perfect Seal.

2. Install cable to bell housing with tool part No. 91-12037. See **Figure 14** (old style cable) or **Figure 15** (new style cable). Tighten retainer nut securely.

3. Wrap the cable end with tape to prevent it from getting dirty as it is installed in the transom. Insert cable end through the shift cable bellows. Once installed, remove the tape and wipe the cable end with Quicksilver 2-4-C Multi-Lube.

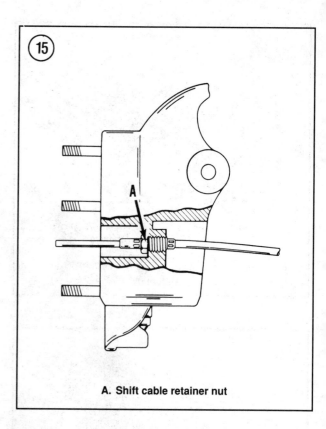

A. Shift cable retainer nut

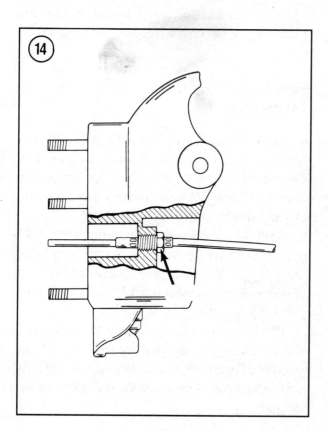

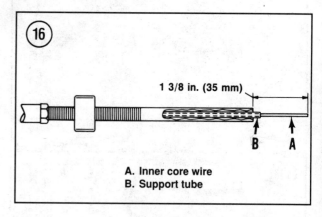

1 3/8 in. (35 mm)

A. Inner core wire
B. Support tube

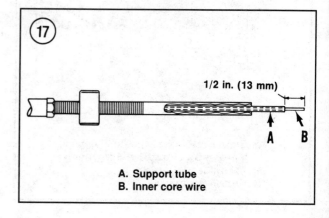

1/2 in. (13 mm)

A. Support tube
B. Inner core wire

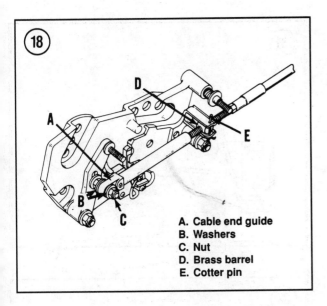

A. Cable end guide
B. Washers
C. Nut
D. Brass barrel
E. Cotter pin

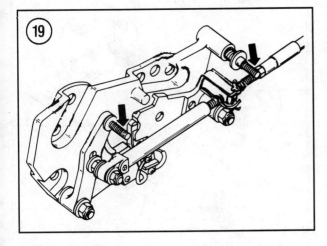

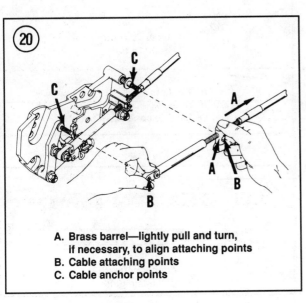

A. Brass barrel—lightly pull and turn,
   if necessary, to align attaching points
B. Cable attaching points
C. Cable anchor points

4. Install the shift cable wrapping, then guide the core wire through the shift slide.

5. Alpha One—Install the inner core wire through the shift cable. Install the shift slide setscrew. Back setscrew off 1/8 to 1/4 turn after it contacts the core wire anchor. Install a new safety wire by wrapping in a figure eight and twisting. Cut off any excess wire. See **Figure 11**.

6. Install the threaded tube finger-tight until it bottoms (**Figure 9**) and tighten the jam nut.

7. Install the stern drive unit (Chapter Twelve). Shift drive unit into FORWARD gear.

8. Slide the support tube over the core wire, then cut the inner core wire to 1 3/8 in. See **Figure 16**. If not cut correctly, the shift operation will be adversely affected.

9. Reposition support tube until only 1/2 in. of the core wire extends from the support tube, then crimp the end of the tube. See **Figure 17**.

10. Slide the cable end guide over the core wire and insert the core wire through the cable anchor. Install anchor screws snugly.

11. Connect the shift cable to the engine shift plate and adjust as described in this chapter.

**Shift Cable Adjustment
(Alpha One)**

1. With the stern drive unit in FORWARD gear, install the drive unit shift cable as shown in **Figure 18**. Tighten nut C until it bottoms out, then back it off 1/2 turn. Install a new cotter pin (E) and spread both ends.

2. Shift the remote control unit into FORWARD gear. Make sure the stern drive unit is in FORWARD gear. Lubricate remote control cable anchor points (arrows, **Figure 19**) with Quicksilver 2-4-C Multi-Lube.

3. Hold remote control shift cable as shown in **Figure 20** and lightly pull the brass barrel outward (A, **Figure 20**) while rotating it to align the cable attachment holes with the shift plate anchor points.

15

4. Once the cable holes are aligned with the anchor points, back off the brass barrel 4 full turns and install on the shift plate (**Figure 20**). Install the washers and tighten the nuts finger-tight.

5. On Alpha One, move the remote control handle to the full REVERSE position and check the shift cutout switch roller position on the shift plate. The roller should be centered (**Figure 21**). If it is not, remove the remote control shift cable from the shift plate and rotate the brass barrel one turn at a time toward the cable end guide until the roller is centered.

6. Once adjustment is correct, tighten the remote control cable attaching nuts (**Figure 22**) until they bottom out, then back off 1/2 turn to allow the cable end guide to pivot freely on the anchor point stud.

7. With the boat in the water and the engine running, shift the remote control handle into full REVERSE. The clutch should engage before the engine starts to accelerate. If the engine accelerates before the clutch engages, loosen the adjustable stud on the shift plate (**Figure 22**) and move it to the top of the slot, then tighten the stud securely.

Shift Cable Removal (Bravo Models)

1. Remove the stern drive unit as described in Chapter Twelve.

2. Remove the 2 anchor screws holding the shift cable. Remove the cable end guide. See **Figure 23**. Disconnect the lower shift cable from the engine shift plate.

> *NOTE*
> *The core wire on early design shift cables must be pulled from the shift cable before the shift cable can be removed from the bell housing. The early cable can be identified by the jam nut (A, **Figure 24**).*

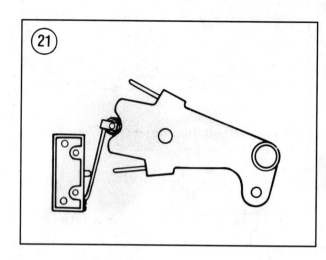

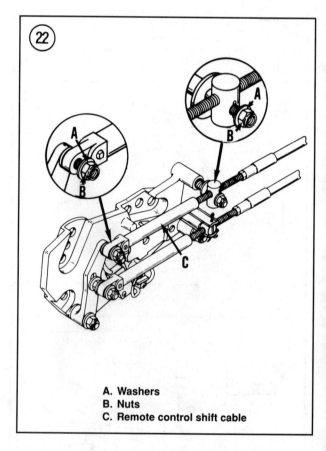

A. Washers
B. Nuts
C. Remote control shift cable

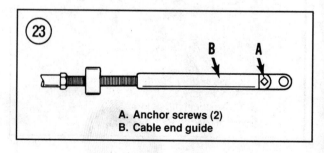

A. Anchor screws (2)
B. Cable end guide

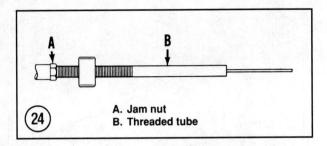

A. Jam nut
B. Threaded tube

24

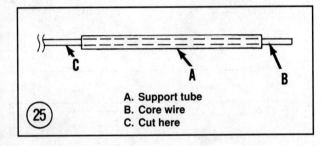

A. Support tube
B. Core wire
C. Cut here

25

26

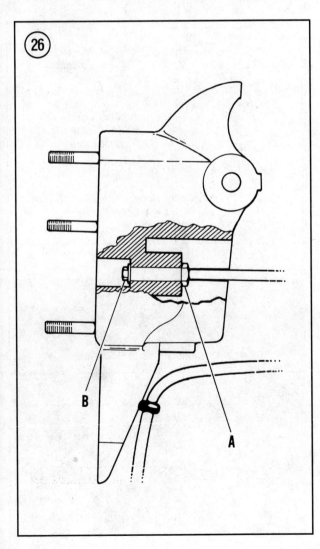

3A. Early design cable:

  a. Loosen the jam nut and unscrew and remove the threaded tube (**Figure 24**).

  b. Cut the support tube from the core wire (**Figure 25**).

  c. Pull the core wire from the shift cable.

  d. While holding the inside nut (A, **Figure 26**) with a wrench, remove the shift cable retaining nut (B, **Figure 26**).

NOTE
*The late design cable assembly can be removed from the bell housing without first removing the core wire. The late cable can be identified by the large retaining nut which will fit over the core wire anchor. See **Figure 27**.*

3B. *Late design cable*—While holding the inside nut, remove the shift cable retaining nut (**Figure 27**).

4. Remove the shift cable wrapping.

5. Loosen the crimp clamp on the shift cable bellows and pull the shift cable through the bellows and out of the bell housing. See **Figure 28**.

27

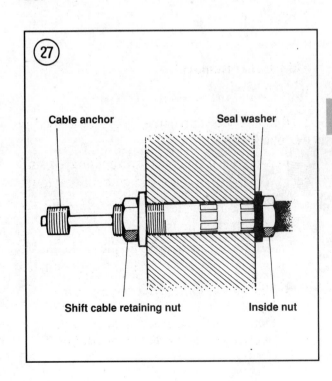

Cable anchor

Seal washer

Shift cable retaining nut

Inside nut

15

Shift Cable Installation
(Bravo Models)

1. On early design cables, remove the core wire, then insert the shift cable into and through the bell housing, shift cable bellows, and transom plate. On late design cables, insert the shift cable and core wire assembly into and through the bell housing, shift cable bellows and transom plate.

2. Apply Quicksilver Perfect Seal to the threads of the shift cable retaining nut. While holding the inner nut with a wrench, tighten the shift cable retaining nut to 65 in.-lb.

3. Install the shift cable wrapping.

> *CAUTION*
> *To prevent water leakage, do not flatten the clamp and bellows when crimping in Step 4.*

4. Install and compress the crimp clamp (**Figure 28**). Make sure the clamp is crimped evenly to ensure a good seal between the bellows and cable.

5. On early design cables, install the inner core wire into the cable.

6. Adjust the cable as described in this chapter prior to installing the stern drive unit.

Shift Cable Adjustment
(Bravo Models)

1. Install the core wire locating tool (part No. 91-17263) on the shift cable as shown in **Figure 29**. Make sure the core wire anchor is up against the locating tool and that the tool is firmly against the face of the bell housing.

2. Install the threaded tube into the cable until it bottoms. See **Figure 24**. Tighten the tube finger tight, then tight the jam nut securely.

> *NOTE*
> *Discard the support tube on early design cables. Do not use the support tube.*

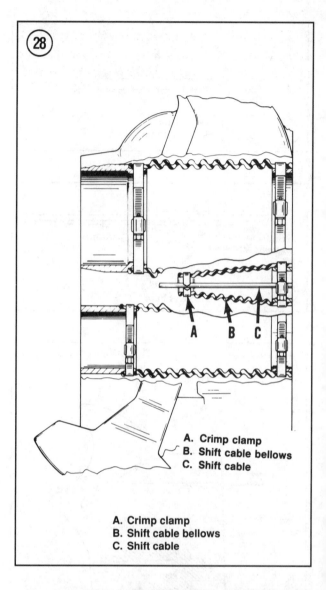

(28)

A. Crimp clamp
B. Shift cable bellows
C. Shift cable

A. Crimp clamp
B. Shift cable bellows
C. Shift cable

(29)

3. Install the cable end guide (B, **Figure 23**) over the core wire. Insert the core wire through the cable anchor and tighten the anchor screws (A, **Figure 23**) evenly to 20 in.-lb.

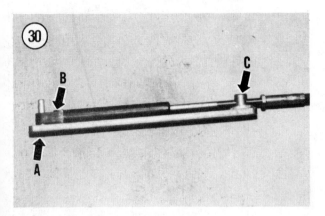

4. Install the shift cable anchor adjustment tool part No. 91-17262 (A, **Figure 30**) on the end of the shift cable (B).

5. Make sure the cable anchor and core wire locating tool are firmly against the bell housing (**Figure 29**).

6. Next, adjust the cable barrel (C, **Figure 30**) so it aligns with the hole in the anchor adjustment tool. Then, hold the cable barrel from turning and connect the cable to the engine shift plate.

GIMBAL BEARING

The bearing and its carrier are a matched set. As such, they must be replaced as an assembly. Whenever the gimbal bearing is removed, replace the tolerance ring.

Whenever the drive unit is removed from the bell housing for any reason, it is a good idea to check the condition of the gimbal housing bearing. Reach into the bell housing and rotate the gimbal bearing to check for rough spots. Push and pull on the inner race to check for side wear. If any excessive roughness or movement is noted, replace the bearing.

Replacement

Gimbal bearing replacement requires the use of bearing tool kit (part No. 91-31220A5). Since removal often destroys the cartridge bearing, be sure you have the correct replacement bearing on hand before attempting this procedure.

1. Install bearing removal/installation tool (part No. 91-31220A5) as shown in **Figure 31**. Use the slide hammer to remove the bearing and carrier.

2. Remove the tolerance ring (**Figure 32**) from the bearing carrier.

3. Assemble the bearing and carrier as shown in **Figure 33**. The bearing grease holes must align with the carrier grease groove.

4. Install and align a new tolerance ring as shown in **Figure 34**. The tolerance ring opening must align with the carrier grease hole.

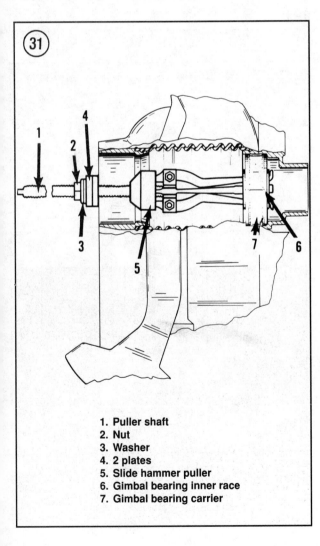

1. Puller shaft
2. Nut
3. Washer
4. 2 plates
5. Slide hammer puller
6. Gimbal bearing inner race
7. Gimbal bearing carrier

15

5. Insert assembly into the gimbal housing, aligning the carrier and tolerance ring grease holes with the gimbal housing grease cavity hole. See **Figure 35**.

6. Assemble bearing removal/installation tool (part No. 91-31220A5) as shown in **Figure 36**. Install the bearing carrier beyond the gimbal housing chamfer by rapping the drive rod with a lead hammer.

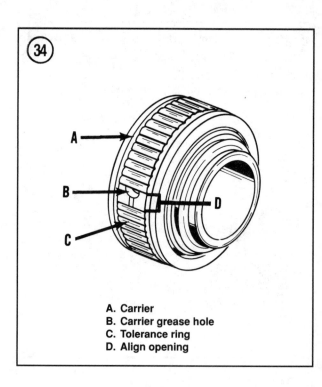

A. Carrier
B. Carrier grease hole
C. Tolerance ring
D. Align opening

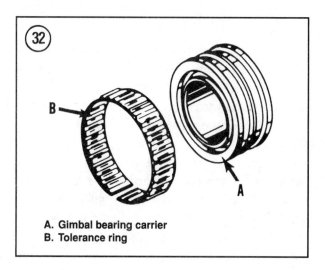

A. Gimbal bearing carrier
B. Tolerance ring

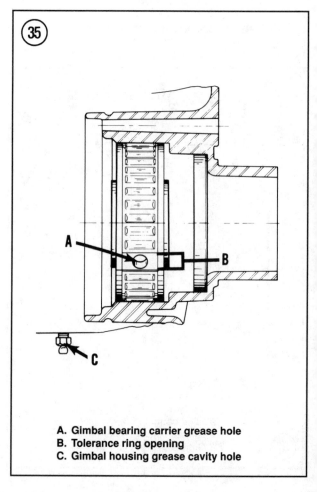

A. Gimbal bearing carrier grease hole
B. Tolerance ring opening
C. Gimbal housing grease cavity hole

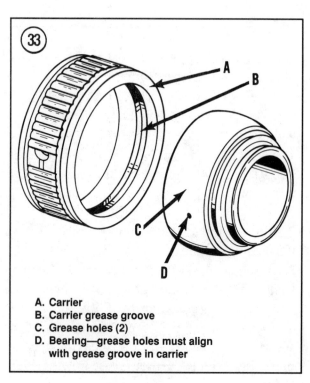

A. Carrier
B. Carrier grease groove
C. Grease holes (2)
D. Bearing—grease holes must align
   with grease groove in carrier

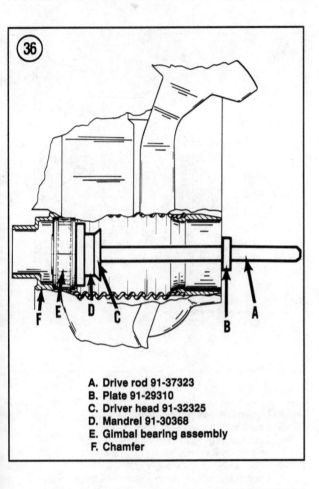

A. Drive rod 91-37323
B. Plate 91-29310
C. Driver head 91-32325
D. Mandrel 91-30368
E. Gimbal bearing assembly
F. Chamfer

BELL HOUSING SERVICE

Removal

1. Remove the stern drive unit. See Chapter Thirteen.

2. Remove the shift cable inner core wire as described in this chapter.

3. Unbolt and remove the trim limit switch and trim position sender.

4. Unclamp and disconnect the water inlet hose at the water tube (**Figure 37**).

5. Remove the water tube cover and rubber grommet (**Figure 38**). Push the water tube through the gimbal housing.

6. Loosen and remove the crimp clamp from the shift cable bellows (**Figure 12**).

CAUTION
Loctite is used in assembling the hinge pins. If necessary to heat the hinge pin to aid in pin removal, use care not to damage the anti-friction (sythane) washers between the bell housing and gimbal ring.

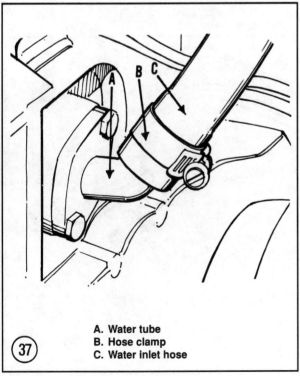

A. Water tube
B. Hose clamp
C. Water inlet hose

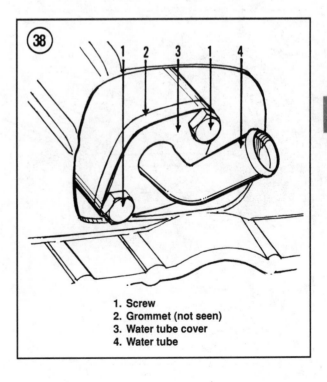

1. Screw
2. Grommet (not seen)
3. Water tube cover
4. Water tube

15

7. Remove the hinge pin on each side of the gimbal housing with tool (part No. 91-78310) and a socket wrench (**Figure 39**). If pin removal is difficult, apply heat at point C, **Figure 39**.

8. Loosen the U-joint bellows front clamp (A, **Figure 40**) and the exhaust bellows rear clamp (B, **Figure 40**) on models so equipped.

9. Pull the shift cable through the bellows, guide the water tube from the housing and remove the

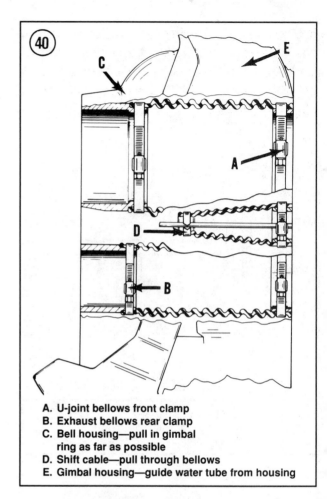

A. U-joint bellows front clamp
B. Exhaust bellows rear clamp
C. Bell housing—pull in gimbal
   ring as far as possible
D. Shift cable—pull through bellows
E. Gimbal housing—guide water tube from housing

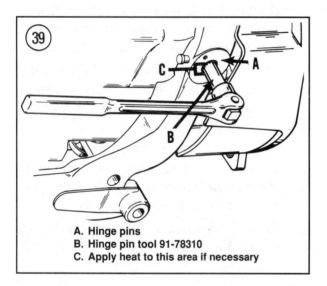

A. Hinge pins
B. Hinge pin tool 91-78310
C. Apply heat to this area if necessary

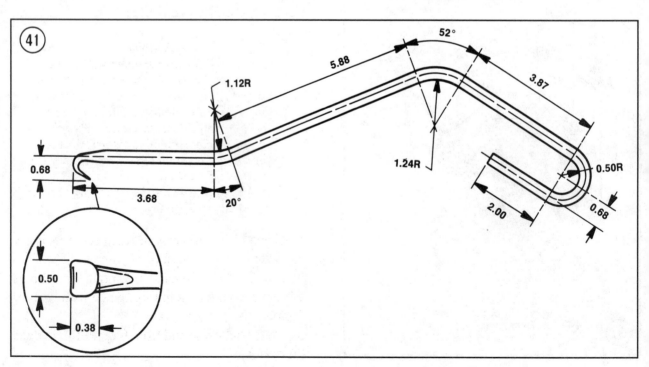

bell housing (**Figure 40**). If the bellows does not come free easily, fabricate a tool to the dimensions shown in **Figure 41** from a 24 in. length of 1/4 in. diameter rod and use it to pry the bellows free.

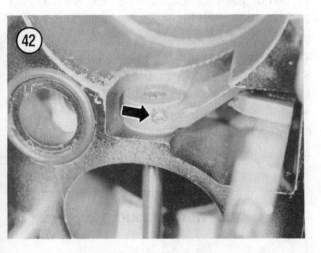

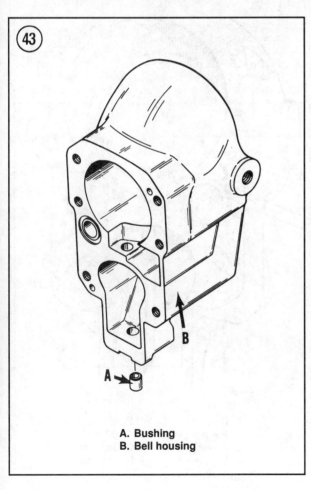

A. Bushing
B. Bell housing

Disassembly

1. Unclamp and remove the U-joint bellows.
2. Remove the shift cable with removal/installation tool (part No. 91-12037) as described in this chapter.
3. Unclamp and disconnect the water hose from the bell housing. Remove the connector.
4. Alpha One:
   a. Remove the upper shift shaft lever screw (**Figure 42**). In some cases, it may be necessary to apply heat in order to turn the screw. Remove the lever and shift shaft.
   b. Check shift shaft oil seal and bushing. Remove and discard the oil seal. If bushing replacement is necessary, remove with a suitable driver.
   c. Check the lower bushing (**Figure 43**). If damaged and replacement is necessary, cut the bushing with a chisel and drive it out with a suitable driver.
   d. Remove and discard the O-ring and rubber gasket (**Figure 44**).

Cleaning and Inspection

> *WARNING*
> *The use of lacquer thinner will cause extremely flammable vapors. Be sure to perform this step in a well-ventilated area, close the container after each use and see that all possible causes of sparks or an open flame (such as motors, stoves, pilot lights, cigarettes, etc.) are removed or shut off until all vapors have dissipated. Avoid prolonged contact with skin or breathing of vapors.*

1. Clean all metal parts in fresh solvent. Blow dry with compressed air.
2. If bellows can be reused, remove the bellows adhesive from the mounting flange with lacquer thinner.
3. Check bellows condition. If doubtful, replace the bellows.

15

4. Clean all mounting flanges in the bell housing and gimbal housing with a wire brush or sandpaper, then wipe with a cloth moistened in lacquer thinner.

5. Check the condition of the shift cable. If casing is cracked or if cable is cut or otherwise damaged or deteriorated, install a new one on reassembly.

6. Check the condition of the water hose. Replace if brittle or damaged.

7. Alpha One:

    a. Check shift lever roller condition and replace entire shift lever assembly if roller lever is worn excessively.

    b. If it was necessary to apply heat to remove the shift lever screw, inspect the washer under the lever for damage; replace as required.

Assembly

Refer to **Figure 44** for this procedure.

1. Alpha One:

    a. If lower bushing was removed, reinstall a new bushing flush with the bottom of the housing. See **Figure 43**.

    b. Install a new shift shaft oil seal with its lip facing downward. If necessary, stake the seal in place.

    c. If shift shaft bushing was removed, install a new one flush with the bell housing surface.

2. Connect the water hose to the water tube and position as shown in **Figure 45**.

3. Reinstall shift cable as described in this chapter.

4. Wipe connector threads with Quicksilver Perfect Seal and reinstall in bell housing. Reconnect water hose to connector and position the clamp screw with its head pointing in the direction of 7 o'clock. Tighten clamp screw securely.

5. Apply a coat of Quicksilver Bellows Adhesive to the mounting surfaces inside the bellows to be reinstalled. See **Figure 46**. Let the adhesive dry for about 10 minutes or until it is not tacky.

6. Install new grounding clips on each end of the bellows (**Figure 2**). The clips prevent the bellows clamps from corroding. The short end of the clip containing the 2 bumps should be installed on the inside of the bellows.

7. Install the exhaust bellows and shift cable bellows to the bell housing. Position the exhaust bellows hose clamp screw at 12 o'clock and the shift cable bellows clamp screw at 3-5 o'clock.

8. Lubricate the metal end of the shift cable with Quicksilver 2-4-C Multi-Lube and insert cable end into shift cable bellows.

9. Insert the water tube through the gimbal housing, routing the water hose, trim limit and trim

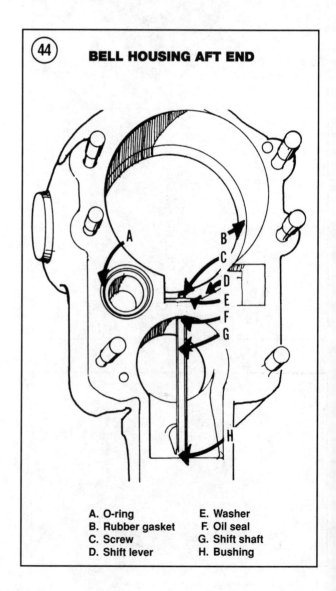

(44) **BELL HOUSING AFT END**

A. O-ring
B. Rubber gasket
C. Screw
D. Shift lever
E. Washer
F. Oil seal
G. Shift shaft
H. Bushing

position sender leads as shown in **Figure 47**. Place remaining hose clamps on bellows.

Installation

1. Position bell housing in gimbal housing and push in place with a steady pressure so that the U-joint bellows will slide onto the gimbal housing flange.

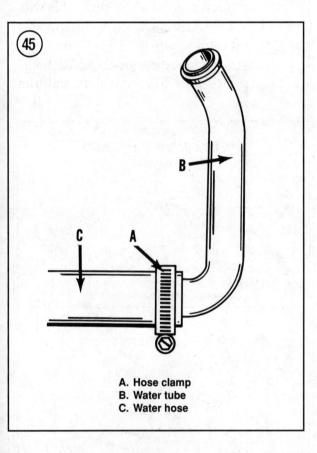

A. Hose clamp
B. Water tube
C. Water hose

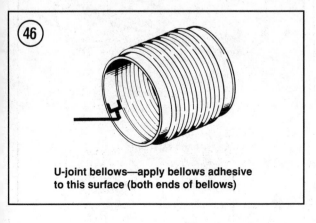

U-joint bellows—apply bellows adhesive to this surface (both ends of bellows)

2. Position the U-joint hose clamp screw as shown in **Figure 48** and tighten the screw securely.

3. Coat hinge pin threads with Locquic Primer "T" and let dry, then apply Loctite 35 to threads. Install sythane washers between bell housing and gimbal ring. Install hinge pins and tighten to 95 ft.-lb. (129 N•m). See **Figure 49**.

4. Install shift cable bellows clamp and tighten clamp screw securely.

5. Install shift cable inner core, then install the upper shift shaft and shift shaft lever.

6. On Alpha One, install a new water passage O-ring and rubber bell housing gasket. See **Figure 44**.

7. Reinstall the trim position and trim limit switches to the gimbal housing.

WATER HOSE AND WATER TUBE

The copper water tube used on 1985-1986 models was replaced by a plastic tube on 1987

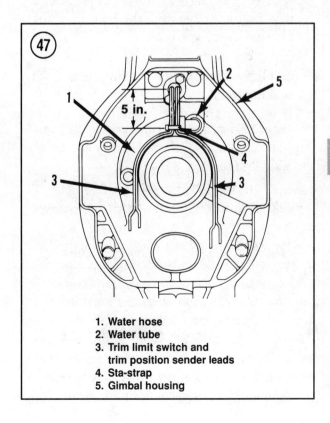

1. Water hose
2. Water tube
3. Trim limit switch and trim position sender leads
4. Sta-strap
5. Gimbal housing

15

and later models (**Figure 50**). The plastic tube provides increased water flow through a more consistent inner diameter and is more resistant to corrosion.

Removal/Installation

1. Unclamp and disconnect the water inlet hose at the water tube (**Figure 37**).
2. Remove the water tube cover and rubber grommet (**Figure 38**). Push the water tube through the gimbal housing.
3. Tilt the bell housing up (**Figure 51**) and loosen the water hose clamp.
4. Remove the water hose. Remove the water tube. See **Figure 52**.
5. Installation is the reverse of removal.

GIMBAL RING, SWIVEL SHAFT AND STEERING LEVER SERVICE

The components can be replaced with or without the engine or transom assembly installed. Both procedures are provided in this chapter.

Gimbal Ring Removal (With Engine and Transom Installed)

This procedure requires the use of a tap and hole saw kit (part No. 91-86191A1) and an access plug kit (part No. 88847A1).

1. Lubricate the upper swivel shaft grease fitting thoroughly with Quicksilver 2-4-C Multi-Lube.

> *NOTE*
> *On Bravo models, two dimples (**Figure 53**) are provided in the gimbal housing (port and starboard) to properly locate access holes. The templates provided with Access Plug Kit (part 22-88847A1) should not be used as they will not work and are not necessary on Bravo units.*

2. Alpha One—Carefully position the template provided with the access plug kit to make sure

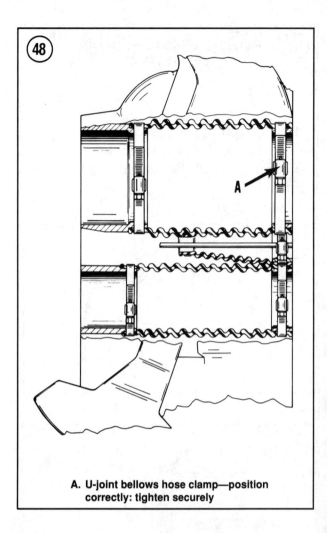

A. U-joint bellows hose clamp—position correctly: tighten securely

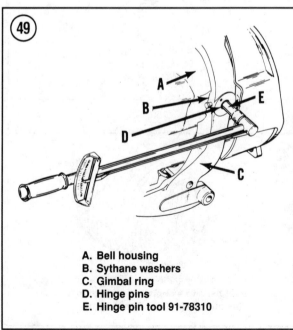

A. Bell housing
B. Sythane washers
C. Gimbal ring
D. Hinge pins
E. Hinge pin tool 91-78310

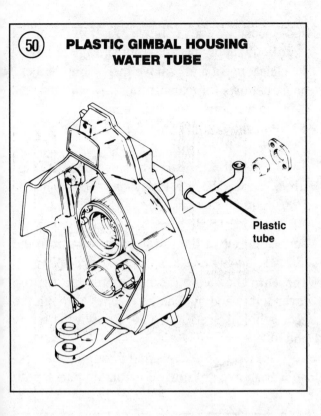

50 PLASTIC GIMBAL HOUSING
WATER TUBE

Plastic
tube

the holes to be drilled are correctly located. If they are not, it will be impossible to remove the upper swivel shaft and the gimbal housing will have to be replaced. Mark the gimbal housing access hole location on each side of the housing with the template.

3. Make sure the stern drive unit is in its vertical position.

NOTE
If tap and hole saw kit is not available, fit the hole saw to be used with a pilot rod instead of a drill bit to keep the hole saw from wandering. Install the pilot rod

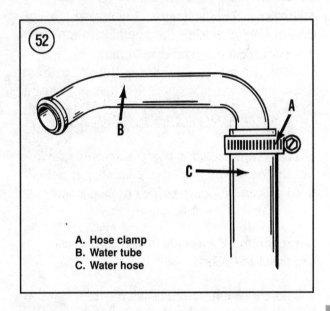

52

B

A

C

A. Hose clamp
B. Water tube
C. Water hose

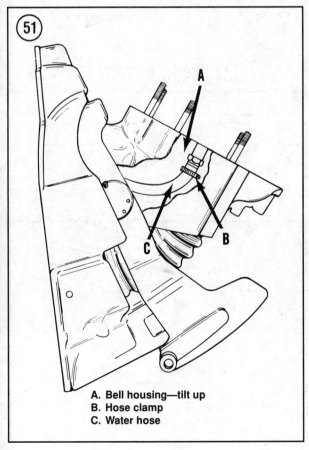

51

A

C

B

A. Bell housing—tilt up
B. Hose clamp
C. Water hose

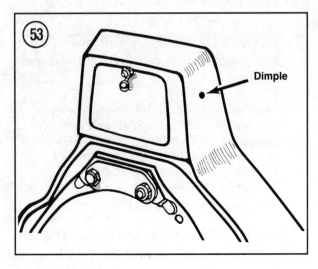

53

Dimple

15

*to protrude no more than 1/4 in. from the saw cutting teeth. See **Figure 54**.*

4. Drill 1/4 in. holes at the marked locations (Alpha One) or at the dimples (Bravo One, Two and Three) on the gimbal housing. The holes MUST be perpendicular to the gimbal housing.

5. Now redrill using a 1 1/8 in. hole saw to cut the access holes at the pilot hole locations. Work slowly and carefully to make the hole as accurate and neat as possible—do not apply excessive pressure while cutting.

6. When holes are drilled, blow all metal chips away with compressed air.

7. Remove the stern drive unit. See Chapter Twelve.

8. Remove the trim limit and trim position switches from the gimbal housing.

9. Remove the power trim cylinders without disconnecting the hoses. See Chapter Sixteen. Suspend cylinders with wire from a convenient place on the unit to prevent stressing the hoses.

CAUTION
Loctite is used in assembling the hinge pins. If necessary to heat the hinge pin to aid in pin removal, use care not to damage the anti-friction (sythane) washers between the bell housing and gimbal ring.

10. Remove the hinge pin on each side of the gimbal housing with tool (part No. 91-78310)

and a socket wrench (**Figure 39**). If pin removal is difficult, apply heat at point C, **Figure 39**.

11. Disconnect and remove the U-joint and exhaust bellows (or exhaust tube). Do not disconnect the water hose or shift cable.

12. Pull the bell housing free from the gimbal housing.

13. Loosen the gimbal ring screws and nut. **Figure 55** shows the new (1987-on) and old (1985-1986) gimbal ring and clamping screws.

14. Remove and discard the lower swivel pin cotter pin. Drive the lower swivel pin from the gimbal housing.

15. Turn the steering wheel until the steering lever screw and nut can be reached through the access holes. See **Figure 56**. Loosen the screw and nut.

16. Use a pin punch inserted through the access hole as shown in **Figure 57**. Rap on punch with

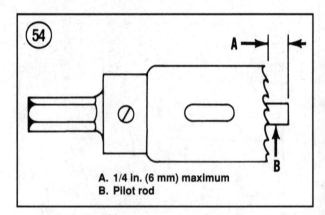

A. 1/4 in. (6 mm) maximum
B. Pilot rod

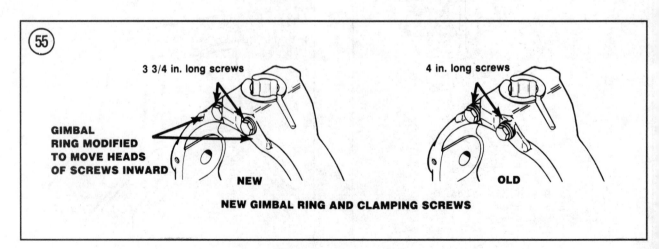

GIMBAL RING MODIFIED TO MOVE HEADS OF SCREWS INWARD

3 3/4 in. long screws

4 in. long screws

NEW

OLD

NEW GIMBAL RING AND CLAMPING SCREWS

a hammer to loosen the nut. Pull down on the upper swivel shaft to provide access for removal as you unthread the nut. Remove the nut from the top of the upper swivel shaft.

17. Remove the upper swivel shaft, steering lever, washers and nut. See **Figure 58**.

18. Remove the gimbal ring.

Gimbal Ring Removal
(With Engine and Transom Removed)

1. Remove the bell housing as described in this chapter.

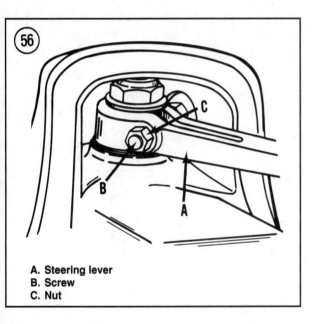

A. Steering lever
B. Screw
C. Nut

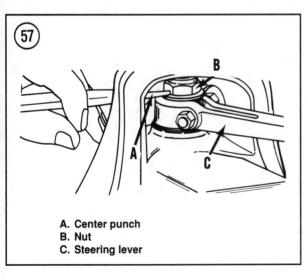

A. Center punch
B. Nut
C. Steering lever

2. Remove the transom assembly. See Chapter Twelve.

3. Remove the exhaust bellows as described in this chapter.

4. Remove the power trim cylinders without disconneting the hoses. See Chapter Sixteen. Suspend cylinders with wire from a convenient place on the unit to prevent stressing the hoses.

5. Remove and discard the lower swivel pin's cotter pin. Drive the lower swivel pin from the gimbal housing.

6. Loosen the gimbal ring screws and nuts. **Figure 55** shows the new (1987-on) and old (1986) gimbal ring and clamping screws.

7. Remove the upper swivel shaft plug. Loosen the steering lever screw (**Figure 56**).

8. Apply downward pressure on the upper swivel shaft to provide access for removal of the

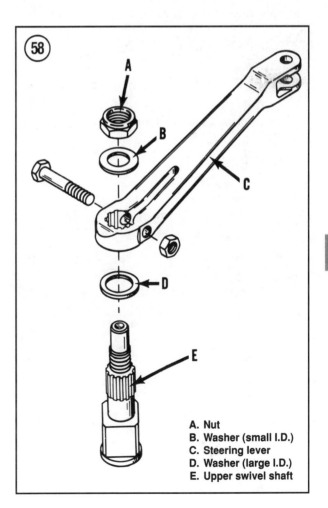

A. Nut
B. Washer (small I.D.)
C. Steering lever
D. Washer (large I.D.)
E. Upper swivel shaft

15

nut. Unthread and remove the nut from the top of the upper swivel shaft.

9. Remove the upper swivel shaft, steering lever, washers and nut. See **Figure 58**.

10. Remove the gimbal ring.

Gimbal Ring Disassembly/Reassembly

1. Remove the gimbal ring as described in this chapter.

2. Remove the oil seals and bearing (**Figure 59**) with driver part No. 91-33492 or equivalent.

3. Clean and inspect the gimbal ring as described in this chapter.

4. Install a new oil seal (lip upward) with driver part No. 91-33492 or equivalent. Install the new bearing, then a second oil seal (lip upward) with the same tool. See **Figure 60**.

Cleaning and Inspection

1. Clean gimbal ring in fresh solvent. Blow dry with compressed air.

2. Check lower swivel pin area where needle bearing rides for pitting, grooving and uneven wear. Replace bearing and swivel pin as required.

3. Check anti-galling (sythane) washers on gimbal ring for excessive wear or misalignment; replace as required.

4. Check gimbal ring upper swivel shaft/bore and hinge pin bores for excessive wear.

5. Check steering lever splines for excessive wear.

6. Check center portion of steering lever retaining bolt. If grooved from rubbing on the shaft, replace the bolt and steering lever.

Gimbal Ring Installation
(With Engine and Transom Installed)

1. If anti-galling washers were removed, align holes in new washers with holes in gimbal ring and epoxy in place.

2. Install a flat washer on each of the gimbal ring screws. Insert screws through holes in rear of gimbal ring. Install another washer on end of screw, wipe screw threads wtih Quicksilver Special Lubricant 101 and thread nuts on, but do not tighten.

3. Apply Special Lubricant 101 to the upper swivel shaft. Install shaft and make sure that it fits completely into the gimbal ring. The shaft shoulder should bottom on the ring when properly positioned. If necessary, clean mating surfaces on ring and shaft with a fine file and coat with Special Lubricant 101.

4. Install the gimbal ring over the bell housing.

5. Install the lower swivel pin and washer in the gimbal housing. Align swivel pin and housing holes and install a new cotter pin. Spread both ends of the cotter pin.

6. Lubricate the lower swivel pin grease fitting with Quicksilver 2-4-C Multi-Lube.

7. Install the screw and nut finger-tight on the steering lever. See **Figure 58**.

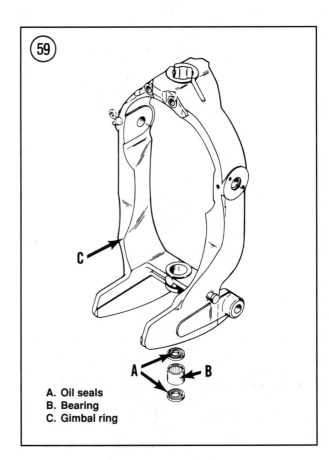

(59)

A. Oil seals
B. Bearing
C. Gimbal ring

8. A new grooved nut is included in the access plug kit. The nut has no threads. To cut the threads properly, install the nut on the upper swivel shaft and tighten it down all the way, then remove it.

9. Fit the steering lever with new nut and washers in place (lever and large ID washer must be installed from inside the boat). Use the access holes to hold the assembly in position.

10. With the gimbal ring in the straight-ahead position, make sure that the flat on the spline of the upper swivel shaft faces forward, then install the upper swivel shaft through the steering lever and thread the new nut in place as far as possible.

11. Use a hammer and pin punch through the access hole to tighten the nut (**Figure 57**) until there is a 0.002-0.010 in. (0.05-0.25 mm) clearance between the lower swivel pin washer and gimbal housing (**Figure 61**).

12. Rap the gimbal ring flanges (A, **Figure 61**) with a soft-faced mallet and recheck the clearance with the feeler gauge, tightening upper swivel shaft nut if required to bring clearance within specifications.

13. Tighten the gimbal ring screws (**Figure 55**) to 25 ft.-lb. (34 N·m).

14. Install the upper swivel shaft plug, then turn the steering lever until there is sufficient access to tighten the lever screw and nut to 60 ft.-lb. (81 N·m).

15. Reinstall the bellows and bell housing as described in this chapter.

16. Reinstall the stern drive unit (Chapter Twelve).

17. Reinstall the power trim cylinders (Chapter Sixteen).

18. Lubricate the hinge pin fittings with Quicksilver 2-4-C Multi-Lube until it can be seen underneath the steering lever. A heavy applica-

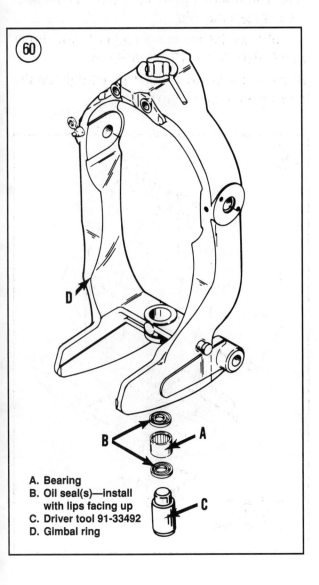

A. Bearing
B. Oil seal(s)—install with lips facing up
C. Driver tool 91-33492
D. Gimbal ring

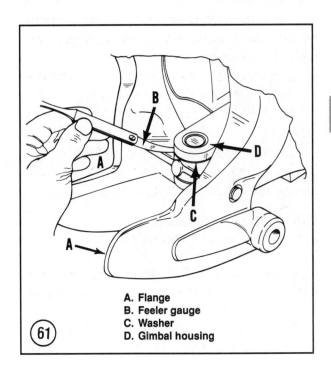

A. Flange
B. Feeler gauge
C. Washer
D. Gimbal housing

15

tion is necessary here to keep metal chips that will be created in the following steps from contaminating the bearings.

20. Position the stern drive unit for a full starboard turn.

21. Apply 2-4-C Multi-Lube to the cutting part of the one-inch NPT tap included in the tap and hole saw kit. Use tap to cut threads in the starboard access hole 1/2 in. ±1/16 in. deep (Alpha One) or 1-1/8 in. deep (Bravo models).

22. Reposition the stern drive unit for a full port turn and repeat Step 21 to thread the left access hole. Use compressed air to blow away all metal chips created by tapping the holes.

23. Thoroughly clean the access hole threads with solvent. Wipe the threads of the 2 plastic plugs included in the access plug kit with Quicksilver Perfect Seal. Carefully install each plastic plug in an access hole with a 5/8 in. Allen-head wrench to prevent cross-threading. The plugs should be installed until they protrude 3/8 in. ±1/16 in. from the housing. See **Figure 62**.

24. Prime and paint any bare metal surfaces.

25. With boat in water and the engine running, turn the steering wheel through the entire range to check for binding. Check for water leakage in the gimbal housing area where the plastic plugs were installed.

Gimbal Ring Installation (With Engine and Transom Removed)

1. If anti-galling washers were removed, align holes in new washers with holes in gimbal ring and epoxy in place.

2. Install a flat washer on each of the gimbal ring screws. Insert screws through holes in rear of gimbal ring. Install another washer on end of screw, wipe screw threads with Quicksilver Special Lubricant 101 and thread nuts on but do not tighten.

3. Apply Special Lubricant 101 to the upper swivel shaft. Install shaft and make sure that it fits completely into the gimbal ring. The shaft

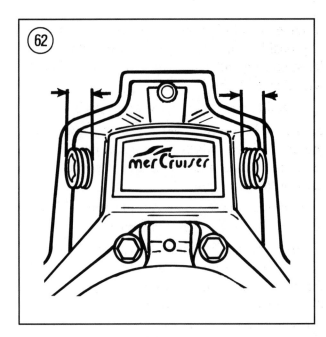

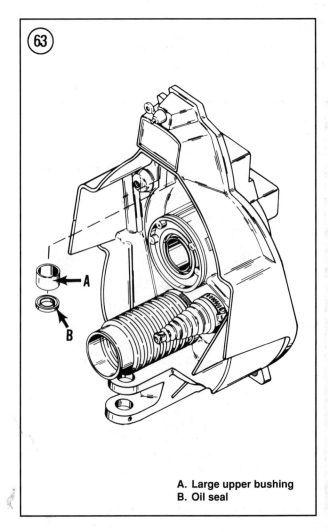

A. Large upper bushing
B. Oil seal

shoulder should bottom on the ring when properly positioned. If necessary, clean mating surfaces on ring and shaft with a fine file and coat with Special Lubricant 101.

4. Install the gimbal ring over the bell housing.

5. Install the lower swivel pin and washer in the gimbal housing. Align swivel pin and housing holes and install a new cotter pin. Spread both ends of the cotter pin.

6. Lubricate the lower swivel pin grease fitting with Quicksilver 2-4-C Multi-Lube.

7. With the gimbal ring in the straight-ahead position, make sure that the flat on the spline of the upper swivel shaft faces forward, then install the upper swivel shaft through the steering lever washer and lever. Install the other washer and nut on the shaft. See **Figure 58** for washer arrangement.

8. Tighten the nut until there is a 0.002-0.010 in. (0.05-0.25 mm) clearance between the lower

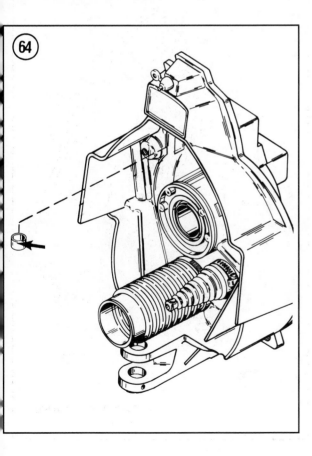

swivel pin washer and gimbal housing (**Figure 61**).

9. Rap the gimbal ring flanges (A, **Figure 61**) with a soft-faced mallet and recheck the clearance with the feeler gauge, tightening upper swivel shaft nut if required to bring clearance within specifications.

10. Tighten the gimbal ring screws (**Figure 55**) to 25 ft.-lb. (34 N.m).

11. Install the upper swivel shaft plug, then turn the steering lever until there is sufficient access to tighten the lever screw and nut to 60 ft.-lb (81 N.m).

12. Reinstall the bellows and bell housing as described in this chapter.

13. Lubricate the hinge pin fittings with Quicksilver 2-4-C Multi-Lube until the lubricant can be seen on the inner and outer gimbal ring surfaces of each pin.

14. Lubricate the upper swivel shaft grease fitting with 2-4-C Multi-Lube until it can be seen underneath the steering lever.

15. Reinstall the transom assembly (Chapter Twelve).

16. Reinstall the engine. See Chapters Six-Eight as appropriate.

17. Reinstall the stern drive unit (Chapter Twelve).

18. Reinstall the power trim cylinders (Chapter Sixteen).

GIMBAL HOUSING SERVICE

1. Remove the bell housing and gimbal ring as described in this chapter.

2. Remove the large upper bushing or bearing and oil seal (**Figure 63**) with a suitable driver.

3. Remove the small upper bushing (**Figure 64**) with a suitable driver.

4. Install a new small upper bushing (**Figure 64**) with a suitable driver until it bottoms in the housing bore.

5. Install a new upper bushing or bearing. Install a new oil seal (lip facing up). See **Figure 63**.

15

Table 1 TIGHTENING TORQUES

Fastener	in.-lb.	ft.-lb.	N·m
ALPHA ONE			
Gimbal ring			
Clamping screws		25	34
Hinge pins		95	129
Steering lever screw/nut		60	81
Transom assembly fasteners		20-25	27-34
Upper shift shaft lever screw	35-40		4-5
BRAVO ONE, BRAVO TWO AND BRAVO THREE			
Exhaust pipe-to-gimbal housing		20-25	37-34
Power steering hose fittings			
Large		20-25	27-34
Small	96-108		11-12
Power trim hose fittings	110		12
Propeller nut		55	75
Steering system			
Cable coupler nut		35	48
Coupler nut lock plate screw	60-72		7-8
Pivot bolts		25	34
Stern drive attaching nuts		50	68
Transom assembly fasteners		20-25	27-34

Chapter Sixteen

Power Trim and Tilt Systems

The MerCruiser power trim system permits raising or lowering the stern drive unit for efficient operation under varying conditions. Early stern drive units used a mechanical tilt system in the form of a series of holes in the gimbal ring. After the unit was set at the desired angle, an adjustment stud inserted through the appropriate holes held it in place.

The power trim system used on 1987 and later models is designated as the Power Trim XD (Extra Duty) system. Modifications in the top cover, gimbal ring and drive shaft housing were made to accommodate the use of longer trim cylinders which increase the drive unit tilt range an additional 6°. This provides extra clearance for launching, beaching and trailering the boat. It also allows the propeller to be brought out of the water for easy replacement on lighter boats.

This chapter covers the MerCruiser low-pressure pump system and the Auto Trim system.

LOW-PRESSURE PUMP SYSTEM

MerCruiser stern drives with transom serial numbers 6216687 and above are equipped with the low-pressure pump system. Prestolite and Oildyne/Eaton pumps are used interchangeably in production installations. Both types of pumps share the same internal valving, oil flow and pressure specifications.

> *CAUTION*
> *Differences in internal valving prevent a low-pressure pump from interchanging with an earlier high-pressure pump. Use of an incorrect trim pump will affect trim operation and can damage the trim system.*

A new Oildyne/Singer trim pump was introduced in late November 1986 as a running change on 1987 models (**Figure 1**). The new pump has a waterproof motor that can sustain a heavy load and stalling without damage. A thermal switch inside the motor shuts it down when the motor is overloaded for a lengthy period and then resets to allow continued operation. The oil reservoir is translucent to provide for a visual inspection of the oil level. An oversized oil fill cap and hole make the addition of fluid easier and more convenient. The new Oildyne/Singer pump is interchangeable with the older Oildyne/Eaton pump and delivers approximately the same trim response. System electrical wiring is essentially the same regardless of the pump used, but different service procedures are required according to the type of pump.

Trim System Bleeding

The trim system is self-purging when the drive unit is raised and lowered 6-10 times after filling with SAE 10W-30 or SAE 20W-40 engine oil.

However, the system should be bled whenever a rebuilt trim cylinder is installed. Use a flare nut wrench when loosening/tightening all fittings to prevent damage to the fitting nut.

1. Position drive unit in the full IN/DOWN position.

2. Remove the fill/vent screw (Oildyne/Eaton pump), oil fill cap (Oildyne/Singer pump) or fill screw (Prestolite pump) and top up as required with SAE 10W-30 or SAE 20W-40 engine oil. See Chapter Four. If both trim cylinders have been rebuilt, the pump reservoir should be filled to reservoir mark (Oildyne/Singer pump) or to the bottom of the screw hole (all others) to prevent it from running out of fluid during this procedure.

3. If the pump is equipped with a manual release valve (eliminated in 1986), make sure that it is completely closed (fully tightened clockwise).

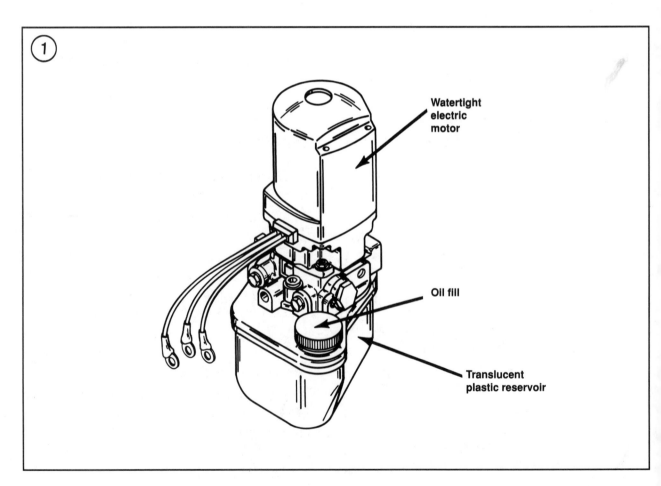

(1)

Watertight electric motor

Oil fill

Translucent plastic reservoir

4. Disconnect the OUT/UP hose from the trim cylinder front connection (**Figure 2**). Disconnect the hose from both cylinders if both were rebuilt.

5. Place the end of the hose(s) in a suitable container and operate the trim pump in the UP direction until no air bubbles are noted in the oil stream emitted from the hose. Reconnect hose(s) and tighten fitting(s) securely.

6. Refill the trim pump as required. See Step 2 and Chapter Four.

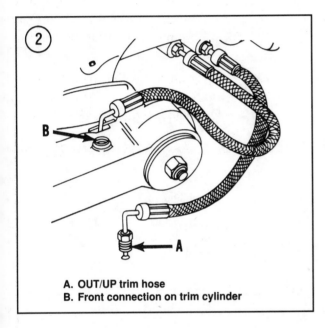

A. OUT/UP trim hose
B. Front connection on trim cylinder

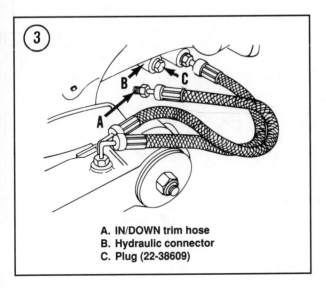

A. IN/DOWN trim hose
B. Hydraulic connector
C. Plug (22-38609)

7. Disconnect the IN/DOWN trim hose from the gimbal housing rear connection (**Figure 3**). Disconnect the hose from both cylinders if both were rebuilt.

8. Install plug part No. 22-38609 or equivalent in the end of each gimbal housing fitting. See **Figure 3**.

9. Place the end of the hose(s) in a suitable container and operate the trim pump in the UP direction to fully extend the trim cylinders.

10. Remove the plug(s) from the gimbal housing fitting(s) and run the trim pump in the DOWN direction until no air bubbles are noted in the oil stream emitted from the hose. Stop the trim pump at that point and reconnect the trim hose(s), tightening the fittings securely.

11. Lower the drive unit to the full IN/DOWN position. Refill the trim pump as required. See Step 2 and Chapter Four.

12. Operate the trim system OUT/UP and IN/DOWN several times, then recheck pump reservoir oil level and top up as required.

Trim Pump Removal/Installation (All Models)

1. Disconnect the negative trim pump lead at the battery, then the positive lead.

2. Unplug the trim harness connector at the pump housing.

3. Use a flare nut wrench to loosen the trim hose nuts at the pump fittings. Disconnect the hoses from the pump. Cap the hoses and fittings to prevent leakage and entry of contamination.

4. Remove the lag bolts and washers holding the pump in place. Carefully lift the pump and mounting bracket from the boat.

5. Installation is the reverse of removal. The black hose connects to the port fitting; the gray hose connects to the starboard fitting. Check pump reservoir and top up as required. See Chapter Four.

16

Trim Cylinder Removal/Installation

1. Position drive unit in the full IN/DOWN position.

2. Disconnect the OUT/UP hose from the trim cylinder front connection (**Figure 2**). Disconnect the hose from both cylinders if both are being removed. Cap the hose and trim cylinder fitting(s) to prevent leakage and the entry of contamination.

3. Disconnect the IN/DOWN trim hose from the gimbal housing rear connection (**Figure 3**). Disconnect the hose from both cylinders if both are being removed.

4. Install plug part No. 22-38609 or equivalent in the end of each gimbal housing fitting. See **Figure 3**. Cap the hose and trim cylinder fitting(s) to prevent leakage and the entry of contamination.

5. Remove the decorative plastic trim caps (if so equipped) from the aft anchor pin on each side to expose the nuts. Hold the anchor pin nut on one side with a wrench and loosen the nut on the other side. Remove the nut and washer, then carefully drive the anchor pin through the trim cylinder eye, catching the other washer. Lower the trim cylinder to the ground. If both cylinders are being removed, continue driving the anchor pin until it clears the other cylinder eye and can be removed. See **Figure 4**.

6. Repeat Step 5 to remove the forward anchor pin. See **Figure 5**.

NOTE
If the bushings were removed from the trim cylinders, use a solution of 1 part liquid soap to 80 parts of water when reinstalling them. Do not use grease or oil, as bushings thus treated may creep out of position during operation.

7. To reinstall the trim cylinder(s), refer to **Figure 5** and install the forward anchor pin through the trim cylinder eye and gimbal housing. Wipe the anchor pin threads with Quicksilver 2-4-C

Multi-Lube and thread the nuts onto the pin by hand.

8. Repeat Step 7 to install the aft anchor pin, referring to **Figure 4**.

CAUTION
If the anchor pin nuts are not bottomed in Step 9, they will back off during operation and the trim cylinder(s) may fall off.

9. Tighten all anchor pin nuts until the washers bottom out against the anchor pin shoulders. See **Figure 6**.

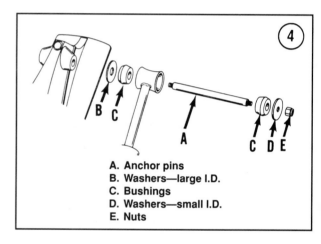

A. Anchor pins
B. Washers—large I.D.
C. Bushings
D. Washers—small I.D.
E. Nuts

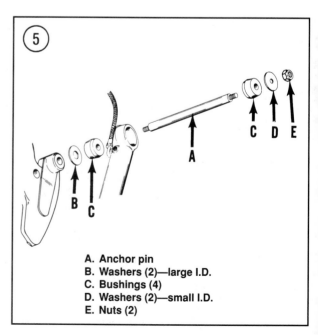

A. Anchor pin
B. Washers (2)—large I.D.
C. Bushings (4)
D. Washers (2)—small I.D.
E. Nuts (2)

Electrical Troubleshooting

Whenever a problem develops in the low-pressure power trim system, the initial step is to determine whether the problem is in the electrical or hydraulic system. Electrical tests are given below. If the problem appears to be in the hydraulic system and cannot be corrected by bleeding the system, refer it to a dealer or qualified specialist for necessary testing and service.

Before troubleshooting any electrical circuit:
1. Make sure the plug-in connectors are properly engaged and that all terminals and wires are free of corrosion. Clean and tighten as required.
2. Make sure the battery is fully charged. Charge or replace as required. Refer to **Figure 7** (Prestolite pump), **Figure 8** (Oildyne/Eaton pump) or **Figure 9** (Oildyne/Singer pump) for all of the following procedures.

All circuits inoperative, solenoids do not click

NOTE
If the 20 amp fuse blows while trimming OUT/UP, check for shorted trim switch leads. This can be caused by chafed insulation which allows the conductor to contact the gimbal housing and short out

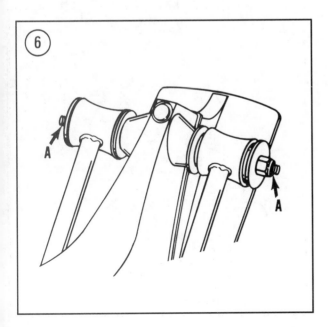

*the area shown in **Figure 10**. If this is the cause of the problem, replace the trim limit switch with part No. 99122A3 (includes the leads) as shown in **Figure 11**, using a sta-strap as indicated.*

1. Check 20 amp and 110 amp fuses. If one or both fuses are blown, locate and correct cause before replacing fuse(s).

2. Disconnect the trim limit switch leads at points 14-17. Depress TRAILER switch, If drive unit can be raised, the trim limit switch or its leads are grounded.

3. Clean and/or tighten connections at points 1, 2, 4, 10, 11 and 12.

4. Separate connector (point 13). Clean as required and reconnect.

5. Connect a voltmeter between point 4 and ground. If no voltage is shown, repeat Step 1.

6. Connect a voltmeter between point 8 and ground. Depress the OUT/UP button. Move the red voltmeter lead to point 6 and depress the IN/DOWN button. If no voltage is shown at one or both test points, check teh trim control for a loose/corroded connection or a damaged power supply lead in the harness.

All circuits inoperative, solenoids click

1. Connect a voltmeter between point 5 and ground. Depress the IN/DOWN button. Move the red voltmeter lead to point 3 and depress the OUT/UP button. If no voltage is shown at one or both test points, check connections at points 2, 3, 4 and 5. If connections are good, replace the solenoids.

2. Disconnect the blue/white lead at the solenoid terminal point 8. Depress the IN/DOWN button. If pump motor operates, there is a short in the wire harness. Repair or replace harness as required.

16

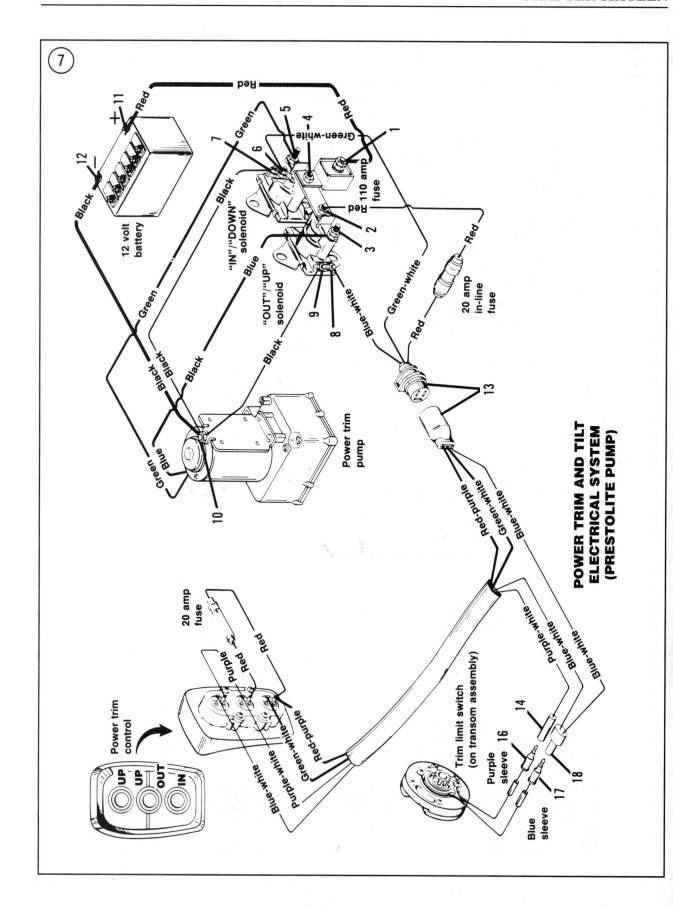

POWER TRIM AND TILT
ELECTRICAL SYSTEM
(PRESTOLITE PUMP)

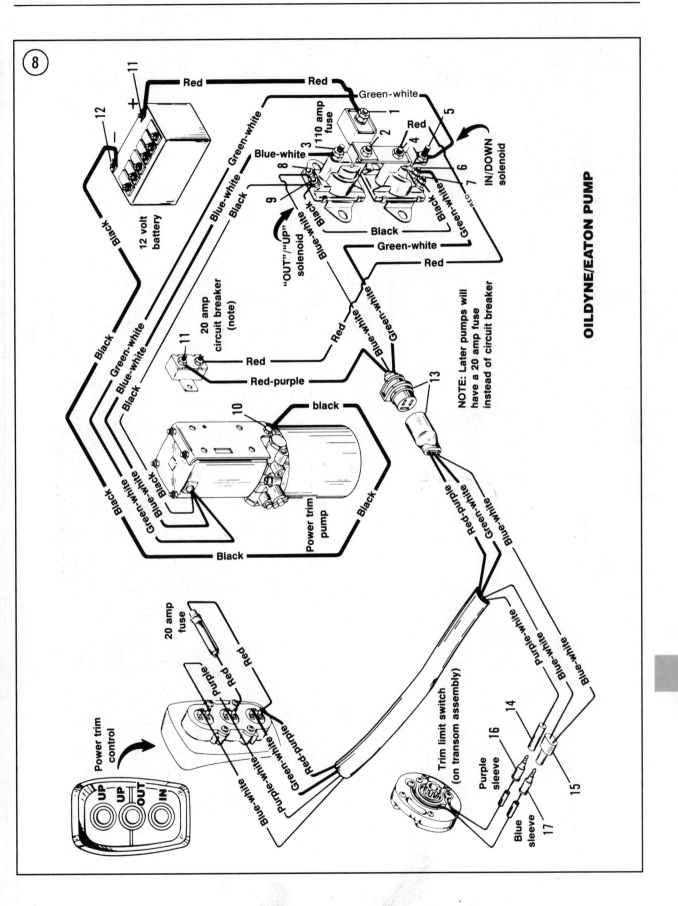

8

11

12

Red Red

Green-white

+

110 amp fuse

1

2

Red

4

5

Blue-white

3

IN/DOWN solenoid

8

6

7

12 volt battery

Green-white

Blue-white

9

Black

Black

Green-white

"OUT"/"UP" solenoid

Blue-white

Green-white

Black

Black

Black

Red

Green-white

Blue-white

20 amp circuit breaker (note)

11

Red

Green-white

Blue-white

Red

Red-purple

13

NOTE: Later pumps will have a 20 amp fuse instead of circuit breaker

OILDYNE/EATON PUMP

10

black

Green-white

Blue-white

Black

Black

Black

Power trim pump

Black

Red-purple

Green-white

Blue-white

16

20 amp fuse

Red

purple

Power trim control

UP UP OUT IN

Blue-white

purple-white

Green-white

Red-p-purple

Blue-white

purple-white

Blue-white

Trim limit switch (on transom assembly)

Purple sleeve

16

14

15

17

Blue sleeve

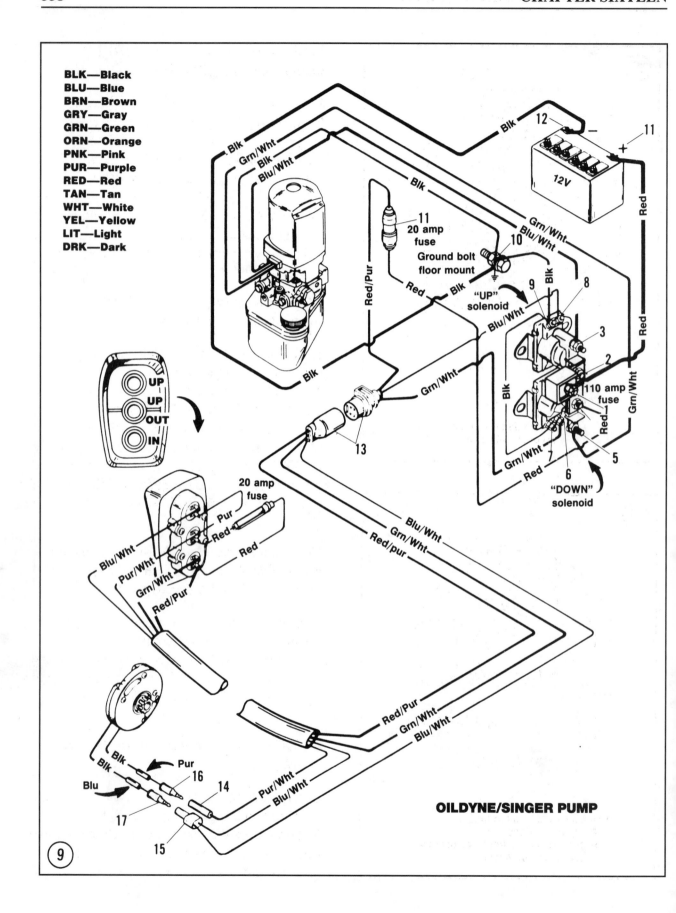

BLK—Black
BLU—Blue
BRN—Brown
GRY—Gray
GRN—Green
ORN—Orange
PNK—Pink
PUR—Purple
RED—Red
TAN—Tan
WHT—White
YEL—Yellow
LIT—Light
DRK—Dark

OILDYNE/SINGER PUMP

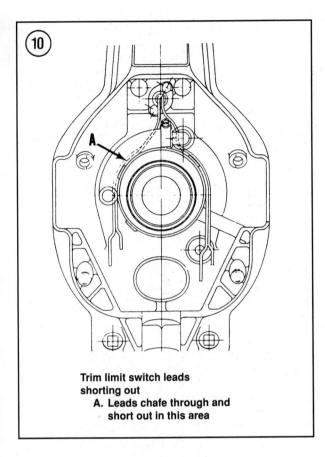

**Trim limit switch leads
shorting out**
  **A. Leads chafe through and
    short out in this area**

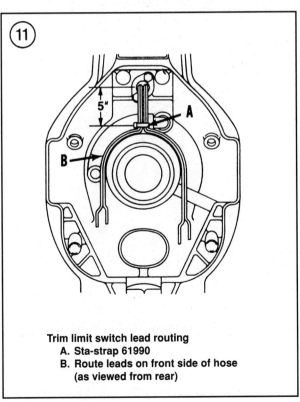

Trim limit switch lead routing
  A. Sta-strap 61990
  **B. Route leads on front side of hose
    (as viewed from rear)**

DOWN circuit inoperative; IN/DOWN solenoid does not click (UP circuit good)

1. Check connections at point 6 and point 7. Clean and/or tighten as required.
2. Connect a voltmeter between point 6 and ground. Depress the IN/DOWN button. If no voltage is shown, check the IN/DOWN circuit for a loose/corroded connection or a damaged IN/DOWN circuit lead. If the connections and leads are good, test the trim switch continuity. If satisfactory, replace the IN/DOWN solenoid.

DOWN circuit inoperative; IN/DOWN solenoid clicks (UP circuit good)

1. Check connections at point 8 and point 9. Clean and/or tighten as required.
2. Connect a voltmeter between point 8 and ground. Depress the OUT/UP button. If no voltage is shown, check the OUT/UP circuit for a loose/corroded connection or a damaged OUT/UP circuit lead. If the connections and leads are good, test the trim switch continuity. If satisfactory, replace the OUT/UP solenoid.

UP circuit inoperative; IN/DOWN solenoid clicks; TRIM and TRAILER switches inoperative (DOWN circuit good)

1. Check connections at point 2 and point 3. Clean and/or tighten as required.
2. Connect a voltmeter between point 3 and ground. Depress the OUT/UP button. If no voltage is shown, replace the OUT/UP solenoid.

OUT/UP trim switch inoperative (TRAILER switch good)

1. Check connections at points 14, 15, 16 and 17. Clean and/or tighten as required.
2. Disconnect the trim limit switch leads at the trim harness. Connect an ohmmeter between lead 16 and lead 17. With drive unit in full

16

IN/DOWN position, the meter should show continuity. If not, check for poor connections or damaged leads. If connections and leads are good, replace the trim limit switch.

TRAILER switch inoperative (OUT/UP trim switch good)

1. Check trailer switch with an ohmmeter. It should show continuity when the switch is depressed and no continuity when switch is at rest.
2. If switch is good, check for loose or corroded connections or a damaged trailer circuit lead.

Trim system functions while unattended

1. Check trim pump harness and trim control harness for a short circuit. Repair or replace as required.
2. If harness circuits are good, check the TRIM and TRAILER switches with an ohmmeter. Each switch should show continuity when depressed and no continuity when switch is at rest. Replace switch as required.

AUTO TRIM SYSTEM

The MerCruiser Auto Trim system was introduced on 1986 260 models as a factory-installed option available from the boat manufacturer. It is available as a factory- or dealer-installed option on all 1986 and later V8 models.

Auto trim automatically adjusts the drive unit trim angle relative to engine speed. Once the boat is on plane, the Auto Trim system them trims out to a preset position that maximizes performance.

The system consists of an auto trim pump (the same as used in low-pressure power trim systems), a solid-state control module, a 2-position mode switch which allows the operator to select manual or automatic trim, a manual trim, control, trim limit switch and a 3-buttom control panel or remote control panel control.

The Auto Trim electrical system is protected by a 110 amp fuse on the pump, a 20 amp in-line fuse at the control module positive battery lead, and a 20 amp in-line fuse at the ignition switch (if switch is a Quicksilver product). If the boat is equipped with the 3-button control panel, a 20 amp in-line fuse is also located at the panel.

Trim Pump Removal/Installation

See *Low-Pressure Pump System* in this chapter.

Trim Cylinder Removal/Installation

See *Low-Pressure Pump System* in this chapter.

Trim Limit Switch Adjustment

The amount of "out" trim capability is controlled by the trim switch. Proper switch adjustment requires the help of an assistant.

WARNING
If trim limit switch requires adjustment, take the following precautions:

a. Use extreme caution not to start the engine.
b. Make sure no one is near the propeller area.
c. Do not place hands where they can be injured by the drive unit movement.

CAUTION
Trim switch adjustment must be made exactly as described in the following procedure. If switch adjustment is incorrect, the drive unit can move out beyond the gimbal ring support flanges during the test run. If this happens, the drive unit may be severely damaged.

1. Make sure the drive unit is in its full IN position.
2. Loosen the trim switch retaining screws. Rotate the switch clockwise to the end of the slots.

3. Place the Auto Trim mode switch in MAN-UAL position and turn the ignition key to RUN.

4. Have an assistant operate the manual trim control switch (do not use TRAILER switch) to trim the drive unit OUT while you slowly turn the trim limit switch counterclockwise until trim cylinders extend 6 1/4-6 3/4 in. (measured from cylinder end cap to centerline of pivot end nut). At this point, retighten the trim switch retaining screws.

5. Turn the ignition OFF. Test your adjustment by running the boat along a smooth stretch of water and trim the boat with the manual trim control until maximum performance is obtained.

6. Once the best trim angle has been found, stop the engine without changing the drive unit trim angle. Measure the distance between the trim cylinder end cap and pivot end (same measurement as made in Step 4).

7. Repeat Step 1 and Step 2.

8. With the Auto Trim switch in the MANUAL position, turn the ignition key to RUN.

9. Have the assistant operate the manual trim control switch to trim the drive unit out while you slowly turn the trim limit switch counterclockwise until the trim cylinders extend to the dimension measured in Step 4. At this point, retighten the trim switch retaining screws.

WARNING
Adjusting the drive unit too far "out" can result in handling difficulties and loss of operational control. Perform Step 10 with caution and if difficulties arise, move the drive trim angle "in" enough to eliminate the problem.

10. Turn the ignition switch OFF. Test your adjustment by running the boat along a smooth stretch of water with the Auto Trim switch in the AUTO position. Run boat at various speeds, through turns with varying water and load conditions. If not satisfied with boat performance, repeat the procedure.

Trim Position Indicator Adjustment

Place the ignition key in the RUN mode and check the Auto Trim indicator gauge. The needle should rest at the bottom of the scale when the drive unit is fully IN. If not, adjust as follows:

1. Turn ignition key to RUN.

2. Loosen the trim position sender retaining screws.

3. Rotate sender as required to position the needle at the bottom of the gauge scale.

4. Tighten the sender retaining screws securely. Recheck instrument reading and turn ignition key OFF.

Electrical Troubleshooting

Whenever a problem develops in the Auto Trim system, the initial step is to determine whether the problem is in the electrical or hydraulic system. Electrical tests are given below. If the problem appears to be in the hydraulic system and cannot be corrected by bleeding the system, refer it it a dealer or qualified specialist for necessary testing and service.

Before troubleshooting any electrical circuit:

1. Make sure the plug-in connectors are properly engaged and that all terminals and wires are free of corrosion. Clean and tighten as required.

2. Make sure the battery is fully charged. Charge or replace as required.

Refer to **Figure 12** for all of the following procedures.

All circuits inoperative in manual and auto modes (solenoids do not click)

1. Check cable at point 13 for a loose/corroded connection or damaged leads. Correct as required.

2. Disconnect the connector plugs at point 47. Clean as required and reconnect snugly.

16

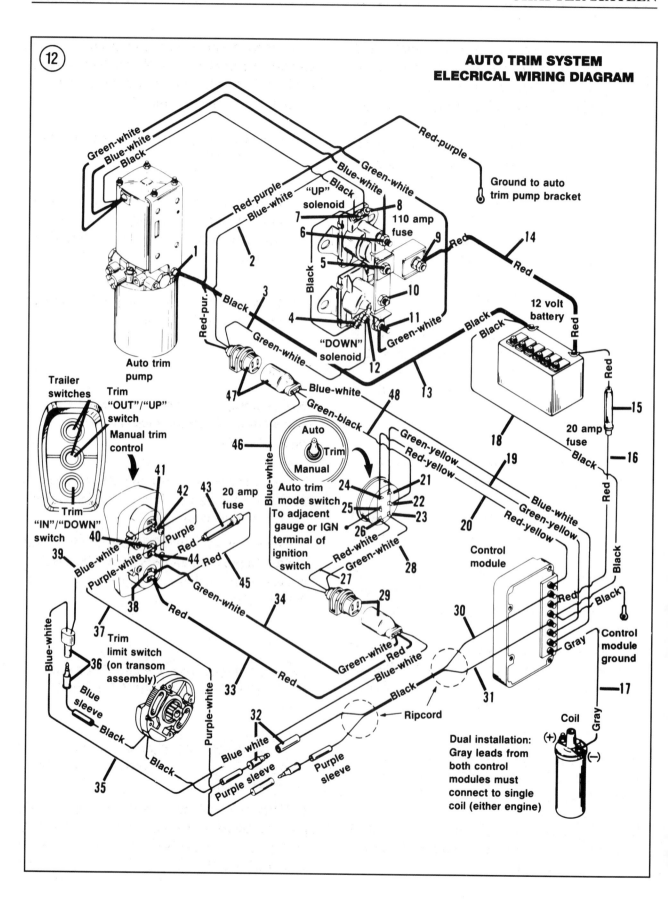

AUTO TRIM SYSTEM ELECRICAL WIRING DIAGRAM

(12)

Green-white
Blue-white
Black

Red-purple

Ground to auto trim pump bracket

Red-purple
Blue-white
"UP" solenoid
Blue-white
Black

Green-white

110 amp fuse

Red

14

Red

Red-pur.
Black
Black

12 volt battery

Black
Black

Red

Auto trim pump

"DOWN" solenoid

Green-white

13

18

Red

15

Trailer switches
Trim "OUT"/"UP" switch
Manual trim control

47

Blue-white

Green-black

48

Green-white

Auto
Trim
Manual

Green-yellow
Red-yellow

19

20 amp fuse

Black

16

46

Blue-white

Auto trim mode switch
To adjacent gauge or IGN terminal of ignition switch

24
25
26

21
22
23

20

Blue-white
Green-yellow
Red-yellow

Control module

Red

Black

Trim "IN"/"DOWN" switch

41
42
43

40
44

20 amp fuse

Purple
Red

Red

45

Red-white
Green-white

28

27

29

30

Control module ground

39

Blue-white

Green-white

34

31

17

Gray

37 Trim limit switch (on transom assembly)

38

Red

33

Red

Blue-white

Black

Ripcord

36

Blue sleeve

Black

Purple-white

32

35

Blue white

Purple sleeve

Purple sleeve

Coil

Gray

Dual installation: Gray leads from both control modules must connect to single coil (either engine)

3. Connect a jumper jead between point 1 and point 7. If the pump operates, the internal circuit breaker is faulty. Replace the pump.

4. Place the ignition switch in the RUN position. Move the mode switch to MANUAL. Connect a voltmeter between point 8 and ground. Depress the UP switch. If no voltage is shown, complete this step and move to Step 5. Move the red voltmeter lead to point 12 and depress the DOWN switch. If no voltage is shown, proceed with Step 6.

5. Connect the voltmeter between point 25 and ground. If no voltage is shown, check for a poor connection in the power lead.

6. Connect the voltmeter between point 26 and ground (mode switch in MANUAL). Move mode switch to AUTO position and connect the voltmeter between point 24 and ground. If no voltage is shown at one or both connections, replace the mode switch.

All circuits inoperative in manual and auto modes (both solenoids click)

1. Check cable at point 14 for a loose/corroded connection or damaged leads. Correct as required.

2. Connect a voltmeter between point 5 and ground. If no voltage is shown, the 110 amp fuse is blown or the solenoid connection is loose or corroded.

3. Disconnect the blue/white lead at point 8. If the pump motor now runs in the DOWN direction, there is a short in the trim harness. Repair or replace harness as required.

DOWN circuit inoperative in manual and auto modes; UP circuit good (DOWN solenoid does not click)

1. Check the connections at points 4, 7 and 12 for damaged leads or a loose/corroded connection. Correct as required.

2. Connect a voltmeter between point 12 and ground. Depress the DOWN switch (MANUAL model). If no voltage is shown, repeat this step at point 22 and then at point 23.

    a. If there is voltage at point 23 but not at point 22, replace the mode switch.

    b. If there is voltage at point 22, check the leads at point 3 and point 48, and the connector at point 47 for an open in the DOWN circuit.

    c. If there is no open in the DOWN circuit, replace the DOWN solenoid.

DOWN circuit inoperative in manual and auto modes; UP circuit good (DOWN solenoid clicks)

1. Check connections at point 10 and point 11 for damaged leads or a loose/corroded connection. Correct as required.

2. Connect a voltmeter between point 11 and ground. Depress the DOWN switch (MANUAL model). If no voltage is shown, replace the DOWN solenoid.

UP circuit inoperative in manual and auto modes; DOWN circuit good (UP solenoid clicks)

1. Check connections at point 5 and point 6 for damaged leads or a loose/corroded connection. Correct as required.

2. Connect a voltmeter between point 6 and ground. Depress the UP switch (MANUAL mode). If no voltage is shown, replace the UP solenoid.

16

Pump motor continues running DOWN in auto mode until internal timer shuts it off (UP/OUT and TRAILER switches inoperative in manual mode)

1. Check connections at point 7 and point 8 for damaged leads or a loose/corroded connection. Correct as required.

2. Connect a voltmeter between point 8 and ground. Depress the UP switch (MANUAL model). If voltage is shown, replace the UP solenoid. If no voltage is shown, continue testing.

3. Check connections at point 32 and point 36 for damaged leads or a loose/corroded connection. Correct as required.

4. Disconnect the trim limit switch leads at point 32 and point 36. Connect an ohmmeter between the disconnected leads. If continuity is not shown with the drive unit in the DOWN position, readjust or replace the switch as required.

5. If continuity is shown in Step 4, check leads 30, 35, 46 and 2 for damage or a loose/corroded connection. Correct as required.

6. If the problem still has not been located at this time, replace the control module.

UP circuit inoperative in auto mode (manual mode good)

1. Check lead 17 for damage or loose/corroded connections. Correct as required.

2. If lead 17 is good, replace the control module.

DOWN circuit inoperative in auto mode (manual mode good)

1. Connect a voltmeter between point 21 and ground while turning the ignition switch to RUN (AUTO mode). Repeat this step at point 22.

2. If voltage is shown at point 21 but not at point 22, replace the mode switch.

All circuits inoperative in manual mode (auto mode good)

1. Connect a voltmeter between point 26 and ground (MANUAL mode). If no voltage is shown, replace the mode switch.

2. Check lead 27 and lead 33 for damage or loose/corroded connections. Correct as required.

DOWN circuit inoperative in manual mode (UP/OUT and TRAILER switches good in auto mode)

1. Connect a voltmeter between point 38 and ground. Depress the DOWN switch (MANUAL mode). If no voltage is shown, replace the manual trim control DOWN switch.

2. Connect a voltmeter between point 23 and ground. Depress the DOWN switch (MANUAL mode). If no voltage is shown, check lead 28 and lead 34 for damage or a loose/corroded connection. Correct as required.

3. If leads are good in Step 2, connect the voltmeter between point 22 and ground. Depress the DOWN switch. If no voltage is shown, replace the mode switch.

UP/OUT and TRAILER switches inoperative in manual mode (DOWN switch good and auto mode functions good)

1. Check the 20 amp trim control fuse at point 43 to make sure it is good. If not, locate and correct the problem before installing another fuse.

2. Connect a voltmeter between point 44 and ground. If no voltage is shown, check lead 45 for damage or a loose/corroded connection. Correct as required.

3. Connect the voltmeter between point 40 and ground. Depress the UP/OUT switch. If no voltage is shown, replace the switch.

UP/OUT switch inoperative in manual model (TRAILER switch good and auto mode functions good)

1. Connect a voltmeter between the switch output terminal and ground. Depress the UP/OUT switch. If not voltage is shown, replace the switch.
2. Check lead 31 and lead 37 for damage or loose/corroded connections; correct as required.
3. If leads are good in Step 2, replace the control module.

TRAILER switch inoperative in manual mode (UP/OUT switch is good)

1. Connect a voltmeter between point 41 and ground. Depress the TRAILER switch. Repeat this step at point 42.
2. If voltage is shown at point 42 but not at point 41, replace the TRAILER switch.
3. If lead is good in Step 3, check lead 39 for damage or a loose/corroded connection.

TRIM CYLINDERS

A Type 3 trim cylinder is used on all models. Trim cylinders carrying a -1 after the part No. (98703-1) stamped on the casting (**Figure 13**) are capable of trimming IN an additional 3° more than those without the -1 (98703). These trim cylinders can be used as service replacements for the older cylinders without the additional capability.

Drive units with the older cylinders can be updated to utilize the additional trim IN capability by replacing both cylinders with the newer -1 cylinders. However, it may be necessary to remove a slight amount of metal from the gimbal ring at the points shown in **Figure 14**. This will provide adequate clearance between the gimbal ring and bell housing when the drive unit is in the full IN position.

The Power Trim XD (Extra Duty) system installed on 1987 and later models provides up to 6° of additional tilt by the use of longer trim cylinders (**Figure 15**). This required a modifica-

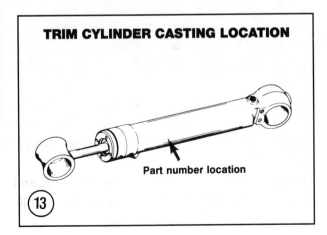

TRIM CYLINDER CASTING LOCATION

Part number location

13

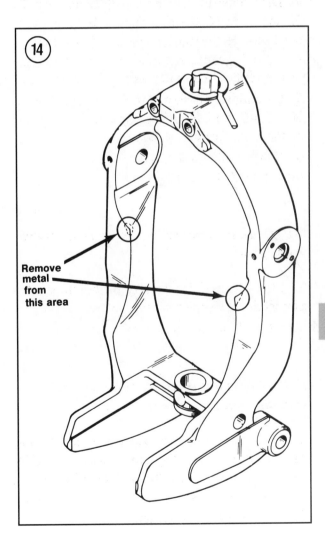

14

Remove metal from this area

16

tion of the drive shaft housing (**Figure 16**) to clear the longer cylinders and hoses when the drive unit was in the fully down position. In addition, modifications were made to the top cover and gimbal ring to provide adequate clearance when the drive unit was in the fully tilted position.

Some 1987 and later boats fitted with a swim platform may not have sufficient clearance to accommodate the extended tilt range. In such cases, a tilt limit spacer kit (part No. 15768A1) can be installed with a spanner wrench (**Figure 17**). Installation of the spacer kit limits the drive unit to the previous trim/tilt range (54°) instead of the 60° available without the spacer.

All 1987 and later models use a longer aft anchor pin to accommodate the use of decorative plastic caps (**Figure 18**).

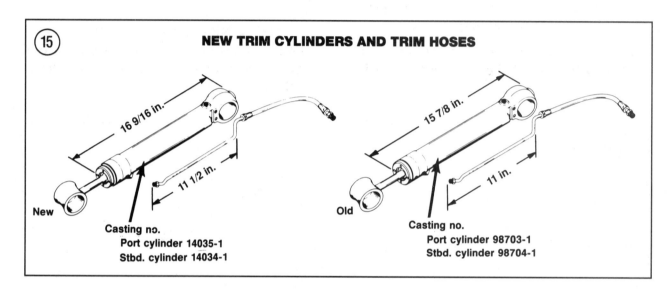

(15) **NEW TRIM CYLINDERS AND TRIM HOSES**

16 9/16 in.

11 1/2 in.

New

Casting no.
Port cylinder 14035-1
Stbd. cylinder 14034-1

15 7/8 in.

11 in.

Old

Casting no.
Port cylinder 98703-1
Stbd. cylinder 98704-1

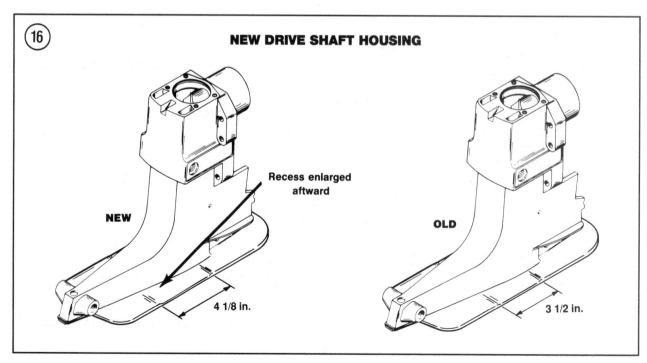

(16) **NEW DRIVE SHAFT HOUSING**

Recess enlarged
aftward

NEW

4 1/8 in.

OLD

3 1/2 in.

Trim Cylinder Quick Test

If a defective or malfunctioning trim cylinder is suspected, this simple quick check will tell you which cylinder (if any) is causing the problem.

1. Disconnect the aft end of both trim cylinders as described in this chapter.

2. Suspend each trim cylinder in the air so that they are on the same horizontal plane.

3. Depress the UP buttom on the control panel while watching the piston rods.

    a. If both piston rods move at the same time and rate of travel, the problem is not in the trim cylinders.

    b. If one piston rod moves after the other, or if one moves at a slower rate of travel, that cylinder is malfunctioning.

4. Service the defective cylinder as described in this chapter.

5. Reattach both cylinders as described in this chapter.

Trim Cylinder Overhaul

Mercury Marine recommends the use of a spanner wrench available from Snap-On Tool dealers to remove and install the end cap. Refer to **Figure 19** for this procedure.

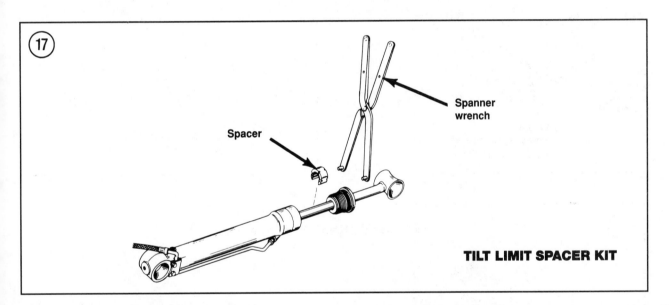

Spanner wrench

Spacer

TILT LIMIT SPACER KIT

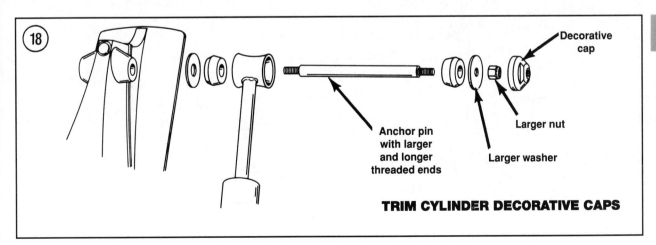

Decorative cap

Larger nut

Larger washer

Anchor pin with larger and longer threaded ends

TRIM CYLINDER DECORATIVE CAPS

16

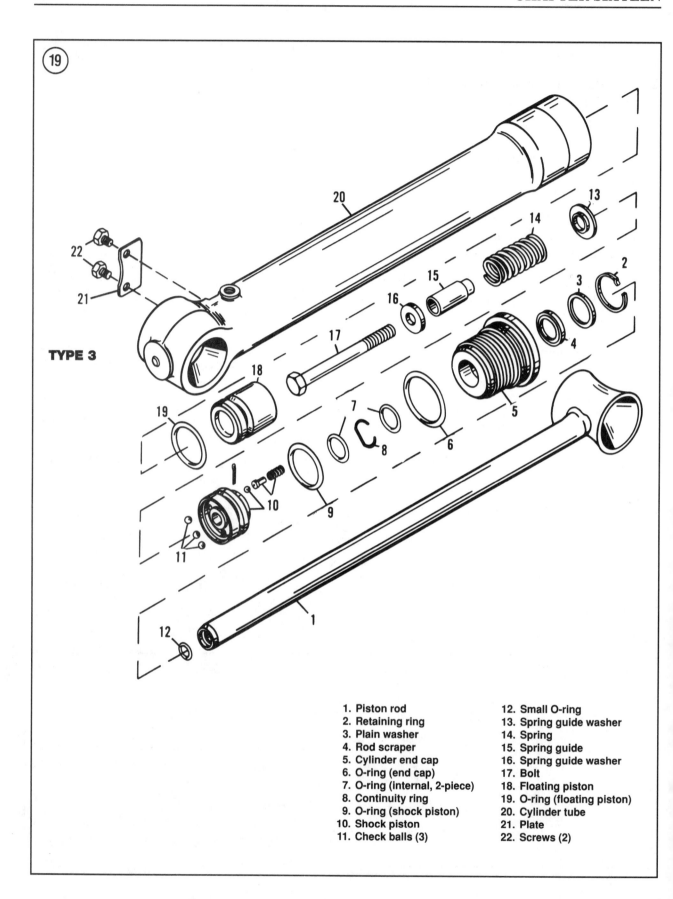

TYPE 3

1. Piston rod
2. Retaining ring
3. Plain washer
4. Rod scraper
5. Cylinder end cap
6. O-ring (end cap)
7. O-ring (internal, 2-piece)
8. Continuity ring
9. O-ring (shock piston)
10. Shock piston
11. Check balls (3)
12. Small O-ring
13. Spring guide washer
14. Spring
15. Spring guide
16. Spring guide washer
17. Bolt
18. Floating piston
19. O-ring (floating piston)
20. Cylinder tube
21. Plate
22. Screws (2)

1. Remove the trim cylinder as described in this chapter.

2. Hold the cylinder ports over a suitable container while extending and retracting the piston rod by hand several times to expel oil from the cylinder.

3. Clamp the piston rod in a vise with protective jaws as close as possible to the pivot end.

4. Remove the cylinder end cap with Snap-On spanner wrench A176, then pull the piston rod

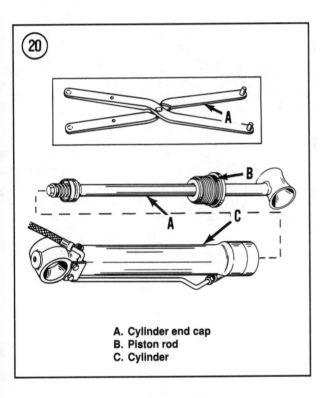

A. Cylinder end cap
B. Piston rod
C. Cylinder

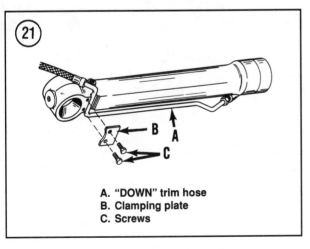

A. "DOWN" trim hose
B. Clamping plate
C. Screws

and end cap assembly from the cylinder (**Figure 20**).

5. Remove the clamping plate holding the DOWN trim hose (**Figure 21**).

6. Use a flare nut wrench to loosen the DOWN hose fitting nut, then unscrew the nut and remove the hose.

7. Place a wooden block on the floor and rap the cylinder sharply several times to remove the floating piston. Remove and discard the piston O-ring.

8. Remove the bolt from the end of the shock piston. Remove the spring guide, spring, spring guide washer, 3 check balls and the shock piston from the piston rod. Remove and discard all O-rings.

9. Remove the end cap from the piston rod. Compress and remove the snap ring from the end cap, then remove the washer and rod scraper.

10. Remove and discard the end cap external O-ring. Remove the internal O-rings and continuity spring.

11. Clean all metal parts in fresh solvent and blow dry with compressed air, if available.

12. Lubricate all parts and the cylinder bore with clean SAE 10W-30 or 10W-40 engine oil.

13. Install the rod scraper and washer in the end cap. Compress and install the snap ring.

14. Install a new O-ring in the rear groove inside the end cap. Install the continuity ring in the middle groove inside the end cap, then install another new O-ring in the remaining groove.

15. Install a new large O-ring on the outside of the end cap, then slide the assembled end cap on the piston rod.

16. Install a new O-ring on the shock piston.

17. Position the 3 check balls in the shock piston. Install the spring guide washer, spring, plain washer and bolt. Install a new small O-ring in the rear of the shock piston.

18. Wipe the shock piston bolt threads with Loctite Type A. Install the shock piston to the piston rod and tighten the bolt to 15-20 ft.-lb. (20-27 N·m).

16

19. Install a new O-ring on the floating piston, then insert the piston assembly into the cylinder (**Figure 22**).

> *CAUTION*
> *If the end cap threads are lubricated with any substance other than grease in Step 20, corrosion may develop due to poor electrical contact between the end cap and cylinder.*

20. Lubricate the end cap threads with grease. Install the piston rod in the cylinder bore. Thread the end cap in place hand-tight, then tighten securely with the spanner wrench. Wipe any excess grease from the end cap.

21. Hand-start the DOWN hose nut in the cylinder fitting. Tighten the nut securely with a flare nut wrench. Install the clamping plate (**Figure 21**).

22. Remove the piston and cylinder assembly from the vise and check for any scratches or other areas where paint has been removed to the bare metal. Such areas should be touched up with paint before reinstalling the trim cylinder to prevent rust and corrosion from developing.

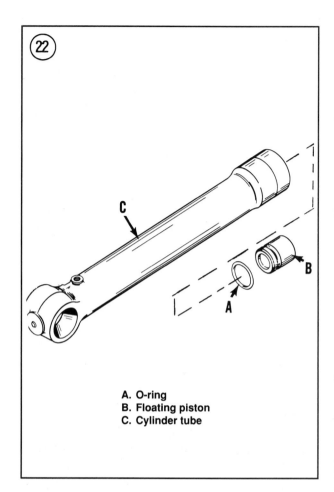

A. O-ring
B. Floating piston
C. Cylinder tube

Chapter Seventeen

Steering Systems

MerCruiser stern drives may be equipped with a manual (non-power) or power steering system. Proper operation of the stern drive steering system is essential for safe boating. The steering system should be rigged *only* by an experienced marine technician and serviced (whenever possible) by one who is equally qualified. The boater should perform routine checks and maintenance to assure that no problems develop. This chapter covers steering safety precautions, steering system troubleshooting and maintenance. **Table 1** (power steering troubleshooting) is at the end of the chapter.

SAFETY PRECAUTIONS

The steering system connects the stern drive unit to the steering wheel (**Figure 1**). When properly installed and maintained, the steering

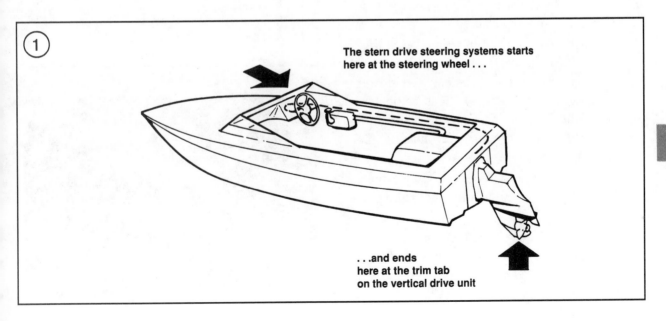

The stern drive steering systems starts here at the steering wheel . . .

. . .and ends here at the trim tab on the vertical drive unit

system gives the boater control over the vessel. A steering system that jams will prevent you from avoiding obstacles, such other boats on the water. If the steering system is loose, the boat will weave regardless of the boater's attempt to maintain a straight course. A steering system failure will cause the boater to completely lose control, resulting in a possible serious accident and even loss of life.

The most important safety precaution you can observe is proper lubrication and maintenance of the steering system. This is especially important whenever the stern drive unit receives a severe blow, such as hitting a piling or other object in the water, or when trailering the boat. Damaged or weak components may fail at a later time while you are on the water. Know what to look for and have any deficiencies you find corrected as soon as possible.

If you must make required adjustments yourself, make them carefully and use only the fasteners supplied with steering attachment kits or equivalent fasteners sold as replacement items by marine dealers. It is also a good idea to have your work rechecked by an experienced marine technician to make sure that no safety hazards exist.

Whenever the engine is removed or other service that affects the steering system is performed, you should make sure that:

a. Cable movement is not restricted. See **Figure 2**. Cable restrictions can result in possible jamming of the system. On power steering models, a cable restriction can cause the drive unit to go into a full turn condition without your ever turning the steering wheel.

b. The engine stringer (mount) does not interfere with the power steering pump and pulley (**Figure 3**).

c. The power steering components and the push-pull cable function freely and will operate the power steering valve only when you turn the steering wheel (**Figure 4**).

MECHANICAL STEERING SYSTEM

A mechanical steering system (**Figure 5**) consists of the helm or steering wheel assembly (A), the connecting cable (B) and hardware (C) that attaches the steering wheel to the steering arm on the inner transom bracket.

Cable Removal/Installation

The steering cable must be serviced as an assembly.

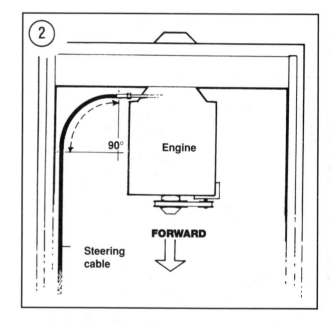

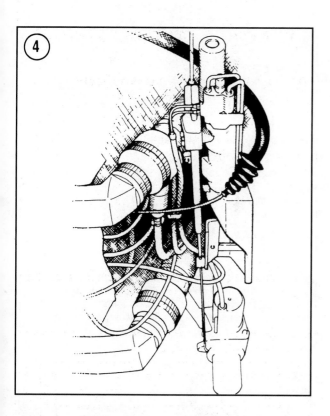

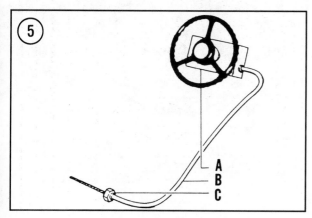

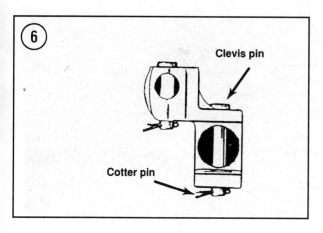

Clevis pin

Cotter pin

1. Remove the cotter pin from the clevis pin which holds the cable to the steering arm. See **Figure 6**. Remove the clevis pin.

2. Turn the helm (steering wheel assembly) to the port full lock position, then remove the cotter pin holding the locking sleeve over the cable coupler nut. See **Figure 7**.

3. Remove the cable. Prior to installation, lubricate the cable with Quicksilver Special Lubricant 101.

4. Insert the steering cable through the steering tube.

5. Move the stern drive steering arm to its center position.

6. Center the steering cable arm. Connect the cable to the steering arm. Install the clevis pin, then install a new cotter pin and spread the ends.

7. Thread the coupler nut on the tube. Hold the tube adjusting sleeve or tube nut with a wrench and tighten the coupler nut to 35 ft.-lb. (48 N·m).

8. Position the locking sleeve on the steering cable and slide it over the coupler nut until the cotter pin hole in the sleeve is between the nut and cable grease fitting. Install new cotter pin and spread the ends. See **Figure 7**.

9. Turn the steering wheel lock to lock. The drive unit should traverse fully in each direction. If not, loosen the adjusting nuts and move the cable guide tube as required to obtain full travel.

10. Turn the steering wheel until the drive unit is centered. If the steering wheel is not centered at this point, readjust the cable guide slightly as described in Step 9 to center the steering wheel.

11. Repeat Step 8 to make certain that both adjustments are correct.

Steering System Lubrication

See Chapter Four.

17

Trim Tab Adjustment

Proper adjustment of the trim tab will provide equal steering effort in both directions. If the boat seems to steer easier in one direction than the other, operate it in a straight line with a balanced load on a stretch of water where wind and current will not be factors. If steering effort is not equal under these conditions, adjust the trim tab as follows:

1. Determine in which direction the steering is easier.

2. Loosen the trim tab bolt.

   a. If steering effort is easier to port, move the trim tab slightly to port.

   b. If steering effort is easier to starboard, move the trim tab slightly to starboard.

3. Tighten the trim tab bolt and recheck the steering effort by running the boat. Repeat this procedure as required to equalize the steering effort.

4. When steering effort is satisfactory in both directions, tighten the trim tab bolt to 28 ft.-lb. (38 N•m).

POWER STEERING SYSTEM

In addition to the components used in the manual steering system, the power steering system uses a power steering pump, oil cooler, control valve/piston assembly and connecting hydraulic hoses. These components are all serviced as assemblies.

The power steering pump is mounted on the front side of the engine and belt-driven off the crankshaft pulley (**Figure 8**). The control valve/piston assembly is mounted on the inner transom bracket (**Figure 9**) and connects to the steering arm and steering cable ram. **Figure 10** shows the relationship of the system components.

The valve spool in the control valve assembly moves about 1/8 in. (total) in response to movement of the steering cable casing. Although the

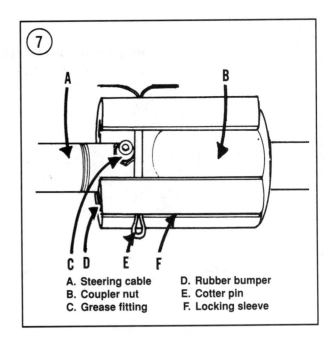

A. Steering cable
B. Coupler nut
C. Grease fitting
D. Rubber bumper
E. Cotter pin
F. Locking sleeve

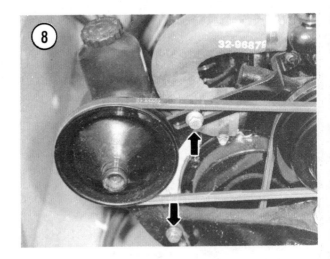

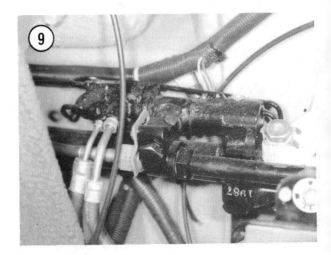

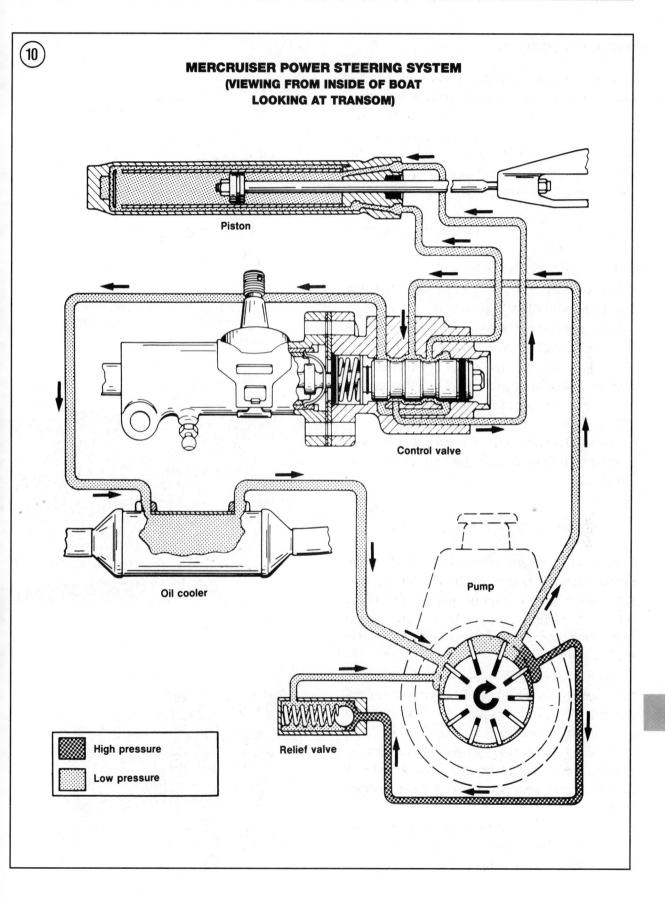

**MERCRUISER POWER STEERING SYSTEM
(VIEWING FROM INSIDE OF BOAT
LOOKING AT TRANSOM)**

Piston

Control valve

Oil cooler

Pump

Relief valve

High pressure

Low pressure

17

amount of spool movement is small, it is enough to direct hydraulic pressure to the correct side of the piston. If the cable casing is restricted at the stern of the boat, it will affect the movement of the valve spool and result in hard steering in one or both directions. Make sure the area around the steering cable casing is clear and that nothing restricts cable movement near the engine. See **Figure 11**, typical. Wiring harnesses and control cables should not be tied to the steering cable.

Fluid Level Check

Although the dipstick is marked with both HOT and COLD lines, this procedure should be performed with the engine at normal operating temperature and OFF. The drive unit position should be straight ahead.

1. Remove the engine compartment cover or hatch.
2. Unscrew the power steering pump reservoir cap and remove the cap/dipstick.
3. Wipe the dipstick with a clean shop cloth or paper towel. Reinstall the cap/dipstick, wait a few moments, then remove again and check the fluid level on the dipstick.
4. If fluid level is below the recommended level on the dipstick shown in **Figure 12**, add sufficient Type F or DEXRON II automatic transmission fluid to bring the level to the FULL HOT mark on the dipstick.
5. Reinstall cap/dipstick in the power steering pump reservoir.
6. Turn the steering wheel from lock to lock several times, then repeat Steps 2-5 as required.

Bleeding the Hydraulic System

A low fluid level and/or air in the fluid are the most frequently encountered causes of pump noise. The power steering system must be bled to correct the problem. It must also be bled whenever a hydraulic line has been disconnected to service the system.

1. With the engine off, check the fluid level as described in this chapter.
2. Start the engine and run at 1,000-1,500 rpm until it reaches normal operating temperature.
3. Turn the steering wheel from lock to lock several times, then center the steering wheel (drive unit centered) and shut the engine off.
4. Remove the power steering pump cap/dipstick and recheck the fluid level. Top up as required.
5. Turn the steering wheel from side to side without hitting the stops. Keep the fluid level in the pump reservoir just above the integral pump casting. If there is air in the fluid, it will appear light tan in color or foamy in appearance.

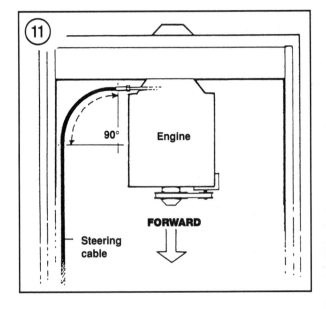

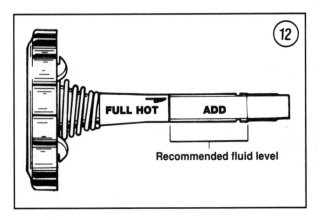

6. Turn the steering wheel to the center position. Start and run the engine for 2-3 minutes, then shut it off. Recheck the fluid in the reservoir. If it still contains air, repeat Step 5 and Step 6 until the fluid does not foam and the level remains constant.

7. When all air has been bled from the system, run the boat on the water to make sure that the steering operates properly and is not noisy.

8. Recheck the fluid level (engine at normal operating temperature) to make sure it is at the FULL HOT mark on the cap/dipstick.

Power Steering Pump Removal/Installation

Metric fittings are used with all pumps. Replacement high pressure hoses must also have metric fittings and metric flare nut wrenches should be used to loosen or tighten the fitting nut to prevent rounding off the corners of the nut. Whenever the return line is removed, a new worm-type clamp should be installed.

All except 4.3L engine

1. Use a metric flare nut wrench to loosen the high pressure (lower) hose at the rear of the pump. Use a suitable screwdriver or cap driver to loosen the return (upper) hose clamp. See **Figure 13**.

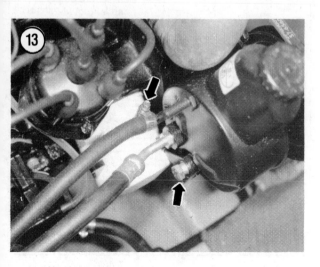

2. Place a shop cloth underneath the fittings and disconnect the lines one at a time. Cap the hose ends and pump fittings to prevent leakage and the entry of contamination. Secure both hoses in an upright position by wiring them to the alternator bracket or other convenient point to prevent fluid drainage.

3. Loosen the pump mounting fasteners and slip the drive belt off the pump pulley. See **Figure 8**, typical.

4. Unbolt the pump and remove the pump/bracket assembly from the engine.

5. If the pump is to be replaced, remove the mounting bracket and install it on the new pump.

6. Position the pump assembly on the engine and install the mounting fasteners finger-tight.

7. Hand-start the high-pressure hose fitting nut, then tighten the nut to 35 ft.-lb. (47 N•m). Install the return hose with a new worm-type clamp and tighten securely.

8. Fill the pump reservoir with Type F or DEXRON II automatic transmision fluid. Rotate the pulley clockwise (as seen from the front of the pump) until no air bubbles can be seen in the fluid.

> *CAUTION*
> *Do **not** pry against the pump or pull the pump outward by its neck to adjust belt tension in Step 9. This can cause internal damage to the pump.*

9. Pivot the pump away from the engine and tighten one mounting bolt to hold the pump in that position.

10. Check drive belt tension. If a belt tension gauge is used, tension should be 75-95 lb.; if the belt deflection method is used, the belt should deflect 1/4 in. (inline engines) or 1/2 in. (V6 and V8 engines) when finger pressure is applied at a point midway in the belt span.

11. If belt tension is not correct, reposition the pump and repeat Step 10. When belt tension is correct, tighten all mounting fasteners seccurely.

17

12. Bleed the power steering system as described in this chapter.

13. Recheck tension of a new belt after the engine has run for 5 minutes.

4.3L engine

1. Unbolt the cooling hose bracket to provide access to one of the power steering pump fasteners. Loosen the pump mounting fasteners and slip the drive belt off the pump pulley.

2. Unbolt the pump and remove the pump from the engine bracket assembly.

3. Use a metric flare nut wrench to loosen the high pressure (lower) hose at the rear of the pump. Use a suitable screwdriver or cap driver to loosen the return (upper) hose clamp. See **Figure 13**, typical.

4. Place a shop cloth underneath the fittings and disconnect the lines one at a time. Cap the hose ends and pump fittings to prevent leakage and the entry of contamination. Secure both hoses in an upright position by wiring them to the coolant hoses or other convenient point to prevent fluid drainage.

5. Hand-start the high-pressure hose fitting nut, then tighten the nut to 35 ft.-lb. (47 N·m). Install the return hose with a new worm-type clamp and tighten securely.

6. Position the pump assembly on the engine and install the mounting fasteners finger-tight.

7. Fill the pump reservoir with Type F or DEXRON II automatic transmission fluid. Rotate the pulley clockwise (as seen from the front of the pump) until no air bubbles can be seen in the fluid.

> *CAUTION*
> *Do not pry against the pump or pull the pump outward by its neck to adjust belt tension in Step 8. This can cause internal damage to the pump.*

8. Pivot the pump away from the engine and tighten one mounting bolt to hold the pump in that position.

9. Check drive belt tension. If a belt tension gauge is used, tension should be 75-95 lb.; if the belt deflection method is used, the belt should deflect 1/2 in. when finger pressure is applied at a point midway in the belt span.

10. If belt tension is not correct, reposition the pump and repeat Step 9. When belt tension is correct, tighten all mounting fasteners securely.

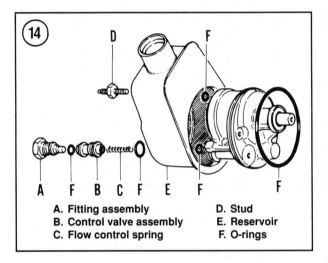

A. Fitting assembly
B. Control valve assembly
C. Flow control spring
D. Stud
E. Reservoir
F. O-rings

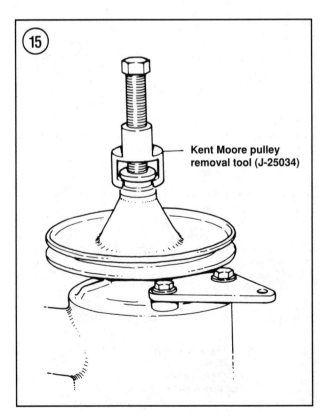

Kent Moore pulley removal tool (J-25034)

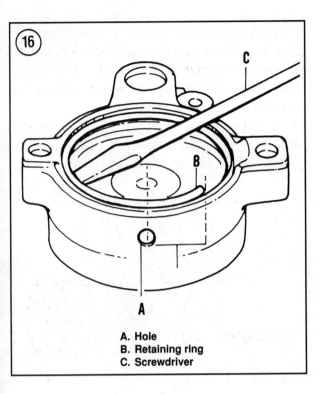

A. Hole
B. Retaining ring
C. Screwdriver

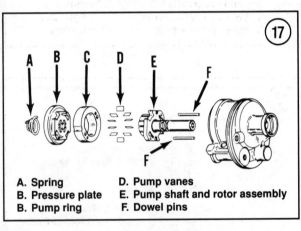

A. Spring
B. Pressure plate
B. Pump ring
D. Pump vanes
E. Pump shaft and rotor assembly
F. Dowel pins

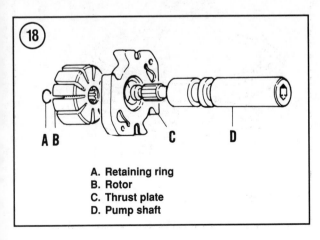

A. Retaining ring
B. Rotor
C. Thrust plate
D. Pump shaft

11. Bleed the power steering system as described in this chapter.

12. Recheck tension of a new belt after the engine has run for 5 minutes.

Power Steering Pump Disassembly/Assembly

The power steering pump can be disassembled, but internal components are not available. If the pump is defective or malfunctioning, it should be replaced. This procedure is primarily of value in cases where the engine has been submerged. In such a case, the power steering pump should be disassembled, all contamination removed and all components lightly lubricated to prevent the pump from corroding. If properly performed, the procedure will save the pump and avoid the cost of a new one.

A new seal should be installed during reassembly. This can be obtained from any local General Motors dealer under part No. 5688044. Refer to **Figure 14** for this procedure.

1. Remove the power steering pump as described in this chapter.

2. Drain all fluid from the pump into a suitable container.

3. Remove the pump pulley with puller part No. J-25034 (**Figure 15**).

4. Remove the fitting and control valve assemblies and the flow control spring.

5. Remove the stud(s).

6. Carefully tap the reservoir from the pump housing. Remove and discard the O-rings.

7. Position the pump body retaining ring as shown in **Figure 16**. Insert an awl in the housing hole and push the ring away from its recess, then pry the ring from the pump body with a screwdriver blade.

8. Remove the pump components shown in **Figure 17**.

9. Remove and discard the 2 housing O-rings.

10. Remove the circlip holding the rotor and thrust plate on the pump shaft. See **Figure 18**.

17

11. Remove the magnet from the pump body (**Figure 19**).

12. Clean all metal parts in fresh solvent and blow dry with compressed air.

13. Lubricate all metal parts with Type F or DEXRON II automatic transmission fluid.

14. Remove and discard the pump shaft seal. Place pump body on a press as shown in **Figure 20**. Position a new oil seal with its metal side facing up and use a 1 in. socket to press the seal in place. Be sure the pump body is properly supported to prevent it from distortion.

15. Install a new pressure plate O-ring in the 3rd groove in the housing, then install the dowel pins (**Figure 21**).

16. Slide the thrust plate and rotor on the pump shaft, then install the circlip (**Figure 18**).

17. Install the pump shaft and rotor assembly in the pump body (**Figure 22**).

18. Insert the pump ring, fitting the 2 smaller holes over the dowel pins. See **Figure 23**.

19. Install the vanes in the rotor slots with their rounded edges facing the pump ring (**Figure 24**). Make sure the vanes move freely.

20. Install the pressure plate with its spring grooves facing upward, then install a new end plate O-ring in the 2nd groove. See **Figure 25**.

21. Install the pressure plate spring and the end plate (**Figure 26**).

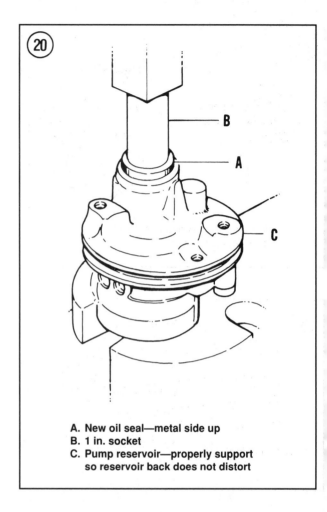

A. New oil seal—metal side up
B. 1 in. socket
C. Pump reservoir—properly support
    so reservoir back does not distort

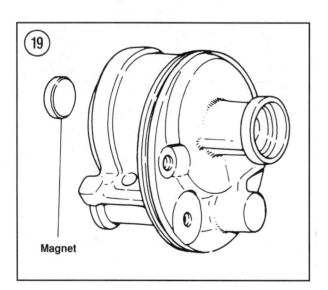

Magnet

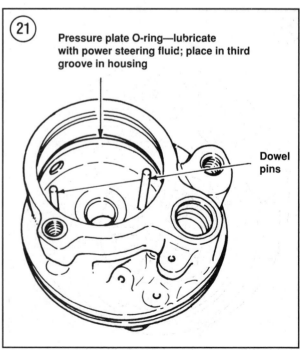

Pressure plate O-ring—lubricate
with power steering fluid; place in third
groove in housing

Dowel
pins

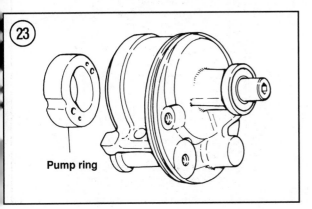

A. Pump shaft and rotor assembly
B. Pump housing

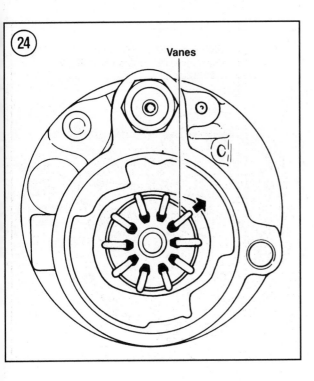

Pump ring

22. Position the housing in a press and apply pressure on the end plate to hold it down evenly. Install the retaining ring and make sure it snaps into its groove around the entire perimeter of the body.

23. Install a new large O-ring on the body and 2 new small O-rings (**Figure 27**).

24. Position the magnet on the pump body housing, then install the reservoir to the pump body and secure it with the studs. Tighten studs to 35 ft.-lb. (47 N·m).

25. Install the flow control spring, control valve and fitting assemblies with new O-rings. Tighten fitting assembly to 35 ft.-lb. (47 N·m).

26. Install the pump to the engine as described in this chapter, then install and align the pump pulley as described below.

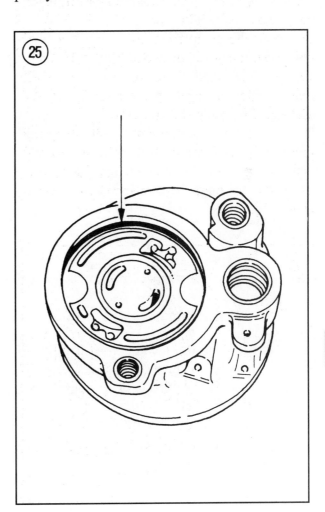

Vanes

17

Power Steering Pump Pulley Alignment

Whenever the power steering pump pulley is removed, it should be reinstalled and aligned with the pump mounted to the engine. This will ensure correct vertical alignment of the pulley groove with the crankshaft or water pump drive pulley and prevent premature drive belt (and steering system) failure.

Refer to **Figure 28** for this procedure.

1. Position the pulley on the pump shaft. Fit the drive belt around its pulleys.

2. Thread the stud from pulley pusher assembly (part No. 91-93656A1) as far as possible into the pump shaft.

3. Position the bearing from the tool assembly over the stud—do not use the spacer included in the kit.

4. Screw the pusher nut onto the tool shaft, then thread the nut and shaft as far as possible onto the stud.

5. Position a long straightedge as shown in **Figure 28** and tighten the pusher nut as required to bring the drive belt parallel with the straightedge.

6. When the pulley is properly aligned, remove the straightedge and pulley pusher tool components.

7. Adjust the drive belt. See Chapter Ten.

Trim Tab Adjustment

See *Manual Steering* in this chapter.

Power Steering Pump Leakage Checks

The power steering system may develop problems such as growling noises, loss of power during low-speed operation or heavy steering effort. It may also require frequent addition of fluid. When any of these problems occur, the most obvious solution is to check for leaks.

Figure 29 shows the common points of pump leakage. If a leak is found at any of the points shown, the pump should be replaced as a unit. In

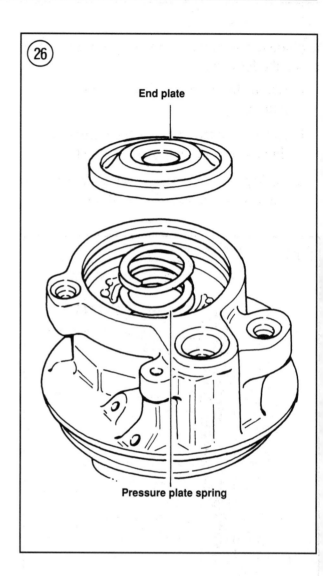

End plate

Pressure plate spring

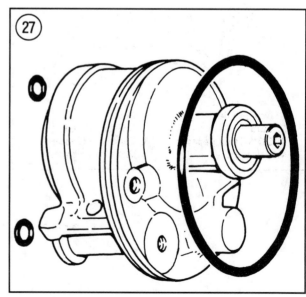

addition to these leakage points, you should also check the following:

  a. Return hose and/or clamp (replace as required).

  b. Cross-threaded or loose high-pressure fitting (correct or replace as required).

  c. Leakage at the control valve or actuator valve spool (replace as required).

  d. Power steering fluid in the cooling system (replace the oil cooler).

Seepage leaks are the most difficult to locate. If you keep the engine clean as suggested in Chapter Four and Chapter Five, it will be much easier to locate such leaks. To locate seepage leaks:

  a. Clean the entire power steering system (pump, hoses, power cylinder/actuator valve and connecting line).

  b. Adjust the pump reservoir fluid to its correct level.

  c. Start the engine and turn the steering wheel from stop to stop several times, then shut the engine off.

  d. Recheck the areas mentioned above for dampness. Correct any deficiencies noted.

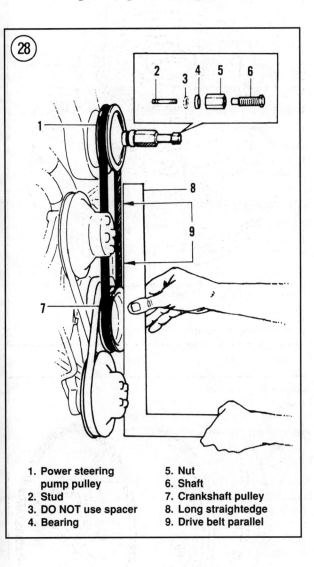

1. Power steering pump pulley
2. Stud
3. DO NOT use spacer
4. Bearing
5. Nut
6. Shaft
7. Crankshaft pulley
8. Long straightedge
9. Drive belt parallel

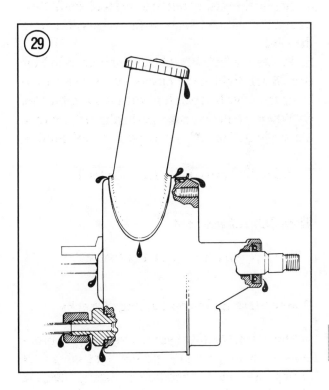

Table 1 is on the following page.

17

Table 1 POWER STEERING SYSTEM TROUBLESHOOTING

Symptom	Likely cause
PUMP	
Chirps or squeals	Loose drive belt
Hissing sound	Normal condition
Rattle or chuckle	Pressure hose contacting other components
	Loose steering linkage
Growl	Steering cable needs adjustment
Whine	Scored pump shaft bearing
Groan	Low fluid level and/or air in the system
Growl	Hose restriction causing back pressure
STEERING SYSTEM	
Excessive loose steering or wheel kickback	Air in system
	Loose steering cable attachment
	Loose or worn steering ball stud
Steering wheel surge or jerk when turning	Loose drive belt
	Low fluid leve
	Actuator spool valve sticks
	Pump pressure insufficient
	Actuator spool valve lacks lubrication
Momentary increase in steering effort during fast turns	Slipping drive belt
	Low fluid level
	Imternal pump leakage
Hard steering	
To starboard	Cable too long or restricted
To port	Cable too short or restricted
Hard steering/no assist	Internal pump or control valve leakage
	Cable movement restricted
	Loose drive belt
	Low fluid level
	Insufficient lubrication
	Excessive linkage friction
	Cable radius too tight at output end
	Actuator spool valve sticking
	Insufficient fluid pressure
	Restricted fluid flow
Low oil pressure	Restriction in hose
	Defective control valve
	Loose drive belt
	Low fluid level
	Air in system
	Defective hoses
	Loose flow control valve screw
Foaming fluid	Air in system

Chapter Eighteen

Corrosion Protection Systems

As the waters in which stern drives are operated become increasingly polluted with waste materials and toxic chemical spills, the problems posed by galvanic corrosion continue to multiply. Galvanic corrosion, which is discussed in Chapter One, has always been with us—it's a fact of nature. But this simple electrochemical reaction is of greater concern today than ever.

More and more boats are plying the nation's waterways, the waterways are becoming increasingly polluted (which greatly accelerates the process of corrosion) and the cost of today's stern drive make damage or destruction by simple neglect on the part of the owner very expensive.

This chapter describes the various corrosion protection systems used on MerCruiser applications. Also provided are simple procedures to minimize damage from galvanic corrosion and a corrosion protection test to determine when aditional protection is necessary.

Table 1 is at the end of the chapter.

CORROSION

Metal immersed or submerged in water is subject to two forms of corrosion—galvanic corrosion and stray current voltage. Metal that remains above the waterline is subject to corrosion from the air, especially in salt water environments.

Corrosion above the waterline is quickly visible but can be minimized by regular use of Quicksilver Corrosion Guard. This clear, non-peeling spray protects external metal surfaces against the ravages of the environment.

Corrosion below the waterline is more insidious and can occur even when you think that you have taken precautions against it.

Galvanic corrosion

As we saw in Chapter One, galvanic corrosion is an electrochemical reaction. When two dissimilar metals share a common ground in a conductive solution such as water, an electric current flows between the two. This causes the most chemically active or anodic metal to erode. Since the drive unit components are manufactured of aluminum (one of the most chemically active of metals), they will be damaged by this process if not protected against it.

Galvanic corrosion is noticed first on sharp edges that are under the waterline. The process is seen in 3 stages. First, the paint blisters, then corrosion appears in the form of a whitish substance and finally, the exposed metal begins to erode. This erosion initially takes the form of pitting on the metal, then whole pieces of the metal just disappear.

Galvanic corrosion can also result from connecting into a shore power hookup while your boat is moored. This ties the aluminum drive unit of your boat (through the wiring) to all the other boats using the same source of shore power. Your drive unit thus becomes part of a large galvanic cell which is interconnected with onshore metal (in addition to the other boats) through the green neutral safety ground lead. The result is accelerated corrosion at a time when it is least expected.

If the drive unit or boat is repainted, do not use an anti-fouling paint containing copper or mercury. Such paints will *increase* the likelihood of galvanic corrosion. Whenever the drive unit is painted or bare metal spots are touched up, be sure to use Quicksilver primer and paint and apply according to the directions on the container.

Stray current corrosion

This phenomenon occurs when an electrical current that is flowing through a metal conductor leaves the metal and passes through water. The current flow thus converts the metal into non-metallic corrosion or, if great enough, simply eats the metal away. The problem is first noticed as a severe case of paint blistering.

This type of corrosion is generally caused by stray current leaking from an improperly insulated circuit. The current tries to ground itself through a path of least resistance—your aluminum drive unit. Lead wires that are immersed in bilge water or wires with weak or deteriorated insulation that are subject to intermittent moisture are common causes of stray current corrosion. So are trolling motors, marine radios, depth finders or other electrical accessories that are incorrectly wired to the engine or boat.

If you have a stray current corrosion problem, it is also possible to transmit it to other boats that do not have the problem. As an example, if you have the problem and are using onshore power at a dock that is not properly grounded, other boats using the same shore power will be subject to accelerated corrosion.

The first line of defense against corrosion is, of course, the use of quality materials and multi-stage painting which incorporates chemical and untrasonic cleaning, zinc chromate priming and paint application that will result in a chip-resistant protective coating. However, even the most meticulous finishing process will not prevent corrosion from developing. To minimuze the potential for damage, there are several forms of protection available.

The second line of defense against corrosion is periodic preventive maintenance (Chapter Four). Proper maintenance procedures including lubrication, flushing and touching up scratches

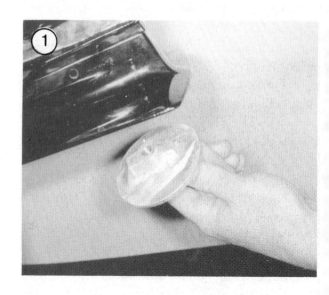

and abrasions will do much to prevent corrosion from becoming a major problem.

ZINC ANODES

The oldest and easiest form of protection against galvanic corrosion is the use of sacrificial anodes. These relatively inexpensive and easily replaceable components provide adequate corrosion protection in most situations where light-to-moderate corrosion conditions exist. Anodes are made of a highly active zinc alloy and take a variety of forms.

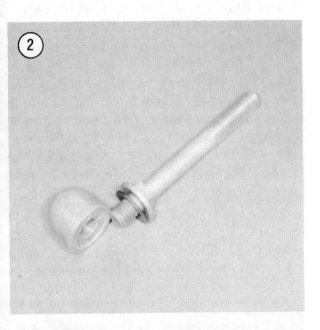

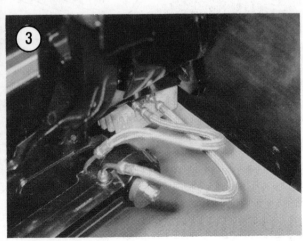

On MerCruiser installations, the trim tab (**Figure 1**) is a primary anode. Other anodes are used on the heads of the gimbal housing attaching bolts (**Figure 2**) or take the form of a plate mounted underneath the transom near the trim cylinder hydraulic fittings (**Figure 3**).

In addition to these, an anti-corrosion anode kit (part No. 71320A3) is available from MerCruiser dealers. This is a large waffle-style anode designed to be attached to the boat and grounded to the drive unit (**Figure 4**). It offers additional protection when a stainless steel propeller is used.

If your boat is fitted with stainless steel after planes (trim tabs), Mercury Marine recommends that you install an anti-corrosion anode kit on *each* after plane to deal with the increased corrosion potential.

While stern drive owners tend to take zinc anodes for granted, there are several things to remember about their use to maximize the protection they offer.

1. Anodes offer no protection when the boat is out of the water. Whenever the boat is put in storage, the drive unit should be thoroughly

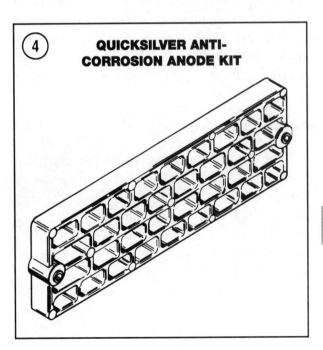

④ **QUICKSILVER ANTI-CORROSION ANODE KIT**

18

flushed with freshwater to remove any polluted or salt water. See Chapter Five.

2. When the boat is moored in the water, the drive unit must be kept in the full down position to make sure that the trim tab remains in the water. If it is not, it will offer no protection against corrosion.

3. Anodes should not be painted. Paint will prevent them from protecting the drive unit against corrosion.

4. Whenever an anode is replaced, the surface to which it is mounted should be scraped down to bare metal and the anode mounting screws fastened tightly. The anode will not do its job unless it makes a good electrical contact with the drive unit.

5. If an anti-corrosion anode kit is installed, be sure that it is grounded to the drive unit.

6. Anodes should be inspected periodically and replaced whenever they are approximately 50 percent eroded. Remember that the trim tab plays a large role in steering and should be in good condition at all times.

7. If an anode appears charcoal gray in color, it may have acquired a dense oxide film. This generally results from being out of the water for a period of time. A simple test with an ohmmeter (R × 1 scale) connected between the anode and stern drive will tell whether or not there is continuity. If the meter shows no continuity, scrape

the anode with a knife and retest. If this provides a reading, the anode is oxidized and should be replaced. Sanding the anode with coarse sandpaper will temporarily restore some of its effectiveness, but the oxide will reform shortly. Service replacement anodes available from your MerCruiser dealer with an "MS" cast into the mounting surface are designed to resist oxidation; they should be used to replace older anodes marked with a "Z."

CONTINUITY DEVICES

In addition to the use of zinc anodes, additional corrosion protection can be obtained by a

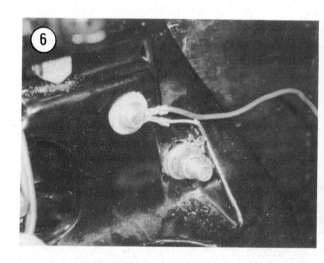

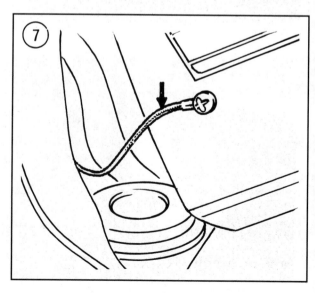

A. Gimbal ring ground wire
B. Hydraulic connector ground plate

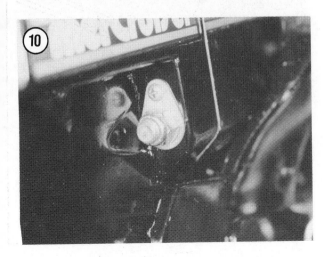

continuity circuit. This is factory-installed on the stern drives covered in this manual. It is also offered in kit form (part No. 99940A1) for installation on older models.

The continuity circuit assures that electrical continuity will be maintained between all components on the drive unit so that those components underwater will receive proper protection against corrosion. It consists of a series of ground wires and ground plates that serve as bridges to connect the separate components. Electrically speaking, the ground wires and ground plates tie the individual components into one large component.

The continuity circuit consists of a steering lever ground wire (**Figure 5**), inner transom plate and engine ground wires (**Figure 6**), a bell housing ground wire (**Figure 7**) and a gimbal ring ground wire located near the trim cylinder hydraulic connections (A, **Figure 8**). In addition to the ground wires, ground plates are installed between the gear housing and drive shaft housing (**Figure 9**), between the drive shaft housing and bell housing (**Figure 10**) and at the trim cylinder hydraulic connector (B, **Figure 8**). On later production models, the ground plate at the hydraulic connector has been replaced by star washers installed underneath each of the connector mounting studs.

Trim cylinders contain an internal continuity ring or spring installed between 2 O-rings in the end cap (**Figure 11**). Whenever a trim cylinder is disassembled, be sure that the continuity ring or spring is reinstalled properly.

When a stainless steel propeller is used, care must be taken to maintain good continuity between the prop and the prop shaft or the propeller will corrode. Periodic removal of the propeller, a thorough cleaning of its hub, the prop shaft all all mounting components, and lubrication of the shaft with Quicksilver Special Lubricant 101 will help maintain good continuity and prevent prop corrosion.

18

A continuity washer (**Figure 12**) is installed between the propeller and spline washer on all models to help maintain continuity. If your drive unit is not equipped with a continuity washer or if you lose it, a new one can be obtained from MerCruiser dealers as part No. 13-42351.

Continuity Test

To assure that electrical continuity is properly maintained between the underwater components, the continuity circuit should be inspected periodically to make sure that all connections are secure and that there are no damaged or missing wires. To check the drive unit for proper grounding, perform the following procedure with the boat in the water and the stern drive in the full down position.

1. Connect the negative (black) lead of a DC voltmeter to the negative battery post. Set the voltmeter on the 0-2,000 millivolt (0-2 volt) scale.

2. Suspend the positive (red) lead of the voltmeter in the water within 6 in. of the drive unit (do not touch the drive unit with the voltmeter lead). The voltmeter should read 3 millivolts or more.

3. Dry the positive voltmeter lead and connect it to each individual metallic component of the drive unit assembly, noting the reading at each connection. The voltmeter should drop to less than 2 millivolts at each connection.

4. If the voltmeter readings are not as specified, one or more components are improperly grounded. Determine which and correct as required.

GALVANIC ISOLATOR

The use of a Quicksilver galvanic isolator (part No. 76664A1) is recommended if your boat is equipped to run on shore power. This relatively small solid-state device (**Figure 13**) series-connects into the boat's safety ground lead in front of all other grounding connections to the vessel (**Figure 14**) and performs the function of an

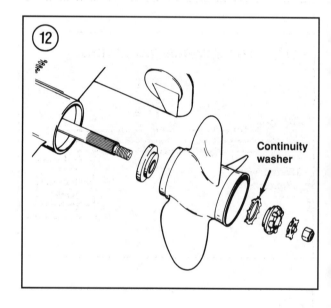

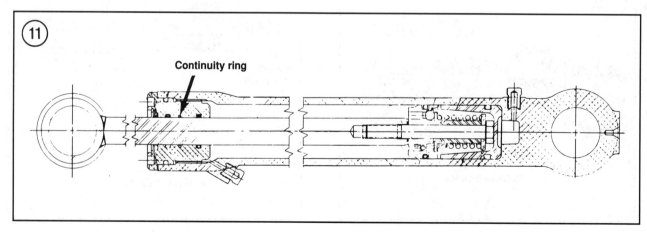

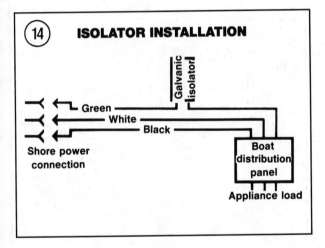

ISOLATOR INSTALLATION

insulation transformer at a fraction of the size, weight and cost involved.

Safety regulations require that any power cable which carries shore power on-board a boat contain a third wire which will ground the electrical and propulsion equipment to the shore. While this serves the purpose of reducing the danger of an electrical shock, it also connects all of the underwater metal components on your boat with similar components on other boats connected into the system, as well as to the pier (if made of steel) and other metallic objects on-shore. In many circumstances, the zinc anodes, continuity circuit and even a MerCathode II system (if installed) cannot cope with the increased potential of galvanic corrosion. Under normal conditions, this situation will cause severe corrosion damage to the drive unit in a period as short as 5 days.

The galvanic isolator isolates the AC shore power ground from the boat, acting as a filter to block the flow of low voltage galvanic currents while still maintaining the function of the neutral safety ground circuit. Electron flow in a dock situation without the isolator is shown in **Figure 15**A; **Figure 15**B shows the same situation with the isolator in use. Should a wiring defect allow AC current to flow in the dockside shore power

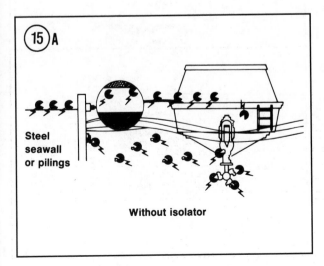

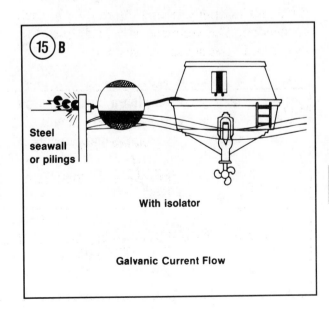

18

ground lead, the isolator will transmit the dangerous voltage to ground. A warning buzzer inside the isolator sounds if the situation occurs.

MERCATHODE SYSTEM

MerCruiser offers the MerCathode II system to provide permanent, automatic protection against galvanic corrosion. MerCathode II is an impressed current system (basic principles are discussed in Chapter One). This solid-state system uses battery current from the boat to impress a reverse blocking voltage that inhibits the flow of galvanic currents.

The MerCathode II system contains a controller unit, anode and reference electrode (**Figure 16**). Battery current from the boat is transmitted into the water through the controller to the anode, which has a platinum surface to prevent it from eroding under the current flow. The reference electrode in the water senses the potential for corrosion and tells the controller the range in which the protective current should be kept to maintain the best corrosion protection.

This method of operation allows the MerCathode II system to compensate for any changes in corrosion potential resulting from variations in water temperature, speed and other factors, including the condition of the paint on the drive unit. An optional MerCathode Monitor can be installed to check system operation at the push of a button.

The MerCathode II system uses such a small amount of battery current that a boat placed in conditions of severe corrosion potential will not require a battery recharge for approximately 5 weeks. Since the system requires water to operate, it automatically shuts off when the boat is out of the water.

The MerCathode II system differs from earlier MerCathode systems in that the reference electrode and anode are integrated in a single housing (**Figure 17**) attached on the bottom of the gimbal housing (the older system required drill-

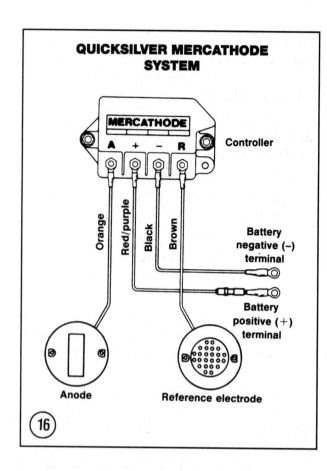

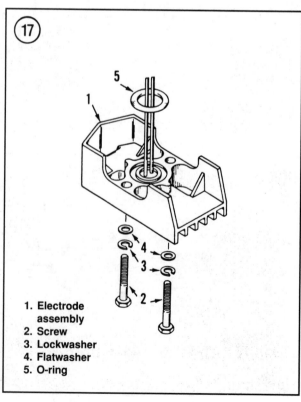

1. Electrode assembly
2. Screw
3. Lockwasher
4. Flatwasher
5. O-ring

ing holes in the transom to install the electrode and anode). The controller is installed directly on the engine. See **Figure 18** and **Figure 19** for typical installations.

Mercury Marine offers the following recommendations to obtain the most satisfactory service from the MerCathode system:

a. Do not paint the integrated electrode assembly. Paint will prevent the system from operating.

b. Do not replace the plastic caps on the gimbal housing bolts (**Figure 20**) with anode heads. This will adversely affect system operation.

c. The MerCathode system draws its power from the engine wiring harness. If a battery switch is installed on the boat, it must be left in the ON position whenever the boat is moored or the system will not provide corrosion protection. If this is not practical, you can remove and discard the red-purple power supply lead from the positive (+) terminal of the controller and install a separate wire between the controller + terminal and the positive battery terminal. A 3 amp fuse should be installed in this wire within 6 in. of the positive battery post.

d. If controller replacement is required, be sure to install a blue unit bearing the same part No. as the one removed. Older (black) units contain different internal circuitry and will not function properly.

e. Perform the *Corrosion Protection Test* as described in this chapter at least once a year to make sure the MerCathode system is working properly.

MerCathode Monitor

The MerCathode monitor (**Figure 21**) can be mounted on the instrument panel and allows

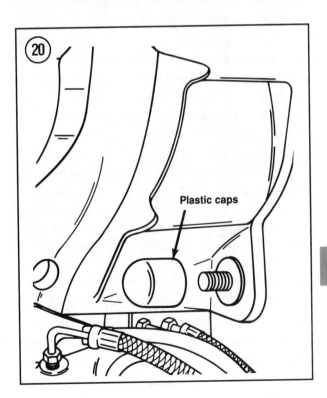

Plastic caps

18

system checks at the push of a button. When installed on a boat fitted with a new stern drive, the green light on the monitor may not come on when the red button is pushed (unless fitted with a stainless steel propeller). This is a temporary but normal condition which exists because the combination of the sacrificial zinc anodes, continuity circuit and new paint on the drive unit are sufficient to provide the necessary protection. If a stainless steel propeller is used, the combination above will not be enough and the MerCathode II system will go into operation immediately.

Once the drive unit has accumulated surface abrasions and scratches which expose bare metal to the water, however, the MerCathode II system will start functioning. At this time, the green light will glow when the red button is depressed. Initially, the light may only flicker but as soon as the MerCathode II system is required to take over full protection of the drive unit, it should glow steadily.

If there is a question about proper monitor functioning, it can be tested as follows:

1. Connect a jumper lead between the minus (–) and the "R" terminals on the controller (**Figure 22**). If the light comes on, the monitor is satisfactory, but the MerCathode II system is not functioning.

2. If the light does not come on in Step 1, disconnect the monitor lead at the "A" terminal on the controller (**Figure 22**) and connect it directly to the positive battery terminal.

   a. If the light comes on, the monitor is satisfactory but the MerCathode II system is not functioning.

   b. If the light does not come on, look for damage to the monitor wiring or loose connections. If neither is found, the monitor is defective and must be replaced.

3. Disconnect the monitor lead from the positive battery terminal and reconnect it to the controller "A" terminal.

CORROSION PROTECTION TEST

The following test should be performed at least once a year to make sure the corrosion protection system is in good condition and the MerCathode II system (if installed) is functioning properly.

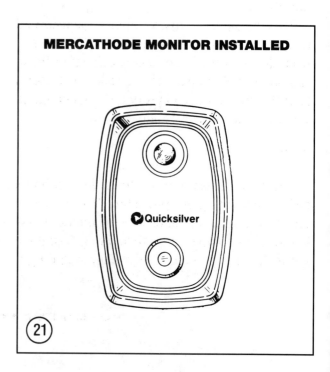

MERCATHODE MONITOR INSTALLED

Quicksilver

(21)

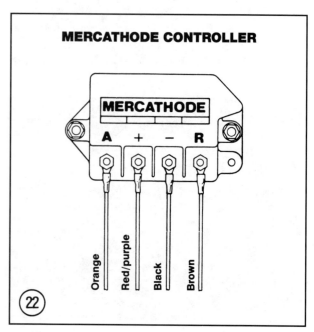

MERCATHODE CONTROLLER

MERCATHODE

A   +   –   R

Orange   Red/purple   Black   Brown

(22)

The test requires the use of a digital multi-meter such as the Radio Shack 22-191 and a Mer-Cathode Reference Electrode Tester part No. 76675A1. Use of a standard analog (needle type) meter will result in inaccurate readings.

If a MerCathode II system is installed, the battery must be fully charged (12.6 volts or more).

New boats will provide higher than normal readings when this test is performed. This results from the combination of a new drive unit finish and sacrificial anodes. This test is most useful after the boat has been in service long enough to acquire minor scratches and abrasions.

Testing

Let the boat rest at moor for at least 8 hours before performing this procedure. This will give the sacrificial anodes and/or MerCathode II system time to polarize the surrounding water. Do not rock the boat excessively while boarding it prior to the test or the test readings will be adversely affected. Refer to **Figure 23** for this procedure.

1. Connect the negative voltmeter lead to the negative battery terminal.

2. Connect the reference electrode lead to the positive voltmeter receptacle in place of the positive voltmeter lead.

3. Set the meter on the 0-2,000 millivolt (0-2 volt) scale.

4. Suspend the reference electrode in the water within 6 in. of the aft end of the drive unit (do not touch the drive unit). The voltmeter should read 750-1,050 millivolts (freshwater) or 880-1,050 millivolts (salt, polluted or mineral-laden water).

5. If the reading is not within specifications, or is within specifications but corrosion can be seen on the stern drive, refer to **Table 1** to disgnose and correct the condition.

Figure 23 and Table 1 are on the following pages.

18

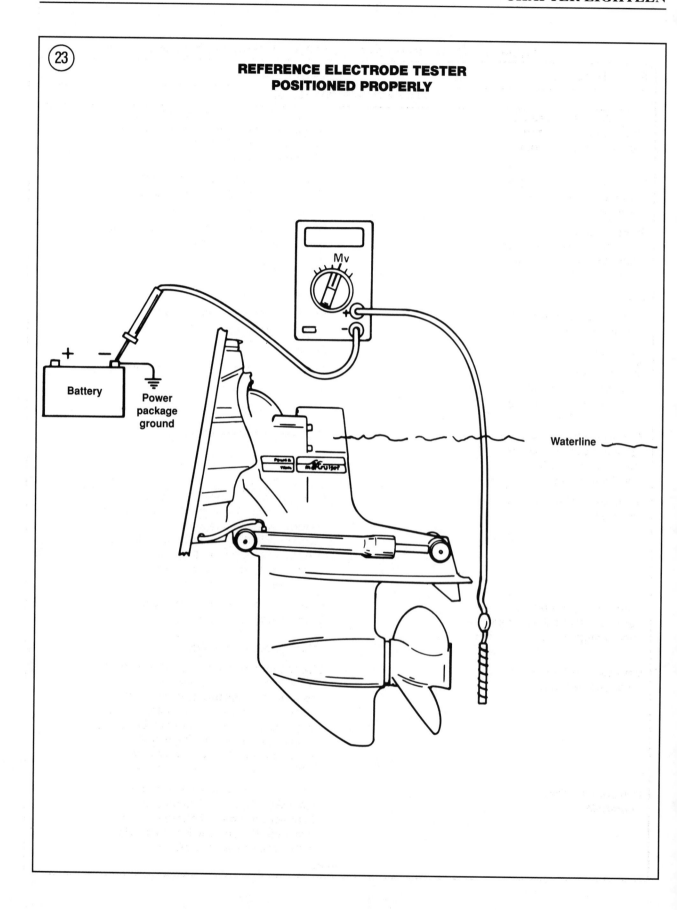

(23)

REFERENCE ELECTRODE TESTER
POSITIONED PROPERLY

Mv

Battery

Power
package
ground

Waterline

Table 1 CORROSION PROTECTION TROUBLESHOOTING

Possible cause	Correction
LOW VOLTMETER READING	
No continuity between drive unit components and negative battery terminal	Check for missing or damaged continuity circuit devices. Make sure connections are clean and tight. Perform Continuity Circuit Test.
Shore power grounding lead not isolated from boat ground	Disconnect shore power and repeat Corrosion Protection Test. If reading increases, install galvanic isolator.
Paint surface on drive unit underwater parts in poor condition or bare metal exposed	Prime and paint underwater metal parts with Quicksilver materials.
Zinc anodes painted	Replace anodes.
Zinc anodes inactive or not properly grounded	Replace oxidized anodes. Clean mounting surfaces to bare metal.
Zinc anodes badly eroded	Replace anodes
Drive unit and/or bottom of boat painted with anti-fouling paint containing mercury or copper	Clean and repaint with proper materials.
Zinc anode heads used on gimbal housing bolts on boat equipped with MerCathode II system	Replace with plastic caps.
No power to MerCathode II controller	Check wiring for defects or loose connections. Connect voltmeter between controller – and + terminals. If battery voltage reading is not obtained, check for blown fuse. If all else fails, substitute a known-good controller.
Poor connection between the brown (reference electrode) and orange (anode) leads and	Clean and tighten the connection. Check wiring for defects.
	MerCathode II controller
Defective MerCathode II reference electrode	Disconnect brown lead from the controller "R" terminal. Connect a voltmeter between the disconnected lead and negative battery terminal. Note reading and repeat test with Reference Electrode Tester. If the same reading is not obtained in both cases, replace the reference electrode.
Defective MerCathode II controller	Connect a jumper wire between the controller "R" and "–" terminals. Connect a voltmeter between the same 2 terminals. If reading is less than 3.55 volts, replace the controller.

(continued)

18

Table 1 CORROSION PROTECTION TROUBLESHOOTING (continued)

Possible cause	Correction
HIGH VOLTMETER READING	
Stray current corrosion	Note reading while disconnecting electrical components one at a time.When high reading is eliminated, the source of the stray current has been located. Correct as required.
Poor connection between brown lead and "R" terminal on MerCathode II controller	Clean and tighten connection. Check for defective wiring.
Defective MerCathode II reference electrode	Disconnect brown lead from the controller "R" terminal. Connect a voltmeter between the disconnected lead and negative battery terminal. Note reading and repeat test with Reference Electrode Tester. If the same reading is not obtained in both cases, replacethe reference electrode.
Defective MerCathode II controller	Replace controller.

Problem	Cause/remedy
NORMAL READING (CORROSION PRESENT)	
Corrosion on entire drive unit Corrosion develops after drive unit is refinished	Trim tab out of water when boat is moored. Aluminum casting was cleaned with steel wire brush (use nylon or bristle brush only). Steel particles were entrapped and formed a small galvanic cell.
Drive unit paint blistering	AC battery charger improperly connected to battery.
Trim cylinder corrosion	Continuity ring or spring missing or not making proper contact.
Corrosion on one individual component but not on others	Test continuity circuit for breakdown in continuity. Install continuity circuit if not so equipped.
Exhaust outlet area corroded	Clean accumulated exhaust gas deposits with marine or auto wax.
Corrosion occurs after unit is removed from storage	Wash exterior and flush interior with fresh water.
Corrosion forms between two metal surfaces	Use Quicksilver Special Lubricant 101, 2-4-C Multi-Lube or Perfect Seal to prevent moisture from accumulating between mating surfaces.
Corrosion occurs even though lubricant was used	Lubricant contained graphite; use Quicksilver lubricants only.
Stainless steel surface corrodes	Foreign matter or contamination covers steel, prevent oxygen from reaching it. This breaks down the protective oxide film and causes oxygen starvation corrosion. If problem is with the propeller, there is a lack of continuity; clean and lubricate surfaces and make sure continuity washer is installed.
Paint blisters but metal is not pitted or eroded	Improper surface preparation prior to refinishing. Resand surfaces to bare metal and refinish with Quicksilver products according to directions.

Index

19

MCM 7.4L AND 454 MAGNUM
(BRAVO ONE DRIVE)

BLK = Black
BLU = Blue
BRN = Brown
GRY = Gray
GRN = Green
ORN = Orange
PNK = Pink
PUR = Purple
RED = Red
TAN = Tan
WHT = White
YEL = Yellow
LIT = Light
DRK = Dark

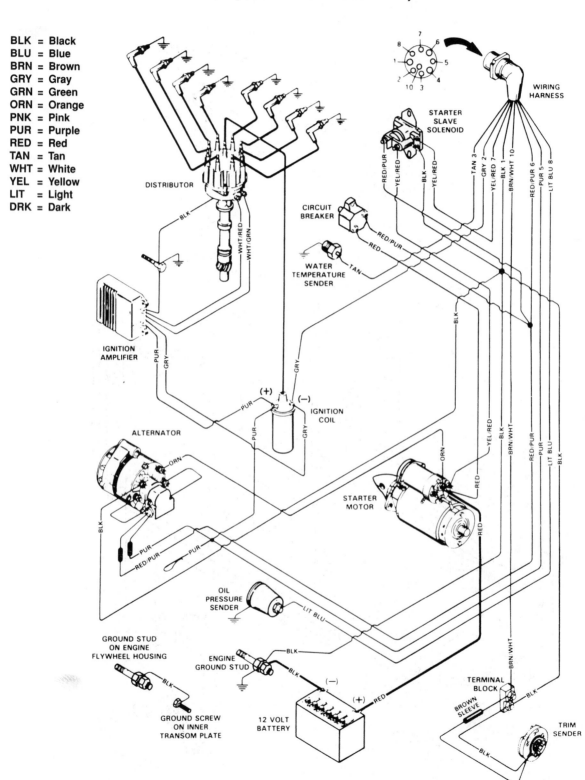

DISTRIBUTOR

WIRING HARNESS

STARTER SLAVE SOLENOID

IGNITION AMPLIFIER

CIRCUIT BREAKER

WATER TEMPERATURE SENDER

IGNITION COIL

ALTERNATOR

STARTER MOTOR

OIL PRESSURE SENDER

GROUND STUD ON ENGINE FLYWHEEL HOUSING

GROUND SCREW ON INNER TRANSOM PLATE

ENGINE GROUND STUD

12 VOLT BATTERY

TERMINAL BLOCK

BROWN SLEEVE

TRIM SENDER

MCM 120/130/140/3.0L ENGINE WIRING
(BATTERY METER CIRCUIT)

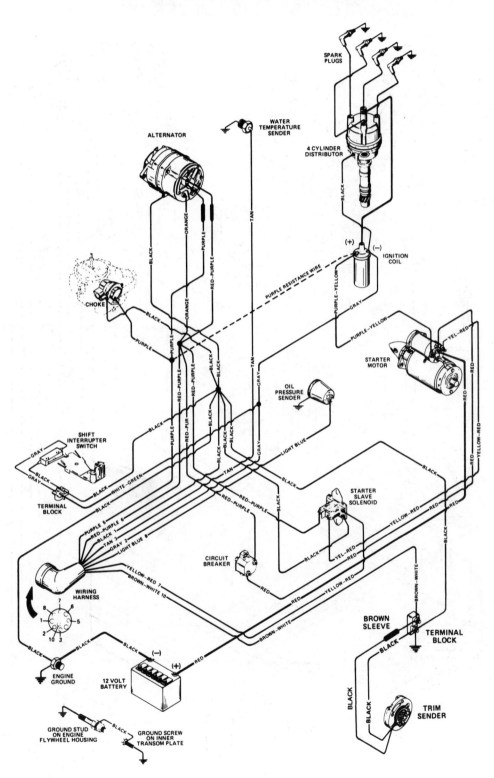

MCM 120/130/140 ENGINE WIRING WITH 90 AMP FUSE AT STARTER MOTOR (ORANGE WIRE) DELCO ALTERNATOR (BATTERY METER CIRCUIT)

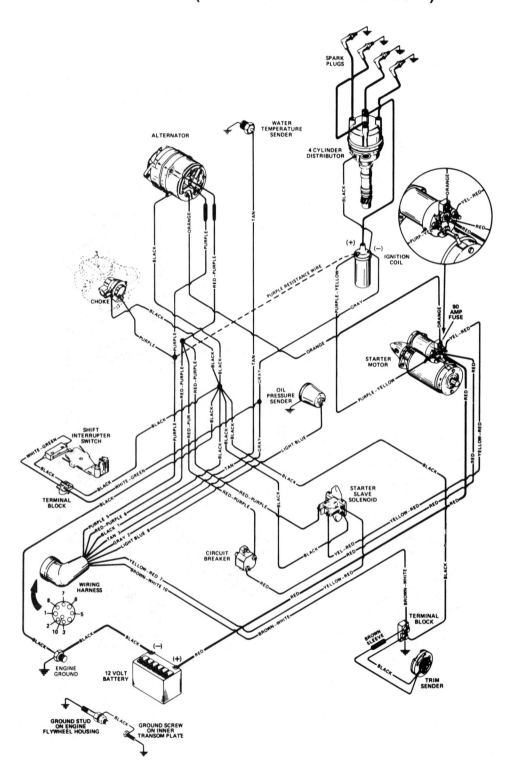

MCM 120/130/140/3.0L ENGINE WIRING WITH 90 AMP FUSE AT STARTER MOTOR (ORANGE WIRE) MANDO ALTERNATOR (BATTERY METER CIRCUIT)

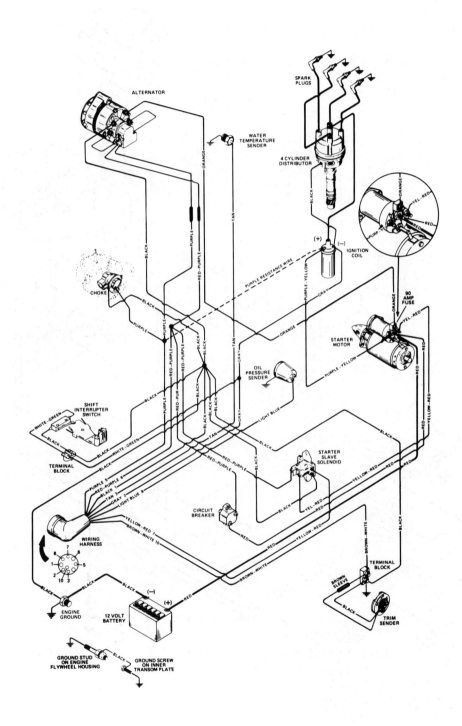

MCM 120R/140R ENGINE WIRING WITHOUT 90 AMP FUSE AT STARTER MOTOR (ORANGE WIRE) MANDO ALTERNATOR (BATTERY METER CIRCUIT)

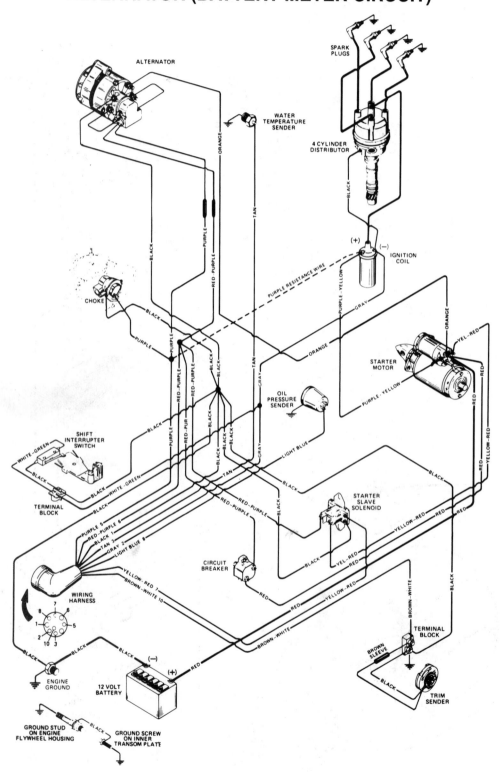

MCM 165/170/180/190 ENGINE WIRING WITH 90 AMP FUSE AT DELCO STARTER MOTOR (ORANGE WIRE) (BATTERY METER CIRCUIT)

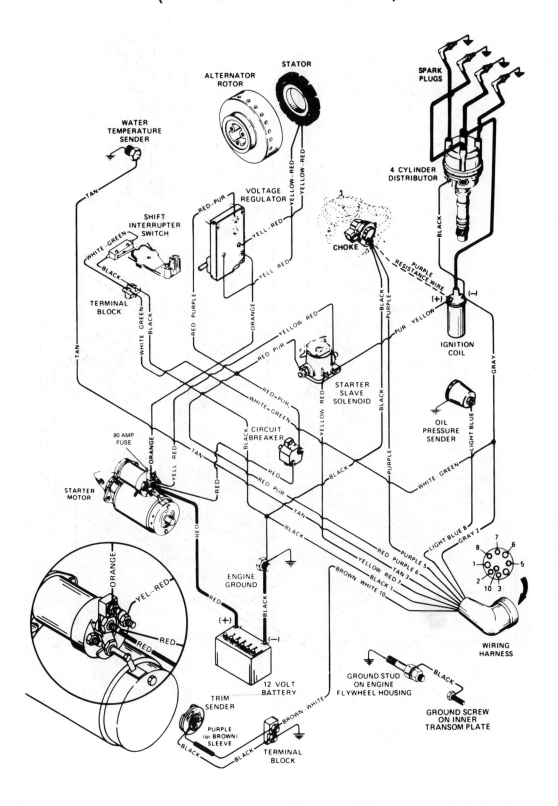

MCM 3.7/3.7LX ENGINE WIRING DELCO STARTER MOTOR (BATTERY METER CIRCUIT)

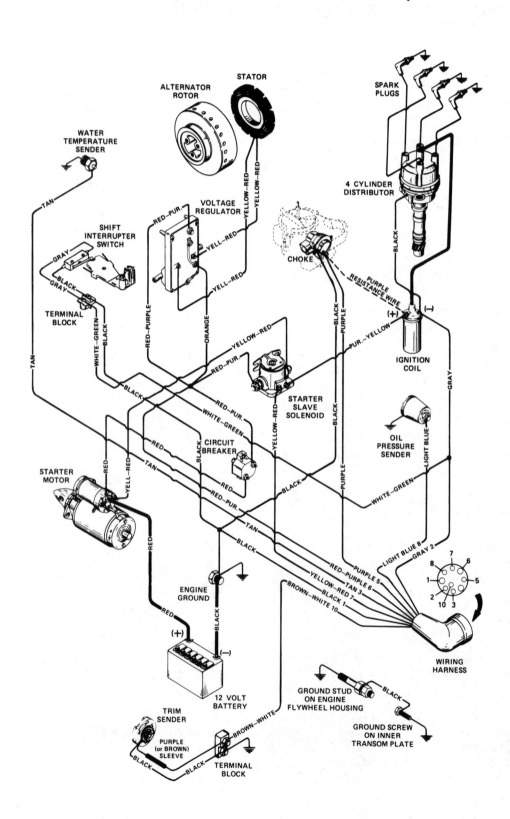

MCM 165/170/180/190 ENGINE WIRING WITHOUT 90 AMP FUSE AT DELCO STARTER MOTOR (ORANGE WIRE) (BATTERY METER CIRCUIT)

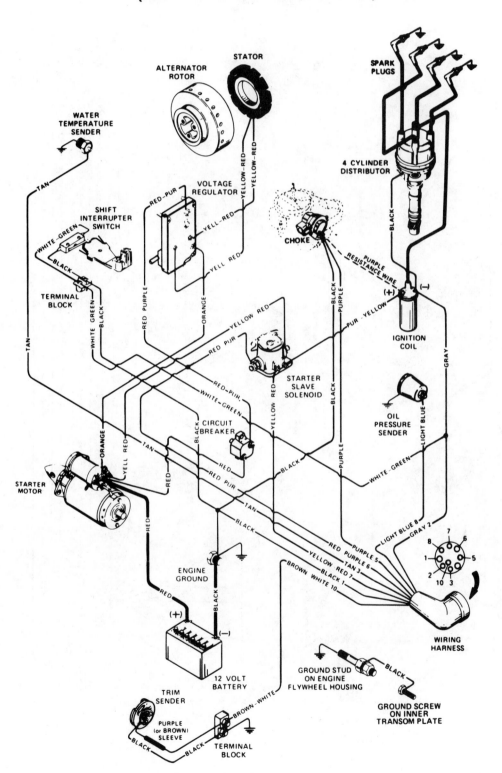

MCM 200/230/260/5.0L/5.0LX/5.7L ENGINE WIRING WITH 90 AMP FUSE AT STARTER MOTOR (ORANGE WIRE) (BATTERY METER CIRCUIT)

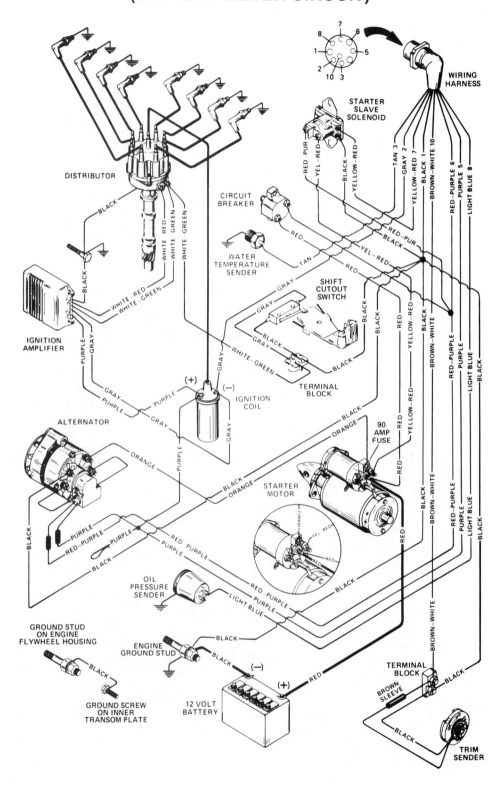

MCM 200/230/260/5.0L/5.0LX/5.7L ENGINE WIRING WITHOUT 90 AMP FUSE AT STARTER MOTOR (ORANGE WIRE) (BATTERY METER CIRCUIT)

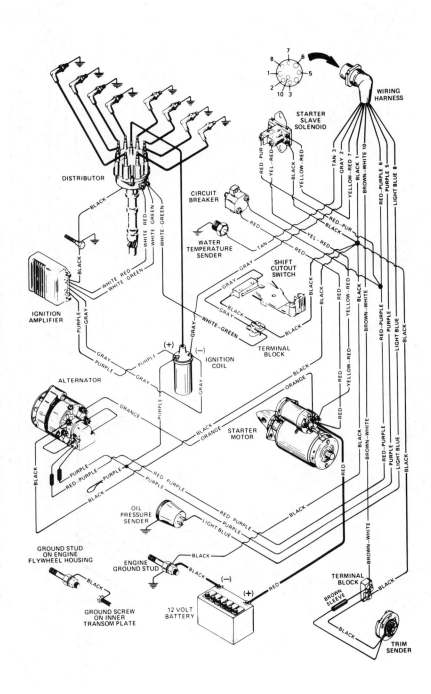

MCM 200/230/260/5.0L/5.0LX/5.7L ENGINE WIRING (BATTERY METER CIRCUIT)

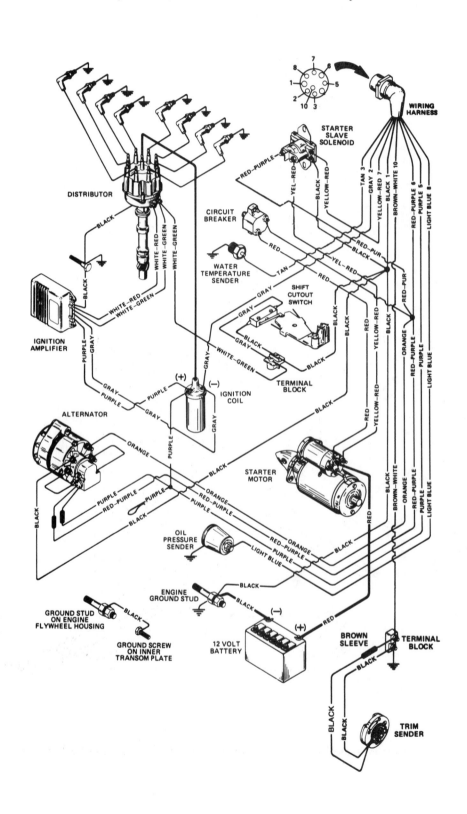

MCM 485 ENGINE WIRING (AMMETER CIRCUIT)

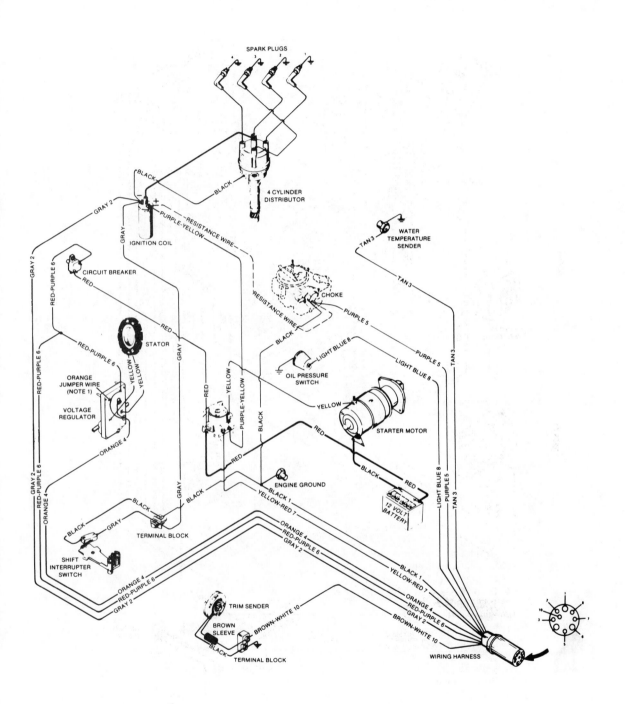

NOTE 1: Remove this wire if ammeter is to be used. Jumper must be left connected if Battery Meter is used.

V6 ENGINE WIRING WITH STARTER MOTOR FUSE

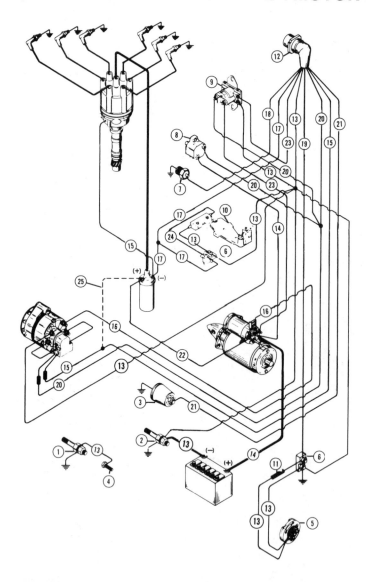

1. Ground stud on engine flywheel housing
2. Engine ground stud
3. Oil pressure sender
4. Ground screw on inner transom plate
5. Trim sender
6. Terminal block
7. Water temperature sender
8. Circuit breaker
9. Starter slave solenoid
10. Shift cutout switch
11. Brown sleeve
12. Wiring harness
13. Black
14. Red
15. Purple
16. Orange
17. Gray
18. Tan
19. Brown/white
20. Red/purple
21. Light blue
22. Purple/yellow
23. Yellow/red
24. White/green
25. Purple resistance wire

V6 ENGINE WIRING WITHOUT STARTER MOTOR FUSE

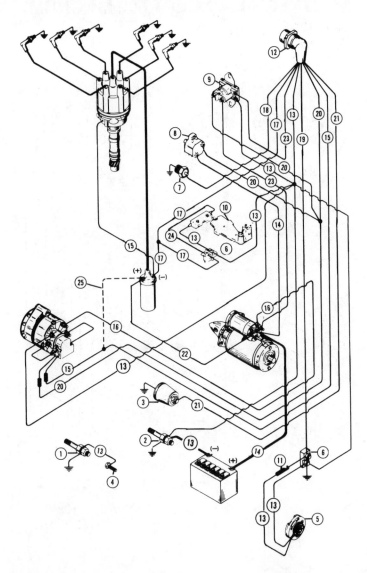

1. Ground stud on engine flywheel housing
2. Engine ground stud
3. Oil pressure sender
4. Ground screw on inner transom plate
5. Trim sender
6. Terminal block
7. Water temperature sender
8. Circuit breaker
9. Starter slave solenoid
10. Shift cutout switch
11. Brown sleeve
12. Wiring harness

13. Black
14. Red
15. Purple
16. Orange
17. Gray
18. Tan
19. Brown/white
20. Red/purple
21. Light blue
22. Purple/yellow
23. Yellow/red
24. White/green
25. Purple resistance wire

ENGINES WITH AUDIO WARNING SYSTEM
(TYPICAL, EXCEPT 502 MAGNUM)

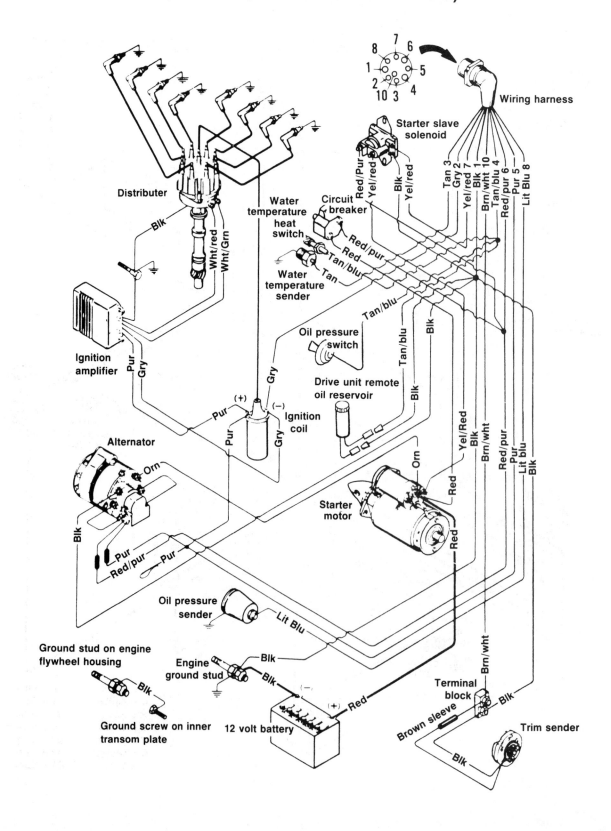

7.4L/350 MAGNUM/454 MAGNUM/502 MAGNUM

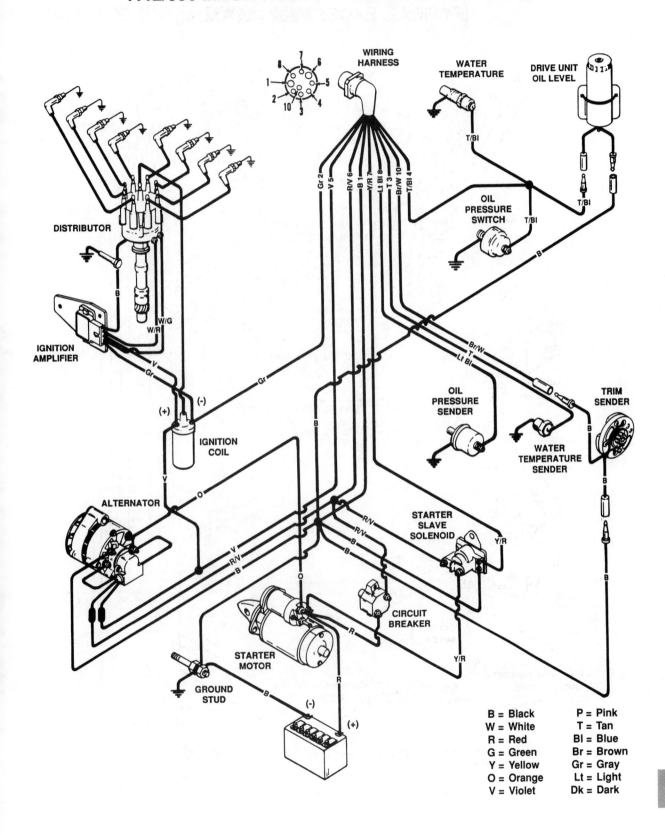

INSTRUMENTATION
(WITH CONNECTOR PLUG)

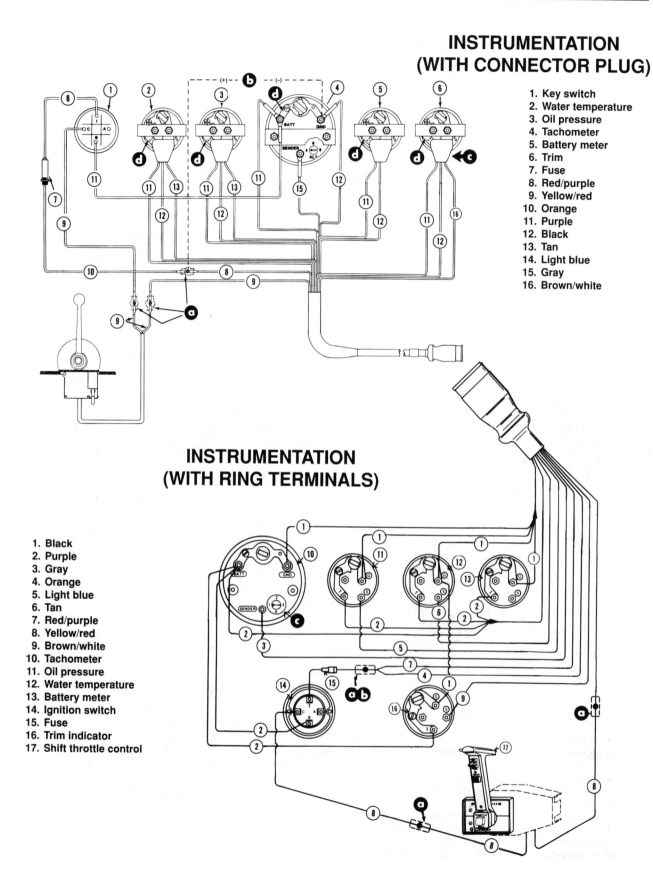

1. Key switch
2. Water temperature
3. Oil pressure
4. Tachometer
5. Battery meter
6. Trim
7. Fuse
8. Red/purple
9. Yellow/red
10. Orange
11. Purple
12. Black
13. Tan
14. Light blue
15. Gray
16. Brown/white

INSTRUMENTATION
(WITH RING TERMINALS)

1. Black
2. Purple
3. Gray
4. Orange
5. Light blue
6. Tan
7. Red/purple
8. Yellow/red
9. Brown/white
10. Tachometer
11. Oil pressure
12. Water temperature
13. Battery meter
14. Ignition switch
15. Fuse
16. Trim indicator
17. Shift throttle control

INSTRUMENTATION FOR AUDIO
WARNING SYSTEM (TYPICAL)

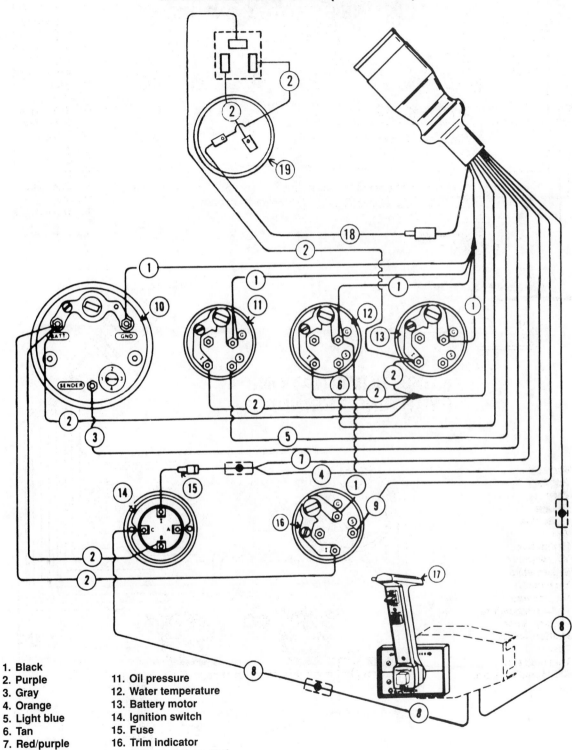

1. Black
2. Purple
3. Gray
4. Orange
5. Light blue
6. Tan
7. Red/purple
8. Yellow/red
9. Brown/white
10. Tachometer

11. Oil pressure
12. Water temperature
13. Battery motor
14. Ignition switch
15. Fuse
16. Trim indicator
17. Shift throttle control
18. Tan/black
19. Audio warning buzzer

20

DUAL STATION
(NEUTRAL SAFETY SWITCH
IN ONE REMOTE CONTROL)

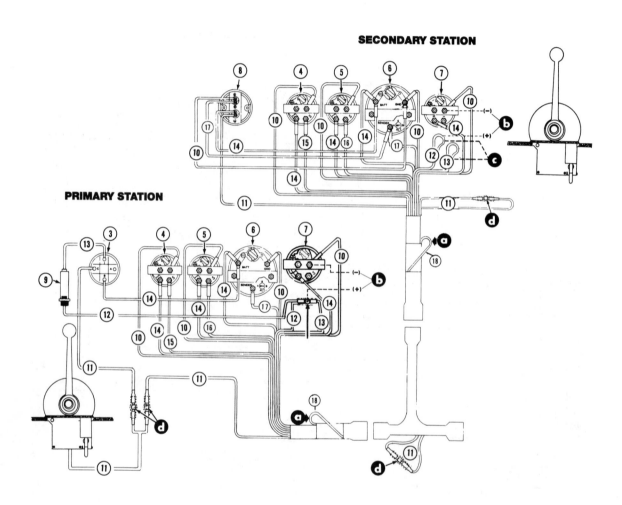

3. Key switch
4. Water temperature
5. Oil pressure
6. Tachometer
7. Battery meter
8. Stop-start panel
9. Fuse
10. Black

11. Yellow/red
12. Orange
13. Red/purple
14. Purple
15. Tan
16. Light blue
17. Gray
18. Brown/white

DUAL STATION
(NEUTRAL SAFETY SWITCH
IN BOTH REMOTE CONTROLS)

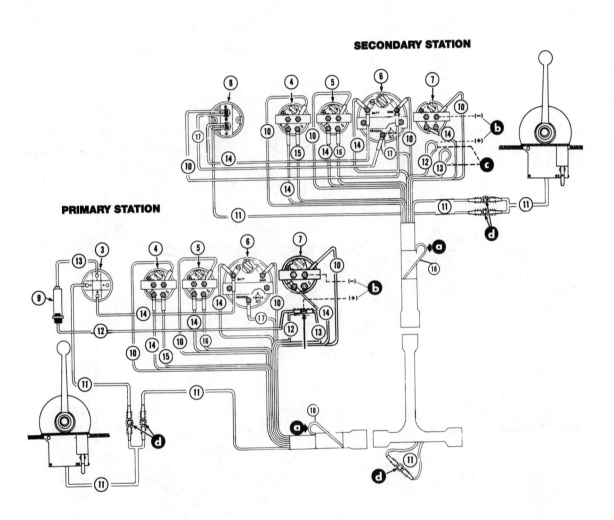

3. Key switch	11. Yellow/red
4. Water temperature	12. Orange
5. Oil pressure	13. Red/purple
6. Tachometer	14. Purple
7. Battery meter	15. Tan
8. Stop-start panel	16. Light blue
9. Fuse	17. Gray
10. Black	18. Brown/white

20

MCM 3.0 AND 3.0LX WITH DDIS IGNITION

BLK = Black
BLU = Blue
BRN = Brown
GRY = Gray
GRN = Green
ORN = Orange
PNK = Pink
PUR = Purple
RED = Red
TAN = Tan
WHT = White
YEL = Yellow
LIT = Light
DRK = Dark

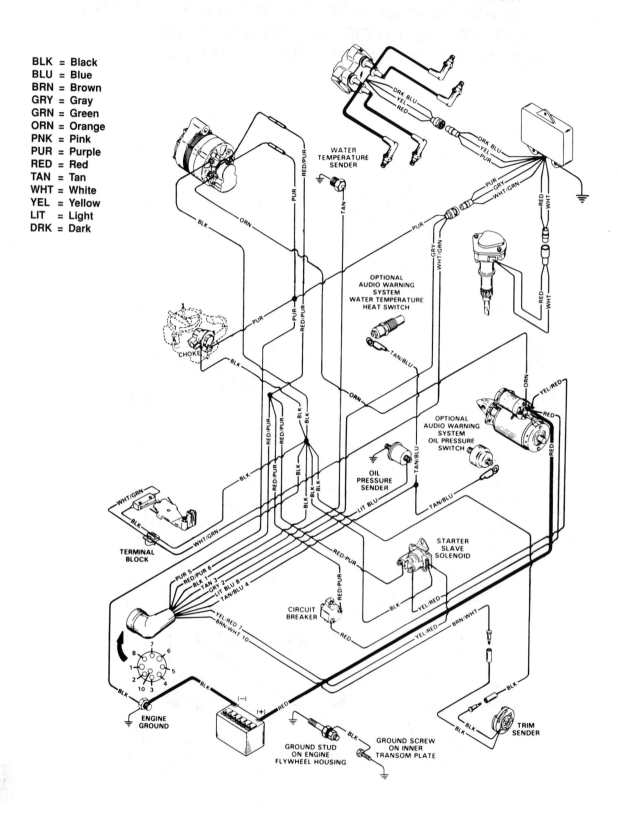

MCM 200/230/260/5.0L/5.0LX/5.7L ENGINE WIRING DIAGRAMS WITHOUT 90 AMP FUSE AT STARTER MOTOR (ORANGE WIRE) (BATTERY METER CIRCUIT) EQUIPPED WITH ELECTRICALLY HEATED CHOKE THERMOSTAT

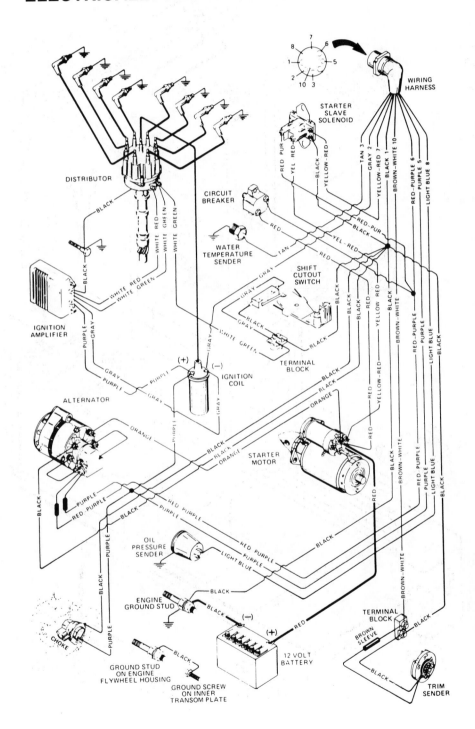

V6 ALPHA MODELS (SERIAL NO. OF000001-ON)

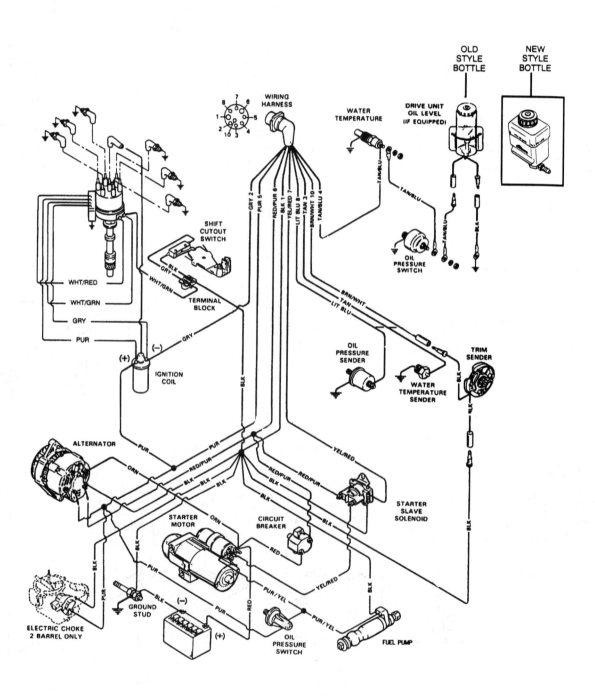

V8 BRAVO MODELS (SERIAL NO. OF000001-ON)

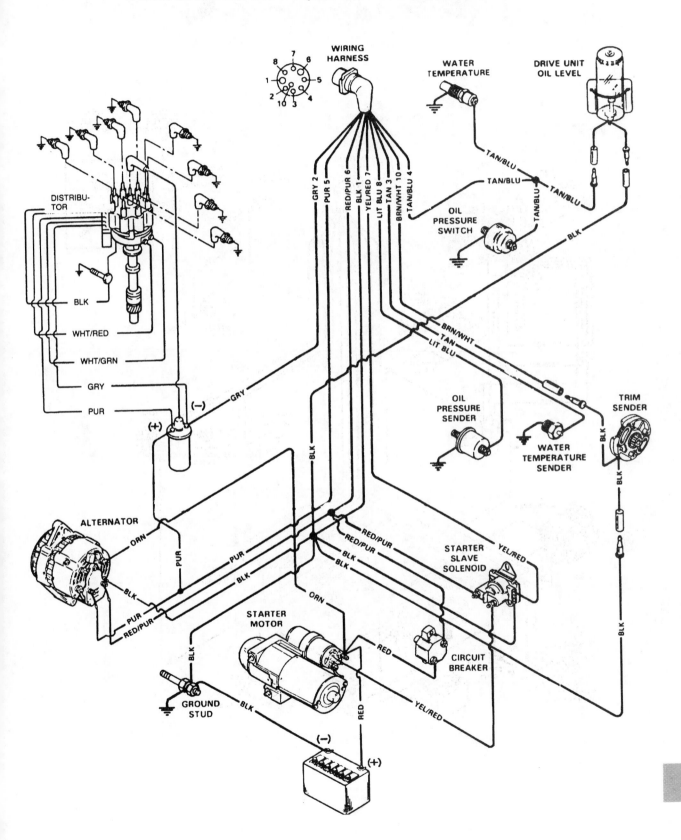

20

V8 ALPHA MODELS (IGNITION MODULE MOUNTED ON EXHAUST ELBOW)

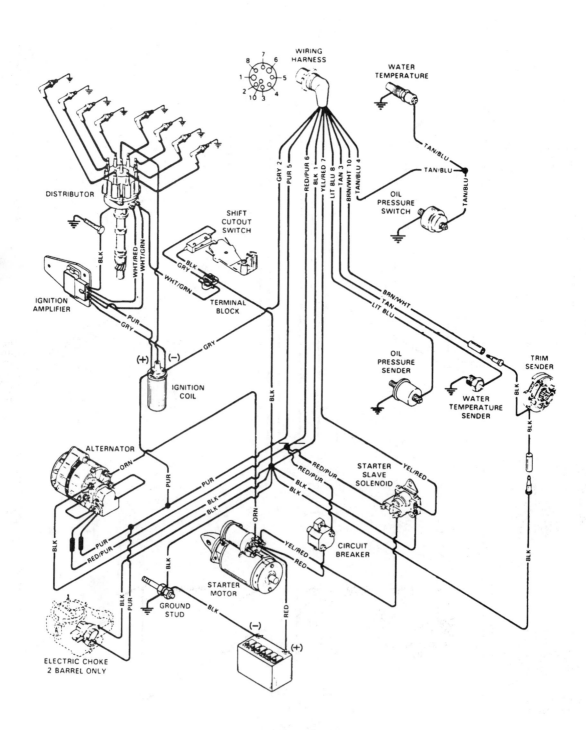

V8 ALPHA MODELS (SERIAL NO. OF000001-ON)

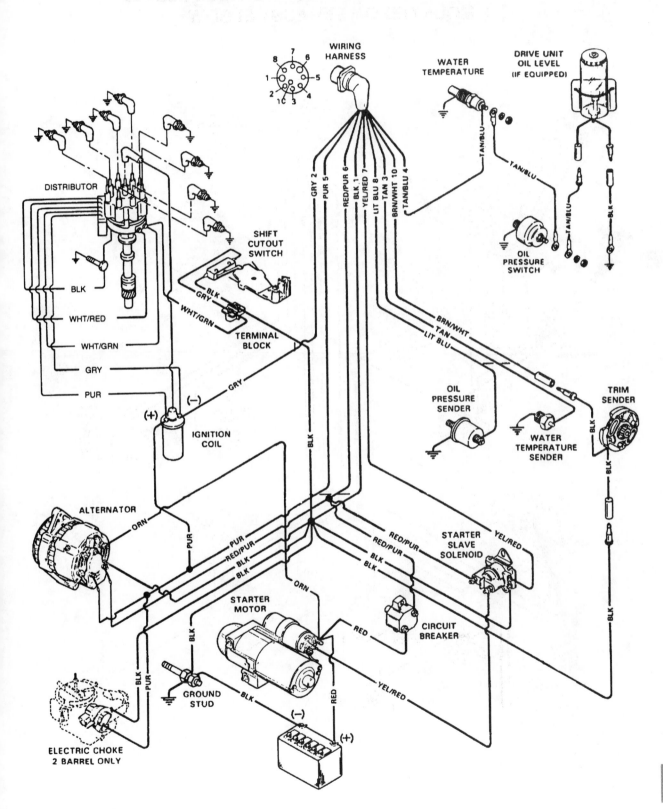

NOTES

NOTES

NOTES